The Independent Writer

JOHN F. PARKER

Vancouver Community College

With the assistance of
Gary Piepenbrink
Researcher

Nancy C. Martinez
University of Albuquerque
Consultant

Harcourt Brace Jovanovich, Publishers
San Diego   New York   Chicago   Atlanta   Washington, D.C.
London   Sydney   Toronto

The Independent Writer

Notes to the Instructor

In order to have a successful and efficient writing workshop in your classroom, two things must happen: you must be free to conduct one-to-one tutorials during class time, and your students must have an abundance of self-directed material to help them improve all aspects of their writing. Such material not only allows you to conduct meaningful conferences with all your students, but it also frees you from having to re-teach fundamentals.

The Independent Writer provides such material in the "Assignment" section to help students in all stages of their writing process, and in the "Workshop" sections to help students choose their content and organization, improve their style, vary their sentence constructions, and eliminate their mechanical errors.

A detailed explanation of converting your classroom into a writing workshop is included in the Instructor's Manual available from Harcourt Brace Jovanovich. You will soon become aware of the following five significant results of implementing a workshop program:

1. Students' writing will improve to such a degree that they will often be able to tell you how much they have improved.

2. You will be able to spend most of the class time in one-to-one or small-group tutorials, becoming part of your students' writing process instead of their judge. When the need arises, however, you will be able to pull the whole class together to give an occasional lecture on a finer point of composition.

3. You will no longer have to take home class-size sets of papers.

4. Your students will learn self- and peer-dependence—writing up to five times more than had you used a traditional, product-oriented method of teaching composition.

5. By the time your students finish your course, they will have become independent rather than teacher-dependent writers.

Writing Programs

You may choose your own method of implementing *The Independent Writer*: from having the entire class work together on similar assignments to placing all students in their own individual programs. For a variety of alternative methods of organizing your class, see the Special Interest Program chart in Appendix A.

Acknowledgments

For their reviews of the manuscript, I want to thank Bruce C. Appleby, Southern Illinois University at Carbondale; Walter H. Beale, the University of North Carolina at Greensboro; and Mary Fuller Hayes, Miami University.

I also wish to acknowledge my wife, Mary, for her understanding and encouragement throughout the entire writing process; Bill McLane, Senior Editor, Margie Rogers, Manuscript Editor, both with Harcourt Brace Jovanovich, for their enthusiastic support; Dr. Harold Kane, Dr. Candice Waltz, and Myles Clowers for their assistance with Chapters 21–23 on "Writing Across the Curriculum"; and the following students who served on my consulting committee at San Diego City College: Monica Blum, Robin Gilmore, Penny Gallagher, Mike Jutras, Karen Klaushie, Charles Nelson, Michael Rutherford, and Alix Stecker. With hours of their caring and thoughtful editing, these students tried to make sure that *The Independent Writer* would be not only clear but also interesting for students across the nation. Finally, I thank Nova Graham for proofreading the final page proofs, and Barbara-Anne Eddy for her support of the project.

Notes to the Student

The Independent Writer will help you to communicate, entertain, inform, and persuade effectively. Like other skills you acquire in life, skill in writing comes from concentrating on the process, rather than on the end product. By developing and practicing a logical, yet simple, process of writing, you will soon be able to produce a desirable product. Think, for a moment, of the process that has gone into perfecting the product of someone other than a writer. For example, an actor rehearses for weeks under the guidance of a director to produce an opening night sensation. A basketball player practices hour after hour under the watchful eye of his coach to perfect a devastating slam dunk. The masterful summation of a young lawyer results from dozens of mock trials before more experienced lawyers and judges. By the same token, you—with the aid of your editors—can produce an exciting and exacting piece of writing that successfully conveys your message and stimulates your intended reader.

It may be useful for you to reflect on how you have, to this point, produced a piece of writing. Have you concentrated on the finished product instead of thinking about the process by which you produced it? In the real world you must take responsibility for your writing as a product. *The Independent Writer*, however, focuses on helping you develop and improve your own writing process to achieve a polished product.

Throughout this book you will learn how to develop your own effective process of writing to deal with a variety of "real-life" writing demands. Although you do not have to follow the steps of the writing process rigidly, you should be aware of what happens in each step:

- During your *prewriting process* you invent or generate an idea that you consider worthwhile.

- During your *drafting process* you begin to compose your piece of writing by selecting appropriate supporting evidence, organizing it in a logical fashion, and developing a tone so that your audience will discover exactly what you want it to know.

- During your *revising process* you ask your peers and writing instructor for their editorial comments so that you can revise, rewrite, and reform anything that does not work. You can accept or reject your editors' comments, but your ultimate aim is to publish your paper—that is, present it to your intended reader or readers.

Although you will be able to experiment with these three steps of the writing process in every assignment in *The Independent Writer*, you should take time to work through the introductory section. It lays the foundation for your becoming an independent writer. Afterward, you will be able to use the entire book with more confidence.

Normally you begin to read a book from the first page and continue through to the end. With *The Independent Writer,* however, you are encouraged to use it as you would an encyclopedia, dipping into it here and there to serve *your* needs. Sometimes you will use it on your own at home, to find out how to write in a particular format or to practice a sentence-building technique; sometimes you will use it with others in a workshop atmosphere at school, to edit each other's papers, or to play a game to eliminate a writing problem. As you become familiar with the book, you will see the usefulness of employing various parts of it to help you get a piece of writing ready for your intended audience.

As you become more involved in improving your writing, you will become aware of the strong and weak aspects of your writing process. Your aim will be not only to build on what is strong, but to correct, modify, or change what is weak. *The Independent Writer* provides ample assignments and workshops with exercises, activities, and games for you to strengthen your writing process.

Contents

Fourth Workshop Section
Mechanical Conventions

Appendixes

Process Writing in a Workshop Atmosphere

WORKSHOP WRITING

You might think, as most students do, that an introduction to a book is unnecessary and that you should go right to Chapter One. This introduction, however, is different. In essence, it provides a step-by-step approach to process writing in a workshop atmosphere. Once you are familiar with this approach, you will be able to enjoy the finer points of *The Independent Writer*. Therefore, take plenty of time and carefully go through the rest of this introduction in order to improve and enrich your writing process.

THE WRITING PROCESS

The writing process involves three general steps: prewriting, drafting, and revising. Writers do not necessarily move from Step One to Step Two to Step Three, ending up very comfortably with a perfect product. During their writing process writers often backtrack, leap forward, and backtrack again. But familiarity with these steps will help you develop *your* personal writing process.

Step One: Prewriting

The writing process begins with the generation of ideas. *The Independent Writer* provides you with specific prewriting suggestions for every assignment. Additionally, you will have opportunities to enrich your prewriting process in four chapters: "Journal Writing," "Brainstorming," "Notetaking," and "Thesis and Topic Statements" (Chapters 24–27). But to begin with, here are some general prewriting methods to think about. You might

1. develop an idea that you have been thinking about (the think/write method);
2. brainstorm a topic by talking with other people (the talk/write method);
3. read until an idea of your own comes (the read/write method);
4. watch a movie, sports event, or other performance; then write about it (the see/write method);
5. write about something in which you have participated (the experience/write method);
6. simply write until an idea comes (the write/write method); or
7. be told what to write about (the assign/write method).

At some point during the prewriting stage, you should begin to control and limit your piece of writing according to six main writing variables: topic, audience, purpose, format, voice, and situation. You will have an opportunity to experience these writing variables later in this introductory section by composing a short piece of writing.

Step Two: Drafting

The drafting stage of the writing process involves the composing of your assignment and the shaping and organizing of it so that it communicates exactly what you want. At this stage of the process, you will be considering the selection and organization of your information, your sentence structure, and your word choice.

The Independent Writer provides specific suggestions for drafting each assignment, as well as finished products of student and professional writing at the end of each assignment. In addition, you will find special drafting help in three chapters: "Beginnings, Middles, and Endings," "Unity," and "Coherence" (Chapters 28–30). Finally, you can refer to other workshop chapters when you require help with a specific writing technique or sentence structure. As you compose, you will probably make many changes, perhaps even write several drafts, before you proceed to Step Three.

Step Three: Revising

Revision is an ongoing process for every writer. In fact, most writers revise their work many times both before and after they show it to others for editorial comments and suggestions. Although you can and should revise your work by yourself, modern research has shown that receiving comments and suggestions from your peers is more helpful. Although at first you may be reluctant to show your fellow students your writing, you will soon discover that this kind of sharing can create a happy working situation; not only do you learn a great deal from your fellow students, but you will also be able to share with them what you know. The learner becomes a teacher and the teacher becomes a learner.

Every assignment in *The Independent Writer* provides a checklist of revising questions for you and your peers to consider; thus, you will always have guidance when you edit a paper. In addition, the First Workshop Section offers two chapters of specific information to make your revising process as smooth as possible: "Self-Editing, Peer-Editing, and Instructor-Editing" and "Unwriting" (Chapters 31–32).

Ideally, the writing process will help you produce a publishable paper. *Publishable* simply means that, in your opinion, your product is ready to present to a final reader. If this reader finds any difficulty in understanding what you have written, the writing process on that particular product is not over, and you may have to take more time to bring it to the publishable stage.

USING *THE INDEPENDENT WRITER*

Besides this introductory section, *The Independent Writer* has one Assignment and four Workshop sections. You are *not* expected to complete everything in this textbook in a single term, so you should become familiar with its contents as soon as possible to see what portions of it can best fulfill your immediate needs. As you go through the textbook, you may find parts that—for you—are too easy, too difficult, or inappropriate. In consultation with your instructor, you both can decide on the parts that are appropriate and challenging and which both of you believe can help you become a better writer.

The Assignment Section: Formats for Writing Nonfiction

The Assignment Section is designed for you to use with the assistance of your instructor-editor and your peers. In this section you can become involved in many real-life projects, all with strategies to shape your writing at each stage of the writing process. Since writing just for the sake of writing often produces bad results, you should always consider a real audience and a real purpose when you write.

You can follow the assignments according to one of the groupings found in the Special-Interest Programs section of the Appendix. Your first task, however, is to begin with the Introductory Assignment on the following page. It will serve to guide you through the steps of the writing process as you do an actual assignment.

The First Workshop Section: Content and Organization

This section presents all the details of the writing process. If you are having any difficulty with any stage of your writing process (prewriting, drafting, or revising), you can read the relevant chapter and do the exercises with a partner (a fellow student at school or a friend or relative at home). If you own, or have access to, a computer, you will also find in this section a chapter on how to implement this textbook and the writing process with word processing.

Once you have developed your own writing process and are able to produce desirable products each time you write, you will no longer need to refer to the chapters in this section.

The Second Workshop Section: Style

This section is also designed for you to work with a partner. It deals primarily with specific techniques that will improve your writing style. Furthermore, each chapter in this section will culminate with a special writing assignment that you can do *for* your partner. You can work on the chapters in any order, as well as complete only those portions of a chapter that you require to help you refine a particular stylistic technique.

The Third Workshop Section: Sentence Combining and Variety

This section is designed for individualized learning; you can work on this section by yourself, at home, or at school. Basically, the exercises in these chapters will help you improve your sentence structure through the use of sentence combining. Suggested answers are provided for all sentence work so that you can check your answers yourself. You should begin with the first two chapters because they will help you develop a common language that is useful when you talk about sentence combining. These chapters also illustrate all the sentence patterns found in the rest of the Third Workshop Section.

The Fourth Workshop Section: Mechanical Conventions

The previous sections of *The Independent Writer* approach writing from a positive viewpoint. Error is seldom mentioned. The Fourth Workshop Section, however, is designed as a handbook so that you can zero in on bothersome writing errors in order to eliminate them from your composing process.

There are two ways to approach this section: (1) During an editing session, your editors may point out spelling, punctuation, and grammatical errors that you have made. If they continually bring the same kinds of errors to your attention, do the chapter dealing with those problems. By working through the chapter with a partner, you can eliminate the errors from your writing. (2) Each chapter in this section begins with a short quiz. Take the quiz and then evaluate your results by locating the correct responses in the Suggested Answers section. Obviously, if you answer the entire quiz correctly, you should not waste your time on the chapter. If you do poorly, you should work on the exercises and games with a partner. Try to find a partner who is more confident about the chapter than you. Your partner, by following the suggestions in each chapter, will become your personal tutor. When you learn writing mechanics and conventions in this way, *you* take control of mastering what you have not yet learned or have forgotten.

INTRODUCTORY ASSIGNMENT

Introduction

Because the best way to learn how to do something is to actually do it, you can learn about the writing process by working through this assignment. Remember these points as you work:

1. *Concentrate on each part of the process* rather than on the finished product. The purpose of this assignment is to familiarize yourself with the format of this book and with the writing process.

2. *Be prepared to try new things*. By working through the steps of this assignment, concentrating on the writing variables, and participating in a workshop atmosphere, you may discover that you are on the way to becoming an independent writer.

3. *Relax*. Modern research has shown that a knowledge of the writing process makes writing easier and more interesting.

Assignment

Write a 125-word piece about some aspect of American society that *concerns* you.

Prewriting Suggestions

As you begin this assignment and start to think about something in American society that you like or dislike, you have already begun the writing process. The following prewriting steps will help you to determine your topic, audience, purpose, format, voice, situation, and thesis statement.

Topic Ideas

The possibilities for specific topics for this assignment are infinite and the methods for choosing one are many. To generate ideas for a topic for this assignment quickly, focus your attention on things in America that you both like and dislike. To help you think more systematically, draw two columns: label one "Like" and the other "Dislike." Now jot down specific aspects of American society, putting them in the appropriate column. Below is what student Joe Davis produced in his two columns.

Like	Dislike
educational opportunities	insanity plea
capital punishment	heroin
democracy	excessive spending by Congress
medical breakthroughs	
particle beam defense system	racism
martial arts	The bomb
free enterprise	obesity
The freedom to go after a dream	55 - mph speed limit
	communism

Broad Topic

After you have written down as many ideas as you can, decide which of these you most like or most dislike. This single idea will be your *broad topic* for the assignment. On a separate piece of paper, record all of your prewriting information, starting with the *broad topic*. Joe wrote:

Broad topic: Heroin

The fact that you have decided on your broad topic does not mean that you are ready to compose your paper, even though without something worthwhile to write about, you will never have a satisfactory product. Before you begin to compose your piece, you should consider the other aspects (or *writing variables*) which will affect your attitude towards your topic and what you say about it. Concentrating on the other writing variables (limited topic, audience, purpose, format, voice, and situation) will help you focus on a particular attitude or point of view, and present a *thesis statement*, which will control the development of your entire piece of writing. (These variables will be discussed in detail on the following pages.)

Limited Topic

Now that you have selected your broad topic, consider narrowing it to a workable *limited topic*. Using your broad topic, you can start to classify or divide it into a more manageable idea. Although there is an entire chapter in *The Independent Writer* on classification and division (Chapter 7), which you can refer to later, narrow your topic by producing a flowchart similar to Joe's partial one shown here. Notice how each

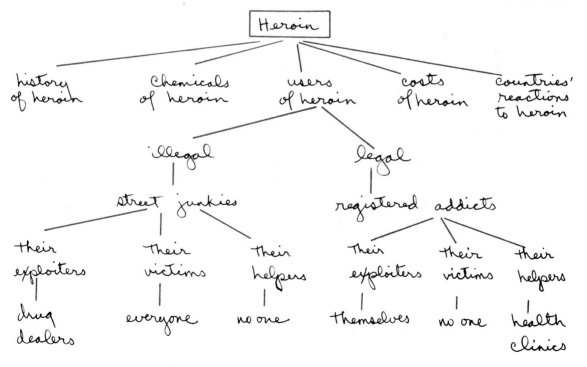

classification or division brings him closer to the topic he wants to write about. Do you see how he could have arrived at a very different narrow topic if he had shifted his focus only slightly (for example, to history, chemicals, users, costs, or, as the following flowchart demonstrates, countries' reactions)?

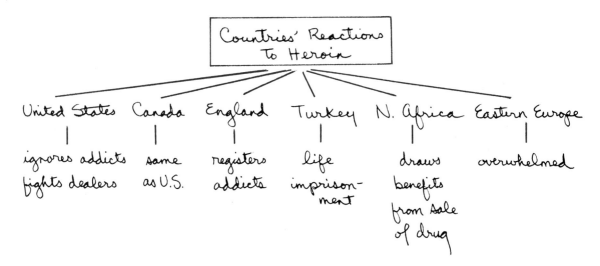

After you have classified and divided your broad topic to the point where you have a workable limited topic, record it on your separate piece of paper. Joe recorded:

Limited topic: Legalizing heroin for a registered addict

Audience

Now that you have selected your limited topic, consider your *audience*. Will your audience be real or fictitious? If real, will you give your intended reader your finished product? Weak writing occurs when a writer has no sense of audience; the writer has written either to no one in particular or to everyone in general. If you have no real person that you want to write to, choose an imaginary audience. Your writing will then have a good sense of direction. Your peer- and instructor-editors should easily be able to sense your imagined audience.

Choose an audience other than your instructor for this course. Because *The Independent Writer* encourages you to make all of your writing real, you should consider your instructor as one of your editors, not as your final reader. For his intended reader, Joe considered the following: his wife, his congressman, a twelve-year-old acquaintance who is completely ignorant about heroin, an imaginary drug addict, and fellow students who may be tempted to try heroin. (Can you see how Joe would have to change his writing style for each intended reader? A single piece of writing could not possibly satisfy them all.) Write down your intended audience as Joe has done, saying whether your audience is real or imagined:

Audience: My congressman. Real. I intend to send it to him.

Purpose

What would you like to tell your reader about the topic? By thinking about the reasons for wanting to write about a particular aspect of American society, you will discover your *purpose* for writing the assignment. Joe considered the following reasons for writing to his congressman: to inform him about Great Britain's program of legalized heroin, to describe a junkie, to argue that heroin should be legalized for registered addicts, to tell him a story about a group of your high-school heroin addicts, and to explain how a junkie feels. Can you see that each purpose would make a different piece of writing even if the limited topic and the audience remained the same? Record your purpose as Joe has done:

Purpose: To convince my audience to introduce a bill legalizing heroin

Format

Consider your *format*. Because you are doing this assignment to familiarize yourself with the writing process, feel free to write in any format appropriate to your purpose: a self-contained paragraph, poem, short story, or other format. The only restriction is that your piece of writing should be short—about 125 words. Joe considered writing either a self-contained paragraph, a poem, or an advertisement.

Are you beginning to see how your consideration of each of the writing variables will make your piece of writing more specific and precise? Can you see that each format would make a different piece of writing even if the topic, audience, and purpose remained the same? Write your format as Joe has done:

Format: Self-contained expository paragraph

Voice

Consider the *voice* you intend to use. Most of the time you will write from your own viewpoint, voicing your opinions openly in a straightforward style. Other times you may pretend someone or something else wrote your piece. For example, there may be times when you wish to satirize your topic, by letting your audience "see" it from a child's viewpoint. You might, therefore, use a child's vocabulary and sentence structure but, despite all the innocence, deliver several lethal blows. If you do this, you are assuming a *persona*. By using a persona, you can often make the expression of your point of view more effective than if you spoke in your own voice. You could also pretend that you are a visitor from outer space because you want to criticize a particular injustice in society that would look strange to an alien. By looking at the injustice from a nonhuman point of view, you can often make your readers see the problem more clearly. Or you could write about hunting from the persona of an animal on the endangered species list. What could be the effect?

Joe considered writing his paragraph from his own point of view, from the point of view of someone who does not know about the existence of heroin or heroin addicts, or from the point of view of the son of an addict. Can you see that each voice would result in a different approach to the topic even if the other four writing variables remained the same? Write your voice as Joe has done:

Voice: My own

If you choose to use a persona, provide several details about it; for example:

> *Voice*: Persona of a Martian who has never heard of heroin or seen an addict

Situation

You should now consider the *situation* surrounding the occasion of your writing experience. If you want to become a good writer (and most people would love to be able to express themselves well on paper), you must forget that you are a student and that you are writing an assignment that will, perhaps, be graded. Rather, you are a writer of a real piece of writing for a real reason to a real audience with every intention of giving it to your intended reader. Once you approach your writing process with this positive outlook, you can consider both *your* situation and *your audience's* situation because both might affect your writing.

Joe first considered his *real* situation as follows:

> *My situation*: I am a good student, husband, and father. I have never tried heroin and never intend to. I respect my congressman and his position of power.

Then he considered his audience's *real* situation:

> *Audience's situation*: My congressman doesn't know me. He has never publicly mentioned the heroin problem in America.

As a result, Joe could make the following assumptions about his audience:

> *Value judgment*: I can assume that my audience isn't aware of the heroin problem in the United States. In fact, I wonder how concerned he is.

Based on his and his audience's real situations as well as the value judgment that he placed on his audience, Joe reflected on how the situation would affect his writing style. He recorded the following details to help him focus on an appropriate style for his piece of writing:

> *Results of situation:* Because I am informed about my topic and my reader is probably uninformed, I should be careful with the terms I use. I shouldn't use jargon (for example, dust, snow, high, etc.). I will have to use clear, general terms. I will also use an objective tone (I better look at Chapter 34) in getting my points across. Also, I will use formal language and medium-to-long sentences. I want my audience to think I am writing directly to him; therefore, I will use second person ("you") whenever possible.

Notice how different the final piece of writing would be if Joe considered the following *imaginary* situation for himself:

> *My situation*: I am an addict who wants to kick the habit.

And the following *imagined* situation for his audience:

> *Audience's situation*: His daughter died as a result of an overdose of heroin.

Joe placed the following value judgment on his imaginary audience:

> *Value judgment*: I do not approve of my audience. I think he is hypocritical because he has never publicly acknowledged the true reasons surrounding the death of his daughter. He is, in fact, totally familiar with the drug scene.

With such an imagined situation, Joe's writing style would have to be quite different from the above real situation.

> *Results of situation*: Because there is a great distance between me and my audience but a close association between my limited topic and him, I'll have to be careful of my word choice. I won't be able to persuade him to my way of thinking if he feels that I don't approve of him. Because I'm pretending to be a heroin addict, however, I'll use jargon terms freely. I'll vary my sentence structure and use sentences of medium-to-short length. My tone will be subjective and I will use second-person point of view.

Can you see how your consideration of various situations will affect your writing style even if the other five writing variables remain constant?

Write your situation, your audience's situation, your value judgment, and a few lines on how your writing style will be affected. The following suggestions should help you record the complex but extremely useful writing variable of situation:

Writer's situation: State your feelings, attitudes, and relationship toward your limited topic and your audience. Make sure you indicate whether the situation is real or imagined. If you are using a persona, provide a situation for the persona as well.

Audience's situation: State your audience's feelings, attitudes, and relationship toward your limited topic and you. State if your audience's situation is real or imagined. If you have an imagined audience, you will have to make up an imagined situation for them. Present only the facts.

Value judgment: For a real audience, interpret the facts as accurately as you can; for an imagined audience, interpret the facts to fit your purpose.

Results of situation: The more you write about how the situations will affect your writing style, the easier your drafting process will be.

Brainstorming

What you have been doing up to now during your prewriting activities is often referred to as *brainstorming*. Throughout *The Independent Writer*, the term *brainstorming* is used to define two methods of generating ideas and supporting evidence for ideas. You may brainstorm either alone or with other people until your idea becomes workable enough for you to begin to write your first draft. When you brainstorm alone, you should imagine storming your own subconscious for ideas and evidence to support them. When you brainstorm with other people, you brainstorm the subconscious of those in your "think tank" for their ideas and supporting evidence. Although both methods are valuable, two or more minds working together will usually produce a larger number of different ideas for you to consider. Furthermore, in a group-brainstorming session, you may often be able to see flaws in your thinking before you begin your first draft.

"*All right, Wilhelm, we have the child walking through the woods.*"

"*Please, Jacob, don't you think we've been using the woods too much?*"

"*Woods are always good, Wilhelm. Now, who does the child meet?*"

"*We did that, Wilhelm.*"

"*Perhaps a dwarf or two?*"

"*How about a wolf, Jacob?*"

Drawing by Stevenson; © 1980 The New Yorker Magazine, Inc.

All of Chapter 25 is devoted to brainstorming techniques. At a later date you will probably study it so that you will have all the techniques at your disposal. In the meantime, go through the following brainstorming technique known as Aristotle's Topics by yourself or with a few of your peers in order to generate support for your limited topic. Record and keep all your brainstorming notes; they will be helpful during both your drafting and revising processes. Do not be concerned about how you record your information—both fragments and full sentences are helpful. Notice how Joe recorded his brainstorming notes. Study them and then begin your own.

ARISTOTLE'S TOPICS	IDEAS
Definition	Heroin is an addictive opiate synthesized from morphine. Heroin addicts fall into two categories: street junkies and registered addicts.

continued

ARISTOTLE'S TOPICS	**IDEAS**
Comparison and Contrast	Street junkies would do anything for a "fix." Registered addicts are treated on medical plans without much expense.
Cause and Effect	Street junkies steal, cheat, and kill. Supervised addicts get cured. If heroin were legalized, black market would disappear. Less crime on the streets.
Supporting Evidence	Diseased junkies die every day. Registered addicts get treatment from governmental departments.

If you do not have much supporting evidence after using Aristotle's Topics, choose another brainstorming technique from Chapter 25 and produce another set of prewriting notes. There are so many different brainstorming ideas to choose from that you are sure to find one or two techniques that will become your favorite methods of generating ideas and supporting evidence.

In order to brainstorm his topic in more detail and to produce more supporting evidence, Joe used three of the techniques from Chapter 25. For his results, see the exercises on Senses Cluster, Newspaper Reporter's Questions, and Absurd Analogies in Chapter 25.

Thesis Statement

Developing a workable limited topic with a consistent point of view is the ultimate reward of a worthwhile brainstorming session. Once you have plenty of supporting evidence, you are nearly ready to draft your paper. In a brainstorming session, you will probably discover what you want to say in your *thesis statement*: the main idea of your piece of writing. Then you will be able to compose a clear, precise thesis statement that you can use to control the rest of your writing. Remember, your audience does not see all of the prewriting that you have done up to now; however, your audience will see your thesis statement.

Compose a thesis statement that clearly focuses on the specific idea contained in your limited topic. A thesis statement is like a contract that you make with your readers. If you do not have a stated thesis, you can hardly expect readers to stay with you for very long, wondering what you are trying to say. If you do have a worthwhile thesis statement they will expect you to fulfill your contract; that is, to support fully the main idea contained in the statement. If you do not provide sufficient support for your main idea, they will feel you have broken the contract. A thesis statement, therefore, should be exact, specific, and precise, and link your limited topic (the subject of your thesis statement) with what you want to say about it (the predicate of your thesis statement) in a complete sentence. In other words, your thesis statement should be a sentence with a complete subject and predicate.

Note: Do not compose your thesis statement until you have set your writing variables and completed brainstorming for ideas and supporting evidence. Composing one too soon limits and stifles your prewriting process.

As you examine Joe's attempts to compose his thesis statement, can you see why he eliminated the first two? What sort of papers would he have composed had he used them?

SUBJECT	PREDICATE
Heroin	affects many Americans
Because the street heroin junkie and the registered heroin addict are both alike and unalike, they	should be treated differently.
Legalizing heroin	will benefit Americans.

If, for this introductory assignment, you have composed a workable thesis statement that controls and limits your main idea, you should begin your first draft. Thesis statements are discussed in further detail in Chapter 27.

Drafting Suggestions

As you write your first draft for this assignment, you may find that other significant ideas emerge. If you discover a new insight or approach to your topic, use it as the basis for another piece of writing and begin the prewriting process again. Never dismiss good ideas. In fact, you should return to the prewriting process to generate more supporting evidence and look forward to the possibility of producing an even better paper.

Listen to Your Inner Voice

Whereas you may receive a great deal of help during your prewriting and revising processes, you will draft your piece of writing alone. The more familiar you become with the contents of *The Independent Writer*, the easier your drafting process will become. Many chapters of the text will help you improve your organization and style. Others will help you improve your sentence structure so that you become familiar with various modes of expression. Finally, other chapters will help you choose vocabulary to reflect the right meaning and exact slant you want. All drafts, however, should echo your inner voice as a writer. Your work must reflect *your* thoughts, not others'. In the end, it matters little that your sentence structure and word choice are accurate and varied if you are merely working with material that your readers already know. Good writing is personal; therefore, express your own opinions and thoughts during your drafting process. By setting your inner voice free during your drafting process, you will soon discover ways of making your writing personal, specific, and, ultimately, original.

Follow Your Writing Variables

Throughout your entire drafting process, follow your writing variables. Keep them in front of you as you compose. Write *to* your audience; consider *your* and *their* situations; keep your purpose clear; maintain your format; keep your voice consistent. If, by any chance, you bog down during a draft, you may find that you need to change one or more of your writing variables. If you do make a single change, draw up a completely new set of writing variables. You may find that other things will be affected when you make even one minor change.

Write a Clear Thesis Statement

Present your thesis statement clearly so that your audience will appreciate and understand what you are writing about. For this assignment you might like to present you central idea near the beginning of your paper; for future assignments you should study Chapter 27 for ways of placing thesis and topic statements effectively in all parts of your work.

Organize Your Presentation

Think about how you are going to develop your thesis statement. You would not want to confuse your reader by organizing your draft following the random method you used to collect supporting evidence during your prewriting process. There are many methods of organization (comparison/contrast, cause and effect, general to particular, and so on); perhaps for this assignment you might use the more straightforward chronological, sequential, or climactic order (if these terms are unfamiliar, see Chapter 29). As you write, present details or arguments to help your reader see what you see, feel what you feel, or share the thoughts that you have.

Write an Effective Conclusion

Conclude your piece by summing up your central idea in a way that you think will interest your reader.

Prepare Your Draft for Revision

In preparation for a revising session, write a relatively clean, double-spaced copy of your assignment and add an appropriate title. The following is an example of Joe's final draft model. As you read it, think about what you as a peer-editor would say to help him revise his paragraph.

Writing Variables
for Introductory
Assignment   Joe Davis

Broad topic: Heroin

Limited topic: Legalizing heroin for a registered addict

Audience: My congressman. Real. I intend to send it to him

Purpose: To convince my audience to introduce a bill legalizing heroin

Format: Self-contained expository paragraph

Voice: My own

Writer's situation: I am a good student, husband, and father. I have never tried heroin and never intend to. I respect my congressman and his position of power.

Audience's situation: My congressman doesn't know me. He has never publicly mentioned the heroin problem in America.

Value judgment: I can assume that my audience isn't aware of the heroin problem in the United States. In fact, I wonder how concerned he is about the problem.

Results of situation: Because I am informed about my topic and my reader is probably uninformed, I should be careful with the terms I use. I shouldn't use jargon (for example, dust, snow, high, etc.). I will have to use clear, general terms. I will also use an objective tone (I better look at Chapter 34) in getting my points across. Also, I will use formal language and medium-to-long sentences. I want my audience to think I am

---

A Few Words about Heroin

Heroin causes more of a versatile range of problems than almost any other single drug. The illegal powder not only causes self-destruction, but also more corruption and violence than any other evil in our society. Prostitution, diseases, robbery, and murder all find strong motives in the drug. After fighting a losing battle to eliminate heroin for several decades, why not consider an alternative approach: legalize it! Legalizing heroin will benefit Americans. While the very words sound absurd, the idea has merit. Consider heroin addicts falling into two categories: street junkies and registered addicts. Street junkies do anything for a fix; registered addicts are treated on medical plans. Whereas a junkie administering his own fix runs the risk of overdosing, breaking off a needle in his arm, and catching hepatitis, the registered addict receiving his injection at a clinic fares well. Recognizing his addiction as a disease, he eventually seeks methadone substitution. Meanwhile, he can always trade a few Coke bottles and afford his fix without having to turn to crime and violence to support his habit. Unfortunately, his street counterpart digs himself deeper and deeper into oblivion and ignores that external help exists. Heroin's major problem being the high street cost, he gambles with his life, totally hopeless in his decrepitude, suffering from starvation and diseases, and resorting to countless crimes to satisfy the exigence of his dealer, often a junkie himself. A legalization of heroin would destroy the illegal drug network and give all junkies a chance to live

writing directly to him;
therefore, I will use second
person ("you") whenever
possible.

Thesis statement: Legalizing
heroin will benefit
Americans.

decently under the control and assistance of health
professionals. Socially, the recognition and registration
of most street junkies, as attempted in Great Britain,
could be the beginning of a thorough and adequate handling
of this plague in our "Ship of State." In addition,
everyone throughout the country would benefit from the
large decrease in burglaries, muggings, prostitution, and
murder.

You are now ready to move on to the next step: the revising process. So that you can experience the rewards of engaging in a peer-editing session, have the following ready:

- All of your brainstorming results
- A list of your writing variables
- A clean, neat, well-spaced copy of your assignment

Revising Suggestions

Professional writers depend on their editors to help them with their revising process: you can use your peers and instructor for this important step in your writing process. Research has shown that when students learn to edit each other's work, their own writing style improves significantly.

If you have never engaged in a peer-editing session, this short introductory assignment is an ideal opportunity for you to learn the basics of editing someone else's writing. Being a skillful editor is not easy; however, if you follow these suggestions, you will be on your way to becoming a successful editor. Remember the more you say about the pieces you edit, the easier it will be for the writers to revise their work.

1. After forming a peer group of three, exchange your completed drafts and lists of writing variables with one member of your group. (Keep your brainstorming notes handy in case one of your editors wishes to see them.)

2. Read the material quickly to get a sense of the writing variables and what the piece of writing is about.

3. Read the draft again, but this time write your reactions directly on the text. To help you make worthwhile comments, keep in mind all of the writing variables of the assignment you are editing; for example, if the intended audience is a twelve-year-old girl or a member of Congress, edit accordingly.

4. Whenever appropriate, use the proofreaders' symbols reproduced on the inside covers. They help speed up the editing process and provide writer and editors with a common language.

5. While editing, give plenty of praise.

6. Check the organization of the paper to see that it makes the meaning and purpose clear. If not, suggest to the writer what should be added, deleted, changed, or moved. You may feel inadequate to suggest that your peers make major changes to their papers, but such content suggestions are far more helpful than pointing out a few spelling or punctuation errors.

7. You might like to answer the following specific questions based on the writing variables and the paper you are editing. Record your answers directly on the writer's draft.

  a. Has the writer expressed the thesis statement clearly?

  b. Does the paper fulfill its purpose?

  c. Has the writer kept the intended reader in mind throughout the entire paper?

  d. Has the writer followed the conventions of the format? For example, a purely descriptive paragraph should not contain exposition, just as a sonnet should have fourteen, not sixteen, lines.

  e. Are the voice and point of view consistent?

  f. Does the style of the piece reflect the writer's and audience's situations?

8. Now answer the following specific questions based on the paper you are editing. Record your answers on the writer's draft.

  a. What do you like best about the paper?

  b. What do you like least? What do you think the writer can do about it? Even if you do not know how to fix a problem, telling a writer that you became confused is extremely helpful. By talking it through after the editing session, the writer and the editor can come up with possible revisions. Perhaps engaging in an additional brainstorming session in order to introduce more supporting evidence into the paper may be worthwhile.

(The answers to the next three questions might be essential in clearing up something that initially confused the editor.)

  c. What further details should the writer add? Why?

  d. What should the writer leave out? Why?

  e. What should the writer rearrange? Why?

  f. Are there any problems with "mechanics": spelling, punctuation, or sentence structure? You may correct any error you see or just say, "I don't think this is right. How about checking it?"

  g. Do the sentences flow logically from one to the other? If not, offer as much help as you can.

  h. Are there enough connecting or transitional words to keep the reader on track?

  i. Is the title interesting?

9. When you have edited one paper from your peer group, you should get the other paper and repeat the above eight steps. Write your comments directly on the paper, even though it will already have been edited by one of your classmates. Read the previous editor's comments as well, and feel free to agree or disagree with those comments as well as to add your own.

10. Read what two of Joe's peers said about his writing variables and his paper. Do you agree with their comments? What more would you have said?

Writing Variables
for Introductory Assignment   Joe Davis

<u>Broad</u> <u>topic</u>: Heroin

<u>Limited</u> <u>topic</u>: Legalizing heroin for a registered addict

<u>Audience</u>: My congressman. Real. I intend to send it to him.

<u>Purpose</u>: To convince my audience to introduce a bill legalizing
heroin

<u>Format</u>: Self-contained expository paragraph

<u>Voice</u>: My own

<u>Writer's</u> <u>situation</u>: I am a good student, husband, and father. I
have never tried heroin and never intend to. I respect my
congressman and his position of power.

<u>Audience's</u> <u>situation</u>: My congressman doesn't know me. He has never
publicly mentioned the heroin problem in America.

How do you know?

Better check this.

<u>Value</u> <u>judgment</u>: I can assume that my audience isn't aware of the
heroin problem in the United States. In fact, I wonder how
concerned he is about the problem.

<u>Results</u> <u>of</u> <u>situation</u>: Because I am informed about my topic and my
reader is probably uninformed, I should be careful with the terms I
use. I shouldn't use jargon (dust, snow, high, fix, etc.). I will
have to use clear, general terms. I will also use an objective tone
(I had better look at Chapter 34) in getting my points across.
Also, I will use formal language and medium-to-long sentences. I
want my audience to think I am writing directly to him; therefore,
I will use second person ("you") whenever possible.

This is good!

<u>Thesis</u> <u>statement</u>: Legalizing heroin will benefit Americans.

Write a more specific thesis statement.

I AGREE!

An interesting idea (I AGREE!)

A Few Words about Heroin   *a catchier Title needed*

WORDY

Heroin causes more of a <u>versatile range of problems</u> than almost

any other single drug. The illegal powder not only causes

self-destruction, but also more corruption and violence than any

other evil in our society. Prostitution, diseases, robbery, and

NOT CLEAR

murder all find strong motives in the drug. After fighting a

losing battle to eliminate heroin for several decades, why not

MENTION YOUR THESIS EARLIER

consider an alternative approach: legalize it! Legalizing heroin

will benefit Americans. While the very words sound absurd, the idea

IDEAS, NOT WORDS, SOUND ABSURD.

has merit. Consider heroin addicts falling into two categories:

street junkies and registered addicts. Street junkies <u>do anything</u> *This sentence*

for a fix; registered addicts <u>are treated on medical plans</u>. Whereas *doesn't*

balance.

LONG *Fix it.*

SENTENCE a junkie administering his own fix runs the risk of overdosing,

(TOO HARD

TO READ) breaking off a needle in his arm, and catching hepatitis, the

registered addict receiving his injection at a clinic fares well.

Recognizing his addiction as a disease, he eventually seeks

methadone substitution. Meanwhile, he can always trade a few Coke

bottles and afford his fix without having to turn to crime and

violence to support his habit. Unfortunately, his street

counterpart digs himself deeper and deeper into oblivion and

ignores that external help exists. Heroin's major problem being the *IS THAT*

These words high street cost, he gambles with his life, totally hopeless in his *HEROIN'S*

are not in *MAJOR*

keeping <u>decrepitude</u>, suffering from starvation and diseases, and resorting *PROBLEM?*

with your

word choice to countless crimes to satisfy the <u>exigence</u> of his dealer, often a

junkie himself. A legalization of heroin would destroy the illegal

drug network and give all junkies a chance to live decently under

the control and assistance of health professionals. Socially, the

recognition and registration of most street junkies, <u>as attempted</u>

Should <u>in Great Britain</u>, could be the beginning of a thorough and adequate

there be *WHAT'S THIS?*

more handling of this <u>plague in our "Ship of State."</u> In addition, *WOW!*

details?

everyone throughout the country would benefit from the large

decrease in burglaries, muggings, prostitution, and murder.

A lot of good things: word choice and sentence variety.
Organization not clear. It's not contrast or cause/effect.
Make your point clearer. Why not start with your Topic sentence?

11. Once you have had your assignment edited twice, read the comments. Then if there is anything you do not understand or agree with, talk to your peers so that you can rewrite, revise, and reform your paper before you submit it to your instructor-editor. If your peers are willing to edit your revised paper, you should certainly let them do so before going on to the next step of the revising process.

12. Present your final revision and your set of writing variables to your instructor for another editing session. How much you have changed them from your originals will depend not only on how helpful your peers have been but on how many of their suggestions you have followed. Remember, the responsibility to accept or reject what your peer-editors suggest is always yours. In Chapter 31 you will discover various ways to engage in peer-editing sessions.

13. Read Joe's revision and note the changes he has made since he had his paragraph peer-edited and the editorial comments and suggestions made by his instructor. The only writing variable that Joe changed substantially was his thesis statement.

A good controversial topic
Well organized - good style
Fine use of vocabulary

Try for a more provocative title.
A question?

Legalizing Heroin

Thesis statement clear

Heroin should be made available to addicts through a controlled legalization. While the idea sounds rather absurd at first, it has merit; the *illegal state of the* drug not only causes self-destruction but also more corruption and violence than any other evil in our society. The

When did heroin become illegal?

time has come, after decades of fighting a losing battle, to consider a solution other than prohibition. Consider heroin addicts falling into two categories: *awk* street junkies and registered addicts. A junkie "shooting" his own fix runs the risk of overdosing, breaking off a needle in his arm, or catching hepatitis from the *an* unsterilized needle. A registered addict fares well; *better* he

introduce cause and effect

receives his injections from a clinic and follows a medical plan that [will eventually support him into seeking methadone substitution to control his disease. Meanwhile, he can always trade a few Coke bottles and afford his injection without having to turn to crime and violence to support his habit.] Unfortunately, his

reform and tighten

street counterpart digs himself deeper and deeper into oblivion and ignores the existence of any external help. Gambling with his life, totally hopeless in his decrepitude, he fears drying out cold

jargon →

turkey, malnutrition, and disease until he finally resorts to crime and prostitution to satisfy the increasing exigence of the "pusher," often a junkie himself. The legalization of heroin would destroy the black-market network and give all junkies a

tighten

chance to live decently under the control and assistance of health *wordy* professionals. The recognition and registration of most street *redundant*

make clear e.g. "using legal heroin"

addicts, finally aware of the presence of an open door, [could be] the *be stronger* beginning of a thorough and adequate *wordy* treatment of this dehumanizing plague. In addition, everyone throughout the country would benefit

make this the penultimate sentence.

from the large decrease in burglaries, muggings, prostitution, violence, and murder.

Your last sentence should focus on your Thesis:
legalizing heroin.

14. In some cases your instructor may ask you to revise an assignment. This can be particularly frustrating, especially if you have already rewritten it several times for yourself and two more times for your peers. For all writers, *writing means rewriting*.

15. You will only really know whether your product works when you present it to your intended audience.

16. Read Joe's final draft, which he sent to his congressman (one way to publish your work). Keep in mind his writing variables. *Note*: You would not give your final audience your writing variables. Why?

Product

```
                    Why Not Legalize Heroin?

     Heroin should be made available to addicts through controlled
legalization. While the idea sounds rather absurd at first, it has
merit; the illegal status of the drug causes more corruption and
violence than any other evil in our society. The time has come,
after six decades of fighting a losing battle, to consider a
solution other than prohibition. Let us compare two types of heroin
addicts: street junkies and registered addicts. A junkie
"shooting" his own fix runs the risk of overdosing, breaking off
a needle in his arm, or catching hepatitis from an unsterilized
needle. Under clinical supervision, a registered addict fares
better. Because he no longer has the pressure of meeting the drug's
high street cost, he can follow a medical plan that could
eventually lead to his accepting methadone, a less dangerous
substitute, or perhaps kicking the habit altogether. By contrast,
his street counterpart digs himself deeper and deeper into
oblivion. Terrified of going "cold turkey" and totally hopeless
in his decrepitude and lack of help, the street junkie faces
malnutrition and disease until he finally resorts to crime and
prostitution to satisfy his expensive habit. The legalization of
heroin would destroy the black-market network and give all junkies
a chance to live decently with the assistance of health
professionals. In addition, every citizen would benefit from the
subsequent decrease in burglaries, muggings, prostitution,
violence, and murder. The registration of most street addicts, and
their treatment by using legal heroin, could be the end of this
dehumanizing plague.
```

Analysis

1. What are some of the differences between Joe's first and final drafts?

2. Compare Joe's final piece of writing with his brainstorming notes. (See Chapter 25 for three results of Joe's brainstorming sessions.)

3. Do you see how the steps of the writing process affected Joe's writing?

4. Is there anything that you think does not work in his final product?

5. In collecting supporting evidence for your piece of writing, did you use the same brainstorming methods as Joe? How useful were they?

6. What method of organization did Joe use to develop "Why Not Legalize Heroin?"? Prove it. What method did you use? Prove it.

7. To what degree did your peers help you revise your paper? To what degree did your instructor help you?

8. For other versions of Joe's paragraph turn to Chapter 37.

ASSIGNMENT SECTION

Formats for Writing Nonfiction

ABOUT THE ASSIGNMENTS

Because the assignments in this section are designed to meet a variety of needs, interests, and levels of ability, *you are not expected to complete all of them during a single term*. Rather, you should do the ones that your instructor or you think will meet your writing goals. Whether you are planning an academic, business, or vocational career, the assignments will help you organize your thoughts and put them on paper in your own unique way. (See Appendix A for alternate ways of completing the assignments in the Assignment Section.)

Each assignment consists of an introduction and specific suggestions on the various steps of the writing process; each is also accompanied by products of a particular mode of discourse, written by students, teachers, and professionals, so that you can see what a finished assignment looks like. You are encouraged to read these products and the accompanying analysis questions before, during, and after you do your own piece of writing.

1

Narrative Paragraph

INTRODUCTION

There are many occasions when you will want to tell or retell a good story. Narration is, therefore, the format that you will probably use most frequently. You can base a narrative on an actual experience, a totally imaginary one, or one that is a mixture of both reality and imagination. In any case, a narrative is an account of events told in such a way that the reader shares the writer's experience.

> ### Assignment
>
> In a paragraph of not more than 200 words, tell of an incident that has happened to you or to someone you know.

PREWRITING PROCESS

1. For your first narrative, choose an amusing, exciting, frightening, or significant incident that happened either to you or in your presence. It should be an incident that you remember well.

Good narrative writing involves bringing the experience to life for your reader through the use of convincing detail. Assume that your reader is prevented from seeing an incident by a high stone wall or some other barrier. You can see both the incident and your reader. Your challenge is to put the essential details of the incident into your reader's mind.

2. Choose a simple incident. Since you are limited to only 200 words, try to structure your narrative so that it fits into a single paragraph.

3. To find a suitable subject for your short narrative, write two column headings: "Incidents Involving Me" and "Incidents I Have Witnessed." Jot down in each column as many significant incidents as you can remember. For example:

Incidents Involving Me	Incidents I Have Witnessed
my first skydive	a car accident
applying for my driver's license	a supermarket robbery
the birth of my first child	my best friend's funeral
my first helicopter ride	an argument between a police officer and a drunk
a child's birthday party that I attended	

4. To decide which incident to write about, determine which one contains the most activity or conflict (a struggle with something or someone). The struggle does not have to be physical; it can be with another person, with nature, with society, or even with yourself.

It is quite possible for a particular incident to have more than one conflict; for example, your story may involve an argument with a truck driver, may take place during a snowstorm, and at the same time may deal with your struggle to control your anger.

5. Go through several brainstorming sessions in order to bring together all the events of your narrative. The following brainstorming techniques from Chapter 25 may be particularly helpful: Newspaper Reporter's Questions, Pentad, Positive/Negative/Neutral Pigeonholes, and Senses Cluster.

6. When you finish brainstorming, look over all your notes. Add additional information as it occurs to you.

7. On a fresh sheet of paper, record the events from your brainstorming sessions as they occurred in the actual situation. If you find gaps in the narrative, you may find it necessary to include additional information (either fictitious or real). Making up a detail is permissible when you write narration. Your task, however, will be to make the fictitious details sound real.

This prewriting activity will make your drafting process easier because you are already developing your method of organization (chronological order).

8. Before you draft your narrative, establish your writing variables. If the narrative is to be part of a larger piece of work (such as a letter), specify both the narrative paragraph and letter formats.

DRAFTING PROCESS

Although your instructions are to write a paragraph, you may need to use several short paragraphs to tell your story. If you provide dialogue, for example, you will need a separate paragraph each time your speaker changes. Or if your story takes place in more than one location, you may want to assist your reader by introducing each new location in a separate paragraph.

In preparing the draft of your narrative, pay particular attention to the following points:

1. Your story should have a beginning, a middle, and an end. Your *beginning* should capture your reader's interest. Which of the following opening sentences would encourage you to continue reading?

- Last month in Ashtabula County I was stung by seventeen wasps on a part of my anatomy that I won't mention and which I'm still having difficulty using.
- I was sitting in my living room, watching television.
- When I noticed smoke coming from my neighbor's window, I phoned the fire department immediately.

Your *middle* should relate events in chronological order. Details in your description of the action should bring the story to life for your reader.

Your *ending* should satisfy your reader's expectations. He or she must not feel that your story has been a waste of time or simply an elaborate trick. Which of these endings would you find unsatisfactory?

- ... and as I ran terrified down the dark alley, with the inexorable footsteps pursuing me, I woke up safe at home in my own bed.

- The snow melted. My uncle relented. And I learned to say "yes."
- The letter came. I had passed.

2. Your narrative should contain, as close to the end as possible, a *climax*—the turning point of the plot. In addition, create as much suspense as possible by delaying the climax. You can do this through the addition of a brief description or the introduction of dialogue. In addition, by using shorter sentences as you approach the climax you may add to your reader's excitement. But make sure that your use of these devices contributes to the plot, or you may lose your story line—and your reader.
3. Use action, reaction, and dialogue to help your reader experience the incident. Describe physical and facial expressions so that your reader can see your subject's emotional reactions, and introduce some actual words that were spoken during the incident.

In the following two passages, note the difference between *telling* an incident and *showing* it.

Telling

After Ran suggested that we have roast duck for our picnic and I indicated in an offhand manner that I thought it would be a marvelous idea, he handed me a wet duck to pluck. As I looked at the duck's tiny lolling head and sleepy eyes, Ran saw my concern and asked if I'd rather not pluck it. I bravely assured him that I'd be happy to do it.

Showing

"Shall we have roast duck?" said Ran.
"Marvelous idea!" I burbled, not really tuned in.
"Fine. Want to pluck it?"
I blanched as he proffered me the damp bundle. All I could see was a tiny lolling head and sleepy eyes.
"Are you squeamish? Would you rather not?" he asked, concerned.
"No, no—happy to do it," I assured him, as a dissonant chord played me sharply. (Anne Baxter, *Intermission*)

4. If you want to "stretch" the truth to make your story better, a quite acceptable practice among writers of narration, add only details that will keep your writing credible.
5. When you have completed your final draft, self-edit by applying the checklists from Chapter 31. Then proceed to the next step of the writing process.

REVISING PROCESS

When you or your peers edit your short narrative, apply the checklists from Chapter 31, as well as the following specific questions:
1. Do the writing variables and the piece of narration complement each other? To

answer this question fully, you must place yourself in the intended audience's position. Remember when you read your peer's draft that you are not the intended audience; you are simply helping the writer get the narrative ready for an audience.

2. Is your story interesting? If not, consider these questions:

  a. Is the first sentence interesting?

  b. Is there conflict?

  c. Is there suspense?

  d. Is there a climax?

  e. Is the final sentence satisfying?

3. Is your story believable? If not, would dialogue or description help to bring the story to life?

4. Is the sequence of events clear?

  a. Have you kept strictly to the story? (If there are any details that do not contribute to the narrative, you should eliminate them.)

  b. Have you told all the important things?

  c. Have you told the story in the same order as it actually happened (chronological order)?

5. Is the point of view clear and consistent? These ideas should help in evaluating consistency.

Person

Stories told in the first person help the reader to believe the incident actually happened to the writer. But whichever person you use, remember to be consistent; do not switch points of view. If you write your narrative paragraph from second-hand information (a story you are telling in which you did not take part), you may choose to write from the third-person point of view. If that is the case, do not switch to "I" or "you."

Tense

Because you will be retelling an event that took place in the past, you should use the past tense. Do not suddenly shift into the present or future tense.

Voice

Use the active rather than the passive voice for narration. *I hit the thief with a bat* is more effective than *The thief was hit with a bat by me.*

6. When you are satisfied with the overall content and organization of your short narrative, present it to your instructor-editor. Afterwards, polish it and prepare a publishable copy for your intended reader.

PRODUCTS

Here are some short narratives. As you read each one, see if you can pinpoint the writer's topic, audience, purpose, situation, and voice. If you were the intended reader, would you be satisfied with the climax? Apply the questions in the Revising Process above to all of the products.

Spooks in the Basement

by Ray McLennan, student

As a child I considered our house a warm, comforting sanctuary from an occasionally hostile outside world. Still, it contained one ominous place: the basement. Silent, cold, and dark, the basement almost certainly harboured a sinister creature of some sort. Even with all the lights on, there were always enough dark corners to shelter such a beast. With spine tingling and pulse racing, I would descend into the gloom to fetch something from the freezer for my mother, never quite sure I would return and wondering how my mother would react if I didn't. Whatever lurked in the basement never threatened when my father or any other comforting adult was present. Instead, it would wait until I was alone or with another equally imaginative youngster before darting out of the shadows. Even then it was impossible to see it directly; a noise or a faint movement in some dark corner was all that ever betrayed its presence, but that was more than enough to send me flying upstairs. Strangely enough, now that I've grown up it never seems to bother me. Perhaps that's because I don't venture downstairs anymore.

Dead Duck

from Intermission *by Anne Baxter*

The picnic spot was beside a smooth flow of river curtained with willows and bottlebrush. Lunch was laid out in small piles on flat rocks.

"Shall we have roast duck?" said Ran.

"Marvelous idea!" I burbled, not really tuned in.

"Fine. Want to pluck it?"

I blanched as he proffered me the damp bundle. All I could see was a tiny lolling head and sleepy eyes.

"Are you squeamish? Would you rather not?" he asked, concerned.

"No, no—happy to do it," I assured him, as a dissonant chord played me sharply.

The body was still warm. Its feathers were starting to dry in sticky points. Cradling it in frozen nonchalance, I sauntered stiffly to the riverbank, ostensibly to dispose of the feathers but actually to hide. I opened my hands to look. The complicated beauty of its coloring stunned me. Feeling numb, I ripped and jerked the feathers, which fell in soundless tufts on the pulpy bank. I pulled every single one, dreadfully nauseated, but like the would-be surgeon, I could scarcely faint at first blood.

The bird was naked now, skinny and pocked, dead as any murdered corpse, and so was I.

I brought it back to be trussed on a stick and cooked above the crackling fire. In minutes it was charred to a grimy kink and I felt years older and very tired. Ran said it tasted fishy from the river.

Paris

by Grace Moseley, student

April 17

Dear Folks,

We arrived in Paris, bone-tired and cranky. The bus ride to the home of my friend did little to improve our mood, nor did the lack of response to our thunderous knocking at her door. Desperately, we went next door and explained our predicament in great detail to the tiny and very wrinkled lady who answered. Eventually, with the help of our Berlitz dictionary and her nine-year-old grandson, comprehension transformed her face. Indicating she would accompany us to Hélène's mother, she painstakingly rearranged the little bun perched precariously on the back of her head, and donned her best black sweater. Relieved, we locked our packs securely in her porch and set off. After what seemed a reasonable distance, we began, amongst ourselves, to question where we were going and finally halted our guide. With her face wreathed in smiles, she spoke at great length—in meticulous French. None the wiser, we set off again, only to twice repeat this performance. Finally, much later, exhausted and desperate, I angrily clamped my hand on the old woman's shoulder. "Where are you taking us?" I bellowed. The expression on the crinkled face was uncomprehending, and at once I felt extremely foolish. Through the help of an English-speaking passerby, we learned that our eighty-five-old guide, thinking we had no money, was walking us six miles across Paris! Tears coursed down my cheeks. Tears of remorse. Tears of fatigue. Later, when a scalding bath and a cup of tea had restored us, we laughed.

Let's hope Brussels treats us better.

Love, Grace

The Discovery

by Mark Roberts, student

A few years ago, while I was at a party, I suddenly found myself very bored and decided to explore my hostess's large house. After covering three floors, I headed up still another staircase to try to find something interesting. I pushed open a hatch-type door and climbed up into what seemed to be a fairly large room. I groped for a light. The room lit up, and I was spellbound. There I stood totally surrounded by the most fantastic model railroad I had ever seen. All around me were trains, tracks, mountains, bridges, little towns, and even tiny figurines, which seemed to be frozen in the positions of all the day-to-day jobs that real people do. I felt like Gulliver himself on one of his travels. This was a storybook land, a creation with all the meticulous detail of a fine watch. In front of me was what seemed to be the control panel. Little buttons. Rows of switches. Blinking lights. This was the nerve center that put this tiny, sleeping, miniature land into motion. Hanging on one of the control levers was an engineer's hat and to my left was a padded chair on rollers. I immediately pictured the creator of this fantasy-land realm sitting in the chair, shuttling back and forth from switch to lever in godlike control of his railroad. An old cliché came to mind as I sat myself in the chair and put on the hat: "The only difference between men and boys is the size of their toys."

ANALYSIS

Spooks in the Basement

1. Who do you think is McLennan's intended reader? Are there any parts that do not seem to be directed to his intended reader? How do you feel reading something that was not intended for you to read? In what ways is this paragraph able to stand on its own; that is, to be read and enjoyed by many readers?
2. What is the tone of his piece—straightforward or ironic? Find proof to support your answer.
3. McLennan used a Positive/Negative/Neutral Pigeonhole graphic to brainstorm. See the results in Chapter 25. Is there any brainstorming detail that you think he should have included in his final product?

Dead Duck

1. Can you feel the warm, unplucked duck? How has Baxter appealed to her readers' senses? Would the scene have been more fully developed by including the sense of smell? If you have ever had a similar experience to Baxter's, then perhaps you have found a suitable topic for this assignment.

2. Try to divide this excerpt into the Positive/Negative/Neutral Pigeonhole graphic (See Chapter 25.)

Paris

1. Moseley involves her parents with her frustrations. When she finds out the old lady is not a thief but is instead trying to be helpful, her readers should be satisfied by her conclusion. In what order has Moseley listed the main incidents of her story?
2. Do you know whether the writer has one or two traveling companions? Why is this probably not a problem for her intended readers?
3. What is your feeling about her repetition of the word "tears"?

The Discovery

1. Roberts implies the climax rather than actually stating it. What is the climax?
2. What does the reader know will be the next thing to happen after the writer sits down and puts on the engineer's hat?
3. Note that the writer has used a lot of description. Do you feel that you know the room?
4. Comment on his use of "seemed to be."
5. Do his minor sentences work; in other words, do they convey clear pictures even though they are incomplete sentences?

2

Descriptive Paragraph

INTRODUCTION

Writing description can be a joyous experience, as you recreate in words what you experience through your senses. Even though you may rarely write a purely descriptive paragraph, there will be many opportunities to include descriptive elements in all other types of writing.

This assignment emphasizes the purely descriptive paragraph as an entity by itself. You will be expected to look at someone or something or to recall someone or something that you saw in the past and write a description without any exposition or narration.

Assignment

In no more than 150 words, describe a person, place, or thing so that your readers can perceive it with all of their senses.

PREWRITING PROCESS

1. To start yourself thinking about description, make a list of some of your most vivid memories. Then classify the list into categories: people, places, and things. Which category interests you most? Using one item from that category, brainstorm by Freewriting in your journal for fifteen minutes nonstop (see Chapter 24).
2. Experiment with your topic by working on one or more of the following brainstorming activities:

   a. Write a few absurd analogies in your journal. No matter what your subject is, how is it like a chair, a monkey, a toaster, a pillow?

b. If you were blind, how could you recognize your subject? Involve all of your senses *except* sight.

c. How would you describe your subject to your mother? To a Martian? To your best friend?

d. Write a journal entry to describe how one color links the parts of your subject together.

e. Observe your subject from various perspectives by listing exactly what you would see:

- Imagine yourself ten feet above your subject. Looking straight down, what do you see?
- Imagine yourself at a great distance from your subject. Look at your subject through binoculars. What is the effect? Now look through the opposite lenses. What can you still see clearly?
- Imagine yourself as a camera that records with scientific precision. Describe exactly what you see.
- Imagine yourself as an impressionistic painter. If the subject of your piece were sitting as a still life, what feature would you highlight? Why? How will you highlight the feature in your writing?

3. From all your brainstorming notes, decide which details you will use in your descriptive paragraph. On a separate piece of paper, record these descriptive details. Think of your blank piece of paper as a canvas ready for your word pictures. Record your descriptions on the page in a logical order—for example, top to bottom, near to far, or unclear to clear. Such a prewriting activity will assist your drafting process; you are already developing your method of organization (spatial order), along with the use of strong, descriptive words.

4. Review your writing variables in order to make this assignment real and worth your efforts before beginning your first draft.

DRAFTING PROCESS

1. To organize your description, start at a focal point and proceed in a logical direction, perhaps using a spatial or climactic perspective. Do not jump indiscriminately from one area to another.

2. A single, exact word (noun or verb) will make a stronger impression than one followed by a string of adjectives and adverbs. Notice how the second sentence in each pair allows readers to use their imagination:

- The noisy, untidy, bad-tempered students have gone elsewhere.
- The barbarians are lurking elsewhere.
- Discarded banana peels, candy wrappers, and assignments are scattered randomly and haphazardly on the floors of the school.
- Discarded banana peels, candy wrappers, and assignments litter the floors of the school.

3. A metaphor might breathe new life into the most mundane subject.

- The cleaning staff raises the dust and rubbish in miniature whirlwinds.
- The cleaning staff tiptoes around the piles of garbage as though crossing a mine field.

Occasionally, a writer will use an extended metaphor or analogy: every detail in the description suggests a comparison between the subject and something else. (See the products in Chapter 36 for examples.)

4. Keep in mind all five senses when you describe your subject.

- The corridors reek of chalk dust, old apple cores, and musty literature.
- Bells, shouts, and shuffling feet echo through the now-empty halls.

5. Consider the overall impression you wish to create and choose your descriptive details accordingly. Do you want your reader to like your subject? to dislike it? to be frightened? to be amused?

The careful writer of description selects details to evoke the desired reaction from the reader. Choose words with connotations or associations that will create the overall impression you are striving for. The word "skinny," for example, will create a different impression from the word "svelte," although both mean "slender."

REVISING PROCESS

See Chapter 31 for suggestions to help you or your peers to revise your descriptive piece. In addition, consider the following specific items:

1. Do the writing variables and piece of writing complement each other? Should you add, delete, or change anything in order to reflect the writing variables?

2. How many senses did you use in the writing? Which ones did you use most effectively? Which additional ones should you have used?

3. Which emotions did you use in the writing? Which ones did you use most effectively? Which additional ones could you have used?

4. Should you add, delete, or substitute any words? Should you add a more precise word, cut out a detail that takes the focus from your subject, or change ineffectual words (*it, this, that, these, those*) for stronger words? Are there unnecessary descriptive words such as *actually, really, quite, kind of*? (See Chapter 64.) Have you overused "to be" verbs? (See Chapter 59).

5. Do the sentences have variety, emphasis, and appropriateness?

6. After you have taken your peers' comments into consideration and before you present your new draft to your instructor-editor, reread it; then close your eyes. Do the words paint the exact picture that you want your intended audience to perceive?

PRODUCTS

Read each of the products to determine its overall effect. Before you read the Analysis, what would you say about the word choice, sentences, images, figurative comparisons, and the writer's own genuineness in each piece? What has the writer done in order to demonstrate a unique style?

Snow

by Pierre Berton

Snow. Snow falling in a curtain of heavy flakes. Snow blowing in the teeth of a bitter east wind off the lake. Snow lying calf deep in the streets, whirling in eddies around log buildings, creeping under doors, piling in drifts at the base of snake fences.

She

by Paul Newcombe, student

She slid gracefully across the backseat of the black and tan Mercedes, opened the door, and stepped out onto the curb. There were no parting acknowledgments, no gestures of farewell to the occupant of the vehicle as she waited until the car disappeared around a corner, several lights farther down the garishly lit boule-vard. At last she turned and walked away, commanding the eyes of the street to follow her imperious swagger. Her jeans were tight and faded, her strides, long and fluid, flowing in smoothly gauged rhythm from sleek, muscular hips. As she moved, the electric blue light of a neon marquee reflected rainbows of loveliness from the fullness of her sequined camisole. Her hair—cropped short—was brown; it accentuated the sharp, angular features of her face: the prominent cheekbones, pin-striped eyebrows, slender nose, and the deep, dark windows of her soul—the telling eyes of a lady of the night.

Dawn in Calcutta

by Desmond Doig

Calcutta, always teeming with people, was almost asleep when we called on Mother Teresa at 5 a.m. It was one of those flat, grey, pre-monsoon mornings when the potholed streets, the peeling build-ings and the crippled trees of the city merged one with the other so that one hardly noticed at first the sleeping bodies along the pavements. They lay in haphazard rows like corpses awaiting burial, covered with taut, dirty sheets, or rags, or paper, or nothing at all. Here and there was grudging movement around small fires from which smoke lifted then hung like a grey canopy over the sleepers. Women cooked frugal morning meals while naked children awoke and swarmed about, and street dogs that detached themselves from the sleeping figures stretched and edged hungrily towards the warmth and the smell of food. The first tram-cars rattled noisily through the empty streets, dilapidated monsters that just hours later would be festooned with people on their way to work.

The Desert

by Marc Attinasi, student

Quiet, humbling, and satisfying, the desert calls to me every weekend. The serene feeling that the desert produces with its blanket of silence and stillness is one of its main attractions. Once in the desert, I become aware of all the subtle noises around me: the whisper of the wind in the trees, the rustling of a snake or a lizard, and the chirping of the birds. They all awaken my senses and open my mind to the world around me. The overwhelming size of the desert and the vast expanse of the surrounding mountains bring me to terms with myself and reinstill in me a realistic self-image. I see the greatness of nature in relation to my smallness and feel rightfully humbled. Surrounded by silence, I feel content; my mind and body are in harmony and I feel at peace with myself and my surroundings. The desert, a wonderful weekend retreat.

ANALYSIS

Snow

1. Notice that Berton not only begins each sentence with "Snow," but also builds each sentence. What is the overall effect?
2. Try writing a similar piece of description, beginning with "Rain."
3. Identify the metaphor in this passage.

She

1. Newcombe has written a paragraph that is essentially descriptive. What parts are not descriptive? Why have they been included?
2. The paragraph does not follow basic paragraph structure (as outlined in Chapter 3); rather, it withholds the identification of its subject until the end. What effect does this create? Was the ending unexpected?
3. What senses does the paragraph involve?
4. Compose an appropriate set of writing variables for Newcombe's description.

Dawn in Calcutta

1. This is the opening paragraph of a biography of Nobel Prize winner Mother Teresa of India. Why does Doig begin this book with a description of Calcutta?
2. What effect does his use of fairly long sentences have?
3. What overall impression of Calcutta do you gain from the paragraph?

The Desert

1. From your reading of this paragraph, can you tell which United States desert Attinasi is describing?

2. What else besides description does the paragraph contain: exposition or narration? Find examples.

3. Is there enough description of the desert to satisfy his reader? Does his description of the desert have the same effect on you as the desert itself has on him? If you know or have visited a desert, how does it affect you?

3

Expository Paragraph

INTRODUCTION

Exposition involves the presentation of information, opinions, explanations, or ideas. As a student, you will probably use the expository format more often than the narrative or descriptive format. You will often find yourself having to explain something, whether it's a chemistry experiment, an historical event, or an interpretation of a short story.

So that you do not confuse pure exposition with narration and description, remember that narration tells a story, description describes something or someone, and exposition explains or argues a point (persuades). Notice the difference:

NARRATION:	Last night I fell in love for the fifth time.
DESCRIPTION:	The girl I love has large blue eyes encircled by golden lashes.
EXPOSITION (to explain):	Many people do not know the meaning of love.
EXPOSITION (to persuade):	Love at first sight is a myth.

Assignment

In a paragraph of not more than 250 words, either explain something you know very well to your reader or try to present your point of view on a topic you feel is important.

PREWRITING PROCESS

1. Choose a topic that is in your range of experience or that you can easily research. Good exposition relies on supporting material based on personal experience or knowledge.

2. Once you have chosen a broad topic, *narrow* it down to a particular limited topic with a specific point of view. Finally, compose a thesis statement. Here, for example, is a breakdown on the broad topic of "education," each one becoming more specific and workable:

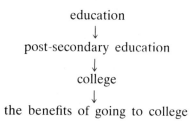

education
↓
post-secondary education
↓
college
↓
the benefits of going to college

As you narrow your chosen topic, you may come up with several very different main ideas that you could express as thesis statements; for example, here are some on "college":

- Not everyone benefits from going to college.
- A college provides a superior education to a vocational school education (or vice versa).
- A college is a good place to meet people.

Can you think of more possibilities for main ideas?

3. Here are some broad topics for you to examine. Narrow two of them. What specific ideas could you write about them? Make up three thesis statements for each of your narrow topics.

defense	sex education	weapons
sleep	food	weather

If you have trouble narrowing a topic, see Chapter 7 for some brainstorming ideas. If you have trouble composing thesis statements, see Chapter 27.

4. There are four specific things to consider when you choose a narrow topic and write a thesis statement for this assignment:

a. *Choose a limited topic suitable for a paragraph.* Your topic of interest might fill volumes rather than a single paragraph, or it might be so limited that a single sentence would say all that could be said about it. So make sure that your main idea can be explained thoroughly in a single paragraph. In your opinion, which of the following thesis statements is the most suitable for a single paragraph? Why?

- Acid rain has become a serious problem in New York State.
- Air pollution is a serious problem in North America.
- Acid rain is threatening our farm.

b. *Choose a limited topic within your scope of experience.* If you write about something that you do not know well, or about which you are unable to gather accurate information, your reader will soon discover your lack of expertise on your chosen subject. Readers do not enjoy reading fuzzy, inaccurate writing. Which one of these thesis statements sounds as though it has come from a personal experience? Why?

- Hawaiians hate mainland tourists.
- There are valid reasons why the people of the island of Kauai distrust some mainland tourists.
- You should not camp alone on secluded Hawaiian beaches.

c. *Choose a limited topic that you consider original.* By writing about something that affects you personally, you ensure a degree of originality. Use this part of the prewriting process to search your mind for an idea that is not hackneyed or worn-out. Such ideas lend themselves to being developed through platitudes. Which of these thesis statements will probably lead to an original piece of writing? Why?

- Women must stand up for their rights.
- Men as well as women should be liberated.
- Much of any liberation movement is, in fact, limiting rather than liberating.

d. *Choose a limited topic of importance to you.* If you are enthusiastic about your idea, you will have a much better chance of stirring your reader's enthusiasm. Besides, you will find that you can say a great deal about your topic. Your problem will then be what to leave out, not what to include—a very comfortable position for a writer. Being able to include specific things that are important to you will help to prevent your writing from being vague. Which of the following thesis statements will probably lead to specific writing? Why?

- Students should be involved in decisions regarding the hiring and firing of faculty.
- Science and engineering students should be compelled to take at least one literature course.
- All students should be compelled to take a writing course.

5. If you are having difficulty finding a limited topic, examine the following controversial statements. Choose one with which you agree or disagree. Would the statement make a good subject for your expository paragraph?

- Women are stronger than men.
- All people should be off the streets by 11 P.M.
- Animals should not live in the same houses as humans.
- If a child breaks the law, his or her parents should be held responsible.
- There is nothing wrong with being fat.
- Sexual preference is nobody's business but that of the participants themselves.

6. To gather material to support your thesis statement, engage in two or three brainstorming sessions by yourself or with your peers. You will find the following

suggestions from Chapter 25 particularly useful for brainstorming an expository paragraph: Talk/Write, Positive/Negative/Neutral Pigeonholes, Positive Cluster, Negative Mandala, Pro/Con Ladder, and Aristotle's Topics.

7. Examine all your brainstorming notes. Concentrate on how you will organize your relevant material (comparison/contrast, cause/effect, chronological order, climactic order, and so on). If in doubt, refer to Chapter 29.

8. Now record your details on a ladder, mandala, flowchart, or other graphic. At this time you may realize the need to add missing details. You may find you will need to do some research before continuing.

This part of your prewriting activities will greatly assist your drafting process because you are concentrating on your method of organizing your supporting evidence.

9. Once you have settled on your thesis statement and have plenty of supporting evidence, decide, if you have not already done so, on the writing variables of purpose and audience for your expository paragraph. If you write for a *real* reason to a *real* audience, the process of writing will no longer be just busywork. For example, convince the members of your club to take a particular kind of action; or inform the readers of your local newspaper of the history of a local landmark slated for demolition; or present a case to anyone over anything that you feel strongly about.

When you decide on your purpose and audience, you will also want to establish your format. You can design your paragraph to be part of a larger piece of writing—for example, a letter or an essay—or you can write it as a self-contained paragraph especially for this assignment.

Finally, consider the situations that surround your writing event (even if you have to invent them), and decide which voice you will use. Before you draft this assignment, record your writing variables so that you can refer to them while you compose.

DRAFTING PROCESS

For your first expository paragraph, you are encouraged to follow *basic paragraph structure*, as follows:

Introduction

The first few sentences of a paragraph should grab your reader's attention and announce your limited topic and your attitude or point of view toward it. In some cases, you can write a single sentence in which you do all three; that is, write an attention-getting sentence that states your limited topic and point of view. In other cases, your introductory sentence will capture your reader's attention, and the following sentence (your thesis statement) will state your limited topic and point of view. To see ways to compose thesis statements and to begin a piece of writing, turn to Chapters 27 and 28.

Which of the following provides the best way of introducing a paragraph? Why?

- I want to tell my fellow students how important exercise is.

- Should parents have to pay for their children's mistakes? I don't think so, for several reasons.
- Drivers who drink are a menace on the highways.
- Is higher education worthwhile? What is the use of spending another four years or more in classrooms with teachers and books when one could be making one's way in the world?

Development

The next step in drafting your paragraph is its development. You must back up your thesis statement through the use of supporting evidence in order to make your paragraph convincing. Decide which types of support to use (facts, examples, reasons, and so on). Notice how one thesis statement might be supported through the use of different types of evidence.

- *Thesis statement*: Drunk drivers are a menace on the highways.
- *Facts*: More than 80 percent of the fatal accidents on American highways involve alcohol.
- *Reasons*: People who have several drinks of any alcohol, even beer or wine, suffer from impaired depth and distance perception and loss of coordination.
- *Illustration through narration*: I used to think there was nothing wrong with driving home after drinking at a party. Then three weeks ago I nearly killed myself.

There are several methods of organizing your supporting evidence (climactic order, cause and effect, analogy, comparisons and contrasts, and so on). Writers sometimes use a combination of methods. To see various methods of organization, read the products at the end of this assignment and the many examples in Chapter 29.

Conclusion

Remind yourself of the thesis of your paragraph. Think of it in terms of a contract that you have drawn up between yourself and the reader. If you have fulfilled your contract during the development of your writing, your conclusion will follow logically. A satisfying conclusion fulfills the expectations you set in motion in your introduction. (You might find Chapter 28, "Beginning, Middles, and Endings," useful.)

In summary, while you draft your paragraph, you should do the following:

1. Consider the basic parts of paragraph structure: introduction (thesis statement), development, and conclusion.
2. Know your purpose for writing. You should be aware of exactly what you are trying to do: explain, inform, or convince.
3. Keep your audience in mind throughout.
4. Know which types of supporting evidence you are collecting and which distinctive method of organization you are using.

As you draft your paragraph, you will probably find yourself substituting one word, phrase, or sentence for another, or perhaps even changing the order of your sentences. You will probably need to revise your first draft by cutting and consolidating or by developing your ideas more thoroughly. You may even need to rewrite your paragraph one or more times. In other words, the process of revising is continuous and occurs even during the drafting process. When you feel satisfied with your paragraph, you are ready to have your work peer-edited.

REVISING PROCESS

When you or your peers edit your paragraph, apply the checklists from Chapter 31 as well as the following specific questions:

1. Can you see the main parts of basic paragraph structure: introduction (thesis statement), development, and conclusion?

2. Have you expressed the thesis clearly?

3. Is it clear whether you tried to inform, convince, or do both?

4. Is there sufficient supporting evidence for your thesis statement?

5. Is the method of organization clearly evident?

6. Are the writing variables implicitly obvious throughout the paragraph? Have you considered the reader? Is the purpose clear? Is the format appropriate? Have you considered all of the implications surrounding the situation? Is the voice used the best one?

7. Do the sentences flow smoothly and logically from one to the other?

8. Should you omit anything in the paragraph because it does not support the thesis statement? Is there anything that you should add?

9. Is there any problem with the point of view?

10. Are there any errors in spelling, grammar, punctuation, diction, sentence structure, and so on?

The following is an example of the results of a peer-editing session of a paragraph entitled "Why College?". Read the abbreviated writing variables first, read the paragraph, and then consider the comments. What would you say to the writer if you were peer-editing this paragraph?

BROAD TOPIC:	Higher education
LIMITED TOPIC:	The worth of higher education *Why not "real"?*
AUDIENCE:	Students who think higher education is pointless. *Imagined.*
PURPOSE:	To convince my audience that higher education is not pointless
FORMAT:	Self-contained expository paragraph
VOICE: *good point*	My own
SITUATION:	I am a returning student; I see many students who do not know why they're in school. *I don't think this is*
THESIS STATEMENT:	Is higher education worthwhile? *a thesis statement.*

Take a firmer stand.
Try to convince your reader.

Why College?

Is higher education worthwhile? What is the use of spending another four years or more in classrooms with teachers and books when <u>one</u> could be making one's way in the world? One of the most important benefits of post–secondary school is the <u>cognition</u> that the <u>termination</u> of school is not the <u>termination</u> of learning. In fact, the process of learning should go on throughout life. Universities, as their names imply, can offer a variety of courses, seminars, discussion groups, and other kinds of <u>get–togethers</u> available <u>no where</u> else. For <u>someone</u> who <u>was having</u> trouble making a decision about the future, a university can be the ideal place to explore several different professional options. There might be the opportunities to take courses from faculties as diverse as <u>law, science, farming, and engineering</u>. At a college or university you will meet not only students your own age but also older people who, after years at home or in the work force, want to upgrade their skills. And if <u>we</u> want to acquire a bachelor's degree in English or mathematics or history rather than <u>training</u> in a specific discipline, (a college or university can expose us to artists from Phidias to Picasso and to thinkers from Socrates to McLuhan.) Do you think you might benefit from some <u>post–secondary education?</u>

point of view weak
Use the "you" point of view throughout

diction problem

wrong word
spelling *point of view* *tense shift*

make parallel

point of view

too much

wrong form

Thesis could be clearer. Be specific.
Why not say "a university education"?

Read the following revised product, noting the changes that the student made as a result of her peer-editing session.

Notice that the revision follows basic paragraph structure. The first three sentences are the introduction, the third sentence contains the thesis statement, the sentences that follow are the development, and the final sentence is the conclusion.

This paragraph takes a much firmer stand than the earlier draft. You may choose to disagree with the opinion offered, but if after reading it you say, "I never thought of it in quite that way," the paragraph has produced the desired reaction.

Often, the final touch for a piece of writing is a suitable title (see Chapter 28). It should indicate the limited topic of your work as well as catch a reader's interest. Perhaps you gave your paragraph a working title, but as you draft and revise, you may feel that it is no longer appropriate. As a result, do not hesitate to change your working title.

Why a University?

Is higher education worthwhile? What is the use of spending
another four years or more in classrooms with teachers and books
when you could be attending a vocational school, working as an
unskilled laborer, or joining the ranks of the unemployed? Consider
the benefits of a university education. One of the most important
is the knowledge that the end of high school is not the end of
learning; in fact, the process of learning should go on throughout
life. At a university you will meet not only students your own age
but also people who, after years at home or in the work force, want
to upgrade their skills. Furthermore, a university, as its name
implies, can offer a variety of courses, seminars, discussion
groups, and other kinds of gatherings available nowhere else. For
someone who is having trouble making a decision about the future, a
university can be the ideal place to explore several different
professional options. If you want to acquire a liberal arts degree,
studying English, philosophy, history, psychology, or the like,
rather than training in a specific discipline, a college or
university can expose you to writers and thinkers from Plato to
McLuhan. As well, there are opportunities to take career-oriented
courses from departments as diverse as law, science, agriculture,
and engineering. So no matter what your interests are, or in which
department you enroll, you are sure to benefit from a university
education.

Now give your expository paragraph to your instructor-editor. Afterwards,
prepare a polished copy for your intended reader.

PRODUCTS

These products have been provided to help you in your writing process as well as
to give you a look at a few finished expository paragraphs. As you read each, examine:

1. the limited topic or thesis statement to see if it is worthwhile and appropriate;
2. the method of development to see if the writer has used basic paragraph
   structure;
3. the paragraph for unity and coherence to see if everything is relevant and flows
   smoothly;
4. the sentences and words to see if they are varied and appropriate to the content
   of the paragraph, to the writer's purpose, and to the intended audience.

Lake Erie: Death or Life?

Dear Sir:

Do we really care about what we are doing to our environment?

There are five Great Lakes, Lake Erie being the shallowest. This lake
is quickly being destroyed by pollution. Industries in both the United
States and Canada have poured their waste, some of it toxic, into the
lake for many years. The many large cities around the lake create
their share of pollution from human and other waste. Slowly but

surely, Lake Erie has been strangled by human incompetence and indifference. Finally, though, someone seems to be paying attention, and the American and Canadian governments have agreed that they will cooperate to try to resuscitate Lake Erie. It is now our turn to see that the governments carry out their promise. The choice is ours: a crystal-clear lake or a moribund swamp.

Let's help Lake Erie rise from the dead.

E. Claire Watters

The SRT-8000 Personal Home Computer

by Richard Pelletier, student

Our country is in the midst of a revolution. You can see it all around you: in schools, libraries, stores, your neighborhood supermarket, and in your own home. It is the computer revolution, and it's everywhere. Do you want your children to be fully prepared for their future? Many concerned parents know that the only way to prepare their children is to introduce them to a home-computer system. That is why many parents choose the SRT-8000 Personal Home Computer System. The SRT-8000, highly recommended by school teachers across the country, is the only home computer that has the Good Housekeeping Seal of Approval. Thousands of software packages make this one of the most versatile home computers on the market today. Our patented Plug-a-Pac learning modules encourage children to learn by making learning enjoyable and entertaining. Experts agree: the only way to prepare your children for the future is to start them early with computer skills; and the computer to start them out with is the SRT-8000 Personal Home Computer.

Memorial Day

by Rev. Donald McCullough

Tomorrow is Memorial Day—a national holiday in which we remember those who have been killed in military service for our nation. It is proper to honor their sacrifice, courage, and patriotism. It is also appropriate to lament the fact that their deaths have not won for us a lasting peace. Where are we today? In 1983 there were 41 wars in the world. There are currently 25,000,000 men under arms worldwide. The nuclear arsenals are staggering. The Soviet Union can destroy every U.S. city of over 100,000 in population 47 times. The U.S. can destroy every Soviet City of 100,000 or more 55 times. The explosive power of the nuclear arsenals of the U.S. and the U.S.S.R. now equals more than three tons of TNT for every person on earth. A single U.S. Navy Poseidon submarine can devastate every city in the Soviet Union with a population over 150,000, and this power represents less than 2% of the U.S. force. And with all this destructive power, the leadership in both superpowers is reviving the cold war approach to diplomacy. As Carl Sagan put it, "We're like two people standing up to our waists in gasoline, arguing because one has a dozen matches in his hand and the other has thirteen—and each threatening to increase his firepower."

Education and Today's Women

by Barbara Thorpe, student

Until recent years, the majority of working women occupied clerical positions, but society's increasing complexity provides many reasons for women to attain higher education. The need for two incomes in many families, along with the higher number of women who are becoming the sole supporters of their families, has challenged women to re-evaluate their education and skills and take positive action to maximize their potential. And, as always, there are those who return to school with the simple desire to learn. Whatever the reason, many women feel compelled to further their education as an integral part of keeping in step with today's society. Technical schools, colleges, and universities are finally attempting to meet the needs of these women.

Toodle, the Engine

by Vance Packard

Social scientist David Riesman devoted a section of his *The Lonely Crowd*, which blueprints the trend to other-directedness, to an interesting analysis of one of the best-selling children's stories of mid-century, *Toodle, the Engine*, issued by the hundreds of thousands as a Little Golden Book. Toodle is a young engine who goes to a school where the main lessons taught are that you should always stop at a red flag and never get off the track. By being diligent in those two respects, he was taught, he might grow up to be a main streamliner. Toodle in his early tryouts conformed to the rules for a while, but then he discovered the fun of taking side trips off the track to pick flowers. These violations are discovered, because of telltale signs of meandering in the cowcatcher. Toodle's waywardness presents the town of Engineville with a crisis, and citizens assemble to scheme ways to force Toodle to stay on the track. Still he keeps going his own way. Finally they develop a strategy to keep him on the track. The next time he leaves the track he runs smack into a red flag. Conditioned to halt at red flags, he halts, turns in another direction only to be confronted by another red flag. Red flags are planted all over the landscape. He turns and squirms but can find no place to romp. Finally he looks back toward the track. There the green and white flag is beckoning "go." He happily returns to the track and promises he will stay on it and be a good engine for ever after, amid the cheers of the citizenry. Dr. Riesman concludes: "The story would seem to be an appropriate one for bringing up children in an other-directed mode of conformity. They learn it is bad to go off the tracks and play with flowers and that, in the long run, there is not only success and approval but even freedom to be found in following the green lights."

ANALYSIS

Lake Erie: Death or Life?

1. The writer has constructed a good paragraph using basic paragraph structure within the letter to the editor. Can you find the parts of basic paragraph structure?
2. What is the thesis statement?
3. What method of organization has the writer used?
4. Is the letter convincing?

The SRT-8000 Personal Home Computer

1. After reading this piece of persuasive exposition, would you buy an SRT-8000 if it really existed? Why?
2. What techniques has Pelletier used to convince his readers?
3. Do you think his word choice and sentence structure are easy or difficult to follow? Support your answer.

Memorial Day

1. This paragraph is the opening paragraph from one of Rev. Donald McCullough's sermons. Does it stand well on its own? What do you think the rest of the sermon was about?
2. Do the many statistics confuse? Why? Remember, the intended audience of the writer only heard the material that you are able to read.
3. How has he organized his supporting evidence?

Education and Today's Women

1. This is a well-written paragraph on its own; however, Thorpe later wished to expand it into a longer paper. At what points do you think she expanded it? What more do you think she said? If ever you have to write an essay and cannot think of a topic, check some of your shorter papers.
2. Does the paragraph explain or convince?

Toodle, and Engine

1. How does Packard develop the paragraph?

2. What effect does this method of development have on the way you read the paragraph?

3. Why are there different levels of word usage, such as "the trend to other-directedness" and "still he keeps going his own way"?

4. What is the moral of the story *Toodle, the Engine*? How does the social scientist, Dr. Reisman, deal with this moral?

5. Can you determine what 'other-directedness" is simply by reading the paragraph?

Narrative Essay

INTRODUCTION

If you have written the assignment in Chapter 1, you already know that narration involves telling a story. In this assignment you will be writing a longer narration, but the suggestions in Chapter 1 still apply.

A narrative essay resembles a short story in a number of ways; in fact, you may have difficulty distinguishing some narrative essays from short stories. However, the narrative essay is a piece of nonfiction, relating the events of an actual incident in

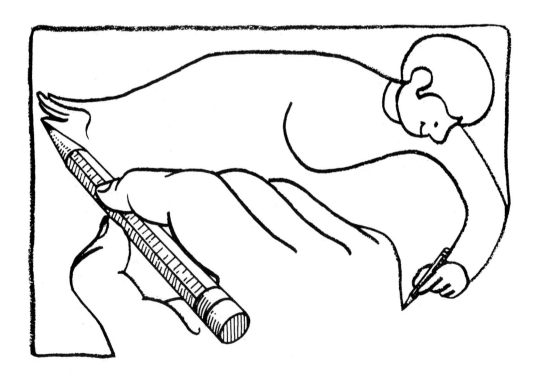

chronological order (as they happened). A short story, on the other hand, is largely fictitious, is not necessarily chronological, and uses literary devices. A short story usually emphasizes character, plot, setting, and theme in more depth than does a narrative essay. A narrative emphasizes the events of the story. The writer controls the content of a short story, whereas the content of a narrative essay controls the writer.

In the hands of many professional writers the narrative essay has become as creative and exciting as any novel or short story. Before you begin this assignment, you should read, just for enjoyment, the narrative essays at the end of this assignment.

Assignment

Write a first- or third-person narrative essay of not fewer than 400 and not more than 800 words.

PREWRITING PROCESS

1. In choosing a topic, which will probably be your biggest concern, keep the following suggestions in mind:

    a. Remember that a narrative may be wholly true and based on an actual event that happened to you or to someone you know, or only partly true, with imaginary additions made to an actual story. You may use either method, but whichever one you use, your narrative essay must *sound* true.

    b. Ensure that your story and its development are right for the length of the essay.

    c. Choose a story with conflict. Either you or your main character must want something. Keep this "something" from your main character until as near to the end of your narrative essay as possible. This should create suspense for your reader.

2. The following activity may generate a suitable topic for a *first-person* narrative essay. On a piece of paper jot down answers to these questions:

- In what true-life situation have I really wanted something?
- What prevented me from having it?
- What was the nature of the conflict?
- Who or what did it involve?
- How long did it take me to get what I desired?

If you have been able to answer all these questions, you have probably found a suitable topic for this assignment.

3. The following activity may generate a suitable topic for a *third-person* narrative essay. On a piece of paper jot down answers to these questions:

- Which of the people I know always seems to be involved in some kind of conflict?
- Do I know of an interesting incident in which this person was involved?
- Who was involved in the conflict?
- What was the nature of the conflict?
- How was it resolved?
- Was there anything that nearly prevented it from being resolved?
- How long did the conflict last?
- Who won?

If you have been able to answer all these questions, you have probably found another suitable topic for this assignment.

4. Once you have a topic in mind, go through several of the brainstorming ideas in Chapter 25. You should find the Pentad invaluable, as well as a Senses Cluster, Newspaper Reporter's Questions, and Positive/Negative/Neutral Pigeonholes. Remember, specific details will make your narrative essay memorable for your readers; therefore, probe deeply in order to record all your thoughts.

5. Because a narrative essay includes several incidents that are linked to a common theme, you should record, on a blank piece of paper, each incident of your story chronologically. The purpose of doing this is to make sure you have not left anything important out of your story.

6. After you have come up with a topic and plenty of supporting evidence, think about a specific audience. Then think of a specific reason for writing a narrative essay, and a definite, real-life situation in which it would be read. Finally, consider writing from a different voice. (If you are having problems, your peers or your instructor-editor may have suggestions about audience, situation, purpose, and voice.) Finally, formulate your writing variables before you proceed.

DRAFTING PROCESS

Before you begin to draft your narrative essay, you may find it useful to write each of the incidents you want to include on separate index cards. If, for example, you were writing about a traffic accident, you might try writing the following ideas on six cards:

- Heavy traffic.
- My girlfriend, Martha, was in the passenger seat.
- Weather conditions
- I was involved in a five-car pileup.
- Martha was taken to the hospital with multiple injuries.
- I was okay.

Arrange the cards in a chronological order and think about the effect that your completed narrative would have on your reader. Then rearrange the cards in a climactic order. Again, think of the effect on your reader. Make another arrangement where you partially reverse chronological order; in other words, have a part of your story told as a flashback. What effect would this order have on your reader?

When you have decided on the best order to tell the events of your story, draft your essay. Although you should be concerned about transition and verb tenses throughout, you will have to be particularly careful if you introduce flashbacks into your narrative. Readers of your narrative essay should know where, chronologically, they are.

1. One way to focus your topic so that your audience will be able to read your narrative easily is to paragraph your essay. Paragraphing, however, creates problems: what should each paragraph contain, how long should each one be? There is no hard and fast rule about length of paragraphs for any piece of writing, but perhaps these ideas may help you in determining the number and length of your paragraphs. At any rate, they will help you focus on the structure of your essay.

    a. Narrative essay paragraphs are generally shorter than those of an expository essay, but avoid paragraphs of one or two sentences unless you can justify their use.

    b. In narration, using shorter paragraphs prior to a climax can create the same suspenseful feeling that shorter sentences do in narrative paragraphs. You may, however, be better off sticking with several terse sentences in a longer paragraph. At any rate, experiment.

    c. Ideally paragraphs should develop a single idea fully and completely. A new paragraph often requires some kind of transitional device to link it to the previous paragraph.

    d. If you use dialogue, you will have to start a new paragraph for each speaker.

2. Because narrative essays are often improved by the use of dialogue, you are encouraged to include it in your work. The only rule about dialogue is to make sure it sounds real—so fit the speech to the speaker. This is where you can legitimately use slang and colloquialisms in writing. But practice artistic economy. Rather than repeat everything your character would say, you might select only what you think is necessary in order to suggest a particular characteristic or to advance your narrative.

Try to avoid strings of "he said," "you said," "she said" as well as the exaggerated "she hissed," "they croaked," etc. Once you have established your speakers and made their style of speech distinctive, you can occasionally present their dialogue without speech tags.

3. Narrative essays are longer than narrative paragraphs, so you will have to be concerned with word and sentence variety. These directions may help you:

    a. Your word choice should be original. Do not repeat similar word patterns or single words unless you want to achieve a particular effect.

    b. Create vivid imagery. Your task is to make sure your reader *sees* what happens in your narrative. Figurative comparisons, expressive verbs, and exact nouns all help. Long lists of descriptive words often do not help much. Which does the better job of painting a word picture?

- He was shy, bashful, and probably embarrassed to be in the same room with her.
- He quickly lowered his head when she entered the room.

   c. Sentences should not all be of a uniform length or structure. Good narrative essayists strive to create the same movement in their sentences that is in the action they are describing. If you are describing a downhill ski race, one long sweeping sentence may be more effective than several jerky ones. What kinds of sentences would you include in a narrative essay about a basketball game?

4. Work for a consistent point of view not only in person but also in style. Once you have established from whose viewpoint or in whose voice the events of the narrative are being told, you should maintain that viewpoint. Also, once you have established a direct or ironic tone for your narrative, you should be consistent.

5. After the first draft of your essay, even before you offer it for peer-editing, you should blue-pencil it. By cutting unnecessary material, you will learn how important the art of selection is to a writer.

6. After one of your early drafts, you should put your essay aside for a few days, then reread it to see if you need to supply explanations, details, or further information, or to delete some material.

REVISING PROCESS

The suggestions in Chapter 31 and the six points that appear in the Revising Process in Chapter 1 apply directly to the narrative essay. They will serve as a guide to you and your peers in editing your narrative essay. You should also consider whether your essay has any distinguishing features:

- Does the writing show a unique style that makes it different from anyone else's work?
- Which sentences are particularly effective?
- Which paragraph is the best?
- To which senses does the essay most appeal?

Your peers should also make comments on the structure of your narrative essay, especially your paragraphing and transitions. Ask them if they are aware of the purpose for which you wrote your long narrative and if your essay is appropriate for its intended audience. If they answer "no" to these questions, ask them for help so that you can make major revisions.

Before you take your narrative essay to your instructor-editor, make sure it is in a publishable condition. Then using the comments from this final editing session, polish your essay for its intended audience.

PRODUCTS

The Girl in the Fifth Row
by Leo Buscaglia

On my first day as an assistant professor of education at the University of Southern California, I entered the classroom with a great deal of anxiety. My large class responded to my awkward smile and brief greeting with silence. For a few moments I fussed with my notes. Then I started my lecture, stammering; no one seemed to be listening.

At that moment of panic I noticed in the fifth row a poised, attentive young woman in a summer dress. Her skin was tanned, her brown eyes were clear and alert, her hair was golden. Her animated expression and warm smile were an invitation for me to go on. When I'd say something, she would nod, or say, "Oh, Yes!" and write it down. She emanated the comforting feeling that she cared about what I was trying so haltingly to say.

I began to speak directly to her, and my confidence and enthusiasm returned. After a while I risked looking about. The other students had begun listening and taking notes. This stunning young woman had pulled me through.

After class, I scanned the roll to find her name: Liani.* Her papers, which I read over the subsequent weeks, were written with creativity, sensitivity and a delicate sense of humor.

I had asked all my students to visit my office during the semester, and I awaited Liani's visit with special interest. I wanted to tell her how she had saved my first day, and encourage her to develop her qualities of caring and awareness.

Liani never came. About five weeks into the semester, she missed two weeks of classes. I asked the students seated around her if they knew why. I was shocked to learn that they did not even know her *name*. I thought of Albert Schweitzer's poignant statement: "We are all so much together and yet we are all dying of loneliness."

I went to our dean of women. The moment I mentioned Liani's name, she winced. "Oh, I'm sorry, Leo," she said. "I thought you'd been told. . . ."

Liani had driven to Pacific Palisades, a lovely community near downtown Los Angeles where cliffs fall abruptly into the sea. There, shocked picnickers later reported, she jumped to her death.

Liani was 22 years old! And her God-given uniqueness was gone forever.

* Names of those involved have been changed.

I called Liani's parents. From the tenderness with which Liani's mother spoke of her, I knew that she had been loved. But it was obvious to me that Liani had not *felt* loved.

"What are we doing?" I asked a colleague. "We're so busy teaching *things*. What's the value of teaching Liani to read, write, do arithmetic, if we taught her nothing of what she truly needed to know: how to live in joy, how to have a sense of personal worth and dignity?"

I decided to do something to help others who needed to feel loved. I would teach a *course* on love.

I spent months in library research but found little help. Almost all the books on love dealt with sex or romantic love. There was virtually nothing on love in general. But perhaps if I offered myself only as a facilitator, the students and I could teach one another and learn together. I called the course Love Class.

It took only one announcement to fill this non-credit course. I gave each student a reading list, but there were no assigned texts, no attendance requirements, no exams. We just shared our reading, our ideas, our experiences.

My premise is that love is learned. Our "teachers" are the loving people we encounter. If we find no models of love, then we grow up love-starved and unloving. The happy possibility, I told my students, is that love can be learned at any moment of our lives if we are willing to put in the time, the energy and the practice.

Few missed even one session of Love Class. I had to crowd the students closer together as they brought mothers, fathers, sisters, brothers, friends, husbands, wives—even grandparents. Scheduled to start at 7 p.m. and end at 10, the class often continued until well past midnight.

One of the first things I tried to get across was the importance of touching. "How many of you have hugged someone—other than a girlfriend, boyfriend or your spouse—within the past week?" Few hands went up. One student said, "I'm always afraid that my motives will be misinterpreted." From the nervous laughter, I could tell that many shared the young woman's feeling.

"Love has a need to be expressed physically," I responded. "I feel fortunate to have grown up in a passionate, hugging Italian family. I associate hugging with a more universal kind of love.

"But if you are afraid of being misunderstood, verbalize your feelings to the person you're hugging. And for people who are really uncomfortable about being embraced, a warm, two-handed hand-shake will satisfy the need to be touched."

We began to hug one another after each class. Eventually, hugging became a common greeting among class members on campus.

We never left Love Class without a plan to share love. One night we decided we should thank our parents. This produced unforgettable responses.

One student, a varsity football player, was especially uncomfortable with the assignment. He felt love strongly, but he had difficulty expressing it. It took a great deal of courage and determination for him to walk into the living room, raise his dad from the chair and hug him warmly. He said, "I love you, Dad," and kissed him. His father's eyes welled up with tears as he muttered, "I know. And I love you, too, son." His father called me the next morning to say this had been one of the happiest moments of his life.

For another Love Class assignment we agreed to share something of ourselves, without expectation of reward. Some students helped disabled children. Others assisted derelicts on Skid Row. Many volunteered to work on suicide hot lines, hoping to find the Lianis before it was too late.

I went with one of my students, Joel, to a nursing home not far from U.S.C. A number of aged people were lying in beds in old cotton gowns, staring at the ceiling. Joel looked around and then asked, "What'll I do?" I said, "You see that woman over there? Go say hello."

He went over and said, "Uh, hello."

She looked at him suspiciously for a minute. "Are you a relative?"

"No."

"Good! Sit down, young man."

Oh, the things she told him! This woman knew so much about love, pain, suffering. Even about approaching death, with which she had to make some kind of peace. But no one had cared about listening—until Joel. He started visiting her once a week. Soon, that day began to be known as "Joel's Day." He would come and all the old people would gather.

Then the elderly woman asked her daughter to bring her in a glamorous dressing gown. When Joel came for his visit, he found her sitting up in bed in a beautiful satin gown, her hair done up stylishly. She hadn't had her hair fixed in ages: why have your hair done if nobody really sees you? Before long, others in the ward were dressing up for Joel.

The years since I began Love Class have been the most exciting of my life. While attempting to open doors to love for others, I found that the doors were opening for me.

I ate in a greasy spoon in Arizona not long ago. When I ordered pork chops, somebody said, "You're crazy. Nobody eats pork chops in a place like this." But the chops were magnificent.

"I'd like to meet the chef," I said to the waitress.

We walked back to the kitchen, and there he was, a big, sweaty man. "What's the matter?" he demanded.

"Nothing. Those pork chops were just fantastic."

He looked at me as though I was out of my mind. Obviously it was hard for him to receive a compliment. Then he said warmly, "Would you like another?"

Isn't that beautiful? Had I not *learned* how to be loving, I would have thought nice things about the chef's pork chops, but probably wouldn't have told him—just as I had failed to tell Liani how much she had helped me that first day in class. That's one of the things love is: sharing joy with people.

Another secret of love is knowing that you are yourself special, that in all the world there is only one of you. If I had a magic wand and a single wish, I would wave the wand over everybody and have each individual say, and believe, "I like me, right this minute. Just as I am, and what I can become. I'm great."

The pursuit of love has made a wonder of *my* life. But what would my existence have been like had I never known Liani? Would I still be stammering out subject matter at students, year after year, with little concern about the vulnerable human beings behind the masks? Who can tell? Liani presented me with the challenge, and I took it up!

I wish Liani were here today. I would hold her in my arms and say, "Many people have helped me learn about love, but you gave me the impetus. Thank you. I love you." But I believe my love for Liani has, in some mysterious way, already reached her.

Of Things That Shine

by Stefani Horton, student

It had been a high-tension day since 4 A.M. when Beau made his standard six-foot bound into the horsetrailer. Los Angeles traffic is merciless for my rickety truck and trailer. Only the floorboards are new so Beau won't fall through.

I forget to breathe when I'm scared. I know I arrived at the showgrounds blue. It didn't help matters when Beau, with his usual six-foot bound out of the trailer, slid on the pavement, unhurt, thank goodness. He thought concrete only grew in washracks. (How clumsy of me to unload him on this giant washrack!) I might have found it funny to see him doing a duck-walk on the unaccustomed footing, but my mind was already ticking off a checklist I knew by rote.

I had memorized my competition pattern to perfection. Deviations would mean elimination. Each movement would be scored strictly, each step must have perfect rhythm, harmonious bend, we must extend and collect with a floating cadence . . . . My coaching rang in my ears, complete with Hungarian accent: "You dare to aspire to classical riding? Sit up! This position comes to us in writings before Christ! Lift your rib cage and follow at the hip, more impulsion! PUSH!!! Ah, better, now a little more bend."

The silk top hat was ready. I'd earned my rank and right to wear it the hard way—bottom up, mucking stalls. My spurs stay packed. Beau has ticklish sides and disapproves of them. The white gloves would not go on till the last minute. The shine on the boots is meticulous. But it is Beau's shine that lights my heart. Cold sculpture can't compare with warm satin in motion. I have spent hours mesmerized by the play of sinew, muscle, and bone wrapped in chocolate-covered satin. I have polished every inch of Beau with adoration. The oil of my hand and my cheek is the formula sought by other competitors.

My breath flutters shallowly as I mount, and my hands tremble on the reins.

In the warm-up ring magic returns. Beau infuses me with awe and confidence. My breath is deep and sure till a supernatural clarity radiates between us. (My coach's words: "They must never see, with the eye, your communication; you are not ready for higher competition until you have telepathy.") Beau's back muscles are resilient. We are ready.

We enter the three-minute holding perimeter under the eye of the judge. She is a veteran of Olympic Gold and eyes us curiously. We have recently started meeting her in the warm-up rings on our surge up. Beau anticipates the sixty-second whistle and moves light as air.

And then it struck. I caught the flash of it as the noise hit. Beau has never been introduced to a Los Angeles garbage truck, let alone one with a trash compressor. A scant twenty yards away on the street, the creature loomed. It flung cans and munched glass, screaming hydraulically.

Beau froze for a fraction of a second. In slow motion I felt his rib cage swell and swell between my calves and then he rose. He lifted to his haunches and then opened up each powerful joint with a massive thrust until he extended straight up. Then he left the ground in leap after magnificent leap! The arcs finally turned forward and rideable while Judge Gurney stopped the time clock. Other competitors milled in the warm-up rings on an eight-minute interval schedule. We had to go on. The whistle blew.

Beau's volatile ancestry was not to be denied. There was a glimmer in his eye as he entered the ring in an unorthodox manner: A full passáge (the show-off gait of stallions at love or war). Our well-rehearsed test was not to be. All eyes upon him, Beau showed his mettle. Our precision was replaced with free form movement. Tail aswirl and flaming nostrils fanned by the bellows of his pumping lungs, Beau reveled. He radiated and the spectators gasped. Every vein stood up in bas-relief on his chiseled body. He danced for the people in pirouettes, perfection of movements never achieved by drill. Finally Beau advanced and froze before the judge. She bowed to Beau amid thunderous applause.

No silver was won that day. Some say we lost.

I KNOW we won.

ANALYSIS

The Girl in the Fifth Row

1. In what ways does Buscaglia's story involve you? In what ways are your instructors like/unlike Buscaglia? Does his story give you an idea for one of your own?

2. What does he do to convince you that his story is absolutely true?

3. Do you think his use of dialogue is effective? What does it contribute to his story?

Of Things That Shine

1. What are the things that shine in Horton's narration?

2. Give examples to show the love and empathy the narrator has for Beau.

3. Find places in the narration where you begin to see the story through the horse's senses.

4. How does the rhythm change throughout the narration—particularly at the climax?

5. What images symbolize the horse? The garbage truck?

6. Is there an educational value to the narration, as well as an entertaining one? Does it change your perspective on the scientific and artistic depth of equestrian sport?

5

Expository Essay: Argumentative

INTRODUCTION

You spend much of your life absorbing and dispensing information: you read and listen to become informed; you talk and write to inform others. In conversations, your purpose changes many times—from wanting only to inform your listeners to wanting to persuade them to your way of thinking.

You can also try to persuade in your writing, though your readers cannot argue back. In order to win your audience to your side, you must learn to argue thoroughly, effectively, convincingly, and logically. An effective piece of persuasive argument is perhaps the most difficult to write but, at the same time, the most worthwhile of any type of discourse.

Most people use the term *argument* in a very narrow sense to mean an oral or written disagreement between two or more persons with differing points of view on a particular topic. But *argument* has a much broader meaning, in that anything you say or write can have an argumentative edge. Therefore, whether you write a recipe, a description, or a friendly letter, you want your reader to taste what you tasted, see what you saw, or enjoy something in the same way that you enjoyed it.

In this assignment, however, you will be writing a purely argumentative essay, one that presents your perception of the facts so that you convince your reader—not necessarily that your point of view is right, but at least that it has merit. In convincing your reader, therefore, you may use some legitimate techniques of argumentation, while omitting illogical persuasive techniques (see "Fallacies," Chapter 65). Using fallacious arguments in writing can be likened to shouting, crying, manipulating, or lying in speech as a substitution for presenting the facts clearly and logically. Writers of propaganda and advertisements may seem to succeed through appeals to emotion rather than reason, but the best arguments are both emotionally effective *and* logically valid because they are based on truth and real experiences.

> ### Assignment
>
> In 500–1000 words, present your argument on a topic about which you feel strongly and want to persuade a reader.

PREWRITING PROCESS

Begin the prewriting process by reading the products and analyses at the end of this assignment.

1. Use the same steps as outlined in the Prewriting Process for Chapter 3 to find a topic for this assignment. An argumentative paragraph can quite easily be turned into an argumentative essay through the use of further supporting details: facts, incidents, reasons, and so on. You may wish, therefore, to look over some of your shorter expositions to see if one of them contains a basis for a good argument.

You may also present yourself with a real-life problem and then proceed to list a number of reasons (arguments) why you could or could not bring the problem to a suitable solution. You should list only items that are, for you, truthful. Here is a small sampling of some problems you might consider as worthy topics for this assignment:

- Should I get married? Divorced?
- Should I lend money to my best friend?
- Should I place my parents in a nursing home?
- Should I continue my schooling or get a job?

2. If you cannot immediately think of a personal situation about which to argue, choose a general topic and narrow it down until you can compose a personal statement about it. For more details on how to narrow topics, see Chapter 27. Your thesis could be in question form, as the examples in Item 1, or it could be a declaration: "I do not believe that I should get married right now."

You can also write in the third person on a general topic, such as "Men and women should not marry until they are twenty-five." Be aware, however, that writing on a general topic can encourage you to use sweeping generalizations and other fallacies. For example, in your argument against early marriage you might make a generalization such as "Few persons are emotionally mature until they reach their mid-twenties." Such untrue or partly true statements weaken your argument; whereas a true, personal statement such as the following will strengthen your argument: "At twenty-three I am certain that I am not emotionally mature enough to take on the responsibilities of a spouse and family."

3. If you are having trouble generating an idea, read the Prewriting Process in Chapter 9, "Cause and Effect," which presents several problem-solving ideas.

4. If you are using this chapter to help you write a paper for the humanities or social sciences, work with Chapters 21–23 as well.

5. Once you have settled on a limited topic, go through two or three of the following brainstorming techniques by yourself or with peers (see Chapter 25): Absurd

Analogies, Pro/Con Ladder, Positive/Negative/Neutral Pigeonholes, Positive Cluster, Negative Mandala, or Seven Controlling Questions.

By filling in your graphic with details of both your and your audience's point of view, you will not be able to ignore your reader's viewpoint when you draft.

6. Draft a statement of writing variables in which you clearly specify your attitude toward your limited topic as well as your purpose and audience. If *you* are not clear about your point of view and which side you are on, your reader will likely be confused as well.

Your statement should be similar to one of the following:

- To persuade our coach that the U. of Y. consistently beats us because of the superior conditioning of their team
- To convince our student services that the printout of students' names for all course sections should include a black-and-white photograph of each student. With such photos available, professors would be able to recognize their students instantly.
- To convince my wife that if she continues to smoke, she will permanently damage her health as well as that of our unborn child

Notice that the statement of writing variables includes that phrase "to persuade" or "to convince" rather than the phrase "to inform" or "to explain."

7. Once you have recorded all of your writing variables, check to see if you need additional facts or evidence to support your thesis statement in order to make your argument more convincing for your reader. There are a number of sources of information:

- Your own experience or observation
- Interviews
- Audio and visual materials
- Reference texts

Nothing is more frustrating than to start drafting and realize that you do not have enough supporting evidence; therefore, take plenty of time during your prewriting process to record all your facts, examples, illustrations, proofs, etc. If you feel that your argument is strong, move into the drafting process.

DRAFTING PROCESS

Your task in writing this essay is to convince your audience that your point of view is correct (or at least reasonable). Because you most probably will not completely convince your reader, you may have to be satisfied if he or she says, "Maybe you're right. I never thought of it quite that way."

1. Respect your audience. Name-calling, insults, and other underhanded tactics weaken your position. Once you have accepted the fact that your reader is as convinced of the value of his or her opinion as you are of the value of yours, you will argue fairly.

2. You should use specific evidence to support your claims rather than unsupported generalizations, distortions, or even false evidence. Try to be positive, rather than negative. In drafting this assignment, remember that you are not involved in an oral debate or in writing a TV commercial. Instead, work from the premise that your opponent is not totally wrong; this will force you to provide much more solid evidence.

3. The more evidence that you produce in support of your argument, the more convincing you will be. As this paper will be only three or four pages long, however, you must be selective. Begin to organize into workable sections all the support you have gathered during prewriting. Choose no fewer than three and no more than five of the most accurate, fair examples that support your argument. It's often a good idea to start with the opposing opinion, presenting it honestly and fairly. Then you can rip it apart (in a thoroughly honest and fair way, of course.)

4. For this assignment, use *basic essay structure*, similar to basic paragraph structure (see Chapter 3). By carefully examining the essay, "If Questions Could Kill," one of the products in this assignment, you will not only see basic essay structure in action, but you will also see a good example of an argumentative essay.

5. The first part of basic essay structure is the *introduction*. Place your introduction with its *thesis statement* in the first paragraph of your essay. Keep your purpose for writing in mind as you draft your opening statements. The following example clearly presents the writer's topic and point of view:

> Everyone should be on guard against the quick responses invited by such narrow and potentially deadly questions [as that posed by the Gallup poll].

6. In the second part of basic essay structure, the *development*, you must convince your reader of your opinion. To gain your audience's support, you should provide a topic sentence for each paragraph and a great deal of supporting evidence (facts, reasons, examples, and so on). Whereas in a single paragraph you are encouraged to use only one or two types of supporting evidence, in an essay you can use a variety of means of support, each paragraph developed with its own supporting evidence.

The same is true of methods of organization (chronological order, cause/effect, comparison, analogy, deductive/inductive reasoning, and so on): you may use a combination of methods to develop your essay, and give each paragraph its own method of development. (Types of supporting evidence and methods of organization are illustrated in Chapter 29.) If your readers can follow the organization of your essay, they are more likely to follow the logic of your argument.

7. The final part of basic essay structure, the *conclusion*, may either take the form of a paragraph on its own or be contained at the end of the last developmental paragraph.

REVISING PROCESS

Once you and your peers have decided on which method of editing you will use (see Chapter 31), you should consider the revising suggestions in Chapter 3 in addition to these specific questions:

1. Have you stated the thesis clearly?

2. Is the thesis statement adequately supported with facts, incidents, reasons, and so on?

3. Is the organization logical? Are the topic sentences for each paragraph easy to find and understand? Which method of organization did you use for each paragraph? Does one paragraph lead to another? Is the overall method for the entire essay clear? Is it obvious that you followed an outline?

4. Is any part of the essay unclear? What can you do to make it clearer?

5. Have you considered the audience? Are there any points mentioned on which the writer and audience agree? Have you treated the opposition fairly?

6. Will your audience be convinced of your opinion? If not, why?

7. Are there any fallacies (see Chapter 65)?

8. When you are satisfied with the overall content and organization of your essay, proofread it for spelling, grammar, word usage, and punctuation. Also, make sure that your essay is an honest account of your opinions. Make sure you have taken your audience's situation into consideration throughout your essay. Now present your argumentative essay to your instructor-editor for additional editing before forwarding it to its intended reader.

PRODUCTS

The *title* catches our attention not only because it startles but because it is an incomplete statement.

The essay follows basic essay structure. The *introduction* includes a quotation: opening with a question involves us immediately. The writer's main claim is quickly established; in the first paragraph she tells us that what we thought was a good idea is, instead, a bad idea. We want to continue to read to see why she thinks the Gallup poll question is nonsense.

The *development* contains three paragraphs. In the

If Questions Could Kill

by Catherine Forster, instructor

Suppose you had to make the decision between fighting an all-out nuclear war or living under communist rule—how would you decide?
—Gallup poll question, June, 1982

The possibility of an all-out nuclear war, which nothing would survive, has become more and more apparent in the Western world; consequently, the Gallup poll question seems at first glance both topical and reasonable. But if we stop to examine the logic of the question posed and the validity of its presuppositions, we would discover that there is no real correlation between its apparent alternatives; in other words, the question is nonsensical. The Soviets say, "Submit or die!"; we reply, "We'd rather be dead than red!" Think, for a moment, if the question were reworded, and directed at the communists. Would they rather be fried than "capitalized"? Everyone should be on guard against the quick responses invited by such narrow and potentially deadly questions.

Although the Gallup poll question is directed at the citizens of the West, it presupposes certain motives and second paragraph, the writer explains why she thinks debating questions of political belief is nonsensical. She supports this claim by providing her reasons. Are they convincing?

The first sentence of the third paragraph fills us with some hope. By developing her paragraph with several facts, she points out that hundreds of thousands of people realize that the Gallup poll question is irrelevant to the real issues at stake: the people must move towards truth and logic and away from blind belief in political ideology.

This paragraph is given the penultimate position because the writer considers it the most important in her essay; it provides the solution to the problem: the many organized professional groups reinforce the ground

impossible alternatives on the part of the Soviets. It supposes, for example, that the Soviets' aim is to bring the Western world under communist domination and that the Soviets could decide to use nuclear weapons in order to bring this about. Now while it is true that the Marxist-Leninist doctrine prophesizes the eventual worldwide rule of the proletariat, Marx said this could only come about by social evolution, not by the use of force. We all know that "stone walls do not a prison make." Nor could force in the form of nuclear weaponry possibly bring about the domination of an ideology. If the nuclear arsenals currently computerized for attack and counterattack by both superpowers were ever set in motion, no populace would be left to debate questions of belief. Aside from the immediately devastating effects, if only two percent of the current nuclear stockpiles were deployed, such destruction of the ozone layer would follow that neither communist nor capitalist, fish nor fowl, would survive to perpetuate their societies.

Disturbing as the implications of the Gallup poll question on nuclear war may be, the same source provides us with some reason for hope. According to Gallup records, when a similar question was asked in 1962 sixty-five percent of the respondents replied that they would "rather fight than submit"; whereas only forty percent of the respondents in 1982 made the same reply. Abstracting the change in statistics, Gallup notes that "the ratio of those who would back a nuclear war has fallen from 6 to 1 [in 1962] to 1.5 to 1 [in 1982]." That there are fewer supporters of nuclear war may seem to be part of the general falling off of belief in our governments. Such a change in statistics, however, along with the participation of not just devoted pacifists, but of hundreds of thousands of people from all walks of life, in antinuclear marches and rallies in 1982, represents a raising of the public consciousness, a trend towards truth and logic and away from blind belief in political ideology.

Further evidence of this change of attitude is seen in the activities of the many recently formed professional groups concerned with disarmament (the Union of Concerned Scientists, Educators for Social Responsibility, Nurses' Alliance for the Prevention of Nuclear War, Concerned Clergy and Laity, Performing Artists for Nuclear Disarmament, and the list goes on). Prominent among these, the U.S. Physicians for Social Re-swell of opinion favoring disarmament.

sponsibility have been meeting for the past few years with their counterparts from over forty countries, including the U.S.S.R., to discuss the difficult roles they would be forced to play in the event of a nuclear war. Reviewing the projected initial and subsequent devastation of even a "limited" exchange of today's super weapons, these physicians have concluded that the best emergency plan would be to have stockpiles of morphine available throughout their countries. That there would be no survivors of an all-out nuclear war has been recognized by doctors of East and West alike.

The *conclusion* sums up the thesis of her entire essay: the rational approach of those in favor of disarmament does much more good than responding emotionally to provocative questions.

Rather than despairing, U.S. physicians have launched a program of public awareness to stress that "prevention"—in other words, disarmament—is the only possible treatment for the fatal disease of nuclear war. Physicians came to this conclusion by asking a productive question, "How can we best preserve life?" Their question and their rational approach to an answer contrast sharply with the gut response invoked by the "Would you rather die or be dominated?" query of the Gallup poll. In these times when we are, quite rightly, fearful and edgy, we would do well to take our doctors' advice, to pause and think about what we value before we rush with bull-like anger in response to the wave of a red flag.

You Could Be Better Than You Are . . .

by Bil Gilbert

Generally we are satisfied with our humanity; *i.e.*, except for an occasional demented Balkan count or shaman, we do not want to be bats, wolves or other beasts. However, that we are accustomed to ourselves does not justify mindless zoological chauvinism: the pigheaded insistence that we are the perfect species in every detail. It is obvious to the fair-minded that other creatures have come by excellent characteristics, some of which are worth our looking into, in design terms. Such major innovations as cold blood, gills and wings, though ingenious, are probably too exotic for our kind, but there are a number of minor, stylistic features developed by other mammals that might be useful and enjoyable for us to possess. Some adaptations that could be worked into the basic human model without drastically altering it come quickly to mind.

Functionally, our noses are disgraceful. In millenniums past they were adequate, if not outstanding organs, but we have let ourselves go to the dogs in this regard and now can barely distinguish very good from very bad smells. In contrast, an ordinary, inbred cocker spaniel can stand in a field and by sniffing learn many interesting things about current but invisible events and beings, what has happened there recently and who will appear within the next few minutes. Even a modest improvement in our olfactory sense would make it virtually impossible to lose scented car keys, checkbooks and golf balls. Wives would know immediately if husbands had been working late, as they claimed, or in fact had been cavorting with the boys' or other girls. Children could not cop false pleas that they had too brushed their teeth and that they had not run through the camellias. By using their noses, many mammals can determine whether others are fearful, hostile, lovable, etc. This would be an area in which we might well specialize, so as to be able to smell out the true intentions of politicians, automobile salesmen, lawyers and the like.

We have also declined badly in regard to hairiness. If we could manage to become as hirsute as even our medium ancient forebears, there would be much less reason than there is to worry about OPEC, the greenhouse effect and the possibility of a Toronto-Montreal World Series. If we were heavily and attractively furred we would have no need to scrag and endanger otters, spotted cats and baby seals. This change might work some hardship on commercial trappers and furriers, but the overall economic consequences would be stimulative. The millions of dollars now spent to clean, conserve and coif our teensy thatches of body hair would be multiplied many times if we had full, luxurious pelts to groom.

Beyond the practical benefit for people who have to work on concrete floors or run in city marathons, hooves would have a similarly good impact on business. The demand for utility, sport and dress hoof protectors might in fact be sufficient to revitalize the ailing steel industry. The loss in terms of boutiques and shoe clerks would be more than compensated for by the return of blacksmiths and their shops, three or four of which would no doubt be needed in every decent shopping mall.

Something full and swishy in the way of tails also would be an economic boon (consider the industries now supported by such minor appendages as earlobes and fingers). But the true benefit here would be aesthetic. No dispassionate observer can compare the back end of, say, a raccoon with that of even a shapely human and not admit that the former is the more handsome. If we could learn to use a tail as expertly as do squirrels and dogs we would be generally more communicative and, in specific activities like oratory and dramatics, marvelously more expressive. Given a long, thick, flexible brush to work with, a Jesse Jackson or a Meryl Streep would upgrade their performing arts in quantum fashion. Physiologists have already suggested that induced human hibernation may be possible in the future and would be desirable for crews making long voyages in spacecraft. The technique would clearly have many domestic uses.

Rather than being shuttled between swimming pools, camps and undeserving grandparents, children during their summer vacations could be stored in cool basements. Rainy vacations at expensive resorts, interminable visits from in-laws and perhaps all of February north of the Ohio River might be passed in pleasant, restorative hibernation rather than in misery.

Many of our fellow mammals are sexually responsive for only a few weeks, once a year. Enormous social changes could be expected if we adopted this arrangement, and therefore the matter should be extensively debated before irrevocable decisions are made. However, some affirmative arguments suggest themselves. There would be only a very limited, seasonal demand for pornography, rock and country and western music, soap operas, poorly lighted and expensive bars, high-heeled shoes, psychiatrists and after-shave lotions. Males would not be obliged to put on unseemly macho displays, nor females to have so many sick headaches. Advertisers would not have to tell fibs about the aphrodisiac qualities of beers, cigarettes and automobiles. Able but sexually unattractive people could become TV anchors, even candidates for President, and generally suffer less discrimination. Education would become the principal function of secondary schools, colleges and universities.

Crimes of passion and thwarted passion would be eliminated during most of the year. The Arousal Season would no doubt be frenzied but not necessarily violent, since the frustrations, ambiguities and hypocrisies of present courtship practices would probably seem a great waste of precious time. Two new holidays would naturally evolve and be cause for universal celebration: the Mating Time and Birthday Weeks. Since they would emphasize our common humanity they might be expected to promote worldwide sister- and brotherhood.

All of which, if nothing else, may be an optimistic way and reason to reflect on the future of genetic engineering.

Roommates

by John Volansky, student

Hey, listen . . . listen to me! Over here in the corner. Yeah, me, the spider on the wall. I'm the house spider and I've been living around here for ages, in peace. Since you two moved in, it's been World War III. My nerves can no longer take this childish bickering. I'm on this web day after day and I hear your fights. Constantly on each other's backs and at each other's throats. John, you are so blunt and belligerent you scare me, and Loretta, your selfishness is enough to drive me out. Can I ask you a question, without you biting my head off, John, and you running to your room, Loretta? Does either of you ever think of anyone but yourself? This selfishness is absurd! It has got to cease or I'm out.

Yes, you heard me right. I want out of this relationship!

Why do the two of you live together? You don't get along! You seem to enjoy your fighting. I can't understand why you two would want to put yourselves through this hell. The other day I was so frightened by your arguing that I shook myself right off my web. I hid in the carpet until you were in bed. I'm afraid to even have a friend over because you two might start fighting again.

This is a warning; either you change your ways or find another spider to live in this apartment. I catch most of the bugs and keep my web neat. I like living here. The location of my web is great and the food supply is plentiful.

Why not work at living together? Talk to each other; it could help. Or maybe one of you could move out. There have to be changes. A spider can only take so much.

ANALYSIS

You Could Be Better Than You Are . . .

1. What is Gilbert's main argument?

2. Examine each of his paragraphs. How are they connected? How do they reflect his overall structure?

3. Is his style straightforward or ironic? Support your answer.

4. How does the inclusion of humor add to or hinder his argument?

Roommates

1. This topic is one to which most readers can relate. Who do you think the student writer is really addressing? Might he also be addressing himself? Support your answer.

2. Why has he chosen to set his argument in a narrative format? Is it effective? Why do you think he chose a persona as the narrator? Is his choice effective? How might he have written about the same topic, using exposition and his own voice?

3. Should the penultimate paragraph be cut or changed? Support your answer.

© 1984 United Feature Syndicate, Inc.

6

Expository Essay: Informative

INTRODUCTION

Some writers believe that there is no such thing as purely informative writing: that all writing, in one way or another, has an argumentative edge. Be that as it may, in this assignment you will be able to write an informative essay to give your reader information about a topic in which you are interested and knowledgeable. In many courses the long informative essay using sources is called a *term paper*. Because your humanities and social science instructors frequently assign term papers, you will probably write more informative essays than any other kind (see Chapters 21–23).

Assignment

In 500–1000 words, write an informative essay that you thoroughly develop by selecting facts, details, examples, or illustrations. If the choice of topic is up to you, make sure you choose one about which you have a great interest.

PREWRITING PROCESS

1. If you have written a short exposition, you can easily add more details, examples, reasons, causes, and so on. This extra development is often the very thing that your reader needs for a full understanding of your thesis. Therefore, look over some of your shorter expositions, especially the ones you still feel strongly about. You may find that you have already worked on a suitable topic for this assignment. All you will need to do is flesh it out, give it a sharper focus, and structure it as a longer essay. You may wish to follow basic essay structure (outlined in detail in Chapter 5).

2. If you have no shorter exposition that you would like to restructure as an informative essay, use the suggestions in the Prewriting Process of Chapter 3 to find a topic for this assignment. Perhaps the only difference is that you can broaden your choices because you now have an opportunity to write up to five times more on your chosen topic. If you are still stuck for a topic and one is not assigned to you, examine your hobbies or clubs and associations to which you belong or sports and other activities in which you are regularly involved.

3. Choose your topic keeping in mind the particular way you are going to develop your essay. Take a few minutes to read the products at the end of this assignment as well as those in Chapters 7–10. From your reading you will be able to see which one you would like to emulate.

4. Use two or three of the following brainstorming methods (see Chapter 25) in order to probe your topic for supporting evidence: Newspaper Reporter's Questions, a Freewriting journal entry, and Seven Controlling Questions. In addition, make a four-part cluster, based on the Four Faces of Knowledge on your topic.

5. An important part of the prewriting process of an informative essay involves research. Readers regard such essays as authoritative; therefore, you may need to take time out either to research your topic more thoroughly or to change it to one you know something about.

Note: If you need to do extensive research, you will have to give credit to your sources. Indeed, you may need to move to Chapter 14 ("Research Reports") instead of continuing in this chapter. At any rate, you are cautioned not to use research material as your own. You do not want to plagiarize (see the Index).

6. If you are using this chapter for a term paper in a humanities or social science course, use the suggestions in this chapter in conjunction with those in Chapters 21–23.

7. Just before you begin to draft your essay, try to bring everything together in a statement of purpose. This sentence will undoubtedly help you compose your thesis statement. The following are examples of ways to express your writing variables:

- Because I feel strongly about my husband's drinking problem (situation), I intend to write a comparison/contrast essay (format) to my husband (audience) to let him know (purpose) how our relationship was before he started to drink heavily and now (topic). I do not intend to use argumentation; rather, I just want to present the facts (further purpose).

- In a history term paper (format) for my professor (audience), I intend to explain the details of the black movements (topic) as though I am an observer from Russia (persona). This essay should show why some blacks feel that they still do not have full citizenship rights (purpose and situation).

- I am writing a letter (format) to my boss (audience) informing him what I think a good working atmosphere should be. I am going to point out to him the possible consequences of his behavior on our office (situation and topic). I want to continue working in this office (purpose).

DRAFTING PROCESS

1. Because the chief purpose of an informative essay is to share your knowledge with your audience, make sure you choose a topic about which you know a great deal. Remember, people usually read informative essays to find out something they do not know.

2. Assuming you have gathered all of your supporting evidence, decide on your overall method of organization (cause/effect, comparison/contrast, general to particular, chronological order, and so on). Spend a few minutes picturing your essay in the form of a mandala, ladders, flowcharts, pigeonholes, etc. (see Chapter 29). The few minutes you spend on this activity will make your drafting process easy. Furthermore, make sure you have included a clear topic statement for each of your paragraphs and develop each in a consistent fashion (see Chapter 27).

3. You may use one or more narrative illustrations in order to develop a single paragraph. Some writers may use one very elaborate narration to develop the thesis statement of their expository essay.

4. You may also use descriptive illustrations to develop a single paragraph. Again, you can use one elaborate description to support your thesis statement.

5. As you draft, decide whether you are going to treat your subject in a straightforward or ironic manner. If straightforward, is your style going to be breezy, colloquial, instructive, or objective? If ironic, is your style going to be comic, mocking, or bitter?

6. Whichever method of organization you choose, make sure you follow basic essay structure: introduction, thesis statement, development, conclusion (see Chapter 5). As you continue to write, you will learn how to use structures other than basic essay structure; for example, you can choose to state your thesis statement at the end of your essay instead of at the beginning.

7. You should now produce a final draft of your informative essay in preparation for a session with your editors.

REVISING PROCESS

1. Besides using the suggestions in Chapter 31 and Chapter 3, the following questions will help you or your peers to edit your work:

a. Have you stated the thesis clearly? Have you included a topic sentence for each of your paragraphs?

b. What part of your essay is clearest?

c. What part is still unclear? Why? What can you do to make it clearer?

d. Are all important points emphasized? If not, which ones need to be emphasized more and how?

e. Which parts seem overemphasized? What should you omit or shorten?

f. Have you separated facts from opinions? As stated earlier, it's nearly impossible to present a paper without any argumentative edge. But attempting to produce a purely informative piece is a useful exercise.

g. Is the point of view clear and consistent?

h. Is the organization easy to follow?

i. Are the sentences too full of information? Too long? Poorly coordinated?

j. Are all the words appropriate? A strong, precise verb can be more effective than a weak verb followed by a string of adverbs and adjectives.

2. Is there anything with which your peers disagree? Can they convince you to make changes? The prospect of massive revision is always harrowing, but sometimes it's the only thing you can do to produce an effective essay.

You can see that this process takes time. Do not think that you can write a coherent 1000-word term paper the night before it is due—even an experienced writer would blanch at such an idea.

3. Before you present your essay to your instructor-editor, make sure that all your facts and writing mechanics are correct. You should strive to make this informative essay uniquely yours in content and style.

4. You have arrived at the point where many professional writers have the most fun: the point where your writing is nearly ready for its final audience. Try to make your essay distinctly yours by testing each sentence and word to make sure it does precisely what you want it to do. One way of doing this is to put your essay away for a few days and come back to it with a fresh, open mind. If you still feel confident about your essay, polish it for its intended audience.

PRODUCTS

The Conquests of England

by David Mueller, student

When we think of Britain, we tend to think of an empire over which the sun never set, a proud and unconquered country that withstood the Spanish Armada, the Napoleonic Empire, and the Nazi menace. In its early history, however, Britain itself was successfully invaded, first by the Romans, next by the Angles and Saxons, then by the Danes, and finally by the Normans.

The Romans, under Julius Caesar, landed on British soil in 55 B.C. At the time, the island was known as Britain and the inhabitants were the same race that populated the European continent. The 55 B.C. invasion was only a reconnaissance, for Caesar was in the midst of conquering Gaul (present-day France) and needed to learn more about Britain. He wrote:

> I thought it would be useful merely to have visited the island, to
> have seen what sort of people lived there, and to get some idea
> of the terrain and harbors and landing places (Caesar 80).

This being accomplished, Caesar left Britain and prepared for his return there. The next year Caesar returned to Britain with a much larger force, intent on mastering the Britons. His military campaign, as far as it went, was successful. The Romans landed in the southeast corner of Britain and penetrated to just beyond the Thames River. Caesar extracted some hostages and a promise of tribute, then returned to Gaul. Caesar's expeditions planted the idea of a new Roman province into the minds of future emperors. Britain, rich in raw materials, metals, wheat, cattle, and slaves, would be a profitable addition to the Roman Empire. Roman legions invaded Britain in 43 A.D. This time the Romans stayed and established their rule over most of the island. However, it was not a quick or easy task. The Romans occupied the plains within five years but could not completely subdue the western region, mountainous and heavily forested terrain. Large garrisons had to be stationed there throughout the Roman occupation. Britain produced a heroine, Queen Boudicca, who led a rebellion against the Romans. In 61 A.D. Boudicca fell heir to the leadership of her tribe when Roman soldiers murdered her family and ravaged their land. With nearly all Britons in the area joining her, she led a devastating attack upon all Romans and all things Roman until she met General Suetanious in battle. The victors say that 10,000 Roman soldiers defeated and killed 80,000 Britons in the fight, and that Boudicca poisoned herself (Churchill 20).

The interior of the Roman province was now secure but Scots and Picts raided Britain from Scotland. The Romans built Hadrian's Wall to keep them out, but it was not wholly effective. Starting about 350 A.D. Germans, who crossed the seas for plunder, also assailed Roman Britain. While trying to fend off the barbarians from Britain, the Empire itself was attacked from several quarters. By 410 all Roman troops had been withdrawn from Britain; in answer to appeals for help, the emperor could only say that "the cantons should take steps to defend themselves" (Churchill 40).

Thus, the British faced Scots, Picts, and Germans without the aid of Rome. The Germans proved to be the strongest; these tribes, Angles and Saxons, were more or less one band of people. They first ventured to Britain for wealth, wine, and women, but, about the year 460, started to settle in Britain (Collingwood 356). The Anglo-Saxon conquest, taking place over the span of a century, left most of present-day England in German control. Winston Churchill puts it best:

> The conflict ebbed and flowed. British victories were gained, which once for a whole generation brought the conquest to a halt; and in the end the mountains which even the Romans had been unable to subdue proved an invincible citadel of the British race (51).

The Germans were thorough in the lands they did conquer; they killed off most of the Britons there, replaced much of the British language with their own, and laid out the civilization we know today as English. The Angles gave to the country their name (Angle land) and the Saxons gave England a dynasty of kings. The people, a mixture of British, Roman, and Germanic blood, were now called English.

Toward the end of the eighth century, the Vikings from Scandinavia launched a wave of plunder and conquest that encompassed all of Europe. The Northmen first raided England in 789 (Churchill 70). Viking warriors, using longboats at sea and horses on land, ranged about England at will. A favorite Viking pastime was the plundering of monasteries:

> The vitality of the Church repaired the ruin with devoted zeal. The Vikings, having a large course of action, allowed an interval of recovery before paying another visit. Iona was sacked thrice, and the monastery of Kildare no fewer than fourteen times (Churchill 71).

In 865 the Danish Vikings invaded in earnest, taking hold of the eastern half of England. They renamed the land they had taken Danelaw, and continued to press into England. The Danish conquest was checked by King Alfred, "the greatest figure in Anglo-Saxon history" (Lunt 23). He, and his successors, eventually reconquered Danelaw and in 954 finally established a king over all of England. In 1013 the Danes, never satisfied, again sent an army across the North Sea. By 1017 the Danish crown had control of England. The Danish lines of kings died off and in 1042 the Saxons were able to put one of their own back on the throne of England (Lunt 53–54). Yet, fate had decreed that Saxons were not to rule the land.

Concurrent with the first Danish invasion of England other Northmen had landed in France. These were the Normans, whose name literally means "northmen." In 911 the king of France ceded to them the Duchy of Normandy (Lunt 54). The Normans, like all Vikings, were a military-minded folk who liked nothing better than a good fight. Since settling in France, they had adopted the language and customs of the French, yet the Normans retained their military vigor.

Normandy and England were closely associated. Edward, the king put up by the Saxons in 1042, had been exiled to Normandy while England was under Danish rule. He brought Norman advisors with him when he ascended the throne of England. Furthermore, he and the Duke of Normandy (William) were cousins. The two men were not alike, however. Edward was a pious man who cared little for politics. William, on the other hand, inherited all the spirit and ambition of his forefathers. It seems that Edward had secretly promised that when he died, William would succeed him as king. Edward died in 1066, but the English lords chose Harold of Wessex as king, instead of William. Harold had no royal blood but he wielded much political power, and the English believed they would be better off with him than with a Norman ruler.

William (later called the Conqueror) reacted immediately. He secured the consent of his king to invade England, got the Pope's blessing, and gathered an army from all over Europe. William landed in southern England on September 28, 1066 (Lunt 58). Realizing that he would have to defeat King Harold's forces in order to be recognized as king, William waited for Harold to take the field against him.

Harold was up north putting down a rebellion. When he heard that the Normans had come, he hurried south with a contingent of professional soldiers. Harold collected some militia in London, then went on to meet William at Hastings. The English drew up in line at the top of a hill, professionals in front, militia in the rear flanks. The Normans had to break this line and scatter the English to win. William had a force composed of cavalry and archers; the English used mainly swords, axes, and clubs. Both sides were approximately equal in number.

The battle started around noon, October 14. The Normans repeatedly charged the English line, each time being thrown back with many men killed. In the interval between attacks, archers rained arrows upon their foes. William saw that after each charge, a few of the English militiamen pursued the retiring Normans and he thought of a tactic that would win the day. After several hours of battle, William ordered his cavalry to feign a retreat; when the English charged after them, the Norman cavalry turned and cut them to pieces. Harold himself was killed by an arrow shot into his eye. The English, though they fought bravely, were beaten.

William the Conqueror then marched on London. England now had no organized force to oppose the Normans and William was crowned King of England on Christmas Day, 1066. William rewarded his nobles with English lands and set up an efficient administration of England.

The Normans founded the British Empire and produced the greatest dynasty of monarchs the country has ever known—the Plantagenets. Though it would, in succeeding centuries, go on to conquer half the world, England would never again be conquered.

Works Cited

Ceasar, Julius.   The Battle for Gaul.   Trans. Anne and Peter Wiseman. Boston: David Gordine, 1980.

Churchill, Winston.   The Birth of Britain.   New York: Dodd, 1956.

Collingwood, R. G.   Roman Britain and the English Settlements.   London: Oxford University, 1937.

Lunt, R. E. History of England. 4th ed. New York: Harper and Row, 1957.

Coke: It's got a Real Sting

by Dewey Gram

For the past decade or so, it has been fashionable to regard cocaine as an innocuous recreational drug, expensive but safe when used in small quantities every now and then—just the thing to give parties an exciting, if illicit, boost. Its only danger, according to this widespread view, lay in the risk of getting caught by the law—and this, as well as its price, lent it an extra glamor that endeared it to the smart set.

But the glamor wears thin... for even the most sparing and occasional of coke-sniffers. The "permissive" view of cocaine has been undermined by the very body that first gave it apparent scientific respectability, the U.S. National Institute on Drug Abuse. In 1977, NIDA declared cocaine a relatively safe recreational drug when "snorted"—taken up through the nostrils—in small doses. But now a revised study by NIDA has labelled it a poison that can kill. Its new report, "Cocaine Pharmacology, Effects and Treatment of Abuse," states that half of all users run the risk of becoming physically dependent on the drug. The institute says that cocaine can produce all the symptoms of physical addiction; until now it has been seen as merely psychologically habituating—in other words, people get coke habits simply because they like it so much. NIDA says this is wrong. "What is surprising is that more people have not died," says Ronald Seigel, a psychopharmacologist at the University of California in Los Angeles, who contributed to both the old and the new reports. "The gram packages of cocaine sold in the U.S. ought to be labelled with a skull and crossbones."

The original NIDA findings, seen as a green light by large numbers of young Americans, almost certainly contributed to the subsequent rapid escalation in cocaine use. The institute estimates conservatively that 22 to 24 million Americans have tried cocaine, and that more become users every day. Cocaine's promise of energy, self-confidence, drive and sexual prowess has especially attracted the "yuppie" generation—the young upwardly mobile professionals. At $100 a gram (an evening's worth for a few friends) or $2,000 to $3,000 an ounce, it has become the status drug—five times more expensive than gold.

Cocaine's sleazy reputation, acquired in the 1960s through its use by heroin addicts, shifted dramatically in the 1970s. Once upper- and middle-class young people discovered that it was the most potent natural euphoriant known, they gleefully adopted it as a "safe" alternative to their parents' crude intoxicant, alcohol. But it has not turned out to be the perfect "soma." Half of the 99 test-case social users followed by NIDA for the past nine years went from using between one and four grams a month to using one to three grams a week. Many of them graduated from snorting to "free-basing"—smoking the purified distillate—or injecting it. Some of them binged, using the drug compulsively until either their bodies or bank accounts gave out. Horror stories—and there have been plenty—have had no deterrent effect. Supplies of good-quality Colombian cocaine are up—$15 million worth enters the U.S. every month. Prices are falling and use is spreading democratically—to lower-income people, to teenagers, to the hinterland.

The prevalent view (at least among rock stars and the young rising middle-class occasional users) has been that there is a minimal risk of physical addiction. But the latest NIDA report is backed by new studies at Stanford University in California which suggest that the orthodox view of what constitutes physical addiction may need to be radically overhauled. Dr. Robin Press, a psychologist at Stanford's alcohol clinic, describes cocaine as a "highly addictive" drug, "although users' symptoms do not fit the traditional profile for addiction." Press says that animal studies showed the extraordinary power of cocaine. "Monkeys will self-administer doses at the rate of up to 60 doses a minute. They will choose it over food, water, or sex, even to starvation, exhaustion or death."

Underlying the cocaine phenomenon is the fact that western culture accepts and tolerates drugs, says Dr. Norman Clinberg of Harvard University. "Drugs are used in every stratum across the board. Nobody in the U.S. is more than one handshake away from virtually any drug they want to get." Press agrees. Cocaine, which is refined artificially from the leaves of the coca plant (which South American Indians chew without any apparent ill effect in its raw state), is no longer the preserve of the rich, she says.

There used to be a joke among coke-users that cocaine is God's way of telling you that you have too much money. Now, however, the message from coke is much more serious as far as addiction goes. It is far too much of the real thing.

ANALYSIS

The Conquests of England

1. Can you find the clearly stated thesis statement in the opening paragraph? Comment on its content.

2. Did you find this essay easy to read? Why? What main organizational method did the student writer employ?

3. Sometimes he told the facts in narrative form. Did you find that it became more exciting to read his informative essay when he did so?

4. The paper is basically informative; however, the writer has included judgments or opinions of his own. Find a few examples. Do these opinions add or detract from the quality of his paper?

5. What do you think of the writer's use of quoted material and the thoroughness of his research?

6. Who do you think is the intended audience? What impression will his essay make on his reader?

Coke: It's Got a Real Sting

1. In his essay, Gram tells his readers a number of facts about cocaine. Which ones did you already know? Which were new? Do you disagree with any of his information? Support your answer.

2. Although his main purpose is to inform his readers, his essay contains a firm argumentative edge. What is it? Does it get in the way of or add to the information contained in the essay?

3. What is Gram's overall organization? Support your answer.

4. What do the direct quotations from the various doctors contribute to the essay?

5. Why does Gram refer to "soma"? Why does he put quotation marks around the word? From the context, what do you think it means?

6. If you were to use the information contained in the article to write about cocaine for your classmates or friends, how would your essay differ from Gram's?

7

Expository Essay:
Classification and Division

INTRODUCTION

To organize your writing, consider using the techniques of classification and division. When you classify, you separate a topic into classes or categories with each class as an independent entity; from there, you can break down the class into divisions or subcategories.

In this chapter you will learn to implement the techniques of classification and division to help you organize an expository essay (or for that matter any piece of writing). As a bonus, you will also discover how classification and division will help you to generate worthwhile ideas by clarifying what you already know and what you still need to research.

Assignment

Write an expository essay of 500–1000 words, using classification, division, or both. (*Note:* if you wish to write a narrative or descriptive essay for this assignment, check with your instructor first.)

PREWRITING PROCESS

As a child, did you ever pick out the onions and mushrooms from your stew and place them along the edge of the plate? If so, you used the techniques of classification and division—you classified the ingredients of the stew into two exclusive categories: the parts you liked and the parts you disliked. Then you separated or divided the two categories from each other, eating the potatoes, meat, carrots, and so on, while leaving the onions and mushrooms.

1. For a few minutes of Freewriting in your journal, brainstorm a possible topic by answering the following questions: Where, in your daily life, do you use classification and division? How do you organize your clothes, records, desk top, kitchen utensils, food, tools, and so on?

2. For a few minutes examine how you would classify and divide *The Independent Writer*. You would obviously classify it as a book, but notice the various subcategories in the following flowchart:

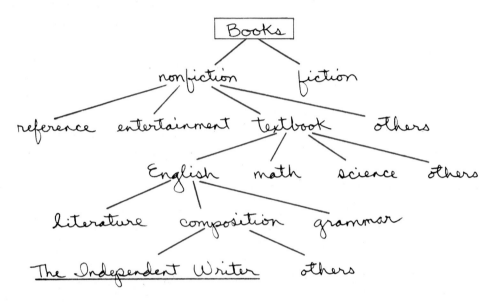

Your flowchart will end with the object you are classifying. You can, however, begin it further back; "books" is one form of "printed material," which in turn is a subcategory of "modes of communication." Draw a similar classification flowchart for one of your other textbooks.

Now examine the division flowchart on page 85 to see how the author has structured *The Independent Writer*.

Draw a similar division flowchart for one of your other textbooks to determine how the author has structured it.

3. Now that you are becoming familiar with classification and division, begin using it as a part of your prewriting process. You might find classification and division useful in choosing a suitable subject for a paper. Of course, if you have already decided on a topic, so much the better. By working on this particular topic, you can use classification or division to clarify your purpose or thesis.

Because some topics that you would like to write about are better suited for classification and others better suited for division, you should note carefully the differences between these techniques before you attempt to narrow your topic during your prewriting process. You would use classification to separate your topic into its various categories, classes, kinds, or types that are whole and independent; you would use division to separate your topic into its individual components or parts that are interdependent. You can, for example, classify a computer system as an IBM, Commodore, Apple, and so on, but you would divide any computer system into its

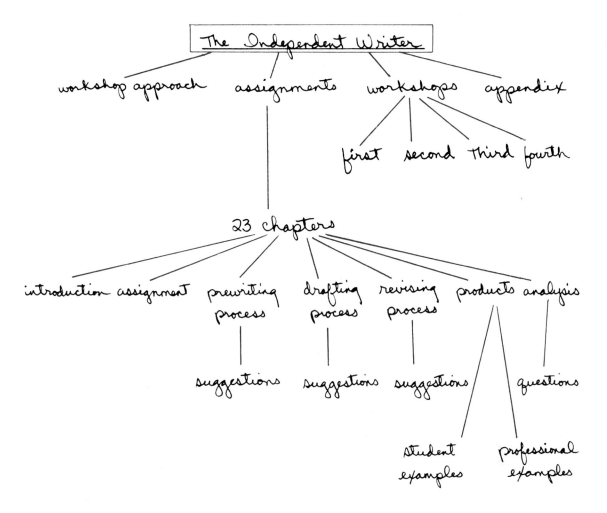

keyboard, monitor, disc drive, printer, and so on. Read Maria's "early" set of writing variables:

BROAD TOPIC:	Computers
LIMITED TOPIC:	Which computer system should our company purchase?
AUDIENCE:	My employer. Real. I intend to give him my paper.
PURPOSE:	To present the facts on all of the available computer systems to help him decide which system to purchase for the office. I want to concentrate on finding the best computer system.
FORMAT:	Proposal
VOICE:	My own
SITUATION:	Everyone in the office has expressed an interest in having the boss buy a computer; two months ago, he said he'd buy one but didn't know which one. This proposal is intended to help him decide.
THESIS QUESTION:	Which computer system should our company purchase?

As you examine her classification/division process, notice how Maria will end up with a specific purpose. By using flowcharts, she was able to classify and divide *computers*, thus presenting her audience with enough facts to make an informed decision.

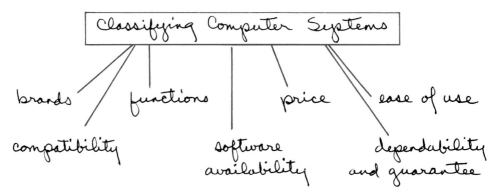

Note: None of the above headings overlap.

Maria continued her flowchart by further classifying the first of the above charts.

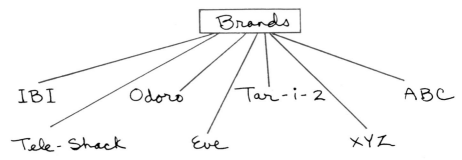

Note: None of the above headings overlap; moreover, Maria could have added others.

Maria continued her flowchart by providing more specific classifications of each kind of computer.

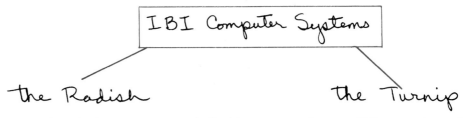

Note: Although there are some similarities among the two IBI computers, the above two are different enough so that the classifications (categories) do not overlap. Only if IBI were to introduce a new system would you add a new category to the classification flowchart.

In order to provide all the necessary information, Maria continued her flowchart by using the division process. Following is her chart for the Radish:

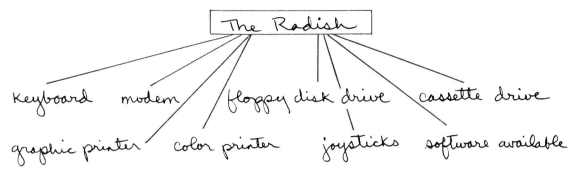

When she continued her work by dividing the Turnip into its parts, she noted two significant differences: its keyboard was two and a half times more expensive than the Radish keyboard, and the Radish software was not compatible with the Turnip system and vice versa. Through her research, she discovered that all the other parts of the Radish system were compatible with the Turnip system—that is, the disc drive, modem, joysticks, and so on. She therefore continued the division process to find out the difference between the two keyboards by setting up comparison/contrast flow-charts. Notice her findings:

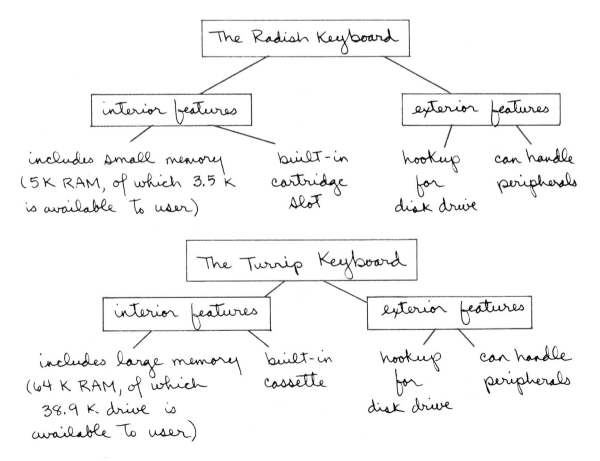

After Maria completed several other classification and division flowcharts of the other computer systems, she had all the necessary facts to make a strong recommendation. After examining all of her flowcharts and discovering which computers had the features her office needed, Maria revised her purpose in her original list of writing variables:

PURPOSE: To recommend that my employer purchase the Turnip from the IBI computer system

In addition, from her flowcharts, she was able to produce a formal outline (partially produced below):

```
                   IBI Computer System's Turnip
          I. Functions
             A. Word processing
             B. Mailing capabilities
             C. Color graphics
             D. Educational games
         II. Software
             A. Inexpensive
             B. Hundreds of programs
             C. Cartridges
             D. Disks
                1. Disk drive
                2. Floppy diskettes
                   a. single density
                   b. dual density
             E. Manuals
        III. . . .
```

During her prewriting, she was able to write the conclusion to her proposal: "Because of its functions, dependability, and price, I recommend that you purchase the Turnip, an IBI computer system, for the office." Armed with her flowcharts, a complete set of writing variables, and a formal outline, Maria moved to the drafting process with confidence.

4. Classify and divide a topic of your own choice by constructing flowcharts similar to the ones above. If you cannot think of a topic, use *police*, *armament*, *love*, or *candy*. Keep classifying and dividing until you have exhausted all but a few possibilities and are able to compose at least one thesis statement which you might easily develop.

To get started, you might first classify "police" into good ones and bad ones. Continue a judgmental classification and division flowchart. Second, you might classify "police" into local, county, state, and federal. Continue classifying and dividing "police" in this way. How else can you classify and divide "police"? From the completed flowchart, produce your formal outline.

DRAFTING AND REVISING PROCESSES

Depending upon whether you are informing or persuading your audience, you should follow the drafting and revising suggestions in Chapter 5 or 6. The only thing that you and your editors need to be aware of is that classification and division should clearly dominate your method of organization.

PRODUCTS

As you read the following products, note the authors' use of classification or division.

On Matters of Love

by James R. Lawson, educator

I fell in love not so many years ago and I found it to be a very frightening experience. It was frightening because I felt that I no longer had control over my feelings and emotions. As a professional researcher, scholar, and social scientist, I found this state of affairs completely unacceptable. I decided to do something about it. I decided to *study* it while experiencing it. This is what occurred.

A search of the literature revealed six classes of love:

Eros	The Love of Beauty
Pragma	Realistic Love
Ludis	Playful Love
Mania	Obsessive Love
Storge (Stor-gay)	Companionate Love
Agape (Ah-ga-pay)	Altruistic Love

Eros, the love of beauty, is where my love for Barbara began. Like the erotic lover, I was powerfully attracted by Barbara's beauty. I took great delight in the color of her hair, her eyes, her smile, her fragrance, her body proportions. My passion for Barbara was ... intense. In fact, too intense, I discovered one day when Barbara slapped my hand away and said, "Is that all you think about?"

I could take a hint. Clearly, Barbara was looking for a different kind of relationship. Perhaps, the kind of relationship found in

Pragma love. The next night in a posh restaurant I explained the joys of pragmatic love. All we had to do, I told her, was analyze our compatibilities ... our social class, education, religion, sexual preferences ... and deeper feelings would follow. She didn't understand at first; I could tell by the look of astonishment on her face. Then, I explained *how* it could be done and she understood immediately. Dramatically, she stood up with her drink in her hand and shouted for all to hear, "*In your computer!*" Then, in her excitement, she spilled her drink on my head, turned, and ran out of the restaurant.

At first, I thought she was in a hurry to get started. Then, I realized it was a game she was playing. My dear Barbara was letting me know she preferred a *Ludic* lover! She wanted a relationship where love is a game and where partners toy with each other, and don't become too attached to each other. I began to treat our relationship more casually. I called less frequently and even pretended I had other lady friends.

Imagine my surprise when Barbara suddenly began to exhibit the behavior patterns of *Mania* love. Mania love is obsessive love manifested by outrageous jealousy and the consuming need of one partner to test the love of the other. Barbara incessantly called me at home and at the office at all hours of the day and night to determine who I was with and whether I still loved her.

I was so upset by this change of events that I decided to resort to a different kind of love: *Storge* love. Storge love is that affectionate kind of love usually reserved for a brother or sister. That companionate love one has for a close friend. Surely, I told Barbara, surely we could be friends. I think she was upset. I remember her screaming expletives as she slammed the door. I never saw Barbara again. The last I heard, she ran off with a ballet dancer from San Francisco.

I still love Barbara with the only love left: *Agape* love, that classic form of love found in all great religions. Agape love is patient, kind, and never demands love in return.

Can People Be Judged by Their Appearance?

by Eric Berne

Everyone knows that a human being, like a chicken, comes from an egg. At a very early stage, the human embryo forms a three-layered tube, the inside layer of which grows into the stomach and lungs, the middle layer into bones, muscles, joints, and blood vessels, and the outside layer into the skin and nervous systems.

Usually these three grow about equally, so that the average human being is a fair mixture of brains, muscles, and inward organs. In some eggs, however, one layer grows more than the others, and when the angels have finished putting the child together, he may have more gut than brain, or more brain than muscle. When this happens, the individual's activities will often be mostly with the overgrown layer.

We can thus say that while the average human being is a mixture, some people are mainly "digestion-minded," some "muscle-minded," and some "brain-minded," and correspondingly digestion-bodied, muscle-bodied, or brain-bodied. The digestion-bodied people look thick; the muscle-bodied people look wide; and the brain-bodied people look long. This does not mean the taller a man is the brainier he will be. It means that if a man, even a short man, looks long rather than wide or thick, he will often be more concerned about what goes on in his mind than about what he does or what he eats; but the key factor is slenderness and not height. On the other hand, a man who gives the impression of being thick rather than long or wide will usually be more interested in a good steak than in a good idea or a good long walk.

Medical men use Greek words to describe these types of body-build. For the man whose body shape mostly depends on the inside layer of the egg, they use the word *endomorph*. If it depends mostly upon the middle layer, they call him a *mesomorph*. If it depends upon the outside layer, they call him an *ectomorph*. We can see the same roots in our English words "enter," "medium," and "exit," which might just as easily have been spelled "ender," "mesium," and "ectit."

Since the inside skin of the human egg, or endoderm, forms the inner organs of the belly, the viscera, the endomorph is usually belly-minded; since the middle skin forms the body tissues, or soma, the mesomorph is usually muscle-minded; and since the outside skin forms the brain, or cerebrum, the ectomorph is usually brain-minded. Translating this into Greek, we have the viscerotonic endomorph, the somatotonic mesomorph, and the cerebrotonic ectomorph.

Words are beautiful things to a cerebrotonic, but a viscerotonic knows you cannot eat a menu no matter what language it is printed in, and a somatotonic knows you cannot increase your chest expansion by reading a dictionary. So it is advisable to leave these words and see what kinds of people they actually apply to, remembering again that most individuals are fairly equal mixtures and that what we have to say concerns only the extremes. Up to the present, these types have been thoroughly studied only in the male sex.

Viscerotonic Endomorph. If a man is definitely a thick type rather than a broad or long type, he is likely to be round and soft, with a big chest but a bigger belly. He would rather eat than breathe comfortably. He is likely to have a wide face, short, thick neck, big thighs and upper arms, and small hands and feet. He has over-developed breasts and looks as though he were blown up a little like a balloon. His skin is soft and smooth, and when he gets bald, as he does usually quite early, he loses the hair in the middle of his head first.

The short, jolly, thickset, red-faced politician with a cigar in his mouth, who always looks as though he were about to have a stroke, is the best example of this type. The reason he often makes a good politician is that he likes people, banquets, baths, and sleep; he is easygoing, soothing, and his feelings are easy to understand.

His abdomen is big because he has lots of intestines. He likes to take in things. He likes to take in food, and affection and approval as well. Going to a banquet with people who like him is his idea of a fine time. It is important for a psychiatrist to understand the natures of such men when they come to him for advice.

Somatotonic Mesomorph. If a man is definitely a broad type rather than a thick or long type, he is likely to be rugged and have lots of muscle. He is apt to have big forearms and legs, and his chest and belly are well formed and firm, with the chest bigger than the belly. He would rather breathe than eat. He has a bony head, big shoulders, and a square jaw. His skin is thick, coarse, and elastic, and tans easily. If he gets bald, it usually starts on the front of the head.

Dick Tracy, Li'l Abner, and other men of action belong to this type. Such people make good lifeguards and construction workers. They like to put out energy. They have lots of muscles and they like to use them. They go in for adventure, exercise, fighting, and getting the upper hand. They are bold and unrestrained, and love to master the people and things around them. If the psychiatrist knows the things which give such people satisfaction, he is able to understand why they may be unhappy in certain situations.

Cerebrotonic Ectomorph. The man who is definitely a long type is likely to have thin bones and muscles. His shoulders are apt to sag and he has a flat belly with a dropped stomach, and long, weak legs. His neck and fingers are long, and his face is shaped like a long egg. His skin is thin, dry, and pale, and he rarely gets bald. He looks like an absent-minded professor and often is one.

Though such people are jumpy, they like to keep their energy and don't fancy moving around much. They would rather sit quietly by themselves and keep out of difficulties. Trouble upsets them, and they run away from it. Their friends don't understand them very well. They move jerkily and feel jerkily. The psychiatrist who understands how easily they become anxious is often able to help them get along better in the sociable and aggressive world of endomorphs and mesomorphs.

In the special cases where people definitely belong to one type or another, then, one can tell a good deal about their personalities from their appearance. When the human mind is engaged in one of its struggles with itself or with the world outside, the individual's way of handling the struggle will be partly determined by his type. If he is a viscerotonic he will often want to go to a party where he can eat and drink and be in good company at a time when he might be better off attending to business; the somatotonic will want to go out and do something about it, master the situation, even if what he does is foolish and not properly figured out, while the cerebrotonic will go off by himself and think it over, when perhaps he would be better off doing something about it or seeking good company to try to forget it.

Since these personality characteristics depend on the growth of the layers of the little egg from which the person developed, they are very difficult to change. Nevertheless, it is important for the individual to know about these types, so that he can have at least an inkling of what to expect from those around him, and can make allowances for the different kinds of human nature, and so that he can become aware of and learn to control his own natural tendencies, which may sometimes guide him into making the same mistakes over and over again in handling his difficulties.

ANALYSIS

On Matters of Love

1. "On Matters of Love" is a copy of a speech given by Lawson at a Toastmaster's banquet. How can you tell that it is a speech? Provide specific examples.
2. Find examples of both exposition and narration. Does the blend of the two genres work?
3. Did you notice how the author has often placed himself in a position of ignorance in matters of love, and Barbara in a place of intelligence? Why has he done this?
4. Besides developing his speech through classification, do you see that the author has also used definition. Was it necessary to use definition?
5. If you were to write an essay on love, how would you classify it?

Can People Be Judged by Their Appearance?

1. In his first paragraph, Berne divides the human embryo into three layers. Draw a division flowchart to illustrate the method of organization. For the rest of his essay, he classifies men into categories. Draw a classification flowchart to illustrate the overall method of organization.
2. Besides employing division and classification as his primary organizational pattern, Berne uses definition, comparison and contrast, cause and effect, and process analysis. Find examples of each secondary method of organization.

3. Considering his audience, justify Berne's use of the large number of scientific words. How does he make their meaning clear to his nonscience-oriented audience? Are his uses of humor geared to this audience? Find a few examples of his use of humor and comment on their success or failure—for example: "cannot eat a menu" and "which may sometimes guide him into making the same mistakes over and over again."

4. Using either the lay terms (*thick*, *wide*, and *long*) or the scientific terms (*viscerotonic endomorph*, *somatotonic mesomorph*, and *cerebrotonic ectomorph*), describe some of the men you know and how they do or do not fit into Berne's classification. Remember that the author himself says that most people are not classifiable in the categories he discusses. After you have completed this exercise, determine whether Berne's classification system is faulty (since it is not intended to include everyone).

5. How can you tell that this piece was written several years ago (1947 to be exact)? Did you notice that it is often sexist? Find several examples of sexist writing. (If you cannot detect the sexist slant, see Chapter 66, Sexist Writing.) If you have not yet found a suitable topic for this assignment, why not try to write an essay entitled "Can Women Be Judged by Their Appearance?" Begin brainstorming by drawing a division/classification flowchart.

8

Expository Essay:
Comparison and Contrast

INTRODUCTION

Some writers and theorists define *comparison* as identifying both similarities *and* differences between two or more things; others suggest it means identifying only similarities, while *contrast* means identifying differences. The latter definition—using both comparison and contrast—is used throughout this textbook.

Assignment

Write an expository essay of 500–750 words in which you develop your topic through comparisons, contrasts, or a combination of both. (*Note*: if you want to use comparison/contrast to develop a narrative or descriptive essay, consult your instructor.)

PREWRITING PROCESS

1. Before you read the next sentence, ask someone to do this prewriting exercise with you; if you attempt to read on before you have a partner, the exercise will not work.

By talking at some length with your partner, attempt to find out all your similarities and differences. Assume that you must write a paper to compare and contrast yourself with your partner. To help you organize your facts, use the two-ladder graphic shown here. When you discover a similarity or a difference, record the detail on the rung of the appropriate ladder as illustrated.

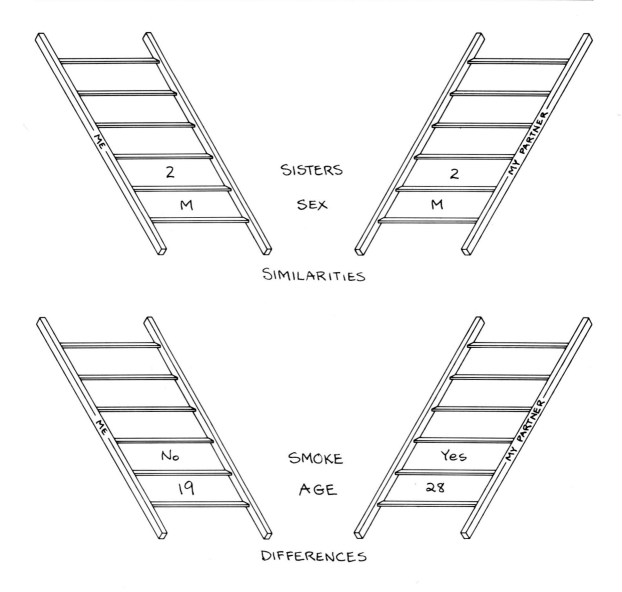

2. For a bit of prewriting fun on a topic of your choice, you might write a dozen lines, each containing a contrast—for example, the following is a paraphrase of a set of contrasts, written by an anonymous businesswoman during the 1970s:

How to Tell a Businessman from a Businesswoman

He's aggressive; she's pushy.
He's good at details; she's picky.
He loses his temper; she's bitchy.
He's depressed about his job; she's moody.
He follows through; she doesn't know when to quit.

He's a man of the world; she's "been around."
He isn't afraid to say what he thinks; she's mouthy.
He exercises authority; she's bossy.
He climbed the ladder of success; she "slept" her way to the top.
If he is well dressed, he's fashionable; she's a clothes horse.
He's confident; she's conceited.
He drinks because of excessive work pressure; she's a lush.
He's enthusiastic; she's emotional.

a. Who do you think is its intended audience? Can you prove it?

b. Which contrasts do you think are accurate and fair?

c. Which are inaccurate and unfair?

d. This piece uses positive and negative slant effectively (see Chapter 37). For your prewriting piece, you might like to write something similar; however, you should try to reverse the attitude and the position of the "he" and "she," for example, "She's positive; he's a blowhard."

e. Or, you might make up a similar set of contrasts, using a variation of "How to Tell a Mother from a Daughter," "How to Tell a Professor from a Student," "How to Tell a Republican from a Democrat," or "How to Tell a Husband from a Wife."

3. You might like to use comparison and contrast to help you come up with a suitable purpose for a paper. By working with an essay topic that Rosa received from her American history professor, you will learn various ways of using the comparison/contrast method of organization. Her exact topic was: "Compare and contrast any two American presidents. Make sure the reader knows why you have chosen the two particular presidents." Read Rosa's "early" set of writing variables:

TOPIC:	Presidents Lincoln and Kennedy
AUDIENCE:	My history Prof. Real. I intend to give him my paper.
PURPOSE:	To compare and contrast the two presidents
FORMAT:	An expository essay, developed through comparisons and contrasts
VOICE	My own
SITUATION:	I don't know that much about either president, but I do know that my professor knows a great deal about them. I want to get a good grade on my paper.
THESIS:	The differences and similarities between Kennedy and Lincoln
THESIS STATEMENT:	There are similarities and differences between Lincoln and Kennedy.

During her prewriting process, Rosa used the two-ladder method to record material that she knew about the presidents. She recorded similarities and differences between the presidents in the spaces on the appropriate ladders; thus, she not only gathered supporting evidence for her paper, but organized its method of development as well.

So that you can participate in this exercise, place the following information on ladders that you draw:

> Abraham Lincoln: 1809–1865; 16th president; born in backwoods cabin; father (Thomas) a pioneer; mother (Nancy) illegitimate; Lincoln was second of three children; both parents illiterate; Lincoln had very little formal education; 6′4″, rawboned, lanky, muscular, backwoods twang, good natured, sometimes moody, charismatic; self-taught lawyer; little known throughout America before he ran for president; professed no particular religious affiliation; married high-spirited, quick-witted, well-educated, aristocratic Mary Todd; they had four sons—all but one died in childhood; Lincoln's greatest crises: Civil War and freeing slaves; delivered many famous speeches, worked on them over long periods of time, e.g., "with malice toward none, with charity for all"; assassinated by John Wilkes Booth in Ford's Theatre (Washington) as his wife sat next to him; myths about Lincoln arose: Old Abe, Honest Abe, Father Abraham; much written about him.

> John F. Kennedy: 1917–1963; 35th president; born well-to-do and quickly moved up the social scale; father (Joseph) banker; mother (Rose) wealthy; Kennedy was second of nine children; both parents educated; Kennedy graduated from Harvard University; served in World War II, wounded; handsome, quick-witted, and charismatic; distinctive Boston accent; became well known before his election; Roman Catholic; married beautiful and wealthy Jacqueline Lee Bouvier; they had three children—one died within two days; Kennedy's greatest crises: Bay of Pigs, Cuban Missile Crisis, Berlin Wall, and civil rights; delivered many memorable speeches, e.g., "Ask not what your country can do for you—ask what you can do for your country"; assassinated by Lee Harvey Oswald in Dallas as his wife sat next to him; myths about Kennedy arose: JFK, someone other than Oswald responsible for his death, linked to sex symbols like Marilyn Monroe; much written about him.

4. If you do not have a topic for your assignment, why not compare and/or contrast the current president with any other president? If you do not know enough about the presidents, you will have to do some research. If that topic does not appeal to you, here are other topics to compare and contrast that you may want to consider: watching a movie on TV or in a theater, a mayor with a governor, a rock star with a country music star, two football teams, an evening and a day college class, a restaurant-made and homemade hamburger, a Ford Granada and a Chevrolet Monte Carlo, working for a large corporation and working for a small business, a female or a male boss, working for a salary or on a commission.

DRAFTING PROCESS

Besides using the drafting suggestions in Chapters 5 and 6, consider the following specific ideas:

1. Whether you compare or contrast, you must decide how to present the facts. You can, for example, discuss several similar aspects of Lincoln and Kennedy by mentioning everything about Lincoln first and then everything about Kennedy. This is the AAA/BBB method of comparing. You can then use the same AAA/BBB method to contrast the two presidents. Or you might mention one fact about Lincoln, and, at the same time, point out how it is similar to or different from Kennedy. You will then be using the ABABAB method. You can use either the AAA/BBB or ABABAB method or a mixture of both when you compare and contrast.

2. Following is a sample paragraph from Rosa's early draft, using the AAA/BBB method:

> Abraham Lincoln, America's sixteenth president, was the second child of illiterate, poor, Kentucky backwoods pioneers. Having next to no formal education, Lincoln virtually taught himself law. At 52, Lincoln—6′ 4″, rawboned, and lanky—was virtually unknown before he ran for president. On the other hand, John F. Kennedy, America's thirty-fifth president, was the second child of well-educated, wealthy Bostonians. Looked after by maids and nannies and schooled in the finest American institutions, Kennedy graduated *cum laude* from Harvard and then enrolled in Stanford. At 43, Kennedy—a handsome, decorated war hero—was well known throughout America before he ran for president.

For practice, write a paragraph to follow the example above. For example, you might like to focus on Lincoln and Kennedy's presidencies, ending with their assassinations. Use material from your ladders as well as any additional knowledge you have of the presidents. Continue to use the AAA/BBB method of organization.

3. Following is a sample paragraph from Rosa's early draft, using the ABABAB method:

> In 1809 Abraham Lincoln was born in a Kentucky backwoods cabin, the second of three children. In 1917 John F. Kennedy was born in a Boston hospital, the second of nine children. While Lincoln's parents were poor and illiterate (Thomas a pioneer; Nancy illegitimate), Kennedy's parents were wealthy and well educated (Joseph a banker; Rose a socialite). Lincoln had no formal education; Kennedy attended America's finest educational institutions: Harvard and Stanford. Both married high-spirited, socially aware women: Mary Todd added an odd touch of aristocracy to Lincoln's homespun, backwoodsy appearance; Jacqueline Lee Bouvier complemented the jet-set image of the handsome Kennedy. The Lincolns always appeared mismatched; the Kennedys were the "beautiful" couple.

For practice, write a paragraph to follow the example above. You might focus on the presidents' wives and end with their sitting next to their husbands at the time of the assassinations. Continue to use the ABABAB method of organization.

4. What are the benefits of the AAA/BBB method for the writer and reader? Of the ABABAB method? If *you* were writing the essay on the presidents, which method would you use? Why?

5. Once Rosa finished her drafts, she was convinced that Lincoln was a greater president than Kennedy because Lincoln had more hardships to overcome than Kennedy and because he was the greater humanitarian. Hence, Rosa changed three of her writing variables:

PURPOSE:	To prove that Lincoln was greater than Kennedy
FORMAT:	An argumentative expository essay, developed through comparisons and contrasts.
THESIS STATEMENT:	Lincoln was a greater president than Kennedy.

Do you think her change in writing variables would produce a more interesting paper? Why?

6. Many writers enjoy pointing out similarities between dissimilar subjects, by employing analogies. If you would like to introduce analogy into your comparisons or contrasts, see Chapter 36.

REVISING PROCESS

Follow the revising suggestions in Chapters 5 and 6. In addition, make sure that you "see" the method of organization: ABABAB or AAA/BBB method.

PRODUCTS

As you read the following products, note the authors' use of comparison and contrast.

We're Going Moose Hunting

by Patrick Michell, student

The act of moose hunting has two extremes. On the one side it has become a passion, and on the other a necessity. In this story there are two people—two hunters; one is a native of the hinterlands, the other an alien from the city.

The city dweller, the affluent, out-of-touch, clean-under-the-fingernails person, is about as informed about moose hunting as he is about rubbing two sticks together. On his vacations this supposedly masculine city dweller flocks to the hinterlands, carrying his dehydrated foods and sophisticated artillery. Traveling by car, boat, or plane, he quickly submerges himself in the deepest and least accessible forest growths. Finally, when there are no more roads or passable rivers or grassy runways, he is satisfied. He is in the densest part of the forest, thinking here, if in any place, is where the moose (terror of the North) resides. He then chops down a parking lot's area of trees to set up his six-by-twelve, fresh-from-the-attic, canvas facsimile of his twice-mortgaged colonial domicile. With the construction of his accommodation complete, he begins his search. Gathering up a couple of pouches of dried roast beef with Yorkshire pudding, two cases of beer, enough ammunition to massacre the Northern native population, and a .44 magnum with 20:1 telescopic ability, he's off. When he is twenty or so yards from the campsite, he begins to huff and puff on his new, latest model, bull moose horn. "Blaaa, Bloooo, Ugh! Ugh! Ugh!" To the residents of the area it sounds like a castrated dog howling in pain; to any unwary moose, it's a definite signal to make tracks in the opposite direction. This poor, stumbling, bug-bitten, and exhausted merchant, shopkeeper, or stockbroker finally decides enough is enough. He spends another two days dismantling his tent and collecting souvenirs in preparation for the trip home.

Vacation is over, hunting is over; silence returns to the forest. Then—only the sharpest ears can perceive it—a faint squishing, like someone silently walking on the ground. The native begins the stalking of his elusive prey.

The moose's pursuer is a clever and simple fellow. He is under six feet tall, has a stocky physique and is lacking two front teeth—all of which works to his advantage. He is an agile hunter; he can pace rapidly through dense forests, glide under fallen trees, and hurdle over thick undergrowth. With the absence of his incisors and the aid of a genuine, hollow goat's horn, he can imitate the call of the moose to perfection. When hunting, he lives on dried meat and fish, makes juniper tea in an old lard can, and sleeps under the night sky. Awake with the first chirps of the forest birds, he sits quietly by a smokeless fire and begins to prepare for the hunt. Closing his eyes, he visualizes past hunts. In thought he recalls his excitement at seeing the first signs of a moose: broken branches, bark-shaven tree trunks, and hoof tracks imprinted on the forest floor. He remembers the nervous breathing he experienced when the moose stood no more than 600 yards in front of him. With the chattering of a squirrel he opens his eyes; he smiles. Quickly he extinguishes the fire; he is ready, and he knows exactly where to begin the hunt. He sets out in a northern direction. He does not expose himself by tracking over twigs or brushing against branches—he avoids these, as he does open areas. Soon he is crouching by the edge of a swamp, his presence concealed by the high grass. As his experience has predicted, his prey stands at the other edge of the swamp, lazily munching on pond grass. The moose, swallowing its last bite, raises its head, looks over the swamp; then proudly it lifts its head higher. Straining in high-pitched moose, it releases a long, mournful bellow: its territory call. There is no answer. The moose lowers its head and begins casually to devour another clump of swamp grass. The hunter collects his breath; his breathing is steady and calm. He slowly rises to a standing position, lifts his old army rifle, and with his index finger gently eases the trigger back. There is no pain, physical or emotional, felt by either. This is the simple, harsh fact of survival in the crisp morning air.

Is a Turtle a Fish?

[19th century debate in the Virginia House of Delegates.]

Mr. Speaker,—A bill, having for its object the marking and determining of the close season for catching and killing turtles and terrapins, has just been introduced by the gentleman from Rockbridge, who asks that it be referred to the Committee on Game, of which I have the honor to be chairman. To this disposition of the bill the gentleman from Gloucester objects, on the ground that as turtles and terrapins are fish, and not game, it should go to the Committee on Fish and Oysters.

On Chesapeake Bay and its tributaries, says the honorable gentleman, turtles and terrapins are frequently captured, many miles out from land, in nets or with hook and line, as all other members of the finny tribe are; and that, therefore, they are fish, and nothing but fish.

I have profound respect for the gentleman's opinion; as a lawyer he has acquired not only a state but a national reputation; but even I, opposing a pin's point against the shield of Pelides, take issue with him. Sir, I am no lawyer, I don't understand enough of law to keep out of its meshes, but I will answer his sophistries with a few, plain, incontrovertible facts, and, as the old saw says, "facts are stubborn things."

Is a turtle a fish? I imagine not. Down on the old Virginia lowlands of the Potomac River, where I come from, the colored people have dogs trained to hunt turtles when they come up on the dry land to deposit their eggs, and when they find them they bark as if they were treeing a squirrel. Now, I ask the House, did any member ever hear of a fish being hunted with dogs?

Who does not know that a turtle has four legs; that those legs have feet; and that those feet are armed with claws, like a cat's, a panther's, or a lion's? Has the gentleman from Gloucester ever seen a fish with talons? I think not.

It is well known that a turtle can be kept in a cellar for weeks, and even months, without food or water. Can a fish live without water? Why, sir, it has grown into a proverb that it can not. And yet the gentleman says the turtle is a fish!

Do we not all know that you may cut off a turtle's head, and that it won't die till the sun goes down? Suppose now a modern Joshua should point his sword at the sun and command it to stand still in the heavens; why, Mr. Speaker, the turtle would live a thousand years with its head off. And yet the gentleman says the turtle is a fish.

Æsop tells the fable of the race between the tortoise and the hare, and we are left to believe that it took place on dry land—the author nowhere intimating that it was a swimming match. Did the gentleman from Gloucester ever hear of a fish running a quarter stretch and coming out winner of the silver cup?

I read but a short time ago, Mr. Speaker, of a man who had a lion, which, he offered to wager, could whip any living thing. The challenge was accepted. A snapping turtle was then produced, which conquered the lordly king of beasts at the first bite. Can the gentleman from Gloucester bring any fish from York River that will do the same?

Again, a turtle has a tail; now, what nature intended him to do with that particular member, I can not divine. He does not use it like our Darwinian ancestors, the monkeys, who swing themselves from the trees by their tails; nor like a cow or mule, as a brush in fly-time; nor yet as our household pet, the dog, who wags a welcome to us with his; nor, finally, does he use it to swim with. And, sir, if the gentleman from Gloucester ever saw a fish who didn't use his tail to swim with, then he has discovered a new and most wonderful variety.

Mr. Speaker, I will not take up more of the valuable time of the House by further discussion of this vexed question. I will have only one more shot at the gentleman,—to prove to him that the turtle is the oldest inhabitant of the earth. Last summer, sir, I was away up in the mountains of Giles County, some two hundred miles from the ocean. One day strolling leisurely up the mountain road, I found a land tortoise or turtle, and picking him up, I saw some quaint and curious characters engraved in the shell on his back. Through lapse of time the letters were nearly illegible, but after considerable effort, I made out the inscription, and read—

ADAM. PARADISE. YEAR ONE.

Mr. Speaker, I have done. If I have not convinced every member on this floor, except the gentleman from Gloucester, that a turtle is not a fish, then I appeal to the wisdom of this House to tell me what it is!

ALEXANDER HUNTER

ANALYSIS

We're Going Moose Hunting

1. As he argues his point, Michell describes the nonnative method of hunting first, the native method second. What would be the effect if he reversed the order?

2. Michell uses the AAA/BBB method of contrast rather than the ABABAB method. Would the latter method have also been effective for this subject matter? Why?

3. The main method that Michell uses in his essay to discuss two methods of hunting is contrast. Can you find three examples of the features of each approach that he includes in developing this contrast?

4. From the first half of the essay pick out particular examples of negative slant; from the second half, of positive slant. The writer's use of slant tells you a great deal about his attitude to his audience. What do you think that attitude is?

5. Note that this writer has a mixed tone in his essay. Is his use of both direct and ironic examples justified?

6. How can you tell that this essay was written from personal experience?

Is a Turtle a Fish?

1. As he argued his point in the Virginia House of Delegates over 100 years ago, Alexander Hunter describes the differences between a turtle and a fish, using the ABABAB method. What would the effect have been had he used the AAA/BBB method?

2. In addition to Hunter's use of comparison/contrast, he also uses definitions to give his speech unity. Find a few examples of his use of definition. Discuss the various methods he uses to define (see Chapter 10).

3. Provide several examples of proof that this argument was written during the last century. In what ways is this piece easy for you to understand? Difficult for you to understand?

4. At what point did you determine that this piece is an example of satire? Point out several examples of satire. Why is Hunter using satire?

5. When Hunter says that he "will answer his sophistries with a few, plain, incontrovertible facts," does he also use sophistries (false reasons that seem to be true)?

6. Hunter uses several allusions. To what is he alluding when he mentions Pelides (also named Achilles), Joshua, Aesop, Adam, Paradise?

9

Expository Essay:
Cause and Effect

INTRODUCTION

Cause and effect is a useful method of organizing a sequence of independent events.

> For want of a nail, the shoe was lost;
> For want of the shoe, the horse was lost;
> For want of the horse, the rider was lost;
> For want of the rider, the battle was lost;
> For want of the battle, the kingdom was lost, . . .
> —*The Real Mother Goose*,
> Rand. 1965, 101.

Cause and effect form a continuum, stretching from the most distant past into the most distant future. In the above nursery rhyme, the cause/effect relationships result in the "fact" that a kingdom was lost because of a lost nail.

You can employ the cause/effect method not only to help you organize your writing, but to reveal a more precise topic. You can use cause and effect in reasoning, solving problems, determining the significance of facts, or predicting possible outcomes.

Assignment

Write a 750–1000-word expository essay in which you employ cause and effect organization. If you wish to write a narrative or descriptive essay using cause/effect development, consult your instructor.

PREWRITING PROCESS

1. You cannot exist without affecting people or things, and they in turn affect you by their existence. Even the air around you changes because of your presence. By asking questions about nearly any statement you hear or make, you analyze a cause or effect. A cause produces an effect; an effect is produced by a cause. People and things are both causes and effects. In other words, everything about you and in you is an example of the cause/effect process. By the use of reasoning, you could, if you had the time and the inclination, trace your existence from the moment of your reading this sentence *back* to your conception or *forward* to your demise.

To find causes, ask the question "Why?" To find effects, ask "So what happened?" If, for example, you had to explain to a police officer why you were speeding, you might produce the following: "I am late getting to school." [Why?] "Because I slept in." [Why?] "Because I didn't hear the alarm." [Why?] "Because I went to bed at three o'clock this morning." [Why?] "Because I was studying." [Why?] "..." Relating the story later to a friend might produce this: [So what happened?] "The police officer felt sorry for me." [So What happened?] "She gave me a police escort to school." [So what happened?] (With boosted self-confidence), "I got an A on my exam." The continuum of cause and effect is eternal.

2. You might like to ask your workshop partner to help you with this following causal analysis exercise. *Warning: feel free to stop the exercise whenever you wish!*

Start with an ambiguous question ("Why am I here?" or "Why am I the way I am?") and see where it takes you. Your partner's job in this exercise is to ask you "Why?" for causes and "So what happened?" for effects. During this exercise, you will set up a continuum of proximate (immediate) causes and ultimate (final) effects. You might even probe the cause of creation, a question that many a genius explores. By becoming more and more precise in questions and answers, you will sharpen your powers of reasoning.

3. For a few minutes list two or three skills in which you excel. If you are an extremely talented piano player, tennis star, or reader, you will have an easy time making up the list. If, however, you feel you do not have any excellent skills, you will have to probe deeper. Maybe you are an excellent listener, talker, eater, sleeper, lover, or friend.

Decide on one skill that you would like to analyze for past causes, present effects, and future effects; for example, Sally feels that she "excels" in watching TV. Using a past/present/future flowchart to analyze her TV watching, Sally kept asking herself questions. Try to make a similar flowchart for your skill. Start with an event, a situation, a decision, a judgment, or a question, and work through to the present. Then work back into the past and forward into the "possible" future. Your flowchart should be similar to the one on page 107.

Note: When you read this flowchart from the bottom up, you must replace the "Why?" with "So what (will) happen (s, ed)" and vice versa to make sense.

When you make a cause/effect flowchart, you should include every cause and effect that occurs to you. But not every point will contribute directly to the development of your thesis. Other causes and effects that Sally thought of included:

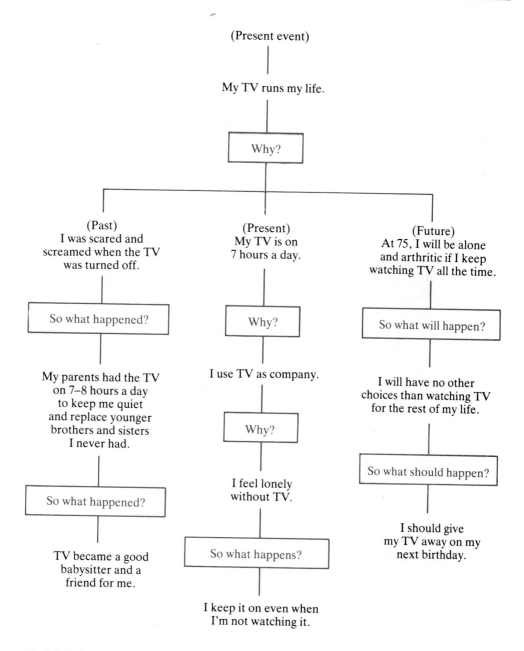

(Present event)

My TV runs my life.

Why?

(Past)
I was scared and
screamed when the TV
was turned off.

(Present)
My TV is on
7 hours a day.

(Future)
At 75, I will be alone
and arthritic if I keep
watching TV all the time.

So what happened?

Why?

So what will happen?

My parents had the TV
on 7–8 hours a day
to keep me quiet
and replace younger
brothers and sisters
I never had.

I use TV as company.

I will have no other
choices than watching TV
for the rest of my life.

Why?

So what happened?

I feel lonely
without TV.

So what should happen?

TV became a good
babysitter and a
friend for me.

So what happens?

I should give
my TV away on my
next birthday.

I keep it on even when
I'm not watching it.

"I didn't have any older brothers or sisters," "My parents had only a grade-school education," "I try to watch *All My Children* every day," "My parents gave me a Betamax for Christmas," "I'll probably have to have my eyeglass prescription changed." Why do you think she excluded each of these from her flowchart?

As she examined the causal relationships in her flowchart, Sally came to the conclusion that her "skill" of watching TV might have undesirable effects. In addition, because she thought that many Americans had become TV addicts for the same reasons she had, she decided to make "Americans watch too much TV" the topic of an argumentative essay. The rest of her writing variables follow:

AUDIENCE: Avid TV watchers. Real. I intend to send my paper to the college newspaper.

PURPOSE: To convince them to give up fruitless and time-wasting TV watching

FORMAT: Argumentative expository essay, using cause/effect

VOICE: My own

SITUATION: I have a love/hate relationship with my TV. I want to describe my addiction to TV so that my readers will relate to what I'm saying.

4. Using the cause/effect method of organization, you might gain insight into a personal problem, which in turn could result in a worthwhile essay topic.

Discuss, with a friend, a personal decision you will have to make; for example, you may be wondering whether you should continue with your education, get married, or buy a car. Describe the causes that could influence your decision; for instance, that all your brothers and sisters had their own cars at 16 or that your widowed father remarried at 65 and regretted it. If you do not explore the causes influencing your possible decisions, and thereby understand the effects, you cannot seek solutions. Once you have talked about your problem for a few minutes, draw a flowchart to illustrate a cause/effect relationship. Use specific cause/effect terms. For an example, see the flowchart on page 109.

Note: In this flowchart, causes are accumulated to produce one effect (or conclusion): "I will have to continue." Can you draw a flowchart where you accumulate effects leading from one single cause?

Because the flowchart on page 109 describes a situation to which you as a student can probably relate, take a few minutes to redraw it on a separate piece of paper with the intention of completing it as it reflects you and your education. When you redraw it, add items that apply to you and delete those that do not. Spend time on this exercise; a complete flowchart *will* result in a well-organized piece of personal writing.

5. You could also use a cause/effect flowchart to explore social or environmental problems, which in turn could lead to a good argumentative essay.

Choose one of the following, make up a flowchart, and compose a set of writing variables. (If you are successful in these prewriting activities, you may want to use the product to draft a piece of writing.)

- If an election is soon to take place, what would be the possible effects of a particular candidate's winning?
- What have been the results of the Great Depression, the women's movement, Watergate, jet travel, or the development of home computers?
- If a nuclear power plant were built near your home, what would be the effects? What could be the effects?

When you construct a flowchart, make sure you identify the causes and effects with precision:

- Make sure you differentiate a cause from an effect.
- Establish whether the cause or effect is past, present, or future.

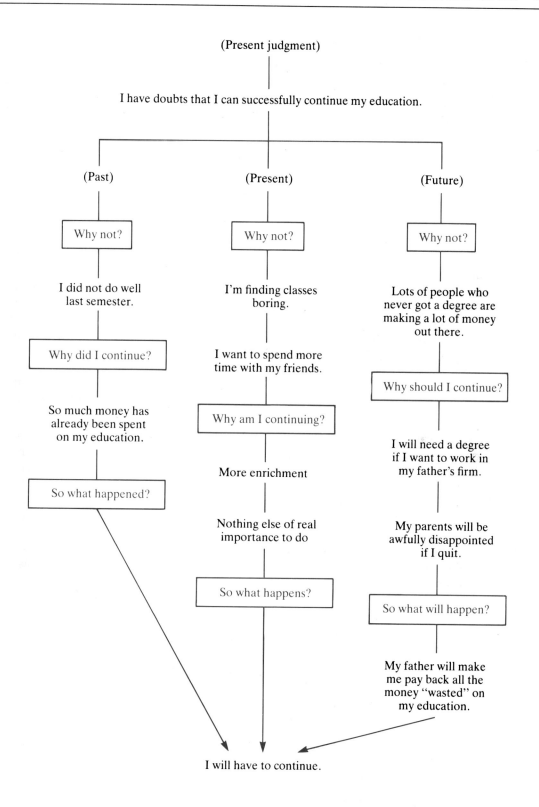

- Distinguish real causes and effects from possible and probable ones.

- Separate proximate causes from ultimate effects.

6. For practice, make up a flowchart to fit the following set of writing variables:

LIMITED TOPIC: The effects of XYZ Factory's pollution
AUDIENCE: Acid Rain Task Force. Real. I will send it.
PURPOSE: To point out that XYZ Factory is contributing to the acid rain problem in the northeastern states
FORMAT: An open letter to the local newspaper
VOICE: Persona of a dead lake in one of the northeastern states
SITUATION: I'm going to write from the future—twenty years from now. Plant and animal life have disappeared. And I believe the destruction was the Task Force's fault because they did not attend to the causes of acid rain when they had the chance.

7. Cause and effect can be eternal in space: a wide spectrum of direct and indirect effects may spring from the same cause (for example, an earthquake or the election of a president). Think of other cause/effect situations that are eternal in space.

8. Cause and effect can be eternal in time: a chain of direct and indirect events may be the repercussions in the future of a past cause (genetics, for example, or the Technological Revolution). Think of other cause/effect situations that are eternal in time.

9. Cause and effect can be eternal in a cycle: sometimes, the process gets "stuck" and the effect becomes the cause, and the cause the effect, which in turn becomes the cause, and then the cause becomes the effect, and on and on (you need experience to get a job, you need a job to get experience). Think of any "Catch-22" situation that creates an eternal cycle.

10. We do not always know the immediate cause(s) of an event or its ultimate effect(s). In fact, a present event becomes a present cause of a future effect. Use your imagination to complete this cause/effect relationship: You cut yourself because of an accident. The effect of the cut is that you miss work. The effect of missing work is that you . . . .

11. Once you have a limited topic and thesis statement for this assignment, you might use any of your favorite brainstorming techniques from Chapter 25 in order to collect supporting evidence.

DRAFTING PROCESS

In all probability your essay will have a strong argumentative edge; therefore, you should use the prewriting and drafting suggestions in Chapter 5. In addition, you might use deductive or inductive reasoning to develop your essay. When you look for causes of a visible effect, you are using *deductive* reasoning; when you project effects of a discernible cause, you are using *inductive* reasoning (see Chapter 29 for details).

REVISING PROCESS

Use the suggestions in Chapter 5. Practicing causal analysis helps writers make logical connections between causes and effects, reasons and results. The intention of this chapter is to emphasize logical thinking; therefore, when you edit a paper that has been developed through cause and effect, check to see that it does not contain false logic. Many of the techniques of false logic are defined and illustrated in Chapter 65.

PRODUCTS

The Way It Was

by Daniel Escher, student

About a year and a half ago I was working in an office, nine-to-five, Monday through Friday. I waited all week to enjoy the Friday night ritual of going out for drinks with my co-workers; however, this ritual was a harmless and enjoyable pastime for everyone else but me. Those first few drinks fueled a vicious cycle that affected my whole life. Once started, I couldn't stop until drunk. I thought my "partying" matched everyone else's but learned that my drinking was typically alcoholic.

Every Friday, for almost a year, I'd accompany the office drinkers to a nearby bar for "happy hour" and we'd stay until we felt the weekend had started on a happy enough note. Everyone else went home to their families; I went to another bar closer to home. That stopover would last beyond the one drink I told myself was the limit; usually I stayed until the bar closed or until I was drunk enough to return to my lonely house and pass out.

I always awoke past noon on Saturdays. After breakfast and buckets of coffee, I'd smoke a joint. Stoned, I'd drive to the gym for a workout and then return home to cool off with a few beers. This started the weekly Saturday binge; those beers took me through a wardrobe change and out the door to continue drinking with friends at dinner and later, with buddies in the bars.

Of course my Sunday morning hangover compounded my guilt of what I could vaguely remember from the previous night. Going to mass helped relieve the guilt, but not the hangover. The hangover, I knew, was best cured by more drinking. Certain bars in my fair city have free give-away beer on Sunday afternoon called "keggers" which I attended as religiously as church. Those Sunday drink-a-thons were very dangerous: I'd drive. And all during the day I would become progressively drunker—from bar to bar, kegger to kegger, oblivious of my depression, seeking escape from the days before and mornings after.

Refreshed and relaxed, my co-workers returned to work on Monday morning; I crawled in the office looking as if I'd barely survived a hurricane. People would ask, "How was your weekend?" I couldn't remember. All I knew was that I wanted to go home and sleep off the hangover. Faced with the darkest day of my week, I wanted to die every Monday. Tuesday I promised myself I'd never drink again. Wednesday I didn't touch a drop of liquor. Thursday night, however, I had forgotten the horrors of Monday and decided a little wine with dinner would do no harm. If I ate alone, I'd drink an entire bottle; if I had a guest, we'd drink two. Once I had a few drinks, I'd make plans for the coming weekend and they'd mirror the weekends before: drinks after work on Friday, joint-gym-beers followed by bars and maybe a disco on Saturday, Sunday keggers.

Friday night drinks were destroying my life, killing me from the liver up, and I knew it.

I saved my life, by the grace of God, on New Year's Eve 1983 when I met a woman who was a nondrinking alcoholic and a member of Alcoholics Anonymous. She told me, "Alcoholism is a disease that blinds you into thinking that you're not an alcoholic. You don't have to drink anymore if you don't want to. You can stop if you're ready." I was ready. Month after month I had been a victim of my drinking and by the time I met this woman I was sick and tired of being sick and tired. The day she took me to a meeting of Alcoholics Anonymous is now my sobriety date—February 7, 1983.

Over a year has passed since my last weekend drunk. I've been set free from the chain reaction of those Friday night drinks by simply not picking up the first drink. Life, I'm learning, can be lived without hiding behind an altered state. I'm living as the AA program advises: one day at a time. The joy of sobriety, for which I am very thankful, gave new meaning to my daily life.

Why Levi's Changed the 501

from **Everybody's Business: An Almanac**
edited by **Milton Moskowitz, Michael Katz, and Robert Levering**

Picture a scene from the Old West, sometime in the 1870s. Weary cowboys in dusty Levi's gather around a blazing campfire, resting after a day of riding and roping on the open range. The lonely howl of a distant coyote counterpoints the notes of a guitar as the moon floats serenely overhead in an unpolluted sky afire with stars.

Suddenly a bellow of pain shatters the night, as a cowpoke leaps away from the fire, dancing in agony. Hot Rivet Syndrome has claimed another victim.

In those days Levi's were made, as they had been from the first days of Levi Strauss, with copper rivets at stress points to provide extra strength. On these original Levi's—model 501—there were rivets on the pockets, and there was a lone rivet at the crotch. The crotch rivet was the critical one: when cowboys crouched too long beside the campfire, the rivet grew uncomfortably hot.

For years the brave men of the West suffered from this curious occupational hazard. But nothing was done about it until 1933, when Walter Haas, Sr., president of Levi Strauss, chanced to go camping in his Levi's 501s. Haas was crouched contentedly by a crackling campfire in the high Sierras, drinking in the pure mountain air, when he fell prey to Hot Rivet Syndrome. He consulted with professional wranglers in his party. Had they ever suffered the same mishap? An impassioned *yes* was the reply.

Haas vowed that the offending rivet must go, and the board of directors voted it into extinction at their next meeting.

Except for eliminating the crotch rivet, the company has made only one other stylistic change in its 501s since they were first marketed in 1873. Responding to schools' complaints that Levi's pocket rivets scratched school furniture, the company moved the rivets to the front pockets. Otherwise the Levi's 501 shrink-to-fit jeans on the market today are identical to the pants that won the West.

ANALYSIS

The Way It Was

1. Make a cause/effect flowchart of the student writer's essay. Do all the pieces of his story fit into your chart?

2. Read his essay again. As you read, however, note the portions that are "causes of his alcoholism," "effects of his alcoholism," "causes of his sobriety," and "effects of his sobriety." Is his supporting evidence complete?

3. This cause/effect essay is an example of mixing exposition and narration. Furthermore, it illustrates what many writing teachers advocate: "Be personal. Writers are not afraid to let it all hang out." What is your reaction to reading Escher's essay? Why do you think he gave permission for his very personal essay to be published in *The Independent Writer*?

Why Levi's Changed the 501

1. It is quite easy to trace the cause/effect relationship throughout this humorous essay. Construct a flowchart that begins with "heat" as the initial cause and "removal of offending rivet" as the final effect. Compare your flowchart with those of your peers.

2. Although the essay is expository, there are narrative elements. Point them out.

3. Criticize the title of this piece. Can you think of a more appropriate one? Why is your title more appropriate?

4. Humor is apparent throughout this piece. Point out several examples of slapstick humor, euphemisms, irony, and overstatements.

5. If you are looking for a topic for this assignment, you might write a cause/effect paper on why the Levi Strauss company moved the rivets from the back pockets of their jeans to the front pockets.

10

Expository Essay: Definition

INTRODUCTION

When you communicate with others, you want them to know exactly what you are saying. But if you try to make sure that your readers understand what you write by including a definition of all the words you use, they would soon lose interest in your material. You can solve this problem by considering your audience and its situation whenever you write and by presenting your material in a way that will make what you want to say as clear as possible.

The author of *The Independent Writer* uses three methods of making sure you understand what you are reading: (1) Instead of defining, a variety of alternative methods has been used within the body of the text—synonyms, alternative terms, examples, literal or figurative comparisons, contrasts, and a listing of parts. (2) Occasionally a formal definition is presented. A formal definition is made up of the *term* (word or words that are being defined), *class* (category to which the term belongs), and *distinguishing characteristics* (the things that distinguish the term from all the other words of the same class). (3) Sometimes, a single term is explained throughout an entire passage (several paragraphs or an entire chapter) by using alternative methods and formal definitions. Because the act of defining continues throughout an entire passage, the definition has been "extended." To see examples of extended definition, turn to the chapters on "Unity," "Style," and "Slant" (Chapters 29, 34, and 37). In this assignment, you will learn how to extend a definition in a piece of your own writing.

Assignment

Write an expository essay of 400–800 words in which you include an extended definition.

PREWRITING PROCESS

Before you begin to choose a topic for this assignment, spend a few minutes experimenting with different ways to define a word.

1. Provide a synonym, an alternative term, an example, a literal and figurative comparison, a contrast, and a list of its parts for two of the following: *thesis statement, leisure time, feminist, sibling, brainstorming, writing variables, capitalism,* and *byte.* Look over the following ways you might explain *thesis statement* without actually defining the term:

Using a synonym

In an essay, you should include a thesis statement (main idea) in your introductory paragraph.

Offering an alternative term

A thesis *statement* is also referred to as a thesis *sentence.*

Providing an example

In his essay "We're Going Moose Hunting," (Chapter 8), Patrick Michell presents his thesis statement at the end of his introductory paragraph: "In this story there are two people—two hunters; one is a native of the hinterlands, the other an alien from the city."

Making a literal comparison

A thesis statement is a sentence that focuses a reader's attention on the content of an entire essay in the same way that a topic statement focuses a reader's attention on the content of a single paragraph.

Making a figurative comparison

A thesis statement is like a road sign that points the reader in the right direction.

Pointing out a contrast

With a thesis statement an essay is easy to write and clear to read; without a thesis statement both writer and reader are in a fog.

Listing parts

A thesis statement should be exact, specific, and precise, linking your topic (the subject) with what you want to say about it (the predicate) in a complete sentence.

2. For the terms in Item 1, provide formal definitions. First, however, check several of the formal definitions in the Glossary of this textbook. As you do so, divide the formal definition into its three parts by inserting the word "term" after reading the term, "class" after the class or category to which the term belongs, and "distinguishing characteristic" after what differentiates the term from other words of the same class; for example:

- A thesis statement [term] is one of the parts of an essay [class] that establishes the main idea of the entire piece of writing [distinguishing characteristic].
- Brainstorming [term] is a group problem-solving technique [class] that involves the spontaneous contribution of ideas from all members of the group [distinguishing characteristic].

If you want to use a term in a special way or alter its accepted meaning slightly, you must provide a formal definition to let your readers know exactly what you mean when you use it. For example, throughout *The Independent Writer* you are often encouraged to use the technique of brainstorming with only one other person or even by yourself. The term *brainstorming*, therefore, is also used in the sense of "storming your own brain" for prewriting ideas.

3. Construct a partial classification flowchart (see Chapter 7) to see if your formal definitions are adequate; for example, examine the following partial flowchart that illustrates a definition of "brainstorming":

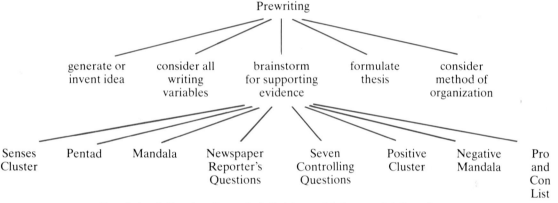

Read the following formal definition with its partial flowchart:

- The workshop approach [term] is a way of learning how to write [class] in which students *actively* engage in the parts of the writing process [distinguishing characteristic].

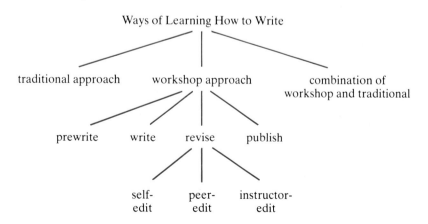

4. Write a formal definition and a partial classification flowchart of the following: *chair*, *thin*, *multimedia*, *romantic love*, *genocide*, *slam-dunk*, *pornography*, and *over-the-hill*.

Be sure that your definition applies specifically to the word you are defining. If, for example, you define "chair" as "an object on which a person sits," you have written a definition which can also apply to a sofa, a bed, or a porch swing, among other things. If you are having difficulty making your definitions precise, use a dictionary.

You might then wish to extend one of your definitions, illustrating it with a formal definition, alternative methods, and possibly the derivation or origin of the term. If so, you have a topic for this assignment.

5. If you have not found a topic for this assignment, examine the Special Writing Assignment in Chapter 39. After you have chosen a topic, go through the following brainstorming techniques from Chapter 25 in order to gather supporting evidence: Senses Cluster, Absurd Analogies, and Seven Controlling Questions.

6. Set down your writing variables in order to make your piece of writing real—for example:

TOPIC:	Senses Cluster
AUDIENCE:	Peer. Real. I intend to give her my paper.
PURPOSE:	To define all five senses and show how to use them in a Senses Cluster
FORMAT:	Informative expository paper
VOICE:	My own
SITUATION:	I think I understand and appreciate the Senses Cluster as a brainstorming technique; my partner doesn't see any sense in it.
THESIS:	Benefits of using a Senses Cluster
THESIS STATEMENT:	An understanding of the Senses Cluster can help a writer to brainstorm many topics.

DRAFTING AND REVISING PROCESSES

Depending on whether your expository paper informs or persuades, you should refer to the suggestions contained in Chapter 5 or 6. However, because you are to use definition as your main organizational method, consider the following suggestions when you draft and revise:

1. Because you will probably follow basic essay structure, you should include in your introduction a thesis statement and a formal, one-sentence definition of the word or phrase. Make sure you include the term, class, and distinguishing characteristic.

2. In the main body of your essay, you should extend your definition by developing your term with examples, illustrations, derivations of the term, comparisons or contrasts, causes or effects, or analogies.

3. In your conclusion, produce a restatement of the formal definition or a climactic example of the term.

PRODUCTS

The following memo is given to English students of a certain California State University:

TO: Students enrolled in English 100, 200, 280
FROM: Department of English and Comparative Literature
SUBJECT: Plagiarism

I. Plagiarism—*handing in written work that is not your own*—is a civil offense in this state (Title 5: State Administrative Code, Section 41301). According to Title 5, it may be followed by expulsion, suspension, or probation. Plagiarism is dealt with swiftly and vigorously in this department. Be sure you understand the consequences. And, above all, be sure you understand what plagiarism is, so that you don't involve yourself inadvertently.

II. Below, you will find four categories of plagiarism. Your instructor will explain the fine points and the discriminations that must be made in categories B, C, D. If he or she does not, and the matter is not clear and self-evident to you, you must be sure to ask. If you have any doubt about a piece of writing you hand in, it is far better to acknowledge your source properly, and to err on the side of being too careful, than it is to risk the chance of being thought dishonest.

III. Plagiarism is any of the following:
   A. Verbatim copying without proper acknowledgement.
   B. Paraphrasing without proper acknowledgement.
   C. Patching together a quilt-work paper from diverse sources, without proper acknowledgement of those sources. Not infrequently in high school a "research paper" is just that—a piecing together of snippets from several sources.
   D. Unacknowledged appropriation of certain types of information or of someone else's ideas. Certain "information" and some types of ideas are in the public domain. Others are not, and sources must be cited. Some are borderline. Only experience gives one a proper sense of the sort of ideas or information that may be reckoned public and those that must be acknowledged. As part of this course, your instructor will spend some time clarifying the distinctions.

IV. In cases of plagiarism, the Department policy is in accord with the stated policy of the University. A plagiarizing student fails the course. Then a memorandum is filed with the Office of Judicial Procedures, where it remains in the active file for a period of five years. The Coordinator of Judicial Procedures notifies the student offender and generally imposes a sanction of disciplinary probation for the first reported offense. A second offense may result in a sanction of suspension from the University for up to two years.

The Virtues of Ambition

by Joseph Epstein

Ambition is one of those Rorschach words: define it and you instantly reveal a great deal about yourself. Even that most neutral of works, *Webster's*, in its Seventh New Collegiate Edition, gives itself away, defining ambition first and foremost as "an ardent desire for rank, fame, or power." Ardent immediately assumes a heat incommensurate with good sense and stability, and rank, fame, and power have come under heavy attack for at least a century. One can, after all, be ambitious for the public good, for the alleviation of suffering, for the enlightenment of mankind, though there are some who say that these are precisely the ambitious people most to be mistrusted.

Surely ambition is behind dreams of glory, of wealth, of love, of distinction, of accomplishment, of pleasure, of goodness. What life does with our dreams and expectations cannot, of course, be predicted. Some dreams, begun in selflessness, end in rancor; other dreams, begun in selfishness, end in large-heartedness. The unpredictability of the outcome of dreams is no reason to cease dreaming.

To be sure, ambition, the sheer thing unalloyed by some larger purpose than merely clambering up, is never a pretty prospect to ponder. The single-mindedly ambitious is an old human type— "Cromwel, I charge thee, fling away Ambition," wrote Shakespeare in *Henry VIII*. "By that sinne fell the Angels"—and scarcely a type that has gone out of style, or soon figures to. As drunks have done to alcohol, the single-minded have done to ambition—given it a bad name. Like a taste for alcohol, too, ambition does not always allow for easy satisfaction. Some people cannot handle it; it has brought grief to others, and not merely the ambitious alone. Still, none of this seems sufficient cause for driving ambition under the counter, in an undeclared Volstead Act.*

By this I do not mean to say that ambition has gone or been driven out of style. It hasn't. Or at least not completely. In our day many people, goaded by ambition, go in for self-improvement programs of one kind or another: speed reading, assertiveness training, the study of books calling for looking out for number one and other forms of aggressiveness. But such activities have always seemed declasse, and the sort of person who goes to est today thirty or forty

---

* The Eighteenth Amendment, prohibiting sale of alcoholic beverages.

years ago might have enrolled in a Dale Carnegie course.* In most respects, it appears that the more educated a person is, the more hopeless life seems to him. This being so, ambition, to the educated class, has come to seem pointless at best, vicious at worst. Ambition connotes a certain Rotarian optimism, a thing unseemly, in very poor taste, rather like a raging sexual appetite in someone quite elderly. None of this, of course, has stopped the educated classes from attempting to get their own out of the world—lots of the best of everything, as a famous epicure once put it—which they continue to do very effectively. To renunciation is thus added more than a piquant touch of hypocrisy.

If the above assertions seemed overstated, consider what seems to me the unarguableness of the following assertions. If one feels the stirrings of ambition, it is on the whole best to keep them hidden. To say of a young man or woman that he or she is ambitious is no longer, as it once was, a clear compliment. Rather the reverse. A person called ambitious is likely to arouse anxiety, for in our day anyone so called is thought to be threatening, possibly a trifle neurotic. Energy is still valued, so too is competence, but ambition is in bad repute. And perhaps nowhere more than in America.

ANALYSIS

Memo on Plagiarism

1. How many different methods of defining *plagiarism* do you notice?
2. Do you now know what *plagiarism* means?
3. What would happen to you in *your* institution if you were caught plagiarizing?
4. Besides its being a "definition paper," this memo illustrates a use of classification/division development. In what ways?
5. What is your reaction to reading this memo?

The Virtues of Ambition

1. Epstein employs several techniques to define *ambition*. Using the suggestions in Item 1 of the Prewriting Process, point out as many examples as you can.
2. Has Epstein used any words or made any allusions that you do not understand? If so, you should use your dictionary or talk to an informed person.
3. Comment on the appropriateness of his title. If you were to change it to a more effective one, what would you choose? Why?
4. If you are looking for a topic for this assignment, you might write about your definition of *ambition*. Your paper might be quite different from Epstein's.

* A self-help class based on the "power of positive thinking."

11

Autobiography/Biography

INTRODUCTION

Writing about yourself or other people can be one of the most fascinating of your assignments. Everyone, in one way or another, wants the world to know who he or she is, and judging from the proliferation of autobiographies on the best-seller lists, a large audience is often eager to find out. If you do not feel comfortable writing about yourself, however, you might write a biography. Many people are more able observers of others than revealers of themselves.

You do not have to write an entire book for either part of this assignment; a short essay will suffice.

Assignment

Part A: Using a specific point of view, write a 300–500-word autobiography.
Part B: Write a 300–500-word biography of someone you know well.

PREWRITING PROCESS FOR PART A

Many student writers may be fearful of writing about themselves because they believe they do not have anything interesting to say. You do not need to have an interesting life to write an interesting autobiography; you can easily catch your audience's attention by your sense of humor, good description, or analysis of everyday life situations.

1. There is no need to tell everything about yourself from your birth to the present; rather, you should attempt to find a thread, an organizational tool, to keep your autobiography unified and concise. This "thread" may be a generalization about your life or a quality or characteristic of yours that you want to emphasize. You will also find that this thread will assist in giving your piece of writing a structure.

In order to find the appropriate thread, you must do a bit of stocktaking of your life to date. You can complete the following brainstorming activity on your own, but you might find it more beneficial to work with another person.

Make up a list of questions to discover if a particular event has occurred at least three times in your life. Here are a few questions to help you get started:

- What types of homes have you lived in?
- What kinds of schooling have you had?
- What sorts of accidents have you had?
- What sorts of illnesses have you had to endure?
- What countries have you visited?
- What is your main quality? Defect?
- What have been your greatest experiences?
- What were the saddest times of your life?
- What were the happiest times of your life?
- What do you enjoy doing when you are with your friends?
- What do you think about but not talk about?

Now either you or your partner should make up other similar questions to discover a particular pattern in your life that might be suitable as a unifying device for your autobiography.

2. When you have completed the preceding exercise, note each time a particular event in your life has recurred. Under each mention of the event, jot down the details of it. Make sure you include the similarities and differences between the recurring events each time they happened. If you have moved several times, for example, each new home may have been larger and better, or smaller and worse, than the one before, or the neighborhood in which the new home was situated may have affected you in different but obvious and dramatic ways. Try reorganizing your material on a ladder, mandala, flowchart, or in some other visual way. (See Chapter 25 for more information.)

3. Assume that your audience does not know you well. In this way you will have to include some details that will make your life distinct from everyone else's.

4. For a bit of prewriting fun, write your autobiography in the form of a birth announcement, predicting what you will be like as an adult, or of your own obituary notice, discussing what you were like. Limit: 50 words.

5. Write a few Absurd Analogies in your journal. Start your entry with one of these. "I'm like a rosebush," "I'm like a tornado," "I'm a watermelon," or "I'm incense."

6. Give ten different answers to this question: "Who are you?" Each answer should be no more than three or four words. When you have recorded ten different responses, circle the one that you consider the real you. Make a half-hour journal entry supporting the topic, "The Real Me."

7. Draw three columns and label them as follows: "The Me Everybody Knows," "The Me Only a Few Know," and "The Me Nobody Knows." Fill in as many probing details as you can. When you finish, decide which column would make the beginning

of the best autobiography. Remember, an effective autobiography is both informative and interesting.

8. Decide to whom you want to tell something about yourself, what you want to tell, why you want to tell it, and in what situation your audience will read it. List your writing variables before you begin to draft your autobiography.

PREWRITING PROCESS FOR PART B

1. As this is to be an informal biography rather than a research report, decide who will be your subject. Mother? Sibling? Grandparent? Boyfriend? Workshop partner? Girlfriend? Or you may know a great deal about a particular athlete, movie star, or other celebrity. The choice of subject is yours.

2. Before you begin, state your purpose for writing the biography. Sorry, but "Because my instructor assigned it" is not a good enough reason.

The statement of purpose should take into account not only your subject but also your other writing variables. As you read these examples of statements of purpose, notice how easy it would be to create an ordinary listing of writing variables from each of them:

- I am going to write a eulogy (format) of a friend of mine who died (situation) recently (topic). I intend to send it to her family (audience) to let them know how much she meant to me (purpose).

- I must present an oral introduction (format) of a speaker (topic) at my club (situation) so that the members (audience) will know a little about him before he speaks (purpose).

- I have been invited to a roast (situation) of a friend of mine (topic) where I have to give a humorous speech (format) to all the guests (audience). I must make them laugh (purpose) by telling them some funny stories in my friend's life. I am going to speak like Bob Hope (persona).

3. Keep your purpose and audience in mind as you gather information for your biography. For some biographies, the audience will be more concerned with factual details about the subject; for others, they will want to get to know him or her more personally. Sometimes you may want to pass judgment on your subject; other times, you will merely want to tell your subject's story.

4. You may wish to choose a major characteristic of your subject and base your biography on that particular quality. For more discussion on choosing a quality or thread, refer to Item 1 of the Prewriting Process in Part A. If you cannot think of a major quality, perhaps you have not chosen the correct subject for this assignment. You should certainly know a great deal about your subject in order to be able to see distinctive features in his or her life.

If you are having difficulty discovering a major characteristic, make up a few questions and, if possible, interview your subject. Here are some examples of questions you might ask:

- What do you think is your best, or worst, character trait?

- What makes you happiest?
- Which countries have you visited?
- How many times have you moved?
- What are you proudest of in your life?
- (If he or she is running for office) What would you do if elected?

5. You might also want to do some reading or to interview other people about your subject (with the subject's permission, of course) before proceeding.

6. For a bit of prewriting fun, write a biography of your workshop partner in the style of *Who's Who*. Post it on the bulletin board so that the rest of your class will know your partner a little better. Limit: 50 words.

7. Write a few Absurd Analogies in your journal. Start your entry with one of these: "My subject is like a fir tree," "My subject is a whirlpool," "My subject is a juicy orange," or "My subject is a viper."

8. Give ten different answers to this question: "Who is my subject?" Each answer should be no more than three or four words. When you have recorded ten different responses, circle the one that you consider the real person. Make a half-hour journal entry supporting the topic, "The Real _____."

9. Draw three columns and label them as follows: "The ————— Everybody Knows," "The _____ Only a Few Know," and "The _____ Nobody Knows." Fill in as many probing details as you can. When you finish, decide which column would make the beginning of the best biography. Remember, an effective biography is both informative and interesting.

DRAFTING PROCESS FOR PARTS A AND B

1. Besides being concerned with structure, this assignment also requires a consistent tone and style. Draft several beginnings of your autobiography or biography until you find the particular style which suits you and the recurring events that you wish to include.

2. After you have finished one draft, you might find it very beneficial to put it away and begin another using a different style. You might enjoy developing a new style you can use for this and other assignments.

3. Examine the following different ways of saying the same thing.

A straightforward style:

I was born in St. Louis on May 1, 1961.

A colloquial style:

I made my debut in these parts on May 1, 1961.

A breezy style:

I came into the world with a little help from my folks on May 1, 1961.

A lecturing style:

My birth took place in the city of St. Louis, the gem of the fair state of Missouri, on the first day of the month of May in the year nineteen hundred and sixty-one.

An ironic style:

The happiest day of my parents' life was May 1, 1961, when they celebrated the arrival of their first tax deduction—me.

A comic style:

My parents shouted "Mayday" in earnest on May 1, 1961, the day I was born.
4. You might like to start your autobiography or biography by composing a concise paragraph. The following is an example:

TOPIC:	John F. Parker
AUDIENCE:	Readers of *The Independent Writer*. Real. To be used in a textbook (this one).
PURPOSE AND SITUATION:	To give you an opportunity to learn a little about the person who is helping you become a better writer
FORMAT:	Expository paragraph
VOICE:	My own
TOPIC SENTENCE:	I wait expectantly to challenge my next highlight.

Highlights to '86

I was born during the Depression to poor but loving prairie farmers who specialized in growing rocks. Besides these piles of white rocks towering amid our spindly wheat fields, my most vivid memories of childhood and teenage days are of fourteen different schools (my family moved a lot): tiny country schools with eight grades in one room, frighteningly spacious city elementary schools, large old high schools, and sterile new ones. At the end of the ninth grade, I was forced to quit school and find a job. I spent a frustrating year as a laborer, getting my fingers stuck between print rollers and cutting off the tips of my fingers with a paper cutter. Deep inside, I yearned for a fuller life, but the reality of my situation didn't allow me to express my inner feelings. I despaired until a friend told me about night school and the possibility of a better life. So at the end of each day I scrubbed off the ink, bandaged my bleeding fingers, and attended night school. In the evening I took grades 10, 11, and 12, managing to graduate in one year. Graduation was a treasured highlight: I could then become a teacher. After teacher training, I was given my own sixth-grade class in Vancouver, Canada. From there I moved up the teaching ladder to the college level while at the same time obtaining a bachelor of arts degree in English and drama at the University of British Columbia and a master's degree in drama at the University of

Washington. Besides teaching English, I've always been a dabbler in theatre—first as an amateur, then as a professional. After seven years as an artistic director of two Vancouver theatre companies, I prepared for my next highlight—a move to London, England. In 1977 my wife, daughter, and three sons all agreed to come along so that I could work as a professional actor in films and television as well as on stage. After three years I returned to Vancouver with good memories and lots of enthusiasm to start yet another career—as a textbook writer. After publishing two books in Canada (*The Writer's Workshop* and *The Process of Writing*), I set off for San Diego where I wrote the book you are now reading—my latest highlight. Before I aim my sights at another career, I will complete another textbook for the American high-school market. And then? Who knows? With my philosophy of living life fully becoming my reality instead of my impossible dream, I wait expectantly, excitedly, yet contentedly, to challenge my next highlight.

Once you have written a similar paragraph for your autobiography or biography, examine it carefully to determine which parts need to be expanded so that you can produce a 300–500-word essay. Which parts of the above paragraph do you think should be more detailed?

REVISING PROCESS FOR PARTS A AND B

1. You and your peers should edit your autobiography or biography according to the instructions in Chapter 31, as well as using the following specific questions:

   a. What is the thread which runs through the essay?

   b. What kind of organization does it have (chronological, climactic, decreasing importance, increasing importance, bad to good, good to bad, and so forth)?

   c. What label would your peers give the style? Ask them to give examples of how you have sustained the style.

   d. What feature of the essay did they find the most revealing?

   e. If your peers are editing an autobiography, what have they learned about you that they did not already know? If they are editing a biography, can they readily recognize the major quality of your subject? They should be able to find several instances that reveal your or your subject's major quality. Ask them to find the direct instances—those which you have stated clearly; then ask them to find indirect instances—those which you have implied or stated subtly.

2. Ask your editors to help you with the answers to the following questions:

   a. Should you omit any words, sentences, or paragraphs from your essay? Why?

   b. Should you add anything? Why?

   c. Should you make any other changes? Why?

d. Will the intended audience see the appropriateness of the purpose and situation for your essay?

e. If you use a persona, will the reader appreciate it?

3. Before you submit your autobiography or biography to your instructor-editor, give it one last proofreading, and then give a polished copy to your intended reader.

PRODUCTS

Footsore

by Gino Nasato, student

I am a foot. I was pulled kicking from warm security on August 16, 1957. It was not so much the cold that startled me that fateful morning, as my realization that I was forever attached to a stumbling lout named Gino Nasato. Still, life was grand during the early months; Gino simply lay on his back and played baby. At the age of eight months, though, our peaceful coexistence was shattered when the lout started to walk. Oh, to describe the pain of those early years brings back horrid memories. I was kicked, I was bumped, I was stubbed, and I was stomped. Self-preservation in mind, I fought back with a vengeance. For the first ten years I tripped him as often as possible. The knees and the elbows hated me for the pain I inflicted, and his poor mother despised me for the clothes she was always mending. Through the high-school years I was continually abused. If I wasn't being butted painfully against a soccer ball, I was risking toes and heels with daring slides into second base. My only hope was that Gino would get a soft desk job after graduating. I hoped in vain.

First, it was logging and those dastardly spiked boots. Tired of logging, Gino went to sea, where hard, slippery, cold steel decks awaited me. I still lose my footing when I think of how that ship rolled. In his twenty-first year Gino decided to go to Europe. The dreams I had—visions of pretty painted toes, French music, and Gino sitting in cafés, resting me on stools. Oh, the naivety of a foot! That bastard shuffled me through Paris subways, blistered me in Athens midday heat, and hobbled me on cobbled streets in Amsterdam. My only respite came when we hit the beaches of Greece. For two glorious months I was in Dr. Scholl's heaven: cool wet sand to leave my autograph in and sparkling surf to soak my calluses. But, alas, it wasn't to last; chasing a pretty face who had cold feet, Gino wound up in Vancouver. As it turned out, that girl didn't have any problems with colds at all. Simply put, she was just a great big heel.

It was about this time that I felt my toes had been stepped on long enough. I formulated a plan with the ankle, and during one of Gino's efforts to kick up his heels, we twisted severely. I was tickled pink when the doctor prescribed one month of total rest, with me kept in an elevated position. Finally, after twenty-three years, I was put on the pedestal I rightfully deserved. With some guidance from me, Gino has finally recognized the prominent role I play in his life. He's now back studying at school, which gives me plenty of time to relax. In fact, things have been going so well lately, I'm thinking of passing on my secrets to other downtrodden feet. I might even start a revolution. After all, just think of all the foot soldiers I could recruit!

Mark Twain by Mark Twain

This has been excerpted from various pieces of autobiographical material.

I was born the 30th of November, 1835, in the almost invisible village of Florida, Monroe County, Missouri. The village contained a hundred people and I increased the population by 1 per cent. It is more than many of the best men in history could have done for a town. Recently someone in Missouri sent me a picture of the house I was born in. Heretofore I have always stated that it was a palace but I shall be more guarded now.

In my schoolboy days I had no aversion to slavery. I was not aware that there was anything wrong about it. No one arraigned it in my hearing; the local papers said nothing about it; the local pulpit taught us that God approved it, that it was a holy thing and that the doubter need only look in the Bible if he wished to settle his mind. If the slaves themselves had an aversion to slavery they were wise and said nothing.

I was some years a Mississippi pilot. I entered upon the small enterprise of "learning" twelve or thirteen hundred miles of the great Mississippi River with the easy confidence of my time in life. If I had really known what I was about to require of my faculties, I should not have the courage to begin. I supposed all a pilot had to do was to keep his boat in the river, and I did not consider that that could be much of a trick, since it was wide.

A pilot, in those days, was the only unfettered and entirely independent human being that lived in the earth. Kings are but hampered servants of parliament and the people; parliaments sit in chains forged by their constituency; the editor of a newspaper cannot be independent, but must work with one hand tied behind him by party and patrons, and be content to utter only half or two-thirds of his mind; writers of all kinds are manacled servants of the public.

I was a soldier two weeks once in the beginning of the war, and was hunted like a rat the whole time. I have shoveled silver tailings in a quartz mill, and I've done "pocket mining." Nature conceals gold in pockets.

I was a newspaper reporter four years in cities, and so saw the inside of many things; and was a reporter in a legislature two sessions and the same in Congress one session, and thus learned to know personally three sample bodies of the smallest minds and the selfishest souls and the cowardliest hearts that God makes.

In October 1866 I broke out as a lecturer, and from that day to this I have always been able to gain my living without doing any work; for the writing of book and magazine matter was always play, not work. I enjoyed it; it was merely billiards to me.

Would I be a boy again? I will answer: 1. Without any modifying stipulations at all, but just simply be a boy again and start fresh? NO! 2. Would I live over again under certain conditions? Certainly I would! The main condition would be, that I should emerge from boyhood as a "cub pilot" on a Mississippi boat, & that I should by & by become a pilot, & remain one. The minor conditions would be these: Summer always; & I would have the trips long, & the stays in port short; & my boat should be a big dignified freight boat—being never in a hurry; & her crew should never change, nor ever die. This is the way I would have it all.

I came in with Halley's Comet in 1835. It is coming again next year, and I expect I'll go out with it. The Almighty has said, no doubt, "Now here go these two unaccountable frauds; they came in together, they must go out together." Oh! I am looking forward to that.

Author's note: In the following product, Grayson is writing about herself in the third person; hence, she is writing a biography.

The Story of R

by Roberta Grayson, student

Take the case of R, from a middle-class family. She has two older sisters and no other siblings. She has little experience with other children prior to beginning school at age six. Shortly after entering school, it becomes apparent that she is not learning to read with the same facility as her schoolmates, even though she seems, in other ways, equally as bright.

Her sight is tested and found adequate, so her teachers just assume that she is "a bit slow." She is branded. When she stumbles over simple words, children tease her, as children always torment those who are different. She begins to withdraw, to see herself as different, to think of herself as dumb. If she could only learn to read well, she would not be different and, perhaps, they wouldn't tease her. Learning to read well, doing well in school becomes all-important. There is no time for playing, no time for movies or music or art. All of her time must be devoted to learning to read well. Still she fails. The jibes become sharper, more painful. The brand, "DUMB," becomes more indelible. If she could just appear to read well, she thinks, then everything would be OK.

She bribes and cajoles her sisters into reading her lessons to her over and over. She memorizes any and everything that she might be called upon to read aloud in class. This works for a while, but when testing time comes, she is caught out. The doubts begin again. Maybe they are right. Maybe she is just plain dumb. The desire to really learn is always there, nagging at her. But she is too busy concealing her inability to read to devote any time to really learning. The teachers pass her from one grade to the next. After all, the poor thing is doing the best that she can.

In high school she withdraws from everyone except a few who will, uncritically, help her with her schoolwork. She would love to drop out of school, but she feels compelled to finish. To fail to graduate would prove "them" right.

After graduation, there is the welcome, busy oblivion of marriage and family. Unhampered by the preoccupation with concealing her inability to read, she discovers that she can learn many things very well indeed. She desires to learn; curiosity is nagging harder than ever. She sets out to learn why she can sometimes read reasonably well and at other times hardly at all. (This common symptom of dyslexia confuses and depresses the dyslexic.)

She studies and soon finds that others share her condition (about 5 percent of the population, with slightly more boys than girls). She learns that the condition has a name, Specific Primary Dyslexia. Now the thirst for learning has a direction, to learn about this condition that has so affected her life. The process begins with communication with people and organizations that might have information. Many painfully written letters begin to bear occasional fruit. She learns that the local community college offers special help to students with impaired sight. They have things like tape-recorded textbooks and readers to give handicapped students tests orally. Perhaps these things can help her. After all, isn't her condition a sort of sight impairment? She certainly doesn't see things as others do.

Hesitantly she enrolls in the community college. She does not volunteer information about her disability easily: some of her teachers never knew. A few knew and didn't seem to care, while others cared, but didn't know how to alter their teaching or testing methods for a dyslexic in their classrooms. Some, however, allowed her to tape their lectures, realizing that was her only means of taking notes. In addition, they worked closely with the support groups of the college so that she could go to them for assistance and do her tests in the student service center with their help.

Knowledge of dyslexia is new to most people, and dyslexic students are even newer to college campuses, but they are beginning to appear and be recognized. They are anxious to learn and they can learn, so methods of circumventing their disability must be found. Soon there will be viable methods devised so that the dyslexic can learn, because there is no known cure for dyslexia.

A Look at Mark Twain

by Flo Manderson, student

The first 36 years of Samuel Clemens's life gave him practical knowledge: as a youngster in Missouri he learned about life in a small town, as a pilot on a steamboat he learned to love the Mississippi River, as a reporter in the West he studied American life, and as a European traveler he studied the world. He used these experiences to become one of the most successful realistic novelists of nineteenth-century America.

Samuel Langhorne Clemens was born November 30, 1835, the third son and fifth child of John and Sarah (Lampton) Clemens, both descendents of Virginians. He was born in Florida, Mo., a village of just 100 people, and, with his birth, increased the population by 1 percent. He later said, "It is more than many of the best men in history could have done for a town."

At the age of 12, Clemens apprenticed as a printer when his father died leaving the family impoverished. The youngster's formal education apparently ceased the following year, in 1848.

When his eldest brother, Orion, became a newspaper publisher in 1851, he invited Clemens to work for him. Young Sam soon became restless, however, and began traveling extensively throughout America. While on a trip down the Mississippi, he arranged to receive navigational training under Horace Bixby, the pilot of the boat. Learning the mysteries of the winding channels of that great river and receiving his pilot's license 18 months later, Clemens thought he found his life's work during the boom period of the steamboat age. For him, the experiences were both instructive and exciting. In addition, he adopted the persona "Mark Twain," meaning mark two fathoms, a term used by Mississippi riverboat pilots in sounding shallows for minimum navigable depths.

The shaggy-headed Mark Twain, whose frontier upbringing and roving career had introduced him to many of the cruder aspects of life, always enjoyed a fun time. A stag party with plenty of drinks and foolish pranks resulted, at least on one occasion, in a night in jail for drunkenness. With great charm, he always spoke his mind when the spirit moved him, yet he was a man of great sensitivity and emotional capacity.

In 1870, Twain married Oliva Langdon from a well-to-do family. After their wedding, they moved to Buffalo, N.Y.; then, shortly thereafter, to Hartford, Conn., where he became a free-lance writer. These were to become his most productive years. "Up to the time of his anchorage in Hartford," as Dixon Wecter noticed, "the most important facts about Mark Twain are the things that happened to him—shaping his development as an artist and feeding the granaries of memory. After that date the chief milestones are books he wrote out of that accumulation" (*Encyclopedia Britannica* 22: 424).

A great humorist and a profound satirist, Mark Twain is accredited with popular and outstanding autobiographies, travel books and novels. *The Adventures of Tom Sawyer* (1876) is one of Twain's most-loved works, certainly his best for a young audience. Shortly after completing the stories of Tom, Twain began *The Adventures of Huckleberry Finn*, his masterpiece, which has been called America's greatest novel. Both these stories are drawn from his boyhood experiences in Missouri, and recreate life along the Mississippi valley before the Civil War.

Twain's writing varies in brilliance because he was a self-trained writer who, at his worst and best, worked instinctively. In his work he looks back over a significant span of American history which he actively participated in. There is no doubt of his unusual powers of invention, especially his genius for creating unforgettable characters. He is as popular today as he ever was during his lifetime, and his writings have become American classics. Along with him, Tom, Huck, and Jim live—on stages and screens throughout the world.

He died April 21, 1910, at the age of 75 years.

ANALYSIS

Footsore

1. This is a witty example of an autobiography using a persona. What do you think his reader's reaction was? Is there anything more about Nasato that you would want to know?

2. Why do you think the author chose to use this persona? If you were to use a persona of a part of your body, what would it be?

3. Can you pick out examples of irony in the piece?

Mark Twain by Mark Twain

1. What is the main focus of the autobiography?

2. Is the collection of Twain facts unified? Support your answer.

3. Is the paragraph beginning "A pilot, in those days..." unnecessary? Why do you think it was included in Twain's autobiography?

4. Do you think the humor in the autobiography is appropriate? Why? (Interestingly, Mark Twain's prophesy proved true. He did die in 1910, the year Halley's Comet reappeared.)

5. After you read the biography of Mark Twain and compare it with the autobiography, what are some of the significant differences in the way the material has been presented?

The Story of R

1. What is your immediate reaction in reading this biography?

2. Why do you think the student writer felt more comfortable writing a biography in the third person to describe her own dyslexic problem? Paradoxically, she gave permission for her essay to be published in *The Independent Writer*.

3. In reality this biography was excerpted from her social science term paper on dyslexia. The biography became a narrative illustration to describe the feelings of a dyslexic. In the essay, she defined dyslexia fully and explored the possibility of a dyslexic obtaining a college degree. Does the biography here stand well on its own? Support your answer with specific comments.

A Look at Mark Twain

1. What organizational thread has the writer used to hold the biography together?

2. What things do you know about Mark Twain that the writer has not included? Should they have been mentioned? Why?

3. Compare the biography with the autobiography of Mark Twain. What are some significant differences and similarities? Support your answer.

The next time you are in a library, bookstore, or drugstore, look at the latest bestsellers. How many of them are autobiographies or biographies of world personalities? Pick one up; you may discover a new source of enjoyable reading.

12

Review

INTRODUCTION

A review is an expository essay in which you give your considered opinion of a work. Unlike the writer of a literary essay, the writer of a review should assume that the reader does not know the book, film, or other material being criticized. Therefore, you should give your reader a general idea of what the work is about, as well as what you think of it. A good review combines information and criticism.

Assignment

Write a review of a book, a film, a play, a TV show, a record, or other work of art in approximately 500 words. Although you may review a sports event, seminar, political rally, restaurant, or any other event, occasion, or place, most of the following suggestions refer to works of art.

PREWRITING PROCESS

1. The main reason for writing a review is to give your opinions about a work of art or other event. Hence, you are expected to be critical. Criticizing a work of art, however, is not just pulling it apart. You should discuss both the parts that, in your opinion, work well and those that do not.

2. Examine a few recent issues of your daily newspaper(s) or national and international journals, and read the latest reviews of books, plays, movies, sports events, restaurants, and so on.

- What kind of information does the opening paragraph provide?
- Does the reviewer provide a summary of the work?

- Has the reviewer used any quotations from the work or event?
- What kind of information does the closing paragraph provide?
- Do you know what the reviewer thought of the work or event?
- Would you go to see or read the work because of the review? Why?

3. A review is the expression of one person's opinion. Theatre critic Wayne Edmonstone puts it clearly:

> I must tell you *what* I think. I must also tell you *why* I think it. I do not tell you what *someone else* thinks I should think. I do not tell you what *you* are to think. It's as simple as that and if all you're looking for is a reflection of your own tastes, prejudices, or preferences, then—with all respect—the place to look is in the mirror.

So when you write, make sure your reader knows exactly where you stand. Be opinionated. Back up your opinions. Be emphatic. Indeed, try to include something memorable—a pun, a witty quote—something that will stick in the reader's mind.

4. To make this assignment more interesting, you might write a review of a show or book, to be submitted to your local or school newspaper. Remember, you will not be writing for the general readership of the newspaper. Your audience for a movie review will be people who go to movies; for an opera, those who enjoy opera; for a boxing match, boxing fans.

5. Once you have chosen the material (show, book, event) you wish to review, plan a brainstorming session to generate supporting evidence. Produce the Pro/Con Ladders, the Pentad, or the Senses Cluster (see Chapter 25). In addition, complete the brainstorming technique called Test Your Prejudice Level. Answer the following questions truthfully and completely:

- What did you think of the material *before* you saw or read it? Had you pretty much made up your mind before seeing or reading it?
- Did you change your preconceived attitude *while* or *after* you saw or read the material?
- What in particular happened to change your preconceived attitude?
- Was there anything external that affected your feelings—for example, was your seat bad, the audience inattentive, your health poor, your mood good?
- Would your attitude change if you were to see or read the same material again?
- What percentage of the audience or spectators felt as you did about the material?
- What do other reviewers think of the material? Do you agree or disagree with them? Why?

6. Experiment with your writing variables in order to come up with quite different reviews. Make up, for example, an audience and situations that are both real and imaginary in order to see which would produce a stronger review.

DRAFTING PROCESS

1. Quickly identify the material you are reviewing by stating the title, author, publisher, theatre, director, channel, musician, event, restaurant, and so on.

2. Consider the purpose and emphasis of the work under review. If it is a nonfiction book, for example, you may want to give your reader some background on its subject; if fiction, you may want to discuss the plot or one or two memorable characters. Ultimately, you must assess a work according to its purpose. Did it succeed in informing, entertaining, or persuading you?

3. Give enough of the plot to interest your readers, so that they can decide whether or not they wish to read, see, or listen to the reviewed work. Do not tell the whole story; a review is not a précis or summary. You should whet your reader's appetite. And if you are reviewing a mystery novel or film, do not, unless you want to be killed by a fan, identify the murderer.

4. The inclusion of a few quotations to show the work's style enlivens a review. Attempt to fit the quotations into your own prose so that the reader can continue smoothly. (Chapter 39 provides examples of how writers can mix quoted material with their own prose.)

5. Because a review is an argumentative essay, you may find it useful to read the Drafting Process of Chapter 5. Remember that you must substantiate what you say by referring to the work you are reviewing.

6. Professional critics sometimes write deliberately controversial, discourteous reviews. As a nonprofessional reviewer, however, you should leave statements like these out of your reviews:

- In *Star Trek II: The Wrath of Khan* the camera lumbers through a standard revenge plot with all the energy of an elephant with a head cold.

- He writes his plays for the ages—the ages between five and twelve.

7. An illustration or a photograph often enlivens a review. Consider including one, if possible.

REVISING PROCESS

After you have written your final draft, you should judge it according to the set of standards outlined in Chapter 31. Then decide which method of peer-editing from Chapter 31 you want to follow. Use the Revising Process from Chapter 5, as well as the following questions, to help you in revising your review.

1. Does the review give enough or too much information about the work or event?

2. Have you expressed your opinion of the work or event clearly? Have you explained why you feel as you do?

3. Has the review convinced your peers? In other words, would they do as you suggest: either see or not see, buy or not buy, read or not read the reviewed material?

4. Does the review include appropriate quotations? Do they fit in well with your own prose?

For further editorial help, present your review to your instructor-editor. Then polish your final copy and send it to your intended reader.

PRODUCTS

Thick Blood Flows at the *Pet Sematary*

by Rita Ringle, student

What do a resurrected cat, a young boy with a scalpel, and the Devil have in common? They're all found in Stephen King's latest novel, *Pet Sematary*.

King's ingenuity has prevailed again. He has taken childhood fears and brought them to life in this book. King knows how to tell a powerful story. His mastery of the English language is stronger each time he publishes another book. He knows how to blend horror with a bit of comedy. The suspense will grab you from the moment you begin reading *Pet Sematary* until the moment you finish it.

The story is about an old, Indian burial ground in Ludlow, Maine, where a town's hidden secret lies.

Louis Creed, a physician from Chicago, moves to Ludlow with his family to start a new job at the local university. Creed learns about the pet cemetery immediately after moving into his new home but doesn't learn about its secret. The action begins when Louis takes on his new job as the university's physician. His welcome is cut short by a tragic accident. Victor Pascow, a student at the university, had been jogging with two friends when a speeding vehicle struck him and sent him head first into a tree. Victor Pascow dies in Louis's arms. Later that same evening when Louis is asleep, he is awakened by the . . . (No, it would not be fair to tell you any more.)

I can tell you about an incident while Louis's wife and children are away on a vacation. Their pet cat dies. Louis buries the cat in pet "sematary." But soon after the burial rites, the cat . . . (No, I can't tell you that either.)

The story truly unfolds when Louis's four-year-old son dies. Louis takes his son to the burial ground in hopes that he can bring him back to life. The blood starts to flow when his son is resurrected. In one scene, the boy's mother is calling for him and he appears in the background, holding one of his father's surgical scalpels. . . .

The story has a climax that will stand the small hairs on your neck on end. If you're a connoisseur of the macabre, this book should satisfy your appetite.

Pet Sematary Buries King

By Danette Bartlett, student

What was supposed to be Stephen King's best horror novel, *Pet Sematary*, has turned out mediocre at best. An ever-tiring buildup of plot, followed with a quick wrap-up, leaves this reader dissatisfied.

How is it that the talented Stephen King can be so cruel as to use only half of his potential? He misuses his talent for bringing across bizarre ideas to the reader and only skims the surface in this novel. For example, he had more graphic explanations in his short story "The Raft" than in this novel.

In *Pet*, King explains the plot early. He outlines what's going to happen so early that he takes away much of the suspense. And if not for suspense, why else does one read a mystery novel?

The story is about a family that moves to a rural house in Maine (where almost all his novels take place). After settling in, Louis Creed, King's main character, meets his new neighbor Judd Crandall. Judd, an elderly man who's lived in the area all his life, immediately informs Louis of the cemetery directly behind his house. Judd talks Louis into taking a hike with him to see the unusual sight. When they arrive at the Pet Sematary, a place designated by past generations of children who couldn't spell, Judd warns Louis he should never go beyond the deadfall in back of the cemetery.

Later, Louis's family takes a vacation and leaves him in charge of their family cat named Church. The next day, the cat is struck by a speeding truck and dies. Louis, upset about whether he's going to tell his daughter the truth about Church, seeks Judd out for advice. Judd takes pity on him and decides to take Louis beyond the deadfall to an old Indian burial ground, a place that supposedly had magical properties to bring the dead back to life. After performing a special burial rite on the cat, Judd leads Louis back to his home and tells him to wait. As you've probably already guessed, the cat returns to life, but he's not quite the same. Walking awkwardly, Church has an awful death smell of rotting flesh about him. Gone is the subtle grace and friendliness he once had. It is replaced with an evil that seeks blood and death. Mind you, all this happens by page 125! So what of the extra 248 pages left? Not much. It's filled with Louis's past life and present anxieties. Extremely boring, predictable material.

In an interview, King was quoted as saying that the story was so scary he had to put it down for a while. Really now! Scary? Hardly. We are swept through his main character's nightmare without ever feeling close to him. While the characters evolved in King's world, I was left out in the cold. In essence, King reveals only more of the same archetypical human nature of man's inability to learn from his mistakes.

I feel that *Pet Sematary* was written purely for money. King usually writes very good stories, but if he starts mass-producing his books to the point that he no longer cares about what is in them, his name will definitely stop appearing in the best-seller's list. I would only hope that in the future Stephen King will take more time and care to give his fans the creativity that they expect.

Heaven help moviegoers if a film is made of *Pet Sematary*. Since it's getting harder to get fans out to see his films, the producers will have to entice big-name stars like Morris the Cat, with a supporting cast of the meow-meow-meow gang! I can hardly wait. Chow-chow-chow!

ANALYSIS

Thick Blood Flows at the *Pet Sematary* and *Pet Sematary* Buries King

1. Has enough plot been related in both reviews to interest you in the book? Too much? Too little?

2. What statement in each review signals the writers' prejudice level? What do you think the writers thought of *Pet Sematary* before they read it? Support your answer. If you have read the book, have these reviewers changed your opinion? Support your answer.

3. Do the writers successfully support their thesis in each opening paragraph?

4. After reading both reviews, do you want to read *Pet Sematary*? Support your answer by referring to the reviews and your own prejudice level toward Stephen King.

13

Literary Essay

INTRODUCTION

There are two different formats that you can use when you respond to a literary work (short story, novel, poem, or play): a review (Chapter 12) and a literary essay (this assignment).

Writing an essay about a piece of literature for an informed reader is perhaps the hardest kind of writing that you will be required to do. Before plunging into this assignment, therefore, you might like to spend a little time working through some of the exercises in "The Reading Process," Chapter 40. There you will be able to respond to and reflect upon pieces of literature, thus gaining experience in writing for your peers or other uninformed readers before becoming involved in weightier literary criticism for your literature or humanities professors.

This assignment suggests a number of specific approaches to the interpretation of literature. Retelling the story, however, is one approach for which you will receive no credit. You should use details of plot only to support particular claims.

In your essay you should resist mentioning what you think of the work; expressing your opinion is *not* the main purpose of a literary essay. In a literary essay you interpret what the work, or a part of it, means; if you wish to criticize its effectiveness, write a review.

Assignment

Write a literary essay explaining your interpretation of one of the pieces of literature in the Appendix or of another piece that your instructor has assigned to you.

PREWRITING PROCESS

Most of the time when your instructors ask you to write a literary essay, they give you specific pieces of literature and specific topics to deal with. At other times you may have a great deal of latitude and be able to brainstorm topics by yourself or with your peers.

1. If you are confused as to what a literary essay is and how to write one, try the following writing activities in your journal before you begin to work with a piece of literature. When you finish, read one of the pieces to two of your peers and ask them whether or not you successfully dealt with an insightful experience.

a. Write a short account of a personal, eye-opening experience dealing with an aspect of the human condition in which you were involved. To start you thinking, consider the following aspects of the human condition: greed, prejudice, love, hate, trust, fear, jealousy, truth, faith. Choose an incident from your life that involved one of the above aspects, and state clearly your opinion or position *before* the experience—for example, you once thought that you were invincible and would never die. Provide the details of the actual experience in which you realized that your original opinion or position was wrong—for example, you were in a nearly fatal accident. State clearly your opinion *after* the experience—for example, you now realize that life is fragile.

b. Write a short account of a time when your first impression of someone or something changed. You might choose a particular food you disliked in the past and now love, a person whom you ignored and now love, a philosophy you did not believe in but now follow, and so on. Choose a subject in which you had a conversion of extremes—from love to hate or hate to love. Describe your past feelings about your subject, the details of the conversion, and your present feelings about your subject.

c. Write a short account of a conflict that you recently had so that two of your peers know exactly with whom or what you were in conflict. Also include the reasons why you were in conflict. Finally, relate the results of the conflict. The most interesting conflicts are ones that involve two or more people, one person against nature or an aspect of society, and one person against himself or herself.

d. Write a short account of a truth about yourself that you had to admit. Provide details about the truth and why you hid it from everyone (including yourself). Then provide details about your life after admitting the truth and bringing it out into the open. Explain the differences in your life-style *before* and *after* admitting the truth about yourself.

You will find that there is very little difference between the way in which you write about literature in a literary essay and the way you write about yourself and your own insights. In a good novel, the author makes characters, setting, and conflict as alive for you as your own life experiences.

2. If you worked through one of the suggestions in Item 1, you have already experienced what it's like to write a literary essay. The only difference is that instead of writing about something in your life, you will be writing about an imaginary character, setting, or conflict.

If the choice of literary selection and topic is up to you, consider examining the influence that the selection had on you, the reasons why you are writing, and to whom you are writing. In other words, choose a selection and topic that are important to you.

In addition, find out how well your audience knows the selection that you are writing about. Consider how the content and approach of your literary essay would change if you were to write to your literature instructor who has been teaching the particular selection for the past five years or to one of your peers who has read the selection only once.

3. If you wish, choose one of the suggested topics following each piece of literature in the Appendix and use it as the basis for your essay.

4. Spend time getting to know the selection that you have chosen, relating to the characters, setting, or conflicts. Doing this is essential before you begin to write a literary essay. If you need more assistance in this part of your reading process, see Chapter 40.

5. By applying a variation of the Pentad and the Pentad Connection methods of brainstorming (Chapter 25) to pieces of literature, you will come to understand and appreciate what you read. Therefore, you are strongly advised to spend a great deal of time brainstorming *before* you begin to draft your literary essay.

6. If you still feel that you have nothing to say after you have read the selection, thought about it, completed a Pentad Connection Cluster, and discussed it with others by using several of the exercises in Chapter 40, you might like to refer to a few secondary sources and read what others have said about the work. You will find a list of suggested resources at the end of this book. Your library should have many others.

If you quote directly from a secondary source, use quotation marks and parenthetical citations as you would for a research essay; otherwise, you will be plagiarizing (see MLA guidelines in Chapter 39). Even if you do not use the exact words from someone else's essay, you should give credit if you use someone else's idea. Your reader may ask you to include a bibliography of the secondary sources you have consulted (see Chapter 39).

7. For a bit of prewriting experience, write a miniature literary essay for an uninformed reader on one of the selections from the Appendix. Here is a mini-literary insight paper. It will, however, make no sense to you unless you first read "The Story of an Hour" in the Appendix. Notice how the quotations are fitted in with the writer's prose.

Monstrous Joy

In "The Story of an Hour," Kate Chopin shows us how *other characters misinterpret Mrs. Mallard's true feelings. To protect* Mrs. Mallard, Richards bears "the sad message" of her husband's death personally. He tells Josephine who, in turn, *conveys the details* to Mrs. Mallard in a *"half concealing"* revelation. The results produce "sudden, wild" hysterics and then, alone, *Mrs. Mallard realizes she is suddenly monstrously joyful.* She is "Free, free, free" of her husband. Yesterday she longed for death; today "her fancy was running riot along those days ahead of her." Josephine, *believing that Mrs. Mallard is grief-stricken*, entices her out of the locked room. When Mrs. Mallard comes out, she has been reborn; she is now filled with "a very elixir of life," feverishly triumphant that she is free. While the reader sees her as "a goddess of Victory," both Josephine and Richards *see only a grieving young woman* with a weak heart. When Mrs. Mallard sees her husband alive, and dies of shock in a split second, she has *no time even to change her expression from that of joy at being free—"Body and soul free."* Only *the reader sees the irony in the last words and understands the real nature of the "joy that kills."* (Italics indicate the thesis statement and its reinforcement.)

You and your peer group members might each write a miniature literary insight paper for each other on one of these topics:

- Mr. Mallard is basically a kind, tender, loving husband.
- Richards and Josephine are the story's messengers.
- The open window represents freedom.
- Weather conditions contribute to the mood of the story.
- The title is significant. With what "hour" does the story deal?

When you have finished your final draft, have a peer-editing session. Use these questions to help in your evaluation:

- Have you mentioned the title and author in the first sentence?
- Have you stated your thesis clearly at the beginning of the paper?
- Can you underline the thesis statement as well as its reinforcement through repetition? (Such reinforcement keeps the reader on track.)
- Are there quotations to support the thesis?
- Have you told too much plot?
- Are you convinced that the insight is valid?
- Does your peers' reading of the miniature paper add to their appreciation of "The Story of an Hour"?

Note: This mini-literary paper does not fulfill the requirements of this assignment; it merely helps you appreciate the form and method of construction of a literary essay.
8. Once you have chosen your selection and found a suitable topic, you should consider your audience and purpose. The audience for a literary essay is always someone who has read the piece of literature and wants to find out how someone else has interpreted it. He or she reads it to gain some new insight both into the story and into the aspect of the human condition with which it deals.

Produce a list of your writing variables before you begin to draft your essay. (If the topic and audience for your essay have been assigned, you will still have plenty of choice in determining the other writing variables.)

BROAD TOPIC:	"The Story of an Hour"
LIMITED TOPIC:	"The Story of an Hour" and the feminist movement

AUDIENCE:	My literature professor. Real. I intend to submit it.
PURPOSE:	To show why women enjoy "The Story of an Hour" more than men. Since "The Story of an Hour" is nearly 100 years old, I want to point out Mrs. Mallard's limited choices.
FORMAT:	Literary essay for the informed reader
VOICE:	My own
SITUATION:	My lit prof said that the women in the class would probably enjoy the story more than the men.
THESIS STATEMENT:	Today, feminists particularly enjoy "The Story of an Hour."

DRAFTING PROCESS

Once you have established your thesis statement and your writing variables, you can begin to draft your essay in the same way as you would any argumentative essay. (See the suggestions outlined in Chapter 5.) The following are a few specific suggestions that you should also keep in mind:

1. At the beginning of your essay, state clearly your thesis as well as the title and the author of the work you are discussing.

2. Be selective in using quotations, plot summaries, and character descriptions; use only those that support your argument. Ask yourself, Does this evidence prove what I want it to prove? If not, you may want to look for stronger evidence or revise your thesis statement.

3. Support every claim that you make with textual evidence. When you quote from most primary sources (short stories, poems, and plays), you must use quotation marks, but you do not have to provide parenthetical citations. For longer primary sources (novels and full-length plays), you might include the page number or act and scene numbers in parentheses *after* quotations. Try to introduce quotations into your own prose smoothly and with variety. For examples of how to do this see Chapter 39.

4. Never retell the plot. Assume that your readers (informed or uninformed) know the story and are reading your essay to learn about some interpretation that either had not occurred to them or that they can profitably be reminded of. For any number of reasons, however, your audience may ask you to include a brief summary of the selection. If, for example, your professor asks you to include a 100-word summary of the plot, you must seriously consider your audience's situation.

5. Preferably, you should write your essay in the third person rather than the first and in the present tense rather than the past. The third person sounds authoritative; the present tense makes the piece of literature seem alive. For example, the use of the first person and the past tense in "In my opinion, Romeo and Juliet loved foolishly, not wisely" is not as effective as the use of the third person and the present tense in "Romeo and Juliet love foolishly, not wisely." Find out, however, what your audience says about person and tense. Some professors prefer that students use the past tense in order to keep the tense of the essay the same as that of the story. However, you can change an original past tense if you include the present verb in brackets: Mrs. Mallard "[carries] herself unwittingly like a goddess of Victory." Whichever tense you use in your literary essay, be consistent.

6. Whenever you are explaining anything, you need to have a knowledge of terms. This is especially important as you draft your literary essay. Some of the literary terms you may want to use are included in the Glossary: metaphor, foreshadowing, crisis, denouement, and so on.

REVISING PROCESS

In revising your final draft, evaluate your literary essay according to the standards outlined in Chapter 31. To help your peers revise your work, use one of the editing methods included in Chapter 31. Make sure that your peers are familiar with the piece of literature you have written about *before* they edit your essay. Consider the following specific items as you and your peers work through the revising process:
1. Have you included a thesis statement and the title and author of the work early in the essay?
2. Have you backed up the supporting evidence with textual proof? Will it thoroughly convince the intended reader? As you and your peers edit, keep the audience in mind. Is the essay for an informed or an uninformed reader? Should you reword anything to suit a particular audience?
3. Have you introduced quotations from the work smoothly into the prose of the essay? Are the conventions of punctuation accurate? Have you varied the techniques of blending your prose with quoted material? (See Chapter 39 for examples.)
4. Is any of the textual evidence unnecessary or irrelevant? Is there any mention of plot for its own sake? You should use any reference to the plot line only as evidence to support a claim (unless the intended audience requires a summary).
5. Have you written the essay in the third person? If not, is there a good reason for the choice of person? Are there any unnecessary shifts in person?
6. Have you used the present tense in all references to the work being discussed? If not, is there a good reason for not using the present tense? Are there any unnecessary shifts in tense?
7. Will the readers have a new or deeper understanding of the story after reading the essay? Will they better recognize or appreciate some aspect of the human condition related in the story?

Because your intended reader for this literary esssay will probably be your instructor-editor, you should consider spending extra time polishing it.

PRODUCTS

The literary works under discussion in the following products are reproduced in the Appendix. You should read each selection *before* you read the essay discussing it. As you read each essay, note that the first writer writes to fellow students, providing his own interpretation of "Agent Orange"; the second writer also writes to students, providing his interpretation of a single aspect of "The Story of an Hour"; the third writer, however, writes to an informed instructor, providing not only her own interpretation of "Because I Could Not Stop for Death" but also blending in quotations of what professional critics have written about the poem.

Topic: Discuss the use of irony in "Agent Orange."

A Defoliation of Children

by *Michael Mooney, student*

The main irony of Elizabeth Brewster's "Agent Orange" lies in the deceptive nature of a defoliant—defined in *Webster's* as "any one of several chemical components that, when applied to plants, can alter their metabolism, causing the leaves to drop off . . . . Their main military objective is to deprive the enemy of cover." Agent Orange supposedly strips life from plants without harming people.

But enough people become strangely ill after the spraying for a doctor to note that: "It's something going the rounds . . . doesn't seem to yield to treatment. . . ." The poet's portrayal of man's attempts to destroy nature contains two ironies. The first involves a father warning his children not to pick lady's slippers because they "were rare / and must be preserved," while the United States Army attempts to wipe out an entire forest. The same quotation can also be taken in a second, different vein: while the children are warned against plucking the flower, the army, like a grim reaper, carelessly plucks the children's youth:

> One of those boys had amused his mother
> when he had told her he was afraid
> he might be drafted when he grew up
> for military service in the American army.
>
> Maybe he wasn't so wrong after all.

The irony intensifies when it is realized that the boy who spoke is a *Canadian*.

In the concluding line, "Hope you are an evergreen," Brewster despairs that our chances of escaping the by-products of mounting public cover-ups and deceptions are slim. Her choice of "evergreen" is perfect, both because it does not succumb to the defoliant and because its name implies lasting health. The line also voices a hope that we might escape such an ironic tragedy, but when "poisons travel / more readily than truth," the hope is a forlorn one.

Topic: Discuss Chopin's use of joy in "The Story of an Hour."

Joy?

by Ken Dick, student

In Kate Chopin's "The Story of an Hour," Mrs. Mallard is completely misunderstood at the "death" and the reentry into life of her husband. Both her sister Josephine and her so-called close friend Richards misinterpret her responses from beginning to end.

After her initial outburst of grief, Mrs. Mallard flees alone to the sanctuary of her room: "she would have no one follow her." The reader now discovers that Mrs. Mallard has loved Mr. Mallard "sometimes," but his "powerful will" always made her feel imprisoned in both her home and her marriage. She has spent many an hour behind a locked door, sitting in her "comfortable, roomy chair" in front of an open, inviting window. Looking out into the square has always made her aware of what she was missing, the true joy of living a full, free life.

Before the announcement of her husband's "death," she can only dream of being free. However, thinking her husband is dead, Mrs. Mallard at last senses an opportunity for a new beginning as she sits in front of her open bedroom window. "The trees that were all aquiver with the new spring life" entice her to freedom; the "delicious breath of rain" and the "countless sparrows" whisper and sing f-r-e-e-d-o-m; even a "peddler . . . crying his wares" indicates that she shall be forever free.

Luxuriating in planning the rest of her promising future, she admits how wonderful life will be without her husband. She can now "live for herself." She can now joyfully open and "spread her arms out" to welcome freedom, with the "possession of self-assertion which she suddenly recognized as the strongest impulse of her being." During all this time, Josephine, on the other side of her sister's door, mistakes Mrs. Mallard's discovery for inconsolable grief.

Yielding at last to the pleas of her sister, Mrs. Mallard leaves her room, "Free! Body and soul free!," and joyously descends the stairs with Josephine, "[carrying] herself unwittingly like a goddess of Victory." The reader clearly sees a born-again woman, a woman with a new lease on life. But Chopin plays a terrible trick on her heroine: she brings Mr. Mallard, very much alive, back onto the scene. Mrs. Mallard dies instantly, her weak heart giving out in shock and utter disappointment.

Her "monstrous joy" may die with her, but it imprints itself on the reader's brain. The reader watches in dismay as Josephine and Richards (and later the doctors) misinterpret the cause of her death as a "joy that kills." Ironically, however, the "heart disease" that killed her has indeed set Mrs. Mallard free at last.

Topic: Comment on the statement that Emily Dickinson's "Because I Could Not Stop for Death" is one of the greatest poems in the English language.

A Magnificent Cycle

by Barbara-Anne Eddy, researcher

Emily Dickinson's poem "Because I Could Not Stop for Death" has been acclaimed as "one of the greatest in the English language" (Tate 206). Dickinson, who "lived an uneventful and secluded life" (Bent 296), was virtually unknown until after her death. That she wrote a poem meriting such high praise should make any reader curious.

At first glance the poem is deceptively simple: a description of a carriage ride, hardly worthy to be called *great*. Only on rereading do we discover what Allen Tate calls "the pattern of suspended action" (207) that lies behind the poem's apparent simplicity.

A characteristic of any great work is that it provokes more questions than it answers; "Because I Could Not Stop for Death" certainly does this. Here are just a few: Is the "I" of the poem already dead, or is she being given a preview of her fate? Why can she "not stop for Death"? In the time-honored tradition that "three's a crowd," why is Immortality on the ride? To whom does the "house that seemed / A swelling on the ground" belong, and why does the carriage pause there? How have "centuries" passed since the carriage ride?

We can puzzle out our answers to these and the many other questions we find in the poem, but its final meaning will always elude us.

> Cryptic and enigmatic, introspective yet mystical, it always escapes our comprehension. That must be the case inevitably, for [Dickinson] really doesn't care about our earthbound opinions and judgement. . . . [She] is seeking to know what the giants of all ages have wanted to know: what is Time and what is Eternity, and what is the relation between them? (Alcock 173)

For her they are one and the same: "The carriage held but just ourselves / And Immortality." In other words, Death and Immortality's sharing the carriage ride "toward eternity" with the poet shows that Dickinson wanted to portray them as companions of equal stature.

Dickinson knows that her presence in God's scheme is eternal, and her poetry states this over and over. Her critics, however, insist on complicating her simple answer. For all his admiration of the poem, Richard Chase objects that "the common sense of the situation demands that Immortality ought to be the destination of the coach and not one of the passengers" (252). But Tate contends that the poem's greatness manifests itself because "the idea of immortality is confronted with the fact of physical disintegration" (251). In other words, Chase contends that Immortality cannot coexist with Death, whereas Tate says that their conflict is the central issue of the poem.

There is no surer measure of the greatness of a work than that we can read it over and over and discover fresh insights at each reading. "Because I Could Not Stop for Death" is certainly a work of this stature. Ranging freely through time and space, it starkly and magnificently portrays the cycle of life and death.

Works Cited

Alcock, Richard A. World Literature Made Simple. Garden City, New York: Doubleday, 1957.

Benet, William Rose, ed. The Reader's Encyclopedia. New York: Crowell, 1948.

Chase, Richard. Emily Dickinson. New York: William Sloan, 1951.

Tate, Allen. On the Limits of Poetry. New York: Morrow, 1948.

ANALYSIS

Agent Orange

1. In what way has the writer illuminated "Agent Orange" for you? Do you appreciate the poem more than you did before you read his essay?
2. Does the writer use effective examples to make his point? Are there other examples of irony in "Agent Orange" that he has missed?
3. For what purpose does Brewster use irony? Does Mooney make clear what he thinks her purpose is?
4. Does he quote effectively from the poem?
5. If Mooney were writing for an informed reader (his literature instructor or examiner), what changes should he make in his essay? Why?

Joy?

1. In what way has the writer illuminated "The Story of an Hour" for you? Do you appreciate the story more than you did before you read his essay?
2. Comment on how Dick blends quotations from the story with his own prose. Are they effective, awkward, smooth?
3. Compare this essay with the mini-essay earlier in the chapter. You will note that

the topics are extremely similar. Are there any differences? Which provides more information? Which is clearer? Which do you prefer? Support all of your answers.
4. If Dick were writing to an informed reader (his literature instructor or teaching assistant), what should he change? Why?

A Magnificent Cycle

1. In what way has the writer illuminated "Because I Could Not Stop for Death" for you? Do you appreciate the poem more than you did before you read her essay?
2. Can you tell that the essay is intended to be read by an informed instructor, who perhaps has taught the poem several times? How? What are some characteristics of this essay that do not appear in the previous two essays? Support your answer with specific details and examples.
3. What is the writer's thesis? Has she developed it fully? Does she keep the reader on track?
4. Eddy relies heavily on secondary sources. Does she use them effectively? Are her quotations well integrated? Has she used the MLA method of parenthetical citation correctly? (Remember, if you can find nothing to say about a piece of literature, you might discover some ideas by reading critics and other authorities.)
5. What do you sense is the writer's opinion of the poem? Justify your answer by discovering what she says.
6. The writer often uses the first person plural *we*. What is the effect of her use of the first person? Would the essay be better if she were to use third person?

Research Reports

INTRODUCTION

When you undertake writing a research report, you must search carefully and diligently for facts on your chosen topic. You should present the research from your personal point of view and should blend your own prose with quotations from authorities. This chapter contains two different kinds of research reports: a *formal* research report in which you use parenthetical citations and provide a bibliography and an *informal* research report that takes the form of a feature article.

Assignment

Part A: Write a research report of at least 1000 words on a topic of your choice.
Part B: Write a feature article of at least 1000 words on a topic of your choice.

PREWRITING PROCESS FOR PART A

1. If you are unfamiliar with what a research report is, how to gather supporting evidence from a variety of secondary sources, or how to set up parenthetical citations and a bibliography using either the MLA or APA styles of citation, you should complete several of the workshop exercises in Chapter 39. There you will be able to learn and apply the principles of writing research reports by working on an extremely short report.

2. In choosing a topic for this assignment, you may find it helpful to speak to your writing instructor or perhaps another instructor for whom this assignment might serve a dual purpose. For example, if your history instructor requires you to research a topic, you might take your research report through the steps of prewriting, drafting, and revising and submit it first as an English assignment; then when it is returned, polish it for resubmission to your history instructor, your intended audience. There are great benefits in doing a research assignment this way: you learn the scholarly techniques necessary to do a research assignment, your writing instructor can credit you with completing an assignment, and your history instructor will have an enjoyable paper to read. But do check this procedure with the instructors concerned *before* you begin working on this assignment. Furthermore, refer to the detailed information about research papers for non-English courses in Chapters 21, 22, and 23.

3. .If you are choosing your own topic for this assignment, it is important that you go through a number of brainstorming sessions to help you choose a worthwhile topic, to narrow it, and to gather supporting evidence. Begin with a classification/division flowchart (Chapter 7), and then work through a few of your favorite brainstorming techniques that you think will produce the most appropriate supporting evidence: Newspaper Reporter's Questions, Seven Controlling Questions, Comparison/Contrast Ladders, Cause/Effect Flowcharts (see Chapter 25).

4. Make a list of your writing variables as in the following example:

BROAD TOPIC:	*Macbeth*
LIMITED TOPIC:	The witches in *Macbeth*
AUDIENCE:	My writing and literature instructors. Real. I intend ultimately to submit it as my term paper for literature.
PURPOSE:	To point out and illustrate why Shakespeare included the witches
FORMAT:	Long research report
VOICE:	My own
SITUATION:	My essay will serve as two assignments: first for my writing class, then for my literature class; it's OK with both my instructors.
THESIS STATEMENT:	Elizabethans believed in the powers of witchcraft; therefore, Shakespeare included witches and references to superstition in *Macbeth* to ensure his audience's attention.

PREWRITING PROCESS FOR PART B

A feature article or saturation report is basically "soft" journalism, emphasizing some topic of current interest. It is also referred to as a "human-interest story." Feature articles are found in newspapers and magazines with strong, forthright titles: "Learning Disabilities Can Be Licked," "The AIDS Epidemic," "Teen Sex," "The Public is Forgetting the SPCA," "War on Cocaine," "Star-Wars Defense System is a Reality." (You might find researching and writing a feature article more enjoyable than working on a traditional research report because of the variety of research methods at your disposal.)

Using reference books is the main way to obtain material for a research report, but it is just one of many ways to research a topic for a feature article.

1. You might like to write your feature article about a place, a group, or an individual that you know reasonably well but would like to know more about. Here are a few suggestions for topics: wigs for men, a controversial political figure, the latest musical trend, your local bakery, a club that you go to, contact lenses, designer jeans, the achievements of one of your college instructors.

2. Once you have a topic for your feature article, consider the other writing variables. Feature articles normally appear in newspapers and magazines and are written for a wide audience, often by free-lance writers who earn their living by this kind of reporting.

Feature article writers have ideas, usually about some current event or interest, and immerse themselves in the topic, gathering information from every source. Then they shape the bits and pieces of research into a unified whole, which often resembles a long narrative.

3. Read the feature article at the end of this assignment and others in newspapers or magazines. Examine them to determine the kind of research the writers used and how they organized their material.

4. Focusing on popular social issues will give universal appeal to your article and certainly interest the average reader. This microcosm-macrocosm approach will give distinction to your report. If you were, for example, to choose "sleeping habits" as your topic, the habits you explore and write about should be universally recognizable. Instead of writing for one particular reader, think of the whole reading world as your audience.

5. The success of a feature article usually depends on its topic, viewpoint, and research, so allow plenty of time for thorough reporting.

In order to write a good feature article, you must become a sponge, soaking up details as you perform various kinds of *firsthand research.* Your research may take you into the library, primarily into the periodical section, but more importantly—in order for you to saturate your topic—you will have to observe and listen, interview and experience, watch TV and listen to the radio, read newspapers and magazines, and collect pertinent articles. Be prepared to spend a lot of time digging into your topic, and enjoy yourself.

6. You should, of course, attempt to make your report as thorough as possible; but because a feature article usually deals with current events, you cannot possibly say all that there is to be said about a topic. Your readers may well have information that you did not include, and in fact they may be able to use your report as the basis for one of their own.

7. Now before you begin your prewriting search for supporting materials, list your working writing variables as in the following example:

BROAD TOPIC:	Family breakdowns
LIMITED TOPIC:	Divorce and children
AUDIENCE:	Readers of my local newspaper. Real. I intend to send it in. (But I have in mind a married couple considering divorce. They are in their thirties with two children. They intend for the father to keep the children and the mother to have visiting privileges.)
PURPOSE:	To point out the effects of a family breakdown on children
FORMAT:	Feature article
VOICE:	Persona of a child

SITUATION: My persona is a child of divorced parents, who hates the fact that she no longer has her mother and father under the same roof. My persona doesn't think her adult readers are very considerate about her feelings. She wants them to realize that they shouldn't place their own feelings before their children's.

THESIS QUESTION: How does divorce affect a child?

8. Depending on your topic and the kind of supporting evidence you need, choose three or four brainstorming techniques: Classification and Division Flowchart (Chapter 7), Comparison/Contrast Ladders (Chapter 8), Cause/Effect Flowchart (Chapter 9), Newspaper Reporter's Questions, Four-Faces-of-Knowledge Cluster, and Seven Controlling Questions (Chapter 25). They may produce several questions that indicate required research.

DRAFTING PROCESS FOR PART A

1. Longer research papers are made up of several parts; depending on the complexity of your paper and the requirements of your reader, you may or may not need all of the following:

Title Page

This includes the title of your report, your name, the name and section (if there is one) of the course for which the paper is written, your instructor's name, the name of your college, university, or employer, and the date. (Your instructor may want you to use a particular layout for the title page, so check before you begin.)

Table of Contents or Formal Outline

Depending on how long or complex your paper is, you may or may not need a table of contents or formal outline. If you do use one, it should indicate the headings of each section and perhaps the page on which each section begins.

Appendices and Charts

If you use material that is essential but which you cannot include in the text because it's too long or too complex, you must present it as an appendix in a separate section between the body of the text and the "Works Cited" or "References." If you are going to include charts, graphs, or other illustrations, place them near or within the part of the text to which they relate.

Parenthetical Citations

Since 1984 the Modern Language Association (MLA) has recommended the practice of placing citations of sources directly in the text, in parentheses. This happy decision closely resembles that of the American Psychological Association (APA). No longer will you have to be concerned about footnotes, *ibid., op. cit.*, and the myriad of fussy scholarly techniques. The key to parenthetical citation is common sense; however, you should spend a few minutes noting the differences between MLA and APA styles (see Chapter 39).

Note: If you include explanatory or supplementary comments that you do not want to include in the body of your text, use a footnote or endnote number beside the particular word and include the comment with the corresponding number either at the foot of the page or at the end of the paper.

Bibliography expressed as ''Works Cited'' or ''References''

At the end of your paper (after any endnotes), you should cite all the books and other materials that you used in compiling your paper. (See Chapter 39 for information on setting up an MLA and APA bibliography.)

2. Before you draft your paper, you should read the research reports at the end of this assignment. Notice particularly the way the writers have fitted in their quotations, the form of their parenthetical citations and bibliographic material, the organization and structure of the reports, and the style.

3. If you have brought to your drafting process all the material you need to compose your paper, begin by sorting your information index cards in a logical manner. As a guide, use your working outline, thesis statement, and individual topic sentences, which will govern the content of each of your paragraphs (or sections).

After you have sorted your cards into a number of piles, flesh out your outline in more detail. Now examine your outline carefully. If it does not look thorough and if you feel you are not going to be able to support your thesis and topic sentences, you should do more research and bring to your drafting process paraphrases, précis, summaries, and quotations. It should also be obvious to you whether your research report is going to be purely informative, argumentative, or a combination of these.

Assuming you have sufficient material to start drafting, you would be well advised to follow the drafting instructions for an informative essay (Chapter 6) or an argumentative essay (Chapter 5).

4. As you compose, include parenthetical citations *after* all direct quotations, paraphrases, précis, and summaries, as well as after any ideas that are not your own.

5. When you finish your draft, put it away for a few days. When you return to it, assume that you were not the writer. Then give it a thorough evaluation, using the checklist in Chapter 31. Plan to present a near-perfect research report to your peers.

DRAFTING PROCESS FOR PART B

1. When you write a lengthy piece such as a feature article, you must think about how you are going to arrange your material. In all probability you will write your report in bits and pieces—conversations you have had or overheard, descriptions, interviews, researched facts, articles you have read, and so on. Once you have collected all your material, you must spend time piecing it together. You may use any sequential order: time, importance, size; however, to give your report variety, you can also use flashbacks and flash-forwards.

2. A feature article is a nonfiction report, but you may wish to use such fictional techniques as scenes, characterizations, and dialogue to add interest and variety.

3. One of the main differences between a feature article and a research paper is the way in which you present the research. You organize and present a research paper formally, whereas in the feature article you blend the research material so subtly and effectively into your own prose that the reader scarcely notices its presence.

Unlike the research essay, the feature article requires no parenthetical citations or bibliography. When you quote, you should include the name of your source in the body of your report. ("According to Moyers, ..." "A leading physician noted. . . ." ". . . seen recently on *Good Morning America*."

4. You can have a great deal of fun with your point of view because it can be as flexible as you want. As long as you prepare the reader for shifts, you can be a participant in the action, remove yourself, and then take part in the action again. This technique will become clear when you read a feature article. Many of them read as narratives.

5. Feature articles often contain illustrative material. Graphs, charts, illustrations, photographs, and cartoons can enrich your article.

REVISING PROCESS FOR PARTS A AND B

Ask your peers, when they edit your paper, to use the checklists from Chapter 31 and the following specific suggestions:

1. For Research Report

   a. Is your research thorough? Have you left any questions unanswered? Are there areas where the research is insufficient?

   b. Are there any signs of plagiarism?

   c. Have you used a consistent style—informal or formal, MLA or APA?

   d. Have you blended the quoted material and your prose smoothly?

   e. Is the use of scholarly techniques correct? Have you punctuated quotations correctly? Have you set up and punctuated all your references to sources correctly?

2. For Feature Article

   a. Ask your editors for their reactions to your article.

   b. Do they think there is anything missing? They just might be able to point you in the direction of another tidbit of information.

   c. Do they think you have focused too much on one area?

   d. Did they get lost because they could not follow your organizational method?

Limit the discussion during peer-editing to these larger issues. If your readers are worried about how you have communicated your content, you may have to go back to the drafting process and plan to meet with your editors another time. It is rare for a student to produce a perfect feature article for the first peer-editing session.

3. When your peer-editors are pleased with your essay, you should put it away for a few days, and then take a fresh, critical look at it. You will then be in a better position to polish it before you ask your instructor-editor to go over it.

4. Presentation is important. Concentrate on the appearance of your paper; in fact, to add an authoritative touch, you should type it (or have it typed) double-spaced on one side of the paper only.

5. Because of the amount of work a research paper entails, you should make a second copy of it before you submit it, in case an editor or your intended reader misplaces the original.

6. The following products and their analysis questions will give you a few more ideas on how a polished research report and feature article should look.

PRODUCTS

The Vampire: Fact or Fiction?

by Rita Ringle, student

What does the word "vampire" mean to you? You probably think of a tall, pale man in a dark suit, wearing a cape and looking ready to attend an opera or a formal dinner. Let us not forget the two fangs, used to bite and draw blood. You may believe he comes from a place called Transylvania and speaks with a slight accent, "I vant to drink your blooood."

This is the way most of us visualize a vampire today. The image comes mainly from Dracula, by Bram Stoker. But let us explore the real origin of the vampire legend. There are many facts and superstitions about the vampire and they come from all parts of the world.

In the myths of the ancient Greeks there is Lamia. When Lamia's children were killed, she went mad. To avenge herself, she went about killing other people's children. She drank their blood and ate their flesh. Once a beautiful woman, she became very ugly. In Latin, the word "lamia" is short for "a sorceress, an enchantress" (Summers, Europe 226).

The Armenians feared a mountain spirit called Dashnavar. This monster sucked blood from the soles of travelers' feet. Dashnavar was particularly dangerous to people while they were asleep. Most travelers slept with their boots on because they feared Dashnavar (Summers, Europe 300).

Much has been written about real vampires. One such writer was an Englishman, William of Newburgh. He wrote that a squire of Alnwick Castle was an evil man who, after he died, did not stay in his grave. He wandered about in the streets at night, betraying his presence by the smell of rotting flesh. When plague erupted, people associated it with the stench and ran, leaving a real "ghost town."

Finally, two young men whose father had died in the plague decided to take action. They broke into the cemetery and dug up the squire's corpse. They found the body just beneath the surface, not six feet deep as it should have been. The two young men were angry, not frightened. One struck the corpse with the sharp edge of his spade, the blood gushed in thick streams, and the body was dragged outside of the town and burned. Immediately, the plague stopped (Summers, Europe 286).

Originally, vampires had nothing to do with bats. If they changed physically at all, it was into wolves. Legends of the vampires and the werewolves were often confused. Then, in the sixteenth century, the Spanish in Mexico discovered small bats that really did drink blood. When the stories of these bats reached Europe, people immediately thought of the vampire. They called them "vampire bats." After that, the bat became an important part of the vampire legend.

Stories about vampires were written before Stoker came out with his. One of the first was written in 1816. In the summer of that year the poet Byron, his friend the poet Shelley, and Shelley's wife Mary were on vacation in Switzerland. They had rented homes near Lake Geneva. Byron's personal doctor, Polidori, was with the group. In the evenings they would get together and tell ghost stories.

Byron began a story about a vampire, but never finished it. Doctor Polidori took over the idea and developed it into The Vampyre. A successful story, it was made into a play. This vampire was called Lord Ruthven (Summers, Kith 207). Alas, this play never made Broadway.

Another such story was Varney the Vampyre, or The Feast of Blood, by James Malcolm Rymer, written in 1847. The story of Varney ran over half a million words. It is one of the longest novels of any kind ever written.

Finally, in 1895, Bram Stoker's novel Dracula was published. It was an immediate success and even today, almost a hundred years later, is as popular as ever.

There really was someone named Dracula. A nobleman from Transylvania, Rumania, named Vlad Tepov was nicknamed Dracul, a word which means "dragon" and also "devil." A warrior of the fifteenth century, he had a reputation for being bloodthirsty and cruel. He had his enemies stuck on sharp wooden stakes. He was also said to have eaten his meals while watching his prisoners disemboweled and mutilated. In Rumania, Vlad Tepov was considered a hero. He was very successful in fighting Turks who were invading their land (Ronay 76). So there really was a Dracula, but he was no vampire.

Another historical character who had a good claim to vampirism was a Hungarian countess named Elizabeth Bathory, who lived during the late sixteenth century. Countess Bathory supposedly had hundreds of people murdered. She used the blood of her victims in "magical" potions, which were supposed to keep her young forever (Ronay 109–15).

Webster's New Collegiate Dictionary defines the vampire as: "1. The body of a dead person believed to come from the grave at night and suck the blood of persons asleep. 2. One who lives by preying on others." There are many types of modern-day vampires in our world today. Vampires sleep in or among us all: people like Charles Manson, Richard Speck, John Collins, and a most recent discovery—Christopher Wilder, who violently killed at least 11 women. These people have all shed blood in preying on others. Did they indeed live "by preying on others"? Also, have you noticed that because so many violently dangerous people have become human monsters, legendary monsters are being portrayed as gentle, even comic, creatures?

Works Cited

Ronay, Gabriel. The Truth about Dracula. New York: Stein and Day, 1972.

Summers, Montague. The Vampire—His Kith and Kin. New York: University Books, 1960.

---. The Vampire in Europe. New York: University Books, 1968.

Webster's New Collegiate Dictionary. 1979 ed.

Child Abuse: A Growing Concern

by Michele Beisner, student

The exploitation of children has existed throughout history, although it has only been in recent years that professionals have labeled certain parental behavior "abusive." Dr. C. Henry Kempe coined the term "battered-child syndrome" in the 1960s, and since that time, clear guidelines for legal intervention to protect the child have been developed by the legislature (Gil, 1983, p. 2).

Child abuse is defined as any act of omission or commission that endangers a child's physical or emotional health and development. This includes physical assault, corporal punishment, physical neglect or inadequate supervision, emotional deprivation, and sexual exploitation (Child Abuse: Intake, p. 1).

Today, the incidence of child abuse and neglect has reached serious proportions. Statistics offer mere estimates of the true incidents of abuse, as thousands of cases go undetected or unreported. In 1980, over 700,000 cases of abuse were reported nationally, 100,000 of these in California alone (Gil, 1983, p. 2). It is estimated that nearly one million American children are suffering from abuse or neglect at any given time and that one fourth of that million will be permanently injured for life as a result of maltreatment.

Contrary to popular belief, child abuse occurs in all cultural, ethnic, occupational, and socioeconomic groups. Although the number of abusers who are psychotic or psychopathic is very small, a poor self-image and lack of self-confidence appear to be common traits.

Perhaps the complexity of those who abuse children can be summarized in this way:

> Child abuse is seldom the result of any single factor. Rather, it is a combination of circumstances, as well as personality types, which precipitate acts of child abuse. When a parent or caretaker is under emotional stress, such as marital problems or joblessness; when he or she has a predisposition towards mistreatment, perhaps as a mistreated child themselves, or one who believes in corporal punishment; when the child happens to trigger his or her contempt or resentment; and when the parent or caretaker has no other outlet for tension, anger, or aggression, abuse usually occurs. (Child Abuse pamphlet, 1976, p. 5)

Clearly, fines and jail sentences alone are unlikely to rehabilitate the child abuser. Thousands of children each year are taken into protective custody temporarily, placed in foster homes, and ultimately returned to the natural parents, only to be mistreated once again.

For this reason, the basic goal of most child abuse programs is to disrupt the generational cycle of abuse. Treatment is aimed towards counseling the entire family, as similarities have been noted between the abused children and their siblings in their shy, gloomy, and passive dispositions. None of the children in a family can possibly escape the effects of the violence being exhibited in the home.

Family therapist Sandra Halperin notes:

> The great emphasis on the individual abusing parent in both sociological and clinical research has *severely* hampered the understanding and treatment of the complex phenomenon of child abuse. A major limitation of most of the clinical and research literature is in the neglect of the importance of the spouse as well as the abused child and his siblings, all integral parts of the family system in which abuse occurs. (1981, p. 90)

Accordingly, she has developed a three-phase approach to treating an "abusive family." Phase one consists of an initial assessment of the entire family unit. Phase two is devoted to individual interviews and treatment. And finally, phase three unites the entire family into group therapy and hopefully a renewal of open communication, understanding, and cooperation within the home. Halperin is confident that "the relationship between parents and children *can* be reshaped. The individuals within the family can learn to share their feelings and expectations more openly with one another, deal with power issues, and together improve communication as a whole" (1981, p. 95).

Social worker Elizabeth Davoren emphasizes the need for parents to be taught "reparenting." Therapy is geared towards several key factors:

- Parents need help to feel good about themselves, to make up for the devastating belittling they have experienced in their own lives;
- parents need someone who will not be led into accepting their low sense of self-worth;
- parents need someone who understands how hard it is for them to have dependents when they have never been allowed to be dependent themselves;
- parents need to feel valuable, and eventually they need to be able to give themselves and to have some role in helping others (1975, p. 39).

Although the rehabilitative techniques of both Sandra Halperin and Elizabeth Davoren have shown great success, they offer little help to those families who cannot afford such extensive treatment and personalized therapy. In response to this need, many community groups and services are becoming available.

Parents Anonymous, a self-help group founded by a former abusing mother, was established in Los Angeles in 1969 (Hurt, 1975, p. 17). The members of this group maintain frequent contact through meetings and telephone calls, continuously striving to assist one another in directing their aggressive feelings into constructive activities.

Additionally, 24-hour crisis lines, homemaking services, community emergency funds, voluntary child care services, and crisis nurseries all offer supportive assistance to parents who often feel alone in their struggle to end abusive patterns of behavior.

Whereas most professionals are concerned with the protection of abused children, it is important to recognize a controversial issue: the rights of parents to rear their child as they see fit versus the right of the child to life, liberty, and the pursuit of happiness. The court system defines the rights of children in the following terms:

- the right to be with natural parents and siblings
- the right to good physical care, with adequate food, shelter, and clothing
- the right to an education
- the right to emotional security
- the right to medical treatment

- the right to protection; to freedom from harm, freedom from injury, freedom from neglect
- the right to protection under the federal constitution (<u>Termination</u>, 1971, p. 9)

When these rights are abused or withheld, professionals and laymen alike have the moral responsibility to report such actions.

   In summary, the incidence of child abuse and neglect is increasing dramatically in the United States and will only be effectively reduced by early reporting and treatment. All too often, the public is reticent in reporting "suspected cases" for fear of making a mistake. This view must be abandoned through recognizing the importance of protecting the abused child, his siblings, and yes, even the unborn child. As Dr. Henry Kempe once stated, "I would rather apologize to a parent because I made a mistake in reporting, than to apologize to a brain-damaged child for not reporting" (Gil, 1983, p. 5).

References

<u>Child Abuse</u>.   (1976).   California Dept. of Justice Information Pamphlet No. 8, Aug.

<u>Child Abuse: Intake and Investigation</u>.   San Diego County Dept. of Public Welfare.

Davoren, E.   (1975).   "Working with Abusive Parents."   <u>Children Today</u>.   Vol. 4, No. 3.

Gil, E.   (1983).   <u>The California Child Abuse Reporting Law</u>. Sacramento: State of California Dept. of Social Services.

Halperin, S.   (1981).   "Implications for a Comprehensive Family Treatment Plan."   <u>Family Relations</u>, Jan.

Hurt, M.   (1975).   <u>Child Abuse and Neglect: A Report on the Status of the Research</u>.   Washington D.C.:   U.S. Dept. of Health, Education, and Welfare.

<u>Termination of Parental Rights</u>.   (1971).   Denver: The American Humane Assoc., Children's Div.

Hear the Children Cry

by *Jeff Clark, student*

   "A mother looks out of a tenement window for her six-year-old son, Joseph. Not seeing him in the area, she runs out frantically to find him. After he turns up, she beats him so hard that she bruises his face."

"A young woman walks angrily back and forth in the kitchen of her suburban home. Her husband is on a business trip, and she is alone with her children. When her two-year-old daughter accidentally spills a glass of water, the mother slaps her repeatedly."

"A well-to-do doctor tells his small son, Bobby, to pick up some toys. The boy refuses. Enraged, the father takes a metal truck and begins hitting the child's head with it. Fifteen minutes later, Bobby is dead."

These incidents, horrible as they sound, are true. They are only three different incidents that were published recently in an article in Family Health, a magazine specializing in medical topics.

These parents come from widely different social backgrounds, but they all have two things in common: they are child abusers and they need help. My purpose in this report is to define child abuse and show that it has reached epidemic proportions.

Child abuse occurs in every socioeconomic, religious, cultural, and racial background, and it is not anything new in society. Since ancient times, children have been abandoned, beaten, abused, neglected, and even killed by their parents. Abraham was fully prepared to sacrifice the life of his son Isaac had God not intervened in the nick of time (Genesis: 22).

For centuries, child abuse has been accepted by society to varying degrees. In fact, for years children have been rocked to sleep with nursery rhymes describing this phenomenon:

> There was an old woman who lived in a shoe;
> She had so many children, she didn't know what to do.
> She gave them some broth without any bread,
> Then whipped them all soundly and sent them to bed.

> Rock-a-bye baby on the tree top. . .
> When the bough breaks, the cradle will fall,
> Down will come baby, cradle and all.

Child abuse can be defined as any act (not necessarily physical) that causes a child needless pain. On the other hand, most Americans would say that the infrequent and not-too-hard spanking given to a child by an otherwise loving parent does not constitute abuse. For all legal purposes in the United States, the occasional spanking is defined as discipline. The difference between the abuser and non-abuser is that the former lets those spankings get out of hand. The abuser is also one who gives punishment that's either uncalled for or is out of proportion to what has happened; for example, few parents would set a child in boiling water if he wet his pants, but many would burn the fingers of a child who plays with matches. Both examples constitute child abuse, however.

According to M. A. Lewis, author of The History of Child Abuse, the first move to protect children occurred in New York City in 1874.

> Mary Ellen, nine years old, was starved and chained to her bed by her adoptive parents. When appeals to city authorities failed, church workers turned to the American Society for the Prevention of Cruelty to Animals. On the basis that Mary Ellen is a member of the animal kingdom, the ASPCA successfully brought action to remove her from her parents' home.

Fortunately, things are changing and people are becoming more concerned. There is still a large number of cases, however, that go unreported. What's holding people back from getting more involved? R. Wright, M.D., suggests there are many answers to this question:

1. lack of understanding of the seriousness of the problem
2. lack of awareness of one's own responsibilities in reporting the abused child
3. disbelief that there could be abusive parents
4. reluctance to expose prosperous families to a court hearing
5. lack of knowledge about how to make the report itself
6. a wish not to become involved with court proceedings
7. a belief that the court will not take appropriate action anyway
8. lack of community facilities which can provide the type of help these parents need

I would like to suggest an additional reason: the fear or discomfort which the reporting person feels when he or she is confronted with a battered child and the parents.

Most people agree that beating a child is an obvious form of child abuse, but few parents know that allowing their baby to cry for long periods of time is also a form of abuse. Prolonged crying may actually be harmful, according to a report presented at the 1976 workshop at the University of Illinois, which found "a marked decrease in oxygen pressure in the arteries of babies, with respiratory distress after crying."

Dr. Lee Salk, professor of Psychiatry and Pediatrics at the New York Hospital-Cornell Medical Center states, "To claim that crying is good for babies' lungs is like saying that bleeding must be good for the veins." He goes on to say, "Children whose cries are answered learn to vocalize well and not to whine and whimper, because they've already found out that verbal behavior is rewarded. A baby repeatedly left to cry alone ultimately learns to give up and tune out the world. This is learned helplessness and possibly the beginning of adult depression."

Since many people dealing with parents of battered children are themselves parents, working with these families makes them confront their own conflicting feelings about discipline. In my own experience, while working with counselors specializing in child abuse, I found it much more difficult for me to tell these parents that I was reporting them for child abuse than it was for them to accept my action. I found that many battering parents are uncomfortable with their own situation and are actually relieved when they are reported to the authorities.

In conclusion, I would like to add that very few parents wake up thinking, Today I am going to abuse my child. Most abusing parents do not want to hurt their children and would respond to help. Yet the estimated incidence of child abuse in the United States in 1984 is 10 per 1,000, or 1.6 million, of whom 2,000 will die.

Child abuse affects all of us, parents and nonparents alike. The child of today is our future for the world tomorrow. If every child is able to look at an interesting world through loving and secure eyes, then our world will be a more loving and secure place in which to live. It must be pointed out, however, that not all countries are lagging behind in protecting their children. The June 1984 circular "The Church around the World" reported that Sweden has adopted a policy that strictly forbids any child abuse, including the spanking of children.

ANALYSIS

The Vampire: Fact or Fiction?

1. From Ringle's research report, what did you learn about vampires that you did not already know? Do you have confidence in her facts?

2. Who do you think her intended audience is? Support your answer.

3. Do you think her final paragraph is a suitable conclusion for her research report? Support your answer.

4. Rita uses the MLA system of citing her sources. How does she let her reader know from which of the two different books by Summers she is citing?

Child Abuse: A Growing Concern

1. Beisner, a nursing student, has chosen a topic both to satisfy a course requirement and to interest a large number of readers. In addition to gathering a number of facts, she often offers her own opinion on the subject—for example, "Although the rehabilitative techniques of both Sandra Halperin and Elizabeth Davoren have shown great success, they offer little help to those families who cannot afford such extensive treatment and personalized therapy." Find other examples of the writer's own opinion.

2. How does this research article compare with "Hear the Children Cry"? Support your answer.

3. Beisner uses the APA system of citing her sources. Why? How does she let her reader know from which of the three different books with the title *Child Abuse* she is citing?

Hear the Children Cry

1. How can you tell that the student who wrote this feature article is himself a father and a counselor?

2. For whom is the article written? Where could it be published? How do you, as a student, feel while reading the article? What did you learn from reading this article?

3. What has Clark left out about child abuse that you think should be included? Often your reading of one feature article may inspire your writing another. Do you have the feeling that you would like to write a feature article on child abuse?

4. You will note that this feature article deals with the same subject as "Child Abuse: a Growing Concern" above. What are the main differences between the two pieces? Which do you think is more successful in putting its point across to the reader? Support your answer with examples.

15

Instructions and Process Analysis

INTRODUCTION

We spend much of our lives reading, writing, or following instructions. We need instructions, for example, to learn how to assemble an object or take it apart, operate a machine, do a project, get from A to B, or prepare a recipe. If you are writing instructions or giving directions, the key is to make sure your reader can follow them. In addition, you may often have occasion to analyze the process or function of something; for example: How does a computer work? How do we elect our President? How are your grades determined for this English course? This chapter contains two assignments: a simple set of instructions and a more complicated process analysis that combines information with more sophisticated instructions.

> ### Assignment
>
> *Part A*: Using only as many words as necessary, write a single set of instructions or directions.
>
> *Part B*: Using only as many words as necessary, write a process analysis to explain how something works or happens.

PREWRITING PROCESS FOR PART A

1. For this assignment, you may use any of the situations mentioned in the Introduction or modify one of these:

   a. Give directions on how to get from your college or university to your home by car, by bus, or on foot.

   b. Share a recipe for a favorite dessert, main course, drink, or other special concoction you make.

c. Explain how to drive a car with a standard transmission, play racquetball, make tacos, write a program for your home computer, change the battery in a quartz watch.

2. To make this a profitable assignment, think about who your final reader might be and your purpose for giving him or her your set of directions or instructions. Your choice of topic for this assignment can be a real test to your creative thinking. Choosing a simple topic is not a challenge for the serious writer. You may need to go through a brainstorming session to determine a suitable topic. When you have chosen your topic, fill this in: "I need to show or explain to _____ how to _____ because _____." Once you have filled in the blanks, think about your format. You may include your instructions in a letter, report, or memo.

3. When you have decided on the topic for your set of instructions or directions, make a checklist of all the material your reader needs to know. Do not be concerned about the order; simply list them as they occur to you. However, if you place your facts, details, examples, and reasons on the rungs of a ladder graphic (Chapter 25), you may begin to see the sequential order of your supporting evidence. Afterwards, use one or two of your favorite brainstorming techniques in order to gather more supporting evidence.

4. Before you start to draft your instructions or directions, take some time to consider the audience and purpose you chose. Determine whether your audience is experienced or inexperienced in the topic you have chosen. For example, anyone may be able to pick up your recipe and produce a tasty drink, but only a computer programmer may be able to follow your set of instructions on how to write a program for a home computer.

Prepare to define any terms the reader may not understand. (To save time, you should have all necessary definitions on hand before you begin your first draft. A knowledge of Chapter 10 will help.)

5. Complete this part of your prewriting process by listing your writing variables. For example:

TOPIC:	Individualized-learning biology lab
AUDIENCE:	My lab partner. Real. I will give him my set of instructions.
PURPOSE:	To explain how to use the system
FORMAT:	A memo
VOICE:	My own
SITUATION:	My lab partner was absent when the lab instructor explained how to use the audiovisual tapes and slides
THESIS:	How to use the individualized-learning biology lab
THESIS STATEMENT:	There are several things you need to know in using the individualized-learning biology lab.

or

TOPIC:	Using toothpaste
AUDIENCE:	My roommate. Real. I'll post it on the bathroom mirror.
PURPOSE:	To get my roommate to stop squeezing the toothpaste tube in the middle.

FORMAT:	A note
VOICE:	I am going to write from the persona of the tube of toothpaste.
SITUATION:	Someone is squeezing the toothpaste tube in the middle. I'm angry.
THESIS:	How to use toothpaste properly
THESIS STATEMENT:	If you'll be good to me, I'll be good to you.

PREWRITING PROCESS FOR PART B

In writing instructions, you inform your reader how to put something together (or perhaps how to take it apart). When writing a process analysis paper, however, your task is somewhat more complicated; you must explain how or why something works. You will find that the process analysis paper will be a more acceptable paper for a college English course than a set of instructions because it requires a degree of critical thinking. If, as you go through your prewriting process, you have difficulty organizing your process analysis paper, concentrate on the subject of your paper for a few minutes. Think of it in terms of its early stages, before it was made, developed, or invented. Write a set of instructions describing how to make, develop, or invent your subject, and then continue work on your process analysis paper.

1. For this assignment, you may use any of the ideas mentioned in the Introduction, or you may modify one of the following:

- For a particular story that you are reading, point out how the author achieves suspense.
- For a particular textbook you are studying, point out how the writer organizes ideas.
- In a tennis match, football game, or chess match you played recently, explore how the opposing player or team pressed the attack.
- When a movie critic goes to a motion picture, what does he or she look for in the film?
- How would you make a popular motion picture?
- Discuss the ingredients, chemistry, and process necessary for developing a love relationship or making people either the best of friends or the worst of enemies.
- How does *The Independent Writer* help a student's writing process?
- How does a bimetal switch on a steam engine work?
- How can one choose the right wine, a new car, a college, or a light beer?
- How is the Olympic swimming, equestrian, or track-and-field team selected?

2. Once you have chosen your topic, apply all of the prewriting suggestions mentioned in Part A. Your format, however, should be that of an expository or perhaps a narrative essay.

3. Do not go to the drafting process until you have a complete set of writing variables and plenty of supporting evidence (from engaging in two or three of the following brainstorming sessions: Cause/Effect Flowchart, Comparison/Contrast Flowchart, Classification and Division Flowchart, Absurd Analogies, Pro/Con Ladder, Four-Faces-of-Knowledge Cluster, and Positive/Negative/Neutral Pigeonholes).

DRAFTING PROCESS FOR PART A

1. Look at the checklist that you made while prewriting (Item 3 of Part A). Number the items in your list in the order you expect your reader to follow them.
2. Now write your first draft, following the order you have set up. Check each item off the list as you include it in your draft.
3. When you have included each item in your draft, read it to see if you have revealed the importance of each step to your reader. Readers should know why they should follow each step in order.
4. If you need to define a term, try to work the definition into your prose smoothly and unobtrusively. In all probability, your reader will not need to learn terminology but will want to be able to follow the instructions or directions as easily as possible.
5. Use simple, direct sentences.
6. Usually you should write a set of instructions in the second person: "After you do that, do this."
7. Keep an appropriate list of transitional words and phrases (outlined in Chapter 30) near you as you write to help you make your instructions coherent.
8. You may want to make a list; in fact, it may be advisable (for ingredients in a recipe, items needed to assemble something, contents of a suitcase you want packed, and so on).
9. Diagrams may sometimes explain instructions better than words, so if you begin to bog down in verbiage, try drawing a graph, map, or diagram.
10. Often one- or two-sentence paragraphs may be clearer than long, complicated ones. Shorter paragraphs also produce more clean space on the paper and make instructions look less complicated for your reader.
11. Make sure in your draft that your reader will understand how each step, fact, or item leads to the next step, fact, or item. There is nothing more frustrating for a reader of a set of directions than to discover, after having completed one step, that something else should have preceded that step rather than followed it.
12. Whenever possible, use active rather than passive voice (see Chapter 57, Exercise Two).
13. You have just read a set of instructions.

DRAFTING PROCESS FOR PART B

1. The first thing you should do in drafting a process analysis is to determine *how* something works or *why* something works. If you are explaining *how*, you would be wise to create a Classification and Division Flowchart, to make sure that you have not left out an important function of the process. If you do not know how to make such a flowchart, see Chapter 7. If, on the other hand, you are explaining *why*, you should create a Cause/Effect Flowchart to make sure that each function logically follows the next. If you do not know how to make such a flowchart, see Chapter 9.

2. If you have produced a complete flowchart, it will serve as an outline from which you can draft your paper.

3. Whether you set your process analysis in an expository or narrative paper, you should use sequential or chronological order. You should, however, break up the dull first-second-third sequential structure by introducing other transitional devices. If, for example, you are explaining why one step must precede another or what effect a particular step will have on the next step, you would use transitions like *consequently* and *as a result* (see Chapter 30 for a list of transitions). In addition, you may break the dull chronology by introducing an extended definition (Chapter 10) or a comparison or contrast (Chapter 8).

4. You can vary your sentence structure for your process analysis more than you can for your set of instructions. Into your strong, clear style of active verbs and short sentences, you may have the occasion to introduce complex, long, and involved sentences.

5. In a set of instructions, you may include diagrams or other visual material to show how to construct something in stages; as well, you may use visual material in a process analysis paper to show how it contributes to the process.

6. Use third person: "Above all, the movie critic gives his or her personal, honest opinion." (In a set of instructions, however, you would use second person: "Above all, give your personal, honest opinion.")

REVISING PROCESS FOR PARTS A AND B

1. Revise your first draft yourself by examining the tone of your piece of writing. Will your intended reader appreciate the tone? A set of instructions or a process analysis should have an efficient, professional air without being condescending. So put your draft away for a day or so, come back to it with a fresh outlook, and see if its tone or style disturbs you.

2. Consider the physical presentation of your piece of writing. Remember, you want your reader to be successful in completing the particular set of instructions or directions. Your points should be easy to find and follow; in other words, do not introduce extra material that might confuse—no matter how interesting the material is. Decide whether it is better to place a diagram, if needed, within your prose or on a separate page.

3. For your process analysis, you must make sure that you have an appropriate introduction that contains the whole idea as well as the parts. In your development you should have disguised routine chronological order with interesting side trips: an extended definition, a cause or effect, a comparison or contrast, and so on.

4. Have you used second person for the set of instructions and third person for the process analysis?

5. You should test your instructions *before* you present them to your reader by following them yourself. As you go through them for the final time, ask yourself: Is it clear? Have I left anything out? Is what I have said in logical sequence?

6. Now give your assignment to your fellow students for them to edit. They should follow the suggestions in Chapter 31 and in the drafting and revising processes above as they read your set of instructions or process analysis. Ask them to make sure that what you have said is clear, relevant, and logically arranged.

7. As in all writing, the final word should be left with you, the writer. It is your piece; it should have your stamp of approval. However, the true test of whether your instructions or directions work is, of course, in the hands of your readers. If they are able to complete your instructions or understand the analysis of your process, your writing works.

8. Once you have satisfied your peers, give your set of instructions or process analysis to your instructor for a final editing session. Then present it to your final reader.

PRODUCTS

Be Prepared for That Job Interview

by Penny Gallagher, student

There was a time when a college graduate could walk into almost any company, have a short talk with the personnel manager, and get a job immediately. Those days have disappeared. Now one job may have dozens or even hundreds of applicants, and the impression you give during the job interview will make the difference between being hired and being rejected.

Placement officers and career counselors recommend the following steps to take in preparing for a job interview:

1. Find out as much as you can about the firm you wish to join from newspapers and other media, friends who already work there, and other sources. Have questions ready for the interviewer about the company's policies and plans.

2. If possible, try to learn about the personality of the interviewer. Again, friends in the company will be your best sources of this information.

3. Apply for a specific position. Be prepared to explain how your abilities make you suitable for the position.

4. Know your strengths, and don't be ashamed to acknowledge them when asked about them for fear of appearing conceited. If you have weaknesses, consider how you will divulge them. You should not accept a job under a false understanding.

5. Stage a mock interview with a friend. Ask him or her to let you know about annoying mannerisms, lack of information, or other defects in your presentation.

6. Dress appropriately for the intended job. Observe how most people who do your prospective job dress and follow their example.

7. Be punctual for the interview. If you are delayed for some reason, phone the interviewer as soon as you can to let him or her know about your problem.

8. Give the interviewer your complete attention.

9. Be enthusiastic about your prospective job.

10. Be prepared to discuss your expected salary. You should not accept a job without knowing what your salary will be.

11. Be prepared to answer questions such as the following:
    a. Why do you want to work for this company?
    b. What are your ambitions?
    c. How long are you prepared to work here?
    d. Why are you applying for this particular position?

12. Ask the interviewer when you will be notified whether or not you have the job. If you are not notified within that time, contact the interviewer and ask if the position has been filled.

Cooling Burnout

by David Stansbury

Presented for your approval—three average college students, each a victim of the same disease. A disease that can take any form, any shape. A disease that can appear suddenly and without warning, to wreak havoc with its victims' lives. These students have just stepped into . . . the Burnout Zone.

Sally's a great girl. She's a pre-med major with a 3.81 GPA. She's the majority whip of the Student Senate and an active member in Young Republocrats. She spends at least eight hours a week working with disenfranchised Lhasa apsos. She has a steady boyfriend and was awarded two scholarships recently. She cries a lot for no apparent reason.

Alex never gets up before noon, and he never goes to bed before the national anthem. Lately he has switched from a filter cigarette to one that tastes more like old socks. He is notorious on campus for not leaving his dorm room except to buy more pork rinds at the nearest convenience store. He has recently been put on scholastic probation and no longer has a measurable GPA. When Alex was a freshman, he thought he was going to enjoy college. That was a long time ago.

Chuck has always planned to work in his father's real-estate agency. His grades are average, and he works 15 hours a week at the local Madras 'n' Stuff clothing outlet. He goes out regularly, either on dates or with fraternity brothers. He has just two more semesters before graduation. He's thinking of dropping out of school.

While the circumstances and symptoms are different in each case, these students are all burned out on school and don't know it. There's something amiss in their lives that's causing them to be depressed. If they fail to acknowledge the burnout symptoms, their problems will almost certainly increase, perhaps irrevocably.

WHAT IS BURNOUT?

You are a good candidate for burnout if you follow a tedious routine that makes you feel trapped. When you feel trapped, you feel anxious. Anxiety drains your emotional, intellectual, and physical resources quickly and extensively. As you weaken and tire, you begin to give up. You become one of the walking dead. Well, maybe not dead. You become a walking potato-head.

To control burnout, you need to know what causes it. Unfortunately, the list of contributing factors encompasses everything that is part of your life: family, friends, lovers, school, work, success, failure, ambition, indolence, opportunity, competition, self-esteem, and the pace of modern life. What's more, burnout can hit over- and under-achievers alike.

Any combination of factors can cause burnout. In fact, the only thing you can count on is that you'll have succumbed to this condition at least once before graduation. As a college counselor, I often see predictable patterns of burnout develop. Your freshman year is filled with excitement of new challenges to be met and new frontiers to be explored. Most of the time you're so busy trying not to act like a freshman that you don't have time to get caught in a soul-deadening routine. Often the toughest problem you face is figuring out where to buy a *College Blue Book*.

By sophomore year—the time of the legendary sophomore slump—you're comfortably ensconced in the campus community. You know the ropes, and you can play the game. Surviving registration lines, bargaining for extended deadlines, and avoiding the cafeteria's meat loaf are old hat. Now you must deal with the realization that you're facing another two or three years of this same damn game.

Sophomore year also marks the time when you experience the sharpest divergence between you and your parents and between your new values and the values of your adolescence. High-school certainties—you were destined to be a lawyer, or you'd postpone sex until marriage—start to fade away, and you're left to make your own rules. It's at this point that you find yourself debating whether to spend your available cash on a mohawk haircut or a subscription to *The Wall Street Journal*.

The momentum picks up again during your junior year. You're into the thick of your major studies, and you're either handling it or trying frantically to develop study habits. At any rate, the end of your academic travails no longer seems that far away. In fact, this may be the first time you can give people a straight answer when they ask what your major is.

In your senior year, however, you might become a lame duck looking for crutches. You're almost done with college, so why bother with studying? At the same time, you dread the "real" world beyond campus. It's too late to retreat into childhood; it's too early to start acting like a middle-aged adult (checking into insurance policies and going to bed by 10 P.M.). All you can do is wait until graduation, with maybe a GRE or a few job interviews to relieve the tedium.

SYMPTOMS OF BURNOUT

So how do you know if you're turning to toast?

- You're ready for bed at six-thirty every night. None of your classes start before noon. Even with 16 hours of sleep, you feel as if you've been lifting houses all day.
- You've cut so many classes that you've forgotten how to get to campus from your apartment.
- You're ill more often than usual. You're constantly touching your forehead to see if you have a fever.
- You recently spent an entire weekend living on beer and Twinkies. The last vegetable you ate was a burrito.
- You blame everyone else for your problems. When your roommate is so stupid, and your parents are so pushy, and your professors are so boring, and your friends are so insensitive, how could anyone expect you to concentrate on school?
- You blame only yourself for your problems. Maybe if you weren't so lazy, maybe if you weren't so dumb, maybe if you weren't such total scum, you'd be able to concentrate on school.
- You realize that your work is slipping, so you decide to give it your all. You study until 3 A.M. every night and take your homework to parties. It doesn't help.
- Your favorite songs are "King of Pain" and "Burning Down the House," and you listen to them constantly instead of working.

FREE ADVICE

The most dangerous aspect of burnout is its tendency to intensify the more you worry about it. If you try to suppress it by working harder, then you just burn out faster. If you ignore it, insidious burnout will just keep hammering away until you crumble under its assault.

If you're suffering from burnout, the first thing you must do is seek perspective. You should definitely talk about the problem. Friends, teachers, and family members may be able to help, but you really need to talk to someone who's not putting any kind of pressure on you. Campus counseling centers usually employ professionals who can help you recover from burnout. These people have seen burnout in all its various forms; they know how to help. If you don't hit it off with a particular counselor, feel free to move on to another one. In short, talk to the people who actually seem to be doing you some good by listening.

Tips for Getting Better

- Remember, you won't be in college forever. A case of burnout is not the end of the world—though it may feel like it.
- Change your routine. Don't blow everything off. Instead, rearrange your schedule so that it is more to your liking—or just different. Don't go for long periods of time without leisure, and conversely, don't let schoolwork pile up into an interminable string of all-nighters.
- Do something that relaxes and pleases you when you do have some time off. That may sound simplistic, but think about the ways you spend your leisure time. You'll probably discover that you do a lot of things out of habit. For example, going out for a beer with the same old crowd may have lost its thrill months ago. If so, it's time to develop some new interests.
- Establish short-term goals with concrete rewards. Finish one assigned book this week, then buy yourself a banana split. Do exactly four hours of library research over the weekend, then treat yourself to a movie. Promise yourself at least one quiet evening alone every week.
- Respect yourself. Your mother was right. You should clean up your room, take your clothes to the cleaners, and eat foods that require a knife and fork. Indulge rather than debauch yourself.
- Plan a trip. Even if it's only for a weekend, do something besides taking your dirty laundry to your parents' house.

- Plan to take a semester off. Work, travel, try a different way of life. This can be an excellent opportunity for you to evaluate your options. In a new location, without the pressure of a daily grind, you may be able to focus on the direction you'd like your life to take. You might decide to completely change your life—or just your major. Or you might decide that you just needed a break and are, in fact, on course and eager to start moving again.

- Change your plans; take a risk. Burnout often indicates a dissonance between your work and your values. If you have chosen a major that doesn't match your talents and dreams, then no wonder you feel alienated, tired, and frustrated.

- Learn to say no. Don't think you have to do what everyone wants you to do. You can accomplish a lot without carving yourself up like a brisket at an Elks' picnic.

- Finally, don't take life—or the occasional case of burnout—too seriously. A little humor and imagination can help you over the hump when the camel gets angry.

ANALYSIS

Be Prepared for That Job Interview

1. Are there any points about job interviews that you feel should have been included in this set of instructions?

2. Are any points included that you feel do not apply? Why?

3. Which is the most important instruction? Why?

Cooling Burnout

1. In this process analysis paper, Stansbury points out clearly how you can tell if you are burning out. Do you have any of the symptoms? What are you doing about your problem? Will this product help you solve it?

2. For which particular age group does Stansbury, a college career counselor, write? If you are not in that age group, how does "Cooling Burnout" apply to you?

3. Comment on Stansbury's writing style. Mention his opening and his three thumbnail case studies, his humor, and his method of organization.

4. If you are still searching for a topic for a process analysis paper, you might pattern one after "Cooling Burnout." Consider one of the following topics: being a middle-aged student, maintaining a 4.00 GPA, or any other topic dealing with your student experience.

5. Stansbury includes a set of instructions for those suffering from burnout. Point out the difference between his process analysis and his set of instructions.

16

Memo

INTRODUCTION

A memo (memorandum) enables easy, fast communication between people in the same club, college, company, or business. Basically, a memo is a concise, informal message from one person to another to make a request, give instructions, make an announcement, answer a question, and so on. It is not unusual for a person to ask that the main points of a telephone conversation be confirmed by a memo. This is often done for verification or clarification. Whatever its purpose, the memo saves time and provides a written record of the date of the communication, the message, the name of the sender, and the name of the recipient.

Assignment

Write a memo to one or more people in your college, university, club, work, or family. Make your memo appropriate to a particular need that concerns you.

PREWRITING PROCESS

1. After you have decided on a suitable topic and audience for your memo, the most important requirement is that you have a complete knowledge of the situation about which you are writing. You may need to do some research for a memo or ask questions as your first prewriting step.

2. You must also be aware of the needs and interests of your readers. Since you will be writing to members of groups to which you belong, you should not find this difficult. (If you wish to write to someone *outside* your group, you should use the format of a business letter. See Chapter 18, Part B.)

3. Begin your prewriting by writing a topic or summary sentence for the memo, outlining the idea of the message as well as stating its purpose. Because memos are normally written in the second person, use the "you" point of view in this summary sentence.

4. Jot down all of the supporting facts and ideas that you wish to include by using the Newspaper Reporter's Questions brainstorming method (see Chapter 25).

5. Before you draft your memo, make sure you complete a full set of writing variables. A knowledge of both your and your audience's situation is essential for a successful memo. Know what you want to achieve by writing the memo and what your audience is expecting. Even if your reader is not expecting to receive your memo, you should include this fact in your set of writing variables.

DRAFTING PROCESS

1. Look over the ideas that you jotted down in your Newspaper Reporter's Questions list. Arrange them in a logical order and in complete sentences.

2. Add necessary transitional devices (see Chapter 30).

3. To make what you have written easier to read, you should now begin to divide your writing into paragraphs. The main difference between paragraph writing for a memo and for an expository essay is that you do not need a topic sentence for each paragraph in a memo. There should be only one main topic sentence for a memo; all the other sentences should support this one statement.

4. Once you have gathered all of your material, decide on how you are going to present it. Your main concern in writing a memo is to ensure that it can be read easily and quickly.

5. Make sure you have included the following captions in the top left corner, seven lines from the top of the paper:

DATE:

TO:

FROM:

SUBJECT:

Fill these in and write your memo under them.

6. Use headings to help the reader see your organization at a glance and to note specific information.

7. Write your points in list form whenever possible; in this way, your memo will be easy to read and easy to refer to.

8. Plenty of white space makes a memo look neater and less overpowering. If you type your memo, you usually single-space.

9. When you have said what you want to say, *stop*. A formal conclusion is not necessary.

10. You need not sign a memo; however, you may initial it at the bottom or after your name in the heading.

11. Apply this checklist to your completed draft, before you have others edit it:

   a. Reread your entire memo. Add, omit, or change anything that does not fulfill your purpose.

   b. Make sure that you have caught your reader's attention and interest. You should use a friendly approach, keep your message brief and to the point, and begin and end on a positive note.

12. Before you have your memo edited, have a little fun by drafting your memo using a persona. You can sometimes achieve a desired effect even better by hiding your own voice. If you wish to retain your original draft, this extra draft may provide you with another element that you can include.

REVISING PROCESS

1. Besides following the suggestions in Chapter 31, your peers should give their opinions on the following specific items in your memo:

a. Are the beginning and ending positive enough?

b. Can you change, add, or cut anything?

c. Did you use the second-person point of view consistently?

d. Is your slant positive rather than negative?

e. Would an illustration, diagram, graph, or picture help?

f Is the end of the memo too abrupt? (Since there is no formal closure for memos, the message must end smoothly.)

g. If your peers were to receive the memo, what would be their reaction?

2. After your peers edit your memo, ask your instructor-editor to give it a final editing. Send your polished memo to your intended reader. The response you receive will soon let you know whether you have written a successful memorandum.

PRODUCTS

As you read these model memos, determine how you would react to receiving each of them. Note particularly the trio of memos on the same topic, each written from a different point of view or persona.

```
DATE:  Feb. 2, 1985
TO:  All Company Hockey Team Members
FROM:  Michael de Hock
SUBJECT:  Next Meeting


I would like to remind all team members that there will be a meeting
on Monday, February 7, at 7:00 p.m. in the board room. (Please take
note of the items to be discussed.)

    Agenda
    1.  Revision of practice-time schedule
    2.  Planning fund-raising activities
    3.  Tips on penalty-killing
    4.  Information on upcoming games

I cannot stress enough that attendance at this meeting is extremely
important. If for any reason you are unable to attend, please
contact me personally at my home (435-5555).
```

DATE: May 18, 1985
TO: All Employees
FROM: Crew Chief
SUBJECT: Early Departures

Situation   It has come to my attention that a few employees
             have begun the bad habit of regularly leaving work
             up to half an hour early. This is unfair to other
             employees who must cover for you until your
             replacement arrives.

Suggestions Day-shift hours are 7:30 a.m. to 3:30 p.m. If you
             need to leave early for a valid reason (school
             commitments, doctor's or dentist's appointments,
             etc.), please let me know as far in advance as
             possible so that I can arrange for someone to
             replace you.

Let's all cooperate to make Max's a pleasant place to work.

Fran

DATE: September 19, 1985
TO: Members of the Basketball Team
FROM: Bob Horton, Captain *BH*
SUBJECT: The Condition of the Locker Room

Problem
Look, guys, that was quite a mess we made in the locker room last
Friday. I know that both Coach Reed and Mr. Desmond were really
upset when they saw the condition of the room.

Solution
I think the whole team should get together and apologize to both
the coach and the custodian and that each member of the team should
agree to clean up the locker room once a week. I don't think that's
too much to ask.

DATE: Sept. 19, 1985
TO: Members of the Basketball Team
FROM: Coach Reed
SUBJECT: The Locker Room

SITUATION: Last Friday some unidentified members of the
                    basketball team left the locker room in an
                    appalling condition. I came in Saturday morning
                    expecting to pick up a few towels and ended up
                    spending most of the afternoon with Mr. Desmond
                    restoring the room to some sort of order.

PROBLEM: The juvenile attitude of some members of the team
                    amazes me. Unfortunately, I don't know which of
                    you actually did the damage, so I must penalize
                    the whole team unless and until those responsible
                    actually come forward and apologize.

SOLUTION: So unless those who made the mess apologize to me
                    and to Mr. Desmond within forty-eight hours, the
                    entire team will be dismissed and tryouts held
                    next Wednesday afternoon for their replacements.
                    Those who own up to causing the damage will be
                    suspended for three games and will not be allowed
                    into the locker room until their suspension is
                    over.

RESULTS: I hope to hear from some (or, if necessary, all)
                    of the team soon.

DATE: Sept. 19, 1985
TO: The Basketball Team
FROM: James Desmond, Custodian
SUBJECT: The Pigsty You Left Last Night

You dodos have gone too far! I told you before that if you left the
locker room in a mess, you wouldn't be allowed to use it any more.
Well, the mess I found last night was beyond belief. Even pigs are
cleaner. I've had it with you animals.

This is your last warning. If the locker room is ever a mess again,
I'll lock it up and throw away the key.

DATE: March 14, 1985
TO: Mike, Ben, Weni, Jessica, Heather, and Julia
FROM: Dad
SUBJECT: The Refrigerator

Problem   There's too much time being spent in front of the
               refrigerator.

Solution   The following are new rules concerning the use of
               the refrigerator:

               1. There are two reasons for opening the fridge
               door:
                   a. Taking food out
                   b. Putting food in
               The fridge is not an air conditioner and should
               not be used as one. No standing in front of the
               fridge door to cool off.

               2. Time periods for opening the fridge door are as
               follows:
                   a. Breakfast—7 a.m. to 7:30 a.m.
                   b. Lunch—12 p.m. to 12:30 p.m. (except school
                      days; then the times will be from 3:15 p.m.
                      to 3:30 p.m.)
                   c. Dinner—5 p.m. to 5:30 p.m. (except Sundays
                      and holidays. Times for these days will be
                      posted the night before.)

               3. The fridge door should not remain open more
               than 10 seconds at any one time. Know the item you
               are getting ahead of time and where it goes when
               returning it.

               4. Midnight raids—Saturdays only! This must be
               cleared with at least one parent 24 hours in
               advance. There are two reasons for this rule:
                   a. Mom and Dad like midnight raids, too, and it
                      gives us plenty of time to get what we want.
                   b. Give Mom and Dad a chance to make sure
                      there are nutritious goodies to eat.

               5. Make sure the light goes out when the fridge
               door closes.

ANALYSIS

Michael de Hock's Memo

1. This memo does not use the layout suggested in the Drafting Process of this assignment. Is it still an effective memo? Why?

2. The sentence in parentheses in paragraph one could be omitted. Why?

Fran's Memo

1. Why would there be a difference in tone between this memo and the previous one? Does Fran make her point?

2. Do the two underlined headings get in the way or do they add to the memo? In what way?

Bob Horton's Three Memos

Bob Horton was asked by his coach and the custodian to write several different memos asking his team to keep the locker room tidy. In addition to his own name, Horton was told he could use the coach's and custodian's names as authors of the memos.

1. Which of Horton's three memos do you think Coach Reed asked him to post? Why?

2. Remember that Horton wrote all three memos, using Desmond and Reed as personae. Examine the tone of each to see the main differences among the memos. Is each appropriate for its persona?

Dad's Memo

1. Dad is, in reality, student Jeff Clark. He is, indeed, a father of six. After reading his memo, how can you tell this fact?

2. Clark posted his memo on the refrigerator door. Can you tell that he has a sense of humor? How? Provide at least two examples.

3. What exactly is his and his audience's situation that caused Clark to write this memo? Do you think his memo is effective or could he have achieved his purpose in a better way?

17

Proposal and Report

INTRODUCTION

In many situations you must submit a proposal in order to obtain approval for a project. Often, once you have completed the project, you must turn in a report outlining its success or failure.

Therefore, in most cases you will be expected to do both parts of this assignment. First, you are to write a proposal where you present either a problem with your suggestions for solving it or an idea with your methods for making it feasible. Second, you are to write a report based on the success or failure of your proposal.

Assignment

Part A: Write a proposal which involves either a problem that you would like to solve or an idea that you would like to see become a reality. The subject of your proposal may concern your college, university, club or organization, work, or family.

Part B: Write a report on the successful or unsuccessful execution of your proposal. (Or, with your instructor's permission, write a report that stands alone.)

PREWRITING PROCESS FOR PART A

1. Decide on a real problem or idea about which to write your proposal. Here are a few topics to get you thinking:

- Propose that a rock band come to your college for a concert.
- Propose to your spouse or parents that you need more financial assistance to help you through college.

- Propose that you and a friend set up a business to sell Christmas crafts. The proposal is to your friend.
- Propose that the company where you work enlarge its storage space by adding a new floor to the building.
- Propose that your college reintroduce an open-door policy regarding admission.

2. If your proposal deals with a problem, jot down all the ramifications of that problem in a Pro/Con list, so that you can easily solve it. If your proposal deals with an idea, jot down all the facts concerning it using the brainstorming technique of Aristotle's Topics, so that you will be able to convince others that it is indeed a worthwhile effort. If necessary, use other brainstorming sessions to gather supporting evidence (see Chapter 25).

3. State your problem or idea in a concise question or a thesis statement. Be specific. Now state your solution or reasons in several single sentences. You will use these sentences as recommendations and support for your proposal, so write down everything that you think is pertinent to the proposed problem or idea. This may involve research. To find support for your proposal, you may need to go to the library or find appropriate persons to interview.

4. Once you have all your data, make a list of your writing variables as in the following example:

BROAD TOPIC:	Summer work
LIMITED TOPIC:	The formation of a summer theater company
AUDIENCE:	Department of Summer Employment. Real. I intend to send it.
PURPOSE:	To request that the Department provide financial backing for our project
FORMAT:	Proposal
VOICE:	My own
SITUATION:	I am one of a group of recent graduates of the theatre department at a local college. Everyone in the group needs summer employment in order to continue our education. The Department of Summer Employment has called for proposals for summer projects for students.
THESIS STATEMENT:	A summer theater in our town would not only give employment to a number of recent graduates but also entertainment for the community as a whole.

DRAFTING PROCESS FOR PART A

1. Your main purpose in writing the proposal should be to gain the interest and support of your audience. Consider what your reader's interests will be. Money? Time? Potential benefits or profits? Do the advantages of your proposal outweigh the disadvantages?

2. Read the proposal at the end of this assignment for an example of layout and organization.

3. Because you will usually need to submit an outline of the proposal, prepare a working outline of your draft. No doubt, as you continue to compose, you will add to your outline.

4. In order for your proposal to be taken seriously, it should be well constructed and written in a businesslike manner. Make sure your word choice, sentence structure, transitions, and paragraphs follow the principles of quality writing.

5. After you have written your first draft, reread and then rewrite it, including any pertinent information that you have left out, omitting any unnecessary repetitions, and changing anything that does not present the facts accurately.

REVISING PROCESS FOR PART A

1. Ask your peers to assume that they are the final reader of your proposal: your landlord, employer, parent, and so forth. They should think of all the reasons why they might turn down your proposal. Carefully consider any reasons they suggest for completely or partially refusing your proposal, so that you can revise it further by adding, deleting, or changing some of its sections.

2. Encourage your editors to use the checklists in Chapter 31. Ask them to comment on your tone and style. If there is anything that they find unclear, prepare to change it.

3. The final responsibility for the acceptance or rejection of the proposal rests ultimately with you; therefore, give it a thorough editing before submitting it to your instructor-editor.

4. Once your instructor accepts your proposal, you may either go to Part B of this assignment or you may submit your typed proposal to its intended reader. If you make the proposal a real one and obtain acceptance, you will feel more successful than if you receive an *A* for a classroom assignment.

PREWRITING PROCESS FOR PART B

There are so many different kinds of reports that in order to gain experience in writing most of them, you will have to take a special course in report writing. In such a course you will learn the characteristics of progress reports, analytical reports, feasibility reports, history reports, procedural reports, informative reports, interpretive reports, status reports, and narrative reports. For this assignment, you can become familiar with the general characteristics of report writing by writing one to follow your proposal assignment.

If you indeed wrote a real-life proposal for the first part of this assignment and if that proposal was accepted, you may be in an ideal situation to write the second part of the assignment. Assuming that the event you proposed has occurred, you should now prepare an analytical report for the same audience that accepted your original proposal. (In some real-life situations, you may be required to submit interim reports to a program manager.)

If you composed a fictitious proposal, you should now assume that the event has occurred so that you can prepare an analytical, formal report.

1. Begin to jot down everything that occurred during the execution of the project. For example, if your theatre group did get financial assistance from the Department of Summer Employment, use a favorite brainstorming technique to record all the facts, so that you do not omit anything in your report. Make sure to list all the details surrounding the event: before, during, and after.

2. Once you have all your necessary information, you should list your writing variables. The following example corresponds to the one used in Part A:

BROAD TOPIC:	Summer work
LIMITED TOPIC:	The formation of a summer theatre company
AUDIENCE:	Department of Summer Employment
PURPOSE:	To report on the success of presenting plays throughout the summer
FORMAT:	Two interim reports plus a final, detailed formal report
VOICE:	My own
SITUATION:	I have been appointed spokesperson for the group. We are all pleased with the results and optimistic that we may do the same thing next summer.
THESIS STATEMENT:	The summer theatre company was a huge success.

DRAFTING PROCESS FOR PART B

1. Formal reports have many parts: title page, letter of transmittal, preface or foreword, abstract or summary, table of contents, list of illustrations, graphic aids, body, bibliography, and appendix. You should also note the layout of formal reports: headings, placement of page numbers, and spacing (look at the product as a guide). When you write your report, determine which of these parts you will need in your report. The following descriptions will be of help to you:

Title Page

Your title page should be set up in the same way as in the product.

Letter of Transmittal

This letter follows the conventional letter format and states its message simply. What you basically need to say is "Here is the report." However, you may include your main conclusion and acknowledgements for any help you received in preparing the report. (Instead of using a letter, you may forward a memo of transmittal.)

Preface

The preface (also called a synopsis) usually includes the summary or abstract, which provides an overview of the entire report, a statement of your purpose in writing the report, and an explanation of the method you used in putting the report together.

Table of Contents

For long reports you should provide a list of your contents with the number of the first page on which each section appears.

List of Illustrations

If you have included several illustrations, photographs, diagrams, and so on, provide a list with the numbers of the pages on which they appear.

Body

This is the main part of your report. It should be written as an expository essay with an introductory paragraph, developmental paragraphs, and a concluding paragraph. The body may or may not contain subheadings.

In the body of the report present the details of the event in some logical order. You may want to begin with an overall assessment of the project, then go on to discuss specific aspects: costs, results, and so on.

In many cases the project will have been a "mixed success"—partially successful, partially unsuccessful. Consider both the positive and negative aspects; then decide if the advantages outweigh the disadvantages. Your decision will form the summary or conclusion of your report. A common method of concluding a report is to give a recommendation for further action.

Bibliography

In some analytical reports, you will need to quote from several sources. In such cases, you will need to present a formal bibliography (see Chapter 39).

Appendix

Instead of interrupting the body of your report with additional relevant material (clippings, pamphlets, letters of commendation, and so on), you should include them in an appendix. Make sure that throughout the body of the report you refer the reader to the appendix for further information, proof, or support.

2. Based on your prewriting material, prepare a working outline for your report. You may add to it as you continue to compose your report.

3. After you have written your first draft, rewrite it, including any pertinent information that you have left out, omitting any unnecessary repetitions, and changing anything that does not present the facts accurately. Although you no doubt wish to present a favorable report, you must be truthful about your findings.

REVISING PROCESS FOR PART B

1. Ask your peers to read your report as though they were the intended reader, using the suggestions outlined in the Revising Process of Part A of this assignment.

2. Ask them to check particularly your organization (to see that you have followed an outline) and your completeness (to see that you have accurately included all facts).

3. Have your editors test to see that your writing passes the checklists outlined in Chapter 31.

4. If you attach a letter to your report, ask your peers to edit it according to the instructions in Chapter 18.

5. When you have satisfied your peers, present your paper to your instructor-editor for a final evaluation.

6. After you have completed the final version of your report, place a cover on it to protect the inner pages. On the cover place your name and the title of your report. Present your report to your final reader.

PRODUCT

Proposal

CONTENTS

HOSPITAL FOOD SERVICE FOR NIGHT STAFF

A Proposal Prepared for
Harry Fenster
Associate Administrator
Jackson Memorial Hospital

by Nancy J. Sadler
Nursing Supervisor

1

I. Introduction

A. *Summary*

Food machines, the only source of food available to the night staff, consist primarily of one entree machine and one snack machine and offer a diet limited in variety and poor in nutrition. The Department of Nursing Administration recommends the acceptance of the enclosed proposal to provide food service to the night staff. Access to the nutritious food presently provided by the Dietary Department will benefit the thirty to forty employees on duty at that time and prove cost-effective to the hospital.

B. *Proposal*

Nursing Administration proposes a change in the cafeteria hours and food service to permit the purchase of food by the employees between the hours of 3:00 A.M. and 4:30 A.M.

2

C. *Procedure*

John Miller, Supervisor of the Dietary Department, supports the proposal and agrees to a ninety-day trial period during which his department will collect corroborating statistics.

II. Proposal for Project

A. *Schedule Changes*

A two-hour change in the schedule of one prep-cook would permit the serving of food to the night staff. Presently the prep-cooks report to work at 5:00 A.M. One prep-cook, beginning two hours earlier, will open the grill and serve a variety of hot meals from 3:00 A.M. to 4:30 A.M. Breakfast preparations will then begin at 4:30 A.M instead of 5:00 A.M.

3

B. *Length of Project*

As previously stated, John Miller agrees to a ninety-day trial period and the dietary staff is prepared to commence nighttime operations the first of June.

C. *Impact on Budget*

Because the above proposal requires no additional staff, implementation will have no impact on labor costs or increase in budgeted salaries. Present statistics suggest the average employee will spend two dollars on food each night. The Dietary Department estimates raw food and supply costs to be forty percent (40¢ on the dollar); thus, estimated revenue will be sixty percent of every dollar spent. Over the ninety-day period the hospital should realize a net profit of $4,320.00 in additional revenues.

4

D. *Breakdown of Expenditures and Revenues*

Expenditures

Salaries (no additions necessary) $0.00

Raw food and service cost (per day) $32.00

(Estimated @ 40¢ per dollar spent per employee)

(Estimated service to 40 employees
each spending $2.00 per day)

     Total (90-day trial period) $2,880.00

Revenues (per day) $80.00

(Estimated @ $2.00 per day per employee.
Estimated service to 40 employees)

     Total (90-day trial period) $7,200.00

     Net profit $4,320.00

III. Conclusion

Nursing Administration hopes that this proposal will meet with your approval and that the Dietary Department can implement the changes the first of the month. We look forward to hearing from you soon.

Report

September 7, 1985

Mr. Harry Fenster
Associate Administrator
Jackson Memorial Hospital
New Wilmington, PA 32067

Dear Mr. Fenster:

The night staff wishes to thank you for the food service provided by the hospital the past three months. Employees look forward to their lunch breaks, and employee morale has never been better.

The Dietary Department made the transition with little or no problem. The statistics that John Miller collected over the past three months show the venture to be profitable for the hospital.

I have enclosed a report for your perusal. John Miller plans to present his financial statement at the next department head meeting. I hope you are as pleased with the results as we in Nursing Administration are.

Sincerely,

Nancy J. Sadler

Nancy J. Sadler
Nursing Supervisor

HOSPITAL FOOD SERVICE FOR NIGHT STAFF

A Report Prepared for Harry Fenster
Associate Administrator
Jackson Memorial Hospital

by Nancy J. Sadler
Nursing Supervisor

CONTENTS

1

I. Introduction

A. *Purpose*

    The Department of Nursing Administration, in collaboration with the Dietary Department, presents this report of the ninety-day trial period during which the Dietary Department made food service available to the night staff.

B. *Revenue*

    John Miller, Supervisor of the Dietary Department, will present a financial statement for the above services at the department head meeting in September.

II. Report of Present Food Service Program

A. *Dietary Employee Schedule*

    The two-hour schedule change in the present prep-cook's workday posed no problems. In fact, the new schedule eliminated transportation problems the prep-cook was experiencing previously.

2

However, a problem in staffing did arise during one weekend due to the illness of a relief cook. Because John Miller utilized one of his per diem dietary workers, service continued as usual.

B. *Employee Participation*

Use of cafeteria facilities and the purchase of food increased as the night staff became aware of the service. The staff was enthusiastic in its praise of the cook and the variety of foods offered. Having had only the selection from the food machines available for months, the staff now enjoys hot soups, omelets, fresh green salads, and frozen yogurt. Employee participation exceeded our original expectation.

C. *Usage by Patients' Families*

Relatives of hospitalized patients also availed themselves of our food service during the night. Their patronage accounted for an unexpected source of participation as well as revenue. Many have expressed their gratitude to the Dietary Department for the new service.

3

D. *Revenue*

Hospital net profit proved to be higher than our proposed estimate. Our low patient census in June, with the subsequent decrease in necessary nursing staff, resulted in fewer profits during that month. However, July and August profits were higher than anticipated, and we exceeded our original estimate by three hundred fifty dollars.

III. Conclusion

Nursing Administration believes the food service program to be successful. The service benefits the night shift employees and many patients' families. The service improves employee morale. The service continues to be cost-effective for the institution.

Recommendation

We respectfully submit our recommendation that the cafeteria continue to be open for employees and patients' families during the night.

4

IV. Appendix

June 14, 1985

Mr. Harry Fenster
Associate Administrator
Jackson Memorial Hospital
New Wilmington, PA 32067

Dear Mr. Fenster:

The nurses on the fourth floor wish to say thanks for opening the cafeteria to us at night. Everyone looks forward to lunch breaks now that we have good food served in pleasant surroundings.

Employee morale is at an all-time high on this floor, thanks to you!

Sincerely yours,

Donna Forbes

Donna Forbes
Head Nurse

5

June 7, 1985

Mr. John Miller
Jackson Memorial Hospital
New Wilmington, PA 32067

Dear John:

It has come to my attention that the cafeteria is now open during the night. On behalf of the in-house physicians and the physicians on call at night, I'd like to say thank-you.

Your department is providing a valuable service, one which the physicians appreciate immensely.

Sincerely,

Samuel P. Foster

Samuel P. Foster, M.D.
Chairman of Medicine

SF/nh

ANALYSIS

Hospital Food Service for Night Staff

Proposal

1. Is the object or purpose of the proposal clear? How can you tell that Sadler is an experienced nurse?
2. Does the proposal have a clear and orderly development?
3. What would you expect the result to be?

Report

1. Does the letter of transmittal fulfill its purpose?
2. Is Sadler's report clearly presented? Do you think the reader would need more information? It so, what?
3. Is there anything about its style with which you are uncomfortable? If so, what? How should it be changed?
4. Is its style appropriate for its purpose and audience?
5. What does the appendix add to the effectiveness of the report?

18

Correspondence

INTRODUCTION

Letters inform, solicit, demand, coax, invite, impress, thank, remind, and perform many other functions that would be difficult to accomplish any other way. A letter's only possible competition is the telephone, but a phone call is not nearly as effective as a letter. The receiver of your letter can reread it at a later time, share it with other readers, make notes in its margins, or marvel at your brilliant turning of a phrase. A letter can also be used as physical proof of intentions, expectations, or promises.

How else, for the price of a stamp, can you get a few minutes of someone's undivided attention? Letters, properly written, are a great equalizer: the letter *you* sent to a company manager could be in the same pile as one from the president's office. Depending on the quality of your letter, it may be saved, treasured, followed, ignored, or thrown into the wastebasket.

Correspondence falls into two basic categories: the personal letter and the business letter. In addition, you might write a letter to the editor of a newspaper or journal—a type which shares many of the characteristics of both a personal and a business letter. This assignment, therefore, has three parts.

Assignment

Part A: Write a thank-you letter, a congratulatory letter, a letter of condolence, an invitation, or a conversational, friendly letter.

Part B: Write a letter of inquiry, reply, request, acknowledgement, or complaint or a letter in which you place an order or enclose a remittance.

Part C: Choose an article from a recent newspaper or magazine and write a letter to the editor, agreeing or disagreeing with what the article says.

PREWRITING PROCESS FOR PARTS A AND B

1. Before you begin either of these assignments, think about them. Can you make one of these letters a real-life one? Maybe you would like to:

- Thank someone for a gift
- Congratulate someone for an achievement
- Console someone after a loss
- Invite someone to a party
- Ask someone to give you a character reference
- Complain about something you have recently purchased
- Ask your congressional representative or governor about some local problem
- Request a particular speaker to come to your club's next meeting
- Adopt an older, bedridden hospital patient
- Write to a Russian student to tell him or her about your feelings on world peace
- Offer your support to an animal-rights organization
- Object to the president of a country because you do not approve of something he or she has done
- Ask how you may help a political party
- Keep a prisoner up to date on what's happening in the country
- Write an anonymous letter to someone for a variety of reasons, such as because he is always cheery, because she is the backbone of the neighborhood, because he keeps the office a friendly place to work, and so on.

2. As you would for any piece of writing, you should go through a series of your favorite brainstorming techniques in order to focus on a topic and gather supporting evidence. The Senses Cluster and the Pentad are useful for personal letters; the Newspaper Reporter's Questions and Pro/Con Ladder are effective for business letters (see Chapter 25).

3. Once you have decided what you are going to write about and to whom you are writing, keep your reader's situation in mind. It may determine the style and tone of your letter.

4. From time to time you may want to write a letter of complaint. It is much more effective than making a phone call. Usually you should direct your complaint to the company president or customer service department. You can find business addresses in *Standard & Poor's Register of Corporations, Directors and Executives*. Libraries also have other listings. Sometimes addresses are listed on the product or on its warranty. If you do not have the name of the manufacturer, thumb through the *Thomas Registry*, which lists the makers of thousands of products.

5. Once you know to whom and why you are writing, jot down your writing variables. These examples may be useful:

LIMITED TOPIC:	A Halloween party
AUDIENCE:	Twenty friends. Real. I intend to send the invitations.
PURPOSE:	I want my friends to come.

FORMAT:	A humorous invitation
VOICE:	I intend to write as though I am the Devil.
SITUATION:	The Devil wants to set the tone that this will be a great party.
THESIS STATEMENT:	You, my dear, have been *chosen* to come over to Gina's house on the last day of October because I am hosting a party that you will n-e-v-e-r forget as long as you ____ .

or

BROAD TOPIC:	Starvation
LIMITED TOPIC:	Starvation in Ethiopia
AUDIENCE:	The Red Cross. Real. I intend to send it.
PURPOSE:	To start my war against starvation in Ethiopia
FORMAT:	A business letter
VOICE:	My own
SITUATION:	I saw a shocking documentary on TV and want to help. Even though I don't have any money to send, I'm sure I can do something.
THESIS STATEMENT:	I want to offer a couple of hours each week to help eliminate starvation in Ethiopia.

DRAFTING PROCESS FOR PARTS A AND B

1. Before you start to draft your letter, remember that the letter your reader holds in his or her hands *is* an extension of you. Make a good impression.

2. In writing a personal letter you have much more leeway than in writing a business letter: in the kind of stationery you use, whether to type or write in longhand, or whether to use formal headings. Your personal letter, though, should be legible and neat. Avoid crowding margins at the right and bottom. You want your letter to be enjoyed and appreciated.

3. In the diagram on page 200, note that the sections that are peculiar to business letters are italicized.

4. There are many different ways to punctuate a letter. The most important rule is to be consistent. Study the combinations of block, modified block, and indented forms with open, mixed, and closed punctuation on page 201.

5. While composing your correspondence, especially business letters, ask yourself: Am I clear, correct, and natural? Notice, for example, the difference between these two requests:

- Have you something about fishing and how to start a project on hatcheries? Any books, pamphlets, or references? Hopefully free.

- I am planning a social science project on salmon hatcheries. Because I know that you are knowledgeable about the fishing industry, I would like your assistance. Would you please recommend any reading references, free pamphlets, film-strips, or other audiovisual aids?

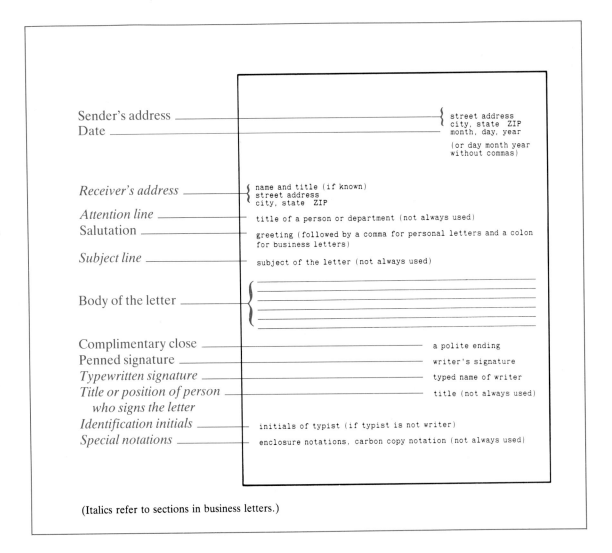

Sender's address ———— { street address
                          city, state ZIP
Date ————————— month, day, year
                          (or day month year
                          without commas)

Receiver's address ———— { name and title (if known)
                            street address
                            city, state ZIP

Attention line ———— title of a person or department (not always used)
Salutation ———— greeting (followed by a comma for personal letters and a colon
                    for business letters)

Subject line ———— subject of the letter (not always used)

Body of the letter ————

Complimentary close ———— a polite ending
Penned signature ———— writer's signature
Typewritten signature ———— typed name of writer
Title or position of person ———— title (not always used)
   who signs the letter
Identification initials ———— initials of typist (if typist is not writer)
Special notations ———— enclosure notations, carbon copy notation (not always used)

(Italics refer to sections in business letters.)

Notice the difference between these two complaints:

- This will acknowledge receipt of your statement. In regard to said statement, there is an error in the billing of the shipment of toothpicks, your Order 18M12, Invoice 38L9.
- Your billing on the enclosed order is wrong; I ordered and received six boxes of toothpicks, not sixty.

Good letters go directly to the point and explain the facts in a natural, yet polite, way. What do you think of this third version of the above complaint?

- I received your billing of the enclosed order. Unfortunately it appears to be wrong; I ordered and received six boxes of toothpicks, not sixty.

Block style, open punctuation

372 Castor Avenue
Seattle, WA 98033
June 1, 1985

Mr. Stéphane Hébert
Save-More Foods
633 Boyer Road
Seattle, WA 98133

Dear Mr. Hébert

SUBJECT: Advertising

_____
_____
_____

Yours very truly

Marie Zuckerman

Marie Zuckerman

Block style, closed punctuation

372 Castor Avenue,
Seattle, WA 98033
June 1, 1985

Mr. Stéphane Hébert,
Save-More Foods,
633 Boyer Road,
Seattle, WA 98133

Dear Mr. Hébert:

SUBJECT: Advertising

_____
_____
_____

Yours very truly,

Marie Zuckerman

Marie Zuckerman

Modified block style, mixed punctuation

372 Castor Avenue
Seattle, WA 98033
June 1, 1985

Mr. Stéphane Hébert
Save-More Foods
633 Boyer Road
Seattle, WA 98133

Dear Mr. Hébert:

SUBJECT: Advertising

_____
_____
_____

Yours very truly,

Marie Zuckerman

Marie Zuckerman

Indented form, closed punctuation

372 Castor Avenue,
Seattle, WA 98033
June 1, 1985

Mr. Stéphane Hébert,
Save-More Foods,
633 Boyer Road,
Seattle, WA 98133

Dear Mr. Hébert:

Subject: Advertising

_____
_____
_____

Yours very truly,

Marie Zuckerman

REVISING PROCESS FOR PARTS A AND B

1. Edit your letters as you would any piece of writing—that is, get rid of excess baggage. Be thorough, be clear, be correct.

2. Before you let your peers read your letter, tell them about your intended reader and the circumstances that caused you to write the letter. If you are writing this only as an assignment, tell them about your fictitious audience and situation so that your peers can assume the reader's position.

3. Ask your peers to help you ensure that you have conveyed your message in as few words as possible and that you have created a favorable impression of yourself.

4. Your editors should be able to answer these questions:

   a. To *whom* is your letter specifically written? Have you considered the reader's situation throughout?

   b. *Why* did you write the letter? Would a telephone call have made your letter unnecessary? Letters should provide more than what a phone call would do: proof, confirmation, a form of receipt.

   c. *When* should your letter have been written? Will your letter reach its destination in time for the reader to act upon its contents?

   d. *What* does your letter contain? Have you included important items like your address, the date, the audience's address, a clear statement of your thesis, the necessary facts and details, a complimentary closing? Have you left out unimportant items like superfluous details, jargon, repetitions?

   e. *How* will your letter accomplish its purpose? Is your message clear and friendly? Will your letter bring the result you want?

5. Ask your editors to verify that you have punctuated your letter correctly and consistently.

6. After you are sure you approve of all parts of your letter, give it to your instructor for a final editing session.

7. Then send it to your final reader.

PREWRITING PROCESS FOR PART C

1. Go through recent newspapers and clip out articles that interest you. Arrange them in the order of their importance to you. Decide which article contains a statement with which you agree or disagree most strongly. Jot down your thoughts about the article in your journal as a Freewriting brainstorming session or try one or two other brainstorming techniques from Chapter 25 in order to gather supporting evidence for your letter. If these brainstorming sessions do not produce enough material for you to write your letter to the editor, then you should find another article.

2. Study the format of the editorial pages and the letters to the editor in newspapers and magazines in your home. What do the letters have in common? When you write a letter to the editor, to whom and for whom are you really writing? Your answers to these questions will help you to determine the audience, purpose, situation, and approach of your letter.

3. Before you begin to draft your letter to the editor, you should list your writing variables in the same way as the following example:

BROAD TOPIC:	Education via TV
LIMITED TOPIC:	Bernice McDonough's opinions on education via TV
AUDIENCE:	Readers of a daily newspaper
PURPOSE:	To disagree with McDonough's opinion and state mine; to focus on the difference between education at home via TV and education at a college campus
FORMAT:	A letter to the editor
VOICE:	My own
SITUATION:	I have just read Bernice McDonough's column, "Let's leave education to the Expert—TV" and disagree with her opinions
THESIS STATEMENT:	I don't think that education via TV *at home* will replace colleges and universities.

4. You might become involved in a debate with someone who disagrees with you. The discussion that follows will give you practice in argumentative techniques that you will need to know when you compose an effective letter to the editor. Like a good argumentative essay (Chapter 5), a letter to the editor should clearly state and support your opinion without using fallacies (Chapter 65).

DRAFTING PROCESS FOR PART C

1. Review Chapter 5 for hints on techniques of argument.
2. Open your letter strongly. You must catch the editor's attention in order for your letter to be published. (See "Beginnings, Middles, and Endings," Chapter 28.) Published letters to the editor are often given titles in the editorial department; you do not have to include a title. If you do not know the name of the editor, "To the Editor" will suffice as a salutation.
3. Make your points clearly and concisely. There is little space in most newspapers for letters; the briefer you are, the more likely your letter will be published intact.
4. Use positive or negative slant wisely and judiciously (see Chapter 37).
5. Use rhetorical devices to make your viewpoint worth remembering (see Chapter 34).
6. End your letter strongly. Leave your readers with your most important thought.

REVISING PROCESS FOR PART C

1. If, in your letter to the editor, you are reacting to something you have read, be sure to clip the original newspaper article to it, so your peer-editors will understand the context of your letter. If you are not writing about a particular article, you may have to explain what you are reacting to.
2. Ask your peers to apply the checklists in Chapter 31 to the final draft of your letter to the editor.

3. Ask your peers to assume that they are newspaper editors. As they read your letter to the editor, they should be concerned with fitting it into the smallest possible newspaper space, using the following guidelines:

   a. What could be removed without changing the original sense?

   b. Do you capture the interest of the readers?

   c. Will the letter convince the readers of the worth of your opinion? Will they appreciate your point of view?

4. After you have rewritten your letter to the editor according to your peers' comments, let your instructor-editor see it.

5. When you have polished your letter to the editor, why not send it to the newspaper? You may see yourself in print in a few days' time. Remember to sign it; editors routinely discard anonymous letters. (If, however, you do not want your name printed, you may ask that your name be withheld or that a pseudonym be used.)

PRODUCTS

Although these letters are set up correctly, not all of them are well written. As you examine each, try to determine what the writing variables are or should have been *before* you read the questions.

---

168 Griffiths Avenue
Brandie, MT 49123
June 18, 1985

Miss Aston Murton
72 Montroyal Boulevard
Winning, MT 49133

SUBJECT: Appointments

Dear Miss Murton:

In reply to your letter of June 16, 1985, I am granting your request for an appointment, which I have scheduled for Friday, June 24, at 9:00 a.m.

I hope that this time is convenient for you; unfortunately, all other spaces have been booked until the beginning of July. Please contact me if any problems arise.

Sincerely,

Michele N. Thyme

Michele N. Thyme
Graphic Design Manager

115-333 Adder Street
Lethe, AL 45001
January 23, 1985

Wylie Electronics
700 Milbourne Avenue
Speedy, IL 58023

Attention The President

Dear Sir

I have always been impressed with the quality of Wylie products and the services that your company provides to its customers.

Last year I received a Wylie clock radio as a Christmas gift. After six weeks of use the power switch did not work properly.

As your warranty policy directs, I returned the clock to your head office for repair, but my claim was refused on the grounds that the warranty was never registered. I was unaware that my warranty was not registered.

This model clock radio is guaranteed for one year, and I feel that mine should be covered under the warranty.

I am sending the clock radio to you and hope the problem can be solved this time.

I appreciate your cooperation in this matter, and I'm sure that I can receive fine service from Wylie Electronics in the future.

Sincerely

Barry Coleman

Barry Coleman

cc: Wylie Repair Manager

3638 Barman Avenue.
San Pedro, CA 92104
Jan. 28, 1986.

Dr. Alice Corveer,
Life Sciences Department,
San Pedro City College.

Dear Dr. Corveer:

This letter is to inform you that, after long and careful
deliberation, I have elected to withdraw from your
Tuesday/Thursday 9 a.m. class. This is not because of lack of
appreciation for psychology.

I have the highest regard for your knowledge of the subject and
your obvious ability as an instructor. Unfortunately, I feel I will
perform much better with a lighter scholastic work load.

I intend to re-enroll in Psychology 100 during another semester and
hope I will be fortunate to have you as the instructor. Thank you
very much for your time.

Sincerely,

Frank E. Brown

Frank E. Brown

To the student who owns this book:

You have finished your first writing assignment, asked a fellow student to edit it for you, and received in return a piece of writing to edit yourself. Yipes! Your first editing job! What do you do? How should you go about editing this unknown student's paper? Well, here's my advice, offered after four months of editing my fellow students' papers: Take it home and read it. Read the writing variables first. Read it again. Are the variables clear? Did the writer follow them? And again, read it. A lot.

Now get your copy of The Independent Writer and turn to the charts in Chapter 31. Compare the paper you are editing with each part of the charts. The lists will help you to plan what to say in your editing comments. I know they helped me. I personally found it expedient to begin with the "superior" list for each category to see where the paper fitted. Maybe the paper had a good central idea but not enough supporting evidence. If that was the case, that's precisely what I told the writer. Continue in this way until you have a clear picture of where the paper stands.

Remember, you are learning how to ask questions and look for ways to improve your writing, too. Believe me, after a while, you will be able to do this fairly quickly.

Another thing to remember when you begin to edit is that people have strengths and weaknesses not only in their writing but also in their ability to edit. In editing for others you may learn a lot about your own writing. So, focus on the areas you are good in, and, as you continue to edit papers, begin to work on the areas you are weak in. Student editors worry about grammar more than anything else. They think they have to correct all the grammar errors, but there is a lot more to writing than that. For example, tell the writer what you liked best about the paper. And then what you liked least. Make a suggestion about how the writer could revise the paper to make it better. Before long, you'll become a very important part in your fellow classmates' writing process. Just as they will be of yours.

I have found that conscientious editing is a great shortcut in improving my writing. But peer-editing can be a lot of fun, while providing students with a chance to exchange ideas. Pretty soon you'll make a lot of good friends, too.

Good luck,

Mike Jutras

September 18, 1984

Letter to the Editor:

Are we to be overwhelmed by the trauma of Olympic Games every four years? Politics and commercialism have taken over this event for the last century, and it's getting worse. The events of the 80s have shown that we are going to lose this most valuable event if we don't soon take firm action.

The original concept of the Olympic Games was to honor the athletes. Various cities would send their best athletes to Mt. Olympus. There they would compete to determine the best, the strongest, the most-skilled athlete in a particular sport. It was an individual competition: man against man. Not city against city. Not country against country. The strength or weakness of an entire nation had nothing to do with an athlete's competitive ability.

Recently both politics and commercialism have all but ruined the Olympic Games. The U.S. boycotted the 1980 games; in retaliation the U.S.S.R. boycotted the 1984 games. The future of this world event looks bleak.

My suggestion is to establish one place that the Olympic Games can be held every year. A place free from politics and commercialism. A place where the money that is spent year after year on building Olympic facilities can be put to good use. Imagine if you had the facilities from Montreal, Moscow, and Los Angeles all at one place. And what if these were all located in Greece near the original site of the games in ancient times? For the three years that the games would not be held, it could become a great vacation spot for the rest of the world! And for the year of the Olympic Games, everything would be ready. With all that vacation money coming in as well as Olympic money from the sponsors, the accommodations would be superb. And all this without suffering the political and commercial trash we have had to put up with every year. The streets of the new Olympia would practically be paved with gold.

Go for it!

Roberta McFarland

Roberta McFarland
804 Turf Sea Circle
Solana Beach, CA 92075

Permanent location for Olympics urged

Recently, both politics and commercialism have all but ruined the Olympic Games. The United States boycotted the 1980 Games; in retaliation the Soviet Union boycotted the 1984 Games. The future of this world event looks bleak.

My suggestion is to establish one place that the Olympic Games can be held every year—a place free from politics and commercialism. A place where the money that is spent year after year on building Olympic facilities can be put to good use.

Imagine if you had the facilities of Montreal, Moscow and Los Angeles all in one place. The hotels, stadiums, and all the other competitive areas—

in one place! And what if these were all located in Greece near the original site of the Games in ancient times?

For the three years that the Games would not be held, it could become a great vacation spot for the rest of the world. And for the year of the Olympic Games, everything would be ready. With all that vacation money coming in as well as the Olympic money from the sponsors, the accommodations would be superb.

And all this without suffering the political and commercial trash we have had to put up with every year.

—ROBERTA McFARLAND
Solana Beach

Well, back to writing letters to the editor . . .

ANALYSIS

Michele N. Thyme's Letter

1. This is a well-written business letter. How does Thyme establish a businesslike tone?

2. This letter uses modified block style, mixed punctuation. The paragraphs are indented. Find several examples of the modified block style. In what respect is the punctuation mixed?

Barry Coleman's Letter

This letter is fairly well written; however, the paragraph "I am sending . . ." could be joined with the previous one. Also, the sentence would be stronger if the passive voice were changed to the active voice: "I hope you can solve my problem."

1. This letter uses block style, open punctuation. What are the characteristics of this style?

2. What does the "cc" indicate? Who else will be reading this letter?

Frank E. Brown's Letter

1. What do you think Brown's audience, Dr. Alice Corveer, thought when she received his letter? If you drop a course, do you send your instructor a letter? Why or why not?

2. What can you tell about Brown from his letter?

Mike Jutras's Letter

1. Since you are the intended reader of Jutras's letter, what is your reaction?

2. Do you agree with Jutras's method of editing?

3. If you were to write a letter to future users of this textbook, what would you want to tell them?

Roberta McFarland's Letters

1. You have the opportunity to read two versions of the same letter: the first is what was sent to the *San Diego Herald*; the second is what was published. What are the significant differences between the two? Was the editing justified?

2. What do you think of the published title?

3. If you are looking for a topic for this assignment, you might react to McFarland's letter. Do you agree or disagree with her sentiments? If you agree, say so and perhaps elaborate on her idea. If you disagree, say why you disagree.

19

Application and Résumé

INTRODUCTION

Sometimes you will be able to get a job through a personal contact, but more often you will be required to submit a partial résumé and a cover letter in answer to a particular advertisement. If you are granted an interview, the employer may ask for a full résumé, listing *all* your previous jobs. In this assignment you will learn to write both a full and partial résumé.

Assignment

Part A: Construct a full résumé containing all the details of your education and employment history.
Part B: Write a partial résumé with an accompanying letter of application.

PREWRITING PROCESS FOR PART A

A résumé is an account of your personal, educational, and employment history. In the full résumé you will be working on in this part of the assignment, you will record *all* the details of your education and jobs. You will also use some of this information in the partial résumé in Part B of the assignment.
1. Writing a full résumé means remembering (or searching for) details of your past. The best way to recall this information is chronologically, backwards from the present (a method some employers prefer, since it allows them to see the most recent, and, therefore most relevant, data first).
2. Professional writers of résumés ask their clients to go through the following exercise, which you can quite easily do yourself. To help you remember all the relevant dates and information, divide a sheet of paper lengthwise into five columns. In the left-hand column write the present year. Label the other four columns accordingly. In each column note whether you were working (and, if you were,

where), going to school (if so, where and what courses you were taking), doing both, or engaged in something else (traveling, unemployed, in the hospital, on vacation) during that time period. The entire exercise will be easy if you work back from the present year to the one in which you completed high school. (If you worked while in school or did not graduate, use the year in which you started working.) You may need to use more than one sheet of paper. Here is an example for one year:

Year	January to March	April to June	July to September	October to December
1985	Part-time freshman student at Univ. of Hawaii. Took 2 liberal arts courses. Worked part-time as teller at Bank of America, Kona Coast, Hawaii	Worked full-time as teller at bank.	Attended full-time summer semester at Univ. of Hawaii. Took 3 freshman courses in liberal arts.	Entered sophmore year at Univ. of Hawaii. Majored in psychology. (present date: 11/5/85)

3. From the above prewriting activity, you will be able to draft a complete full résumé.

DRAFTING PROCESS FOR PART A

1. When you have collected your history, you must select and arrange neatly what you will include in your finished résumé. Do not mention periods during which you were not working or attending school, and unless your work or school record is very brief, do not include anything you did for less than one month.

2. Arrange your educational information chronologically under the heading, "Educational Data," and your employment information under the heading "Employment Data." In addition, you might include, if applicable, a heading entitled "Other Data." Under this heading, you could include a list of awards you have won, community service projects on which you have worked, military service goals and ambitions, and so on. (For suggested arrangements, see the full résumé at the end of this chapter.)

3. Some personal data are also necessary in your résumé. These should include your name, address, and telephone number. Although the law states that you do not have to give your age, height, weight, marital status, sexual preference, state of health, or other personal facts, you might consider presenting some personal details that might be pertinent to the job. You might be asked to provide the names, addresses, and telephone numbers of two or three people whom you know (not members of your family) who have agreed to provide a character reference for you to any prospective employer. (If your references choose not to have an employer call them, you can state "References Available on Request" on your résumé and then ask your references for a letter if an employer asks you for one.)

REVISING PROCESS FOR PART A

When you edit your full résumé yourself according to the above suggestions or give it to your peers and instructor for editing, be sure you still have all the raw data you gathered while prewriting. Your editors might recommend that you insert something you excluded or take out something you included.

Periodically through your career, especially after a change in jobs or the completion of a course, update your full résumé. If you do this regularly, you will be sure of having all the pertinent information available when you need it.

After your instructor-editor sees your full résumé, keep it in order to take it with you to future interviews. Usually you will never send a full résumé with a letter of application. Why?

PREWRITING PROCESS FOR PART B

Since full résumés came into widespread use, employers have complained about the amount of information they have to search through to find out what they want to know: "Has the applicant worked in the position I want to fill or in a similar one? When? Where? For how long?"

To answer this complaint, astute applicants and personnel consultants began to construct a *partial résumé*, tailored to a specific job, accompanied by a letter of application. Once you have written your full résumé for Part A of this assignment, you should have no trouble writing a partial résumé.

1. If you are looking for a job at the moment, you can make this assignment serve a real-life purpose. If by chance you are a successful applicant, your success will be all the more satisfying. Even without actually wanting a job, you can probably find an advertisement or two in the classified section of your local newspaper to which you could tailor your résumé. (Some newspapers print a "Careers" section of advertisements in professional and technical fields.) Besides consulting newspapers, look on local and campus notice boards and at unemployment offices. Here are a few sample ads to which you might want to reply if you choose not to respond to a real-life advertisement:

Mother's Helper
Reliable person needed to live in, help with housework, and care for two small children. Box 27.

Max's Pizza
3400 Major St. Applications for part-time and full-time work now being accepted. In writing please.

Tutor
High-school student needs tutoring in Grade 11 English and math. Box 113.

Teacher's Aide
Elementary school needs parents or others to help teachers with exceptional children. Experience preferred. Submit application to Box 80.

---

2. Study the job descriptions of the ads you have selected. Choose the one that you would like to answer and the job for which you feel most qualified.

3. Work on your partial résumé before you write your letter of application. Keep the following items in mind when you begin to draft your resume:

- What are the objectives of the job?
- In what ways do you qualify for the job?
- What direct experience do you have? (In answering this, point out the previous jobs you have had that are similar to the job for which you are applying.)
- What indirect experience do you have? (In answering this, consider other jobs you have had that have something in common with your intended new job.)
- Select pertinent educational experience from your full résumé.
- Mention pertinent hobbies, activities, or interests.
- State that the salary is negotiable.
- Have references ready if requested.

4. Because being hired for a particular job could change your life-style significantly, you should spend time in some useful brainstorming techniques. The most helpful techniques for a résumé are probably the Newspaper Reporter's Questions and the Pentad, with you and the prospective employer as the main characters in your brainstorming lists. (See Chapter 25 for other brainstorming techniques.)

5. Make a list of your writing variables as in the following example:

BROAD TOPIC:	A job
LIMITED TOPIC:	A job as a tutor
AUDIENCE:	A prospective employer. Real. I intend to send it.
PURPOSE:	To be a successful applicant; to focus on me, the math tutor
FORMAT:	A partial résumé and cover letter

VOICE:	My own
SITUATION:	The employer needs someone like me; I am qualified.
THESIS STATEMENT:	I want to be a tutor of mathematics.

DRAFTING PROCESS FOR PART B

1. Your partial résumé should be, if possible, no more than one page long.

2. Your list of educational and employment data should be structured in your partial résumé as it was in your full résumé.

3. Your letter of application should resemble a business letter. (See Chapter 18, Part B, for more information on business letters.) You should give some information about the advertisement you are answering, in case the employer has advertised more than one position; how you found out about the position (newspaper, bulletin board, personal contact); for what position you are applying; why you believe you are suitable for the position; and when and where you are available so that the employer can contact you. In addition, you might include details about your willingness to travel and your availability to begin working for the employer.

4. If your experience is limited or unrelated to the job for which you are applying, state this honestly in your letter of application and indicate that you feel that you have personal qualities to compensate for your lack of experience. You might write something like this, for example:

> Although my actual experience with computers is limited to academic courses, the work that I did with them in the data-programming course I took in college convinced me that I had a penchant for data processing. I know that my up-to-date skills and knowledge of state-of-the-art equipment would make me an asset to your firm.

It would be a good idea if your peers could pretend that they are the employer and conduct an interview with you. Such an interview could bring to your attention points you did not mention in your partial résumé.

5. After you have polished your work according to the suggestions of your peers, make a very good-looking copy of it (preferably on a single page) and let your instructor edit it.

6. When you have perfected your partial résumé, plan to use it to answer several similar ads by making photocopies and keeping them on file. Make sure you type your résumé (or have it typed) in order to add a professional touch.

7. Accompany your partial résumé with your letter of application.

8. Now send your letter of application and partial résumé in a suitably addressed envelope to your prospective employer. Good luck.

9. Before you go for your job interview, you might find it useful to read "Be Prepared for That Job Interview" in the products of Chapter 15.

PRODUCTS

Full Résumé

Personal Data

Maria M. Fernandez
623 Fifth Street
Sedro, CA 92104
(619) 283-7371

Social Security No. 100-4323-102

Excellent health

Educational Data

High School: Benedictine Abbey High School in the Philippines, 1975-79.

Cora Dolorosa Secretarial School, 1979-80, secretarial certificate. Special courses: business management, office procedures, accounting, typing and shorthand.

Night school, 1979-80, basic English.

University of California at Santa Barbara, 1980-1983. Finished three years of a liberal arts program. Specialities: Spanish, English, French, and history.

Employment Data

October 1985 to present—Government of Mexico, Department of Environment and Resources; Supervisor: Mr. Manuel Cardoza; Position: personal secretary.

May 1985 to October 1985—Office Finders Inc., Temporary Personnel Department; Supervisor: Mrs. Dorothy O'Connor; Duties: typing and file keeping.

January 1985 to April 1985—Government of Mexico, Department of Fisheries and Oceans; Supervisor: Mr. Pedro Aguilar; Position: personal secretary.

January 1984 to October 1984—C & M Inc., Philippines; Supervisor: Mr. Bi Quan; Position: personal secretary.

Other Data

Speak English, Spanish, Tagalog fluently, some French.
Enjoy reading, cooking, swimming, dancing.
Free to travel, if required by job.

Letter of Application

> Secretary/Receptionist
>
> Needed for one-person office of small engineering firm. Must be able to work without supervision. Typing speed at least 45 wpm. Engineering experience helpful but not essential. Knowledge of spoken and written Spanish essential to communicate with clients in Philippines.
> Apply to:
> Mr. Jerry Marks
> Marks and Associates
> P.O. Box 5077
> Portland, OR 93489

```
            623 Fifth Street
            Sedro, CA 92104
            March 16, 1986


            Mr. Jerry Marks
            Marks and Associates
            P.O. Box 5077
            Portland, OR 93489


            Dear Mr. Marks:


            I am submitting my résumé in response to your advertisement in last
            Friday's Sedro Journal, indicating that your firm is looking for a
            secretary/receptionist. I am willing to move and begin work
            immediately.


            My father was a civil engineer in the Philippines, so I am very
            familiar with the vocabulary of engineering. As a Filipino, I have
            spoken Spanish, as well as Tagalog, since childhood; thus, I do not
            believe I would have any trouble communicating with your clients.


            I can be reached at any time by calling (619) 283-7371. Please leave
            a message if I am not there, and I will return your call promptly.


            I hope to hear from you soon.


                          Sincerely,

                          Maria M. Fernandez

                          Maria M. Fernandez
```

Partial Résumé

Maria M. Fernandez
623 Fifth Street
Sedro, CA 92104
(619) 283-7371

Work History (Submitted in Confidence)

October 1985 to present: Government of Mexico, Department of
  Environment and Resources; personal secretary

May 1985 to October 1985: Office Finders Inc., Temporary Personnel
  Department; responsible for typing and file keeping

January 1985 to April 1985: Government of Mexico, Department of
  Fisheries and Oceans; personal secretary

January 1984 to October 1984: C & M Inc., Philippines; personal
  secretary

Education

University of California at Santa Barbara: Spanish, English,
  French, history

Coro Dolorosa Secretarial School: secretarial workshop, business
  management, office procedures, accounting, typing (graduated at
  75 wpm)

Benedictine Abbey High School: Philippines

Other Data

Speak English, Spanish, Tagalog fluently, some French
Enjoy reading, cooking, swimming, dancing
Salary is negotiable
Excellent references available on request

HERMAN

"Your job application says
you like meeting the public."

ANALYSIS

Full Résumé

1. Are there details that you think Fernandez did not need to include in her full résumé? Why?

2. After reading her partial résumé, do you notice any details which should have been included in her full résumé?

Letter of Application and Partial Résumé

1. How do her letter of application and résumé create a favorable impression?

2. How does she indicate that she has read the advertisement?

3. Does she appear qualified for the job?

20

Exam Essays

INTRODUCTION

Exam time can be a nerve-wracking time for most students. This assignment is designed to give you strategies in writing exam essays, so that you will be able to go into the exam room with confidence.

> ### Assignment
> Write an exam question as an in-class assignment.

Your writing instructor may provide you with a series of exam topics, expecting you to hand in a completed paragraph or essay within a specific period of time. Alternatively, you might like to ask one of your other instructors to provide an exam question. At the beginning of the writing class, read the question and write your answer to it. This kind of practice in writing for other disciplines (Chapters 21, 22, and 23) can be very useful to both you and your subject instructors. If the preceding suggestions are not feasible, choose one of the following topics, give yourself exactly one hour, and practice writing an exam essay.

Selected Exam Topics

1. Analyze the drawing on page 227.
2. Prove that Freudian theory is obsolete.
3. Explain how *The Independent Writer* has helped you become a better writer.
4. Contrast Piagetian theory with traditional learning theory.
5. Relate the information on rhythm and meter in the Glossary to your favorite song.

6. List the changes that the institution of marriage has undergone in the last fifty years.

7. Discuss the differences between writing fiction and nonfiction. Base your answer on examples from the work of a favorite author who writes both fiction and nonfiction.

8. Use any question given in the Drafting Process.

PREWRITING PROCESS

1. The best thing to do before you write an exam is to try to predict what the questions are going to be. Your instructors do drop hints, even suggestions, as to what will be on their exams. Remember, they do not want you to do poorly. They find an excellent exam essay much more enjoyable to read than a failing essay.

Before you write essay exams, predict a few questions and do some dry runs at home. Think of how relieved you will feel if you predict the exact question on the exam! Even if you are only half right, you are better off than if the exam question completely surprises you.

2. Being well prepared for an exam is the best prewriting advice. There is nothing quite like the feeling of entering the exam room with confidence, knowing the material so well that you can add some of your own ideas and thoughts on the topics instead of simply repeating the facts from lectures and textbooks. Make sure, therefore, that you review each course throughout the term, preferably each week. Use the SQ3R method, outlined in Chapter 40, to give you confidence.

3. You should also be well rested when you write an exam. If you have studied and prepared during the entire term, there should be no need to study the night before. You will be in a far better condition for the exam if you listen to music the night before and go to bed early.

4. Enter the exam room with the proper tools: pens, pencils, an eraser, a ruler, a dictionary (if permitted), and any other required materials. You might want to bring a watch to enable you to monitor the amount of time you spend on each question. In this way you will be sure to leave yourself enough time to complete the whole exam.

5. When you receive your exam, read over the entire paper. Underline all the significant words in the directions. (Missing the "or" in a question that tells you to do "1, 2, or 3," could be disastrous.) If you read through the whole exam, you are bound to find something you feel competent to answer. It's a good idea to answer first the questions that you know; this gives you a sense of accomplishment.

6. Check to see whether you are expected to list your answers, write paragraphs, or write essays. Also, observe the value of each question and write accordingly. To spend the majority of your time on the first half of the exam, which is worth only twenty points, and then to find that the second half is worth eighty points shows poor planning and might cause you to panic.

7. State your thesis in a clear, workable statement; quickly list your supporting evidence in some logical outline or visual form (ladder, mandala, flowchart); and, finally, decide on your method of organization before you draft your exam essay.

DRAFTING PROCESS

1. For an effective means of guiding your answer in the right direction, begin your essay by rephrasing the question. Following are two examples:

Essay Question

In a 500-word essay explain what you would do to bring about world peace.

Thesis Statement

There are five things that I would do to bring about world peace. (*Note*: Do not use weak openings like "In this essay I am going to . . ." or "My purpose in writing is to . . .".)

Essay Question

Briefly point out how you would dissect a frog. You may use illustrations.

Thesis Statement

There are three main steps in dissecting a frog. (When you write, plan to describe each step in about fifty words or so.)

2. Learning how to approach an exam essay question by focusing on the key words in the question will produce a better paper and a higher mark. The following is a guide to some key words, their meanings, and strategies for answering each type of question.

KEY WORDS	QUESTIONS AND STRATEGIES
Analyze	*Analyze the drawing on page 227 of this chapter.* "Analyze" literally means "to take apart." In order to analyze something, you must examine and discuss it one part at a time, and be able to say how each part contributes to the whole. Chapter 15 deals with process analysis. See the Products section for examples of answers to this question.
Compare	*Compare Darwin's theory of natural selection with Lamarck's theory of the inheritance of acquired characteristics.* When you compare, you should look for qualities and characteristics that resemble each other. The term "compare" is usually accompanied by "with," implying that you are to emphasize similarities. However, you can also mention differences. Chapter 8 deals with comparisons.
Contrast	*Contrast the laws pertaining to consumer protection fifty years ago with those in effect today.*

When you are asked to contrast, you should present differences, although you may also mention similarities. Focus, however, on the things, qualities, events, or problems that you can contrast. Chapter 8 deals with contrasting.

Criticize

Criticize the defense policy of the United States.

When you are asked to criticize, you should not merely find fault but give *your* opinions about both the merits and demerits of something. Take a strong stand, but present all the facts; in other words, for the above question, you should discuss the reasons why the defense policy is what it is. Chapter 12 deals with criticizing. (See also Review in this list.)

Define

Define the term "logarithm."

When you are asked to define, you should be aware of the many ways you can define: give a formal definition; provide synonyms, examples, comparisons, contrasts, and so on; or extend your definition throughout your entire answer (Chapter 10). Always provide clear, concise, and authoritative meanings. Make sure to give the limits of the definition as it applies to the subject you are answering.

Describe

Describe the events surrounding D Day (June 6, 1944).

When you describe, you should recount, characterize, sketch, and relate in chronological, sequential, or spatial order (Chapter 29). You might also describe in story form (Chapter 1, 2, or 4).

Discuss

Discuss Jesse Jackson's role in the Democratic presidential race of 1984.

The term "discuss" appears often in exam questions. You should analyze, examine, and present the pros and cons regarding the problems involved in the question. You will receive a good mark if your details are complete and thorough. Chapter 6 will provide help in dealing with techniques of discussion.

Enumerate

Enumerate the best ways in which students can learn about computers.

When enumerating, you should write in list or outline form, giving points concisely one by one. Making a Classification and Division Flowchart first will help you enumerate (Chapter 7).

Evaluate

Evaluate the income-tax policy of the United States.

After explaining the problem clearly, you should judge its advantages and disadvantages. Mention both the appraisal of authorities and your personal evaluation. See Chapter 6.

Explain

Explain the phlogiston theory in no more than 100 words.

If you know Chapter 3 well, you will know that you are expected to write an expository paragraph when asked to explain. It is important that you explain clearly and concisely. You should appear to your reader as an authority on the subject; therefore, write with conviction.

Identify

Identify the causes of the increase in cases of herpes.
Generally, when identifying, you should state dates, people, places, or events that set the particular fact or figure apart or make it outstanding. By using Cause/Effect Flowcharts to answer the above question, you should identify the reasons for the increase in herpes cases (Chapter 9).

Illustrate

In "The Story of an Hour" how does Chopin make it obvious that Mrs. Mallard is relieved that her husband is dead?
A question on an English or history exam that asks you to illustrate with specific, concrete examples usually requires that you explain or clarify your answer by presenting quotations from the text (seldom from diagrams). Your opinion by itself is not what is required. If you are not able to bring a primary source (in this case, a copy of the story "The Story of an Hour" from the Appendix) into the exam room, you will have to paraphrase rather than give direct quotations to support your claims. See Chapter 32 for information about paraphrasing.
Note: Begin your essay by rephrasing the question; for example, "In 'The Story of an Hour' Chopin makes it obvious that Mrs. Mallard is relieved that her husband dies; here is the proof." Then follow basic essay structure (Chapter 5). By rephrasing the question in this way, you will find that all you have to do is provide illustrations to prove your claim. Chapter 13 provides further help in dealing with questions where you are asked to illustrate.

Interpret

Interpret the reasons for the East European boycott of the 1984 Olympics.
When you interpret, you provide facts, offer comments, and pass judgment about the subject. You should look at all sides of the subject to ensure you have given a fair interpretation. See Chapter 7 to ensure that you will be thorough.

Justify

Justify the internment of Japanese Americans during the Second World War.
You must prove a point or statement when you are asked to justify. Show evidence for your decisions. You must convince your reader that you are right. Chapter 5 will help you argue your point of view.

List

List five symptoms of diabetes mellitus.
The term "list" can be ambiguous. Are you to write an essay, or are you to present a list? If you are asked to write an essay, obviously you must enumerate in paragraph form (Chapter 6); but if you are not, you should present a brief, itemized series. Indicate that you are presenting a list because that is what is asked for in the question.

Outline

Outline the significant details in the political relationships between the United States and Central America.

When you are asked to outline, you should describe under main and subordinate points, omitting minor details and stressing the classification of things (Chapter 7). Generally, you should present your points in order of their importance—from least important to most important.

Prove

Choose some sociological issue in which you participate and prove that you are correct in your participation—for example, living with someone without marrying, being a single parent, marrying someone of your sex.

When you prove something is true, you must provide clear, logical reasons and factual evidence. Chapters 5 and 6 will help. Make sure you do not argue illogically (Chapter 65).

Relate

Relate the discovery of Alaskan oil to future dependence on Middle Eastern oil.

When you are asked to relate one thing to another, you should emphasize the relationships, connections, or associations between them. Beginning with Cause/Effect Flowcharts will help you relate more clearly (Chapter 9).

Review

Review Laurence Olivier's film of Hamlet.

A review demands critical examination (Chapter 12). Do not mention only the bad points, but what you liked as well. Jot down what you wish to discuss: the acting, the scenery, the costumes, the sound, and so forth. Then organize your points in a satisfying sequence and briefly analyze or comment on each.

Summarize

Summarize the causes of the Iran/Iraq War during the 1980s.

To "summarize" means that you are to condense. You may, at times, be given a longer passage to summarize; however, if you are given a question like the one above, you should present only the main facts. Illustrations and elaborations should be left out. (Chapter 32)

Trace

Trace the route of the pioneers who established the Oregon Trail.

Obviously a map or diagram would help to answer this question; but if you are asked to write an essay, you should give a description of the pioneers' progress from the point of origin to their final destination and explain the historical significance of their journey in establishing the Oregon Trail. Use chronological order. Chapter 6 will help you gather information.

Do not be afraid to tell your reader in what way you are interpreting a question. Terms are always open to interpretation. If you have misinterpreted the term, but have explained what you are doing and have answered with conviction, you will receive more credit than if your reader has to figure out what you are trying to do. Furthermore, do not be afraid to include your own insight. Every instructor wants to know that you fully understand the subject matter. Your ability to identify cause/effect relationships and speculate on their significance is a very good indication of your grasp of the material.

REVISING PROCESS

During an exam, you will not be able to receive any editorial help from your peers. Instead, you will have to check your paper yourself. When you have finished writing, reread the questions, then reread your answers. Ensure that

- you have answered all the questions,
- you have not forgotten any important points,
- you have corrected any careless errors, and
- your answers are easy to read. If they are not, recopy them if time permits. Readers appreciate both accuracy and neatness.

After your exam is returned, look it over and learn from it. Find your strengths and weaknesses; build for your next exam by eliminating your weaknesses.

PRODUCTS

Note: Art-history instructor Dick Grooms presented the following essay question to his art interpretation class with a photocopy of Dürer's *St. Jerome* (see p. 227). He did not tell his students the name of the artist, the date of the engraving, the techniques used, or any other information. For *The Independent Writer* he provided two responses with his comments. As you read the exam papers, can you tell which paper received an *A*, and which received a *C*?

Essay Questions

As you "read" (analyze) the picture, tell what you see as well as what the picture says to you.

Student Answers: One

When looking at the engraving, *St. Jerome* by Dürer, there are many things that catch the eye and are impressive. One of the most remarkable of these things is the great variety of textures that one can see. Dürer carefully records how the light reflects off the great variety of surfaces in the room. The wooden ceiling and the lion's form are especially notable for this. Nevertheless, the picture is not only a textural picture for it also has very clearly delineated forms, which may in part be a result of the medium but also could be an important part of the character of the artist. One gets the impression that the artist admires the sort of clearheadedness that allows a sharp distinction between things and a close observance of details. This is very different from many modern artists who sacrifice detail and form to expressiveness and generalizations. Dürer seems to put little effort into the overall composition of this engraving. The perspective of the room defines the space to an extent, but it looks arbitrary and there

seems to be no central focal point. One would assume that Dürer wanted St. Jerome to be the focal point, yet this figure is dwarfed by that of the lion and the aura about his head does not stand out as much as it should because of the bright, patterned light of the windows. Even the object in the upper right-hand corner (it could be a brass pot—I'm not sure) is substantially larger than St. Jerome's head. It seems that the artist put so much energy into the finely rendered details of the image that he forgot about the general composition.

Apart from the details and textures, the subject matter of the engraving is very interesting. The most puzzling part of the whole picture is the great lion in the front. The presence of such a ferocious wild beast in the writing room of a scholar makes no sense whatsoever. Perhaps it was meant as a symbol of how it could be conquered or subdued by the activities of the scholar. Perhaps Dürer believed that "the pen is mightier than the sword" and attempted to show this by illustrating the king of the beasts asleep, by a fox, at the feet of an intense scholar.

The skull on the window ledge is another puzzling element of this picture. Perhaps, however, it is tied in with the age of St. Jerome, the hourglass above his head and the crucifixion of Christ on the desk. All these symbols point to the fact that the physical body can only last for a certain time. This contrasts strongly with the glow of St. Jerome's head and the concentration of his writing that indicates the presence of a strong, unfailing intellect.

Dürer wants to show the superiority of the mental and spiritual world over the physical one. This is very much like the Protestant way of thinking and so it makes sense that we should find it here in the work of a German artist of the sixteenth century.

Despite the lack of a coherent composition, therefore, Dürer's engraving is successful in portraying the feelings of people at the close of the Middle Ages and is also admirable for its amazing textural qualities that must have taken a great amount of technical skill to reproduce.

Student Answers: Two

Firstly, this piece of art work does not look like a painting, but rather an etching on wood. There is a considerable portrayal of depth of field; the animals in the foreground are larger in perspective than the man sitting in the back of the room writing. The cushions along the side shelf correspond to the movement of the ceiling and the floor on the far left-hand side of the room. The eye is taken from the top left corner of the ceiling and is moved to the top right-hand corner and down the back of the wall where one focuses on the elderly man's head. This is probably accentuated by clear space, or glowing quality seen on the top of his bald head.

The room is simply decorated—a hat is on the far wall beside a sand clock. A few shelves are placed along the wall. A table and two chairs are seen. The style of the furniture probably signifies a certain time period, that being around the 15th century. Religious influence is recognized by the Christ figure on the table.

The images are very finely detailed, the fur on the lioness is very precise and exact, even the man's beard, is finely detailed. The idea of daylight is portrayed by the light shining through the windows, casting shadows on the wall and floor near the foot of the table.

It's a very quiet picture. Little movement is seen or felt. The animals are lazily doing nothing. The main movement is probably simply the motion of the fingertips, and the sound heard is the scratching of the pen. The skeleton's head on the window sill adds to stillness of the room. The skeleton's head could symbolize the nearness of death. It is not presented in a gloomy, morbid setting. Despite the fact that the room is still, the light from the window, the smile on the lionnesses face, the casual tidyness of the room gives a feeling of light-heartedness.

Archetecturally, the ceiling, the far wall, and floor appear to be wood, while the side wall with the windows appear to be made of brick. The ceiling is partly being held up by a simple style pillar. The room is probably larger than what is shown, as if in front of the animals looks like the beginning of a rug.

Absence of color is clearly depicted; even the shades of grey are very limited which takes away from an emotional impact it could otherwise give.

Mr. Groom's Analyses and Grades

One

Well-reasoned interpretation and evaluation. Quite perceptive and well-informed analysis. I'm sure that if you had an opportunity to edit your answer, you would have been able to eliminate the occasional examples of wordiness. Congratulations on citing not only the artist, but also the name of the engraving. Grade—A.

Two

You made some worthwhile points, but generally you were not very observant of all that is in Dürer's engraving. For example, the lion is obviously male, not female. The date 1514, which is *in* the engraving , lets you know that it was engraved in the sixteenth, not the fifteenth, century. Your analysis included superficial and irrelevant evidence. You need to supply solid supporting evidence in an analysis. Also, I've noted several spelling mistakes, grammatical errors, and an excessive use of the passive voice. The use of the active voice would make your reading of the print more vital. Grade—C.

21

Writing for the Humanities

INTRODUCTION

In writing papers for courses other than composition, students will often ignore the important prewriting and revising processes, sometimes starting their papers only a few days before they are due. Because they have left no time for revision, they frequently turn in—and are graded on—their first drafts.

For some curious reason, students in courses other than English assume that their professors do not worry about style and will give them high marks as long as their content is correct. It is true that professors of the humanities and sciences expect accurate content, but they also have a right to expect unified, coherent, and well-organized papers from their students.

In this and the next two chapters you will have the opportunity to apply the theories of process writing to everything you write across the curriculum. In this chapter you will find an array of assignments with suggestions on how you can use the three steps of the writing process for a variety of humanities papers. But this chapter is quite different from the preceding ones in that it is filled with extensive cross-referencing.

It seems logical for the composition classroom to become central to successful writing across the curriculum. Therefore, each time you are assigned a piece of writing *for a humanities course*, turn to this chapter first. As you approach this chapter, concentrate on the particular type of format you have been asked to use: a contemplative paper for history, a literary essay for literature, a review for humanities, a summary of a seminar session in art, a paraphrase of a theatre history document, a process analysis of an advertisement, a research paper for a law class, a comparative essay for religious studies, and so on.

When you have settled on the kind of paper (format) that you need to write and have found it mentioned in this chapter, you will be asked to proceed in one of three ways:

- Remain within this chapter and follow the general and specific prewriting, drafting, and revising suggestions that are offered. You will also be able to read a product that illustrates the format.

- Use some of the general and specific suggestions within this chapter *in conjunction* with other chapters throughout the book. You will be told which other chapters to consult, as well as be referred to a product that illustrates the kind of paper you are writing.

- Sometimes, after you have read a few general suggestions, you will be asked to leave this chapter and continue in another one. However, when you work in another chapter, keep in mind your humanities topic and apply all of the suggestions to that limited topic. You will be able to adapt the suggestions in all of the assignment chapters quite easily to your humanities paper. In the Products sections of the other chapters you will often find a product that illustrates writing for a humanities class; for example, Chapter 6 ("Informative Essay") contains a term paper by a history student on the invasions of Great Britain.

You should be able to use the workshop approach contained in *The Independent Writer* for all of your writing, enabling you to produce successful papers that demonstrate your skill in reading, writing, and thinking critically, as well as your mastery of content. You will soon find that all the papers you produce will be well organized, mechanically correct, and stylistically interesting.

Assignment for Parts A to F

Produce an appropriate piece of writing on a topic of your choice or one assigned by your instructor *for a humanities course*, such as literature, history, philosophy, art, law, theatre, music, or librarianship.

Part A

A *humanities term paper* demonstrates that you know a body of information on a specific topic that was handled fully in class sessions, in the textbook, and in some assigned reading. The term paper will usually take the form of an informative expository essay. If you have to write such a term paper, work through all of Chapter 6 and then *return to the revising suggestions in this chapter*.

Part B

A *humanities research paper* presents information on a specific topic that *was not* handled fully in class sessions or in the textbook. You would need to develop the topic by researching extensively. Depending on whether your professor wishes scholarly citations or a nonscholarly approach, you should produce a long research report or a feature article. If you are writing the former, work through Chapter 14 (Part A) and Chapter 39; if you are writing the latter, work through Chapter 14 (Part B). In both cases *return to the revising suggestions in this chapter* when you have finished your work in the appropriate chapter.

Part C

An *analysis paper* presents relationships between the various parts of a primary source, so that other people who have seen, heard, or read the work will benefit from your critical analysis. Primary sources include fiction (novels, poems, short stories, scripts), nonfiction (books or documentaries), and works of art (paintings, sculptures, concertos, plays, films, and so on). If you have to base your analysis paper (also called a critical analysis, literary paper, or insight essay) on a written primary source, work through Chapter 40 before going to Chapter 13. If you have to base your analysis paper on a work of art, work through Chapter 13 (applying the process approach to your subject), but read the Products in Chapter 20 instead of those in Chapter 13. Whether the subject of your analysis paper has been written, painted, or sculpted, you should refer to Chapter 15 (Part B) and read about process analysis. Then *return to the revising suggestions in this chapter.*

Part D

A *researched literary essay* presents an analysis of several critics' interpretations of a primary source. You should, however, include your interpretation as well. As in an ordinary analysis paper, you can assume that your audience has read the primary source, but not the secondary sources (reference works, biographies, critical studies) you refer to. Hence, you will need to give full credit for your quotations from secondary sources by including parenthetical citations as well as a bibliography. Unless your professor gives you other instructions, use the MLA guidelines outlined in Chapter 39. Work through Chapter 40 and follow the composing process outlined in Chapter 13. Read the researched literary essay in Chapter 13 entitled "A Magnificent Cycle." Then *return to the revising suggestions in this chapter.*

Part E

A *critique* (review) presents your critical evaluation of a primary source in terms of how well you believe it fulfilled its purpose. Generally, you write a review to people who have not seen, heard, or read the work. Work through Chapter 12, where you will also be able to read several completed reviews. Then *return to the revising suggestions in this chapter.*

Part F

A *contemplative paper*, in which you are expected to demonstrate a knowledge of course content by reflecting and speculating on a single hypothesis, is often at the heart of many humanities courses. The hypothesis often centers around what you would do if two specific ideas or theories confronted each other.

Because none of the chapters in *The Independent Writer* deals specifically with contemplative papers, most of the information in the rest of this chapter applies specifically to Part F. The suggestions in the Revising Process apply to all humanities papers, however.

Kinds of Contemplative Papers

A contemplative paper blends personal opinion with established researched information into a coherent essay. In the hands of someone who has control of the subject, the result of the blend is often highly original—for example, Bill Moyers's television documentary in which he contrasted *and compared* Franklin Delano Roosevelt and Adolf Hitler. The differences between these two adversaries has been well documented; to hear Moyers point out their similarities was illuminating. Following are other topics for the most common type of comparison/contrast contemplative papers:

- Are the people of Russia better off now than they were before the 1917 revolution?
- Compare and contrast the thoughts of Hamilton and Jefferson in terms of their views on the Constitution, the banking system, and relations with France.
- Ben Jonson was a better comedy writer than Shakespeare.

Note: If you are doing a comparison/contrast contemplative paper, work through Chapter 8 and then *continue with this chapter.*

A second type of contemplative paper attacks or defends someone's views: those of authors, politicians, philosophers, and so on. Again, you are expected to merge your opinions with those of others into a coherent whole on such topics as:

- If you had only one book to read, it would be . . . .
- Descartes or Hume, that is the question.
- In *The Birds* Aristophanes was wrong. He should have brought Euripides instead of Aeschylus back from Hades.
- Even though Richard Nixon will probably always hold the title of America's most dishonest President, he did a lot for America.

A third type of contemplative paper presents a personal approach to a controversial problem or question. The writer quickly passes judgment on accepted solutions and dwells on offering alternative (and better) ones. Here are typical topics for such reflective papers:

- Why did Ronald Reagan win the 1984 presidential election?
- Socrates should not have drunk the cup of hemlock.
- The judges were right; Socrates was corrupting the youth of Athens.
- If Shakespeare were living today, he would earn his living writing for Madison Avenue.
- There *is* a sixth sense.
- Is "sin" a religious invention?

The writers of such papers will be expected to demonstrate a knowledge of research in order to offer viable solutions and answers.

A fourth type of contemplative paper presents a hypothetical situation in which a writer blends research and imagination. "What if?" is at the heart of topics in these speculative papers:

- If Francis Bacon indeed wrote Shakespeare's plays, then . . . .

- What would the world be like if Nazi Germany had won the Second World War?
- What would America be like if we followed Plato's suggestions in *The Republic*?
- What would have happened in *The Great Gatsby* if Gatsby and Daisy had run off together?
- What kind of plays would Shakespeare have written if women, instead of boys, had been allowed to act the female roles?
- What would have been George Orwell's views of the world at the end of the year 1984?

PREWRITING PROCESS FOR PART F

1. Because the topics for contemplative papers are challenging, start early. Give yourself time so that the material you are focusing on has time to interact with your own philosophies and opinions. Wonderfully original contemplative papers usually emerge from people who have spent lifetimes thinking about their topics. No wonder many students panic when they have three weeks to write a 1000-word paper on a topic such as this one for theatre history: "Without Molière and Racine French Neoclassicism would have died a natural death."

2. In most contemplative papers you will be expected to convince your audience; therefore, you should have a good understanding of the argumentative essay. If you do not, turn to the Prewriting Process suggestions in Chapter 5 before returning to this chapter.

3. So that you enrich your limited topic, go through several of your favorite brainstorming techniques, especially Brainstorming across the Curriculum (Chapter 25). You should now have plenty of material to begin your drafting process. However, use this checklist to see if you are indeed ready to continue:

- Have you decided on the exact purpose of your contemplative paper—for example, are you comparing and contrasting, defending or attacking , solving or answering, or speculating? Or are you combining two or more purposes?
- Have you considered your audience and its situation? In what ways will your audience influence the way you write—for example, word choice, sentence structure, scholarly citation, and so on? What can you assume that your audience knows? Is there additional material that you need to read and summarize so that you can include it in your prewriting notes because your readers will need it?
- Have you tested your thesis statement (Chapter 27)?
- Have you considered your method of organization (Chapter 29)? You want all of your excellent material to have an impact on your audience. The main way of achieving this is to follow a coherent method of organization throughout your drafting process. Therefore, do not begin to compose until you have determined your organizational strategy. (Once you have chosen a method, you are not locked into it. Change anything that does not work for you.)

4. Have the following ready so that you spend a comfortable time in your drafting process:

- All brainstorming results
- Research notes (preferably on file cards)
- Full details on all of your quotations: author, title, publisher, place of publication, publication date, page numbers
- A full set of writing variables
- A thesis statement
- A thorough understanding of the method of organization that you have decided best suits your paper
- A list of transitions that you will use as you compose (pages 348–349 from Chapter 30)

DRAFTING PROCESS FOR PART F

Read the suggestions in the Drafting Process of Chapter 5 and the following ones before you draft your paper.

1. You must remember that your readers probably will have heard, read, and seen the material you are writing about. In order to make your argument fresh, therefore, you must synthesize this material from textbooks, classroom lectures, and discussions in order to formulate a logical argument that does not lose your readers. By taking a strong stand and letting your opinion and not your references dominate your essay, you will produce an original contemplative paper that will make your readers say, "That's really interesting! I never thought of it that way."

2. Because a contemplative paper has no correct response, realize that it does not have a wrong response either. That's a comforting thought! It could, however, have an incomplete response. You should not take your readers along a logical route and then derail them, bring them back to the same place as though the whole journey were a waste of time, or lead them to a dead end. You should present your hypothetical argument in a logical fashion and avoid fallacies (see Chapter 65). If your audience finds one weak link in your thinking, your whole premise might collapse.

3. Contemplative papers are difficult to write. Because you may be defending or attacking an established interpretation, viewpoint, or belief that your audience agrees with, make sure you define your terms accurately so that your readers know how you have interpreted them (Chapter 10).

4. If you begin to get bogged down in the logic of your argument, draw several Cause/Effect Flowcharts like those in Chapter 9. Flowcharts can clarify foggy thought.

5. In most contemplative papers you must deal with two aspects of your topic at the same time; therefore, you might develop the entire paper as a parody (Chapter 38). By so doing, you will demonstrate an acute knowledge of one of your topics *without* actually mentioning it. Parody is difficult, but if you succeed, you will be satisfied with the knowledge that you have achieved a high level of excellence. For some of the above topics for contemplative papers, note how you might use parody: use modern American slang to point out Plato's philosophy; write a new chapter for *The Great Gatsby* in which Gatsby manages to sleep with Daisy (actually, A. R. Gurney based his play, *The Golden Age*, on that exact premise); write in the style of Hitler's *Mein Kampf* to advocate a single world government; rewrite a portion of a Shakespearean comedy in the Jonsonian style; use the style of the King James Bible to argue your points about "sin"; use Orwell's style from *1984* to give a synopsis of 1984.

REVISING PROCESS FOR ALL HUMANITIES PAPERS

Use the following revising suggestions for term, research, analysis, literary, critique, and contemplative papers:

1. If you are able to revise your assignment for a humanities course within the workshop atmosphere of your composition class, you will be in an ideal position. Engaging in peer- and instructor-editing sessions will be a tremendous help in bringing your paper to a publishable condition for your humanities professor.

The one main difficulty may be that your peers (and sometimes your composition instructor) will not understand or appreciate the content of your paper. But do not despair. You may find that in order to give a clearer explanation so that your editors understand what you are proposing, you will have to provide more concrete examples, and in order to explain your purpose so that they will appreciate what you are trying to accomplish, you will have to focus and sharpen your paper.

It would be very appropriate for you to include an "Acknowledgement" such as the following at the beginning of your paper:

> I want to especially thank Professor John Darley for giving me the opportunity to workshop this Philosophy 101 paper in his English 101 class and for his suggestions on how to revise it. Also, I would like to thank Busher Amini, Margaret Pennolton, and Ho Grinoldi (my workshop peer group) for their help and suggestions during my revising process. Finally, I want to thank my father who helped me brainstorm for a suitable topic.

The results of your having taken your paper through peer- and instructor-editing sessions will be evident when you let your intended audience read your humanities paper. You editors may question your content, but they should not have difficulty with your syntax, organization, style, and so on.

2. Depending on the format you have used, you should encourage your editors to use the specific revising suggestions illustrated throughout the various assignments in *The Independent Writer* in conjunction with the following:

  a. *Consider your audience.* In truth, your professor knows more about the topic of your paper than you or your editors; therefore, consider your audience in terms of another reader as well—an intelligent reader, who would like to read and understand your paper. Writing for an additional reader prevents you from omitting certain points just because your professor knows those facts, thus allowing your paper to be self-explanatory and independent. Your editors, therefore, should put themselves in the place of your general audience rather than in the place of your specific humanities professor.

b. *Summarize your references.* Except for a literary essay, where you can assume your audience has read your primary source, you should include a summary of all books and articles you have referred to throughout your paper. In other words, you should assume your audience has not read what you have read. If you have bogged down in details, thus losing the thread of your argument, your editors should suggest that you practice the 25-word summary in Chapter 32 so that you include only the salient features of your primary sources. You should also let your readers know why you are including your references. Doing so will help keep them on track.

c. *Use a distinct method of organization.* Because a humanities paper tends to be on the long side, it is important that your readers know quite early your method(s) of organization. Your editors may refer you to aspects of Chapter 29 to brush up on your organization. If you make your methods clear as early as possible and use appropriate transitional devices, your editors should be able to let you know how you have organized your paper without your telling them. A hit-and-miss development will result in confused readers—both editors and your final audience.

d. *Include a satisfying conclusion.* A humanities paper usually requires a lot of time and concentrated energy on the part of your editors. When, for example, you have included a logical conclusion to your detailed argument, they will be pleased that it makes complete sense because they now share with you the same thoughts. If your editors have this same sense of accomplishment, you will know you have produced a successful paper. If they have become derailed because you have gaps or contradictions in your argument, listen attentively to their suggestions so that you can rewrite your paper for your final audience.

3. If possible, engage in a final instructor-editing session after satisfying your peers.
4. To help you in the final presentation of your paper to your intended audience, see the Products section at the end of this chapter.
5. After your audience has read your paper, share his or her reactions with your peer- and instructor-editors.

PRODUCTS

In addition to the following product to illustrate a contemplative paper for a humanities class, you should read some products from other chapters that have many characteristics of typical humanities papers—for example:

- Contemplative paper for humanities: "If Questions Could Kill" (Chapter 5)
- Contemplative paper for humanities: "You Could Be Better Than You Are . . ." (Chapter 5)
- Researched term paper for history: "The Conquests of England" (Chapter 6)
- Analysis paper for philosophy: "On Matters of Love" (Chapter 7)
- Term paper for literature: "A Look at Mark Twain" (Chapter 11)

- Critiques for a book: "Thick Blood Flows at the *Pet Sematary*" and "*Pet Sematary* Buries King" (Chapter 12)
- Literary essays for literature: "A Defoliation of Children" and "Joy?" (Chapter 13)
- Researched literary essay for literature: "A Magnificent Cycle" (Chapter 13)
- Researched term paper for literature: "The Vampire: Fact or Fiction?" (Chapter 14)
- Analysis for art: Dürer's *St. Jerome* (Chapter 20)

Following is an example of a contemplative paper for philosophy.

Question: Should people from the Eastern Hemisphere immigrate to the Western Hemisphere?

The Dark Side of U.S. Hospitality

by Alix Stecker, student

Acknowledgement

I wish to thank Lee and May Vang, a Hmong family, and the social workers from the Linda Vista Community Center for providing me with most of the facts that I have put into my paper.

Introduction

The massive immigration from the Eastern Hemisphere to the Western Hemisphere often presents a problem of adaptation for refugees. The new climate, the different culture, and the gradual loss of the deepest beliefs and ethnic values considerably slow down the immigrants' ability to adjust to their new way of life. The Hmong situation is particularly critical and presents a moral dilemma to Western civilizations: "From a preliterate animistic world governed by the spirits of mountain, forest and field, and by tradition handed down verbally, they have come virtually overnight to about a dozen American cities" (Monagan 38).

Who Are the Hmongs?

Background

The Hmongs originally settled in central and southern China; subsequently, the Hmong tribe (or Meo) was driven southward by the Han-Chinese during the nineteenth century and concentrated mainly in the mountains of Laos, Thailand, northern Vietnam, and Burma. During the Vietnam War, the Hmongs became the "backbone of U.S.-supported guerilla resistance against Communist forces" (Hamilton-Merrit 96). So the story goes, the CIA used to throw rice supplies by helicopter on the path leading to the battlefield. The starving Hmongs, when meeting the enemy, fought fiercely to defend their families and helped the American army on the ground.[1]

The Hmong Situation in 1984

From a population of 1,600,000 during the Vietnam War (Atlas of Man 231), they have decreased to about 150,000 (Monagan 36). This massive loss is mostly the result of the extensive attempt, by the Pathet Lao, to exterminate the Hmong tribe using the "Yellow Rain" chemical warfare. At the end of the war, the American and French governments each received about 50,000 Hmong refugees who settled principally in large cities and proceeded to adjust to an entirely new existence. The remaining tribe, about 50,000 people, are still dying every day from starvation, disease, and lack of medical supplies in Thai refugee camps. They are waiting to be saved by the Western countries and are dreaming of freedom, a decent life, and family reunion.

Adjustment to New Climates

The Hmongs are mountain people; they used to live a rural life in their hillside settlements, supporting themselves mainly by cultivating rice by the slash-and-burn method, by growing vegetables, and by raising chickens. They also used to grow opium for the trade.

If the French Hmongs, who settled in French Guiana, have been almost decimated by malaria and other tragic diseases to which their systems were not immune, the American Hmongs have adjusted fairly well to the American climate. Although they appear vulnerable, their fragility is mostly due to the malnutrition and gassing they endured during the Vietnam War. Many Hmong families settled in California; in San Diego, for example, the community of Linda Vista houses about 500 Hmong families who, with the help of local social services, learn English, look for jobs, send their children to school, and try to make their way through the American way of life.

Contrast of Cultures

The Language Barrier

Not only do the Hmongs not understand the world in which they have been thrown, but they also cannot express their concern or ask for explanations from their new neighbors. The lack of adequate communication is constantly slowing down the process of their social adjustment. Imagine, for example, the fear of a Hmong woman about to give birth in her natural squatting position and being held on her back by two hospital nurses, using strength instead of comforting words. In many instances, the contractions stop, and the doctor has to do a Caesarean operation.

When Feelings Get Hurt

"[The Hmongs] are constantly worried by the threat of disease and sudden death . . . . [They] think of themselves as constant prey to the whims of the spirit world" (Atlas of Man 231). When a member of the tribe is sick, family and friends gather around a shaman who tries to control the evil spirits with songs, dances, and trances. The shaman usually gives the sick person a bracelet with an amulet that should never leave him (or her) and that grants protection in the greatest difficulties, as long as the amulet is in place. At the hospital, however, the nurses often sever the bracelet, which looks like a piece of rag, when they have to stick an I.V. needle into their patient's wrist and do not realize that they are inadvertently offending the Hmong spirits, while bringing a deep feeling of despair to the patient. The Hmong people are very sensitive to vexation and humiliation; other examples of situations where Hmong feelings get hurt are the times when their children receive punishment at school. One day a Hmong child of Linda Vista came home with his sloppy work taped on the back of his shirt. The insult of carrying inscriptions on one's back is considered the ultimate humiliation for a Hmong; the family withdrew him from school and felt totally cast out.

After six to ten years in this country, most Hmongs are still unemployed. On the job market the unskilled, illiterate Hmong is not worth much, and the head of the Hmong family struggles to be able to feed three or more generations of direct and indirect family living under the same roof. The women usually take care of the numerous children while tending a vegetable garden and working on their "padaos," pieces of intricate patchwork and stitchery that they sell at the flea market on the weekends. The men are willing to accept any type of job to help their family survive; the tightening of government welfare policy leaves many of them in distress, dependent on the charity of their already very poor neighbors.

Psychological Issues

The Discouragement

The Hmongs came to the United States hurt, weak, and alone, yet hopeful that their American friends would take care of them. The war had destroyed entire families. Though the usual Hmong family included several wives with their sets of children, U.S. legislation permitted only one wife per household to come with the husband. The rest of the family were literally scattered on various continents. No wonder the Hmongs feel very isolated. Within their "partial" families, dissension has started between the parents and their children. The children, learning the American way of life, begin to refuse to follow their parents' traditions and beliefs. Like many other immigrants, the Hmongs came with very old and unchallenged cultures; however, before long they too will become assimilated in the American melting pot. But for most of them, life never seems to get better; relative physical security only hides a great moral distress that reaches unprecedented proportions with the Sudden Death Syndrome.

The Sudden Death Syndrome

In the United States, the attention of the media was soon alerted by the inexplicable cases of sudden death in the Hmong community. The victims, usually young men, were dying during their sleep, without any known cause. They all were in good health, and the pathologists could never point out any abnormality in their vital organs or any sign of lethal disease or infection. Some researchers attributed the "Sleeping Death" to stress: "The disorientation of the Hmongs did not stop with the war; it is provoked again and again by the details of a world beyond their time" (Monagan 37). Possibly, the Hmongs, when recalling the Vietnam War trauma in their dreams, are literally frightened to death. Their fear, however, may be exacerbated by the feeling that, in the totally unfamiliar and incomprehensible world which surrounds them, their family structure and tribal values are slowly being dismantled.

Conclusion

Did the immigration to Western countries fulfill the Hmongs' hope for a better life? While the Hmong race would be totally extinct by now without the support and hospitality of the West, the immigration seems to have hit them with a last low blow. These noble and fiercely independent people do not appear to be comfortable in our highly urbanized and automatized environment. Tragically, the Hmong population keeps decreasing, and the Hmongs' adjustment problems might never find a solution other than the complete disappearance of the Hmong into the anonymous mass of the hopelessly poor.

Notes

[1] The Hmongs' stitchery work often illustrates the Hmong tribe walking toward large bags of rice thrown to them from U.S. helicopters. They also show the battlefield at the end of the path.

Works Cited

Atlas of Man.   St. Martin Press, 1978

Hamilton-Merrit, Jane. "Tragic Legacy from Laos." Reader's Digest 119 (Aug. 1981).

Monagan, David. "Curse of the Sleeping Death." Reader's Digest 90 (Apr. 1982).

ANALYSIS

The Dark Side of U.S. Hospitality

1. After reading this contemplative paper, what do you think the United States should have done for the Hmong people? Does the student writer present her point of view clearly or does she just state the facts? What things did you learn from Stecker's paper of contemplation?

2. Comment on the organization of the paper. What do the headings add? Do they get in the way? Is each section developed thoroughly? Do you notice an overall cause/effect method of organization?

22

Writing for the Social Sciences

INTRODUCTION

Because most of the Introduction to Chapter 21 applies to this chapter as well, you should read it before continuing.

Many social science professors give assignment topics early in the term to give you an opportunity to research a particular topic. They may also expect you to write about the facts you have learned from lectures, films, textbooks, outside reading, discussions, and seminars.

Each time you are assigned a piece of writing *for a social science course*, turn to this chapter first. As you approach this chapter, concentrate on the particular type of format you have been asked to use: a case study for a health project, a process analysis of an archeological dig, a critique of the U.S. defense budget for a political science class, a research paper to compare and contrast several ways to teach reading, a term paper for a psychology class that points out the significance of having nightmares, and so on.

As explained in detail in the Introduction to Chapter 21, when you settle on the format that you need to write and find it mentioned in this chapter, you should proceed in one of three ways: (1) remain within this chapter; (2) work in this and another chapter; or (3) go to another chapter.

Assignment for Parts A to E

Produce an appropriate piece of writing on a topic of your choice or one assigned by your instructor *for a social science course*, such as anthropology, political science, psychology, sociology, education, or economics.

Part A

A *critique* for many social science courses presents your critical evaluation, both negative and positive, of a short article—often one suggested to you by your professor. Because you usually have to present a summary of the article, you should begin with Chapter 32 to help you to paraphrase or to write a précis or summary of the piece. Once you have determined its thesis, you should concentrate on critiquing the article. Work through your writing process in Chapter 12, where you will also be able to read completed critiques to see how writers support their views with evidence. Then *return to the revising suggestions in this chapter.*

Part B

A *process analysis paper* presents relationships between the various parts of a theory, details of a set of tables, explanations of a series of graphs, and results of the work of a social scientist. Work through the writing process in Part B of Chapter 15, where you will also be able to read process analysis papers. Then *return to the revising suggestions in this chapter.*

Part C

A *social science research paper* presents information on a specific topic that was *not* handled fully in class sessions or in your textbook. You would need to develop the topic by researching extensively. Depending on whether your professor wishes scholarly citations or a non-scholarly approach, you should produce a long research report or a feature article. If you are writing the former, work through Chapters 14 (Part A) and 39, applying the suggestions to your social science topic; if you are writing the latter, work through Chapter 14 (Part B) in the same way. After completing your prewriting and drafting processes, *return to the revising suggestions in this chapter.*

Part D

A *social science term paper* demonstrates that you know a body of information on a specific topic that was handled fully in class sessions, in the textbook, and in some assigned reading. The term paper could take the form of an informative expository essay. If you have to write such a term paper, work through all of Chapter 6 and then *return to the revising suggestions in this chapter.*

Some term papers, however, require that you do extensive reading, researching, observing, and thinking over a period of time before you write. If your assignment is the latter type of term paper, you should *follow the prewriting and drafting suggestions for Part D in this chapter in conjunction with those in Chapter 14 (Parts A and B).*

Part E

Case study papers are common in sociology, psychology, education, anthropology, and political science. A case study will test your ability to present descriptive details of people; for example, a social worker would have to observe a couple who wish to adopt a child and present detailed observations to a committee, or a teacher would have to observe a student who is having extreme problems in the classroom and present a case study to the school's counselor. To write a satisfactory case study, you should *begin with the suggestions in Chapters 2 and 11 (Part B).* But remember that a case study is more than a descriptive essay with a few biographical details; it tests your ability to analyze and to present your case, as well as your powers of observation. You should, therefore, *follow the prewriting and drafting suggestions for Part E in this chapter* when you write a case study.

PREWRITING PROCESS FOR PART D

1. Because of the length and detailed content of a social science term paper, you will have to work on several prewriting fronts at the same time: brainstorming sessions to narrow your topic; summaries of what you read, see, and hear; library research to gather reference material; and journal entries to test your ideas. As you gather your material, you should try to discover a controlling feature to narrow your topic.

2. Remember, you will not be expected to use all the information you know or have found in writing your term paper. Rather, you should focus your paper and use only that information which contributes to your overall method of organization. As you move through your prewriting activities, therefore, keep in mind that you should have a definite thesis statement or controlling question before you begin your drafting process. If you do not have a sense of direction, your paper, even though it may contain more than ample material, will ramble aimlessly.

3. When you have gathered all of your material, you should categorize it by answering several questions that will result in a controlled thesis for your term paper. The authors of *Writing in the Arts and Sciences* (Maimon et al.) suggest that writers of social science term papers ask seven controlling questions. You should complete the Seven Controlling Questions brainstorming technique in Chapter 25 before you proceed to the drafting process of your term paper. By organizing all of your material according to the seven questions, you can decide which question or combination of questions will control your essay and give it unity and coherence.

4. By now you may have a great deal of material and no doubt could begin to draft an informative term paper. However, at the heart of social science term papers is controversy. Your informative paper will probably be more interesting to read if it has a strong argumentative edge to it; however, your argument must be well documented and not based on supposition or, worse yet, unfounded assertions. (For more information about argumentative techniques, see Chapter 5.) Look over your brainstorming notes to see if you have introduced controversy. If you cannot find any, try to introduce a natural (not artificial) controversy into an aspect of your prewriting. Be truthful, but do not hesitate to think extreme thoughts. You can always chop them down to size during your drafting process.

5. Before you draft, use this checklist to see if you are ready to continue:

- Have you decided on the exact purpose of your term paper—for example, are you proving, explaining, arguing, or analyzing? Or are you combining two or more purposes?

- To what degree is your paper controversial? Are you wanting to win your audience to your way of thinking? If so, how do you plan to achieve this?

- Have you considered your readers and their situation? In what ways will your audience influence the way you write—for example, word choice, sentence structure, scholarly citation, and so on? What can you assume that your readers know? Is there additional material that you need to read and summarize so that you can include it in your prewriting notes because your readers will need it?

- Have you tested your thesis statement (Chapter 27)?
- Have you considered your method of organization (Chapter 29) so that your excellent material will have the desired impact on your audience?

6. Have the following ready so that you spend a comfortable time during your drafting process:

- All brainstorming results
- Research notes (preferably on file cards)
- Full details on all of your quotations: author, title, publisher, place of publication, publication date, page numbers
- A full set of writing variables
- A thesis statement
- A thorough understanding of the method of organization you have decided best suits your paper
- A list of transitions that you will use to compose (pages 348–349 from Chapter 30)

DRAFTING PROCESS FOR PART D

Read the suggestions in the Drafting Process of Chapters 6 and 14 (Parts A and B) and Chapter 5 if you are introducing argument, as well as the following suggestions before you draft your paper.

1. Make sure you define your terms early in your paper (see Chapter 10).

2. Even though you have formulated a controlling question to narrow your topic, you may want to let your audience know that you are dealing only with one or two aspects of the topic. Feel free to state its limitations quite early in your paper: "This paper will deal only with the effects of dyslexia on college students," or "This paper will not cover all the causes and effects of dyslexia." At the same time, however, you might like to include a summary of relevant material surrounding your topic. In this way you set your controlling problem in a workable framework—for example, "Because there are so many forms of dyslexia, it remains one of the most difficult learning disabilities to diagnose."

3. If you are introducing anything controversial in your paper, present your point of view early—for example, "Professors and students alike are usually unaware that there are dyslexic students in their classes. Through years of being ignored or feeling embarrassed, the dyslexic students have learned not to bring attention to themselves." Since you have introduced controversy, your paper will no longer be strictly informative; therefore, you should begin to use the drafting suggestions in Chapter 5.

4. If you find it necessary to back up your point of view by citing authorities, you will need to introduce quotations into your own prose. For suggestions on how to do this, see Chapter 39.

5. Keep your attention on your method of organization. Use the transitions listed in Chapter 30 so that your readers will follow your organization.

6. When you have completed your final draft of your term paper, present it to your peers for them to edit. Use the revising suggestions in this chapter; they apply to all social science papers.

PREWRITING PROCESS FOR PART E

Follow the prewriting suggestions in both Chapters 2 and 11 (Part B), keeping in mind the topic for your case study. Then complete the following:

1. After you have gathered all of your observations, you should list them in categories: physical appearance, behavior, environment, and so on (see Chapter 7). Perhaps some categories will not be appropriate for your case study; therefore, you should not include them.

2. Generally, you should not introduce narration or exposition into your objective description unless you include your subject's dialogue in order to demonstrate particular characteristics.

3. Make sure that you separate subjective judgments, interpretations, or explanations from your observations; generally, you should provide only objective observations. Note the difference between objective and subjective observations in these examples:

> OBJECTIVE: The parents leave the home at 7 A.M. for their jobs. They do not make their beds or do the dishes before they leave.
>
> SUBJECTIVE: The prospective parents are obviously hardworking, but they dislike housework.

Try to find out whether or not your audience (a committee or one of your co-workers) would appreciate your written opinion as a part of your case study. You might be required to let your reader make the ultimate inferences and decisions—strictly from your objective description of the case. But be prepared to provide your subjective opinions in conference if called upon.

4. You should, however, present any theories that have a bearing on the case. By comparing or contrasting the subject of your case study with examples from your researched material, you will help others to reach a correct decision—for example, "According to Bowers, 'At least one adoptive parent of a preschool child should be at home during the day to provide a sense of stability.'"

5. Use as much of the prewriting checklist material found above in the Prewriting Process for Part D as you think necessary.

DRAFTING PROCESS FOR PART E

Besides using the drafting suggestions in Chapters 2 and 11 (Part B), use the following:

1. While you write, keep in mind your readers and their situation. Although you have to separate objective observation from subjective inference in formal case studies, your professor may require that you divide the page into columns so that the reader can see both observations at a glance. (See the case study in the Products section.) Keep asking yourself: Why did my subject do this? What is the significance of that particular action? What does my professor want me to learn from this case study?

2. When you have completed your draft, check for two things: that your introduction presents the reason why you are writing the paper, and that you have a unifying thread running through your case study.

3. If you find it necessary to back up your point of view by citing authorities, you will need to introduce quotations into your own prose. For suggestions on how to do this, see Chapter 39.

4. Because your method of organization will probably be chronological, use the transitions listed in Chapter 30 so that your reader will be aware of how events follow one another.

REVISING PROCESS FOR ALL SOCIAL SCIENCE PAPERS

Most of the revising suggestions for humanities papers also apply to social science papers; therefore, refer to the information provided in Chapter 21. In addition, note the following:

1. Depending on the format of your social science paper, you should consider

- whether you have used appropriate subheadings (with your professor's permission) to divide your paper into its important sections;
- whether the tone is appropriately impersonal (first person, however, is sometimes appropriate in some social science papers);
- whether you have overused passive voice in place of the forceful active voice (see Chapter 57);
- whether you have used too many abstract concepts (watch nouns ending in *-tion*, *-ism*, and *-ance*);
- whether you have used weak rather than strong verbs (see Chapter 64); and
- whether you have used the present tense to describe past events or whether you have mixed present and past tenses (see Chapter 57).

2. Because the material in your social science paper may be unfamiliar to your peers and perhaps to your composition instructor, they may not understand your use of technical vocabulary. Because your audience will be specialists, you are permitted (even expected) to use specialized words. However, you should not overuse jargon. Defining your vocabulary, when called upon by your editors, will help you weed out imprecise jargon.

3. Because you have probably used the APA style to refer to your researched references, your editors, who will be more familiar with the MLA style, will need to refer to the APA information in Chapter 39, as well as an APA style sheet (your social science professor can probably provide one for them to examine).

4. If your editors have the time, they could help you by presenting a summary or an outline of your paper (see Chapter 32). If you have omitted or not stressed an important point in your paper, your editors will have difficulty presenting a clear summary or outline. In some social science classes, you may be required to submit a formal outline with your paper. If that is the case, your editors should carefully compare your outline with the content of your essay.

5. To help you in the final presentation of your paper to your audience, see the product paper for social science courses at the end of this chapter.

6. Once you have satisfied your peers, present your social science paper to your instructor-editor for a final editing session. Then present a clean (typed) copy to your intended audience.

7. After your intended audience has read and commented on your paper, make sure to share your reader's comments with your editors.

PRODUCTS

In addition to the following product to represent writing in the social sciences, you should read those in other chapters that have many of the characteristics of typical social science papers—for example:

- Case study for sociology: "The Way It Was" (Chapter 9)
- Case study for education: "The Story of R" (Chapter 11)
- Research paper for psychology: "The Vampire: Fact or Fiction?" (Chapter 14)
- Term paper for psychology: "Hear the Children Cry" (Chapter 14)
- Researched term paper for nursing: "Child Abuse: A Growing Concern" (Chapter 14)
- Process analysis paper for psychology: "Coke: It's Got a Real Sting" (Chapter 6)
- Process analysis paper for psychology: "Can People Be Judged by Their Appearance?" (Chapter 7)
- Process analysis paper for psychology: "Cooling Burnout" (Chapter 15)
- Proposal and report for nursing psychology: "Hospital Food Service for Night Staff" (Chapter 17)

Following is an example of a case study.

Observation II

by Charlene B. Little, student

Sarah is a three-year-old girl at Aunt Mary's Preschool, New Orleans, La. I chose her as a subject because, although she has never spent any time alone with me, she has seen me enough times to ignore me during an observation. The observation was done right after lunch in the playground. The teacher, as well as many children from ages two through four, was present. Except for a brief run around one end of the enormous sandbox, all activity takes place in the sandbox.

TIME	FACTS	INTERPRETATION
12:00	Sarah runs rapidly under gym equipment, across sandbox to pick up a plastic kitchen pot in each hand.	Sarah's ability to run through deep sand shows evidence of good development of gross motor skills (Berger, 1980, p. 282).
	Sarah tells Elizabeth enthusiastically, "I'll be your friend!" She sinks down smoothly and begins to put sand in pots. She winces visibly backward as Elizabeth threatens to throw a sand toy.	Her language development is typical of three-year-olds. She uses grammar that utilizes the subject, verb, and object word order (p. 316).
	Sarah stands up suddenly and runs back through the sandbox, jumps down onto the blacktop and attempts to hitch a ride on the back of Frankie's tricycle. She eagerly chases him around the sandbox to the playhouse.	Sarah demonstrates mastery play in attempting to mount the back of a moving tricycle (p. 276).
	Sarah looks through playhouse window at girls inside.	Looking in the playhouse window is indicative of one of the stages of social play called onlooker play (p. 343).
12:03	Sarah climbs back into sandbox and picks up the discarded pots. Katy and Frankie join her. Sarah shares one pot with Frankie but not with Katy. Frankie says, "Let's get out of here." Sarah replies, "Yeah!" Sarah and Frankie move to another area of sandbox near the sidewalk. Sarah watches an elderly lady stop to talk to the children as Frankie disappears.	
	With a shovel, Sarah pours sand on children playing outside and below the level of sandbox. She is rebuked by the teacher.	Pouring sand on another child is an example of aggression typical for three-year-olds (p. 357).
	She plays with pots by filling them with sand and dumping them.	Filling and dumping sand into pots is a classic demonstration of sensorimotor play (p. 276).
12:06	Sarah pours sand on the ledge from a teapot with her right hand to make a mound.	Sarah illustrates a stage of social play called solitary play by sitting and playing in the sandbox contentedly alone (p. 343).
	She carefully watches several boys playing outside and below the level of the sandbox.	The mounds of sand made on the ledge of the sandbox were made by

TIME	FACTS	INTERPRETATION
	Sarah pours sand from one pot to the other.	pouring with the right hand and indicate specialized brain function and hand preference (p. 289).
	She quietly watches the teacher leave to assist Frankie.	
	Sarah makes a new mound on the ledge with the pot in her right hand, sitting and bending easily at the waist.	
	She pats mound with her left hand.	
12:09	Slowly and deliberately, Sarah pushes the mound off the ledge with two hands simultaneously.	
	She experiences flatulence.	Sarah's spontaneous "I made a sound" shows very good left hemisphere development. Unlike "Happy Birthday," which can be memorized, she is able to associate a word with a normal, but unexpected, bodily function (p. 289).
	Sarah says casually, "I made a sound."	
	She continues to play.	
	Sarah balances the pots open-end to open-end.	
	She pours sand on top with her right hand and begins to sing "Happy Birthday."	The re-creation of a birthday party shows that Sarah is capable of symbolic thought while indulging in creative play (p. 300-301).
	She cuts sand on top of the pot with a twig.	Singing "Happy Birthday" to herself is a kind of monologue and is an illustration of egocentric speech (p. 319).
12:12	Elizabeth comes to sit nearby and plays with her own sand toys.	Sarah's ability to sing and bake an imaginary cake illustrates that she is in the midst of a developmental shift. She is able to talk and do something at the same time (p. 322).
	Sarah sings "Happy Birthday to Frankie" and says, "Blow out the candles." The pots collapse.	
	She puts the pots end to end again and pours sand on top to make a mound.	Her singing of "Happy Birthday" shows inner speech capability and enhanced memory. Sarah shows evidence that birthday parties are memorable (p. 322).
	Sarah lifts off the top pot and sets the bottom pot on top to press down the mound.	
	She continues singing; Frankie joins in from the monkey bars, but she gives no evidence that she hears him.	
	Sarah cuts the sand pile with a twig.	Elizabeth and Sarah take part in social play that contains elements of both parallel and associative play. Both are playing side by side. But Sarah is having a birthday party, while Elizabeth is playing tea party. Elizabeth blows out the candles even though, up to that point, she was involved in her own activity (p. 343).
	She turns to Elizabeth and says, "Blow the candles."	
	Elizabeth blows on the sand pile.	

Reference

Berger, K. S.   (1980).   The Developing Person.   New York: Worth.

ANALYSIS

Observation II

1. How accurately has the student writer described and interpreted Sarah's actions? Did you find any places in her case study where you were confused?

2. Throughout the "Interpretation" column, Little refers to the particular pages from *The Developing Person*. Even without reading this book, can you anticipate the type of material you would find there?

3. Comment on Little's organization. Is it clear?

23

Writing for the Natural Sciences

INTRODUCTION

Even though writing for a natural science course is different from writing for other courses, you are encouraged to read the Introduction to Chapter 21 before you continue in this chapter.

Many natural science professors give assignment topics early in the term to give you an opportunity to research a particular topic. They may also expect you to write about the facts you have learned from lectures, films, textbooks, outside reading, discussions, and seminars. Each time you are assigned a piece of writing *for a natural science course*, turn to this chapter first. Although you may have to write similar papers to those already outlined in Chapter 22 (social science), the most common writing assignments you will have in your natural science courses are a notebook for formal laboratory reports and a review paper on scientific research.

Assignment for Parts A and B

Produce an appropriate piece of writing on a topic of your choice or one assigned by your instructor *for a natural science course*, such as physics, chemistry, biology, meteorology, astronomy, geology, health sciences, mathematics, data processing, computer science, geography, and physical education classes.

Part A

A *laboratory report* for a natural science course is roughly equivalent to a term paper for a social science course; the writing process, however, is quite different. In most cases you place all laboratory reports in your lab notebook. A lab notebook for a scientist serves the same purpose as a journal for a writer. You keep a journal in order to strengthen your writing process; you keep a lab notebook to summarize your observations of specific experiments. A journal is usually private; a lab notebook, however, is public: your lab partner may collaborate in writing it, and your instructor will grade it and evaluate your understanding of the work you have done. A well-written journal serves as an endless source of future writing topics; a laboratory notebook serves to refresh your memory for periodic lab practicals (tests), as well as to record details for later written reports or reviews.

Whereas you might rewrite several portions of your journal in order to sharpen details and improve their overall style, you should never recopy your lab notebook; it would leave the impression that you have altered your results.

Assuming you do not have a commercial lab notebook with a built-in, standardized format, you will be expected to record an experiment under several labeled sections: title, purpose, materials/methods, procedure, results, and conclusions. You may include drawings, diagrams, tables, and graphs, as your experiment warrants.

Part B

A *scientific review paper* is a kind of research report that students of the natural sciences must often write. Although it has many similarities to a humanities or social science research report (Chapter 14, Part A), the scientific review paper, with its objective tone, bears little resemblance to a critical review (Chapter 12).

A scientific review paper informs rather than persuades its readers. The writer should focus on a particular subject in a limited scientific area and explain it in a clear and understandable manner. A review paper is not personal or opinionated; neither does it introduce new or original material. It summarizes recent research on a chosen scientific topic; readers may review an entire topic quickly in this digest form and then use the bibliography listings to find the original research material.

PREWRITING PROCESS FOR PART A

Experiments in science are often complicated and difficult to complete in the allotted time. Prior preparation is a must. Many instructors require that a laboratory report be prepared even *before* doing an experiment, so that only collecting data and compiling results remain for the laboratory period itself. You will notice, therefore, that when you are engaged in writing a laboratory report, you will blend the prewriting and the drafting processes.

Prewrite your report with three readers in mind: (1) yourself, in order to use the condensed "Procedure" section in doing the experiment and the "Results" section to record your observations; (2) a new student, who should be able to understand the general concept of the experiment as well as its specific instructions; and (3) your instructor, who will evaluate not only your results but also the clarity with which you observed, reported, and discussed them.

DRAFTING PROCESS FOR PART A

Form and structure (and, of course, technically accurate information) are of prime importance. The format below is recommended for a standard laboratory report.

Title

Include key words that explain the experiment cogently.

Introduction and Purpose

Provide relevant background information briefly and introduce the purpose of the experiment.

Methods and Materials

Explain in a general summary form how you intend to perform the experiment. List special equipment or materials. It would be appropriate to include diagrams of apparatus and methods of collecting data.

Procedure

List the steps in enough detail that you can complete the experiment with no further reference to the original laboratory text.

Results

Prepare blank tables, graphs, and other data displays so that you can include your observations and compiled steps during the lab period.

Conclusion and Discussion

Considering your expressed purpose (above), allow enough space to evaluate your results and summarize the success of your work and/or recommendation for further work.

References Cited

Cite all literature you used for the report (include your own lab notebook and textbook).

Your prewrite need not be drafted in the same sequence as the final presentation above, and, in fact, it often seems to flow better if you "jump around" somewhat.

1. Even though for most writing assignments you would not begin with a title, for a laboratory report it is recommended you start with a *Title*. It gives both you and your audience a focus. It should command attention and provide just enough key words to allow an instant grasp of what is to follow—for example:

- Preparation, Purification, and Characterization of Acetanilide
- Simple and Fractional Distillation—A Comparison of Efficiencies
- Isolation of Human T-cells from Herpes Lesions

2. While you write the *Methods and Materials* section, remember that your audience should be able to repeat your experiment; therefore, you must provide descriptions of *all* equipment and materials. Be specific to the point of giving the model number and size of specialized equipment. Inclusion of labeled drawings and photographs is in order. You might include corresponding flowcharts to illustrate the steps of the process. Always give a very compact overview of the experimental technique; sometimes it will suffice in the descriptions of equipment and materials to refer to the original laboratory text. Remember to coordinate this writing with your "Introduction and Purpose" section, which is usually written later. Note the following examples of a "Methods and Materials" section:

> The reagents are mixed in water solution and heated to boiling for 20 minutes. Crude product is filtered from the cooled solution then recrystallized from hot ethanol/water after decolorization with activated charcoal. The pure product is air dried, weighed, and characterized by melting point and mixed melting point.
> Apparatus is set up as in Moore and Dalrymple's lab textbook, pp. 131 and 133. Temperatures are read for every 10 drops of distillate collected, and temperature/volume graphs are prepared for both techniques. Samples of distillate are taken at intervals of 10 ml for composition analysis by vapor phase chromatography.

3. Do the *Procedure* next. It is a chronological ordering of specific operations. Do this in list form, and be sure to include the steps in collecting, compiling, and displaying your data—for example:

   a. Prepare 2 sets of 5 test tubes with 0.2 ml each of these halides:
   - *n*-butyl chloride
   - *n*-butyl bromide
   - sec-butyl chloride
   - tert-butyl chloride
   - crotyl chloride
   b. Keep stoppered—nasty smell, might evaporate!
   c. Obtain 15 ml each of
   NaI in acetone (Solution A)
   1% $AgNO_3$ in ethanol (Solution B)
   d. Add a 2 ml portion of Solution A to each tube in one set of the test tubes, and Solution B to each tube in the other set.
   e. Watch for rapid changes in color or the formation of precipitates!
   f. Note times and changes in data table.
   g. Prepare list of halides in order of reactivity toward Solution A and Solution B.
   h. Explain results, using "Introduction and Purpose" as a guide.

4. Now address your *Results* section. Prepare appropriate tables, graphs and other titled blanks for your observations. Later in your drafting process, you will work with your actual data and make this section coherent and complete. Here is a finished "Results" section for a chemical experiment. *Note*: All parts were *prewritten* except the ones in parentheses, which were added as calculated results.

a. Crude acetanilide

wt. of paper + product	(6.31)g
wt. of paper	(0.41)g
wt. of product	(5.90)g

b. Recrystallized acetanilide

wt. of paper + product	(5.74)g
wt. of paper	(0.42)g
wt. of product	(5.32)g

c. Yield calculations based on aniline starting material

$$\text{theoretical yield} = (4.60)\text{g aniline} \times \frac{135 \text{ g acetanilide}}{93 \text{ g aniline}} = (6.70)\text{g acetanilide}$$

$$\% \text{ yield} = \frac{(5.32)\text{g}}{(6.70)\text{g}} \times 100\% = (79\%)$$

d. Melting points

crude:	(110–113)°C
recrystallized:	(113.8–114.0)°C
authentic:	(113.9–114.0)°C
mixed:	(113.8–114.0)°C

5. Now write your *Introduction and Purpose*. You should include necessary background information and your purpose for writing the report. Define key words and present the scope and design of the experiment. Make your "Introduction and Purpose" a compact paragraph or two no matter how much primary material you find related to the experiment. The original laboratory textbook should be a good source of material for you. Be sure that you connect this section smoothly to the "Methods and Materials" section that follows in your report.

6. Your *Conclusion and Discussion* should refocus attention on the original purpose by pointing out how the results validated some original premise (or, in case they did not, how they might be understood in an alternate context).

Do not be glib ("The experiment didn't work too well!"). Use your results specifically in your discussion—for example:

> The gradual slope of the temperature/volume graph showed that the simple distillation technique provided poor separation of liquid mixtures. Peak height chromatographic data confirmed this. By contrast, the ⟋ shaped graph and clearly resolved chromatograms of the fractional distillation technique underscored its efficacy as a separation technique. In my opinion, a longer distilling column would have made the results even better.

7. Finally, you must cite your *References*. You must make sure you use the correct method of citation. No doubt your natural science instructor will want you to use one of the scientific systems rather than the APA style as outlined in *The Independent*

Writer. At any rate, check with your reader before you use a method of your own choice.

8. Before you move to the revising process below, make sure that you are satisfied with your final report.

PREWRITING PROCESS FOR PART B

1. Writing a review paper takes time, so begin early. Finding a topic can be extremely time-consuming: you should select one that is appropriate to the course, suitably limited in scope, and currently under active investigation. In addition to finding a topic, you will no doubt unearth a great amount of supporting evidence for your thesis, if you are indeed proposing one.

2. Find a topic that is interesting to you. Newspapers in virtually all major cities have regular science columns, and television and radio reports of current scientific topics are daily fare. In some cases you may want to follow an original "lead" back to a working scientist in your own community; a meeting or consultation is often surprisingly easy (and fascinating) to arrange.

Recent journal articles in various periodicals tend to report research that is at least a year old; textbook information is usually thorough in its coverage but often more than ten years old. Try *Scientific American*, *Science News*, *Science*, *National Geographic*, *Natural History*, *Science 80*, *Omni*, *Discover* and many others. Some of these provide periodic indexes that list all the titles published over a year's time or more.

3. When you have found a reference in the periodical's table of contents of an article that interests you, locate the article and read the abstract and introduction carefully. Notice when the article was written. From this brief reading you will be able to tell whether you want to finish reading the article or move to another.

If you decide to stick with the article, jot down a few related questions that you might wish to use in order to narrow your topic for your review paper. Furthermore, check carefully all of the references contained in the article so that you might do additional reading. Finally, read the conclusion, also called the "Discussion Section." This final section of the article often contains more details than the abstract, as well as additional references. If all goes well during this specific prewriting activity, you should jot down a few details on your narrow topic. If you have produced a few sentences that are clear and provide a sense of direction for your own review, you should continue in a more specific manner.

4. Now might be a good time to locate and read a published scientific review that contains material on your topic. The advantage of choosing a topic related to an already-published review paper is that you will see how to set up such a paper.

By using an index service such as *Science Citation Index*, *Chemical Abstracts*, or *Index Medicus*, you will soon be able to locate several current scientific reports—all related to your topic. What would it mean if you could not find any recent research reports on your topic? What should you do about your proposed topic?

5. As you read the reports that you have found, summarize (rather than quote directly) the portions that focus on your narrow topic. During your drafting process you will use these summaries, because scientific review papers usually do not contain direct quotations.

6. Once you have gathered several summaries that detail the accounts of your narrow topic in terms applicable to you, you should submit your material to several controlling questions. Use the Seven Controlling Questions brainstorming technique outlined in Chapter 25.

7. By arranging your notes according to the controlling questions, you should have a working outline for your drafting process. Each controlling question, if converted to a statement, becomes a subheading.

8. Most scientists would suggest that you begin to draft your review paper *before* you complete your research. Using this method, you will get an idea of what your finished product will look like, and you will also discover whether your topic is too broad or too narrow for the assigned essay length. Therefore, move to your drafting process now, but plan to return to one of the prewriting brainstorming techniques in Chapter 25 (Four-Faces-of-Knowledge Cluster, Pro/Con Ladder, Newspaper Reporter's Questions) in order to obtain more supporting evidence.

DRAFTING PROCESS FOR PART B

1. Because you will have a paper that has several independent subheadings in its body, you can begin your drafting process with any one of them. When you complete the body of your review, you will write the more important introduction and conclusion. (See further discussion of these two sections in Item 8.)

2. Sort through your prewriting notes and place them into piles under each of your subheadings. You might use the cut-and-paste method of composition; that is, glue portions of your notes on blank pages. You should, however, leave plenty of room so that you can expand on your notes, add connecting paragraphs to them, and even insert notes to yourself to do further research.

3. When you have completed the body of your review, ask two of your peers (who have an understanding of the specialized scientific terminology that you may be using) to edit what you have done so far. They should read for content only; later you can work on sentence structure and grammar. Discuss the paper with them by asking them leading questions: Do you see the point of my paper? Is the research important to you? Do you understand what you have read? Is the background information useful?

4. According to the results of this preliminary editing session, you should continue in your drafting process to fill in holes, answer questions, explain unfamiliar terms, provide simpler examples, introduce transitions, and provide diagrams.

5. Concentrate on the tone of your review. Because a review informs, your paper must sound authoritative. Avoid using "I think," "I assume," and "I feel."

6. Most scientific reviews have three kinds of headings: center the title and major subheadings on the line; underline minor subheadings and place them flush to the left-hand margin; and underline other categories and indent them from the left-hand margin. Notice the spacing and the use of capitalization in the following example of the three kinds of headings:

Title and Major Subheadings

Minor subheadings

Other categories

7. Use the appropriate method for citing your references (as suggested by your natural science instructor) throughout your review paper. If you are allowed to use the APA style, see Chapter 39.

8. When you are satisfied with the body of your paper, write your introduction and conclusion. Do you remember how long it took you to understand the original articles and reviews that you read during your prewriting process? Do you also remember that you read the introductions and conclusions first? Well, you should also remember that your intended readers will probably read your introduction and conclusion before they read the body of your review. From this reading, they will decide whether they want to continue. As a result, you must spend time ensuring that your introduction and conclusion accurately reflect the final version of your review. When you write your introduction, you may either choose to state the importance of the problem that is the subject of the paper or you may refer to the recent research on the topic and the aspect of it that you will be stressing.

When you write your conclusion, remind your readers of the major research steps that you described in the body of the review. Then establish what these results mean and why they are important. This is perhaps the only place in your review where you can legitimately show personal concern. You should include a short statement to the effect that further experimentation may be needed on your chosen topic before a final decision can be made or a final conclusion reached.

9. Finally, proofread your review for surface errors. Standard typewriters seldom contain scientific symbols; therefore, you will probably have to draw them neatly in the blanks that you have provided. Precision in your written work reinforces your precision in the laboratory.

REVISING PROCESS FOR ALL NATURAL SCIENCE PAPERS

Ask your editors to consider the revising suggestions in Chapter 14 (Part A) and those in Chapter 22, as well as the suggestions that follow.

1. Your editors may be tempted to offer suggestions for extensively revising your "Methods and Materials" and "Results" sections in your laboratory report. As these sections describe your experiment exactly as you did it, you should not change them despite your editors' wishes. However, if your editors are confused about any material in your scientific review, you should find out why they have a problem and, if necessary, reform your prose.

2. To help you in your final presentation of your paper to your audience, see the product papers for natural science courses at the end of this chapter.

3. Once you have satisfied your peers, you may obtain a final editing from your English instructor. Then present your paper to your intended audience.

4. After your intended audience has read and commented on your paper, make sure to share your readers' comments with your editors.

PRODUCTS

Following is an example of a laboratory report.

Steam Distillation of Essential Oils

by Harold Kwan, student

Introduction and Purpose

Steam distillation is the separation of a mixture into its components that are not mutually soluble; one of the components is water. It provides a means of distilling a volatile compound at a temperature far below its normal boiling point. Steam distillation is useful in the separation of a water-insoluble organic compound that is present in a large amount of nonvolatile material.

In a mixture of nonsoluble compounds the vapor pressure above the mixture is the sum of the partial pressures of the components $P_T = P_A + P_B$; each exerts its own vapor pressure independently of the other. Since the vapor pressures are additive, the boiling point of the mixture ($P_T = 1$ atm) is lower than the boiling point of either of the components.

Steam distillation is a useful alternative to extraction for the isolation of volatile organic compounds, such as essential oils from plant material. Extraction with solvents removes gums and fats as well as the volatile oils; the latter are separated selectively by steam distillation.

The purpose of this experiment is to steam distil an essential oil from a widely used spice—anise. The major constituent will be characterized as a derivative.

Methods and Materials

1. For diagram of apparatus, see Experimental Methods in Organic Chemistry, Moore & Dalrymple, p. 92.
2. For general method, see same reference, p. 94.
3. For equation for derivative reaction, see same reference, p. 94.

Procedure

1. Anethole from anise
   - Weigh out 10.0 g ground anise seeds into a 500-ml, 3-necked flask.

- Add 150 ml H_2O.
- Heat with flame until steady distillation (1 ml/min).
- Add H_2O from dropping funnel to maintain volume in flask.
- Collect distillate until no further cloudiness is observed in new drops (at least 100 ml total).
- Pour distillate into separatory funnel.
- Extract with 5 ml methylene chloride. WATCH OUT—organic layer on bottom this time!
- Repeat extraction.
- Dry with Na_2SO_4 if necessary (tell by possible cloudiness in the solution).
- Evaporate methylene chloride on steam bath, in fume hood.
- Weigh oily product anethole.
- Calculate percent yield.

2. Derivative of anethole
   - Dissolve 0.5 g $KMnO_4$ in 10 ml H_2O.
   - Add this to anethole in test tube.
   - Boil for 20 min.
   - Add 1 ml dilute H_2SO_4 and 1 g $NaHSO_3$ until no brown color is left.
   - Collect white solid by filtration.
   - Take mpt. in a sealed capillary.

Results

1. Weight of plant materials (anise seeds) 10.0 g
   Weight of pure oil (anethole)   0.847 g

$$\text{Percent yield anethole} = \frac{0.847}{10.0} \times 100 = 8.47\%$$

2. Derivative melting point 180–182°C
   Authentic melting point 184°C

Conclusion

- Indeed, steam distillation works, and it is fun too!
- Anise seeds contain about 8.5% anethole. I am confident of its purity because of the derivative melting point.
- It might be fun to try an extraction method to isolate the anethole and compare the yield with the one I found.

References

Experimental Methods in Organic Chemistry 3rd ed.   Moore & Dalrymple.
Organic Chemistry 4th ed.   Morrison & Boyd.

Following is an example of a scientific review paper.

Caffeine Alkaloids and Their Effects: Stimulating Food for Thought

by Thaddeus J. Hille, student

Abstract

Caffeine is introduced as an alkaloid of the chemical family of xanthines. Several natural plant sources of the family are listed from around the world, and information on extraction methods and historical uses is provided. Emphasis is placed on the physiological effects of xanthines (both short-term and long-term), and the recent literature on clinical tests in animals and humans is reviewed. A bibliography is included.

Introduction

Caffeine is a bitter tasting, moderately potent drug, chemical formula $C_8H_{10}N_4O_2$, of which the prominent dietary sources are coffee and tea. But it is one of the few drugs used to adulterate the general food supply, a dubious distinction shared by alcohol, quinine, and fluoride. That caffeine is a teratogen (causes birth defects) in mammals such as rats, rabbits, and hamsters is acknowledged by the science community, food industry experts, and government officials. Caffeine is known to cross the placenta by way of the blood and enter the human fetus. Further, it has been found in human breast milk. The U.S. Food and Drug Administration (FDA) has warned that pregnant women should avoid caffeine-containing products or use them sparingly. While it is the general consensus that caffeine, in moderate amounts, is safe for consumption by the general population, some people are particularly sensitive to its numerous presumable effects. These sensitivities, coupled with caffeine's possible impact on human reproduction, dictate prudence in its use and perhaps abstinence altogether in some cases.

Caffeine Alkaloids and Other Xanthines

The caffeine alkaloids—known variously as caffeine, thein, guaranine, methyltheobromine, and theophyline—are chemical compounds found mostly in plant but also in animal tissue. As organic bases, they neutralize acid and are alkaline in nature. While found in some cone-bearing trees and some other lower plants, they are most prominently and widely distributed in the seeds, leaves, and bark of flowering plants. Alkaloids are by-products of plant metabolism with no known role of value to the plant per se. They are known to repel some insects when contained in some plants and are transported in solution by way of vascular conduction along with nutrients, hormones, and other by-products.

The value of alkaloids to people lies in their drug effects, which vary. Heroin, morphine, and codeine are derived from the opium poppy. Tetrahydrocannibinol (THC) is the active alkaloidal ingredient of marijuana and has psychotropic as well as other effects. Nicotine, once used medicinally and of value as an insecticide, is an alkaloid contained in tobacco. Caffeine is added to cola drinks and commercially prepared foods such as pudding, baked goods, candy, and frozen dairy products; sometimes it is called "natural flavoring" on the product label. One or another caffeine alkaloid is an ingredient in about 2,000 nonprescription drugs and also in many prescription drugs. Laws in the United States do not require the labeling of caffeine on food and beverage containers, the lack of which is a point of contention with some consumer interest groups.

The group of alkaloids to which caffeine belongs is the xanthines. Theobromine (contained in cocoa along with some caffeine) and theophyline (contained in tea along with caffeine and some theobromine) are also xanthines, cause some of the same effects in humans, and are closely related.

The primary botanical sources of xanthines are coffee, tea, cacao, cola, maté, guarana, and yoco. They are mainly tropical or semitropical evergreens. As an item of international commerce, coffee leads the list in value, and was second only to petroleum in 1970. World coffee imports have increased from 1 million tons per year at the beginning of the 20th century to over 4 million tons per year currently. Approximately a third of the world's people drink coffee. The United States, with less than 5% of the world's population, consumed more than a third of world coffee imports in 1971.

Coffee

The use of coffee as a beverage is thought to have originated in Kefa, Ethiopia, in the 15th century A.D. A shepherd, so the story goes, noticed that after his sheep had eaten the berries of wild coffee plants, they were hyperactive all night. Mindful of the long hours of prayer required of him, he tried the berries himself. Until the close of the 17th century, the world's supply came almost entirely from the province of Yemen in southern Arabia. Nowadays, Brazil, Columbia, and the Ivory Coast are the leading producers.

Coffea arabica L and Coffea robusta[1] are the two main cultivars yielding coffee; the former is grown mainly in Latin America and has a lower caffeine content of approximately 0.8–1.5% in the green, unprocessed state, and the latter has a caffeine content of 1.6–2.5% and is grown mostly in Africa. Both are also grown in Asian countries such as India and Indonesia.

Decaffeinated coffee

Because of the undesirable effects of caffeine, increasing amounts of decaffeinated coffee are being consumed. Two methods employed in decaffeination are: (1) coffee beans are soaked in hot water into which the caffeine enters into solution, after which a solvent separates the caffeine from the water; or (2) solvent is applied directly to the beans. The hot water method is preferable because residue of the solvent is not left behind on beans.

Trichloroethylene, a notorious industrial solvent, was used to decaffeinate coffee until 1975 when it was determined to be carcinogenic (cancer causing). Methylene chloride was and/or is used with certain attendant problems. Ethyl acetate, which is a naturally occurring substance found in some fruits and vinegar, has been authorized for use as a solvent by the FDA. Authorization was based on data contained in a petition filed by General Foods Corporation, maker of Sanka coffee (Better Nutrition, 1982, p. 26).

Tea

Tea is made from the young leaves and leaf buds of Thea (or Camelia) sinensis and is drunk by perhaps half of the world's people. Its use as a beverage dates back to as early as 2737 B.C. in China. Black (fermented) tea comprises 98% of international trade, but green tea is the beverage of choice in China, Japan, and Taiwan. Tea contains caffeine,[2] small amounts of theophyline and theobromine, and appreciable amounts of B-complex vitamins. Caffeine is one of the constituents of the "cream" or precipitate that rises to the top as a tea infusion cools. In addition, tea contains tannin and fluoride, agents supposed to be effective against tooth decay. There are more than a thousand varieties of this plant.

Cacao

Theobroma cacao L[3] is a South American tree, the seeds from which are ground to form chocolate liquor. Cocoa and chocolate are products derived from this process, differing mainly in fat content. In chocolate, the fat or cacao butter content is retained or even added to, whereas cocoa is essentially defatted. Theobroma means "food of the gods" in Greek. Cacao beans were used in making an unsweetened, cold beverage and as currency by the Maya and Aztec Indians before being brought to Europe in the early 1500s. Like coffee, it is cultivated as an understory crop to protect it from too much sun. The cacao bean (or seed) contains 30–50% oil, 15% carbohydrates, and 15% protein. Cacao butter is one of the most stable fats known, containing antioxidants that discourage rancidity and allow for a shelf life of two to five years.

Maté

Maté, also known as Paraguay tea, yerba maté, St. Bartholomew's tea, and Jesuit's tea, is derived from the shrub Ilex paraguariensis St. Hill., a holly related to the one commonly used for Christmas decoration. It grows wild near the Uraguay, Panama, and Paraguay Rivers and is cultivated in Argentina. It contains caffeine and tannin. A sweet drink is made from maté and sugar.

Guarana and yoco

Guarana and yoco are used to make beverages and food and are derived from Paullinia ssp.[4] The seeds of P. cupana H.B.K. are made into a dried paste that has a caffeine content approximately three times that of coffee or not less than 4%. The Guarini Indians originated its use in making a beverage. The seeds of P. sorbilis are also used, whereas the bark of P. yoco is used. Guarana is eaten in solid form and contains tannin. Paullinia ssp. are indigenous to the Amazon Valley of Brazil.

Cola

Cola acuminata and C. nitida Schott & Endl are trees native to tropical West Africa and belong to Family Sterculiaceae. They are cultivated extensively in the American tropics and are also found in the West Indies, West Africa, India, and Ceylon. The seeds are consumed throughout the world for their stimulating effects. They are also used in the manufacture of cola beverages and are a source of caffeine for over-the-counter and prescription drugs. Kola or guru nuts contain caffeine and theobromine.

Effects of Xanthines

Short-term effects

The xanthines are vasodilators, meaning that they dilate or enlarge the blood vessels. This is brought about through their characteristic relaxing effect on the smooth muscles governing blood vessel size. Their effect on blood flow to the brain is just the opposite though; xanthines are vasoconstrictors of the blood vessels supplying the brain. This paradoxical behavior can be explained partly by the fact that while the diameter of the blood vessels in general is regulated by smooth muscles of the arterioles, blood flow to the brain is determined by carbon dioxide, oxygen, and metabolic by-product concentration levels. Xanthines have been prescribed in cases of inadequate blood flow, particularly in veterinary practice. Caffeine is prescribed to relieve headaches following spinal punctures and is contained in headache remedies.

The xanthines have a relaxing effect on the smooth muscles, including bronchial muscles. They are used to counter difficulty in breathing of the mother during childbirth, and they are used to overcome cessation of breathing of premature infants (Murat, 1981, p. 984). In addition, they are commonly found in asthma medications.

The charge that caffeine is responsible for heart disease has not been substantiated, but it is common knowledge that excessive amounts cause alarming irregularities of heartbeat. The effect of moderate amounts on blood pressure is more open to question[5] (Galton, 1982, p. 27; Murat, 1981, p. 985). A U.S. government study conducted in Framingham, Mass., since 1949 has shown no increase in anginal chest pain, onset of heart disease, or heart attacks or stroke from drinking coffee (Galton, 1982, p. 28).

Referring to coffee, William Harvey, the 15th century medical doctor and discoverer of the true nature of circulation of the blood and of heart action, said, "This little bean is the source of happiness and wit!" He bequeathed 56 pounds to the London College of Physicians (Coffee Brewing Institute, 1963, p. 13). Perhaps the xanthines' favorite physiological effect is "to produce a more rapid and clearer flow of thought, and to allay drowsiness and fatigue. After taking caffeine, one is capable of a greater sustained intellectual effort and a more perfect association of ideas" (Gilman et al., 1970, p. 359). Caffeine has been associated with increased attention span, but it has also been implicated in low school performance and symptoms of psychiatric disorder when taken in excess (Zandler, 1982, p. 51).

The effects of the xanthines on the human organism are numerous; they include diuretic, basal metabolism increase, gastric acidity increase (irritating to gastric ulcers), decrease of reaction time (faster reflex action), and inhibition of iron and B-complex vitamin utilization.

Caffeine poisoning

Symptoms of caffeine poisoning are heartbeat irregularity, convulsions, restlessness, excitement, urinary frequency, tinnitus (ringing of the ears), nausea, vomiting, and tremors. These symptoms can be brought about by as little as one gram; the fatal dose is approximately 10 grams. Treatments for caffeine overdose include emesis induced by ipecac (a South American shrub of Family Rubiacaea), gastric lavage, and dialysis (Merck & Co., Inc., 1982, p. 2436).

Long-term effects

John Minton, M.D., conducted a study clearly implicating xanthines with nonmalignant breast disease. Out of 88 women so afflicted, 37 out of 45 women who quit xanthines experienced total disappearance of lumps. Seven of the remainder showed improvement (Galton).

Studies commissioned by the government (e.g., the Collins study) have established a link between prenatal consumption of caffeine and birth defects in rats (missing toes or parts of toes). Another study, in which one group of pregnant rats was fed regular coffee and the other decaffeinated, yielded results equal for both groups.[6] Both groups' offspring displayed behavioral abnormalities and lower brain, liver, and overall body weight. Both groups' offspring did recover from low birth weight after 30 days.

Government's attitude toward caffeine

The Commissioner of the FDA had this advice:

> Today I am advising pregnant women to avoid caffeine-containing foods and drugs, or to use them sparingly. We know that caffeine crosses the placenta and reaches the fetus. We know that caffeine is a stimulant and has a definite drug effect. As a general rule, pregnant women should avoid all substances that have drug-like effects, so while further evidence is being gathered on the possible relationship between caffeine and birth defects, a prudent and protective mother-to-be will want to put caffeine on her list of unnecessary substances which she should avoid. (Leepson, 1980, p. 740)

The FDA has asked the U.S. Public Health Service to advise pregnant women of the risks of caffeine through its maternal and child health projects, community health centers, and other programs. It has called on the U.S. Surgeon General to urge health professional organizations, such as the American Medical Association (AMA) and American College of Obstetricians and Gynecologists, to notify respective members of the possible risks of caffeine. And, in addition to ordering further testing, the FDA has announced its intention to remove caffeine from the Generally Recognized As Safe (GRAS) list and put it on an interim list pending results of these tests (Leepson, 1980, p. 745).

Conclusion

Caffeine has both good and bad, therapeutic and toxic, effects. As with many things in life, it is neither all good nor all bad, but somewhere in between. Moderation (and/or abstinence sometimes and in some cases) and knowledge of the foods and drugs we take in are in our best interest.

Notes

[1] The science of taxonomy places plants and animals in biological units or categories (taxa, singular taxon) based on their appearance, evolution, etc. Greek or Latin words are used and recognizable regardless of one's language. The first capitalized word designates the genus (a noun) from which the common name is often derived. Following it is the species (adjective) to describe the particular member of the genus.

[2] Most caffeine content tables list tea as having less caffeine than coffee. Other informed sources indicate the reverse. According to this source, the caffeine content of tea leaves is approximately 2.0%, or approximately twice as much as coffee, but the beverages as finally prepared contain approximately equal amounts (Gilman et al., 1970, p. 368).

[3] The letter following the species designates the person responsible for naming it. In this case, "L" stands for Carolus Linnaeus, a 17th century Swedish scientist, who developed principles of taxonomy.

[4] "ssp." following the genus indicates reference to more than one species of that organism.

[5] No undesirable side effects noted—specifically, no rise in blood pressure.

[6] These results are highly subject to interpretation. Since decaffeinated coffee has a relatively minute amount of caffeine in it (approximately 3 mg/cup), caffeine may have played an active part in results obtained in both groups. Or as other studies have shown, active constituents of coffee other than caffeine may be at work (Groisser et al., 1982, p. 829).

References

Better Nutrition.   (Sept. 1982).

Coffee Brewing Institute.   (1963).   There's a Story in Your Coffee Cup.   New York.

Encyclopaedia Britannica.   15th ed. (1982).   Chicago.

Galton, L.   (July 1982).   The Caffeine Controversy: More Than a Hill of Beans? 50 Plus, 26–9.

Gilman, A. G., Goodman, L. S., and Gilman, A.   (1970).   The Pharmacological Basis of Therapeutics.   4th ed.   New York: MacMillan.

Groisser, D. S. et al.   (1982).   Coffee Consumption During Pregnancy: Subsequent Behaviorial Abnormalities of the Offspring. Journal of Nutrition, 112(4), 829–32.

Leepson, M.   (1980).   Caffeine   Controversy.   Editorial Research Reports, 11, 739–55.

Merck & Co., Inc. (1982). <u>Merck Manual</u>. 14th ed. Rahway, NJ.

Murat, I. et al. (Dec. 1981). The Efficacy of Caffeine in the Treatment of Recurrent Idiopathic Apnea in Premature Infants. <u>Journal of Prediatrics</u>, 984–89.

Zandler, R. H. (May/June 1982). Are You a Caffeine Addict? <u>Saturday Evening Post</u>, 50–53.

ANALYSIS

Steam Distillation of Essential Oils

1. As an organic chemistry student, could you repeat this experiment? If not, why?

2. Which parts of the lab report did Kwan prepare before he entered the laboratory? Which within the laboratory? Support your answer. Hint: See directions in the Drafting Process for Part A.

3. From the point of view of correct composition, evaluate this lab report. Comment on Kwan's sentence structure, word choice, clarity of style, and so on.

4. How does his method for citing references compare with those required by your natural science instructor?

Caffeine Alkaloids and Their Effects: Stimulating Food for Thought

1. Has the student writer organized his scientific review in an easy-to-read manner? Support your answer.

2. Does the abstract suitably summarize the contents of the review?

3. Do you think a formal outline is needed? Construct one of this review.

4. Comment on Hille's use of notes at the end of his review and his inclusion of parenthetical citations. Are the notes necessary?

5. How does his method of citing references compare with those required by your natural science instructor?

6. After reading this scientific review, do you think the writer was justified in drawing a noncommittal conclusion? Would you have drawn a stronger conclusion? What would it be?

WORKSHOP
SECTIONS

INTRODUCTION TO THE WORKSHOP SECTIONS

The four workshop sections are designed to help you perfect your writing process so that you communicate exactly what you want to say to your audience every time you write. The sections serve, more or less, as a resource center. Instead of your having to go to your instructor or a drop-in center for help in various stages of your writing process, you can "drop in" to the various sections, chapters, exercises, games, lists, or special writing activities, and solve your problems at your own pace.

You will quickly discover your own way of working through portions of the workshop sections, but the text suggests you begin alone or with a partner. Although you can certainly learn a great deal by yourself, research has shown that you learn more easily and more thoroughly using the buddy system—that is, working with someone else (a fellow student, friend, or relative). By talking through a difficulty and by using the suggestions in the workshop sections, you are sure to become quickly enlightened. By completing various exercises and checking your answers in the Suggested Answers sections, which follow each workshop section, you will soon increase your confidence in writing.

Specifically, the four workshop sections will help you with your content and organization (First Workshop Section), your writing style (Second Workshop Section), your sentence structure (Third Workshop Section), and your mechanics (Fourth Workshop Section). The more familiar you become with the various offerings in the four sections, the easier it will be for you to use them to help you; therefore, take a few minutes to read the introductions to each of the sections in order to see what each section has to offer you. It is a good idea to note particular chapters that you want to study in more detail. To make this process easy and systematic, check off the appropriate chapters on the Progress Chart found at the end of *The Independent Writer*.

Content and Organization

ABOUT THE FIRST WORKSHOP SECTION

The First Workshop Section emphasizes prewriting, drafting, and revising as it focuses attention on content and organization. If you have something worthwhile to say and if you organize your content in a logical manner, you will know that, initially, your writing works. In the other workshop sections, you can perfect your style, sentence variety, and mechanics.

Although you will soon discover your own way of working through the chapters in the First Workshop Section, you should attempt, whenever possible, to work with a partner. By talking through the various exercises with someone else, you will move through them quickly and with confidence.

The prewriting chapters (24–27) will help you locate worthwhile limited topics and supporting evidence. As well, you will learn how to compose thesis and topic statements that will help you and your reader focus on your content. The drafting chapters (28–30) will help you develop and organize your topic so that it is unified and coherent. The revising chapters (31–33) will help you edit your completed draft in order to get it ready for your intended audience.

24

Journal Writing

INTRODUCTION

As a young actor in Hollywood, Charlton Heston kept a journal. In 1978 he brought those otherwise unrecorded experiences together to create a fascinating best-seller, *The Actor's Life.*

During most of her productive life as a writer, Anaïs Nin kept an exhaustive journal where she recorded the impressions of the world as received through the network of her own sensitive nerves and emotions. The result of her efforts, which began to be published in the 1960s, runs to many volumes as *The Diary of Anaïs Nin.*

Popular children's novelist Judy Blume recently brought out a unique diary that contains no dates. Only the occasional quotation appears. Thus, she encourages the owners of her book to write down their own feelings, reactions, and sensations. She, in fact, encourages journal writing.

> *For at least ten minutes each day, in or out of class, write in your journal.*

SOME QUESTIONS AND ANSWERS

What is a journal? A book in which you write about your feelings, thoughts, and experiences.

Who will read my journal? Only you. Or anyone to whom you care to show it. Journal writing allows you to explore thoughts and ideas and to experiment with language without worrying about evaluation.

What is the point of writing in a journal? To get in touch with yourself. The more you write about your feelings, thoughts, and experiences, and the more you experiment with paragraphs, sentences, and words, the more comfortable you should be with all of your future writing assignments. As you continue your journal entries, you should become more adventurous and you should stretch your writing in untried ways so that your journal becomes more and more valuable to you. Discover your strengths; learn to develop your own unique way with words by experimenting in your journal. So that you can find a particular piece of writing quickly, you should date and label (or title) each journal entry.

Why is it necessary to write every day in my journal? Your goal should be to create a habit of writing. If you want to swim well, for example, you need to get into the water and practice swimming. Your journal writing is one way to practice your writing skills every day.

May I use any of my journal entries for other assignments? Certainly. You will find that in a future assignment you will be able to refer to your journal for an idea, a particular sentence, even a turn of phrase. Also, a journal is an ideal place to record your brainstorming ideas during your prewriting process.

What do I do with my journal at the end of the school term? That is up to you. If you have begun the habit of journal writing, you will probably keep it up long afterwards.

JOURNAL WRITING

Once you are in the habit of writing in your journal, it should not be difficult to identify something you want or need to write about. But here are some suggestions to get you started.

1. Start with one of these openings and write about *yourself*. Do not be concerned about how your piece will end—just write.

- People always thought I was strong (weak).
- I would rather not be a lender (borrower).
- I am (not) a victim of others.
- I do (not) intend to get married.
- I often (seldom) become embarrassed.

If you prefer, create your own opening.

2. Describe yourself to an imaginary reader. Tell about the following:

- Your favorite song
- Your favorite singer
- Your favorite teacher
- Your least favorite person
- Your likes and dislikes
- Your ambitions

Add to the list.

3. Recall a past event, such as one of the following, and list all the details that you can remember:

- An event from childhood

- A highly emotional event
- Your last birthday
- The most scary time of your life
- A sad event

4. Use your senses to describe the place where you are writing. Record everything you hear, see, feel, and smell. From time to time repeat this entry, but change your writing location.

5. Recall a recent newspaper headline or news item. What was your reaction?

6. Think about a familiar saying such as one of the following:

- A bird in the hand is worth two in the bush.
- Most people are nicer to total strangers than they are to their loved ones and to themselves.
- You are what you eat.
- Success is a journey, not a destination.
- With ordinary talent, and extraordinary perseverance, all things are attainable.

Explain why you agree or disagree, or describe an incident that illustrates the saying.

7. Write a piece that concludes *logically* with one of the following statements, or make up your own concluding statement *before* you begin your piece of writing.

- And the blind man in the pool said, "Life's been good to me."
- There is no such thing as a well-adjusted slave.
- No one can bring you peace but yourself.
- But she (he) promised me that she (he) would come through.
- It's impossible to go back in time.

8. You may also use your journal to practice sentence variety and sentence combining. If you would like to master a particular sentence pattern that you have studied in the Third Workshop Section, rewrite any past journal entry using that sentence pattern as often as possible. Remember, there are very few English sentence patterns to master, and once you have control of them, you will have all the tools that professional writers have. Writing with the knowledge of all of the sentence patterns is like playing tennis with a fully strung racket; writing with only a few sentence patterns at your disposal is like playing with half the strings missing.

9. To develop and enrich your writing style, you might follow the suggestions in one of the special writing assignments in the Second Workshop Section of the text, namely, Chapters 34 to 40. By practicing these assignments in your journal often, you will soon notice that your modes of expression will increase; hence, you will have a far richer writing style.

10. You might keep a portion of your journal to record your experiences of using a writing process. Comment on any of the following:

- Your attitude to writing in general and how it changes throughout the term

- Your feelings about using the prewriting, drafting, and revising stages of the process
- Your concerns about using and mastering a particular rhetorical device or sentence element
- Your improvement, as you see and feel it
- Your improvement, as you watch and listen to your editors
- Your improvement, as you note the reactions of your intended readers

> From time to time, write a running commentary in your journal of an entire assignment you are working on; for example, after you have brainstormed a topic, make a journal commentary on your brainstorming activity. After you draft the paper, comment on your drafting process, and so on.

FREEWRITING

Freewriting is a good solitary brainstorming method to generate ideas for writing assignments.

1. Begin by writing down one of the more important aspects of the human condition, such as *love*, *fear*, *death*, *greed*, *loneliness*, or *birth*. Or write the word of your broad or narrow topic, such as *abortion*, *democracy*, *the honeybee*, *China*, *Napoleon*, *the Mississippi River*. Write the word over and over until something else comes into your mind, then continue writing about that thought. Plan to write nonstop for at least ten minutes. If you get stuck, go back to writing the original word until something new comes into your mind. You may write messages to yourself about your topic, such as "I don't know enough about Napoleon and the Battle of Waterloo, so I will have to do some research before I start drafting my essay. I do know a lot about Napoleon's retreat from Moscow. . . ."

2. What are your feelings about some of the more profound theories, ideologies, religions, and so on? Start with a word like one of the following and then write: *monogamy*, *numerology*, *psychiatry*, *capitalism*, *alienation*.

INSTANT WRITING

As an alternative to solitary journal writing and freewriting, try instant writing. Practicing to write on demand at least once a week should not only prepare you to produce better exam essays (Chapter 20) but also give you an additional opportunity to have a piece of writing edited.

For each of the instant-writing exercises, plan with your partner the exact details surrounding the writing experience. Consider the following:

- The exact day and time the writing will take place
- Which of the following instant-writing exercises you will do

- How much time to allot for each session—never more than ten minutes
- How the piece of writing will be edited
- Whether a rewrite will be beneficial or desirable

Until you and your partner make up your own topics for instant-writing exercises, use the following suggestions:

1. *What's the problem?*

   - Exchange questions with your partner. Make them as personal as you wish; for example, "My father drinks a lot; I think he may be an alcoholic. What should I do?"
   - To the best of your ability, answer, in a journal entry, the question posed by your partner.

2. *What's the answer?*

   - Exchange questions with your partner, basing your questions on a course that your partner is studying; for example, "Point out two reasons why the German people accepted Hitler as their leader."
   - Answer the question you are given as though it were an exam question.

3. *If I were . . . .*

   - Use the following: "If I were _____, I'd _____." Fill in the first blank only and exchange beginnings with your partner. Use your imagination; for example, "If I were a toad, the richest person in the world, a horseshoe, or my mother, I'd . . . ."
   - Using your partner's beginning, write either a serious or humorous ending.

4. *The story isn't over.*

   - Ask your partner to choose a short story, novel, play, film, television show, or radio play with which you are both familiar. (If you do not know your partner's choice, keep asking until your partner names one you know.) Ask yourself: What will the main character in the story be doing one year after the story ends?
   - Use your imagination to extend the story. Try to copy the original style.

5. *Haiku*

   - Try your hand at writing haiku, one of the simplest verse forms. It has only three lines; the first line contains five syllables, the second seven, and the third five. The haiku is used by the Japanese for brief descriptions or to convey the essence of a mood. It can make a pleasant instant-writing exercise for you and can help you appreciate the importance of choosing words to evoke an exact image. Read these examples of Haiku, noting particularly the 5-7-5 rhythmical pattern.

   A buzzing bully,
   The Bee, possesses clover,
   A private domain.

Storm clouds in the sky,
Armed with lightning, growl warning
Of Apocalypse.

Crimson dragonfly,
As it lights, sways together
With a leaf of rye.

Note that the first and third lines *can* rhyme.

- Exchange topics for a haiku with your partner.
- Write a haiku and compare it with your partner's.

6. *Sentence patterns*

- Exchange topics and one sentence pattern with your partner; for example, "Write on the topic of abortion, using a verbal phrase in every sentence."
- The more familiar you are with the Third Workshop Section of this book, the easier you will find this exercise.

7. *A word*

- The object of this exercise is to use a given word and all related words in the piece of writing. Exchange topics and a single word with your partner; for example, "Write on the topic of mountain climbing, using the word *serene* and all words with the same root."
- You may use your dictionary if you are unfamiliar with the word or if you do not know all of the related words. Words associated with *serene* are *serenity*, *serenely*, *sereneness*.

8. *Almost freewriting*

- Although the choice of topic is not free, the procedure of this instant-writing exercise is similar to that of freewriting.
- Exchange a single word with your partner, for example, *money*, *sports*, *clothes*. The object of this exercise is to write about that word for a specified number of minutes. If you cannot think of anything to write, keep returning to the word and simply write *it* down until something comes into your mind.
- In analyzing your efforts, note how many times you were not able to think of anything to write; that is, how many times you had to list the single word.

9. *Found poetry*

- Independently, you and your partner find a part of one of the products in *The Independent Writer* (especially a sentence or two that you may not fully understand or appreciate). Exchange and rewrite the portion on a clean page as a poem. Experiment by repositioning words until you find an arrangement that either makes the meaning clear or brings forth an appreciation of the setting. You may leave out parts of a sentence or combine sentences. Read the following example of the second sentence from the product "Dawn in Calcutta" (Chapter 2):

- *Original sentence*
  It was one of those flat, grey, pre-monsoon mornings when the potholed streets, the peeling buildings and the crippled trees of the city merged one with the other so that one hardly noticed at first the sleeping bodies along the pavements.

- *Found poem*
  Morning—flat and grey.
  Potholed streets,
     Peeling buildings,
      Crippled trees.
  Bodies everywhere,
  Sleeping
       a
       l
        o
        n
         g
         the pavements.

10. *The unknown*

- With your partner arrange to write a mystery piece.
- Do not discuss the subject or the format either *before* or *during* the actual writing.
- One of you should write an opening sentence, then pass it on for the other to add a second sentence. When the second sentence is completed, pass the piece of writing back to your partner for a third sentence to be added. The assignment is completed when one of you writes "The End."
- In your evaluation discuss the effectiveness of the piece, the difficulties encountered, any errors that you detect, and so on.

25

Brainstorming

INTRODUCTION

Few writers are lucky enough to have an inspired, full-blown idea spring into their minds in a beautifully complete and organized manner. Most writers, after years of collecting information from personal experiences and observations, have only an inkling of what they want to write about their idea. In order to generate support for their idea, they use one of two methods: they either think about it by themselves, or they talk about it with several people until their idea becomes workable enough for them to begin to write their first draft. Throughout *The Independent Writer* the term *brainstorming* is used to define both of these methods. When you use the former method, you should imagine storming your own subconscious for an idea and evidence to support it. When you use the latter method, you brainstorm the subconscious of those in your "think tank" for their ideas and supporting evidence. Although both methods are valuable, two or more minds working together will usually produce a larger number of different ideas for you to consider. Furthermore, in a group brainstorming session, you may often be able to see flaws in your own thinking.

When you plan a brainstorming session (either alone or with others), allow the creative process to surround you, your writing process, and your ideas. When you brainstorm during your prewriting process, record everything that you are thinking about, no matter how obvious, ridiculous, or peculiar the idea or the supporting evidence may seem.

Note: You should engage in brainstorming sessions during your drafting and revising processes as well. Details appear in Chapters 29 and 31.

Whether you participate in a brainstorming session with an entire class led by your instructor, with a peer group, with a partner, or by yourself, you should devise a way to record your ideas. The purpose of brainstorming is for you to produce an honest, perceptive, specific, detailed, and useful collection of related ideas and supporting evidence. You do not need to attempt to organize your collection, although a certain amount of organization is often the result of a good, prewriting brainstorming session.

When you have recorded your brainstorming session, you will often be able to link certain items together, to recognize forceful details, to eliminate useless details, to see the need for further additions, and to start another brainstorming session. One thing inevitably leads to another if you allow it to. Everything you say or think contains endless possibilities for more ideas and more supporting evidence.

Note: Keep the records of your brainstorming sessions; they can be very useful during later drafting and revising sessions. If you detect a weakness in your completed paper, you may want to check earlier brainstorming notes and continue brainstorming for further ideas and supporting evidence.

There are many methods of brainstorming. For your first few papers, use as many methods as possible in order to familiarize yourself with the mechanics of each one. Ultimately you might use a combination of techniques or even devise a new one to suit your needs. There are, however, four points to remember when you brainstorm: (a) there are no rules to follow; (b) there is no special order to follow; (c) record everything you think of about your topic; and (d) keep everything. As a result of a thorough prewriting brainstorming session, you will have a mass of material, all of which is related in some way to your topic.

The following exercises are designed for you to learn specific brainstorming techniques; they are organized into three types:

1. Those that help you generate ideas to clarify and limit your topic

2. Those that help you generate supporting evidence for a chosen topic

3. Those that help you organize your thinking, as well as generate ideas to limit or develop your topic

How you implement the various brainstorming techniques in your prewriting process (by yourself or with others) will depend on your needs.

Note: To learn how to benefit from using all of the brainstorming methods, you should do the following exercises with at least one other person. By asking each other questions, you can easily clear up anything that may confuse you.

BRAINSTORMING TECHNIQUES THAT HELP YOU CLARIFY OR LIMIT YOUR TOPIC

EXERCISE ONE
Think/Write

This exercise is especially useful when you are alone and know *you will soon begin to write an assignment.*

Most of *The Independent Writer* emphasizes that you go through various steps as you write. Because *content* is the most important aspect of your writing, in the first step of your writing process you should generate an idea and then refine and enrich it so that you can develop it fully.

Professional writers are seldom told what to write about; they create their own ideas. With this in mind, you should reflect on where ideas come from. After reading the following excerpt from Dr. Wayne Dyer's *Pulling Your Own Strings*, you should have no reason to say, "I can't think of anything to write about."

... the storage capacity of your grapefruit-sized brain is staggering—conservatively estimated at ten billion units of information. If you want to find out what you *do* know, Michael Phillips suggests this little exercise. "Suppose that you sat down with paper and pencil to write out everything you remembered, including names of people you know or have heard about, experiences from childhood on, plots of books and films, descriptions of jobs you've held, your hobbies, and so on." But you'd better have a lot of time for proving this point to yourself because, as Phillips goes on to say, "If you wrote 24 hours a day, you'd be at it for an estimated two thousand years."

Take a few minutes for you and your partner to list some of the things that have been on your minds—things that concern you. They may be about society, the environment, politics, or about very personal problems.

Share with your partner a topic from your list that you have been thinking about and would like to write about. Explain why you want to write about it. For whom would you like to write? You might like to use one of the many brainstorming techniques in this chapter to develop your topic, rather than begin to draft your paper immediately.

EXERCISE TWO
Talk/Write

This exercise is especially useful if you like to talk through your ideas, rather than write them out.

Sometimes you can brainstorm a topic by talking with one or more people. By listening to other people voice their opinions, you are often able to clarify your own opinions. Where do you do your best brainstorming: in a classroom, around your dinner table, at a party?

Choose a topic from one of those sessions, and brainstorm it by talking about it with your partner. If you cannot think of a topic, look over the following list. Find one on which the two of you have differing opinions, and brainstorm it to the point where you could use it for an assignment. Before you draft, however, you might like to brainstorm further by using one or two other techniques.

- Should both men and women be allowed maternity leave from work after the birth of their child?
- Should credit cards be banned?
- Is there anything wrong with being bisexual?
- Should service-sector personnel (bus drivers, pilots, post office, and telephone workers) be allowed to strike?

EXERCISE THREE
See/Write

This exercise is especially useful if you would like to write about a number of activities that you see.

Tell your partner about something that you see on a regular basis—for example, a particular sports event, a television show, and so on. Why specifically do you watch the event or show? What events or shows would you not see on a regular basis? Why?

Share with your partner something you have seen recently that you would like to write about. To whom do you want to write? Why?

Afterwards, you may like to participate in another brainstorming activity to find more supporting evidence for your ideas.

EXERCISE FOUR
Experience/Write

This exercise is especially useful if you want to write about a number of activities that you are involved in.

Tell your partner about some of the things that you enjoy doing—for example, dancing in your favorite disco, hunting, making something with your hands, and so on. What about the experience do you particularly enjoy? Why? What are some of the things that you do not enjoy—for example, having a tooth filled, eating raw oysters, doing a repetitive job, and so on? What about the experience do you particularly dislike? Why?

Share with your partner something you have experienced that you would like to write about. It may be something that you enjoyed or disliked. To whom do you want to write? Why?

Afterwards, you may like to participate in another brainstorming activity to find more supporting evidence for your ideas.

EXERCISE FIVE
Read/Write

This exercise is especially useful if you want to write about what you have read.

Tell your partner about your reading habits. Which newspaper do you read? What parts of the paper do you read regularly? Do you have favorite columnists? Which magazines do you read? Other than required course books, name the last three books you have read. Who are your favorite authors? Why are they your favorites?

Share with your partner something you have read recently that you would like to write about. To whom do you want to write? Why?

Afterwards, you may like to participate in another brainstorming activity to flesh out your ideas.

EXERCISE SIX
Assign/Write

This exercise is especially useful in helping you write an assignment quickly.

As a student, you will use this method in most of your classes. Chapter 20, "Exam Essays," offers several useful suggestions on how to write on an *assigned* topic.

If you have such an assignment coming up for one of your courses, ask your partner to predict an essay question. Explain how you would attempt to answer it. Perhaps you might then participate in one or two other brainstorming techniques in order to accumulate more supporting evidence and to make drafting easier.

EXERCISE SEVEN
Write/Write

This exercise is especially useful in finding out what you want to write about.

A number of writers believe that they do not know what they want to write about until they start to write. In fact, they write to *find* a topic. If you have begun to keep a daily journal, perhaps you know how it feels to sit down without a thought in your head and write. As you write, however, thoughts do come. From a ten-minute session of journal writing, a worthwhile idea might emerge. By pursuing an idea that seems a possible writing topic, you write all your thoughts about that idea as they occur to you.

One of the most important brainstorming sessions you can engage in, therefore, is to keep a daily journal. (See Chapter 24 for more details.)

EXERCISE EIGHT
Free Association Cluster

This exercise is especially useful in gathering more ideas that can produce a limited topic to write about.

Free Association is similar to playing a word association game. In word association you say the first word that comes into your mind when you hear a word; for example, "What is the first word you think of when you hear *fire, cat, vegetable*?" In Free Association, on the other hand, you continue generating words or phrases from your own responses; for example, to *fire* you might add *engine*, to *engine* you might add *siren*, to *siren* you might add *don't like loud noises*, and so on until you have a mass of material.

If you get stuck along the way, go back to an earlier word and begin the process again; for example, to *engine* you might add *good condition*, and then continue the Free Association technique from this response.

So that you do not lose any of your material, gather it by using a clustering method similar to the partial Free Association Cluster on page 287. Note that the cluster began with the word *fire*; if you wish, continue the clustering process.

When you complete a Free Association Cluster, connect various entries to see if you can come up with a suitable limited topic for a writing assignment. What from the cluster shown here might be a suitable limited topic? When you have a limited topic, choose one or two other brainstorming techniques to gather supporting evidence.

After choosing the same word as your partner, independently begin a Free Association Cluster. Keep the cluster going until you come across a topic that might be a worthwhile limited topic. Afterwards, compare your limited topics and clusters. If you cannot agree on a word, use *ladder, money,* or *health.*

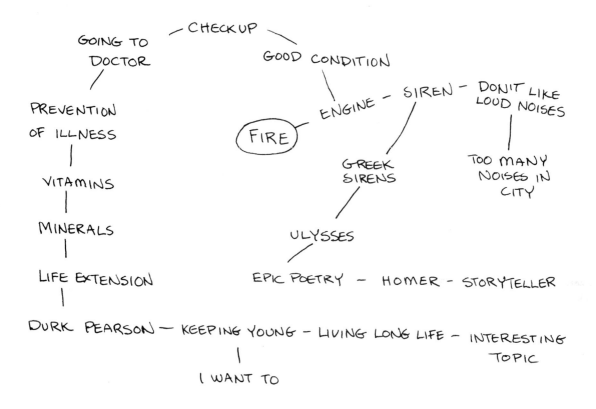

EXERCISE NINE
Absurd Analogies

This exercise is especially useful for creative writing projects, poetry, short stories, drama, narratives, reviews, and literary analyses.

When you start to compose a paper in earnest, you may illustrate an idea, problem, or event by using analogy; in other words, comparing something unknown (or imprecisely known) to something known. You are encouraged to write in your journal, using Absurd Analogies as a brainstorming technique. Compare your topic to anything—literally *anything*. Do not be concerned about creating a false analogy (one that cannot be compared or tries to prove instead of illustrating); the purpose of this exercise is for you to stimulate your imagination and have some fun.

When you create an Absurd Analogy, list an aspect of your topic (thing, activity, problem, event) and say that it "is like" another thing, activity, problem, or event that you know. For his topic on "Heroin," in the Introductory Assignment of this text, student Joe Davis compared the act of a junkie's finding cash for heroin to sports fishing, to eating a chocolate sundae, to running a marathon, and to building a tree house. "How absurd!" you may be saying. "There is nothing that these acts have in common with heroin addicts." Nonetheless, Joe continued to work on his Absurd

Analogies. Read the results of one of them. He began with "A junkie's finding cash for heroin is like a sportsman's fishing." Then he started to break down the activity of sports fishing into its parts.

For example:

> being full of expectations
> wanting to make a big catch
> looking into the dark water
> putting on bait
> throwing in the line
> waiting
> having lots of free time
> hooking a fish ...

To write an Absurd Analogy, you should use many of the terms and suggestions from your list to describe the activity of your topic in terms of the analogy. Read what Joe produced.

> A junkie's finding cash for heroin is like a sportsman's fishing. When a junkie baits his hook to catch the unsuspecting, he'll use any line to lure his prey into his net. When he catches his fish, he'll not let go, even if the victim gasps and tries to slither to safety.
>
> After he has picked the bones clean, the junkie will toss aside the skeleton of his poor fish. Ever ready for his next catch of the day, the addict waits patiently to snare from the sea of humanity anything that stirs: a whale loaded with blubber, a stupid sucker, a young fry . . . .

Absurd Analogies are fun; they test your creative powers. You may also unearth new and pertinent ideas, as well as hit on an interesting way to develop your topic.

Produce a few Absurd Analogies for an aspect of a topic of your choice. Ask some of your peers to read them over so that you can get their reactions. If you cannot think of a topic and an Absurd Analogy, choose one from the first column and then one from the second.

POSSIBLE TOPICS	ABSURD ANALOGIES
Writing an essay	Eating an ice cream sundae
Disney World	Peeling a grape
The crisis in the Middle East	Getting a vaccination
A computer	A canoe
A problem you have	Any musical instrument
Break dancing	Playing cards (poker, bridge)

What parts of your Absurd Analogies would you find most useful if you were to begin writing? What parts would not be useful? Why? What could you do to make those parts more useful—compose another Absurd Analogy or choose another brainstorming technique?

BRAINSTORMING TECHNIQUES THAT HELP YOU GENERATE SUPPORTING EVIDENCE

EXERCISE TEN
Random Lists

This exercise is especially useful for gathering a great deal of supporting evidence.

To ensure that you do not forget to do certain things, perhaps you have already begun the habit of making lists—for example, a Christmas list, a packing list, a preparation list, and so on. The random order of the list usually depends on which item or person you thought of first and which you thought of last. If a special order is important to the list, you will recopy the list according to a plan that serves your needs—for instance, from particular to general, chronological, climactic, sequential, and so on (see Chapter 29).

Making a Random List can also help you gather supporting evidence for a future piece of writing. Assume that you and your partner have to write a paragraph to explain how you prepare to move, study chemistry, or prepare for a trip. Independently, make a Random List of about twenty items. Afterwards, compare your lists to see if you have thought of the same items. You might like to suggest a method of reordering the items as they would appear in the paragraph.

Do you now have enough material to begin your drafting process, or should you participate in another brainstorming session?

EXERCISE ELEVEN
Senses Cluster

This exercise is especially useful for descriptive and narrative prose, literary analysis, reviews, poetry, and drama.

By creatively thinking about your topic and its sound, sight, taste, smell, and feel, you will often enrich an otherwise drab piece of writing. To help you gather words and phrases that link and extend your topic and senses, jot them down in the form of a cluster. How detailed your Senses Cluster will be depends on how creatively you, and those helping you, brainstorm. Before he wrote his introductory assignment, Joe Davis produced the following Senses Cluster about a junkie. Can you add to it?

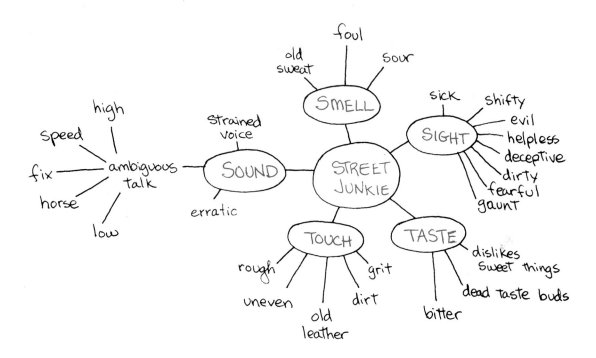

After choosing a specific topic that you might use for a piece of writing, enrich it by using a Senses Cluster. If you cannot think of a topic, use: a piece of cake, a break dancer, the hero of a specific movie, or a particular location around your campus.

What parts of your Senses Cluster would you find most useful if you were to begin writing? What parts would not be useful? Why? What could you do to make those parts more useful—continue the Senses Cluster more creatively, or choose another brainstorming technique?

EXERCISE TWELVE
Positive/Negative/Neutral Pigeonholes

This exercise is especially useful in developing observation techniques, narrative essays, comparison/contrast essays, argumentative and persuasive writing, and literary analysis.

When you are trying to add details to an incident or event, you might find it useful to list all the associations (events, characters, conflict, dialogue, setting, descriptions, and so on) in three columns with several pigeonhole boxes under them. In the "Positive" column include good, happy, warm, and fun associations; in the "Negative" column include bad, sad, frightening, and angry ones; in the "Neutral" column include vague or inconsequential ones. Probe deeply.

Record the events as they occur to you. Do not worry about logical order. Examine the following partial results of a Positive/Negative/Neutral brainstorming session on the topic of a student's fear of basements.

POSITIVE	NEGATIVE	NEUTRAL
Not frightened with Father	Ghosts waited for me	Did ghosts really live in basement?
Food in freezer	Worse fear with a friend	Pretended not to hear Mother
Happy to be upstairs	Creaks and groans	Pretended to be ill
Lights turned on	Still fear dark and basements	Is fear of the basement justifiable today?

After you complete the session, try to connect some of the pigeonholes because they may have a comparison/contrast or cause/effect relationship. Note the above connecting lines. What relationship between the items do the lines indicate? Can you draw further connecting lines?

After choosing a specific topic that you might use for a piece of writing, enrich it by using Positive/Negative/Neutral Pigeonholes. When you finish, connect some of the pigeonholes by drawing relationship lines. If you cannot think of a topic, use: watching a movie on a home video, an incident that recently happened to a friend of yours, a holiday, a family conflict, or an incident that you empathized with in a movie you saw.

What results of your brainstorming session would you find most useful if you were to begin writing? What parts would not be useful? Why? What could you do to make those parts more useful—continue adding more pigeonholes or relationship lines, or add one or both of the next two brainstorming techniques?

EXERCISE THIRTEEN
Positive Cluster

This exercise is especially useful for argumentative and persuasive writing.

To probe your limited topic deeply, you might select a single point of view and think only of your topic and its positive associations. Notice how one student decided to connect his topic of "The Rewards of Going Back to School" to seven positive characteristics of the human condition. Can you add to this partial Positive Cluster?

After choosing a limited topic that you might use for a piece of writing, enrich it by using a Positive Cluster. Use the same seven aspects of the human condition as in the cluster shown here, or choose your own positive divisions. If you cannot think of a topic, choose one of the suggested topics in Exercise Twelve.

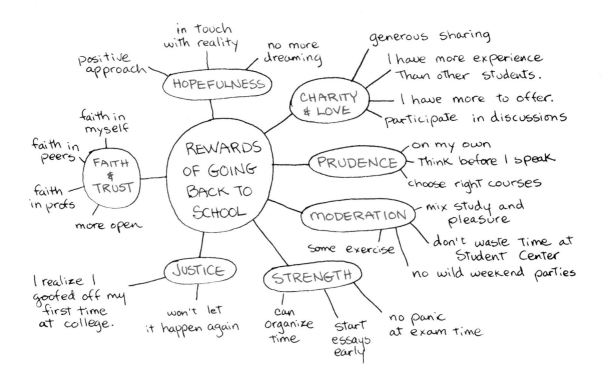

What parts of your Positive Cluster would you find most useful if you were to begin writing? What parts would not be useful? Why? What could you do to make those parts more useful—add more details to one or more arms of your cluster, or choose another brainstorming technique (such as the Negative Mandala)?

EXERCISE FOURTEEN
Negative Mandala

This exercise is especially useful for argumentative and persuasive writing.
  When you brainstorm, you can use just about any organizational device to record your ideas. By focusing only on the negative aspects of your limited topic and by recording them in the form of a mandala, you will already be thinking about the organization of your piece of writing. If you were to focus on the negative aspects of the same topic you used in the previous exercise, you could collect supporting

evidence for a good contrast paper. You could use, for example, the topic "The Negative Aspects of Going Back to School." Notice how one student decided to connect this topic to seven negative characteristics of the human condition. Can you add to this partial Negative Mandala?

LAZINESS

BOREDOM

- not interested in student politics and clubs
- not much relevance to real world in school work
- rather be doing fun things than homework
- info easier to get from TV than from books

ANGER

- Young students annoy me sometimes.
- too many assignments due on same date
- happens too often

OVERWORK

- Profs expect too much.
- Just too much to learn in one term

THE NEGATIVE ASPECTS OF GOING BACK TO SCHOOL

- Some students find studying easy.
- Many students already know each other and are friends.

ENVY

- I feel like I'm in prison: cells, bells, security guards.
- prescribed lessons & texts
- everyone expected to learn at same speed

RESTRICTIONS

- Some Profs talk down to students.
- I have more experience than most students.

EXCESSIVE PRIDE

After choosing a limited topic that you might use for a piece of writing, enrich it by using a Negative Mandala. Use the same seven aspects of the human condition as the mandala shown here, or choose your own negative subheadings. If you cannot think of a topic, choose from the ones in Exercise Twelve.

What parts of your Negative Mandala would you find most useful if you were to begin writing? What parts would not be useful? Why? What could you do to make those parts more useful—add more details to one or more sections of the mandala, or choose another brainstorming technique (such as the Positive Cluster)?

EXERCISE FIFTEEN
Pentad Cluster

This exercise is especially useful in narratives, literary analyses, short stories, and plays.

Specific details will make a story memorable; therefore, probe deeply in order to record all your thoughts. The Pentad (devised by Kenneth Burke) allows you to explore five aspects of a topic:

- Act—What was done?
- Agent—Who did it?
- Agency—By what means or with what was it done?
- Scene—Where and when was it done?
- Purpose—Why was it done?

In order to see how to use the Pentad, study the following partial cluster based on the topic "Traveling from France to Spain." Can you add to the Pentad Cluster?

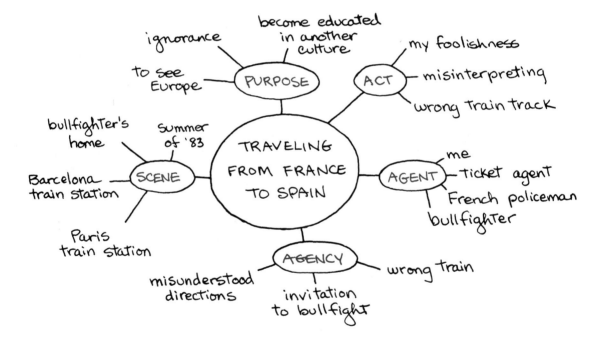

After choosing a specific topic that you might use for a piece of writing, enrich it by using a Pentad Cluster. Use the same five points as the above cluster. If you cannot think of a topic, use: a conflict that you were involved in, your first or last day of high school, the first or last meeting of someone close to you, or a visit to the dentist.

What parts of your Pentad Cluster would you find most useful if you were to begin writing? What parts would not be useful? Why? What could you do to make those parts more useful—add more details to one or more of the arms of the cluster, or choose another brainstorming technique?

EXERCISE SIXTEEN
The Pentad Connection

This exercise is especially useful in developing literary essays.

Assuming that you know the basic mechanics of the Pentad, you are ready to work on this brainstorming technique to examine short stories, novels, and plays.

First, use the five points of the Pentad in order to understand the plot line or "surface" of the story. If you do not know exactly what is going on *in the lines* of the piece of literature, you will find it very difficult to know what is going on *between the lines*. Because you are now using the Pentad as part of your *reading process*, note how different the questions are from those in Exercise Fifteen.

• PLOT (ACT):	What happens?
• CHARACTERS (AGENTS):	Who are the characters and what sort of people are they?
• SCENE (SCENE):	What is the specific setting—time, place, atmosphere?
• FORM & LANGUAGE (AGENCY):	What literary devices and style does the author use?
• MOTIVATION (PURPOSE):	Why do the characters do what they do?

Apply the Pentad to the short story, "The Story of an Hour," found in the Appendix of *The Independent Writer*. When you have finished, you should have a reasonable understanding of the text of the story. Now use the Pentad Connection to analyze the subtext. In this method of brainstorming, you are encouraged to connect two parts of the Pentad, seeing how one part interrelates with the other in order to get a deeper meaning of the story; for example, when you have established the plot as simply as you can, connect it to the "characters" to see how they make the plot more relevant. Then connect the plot to the "scene" to see how it makes the plot more relevant, and so on with "form and language" and "motivation."

When you have done this for the plot, go through the same routine with the other four parts of the Pentad. When you finish the Pentad Connection, you will have twenty brainstorming entries, each one shedding light on the subtext of the piece of literature you are reading.

Without doubt, using the Pentad Connection will prepare you to discuss the piece of literature with others, to listen to a lecture by your literature instructor, and to become an independent reader, developing in your own mind a fuller interpretation of what you have read.

You should now do a cluster of a Pentad Connection for "The Story of an Hour." When you finish yours, compare it with the one on page 296, noting the differences. Remember, the purpose of this brainstorming session is to clarify *your* thinking, not that of others. To a casual onlooker, such a cluster looks like nonsense; to you, it's the beginning of a literary essay.

All characters believe Mrs. M dies of joy at seeing her husband alive. We know she dies of grief and the instant loss of her freedom.

CHARACTERS

Chopin alludes to the fact that in all marriages one partner must give up freedom. Her story demonstrates the results of marriage.

PLOT

The reader discovers characterization more from what is not said than what is said.

CHARACTERS

SCENE

Chopin spends most of her energies in painting a precise setting. Then she merely places her plot & characters into this setting.

MOTIVATION

In order to understand the story and why Mrs. M dies, the reader must read and think about each short paragraph.

FORM & LANGUAGE

Extremely short paragraphs, heavy emphasis on description, little dialogue.

Each paragraph forwards the story at a tremendous pace; e.g., penultimate paragraph: the protagonist dies.

PLOT

The setting symbolizes Mrs. M's behavior clearly.

SCENE

FORM & LANGUAGE

Although the reader does not predict the surprise ending, he/she reads with the feeling of suspense. Each short paragraph brings the reader closer to a full understanding of Mrs. M's actions.

They all misinterpret Mrs. M's "monstrous joy."

CHARACTERS

SCENE — The setting of the enclosed, locked room and the open, inviting window represent Mrs. Mallard's story. Springtime and new growth invite her to freedom.

FORM & LANGUAGE — By writing from Mrs. M's point of view, Chopin invites us to understand the significance of the plot.

MOTIVATION

Mrs. M goes into her room, away from her sister & Richards. She takes us with her so that we can see her mixed feelings: sadness at the loss of her husband, joy that she's now free.

Mrs. M has been stifled through her whole marriage to Mr. M. When she thinks he dies, she's filled with joy for her future.

MOTIVATION

Mrs. Mallard finds out her husband dies & feels free; she discovers him alive and dies.

PLOT

THE STORY OF AN HOUR

FORM & LANGUAGE

PLOT

The story and the setting can easily be divided into two: those that represent freedom & those that represent bondage.

SCENE

Springtime in a well-to-do home. Mrs. M's room with its open window facing an open square is the main setting.

CHARACTERS

FORM & LANGUAGE

The author has emphasized setting more than characterization and plot so that the reader can imagine the characters more and can feel the full impact of the events of the story.

The closed room symbolizes Mrs. M's life with Mr. M.

The open window symbolizes her joyous future.

CHARACTERS

MOTIVATION

Josephine really doesn't know her sister. Both she and Richards protect Mrs. M for the wrong reasons.

MOTIVATION

The setting clearly demonstrates why Mrs. M reacts the way she does. It is obvious that she has spent many hours in front of her open window— hoping & praying for freedom.

Mrs. Mallard— weak heart
Josephine - her helpful sister
Richards - friend of Mr. M
Mr. Mallard - dominated Mrs. M

PLOT

Demonstrates the eternal battle of the sexes - also how people misinterpret other's actions and reactions.

SCENE

The setting indicates a well-to-do family. The closed room reveals Mrs. M's true feelings.

FORM & LANGUAGE

Even though the story deals with freedom & death, there is very little action and dialogue. The reader is able to imagine past events that have formed the characters.

EXERCISE SEVENTEEN
Four-Faces-of-Knowledge Cluster

This exercise is especially useful for developing informative essays, research papers, feature articles, reports, proposals, résumés and letters of application.

When working on this brainstorming technique, use the following faces:

☺ I know everything about this aspect of the topic.

🙂 I feel pretty confident about this aspect of the topic.

😐 I'm a little shaky about this aspect of the topic.

🙁 I don't know anything about this aspect of the topic.

Examine this partial Four-Faces-of-Knowledge Cluster on the topic of "English Invasions" before you do yours.

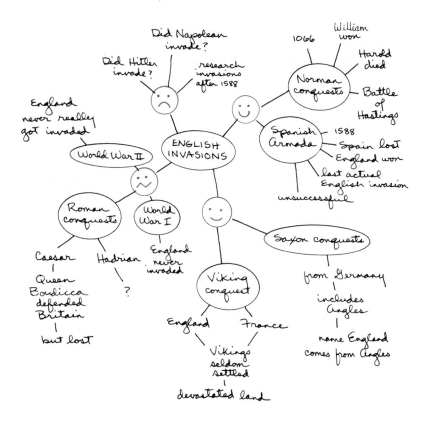

After choosing a limited topic that you might use for a piece of writing, develop it by using a Four-Faces-of-Knowledge Cluster. If you cannot think of a topic, use: the

Jacksons' Victory Tour, acupuncture in the United States, or the victories of a favorite sports champion.

After completing your Four-Faces-of-Knowledge Cluster, discuss with your partner what you need to research before you begin a draft. As well, talk about where you would go for information—library, newspapers, people, computer data bank.

BRAINSTORMING TECHNIQUES THAT HELP YOU ORGANIZE WHILE YOU GENERATE IDEAS

Perhaps nothing in your writing process ever fits neatly into perfect steps. You may blend two steps, repeat one, or move from drafting back to brainstorming. The following brainstorming methods are useful in generating ideas, but you might like to do them in conjunction with other brainstorming techniques. These methods have a built-in bonus that will help you during your drafting process. If done thoroughly, they will practically organize your paper for you.

EXERCISE EIGHTEEN
The Pro/Con Ladder

This exercise is especially useful in developing the argumentative essay.

On a piece of paper draw two ladders, each with ten rungs. Label one ladder "Pro" to indicate support *for* your argument; the other "Con" to indicate support *against* your argument. Under the ladders draw a box in which you will write your limited topic. By filling in as many rungs as you can on *both* ladders, you will see your argument from both your point of view and your reader's. Thus, when you draft, you will not be able to ignore your reader's viewpoint. Study the following partial Pro/Con Ladder. Can you complete it by adding fictional details?

After choosing a limited topic that you might use for a piece of writing, develop it by using a Pro/Con Ladder. If you cannot think of a topic, use: "My brother/sister should quit drinking," "I should get a job," "I should buy a car."

What parts of your Pro/Con Ladder would you find most useful if you were to begin writing? What parts would not be useful? Why? What could you do to make those parts more useful—add more rungs on the ladder, or choose another brainstorming technique?

In addition to the brainstorming ideas in this exercise, spend time on working through the prewriting suggestions found in Chapter 8.

EXERCISE NINETEEN
Aristotle's Topics

This exercise is especially useful in developing comparative/contrast or cause/effect essays.

In his *Rhetoric* Aristotle provided instructions for public speakers in fifth-century B.C. Greece. Today you can still use his "topics" to organize your ideas. Put simply, you should define your limited topic, compare and contrast it, point out its cause and effect relationship, and provide evidence to support your idea.

Before you work on this brainstorming technique, examine Joe Davis's treatment of Aristotle's Topics in the Introductory Assignment, page 12. Then make a similar list on some aspect of a topic of your choice. Try to provide as many related ideas as you can, even though you may not use them in your final piece of writing. If you cannot think of a topic, use one of these: attending college or university, moving oil by tanker or pipeline, democracy in America and in Argentina, or blacks in America and South Africa.

What parts of your list would you find most useful if you were to begin writing? What parts would not be useful? Why? What could you do to make those parts more useful—continue probing your mind, use a portion of Aristotle's Topics, or choose another brainstorming technique?

EXERCISE TWENTY
Newspaper Reporter's Questions

This exercise is especially useful in developing expository papers—informative, argumentative, and persuasive.

By using the traditional newspaper reporter's investigation techniques in relation to your topic, you could produce an extensive and useful list of supporting evidence. Before he started on his controversial argumentative essay on the limited topic of legalizing heroin, Joe Davis produced the following extensive list by using the Newspaper Reporter's Questions. As you examine the Who-What-When-Where-Why-How list, note its details and its usefulness.

Legalizing Heroin

WHO?street junkies/registered addicts/pushers/black marketeers/victims

1. What kind of people are involved with the problem?

   • Literally everyone is affected if we do not legalize heroin.

2. How does this affect the problem?

   • Need leadership to solve the problem

3. How much do the involved parties mean to one another?

   • Black market gets fat off suffering addicts.
   • Government doesn't care enough.

4. What is each person's relationship to the problem?

   • Street addict would love legalization.
   • Registered addict knows it works.
   • Pushers and black market will be out of luck.
   • Government concentrates on the black market.
   • No more victims.

5. Is the problem of equal importance to everyone involved?

   • Definitely not

6. Who has the most at stake?

   • Desperate addicts

7. How do others see the problem?

   • Great Britain recognizes benefits of legalizing heroin.
   • East Europe is overwhelmed.
   • Turkey locks up addicts and throws away the key.
   • Some South American countries get rich on heroin sales and want the problem to remain.

8. Are the same people involved with the problem now as when it started?

   • More people are involved
   • Organized crime is involved
   • Other countries get rich at America's expense.

9. Are there more or fewer people involved?

   • Since heroin was made illegal in the 1920s, the problem has increased; therefore, more people are involved.

WHAT? heroin/methadone/money/crime/prostitution/murder
1. What are the details of the problem?

  - Illegal heroin results in crime.
  - Legal heroin reduces crime.

2. Do all those involved agree on what the details are?

  - Obviously not; therein lies the problem.

3. Are some details more important than others?

  - Most would like to ignore the problem and pretend it doesn't exist.
  - We all pay a heavy price; our society would be different if heroin were legalized.

4. Is there a particular order of details?

  - Street junkie, then registered addict, then addict on methadone, then someone who has kicked the habit

WHEN? timelessness/present/past
1. Why is time important to the problem?

  - Because heroin addiction is on the rise
  - Because crime is running rampant

2. How does time affect the problem?

  - Drug addiction is becoming an accepted institution in America.
  - Institutions are hard to topple.

3. When is a bad/good time for the problem?

  - Now is a good time to legalize heroin and topple the black market.

4. Does the problem have a general chronology?

  - Heroin made illegal in the 1920s
  - Black market and pushers and crime increased
  - Powerful and rich people involved
  - Laundered money, huge bank accounts exist
  - Young people lured into addiction
  - Americans fear heroin and its effects.

WHERE? back alleys and cheap hotel rooms/sanitary clinics
1. Does the problem always occur in the same place?

  - All over, in all walks of life

2. Does problem reside mostly with you and/or others involved with it?

  - Not me directly, but I am concerned about being burglarized by a crazed junkie.

3. Does it only exist where you are?

  - I think heroin addiction exists all over America.

4. Does it get better in some places?

- Great Britain

5. Worse in others?

- Turkey, Mexico, Russia?

6. What and who determine where it occurs?

- Lack of government direction keeps America filled with street junkies.
- Black market preys on addicts and innocents.

7. Does the place of occurrence contribute anything to the problem?

- Street junkies feel total abandonment.
- A registered addict is aware of the return of self-worth.

WHY? reasons surrounding problems

1. Why does the problem exist?

- Prohibition caused heroin to go underground.
- Out of control of proper authorities
- In control of criminals

2. Is someone allowing the problem to continue?

- The government and the American people

3. Why does it qualify as a problem?

- Because heroin causes so much suffering

4. Why does it continue?

- Because the government concentrates efforts on dealers and ignores addicts

5. Why will it eventually end?

- When Americans have had enough

6. Why will it perhaps never end?

- If the dealers gain more power

7. Why don't we end it right now?

- Not enough people are protesting.
- The government isn't taking the initiative.

HOW? do anything for a fix

1. How does the problem happen?

- Addicts can't support their habit by honest means; therefore, they resort to crime.

2. How could it be prevented?

- Heroin could be freely given to registered addicts.

3. Who causes it? How? What causes it? How?

- Dealers because of their action
- Government because of its inaction

4. Is there a sequence of events that makes it happen?

- By legalizing heroin, the government could destroy most of the illicit drug-dealing and crime-related activities.

5. How are they related?

- Through normal cause and effect

6. How did it begin?

- Government made heroin illegal

7. How did/will it end?

- Government will have to make heroin legal to registered addicts.

Make a similar Who-What-When-Where-Why-How list on a narrow topic of your choice. Remember, try not to be superficial, but keep asking a series of related questions similar to the above list. If you cannot think of a topic, use: a current social problem in your community, a family conflict, an incident involving one of your faults or weaknesses, or a topic that you have to write about for a subject other than English.

What parts of your list would you find most useful if you were to begin writing? What parts would not be useful? Why? What could you do to make those parts more useful—continue one aspect of the list more creatively, or choose another brainstorming technique?

EXERCISE TWENTY-ONE
Seven Controlling Questions

This exercise is especially useful for informative and argumentative papers, research reports, and term papers for noncomposition courses.

Use the brainstorming technique of Seven Controlling Questions *after* you have gathered all of your supporting evidence through using other brainstorming methods. This technique can act as a means not only to let you know if you have enough support to develop your limited topic, but also to provide an organizational tool for your drafting process. A brainstorming session in which you use the Seven Controlling Questions should result in your composing a single question that controls your entire essay.

For her paper on "Dyslexia," a writer answered the following questions (substitute "dyslexia" or "dyslexic student" for X):

1. What are the causes of X?

2. What are the theories of X?

3. What are the characteristics or symptoms of X?

4. What are the capacities for and likelihood of change in X; and what are the effects of any change in X?

5. What are the characteristics of the family or social group of X?

6. What are the similarities or differences in X, depending on the environment?

7. What is the history of X?

Using the material gathered from other brainstorming sessions, the writer was able to answer all the questions. After answering them, she decided to focus on Questions 3 and 4 and write her paper on the controlling question: "How can a student with dyslexia obtain a bachelor of science degree?" At this early point in her prewriting process, she intended to present the characteristics and symptoms of dyslexia from personal experience (she is dyslexic), and to demonstrate how a student with this handicap could—with the cooperation of the counseling department and the professors—study, complete class projects, sit for exams, and write term papers.

After choosing a limited topic that you might use for a piece of writing and after gathering a certain amount of supporting evidence through other brainstorming methods, apply the Seven Controlling Questions to your material so that you come up with *one* question that controls your entire essay. Use the same seven questions listed above; however, substitute your limited topic for X. If you cannot think of a topic, use: a problem that you are trying to work through, a topic that has been assigned in a noncomposition class, a disability, a moral dilemma, or a religious matter.

From the Seven Controlling Questions that you used, which question or combination of questions was most useful in allowing you to come up with a new question to control your essay? What is your controlling question? What method of organization can you use to develop your controlling question? (See Chapter 29.)

EXERCISE TWENTY-TWO
Flowchart

This exercise is especially useful in limiting topics and organizing most writing involving classification and division and cause and effect.
You and your partner should spend time examining the prewriting suggestions in Chapters 7 and 9 in order to see how the use of flowcharts can produce a limited topic, supporting evidence, and a method of organization. Afterwards, practice making several flowcharts on topics of your choice.

EXERCISE TWENTY-THREE
Brainstorming Across The Curriculum

Make sure you do this exercise with a workshop partner so that you can discuss your results in detail.
To illustrate how you would write on the same topic for several courses, spend a few minutes brainstorming one of the following broad topics: babies, jewelry, sailboats, sex, the pyramids, or peas.

Assume that you are to write five different papers *on the same topic* for five different courses. Choose one of the topics and five of the following courses: anthropology, anatomy, sociology, biology, physics, chemistry, zoology, philosophy, graphic arts, geography, history, humanities, literature, computer science, business administration, mathematics, religious studies, music criticism, theatre history, psychology, health, political science, journalism, art criticism, economics, or any other course you may be taking.

Keeping in mind the course you are writing for, narrow your topic to a workable thesis statement or a question that limits or controls your paper. Because this brainstorming exercise is experimental and because you will probably not complete any of these papers, stretch your imagination to create limited topics that are as dissimilar as possible. *Keep in mind that the purpose of this brainstorming activity is for you to apply what you have been learning in your composition class to courses across your curriculum.* When you have narrowed your topic, invent a purpose, a suitable format, an appropriate audience, and real or imagined situations for your proposed pieces of writing. For example, note how one student narrowed the broad topic "babies":

> *Psychology*: A research paper that illustrates "What would a male child of six be like if he were raised by apes from the time he was a baby?" After reading *Tarzan: Lord of the Apes*, I decided to investigate whether such a thing were possible. My psychology professor has required that we write to our fellow class members.

> *Sociology*: A term paper to point out the effects of the baby boom in our state on the educational facilities, with suggestions to the Board of Education about what it should do to prepare for the children's proper education.

> *Nursing*: A report to prove that a fetus aborted at twelve weeks has the same number of cells as a full-term baby. I will write to members of pro-choice organizations.

> *Art History*: An essay analyzing the main characteristics of artists' treatment of babies in early Renaissance paintings. My professor is an authority on this period, so I will have to do thorough research, as well as offer my own detailed observations.

> *Anatomy*: A formal laboratory report to determine the effects of certain stimuli on babies during their first five days of life in a hospital nursery. Because my readers will be my professor and fellow students, I must provide an exact description of my methods so that they could replicate my procedures.

Once you have narrowed a single topic for use in five different courses, choose one and continue to limit the topic, give it direction, and focus it so that you can develop an original piece of writing from a strong point of view. You will succeed by engaging in one or two of the many brainstorming techniques discussed in foregoing exercises.

When you write a paper for a humanities or science course, you usually do not know everything you want to say *before* you brainstorm, let alone before you compose. Therefore, as you brainstorm, keep limiting your topic. Always record both the things you know and those you need to find out. A question mark (?) next to an idea from a brainstorming session is a useful device to indicate what you have to research. Through experimenting and researching, as well as through writing a few early drafts of your paper, you will discover additional gaps in your knowledge. You should quickly realize the truth in the maxim that people write to discover what they want to say. So never start to write your paper until you have completed a few solid brainstorming sessions.

In the following partial cluster, examine the student's use of the Newspaper Reporter's Questions from Exercise Twenty for the topic of the effects of certain stimuli on babies during their first five days of life in a hospital nursery.

The results of such a brainstorming session will soon show you which items to delete because they seem unimportant, which to emphasize, and which to research. Also, you may discover important relationships forming (causes and effects, comparisons and contrasts) that will help you organize your piece of writing.

From the results of her brainstorming session, the student planned a pigeonhole chart to record her observations for her five-day experiment. She made up a similar chart for each baby in her control group (Baby B, C, D . . .). Examine the partial chart shown here.

Reactions to Specific Stimuli on Different Days

		DAY 1	DAY 2	DAY 3	DAY 4	DAY 5
Details of Baby A: **Male** **Black** **Born 6:02 a.m. March 1, 1985**	Light -eye squint					
	Dark -cries when light goes out					
	Voices -enjoys nurses' voices					
	Noises -screamed when tray dropped					
	Music -gurgles when soothing music plays					

There are other stimuli that the student could have added, but in order for her audience to be able to replicate the exact experiment described in her laboratory report, she limited her paper to only five. At the conclusion of her five-day experiment, the student was able to draft her report with confidence.

You should now brainstorm your limited topic until you can confidently begin to compose your first draft.

Discuss with your partner some of the results of your having worked through the material on this exercise.

SUMMARY

If you have taken time to go through the preceding brainstorming ideas, you will have amassed a great deal of raw, unorganized, and often useless material. But you also have probably unearthed a number of worthwhile things you will want to say about your topic. Brainstorming sessions help you to focus your attention on your thesis—that part of your limited topic that you want to develop. In addition, they may provide clues on how to organize your information in the most effective way.

26

Notetaking

INTRODUCTION

Professors in both humanities and science courses lecture on topics in their field of expertise, use visual aids, and give reading assignments from textbooks and other related material. Without a written record of what goes on during your classes, you will not be able to remember needed details for future essays, exams, and discussions. However, if you have a system of recording what you hear, see, and read, you can help yourself recall what you have experienced.

In order to take the best possible notes on what you hear and see in humanities and science courses, practice the following strategies before, during, and after each class period.

Before the period you should prepare by reading your text and any assigned reading. Anticipate what will take place during the lesson by listening or looking for key phrases like "The main point is . . . ." and "You will need to remember . . . ." Always have paper and pen or pencil ready to take notes.

During the period you should integrate what you hear and see with what you have previously read by summarizing or making an outline during the period. In addition, you should make a conscious effort to take notes on the discussions, seminars, and labs you participate in. With practice, you can engage in a discussion and take notes at the same time. In fact, by taking notes, you will stay alert and active, and become a shaper of the organization of the discussion. By taking notes during a discussion, you will formulate questions for which you need to find answers. Remember, the stupid question is the one you don't ask. The notes that you take do not have to make sense to anyone but you; but whenever possible, write in full sentences rather than fragments: a phrase that is very clear at the time might mean little to you the next day.

After the period you should rewrite your notes. Provide more details from memory or from your textbooks. Make a notation of the areas in which you are confused, so that you can do extra study and research.

The main result of producing a set of useful notes is that if you have to write an essay, present a seminar, or prepare for an examination, you will have plenty of material for your prewriting process. When you write, use the material in your notes to discover ideas for topics and to provide supporting evidence.

Note: Because there are many methods of taking notes, you should do several of the following exercises *with a partner*. If you and a peer are in the same chemistry class, for example, you should both plan to take notes according to the suggestions in one of the following exercises on exactly the same material and compare your notes at a later date to see whose are more thorough. Eventually you will settle on a few ways of taking notes that will suit your future needs.

EXERCISE ONE
Unwriting

1. Plan to write a paraphase, précis, summary, or outline of the material contained in a chapter, lecture, film, experiment, or discussion (see Chapter 32).
2. Plan to write a 25-word summary of the contents of a chapter, short story, graph, diagram, or mathematical theory, of a one-to-one tutorial you had with your professor, or of some other event (see Chapter 32).
3. Plan to write a thesis statement of the entire contents of a lecture, chapter, film, student presentation, talk by a guest speaker, or other event (see Chapter 27).

When you compare notes with your partner, do so in order to discover ways of improving your methods of notetaking. Ask questions. Listen to answers. Plan to improve.

EXERCISE TWO
Visualize Your Notes

Independent of your partner, record the same material of a lecture, film, or chapter in the form of a cluster, flowchart, ladder, mandala, or a network of pigeonhole boxes. See examples of these graphics in Chapter 25. As you need to record more material, you simply increase the size of your graphic: give your cluster more arms, your ladder more rungs, and so forth.

Start your graphic in the middle of a page so that you can record information in any direction. After a few attempts at visualizing your notes, you will know which form of graphic to use as you listen to what is said during the first few minutes of a lecture or documentary film, or as you read the opening paragraph of a chapter. For example, if you detect that the original material has been organized in sequential or chronological order, you might record your notes on a ladder; with a cause/effect order, you might use a flowchart; and so on.

When you complete your graphic at the end of the session, you might like to connect particular ideas to show their relationship by drawing in lines of a different color. Afterwards, you might like to convert the graphic, which can easily become a maze of arrows and jottings, that only you can make sense of, into a coherent summary.

When you and your partner compare your completed graphics and summaries, discuss their effectiveness and completeness. Determine whether you used the graphic that best complements the material.

EXERCISE THREE
Write Yourself a Note

Write a memo to yourself (see Chapter 16). The subject of your memo could be something like "Things to remember from today's lecture on 'The Causes of the Second World War.'"

Afterwards, exchange memos with your partner to see who wrote the more effective and useful memo. By keeping a complete set of memos on a lecture course, you will find it easier both to study for exams and to find ideas and supporting evidence for term papers.

EXERCISE FOUR
Predict the Content

Predict what will happen before you hear, see, or read the material by listing your expectations or the specific questions you need answered. Students who know the content of their courses are never surprised by a particular lecture; they have anticipated its content and have left plenty of room in their notes so that they can insert additional comments while they are listening to the lecture.

Before you and your partner go into the same lecture, exchange sealed envelopes in which you have written your predictions of what will happen during the period. Try to list specific expectations or questions that you expect will be dealt with. During the period, take notes in a method of your choice. Afterwards, meet, break the seals of your envelopes, and discuss how accurate your predictions were. Determine how you might predict more accurately.

EXERCISE FIVE
Draw Relationships

With your partner, draw relationships between two or more of your courses, even those that at first glance may seem unrelated. Instead of making notes in one period as though you are taking only one course, jot down ideas that link two courses. Later, make journal entries, which you can share with your partner, that, for example, link an artistic and a scientific event, that signify a particular relationship between physics and humanities, that show how a biological discovery affects a playwright's theme, and so on. By talking about them with your partner, you can test your ideas to see if you are on the track of some original thinking. Such discussions can ultimately produce original papers.

SUMMARY

After reading some of the products of your early notetaking sessions, you may become aware that they do not make complete sense. In addition, perhaps you can no longer remember details of what you heard, saw, and read. To help you dig information out of your memory, try making a freewriting or word association journal entry in order to record everything of importance (Chapters 24 and 25). If you still have holes because your memory is completely blank, you will know that for the next lecture you will have to pay closer attention and take clearer notes.

27

Thesis and Topic Statements

INTRODUCTION

When you write, you choose a general or broad topic to write about, narrow it to a workable size, then focus your limited topic with a particular point of view. You present your point of view within a statement or sentence called a thesis statement, which controls the development of an entire essay. Your thesis statement will probably contain several ideas or elements that you will want to write about in your essay; you usually treat each idea in a separate paragraph and express that idea or element in a statement or sentence. A topic statement, therefore, controls the content of a single paragraph.

When you include clear thesis and topic statements in your writing, you use them not only to help you develop and structure particular portions of your prose but also to guide your readers through those portions. Thesis and topic statements are like road signs. When road signs are well posted, both driver and passengers enjoy the scenery and arrive at their destination without getting lost. When thesis and topic sentences are explicitly stated by a writer, readers enjoy the details and arrive at a clear understanding of the piece without losing their way.

If you have completed the Introductory Assignment at the beginning of this textbook, you have already been introduced to the process of moving from choosing a broad topic to formulating a thesis statement based on all of your writing variables. In this workshop, you can reinforce your understanding of the important prewriting concepts surrounding thesis and topic sentences.

So that you begin this workshop with a clear understanding of the terms used in this chapter, you and a partner (classmate, friend, relative) should study and discuss the flowcharts on pages 313 and 314 that illustrate the development of a topic.

EXERCISE ONE
Why Write a Thesis or Topic Statement?

Writers need a controlling idea in the form of a sentence both to limit the ideas discussed and to order the structure of an essay or paragraph. The following

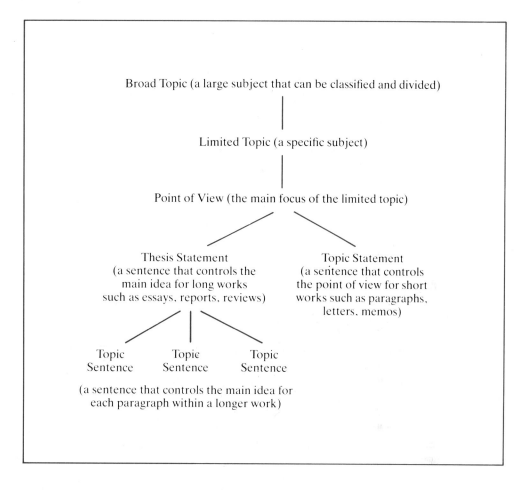

Broad Topic (a large subject that can be classified and divided)

Limited Topic (a specific subject)

Point of View (the main focus of the limited topic)

Thesis Statement
(a sentence that controls the
main idea for long works
such as essays, reports, reviews)

Topic Statement
(a sentence that controls
the point of view for short
works such as paragraphs,
letters, memos)

Topic
Sentence   Topic
Sentence   Topic
Sentence

(a sentence that controls the main idea for
each paragraph within a longer work)

paragraph demonstrates an uncontrolled piece of writing. The ideas and details are fine, but the piece is aimless—neither the writer nor the reader really knows precisely where the paragraph is going. Either you or your partner read it aloud and find evidence that both writer and reader are crippled because the paragraph contains no controlling sentence.

A crack of thunder startled my cat, Minette. Then the winds tumbled my ice plants and ivy on the patio. I scrambled to close the car windows. Minette dashed under the bed. Meanwhile the hail began to pummel my May roses, scattering pink, yellow, and red petals. And even before that, the first icy pellets stung my arms as I reached to rescue the hanging baskets. I had known, of course, that this storm was coming. The smell of sulphur had assaulted my nose and the sudden, prickly chill of a thundershower had made me wish for a sweater and some coffee instead of the ice tea I was drinking as I watched the inky thunderheads boil up over the mountains and down into the valley. Poor Minette—she can bear cloudbursts, mild earth tremors, and blizzards, but she trembles at the faintest thunderclap and heads for her safe place under my bed. Fourth-of-July fireworks affect her the same way. But like me, she always waits until the last moment before she dashes for cover.

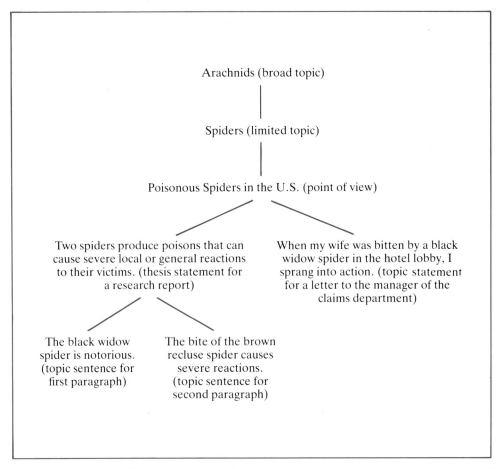

Now read the following aloud; notice how the topic sentence limits the content of the paragraph by telling you exactly what to expect.

The onslaught of a desert storm hypnotizes woman and beast. I sit on the patio with my cat Minette in my lap and a glass of ice tea in my hand, watching inky thunderheads boil up over the mountains and down into the Rio Grande Valley. We both know we should move—Minette to the safety of her favorite hiding place and me to close the car windows and take down the hanging plants. But we sit mesmerized, wrinkling our noses as the smell of sulphur grows stronger and a damp chill rides in on the rising desert wind. Suddenly a crack of thunder breaks the spell. Minette hurtles for her cat door and disappears into the house. I scramble to close the car window and rescue the ice plants and ivy. Icy pellets sting my arms; a cloud of pink, yellow, and red petals whirls into the air as wind and hail pummel the roses. The storm has us in its power.

1. The opening topic sentence controls the content of the paragraph. Find words and ideas in the rest of the paragraph that reinforce "hypnotizes woman and beast."
2. The writer has used climactic order to structure the content. Point out the features of climactic order.

3. What items did the writer omit from the original paragraph? Why?

4. Independent of your partner, both of you should write another version of the first paragraph. Use this topic sentence to get you started: "A desert storm affects animals more than people."

5. Read each other's completed version and comment on the results of how well you both controlled the content of the paragraph. Although it is still early in this workshop, do you see how establishing a topic sentence makes your writing process easier?

EXERCISE TWO
How to Limit Your Topic and Create a Point of View
and a Thesis or Topic Statement.

The crux of coming up with a suitable point of view and ultimately a successful piece of writing depends on your choosing a broad topic that interests you, narrowing it down to a manageable size, and considering your limited topic in terms of the other writing variables: audience, purpose, format, situation, and voice. Using each writing variable to flesh out your limited topic, you will arrive at the precise point of view you want. Assume, for example, that your broad topic is *oceans*.

1. Independent of your partner, both of you should list a possible response for each writing variable as in the examples that follow. (Instead of using the ones provided, make up your own examples.) In addition, you should record a specific point of view on which your writing will focus. Finally, attempt to write either a thesis statement (for a longer work) or a topic statement (for a shorter work or for a paragraph in a longer work).

TOPIC:	Surfing in the ocean
AUDIENCE:	My best friend. Real. I intend to send it.
PURPOSE:	To invite him to surf with me
FORMAT:	A letter
VOICE:	I am going to pretend that I am the ocean, inviting him to surf.
SITUATION:	Both my friend and I love to surf.
POINT OF VIEW:	I think it would be fun to enter a Sunday surfing contest.
TOPIC STATEMENT:	Listen, Pedro, to the power of my waves, the thrill of the crowds, the excitement of a Sunday surfing contest.

TOPIC:	Food in the ocean
AUDIENCE:	My biology instructor. Real. I will hand it in.
PURPOSE:	To convince her that oceans can be used more efficiently to feed the hungry
FORMAT:	A scientific review paper
VOICE:	My own
SITUATION:	To fulfill a required biology assignment
POINT OF VIEW:	I think the ocean's food supply is unending.
THESIS STATEMENT:	The latest scientific research demonstrates that the oceans of the world could feed all the people of the world indefinitely.

TOPIC:	Ocean pollution
AUDIENCE:	The governor of our state. Real. I may send it in.
PURPOSE:	To protest the presence of oil tankers off our coast
FORMAT:	An argumentative essay
VOICE:	Future generations
SITUATION:	The governor is not as concerned with ecology as I am.
POINT OF VIEW:	I think we're gambling with our oceans; the possibility of ocean pollution is very real.
THESIS STATEMENT:	Compare the ruined shores of our state now—in the year 2018—with their condition in the year 1985.

If you get stuck in formulating your point of view, thesis statement, or topic sentence, return to your writing variables. Perhaps you should change one or more of them in order to focus your ideas more specifically.

2. Compare and discuss your list with that of your partner. If you cannot easily predict what kind of a piece of writing will result from the exercise, make suggestions for changes.

EXERCISE THREE
Composing Thesis and Topic Statements

Generally, you express your limited topic in the form of a thesis or topic statement. Although both thesis and topic statements should be clear, unified, precise, and limited, thesis statements control the development of an entire essay while topic statements present a narrower focus on the content of a single paragraph. You should usually place a thesis statement at the beginning of a work and a topic statement anywhere within the paragraph.

1. With your partner, discuss the differences between the following thesis and topic statements:

THESIS STATEMENT:	The issues during the 1984 presidential campaign involved the deficit, defense, and unemployment.
TOPIC STATEMENT:	The Republican candidate was the incumbent president, Ronald Reagan.
THESIS STATEMENT:	When I go out to dinner, I go either to an Italian or a Chinese restaurant.
TOPIC STATEMENT:	Using chopsticks is easy if you follow a few simple instructions.

2. Look over the following list of questions. Independent of your partner, answer each question yes or no. Determine which one(s) you both disagree with, and narrow the subject to the point where you could use it as a limited topic for an assignment.

- Are men and women really equal?
- Should we forget the space program and spend money on improving the earth?
- Is there anything wrong with interracial marriages?
- Should all hospitals be free?

- Should professional athletes be allowed to compete in the Olympics?
- Is it right for police to place undercover agents in high schools or on college campuses?

Using one of the above (preferably one in which your responses differ), independently compose a set of appropriate writing variables for a long piece of writing. Record a specific point of view on which your writing will focus. Then compose a thesis statement for your entire piece. Finally, compose a topic statement for two or more of your developmental paragraphs.

3. Compare and discuss your thesis and topic statements with those of your partner. If you were to write the entire piece, can you readily see how they will become road signs for your readers so that they will easily find their way through your essay? Should any aspect of your thesis and topic statements be changed to make the journey easier for your readers? Why?

EXERCISE FOUR
Placement of Topic Statements

1. *At the beginning.* The most common place for your topic statement is in the first sentence of the paragraph. After reading your opening statement, your readers will expect to see supporting evidence in the form of details, examples, reasons, explanations, and so on. The following example is a refocusing of the paragraph in Exercise One:

> The onslaught of a desert storm hypnotizes my cat, Minette. She knows she should move from my lap to the safety of her favorite hiding place, under my bed. But she sits mesmerized, wrinkling her nose and watching the inky thunderheads boil up over the mountains and down into the Rio Grande Valley. She twitches as the smell of sulphur grows stronger and a damp chill rides in on the rising desert wind. A sudden crack of thunder breaks the spell. Minette hurtles for her cat door and disappears in the house.

2. *At the end.* The second most common position of the topic statement is in the last sentence of the paragraph. Your reader will read all of the details, examples, and other developmental techniques first because you will have built them up to your main idea.

> As the desert storm begins to build, my cat, Minette, knows she should move from my lap to the safety of her favorite hiding place, under my bed. But she sits mesmerized, wrinkling her nose and watching the inky thunderheads boil up over the mountains and down into the Rio Grande Valley. She twitches as the smell of sulphur grows stronger and a damp chill rides in on the rising desert wind. She waits until the first crack of thunder breaks the spell before she hurtles for her cat door and disappears in the house. Indeed, the onslaught of a desert storm always hypnotizes Minette.

3. *At the beginning and the end.* Sometimes you might use both the first and last sentences to show your complete point of view. In other words, each sentence could contain only a part of your main idea. You could also use the last sentence to merely repeat, for emphasis, the topic that you expressed clearly in the first sentence.

> <u>As the desert storm begins to build, my cat, Minette, acts strangely.</u> She knows she should move from my lap to the safety of her favorite hiding place, under my bed. But she sits mesmerized, wrinkling her nose and watching the inky thunderheads boil up over the mountains and down into the Rio Grande Valley. She twitches as the smell of sulphur grows stronger and a damp chill rides in on the rising desert wind. She waits until the first crack of thunder breaks the spell before she hurtles for her cat door and disappears into the house. <u>Indeed, the onslaught of a desert storm always hypnotizes Minette.</u>

4. *In the middle of the paragraph.* If you place your topic sentence in the middle of the paragraph, you would place some details to lead up to your main idea and some additional details to follow it. A slight variation of this technique is to place the topic sentence as your second sentence after an attention-getting opening.

> She knows she should move from my lap to the safety of her favorite hiding place, under my bed. But she sits mesmerized, wrinkling her nose and watching the inky thunderheads boil up over the mountains and down into the Rio Grande Valley. She twitches as the smell of sulphur grows stronger and a damp chill rides in on the rising desert wind. <u>Indeed, the onslaught of a desert storm always hypnotizes my cat.</u> But when the first crack of thunder breaks the spell, Minette hurtles for her cat door and disappears into the house.

5. *Not stated, but implied.* Rather than stating your main idea explicitly, you might imply what it is by the details of the paragraph. You must, however, always have a controlling idea in mind when you write—whether you state it or imply it.

> My cat, Minette, knows she should move from my lap to the safety of her favorite hiding place, under my bed. But she sits mesmerized, wrinkling her nose and watching the inky thunderheads boil up over the mountains and down into the Rio Grande Valley. Even as the smell of sulphur grows stronger and a damp chill rides in on the rising desert wind, she merely twitches a few whiskers. But when the first crack of thunder breaks the spell, Minette hurtles for her cat door and disappears into the house.

With your partner, comment on the different effects of moving the topic sentence in the above exercise.

The best way for you to determine the effect of moving your topic sentence to different places in your paragraphs is for you to do a similar exercise. It's time-consuming, but if you seriously want to improve your writing style, you must experiment. How do you know what the effect of the placement of a topic sentence is going to have on a reader until you have moved it in several positions?

EXERCISE FIVE
Discovering and Evaluating Thesis and Topic Sentences

1. Ask your partner to assign you a model essay to read—for example, ''A Magnificent Cycle'' (Chapter 13), ''If Questions Could Kill'' (Chapter 5), or ''The Girl in the Fifth Row" (Chapter 4). Your task is to discover and evaluate the thesis statements. In addition, comment on how well the writer developed the thesis statement. Finally, discover and evaluate the topic statements from each of the paragraphs within the essay. Comment on the effect of the placement of each of the topic sentences. Discuss your findings with your partner.

2. Ask your partner to assign you a model paragraph to read—for example, one from Chapter 2, 3, or 29. Your task is to discover and evaluate the topic statement. Also, note the effect of the placement of the topic statement. Discuss your findings with your partner.

EXERCISE SIX
Making up a Thesis Statement and Topic Sentences

Thesis statements and topic sentences have already been alluded to as road signs. In this exercise they will be likened to contracts. When you write a clear thesis statement or topic sentence, you enter a contractual agreement with your readers. You say you are going to do something; they have every right to expect you to keep your bargain. When you state your thesis statement and topic sentences explicitly, you cannot help honoring your contract.

Read the following limited topics and points of view carefully, and, on a separate piece of paper, make up an appropriate thesis statement and an appropriate number of topic sentences. Remember that each should be a complete sentence that controls the ideas to be discussed.

Example

LIMITED TOPIC:	Gift giving in my family
POINT OF VIEW:	I know that gift giving in my family can be joyous and disastrous.
THESIS STATEMENT:	At Christmastime in our house, gift giving has not only been a joyous affair but, at times, disastrous.
FIRST TOPIC SENTENCE:	My dad always gives the right gift to everyone on his list.
SECOND TOPIC SENTENCE:	My mom never seems to manage to give an appropriate gift.

1. LIMITED TOPIC: Importance of good nutrition
POINT OF VIEW: I am sure that good nutrition can add years to your life.
(Make up one thesis statement and three topic sentences.)

2. LIMITED TOPIC: Different kinds of fishermen
POINT OF VIEW: It would be interesting to compare a commercial fisherman with a sports fisherman.
(Make up one thesis statement and two topic sentences.)

3. LIMITED TOPIC: My domain
   POINT OF VIEW: I love my one room, which serves as kitchen, living room, and bedroom.
(Make up one thesis statement and three topic sentences.)

4. Ask your partner to present you with two other limited topics and points of view so that you may continue this exercise.
5. Ask your partner to refer you to a model essay in the text. Read the essay, then list the thesis statement and topic sentences. Examples of model essays are "We're Going Moose Hunting" (Chapter 8), "Footsore" (Chapter 11), or "Cooling Burnout" (Chapter 15).
6. Discuss the entire exercise with your partner until you understand perfectly how a thesis statement controls the ideas of an entire long piece of writing and how a topic sentence controls the ideas of a paragraph within a long piece.

EXERCISE SEVEN
Test Your Ability to Compose Thesis and Topic Statements

All you have to do for this exercise is compose a point of view and a thesis statement or a topic statement for each item below. When you finish, you should compare your statements with those of your partner.

A. On a separate piece of paper write a point of view and a thesis statement for each of the following suggestions for essays or longer pieces.

1. LIMITED TOPIC: Arresting drunk drivers
   AUDIENCE: Readers of *Time* magazine
   PURPOSE: To argue the need to jail drunk drivers and take away their licenses until their trials
   FORMAT: Argumentative essay
   VOICE: My own
   SITUATION: I was hit by a drunk driver, who was released the next day.
   POINT OF VIEW: _____
   THESIS STATEMENT: _____
2. LIMITED TOPIC: Writing an essay can be a horrifying experience.
   AUDIENCE: My writing instructor
   PURPOSE: To explain my trauma over writing an essay
   FORMAT: Informative essay
   VOICE: My own
   SITUATION: Every time I have to write an essay, I go into shock. My instructor thinks writing an essay is a breeze.
   POINT OF VIEW: _____
   THESIS STATEMENT: _____
3. LIMITED TOPIC: The problem of mid-term school parties
   AUDIENCE: Fellow students

PURPOSE:	To explain how to party your way through school and flunk out, without even trying
FORMAT:	A set of instructions
VOICE:	Persona of a partying student
SITUATION:	I notice that a large number of students are not really interested in school. I am, and I intend to satirize these party types.
POINT OF VIEW:	_____
THESIS STATEMENT:	_____

4. On a separate piece of paper make up your own set of writing variables and thesis statement on the broad topic of *restaurants*.

5. On a separate piece of paper make up your own set of writing variables and thesis statement on a broad topic of your choice.

B. On a separate piece of paper write a point of view and a topic statement for each of the following suggestions for paragraphs or shorter pieces. Also, indicate where you would place your main idea: at the beginning, end, middle, or beginning and end, or implied instead of stated.

1.
LIMITED TOPIC:	Last year's clothes don't fit me anymore.
AUDIENCE:	My wife
PURPOSE:	To ask her to help me change my eating habits
FORMAT:	Love letter
VOICE:	Persona of myself when we were first married
SITUATION:	I used to be slim. I know my wife isn't as attracted to me as she used to be.
POINT OF VIEW:	_____
TOPIC STATEMENT:	_____
PLACEMENT:	_____

2.
LIMITED TOPIC:	Violence on the NBC television show, *The A-Team*
AUDIENCE:	Readers of *Parent* magazine
PURPOSE:	To praise the hell-bent action on the show
FORMAT:	Short review
VOICE:	My own
SITUATION:	I think the violence is so exaggerated that kids won't take it seriously.
POINT OF VIEW:	_____
TOPIC STATEMENT:	_____
PLACEMENT:	_____

3.
LIMITED TOPIC:	Violence on the NBC television show, *The A-Team*
AUDIENCE:	Readers of *Parent* magazine
PURPOSE:	To protest the violence on the show
FORMAT:	Short review
VOICE:	Persona of a young child
SITUATION:	I think the violence causes damage to kids who watch the show.

POINT OF VIEW: _____

TOPIC STATEMENT: _____

PLACEMENT: _____

4. On a separate piece of paper make up your own set of writing variables and topic statement on the broad topic of _cramming for exams_.

5. On a separate piece of paper make up your own set of writing variables and topic statement on a broad topic of your choice.

If one or more of the above items interest you, you might write an entire essay or paragraph at a later time.

28

Beginnings, Middles, and Endings

INTRODUCTION

Most writers find that beginning and ending their pieces of writing are their most difficult tasks. The King of Hearts' advice in *Alice in Wonderland*, "Begin at the beginning, go on until you come to the end, and then stop," is much harder to follow than would appear at first glance.

The drafting process is usually a solitary task (no one but you can compose your first draft), but you can still storm your brain for a few more ideas. By asking yourself a few questions while you draft, you will stretch your creative powers. Some writers like to begin with the middle part of their draft, complete the ending, and finally write a beginning. No matter what your drafting process, you might answer the following questions about your beginning and ending before you compose them:

- What do you want to accomplish at the beginning and end of your piece of writing?
- For your beginning, do you hope to capture your reader's attention? If yes, how will you introduce your limited topic, point of view, and purpose for writing?
- At the end, do you want to sum up your piece in a new and interesting way so that your reader will think about what you have written?

In addition, your beginning and ending should enclose a middle section that you should make as informative and interesting as you can. (Middles are discussed more fully in Chapter 29.)

This workshop deals with ways to compose beginnings, middles, and endings for paragraphs and essays. Specialized formats such as letters, proposals, memos, and résumés are not specifically dealt with in this workshop.

EXERCISE ONE
Beginnings

From your own experience you know how important first impressions are. Discuss with your partner some of the following first impressions:

- What attracted you to your best friend?
- What attracted you to your workshop partner?
- If you saw a record album by a group you did not know or had not heard before, what would cause you to buy the album?
- What makes you pick up or not pick up a magazine from a book rack?
- What kinds of opening sentences attract you to a piece of writing?

Consider, too, in your discussion the people, clothes, music, and books that you have rejected because of your first impressions of them.

Every writer strives to compose a catchy sentence or two that grabs the reader's attention. In his *How to Live to Be 100—Or More*, George Burns speaks for those who hate writing beginnings:

> Well, I'm going to write another book. This is my fourth one, and I've learned that the most important thing about writing a book is to have a great first chapter to grab your readers. If you've got that, from then on everything flows. I've also learned that writing a first chapter is not easy. I've been sitting here for three hours and nothing's happened. So I'm going to make this my second chapter.

Many writers, finding themselves unable to write an attention-getting opening, will compose an entire essay before they draft the beginning. They may not even think of a title for their work until they have completed it.

The following are some of the many types of beginnings that you could develop for a single paragraph on the topic of *Lake Erie*.

1. The *statement*, the most commonly used opening, does not exactly serve as an attention-getter, but it does state what you are going to write about: "There are five Great Lakes, Lake Erie being the shallowest." Once you have said this, you are ready to write your topic statement: "This lake is quickly being destroyed by pollution." Your readers now expect that the body of your paragraph will provide examples of how Lake Erie is being destroyed. If your readers are interested in the pollution problems of Lake Erie, you have gained their attention.
2. The *generalization*, another common introduction, simply introduces your paragraph with a broad statement: "Water pollution is a widespread American problem." You can then state your particular thesis in the topic statement: "In Lake Erie pollution has reached epidemic proportions." What do you think will follow?
3. Use the *scare-headline tactic* judiciously: "You could be dead before the end of this decade." The reason, water pollution, will of course be introduced in the topic statement.
4. The *question*, another frequently used method of introduction, asks one or two questions: "Do you care about saving Lake Erie? What can you do?" What do you think will be included in the paragraph that follows this beginning?
5. The *summary*, a useful introduction, tells your reader of several possible approaches and then, in the topic statement, presents the one to be dealt with in the paragraph: "There are probably half a dozen steps that must be taken to bring Lake Erie back to life. To me, the most important one is to stop the dumping of chemicals now."

6. The *quotation*, if it is apt, can give authority to your paragraph: "Our member of Congress said, 'Americans and Canadians must work to save Lake Erie from certain death.'" How does this beginning hook the reader and indicate what will follow?
7. The *analogy*, a comparison that will be sustained figuratively throughout the paragraph, can result in an accomplished piece of writing: "Lake Erie lies helpless and gasping while the factory towns ignore its cries for help."

With your partner choose a topic that you both know something about, making sure that you can narrow the topic to several different points. Then write a beginning for your topic in each of the seven styles outlined above. When you have both completed your seven beginnings, discuss their effectiveness, and try to decide which one would probably produce the best paragraph.

You should use the same tactics as noted above when you write a beginning for an essay; however, your beginning usually takes the form of an introductory paragraph. Your introductory paragraph should do two things:

- Present a thesis statement that controls your specific topic (see Chapter 27)
- Convince your readers that they will not waste their time by reading your entire essay

The Far Side

Reprinted by permission of Chronicle Features, San Francisco.

Assume that you and your partner are going to write an essay about Lake Erie. Following the above seven suggestions for beginnings, write seven opening paragraphs—for example, the following paragraph is a variation of the first suggestion:

> There are five Great Lakes, Lake Erie being the shallowest. This lake, however, is quickly being destroyed by direct and indirect pollution.

This opening paragraph indicates that the middle part of the essay will have two paragraphs: one detailing the direct pollution problems—runoff from factories; the other detailing the indirect pollution problems—acid rain. Each of your other six introductory paragraphs should clearly indicate how you should structure the rest of the essay.

The next time you are engaged in revising a piece of your writing, check your beginning. If you have begun with a weak opening, such as "I feel," "I think," or "In this essay I am going to," return to this exercise for an idea on how to compose a better beginning.

For a few minutes, examine with your partner the beginnings of a few of the products in the Assignment Section. Determine the method used for each.

EXERCISE TWO
Middles

When you are in the middle of something, whether it be a sumptuous feast or a good book, you should have a sense of purpose and direction. Spend a few minutes with your partner discussing some of the "middle periods" you have experienced. Use these suggestions to talk about the middle period of an experience:

- What do you expect to accomplish during your middle age?
- What do you feel when you are in the middle of a mystery book, a romantic movie, or a close game?
- Of all the things you do, which offer the best "middle" times?

If in writing about "Lake Erie" you started your paragraph with "There are many things in Lake Erie that need to be cleaned up," you might develop the middle of your piece of writing by providing *examples* of what needs to be cleaned up. You could organize your paragraph through *order of importance*. In this way, your paragraph might make one or more of the following points:

- The pollution in Lake Erie becomes more serious every day.
- The pollution problem of Lake Erie has been allowed to continue for far too long.
- Through our shortsightedness we will be passing on a moribund Lake Erie to our children.
- The British saved the Thames; let us save Lake Erie.
- Several lives have already been lost because of the pollution in Lake Erie.

Select a few of the beginnings you developed in Exercise One and have your partner tell you how he or she would develop the middle part of the paragraph. (If either of you finds this difficult, refer to Chapter 29.)

EXERCISE THREE
Endings

Life is filled with beginnings and endings. With your partner, discuss some of the final moments you have experienced. Use these suggestions as the basis for your discussion:

- How does one of your favorite songs end?
- What happened during the last moments of saying farewell to a friend or acquaintance of yours?
- Of a few recent movies that you have seen, which ending do you remember most vividly? Why?
- What do you look for in the ending of a novel?

Ending a piece of writing can be a difficult task. From the time you first started to write paragraphs, you were probably told that your conclusion should summarize your writing in a new and interesting way. Frankly, this suggestion can be frustrating. What kind of ending qualifies as "new and interesting"? Novelty for its own sake has no place in good writing.

The best ending a piece of writing can have is one that satisfies the expectations your beginning and middle have built up in your reader. Imagine your surprise, perhaps even disappointment, on Christmas morning when you open a gift from a special person. Through suggestions and hints prior to Christmas, you are convinced that you will receive the very thing you desire—a digital wristwatch. But when you open your gift, you find an alarm clock. In the same way, if you have led your reader to expect a conclusion to a paragraph listing the dangers of smoking and if you provide the statement "Marijuana can be habit forming," you have let your reader down. No matter how well written your piece is, a poor conclusion will lessen its impact for a reader.

As you move towards your conclusion, keep an eye on your limited topic in general and on your point of view in particular. In that way, your conclusion should satisfy you, your purpose, and your reader.

1. Working with your partner, match these paragraph endings with the seven sample beginnings given in Exercise One:

- The choice is ours—a crystal-clear lake or a moribund swamp.
- If we can bring Lake Erie back to life, there will be hope for other Canadian waterways.
- If Lake Erie dies, abandon hope.
- We cannot let our government shirk the challenge of resuscitating Lake Erie.
- Will Lake Ontario be next on the death list?
- If governments and industries follow my suggestions, Lake Erie can survive.
- Don't let Lake Erie breathe its last.

2. Compose three different endings for one of the beginnings that you and your partner were working on in Exercise One. Avoid an ending that merely sums up and adds nothing of interest—for example, "And these are the many things that need to be cleaned up in Lake Erie." Discuss the appropriateness of each of your endings, and then decide on the best one.

For a few minutes, examine with your partner the endings of a few of the products in the Assignment Section. Use the same products you used in Exercise One. Discuss the effectiveness and appropriateness of the endings.

EXERCISE FOUR
Titles

Many writers think of a title before they begin to write; others use a "working title," which they may or may not use for their finished work; still others do not even think of a title until they have completed their work. No matter what method you use, a good title is important, as comedian George Burns found out:

> My publisher called and said, "George, we want you to write a book, and we've got a great title for it: *How to Live to Be 100—Or More!*"
>
> I said, "I don't like that title. How about *If I Can Do It, You Can Do It?*"
>
> She said, "Too vague. What's wrong with *How to Live to Be 100—Or More?*"
>
> "How about *The George Burns Health and Exercise Book?*"
>
> "Dull."
>
> "Then how about *Long Life Is a Many-Splendored Thing?*"
>
> "You've got to be kidding."
>
> Then I said, "How about—"
>
> Interrupting, she said, "Look, George, you're getting a very big advance—do you want to write this book or don't you?"
>
> "How about *How to Live to Be 100—Or More?*" I asked.
>
> "George, you just came up with a great title!"
>
> "Thank you," I said.
>
> There's nothing like having a publisher with an open mind.

In composing a title, you should not merely put down the name of your limited topic or repeat a part of your thesis statement, you should catch the readers' attention and let them know what to expect from the work.

1. Draw on your own experience and discuss the importance of titles with your partner. Use the following questions as a basis for discussion:

- Which musical group do you think has the most suitable name? Which one do you think does not suit its name? Why?

- What titles can you think of that are deliberately unsuitable for the book, group, film? Why do you think the authors chose an obviously unsuitable title? What is the intended effect on the audience?

- What titles can you think of that are the opposite of their content—for example, a passive title for a violent story, an understatement for a powerful piece? What is the effect on the audience?
- What are the different names that people call you? Which one(s) do you like? Which do you dislike? Why? Which name is the *real* you?
- What kind of title would make you pick up a book? Why?
- Have you ever decided to see or not see a film or play simply because of its title? What aspect of the title attracted or repelled you?

2. Provide two or three titles for the piece of writing that you have been working on in the last few exercises. Discuss their effectiveness and suitability with your partner. (If you want to see a paragraph that uses one of the beginnings and endings quoted in the workshop, turn to "Lake Erie: Death or Life?" in the products at the end of Chapter **3.** What do you think of the title?)

EXERCISE FIVE
Narration and Description

The foregoing exercises have dealt with exposition; in this exercise you can work on various ways to enliven beginnings, middles, and endings for your narrative and descriptive writing.

1. Assume that you and your partner are going to write a narrative about a seaside resort, dude ranch, or luxury hotel/casino.

    a. Independently, each of you should compose two different beginnings.

    b. Compare them and determine which one of the four beginnings would probably make the best opening.

    c. Discuss two ways of developing the beginning, determining which of the two would provide the best middle.

    d. Then, independently, compose two different endings each for the one beginning you chose.

    e. Compare them and determine which one of the four endings would probably be the best conclusion.

    f. Then, independently, compose two different titles.

    g. Compare them and determine which one of the four titles would probably be the best title.

2. Repeat this exercise, writing a description of one your instructors.

29

Unity

INTRODUCTION

When you draft a piece of writing (expository, descriptive, or narrative), you must make sure everything within it is unified; in other words, everything should deal with the same limited topic and contribute to supporting your point of view and thesis statement. Every word and sentence should become an inseparable part of the whole.

During prewriting brainstorming sessions, you learned how to collect the evidence you needed to support your limited topic. In some brainstorming sessions you may have begun to organize your material while you collected it. During your drafting process, you should check over all of your brainstorming notes to see which items fulfill your writing variables. To have a unified draft, you should retain all the relevant points and use them in your work; at the same time, you should discard all the irrelevant ones, which may cause disunity.

From the mass of material you have gathered during brainstorming, you should decide what types of supporting evidence you will need in order to develop your piece of writing. Your decision depends on which types serve your purpose best. To describe the view from your window, you will need to use *details* (the oak tree in the front yard, the private hedge by the side of the house, the crabgrass in the lawn). If, however, you were writing an argumentative essay about the dangers of nuclear power, you would have to collect *reasons* why nuclear power might be dangerous (risk of serious accidents at power plants, problems with the storage of spent fuel, contamination of air and water). Other types of supporting evidence are *facts*, *results*, *incidents*, *illustrations*, *questions*, *lists*, and *quoted material*. You will find examples of all of these types in this workshop.

Note: Although this workshop stands independently, the suggestions will be more meaningful if you have a thorough understanding of thesis and topic statements (Chapter 27) and ways to begin a piece of writing (Chapter 28).

EXERCISE ONE
Visual Organization

If you find that your prewriting material is disorganized and that you really do not know how to begin to unify your first draft, determine how your supporting evidence for your limited topic would fit into one of the following graphics:

- Single ladder
- Double ladder
- Mandala
- Flowchart
- Boxes or pigeonholes

The more you write, the more ways of listing evidence you will discover and want to try.

1. With your partner, study several of the graphics in Chapter 25. What kind of supporting evidence has been used in each graphic (details, examples, reasons, and so on)?

2. After you have studied several of the graphics, take a batch of your own brainstorming notes and list them on an appropriate graphic. Make sure you can identify the main kind of supporting evidence you are listing.

3. With your partner, study the following graphic of a mandala.

If you were to use this mandala to write a paper for a sociology course that required headings and subheadings, how would you organize the material in this mandala to help you draft your essay? Hint: On the outside of the circle various job categories are listed, and within the segments of the mandala are subdivisions showing particular types of positions.

Once you find a logical organization, you should check your brainstorming notes that correspond to each subdivision. If you cannot say at least six things about each particular job, you should brainstorm for more supporting evidence.

If you completed a similar mandala on another limited topic, you should find it easy to compose a thesis statement as well as topic statements for each paragraph of your essay.

4. Use one of the following thesis statements (or one of your choice) and, independent of your partner, construct a mandala with the thesis statement in the middle. You should both use the *same* thesis statement so that you can compare mandalas; therefore, take time to choose a thesis statement that you both agree upon.

- Everyone (or no one) needs a vacation every year.
- The national parks of the United States offer magnificent sights for vacationers.
- Too many people never have a chance to take a vacation.
- If you cannot afford a vacation, think of all the things you can do instead.
- My vacation last summer was the best (the worst) one I've ever had.
- Vacations take too much time, too much money, and too much energy.
- I'm too tired to take a vacation this year.

5. Compare your word mandala with your partner's. Should you add or delete anything? How many segments does your mandala have? If each segment were to become a paragraph, would you have at least six pieces of supporting evidence to support each topic sentence? Besides the introductory and concluding paragraphs, how many paragraphs would your essay contain? If you were to turn your mandala into an essay, would it be narrative, descriptive, or expository?

6. In addition to using graphics, you might find it easy to organize a piece of writing by drawing cartoons or pictures, gathering pictures and making a collage, or drawing a line or bar graph. No doubt, while you create your visual display, you will have to decide the order of your cartoons or pictures. Indeed, while you create, you will be making a number of visual statements. From a completed visual display, you should be able to write your first draft from what you see.

Assume that you must write an essay on the topics mentioned below. Independent of your partner, decide in what way you would list supporting evidence: single ladder, double ladder, mandala, flowchart, pigeonhole boxes, cartoons or pictures, collage, or line or bar graph.

- The life story of a sports figure
- Education in the United States contrasted with education in Haiti

- The food value of several cereals
- Duties of a member of Congress
- What the media said about the U.S. boycott of the 1980 Olympics and the Russian boycott of the 1984 Olympics
- Different kinds of bees
- The history of the fork as an eating utensil
- Ways to eat with a fork
- Ways to study
- What great world thinkers have said about reincarnation

When you finish, compare and talk about the suitability of your choices with your partner.

EXERCISE TWO
Comparison and Contrast

A piece of writing can achieve unity by pointing out similarities and differences between two subjects. Because there is an entire chapter on comparison and contrast (Chapter 8), refer to it if you have difficulties or are confused while completing the following exercises.

1. One method of organization is to point out similarities (comparisons) and differences (contrasts) between two topics. You might first talk about Subject A and then talk about Subject B. That would produce a paper using the AAA/BBB method. If you were to mention items from Subject A and at the same time point out similarities or differences to Subject B, you would be using the ABABAB method. You can use the AAA/BBB or ABABAB method for either comparison or contrast. Furthermore, it is possible to write a *comparison/contrast* paper in which you use either method to point out similarities *and* differences.

What are the benefits of the AAA/BBB and ABABAB methods both for the writer and the reader?

1. Choose two things to compare or contrast.

- Life in America and life in a country of your choice
- Life in your grandparents' time and life now
- Grade schools and colleges
- Military and civilian life

(Or choose your own comparison or contrast topic.)

2. Draw two columns, labeling each with the appropriate topic. List similarities or differences between the two topics. Whenever you put something in one column, add a similar item to the other one. (Instead of using two columns, you might want to draw a double ladder, as illustrated in Chapter 8.)

Life in Grandparents' Time	Life Now
Slower	Faster
Clean, fresh air	Smog in the air
Clean streets	Debris in streets
Safe to walk streets	Crime-infested streets
Lots of reading	Less reading
Entertainment mainly at home	Entertainment outside of home

3. Exchange your lists. Discuss their completeness and decide on the better method for organization of your paper, the AAA/BBB or the ABABAB method.

4. If you like, you can make a collage of pictures contrasting or comparing two things or places. Then point out the differences or similarities to your partner. A good collage will provide an excellent foundation for an essay. The following are examples of topics for collages contrasting bathing habits:

- Pictures of people bathing in beautiful bathrooms and people bathing in muddy rivers
- Different styles of bathtubs
- Different customs of bathing
- The history of bathtubs
- Types of shower systems

EXERCISE THREE
Cause and Effect

You could solidly unify a piece of writing by presenting either the causes of the effects or the effects of the causes (see Chapter 9).

1. Find two pictures: one showing a cause of a problem; the other an effect. For example, you could point out the problems of finding reasonably priced accommodations (cause) by illustrating that some students are forced to live in campers on parking lots (effect). Give the pictures to your partner. (If you cannot find pictures, draw them or provide a word picture.)

2. Your partner's task is to find or draw pictures or write word pictures that explain *how* the effect resulted from the cause. For example, a cause/effect relationship would be clear with pictures of the university's building program, of the increase in student population, of students coming from all over the nation, of the city's lack of rent control, and so on.

3. Your partner should then give you an oral explanation of the cause/effect relationship, outlining the sequence of events that led from the cause to the effect.

4. Repeat the exercise, working back from effect to cause. Explain the effect and cause relationship orally, pointing out the effect (students camping in parking lots) first and the cause (high-priced accommodations) last.

5. Decide which order was better—cause and effect or effect and cause.

6. Repeat the exercise with a different topic.

Before you leave this exercise, see the flowcharts in Chapter 9, which you might find useful in helping you organize a cause/effect paper.

EXERCISE FOUR
Sequential Order

In arranging supporting evidence in sequential order, you place items in a list of instructions in the order in which they occur.

Choose one of the following topics with your partner or make up a topic of your own. Together, make up a list of supporting evidence. Then, independently of your partner, organize the list in sequential order.

- How to pass first-year psychology
- How to prepare an omelet
- How to serve in racquetball
- How to change the oil in your car
- How to hold a golf club
- How to make chili
- How to hang glide
- How to eat spaghetti

With your partner, discuss the logic of each of your methods of organization. You might want to look at the single ladder (Exercise Eighteen) and pigeonhole (Exercise Twelve) graphics in Chapter 25, with a view to using them to help you organize a paper in sequential order.

EXERCISE FIVE
Spatial Order

In arranging supporting evidence in spatial order, you place descriptive details in terms of how you want your reader to *see* them: near to far, far to near, right to left, top to bottom, and so on.

1. Describe orally the room in which you eat most of your meals so that your partner can draw a map of it. (You are not allowed to look at your partner's map *during* your description.) In your description you must mention at least twenty things to be included in the map. Begin with the dimensions of the room, giving the location, number, and size of the doors and windows. Then describe the exact position of the table so that your partner can position everything else in relation to it. To assist you, use directional words like *next to*, *above*, *opposite to*, and *behind*.

2. When your partner has finished the map, see how accurately your description of the room has been interpreted. If there are glaring mistakes, discuss why they occurred.

3. Repeat the exercise, reversing the roles.

Note: You can also use the pigeonhole graphic in Chapter 25, Exercise Twelve to help you organize a paper in spatial order.

EXERCISE SIX
Chronological Order

In arranging supporting evidence in chronological order, you arrange events in a time sequence. If you introduce events out of order (flashbacks or flash-forwards), you should prepare your reader for the shift in time.

1. Tell your partner a story from the first-person viewpoint (I) or the third-person viewpoint (he or she). Use a chronological order. To keep your narrative coherent, you might like to repeat key words like the names of your characters and *I*, *my*, *him*, *she*, and *they*. Also use transitional devices like *although*, *as*, *in order that*, *then*, and *since*.

2. Have your partner number each new event as it occurs in your story.

3. Discuss with your partner the order of each of your events. Did your story have a beginning, middle, and ending? Was there an apparent order? Were the events presented in the best order? In what other order could the story have been told?

EXERCISE SEVEN
Climactic Order

In arranging supporting evidence in climactic order, you should arrange the events in order of their importance for your purposes.

1. Choose one of the following statements or decide on a statement of your own and ask your partner to provide orally six or seven reasons, facts, and examples to prove the statement. (Allow a few minutes for preparation.)

• Some of the local parking regulations should be eliminated.

• Many students do not deserve the opportunity to go to college.

• Mixed marriages don't work.

• In all marriages, one partner has to give up something.

Make sure your partner takes a strong stand, either for or against the idea expressed. The argument should open with one of the above thesis statements (or one of your own) and then have *particular* examples to prove the statement. Use transitional words like *furthermore*, *similarly*, *moreover*, *in addition*, and *finally* to help organize each idea coherently according to its importance.

2. When your partner finishes his or her proof, challenge any piece of information that you thought was either incorrect or inappropriate. Remember when you write an argumentative essay that if a piece of supporting evidence is not absolutely accurate, you should research and correct it or omit it.

3. Discuss the order of each item of proof. If your partner began with the least important item and ended with the most important, the result would be a climactic ending. If he or she organized from the most to the least important item, the beginning would have the greater impact. Which method did your partner use? Was it effective? Should any item be moved?

4. Now reverse the exercise so that you prove a statement.

The pigeonhole (Exercise Twelve) and single ladder (Exercise Eighteen) graphics in Chapter 25 will help you to organize your evidence in climactic order.

EXERCISE EIGHT
Familiar to Unfamiliar

In this method, you will be explaining something with which your audience is unfamiliar, but you will use characteristics, terms, and examples of things they know. Start with the features of the familiar object, then relate them with those of the unfamiliar item.

1. Orally, explain one of the following technically difficult subjects or abstractions to your partner: a lymph node, the DNA molecule, laundered money, clairvoyance, laser beams, continental drift, Darwin's theory of evolution, or one of your choice. Take a few minutes to decide on something familiar that you can compare your subject to; for example, a lymph node is similar to a filter. To help you in your explanation, use transitional expressions like *similarly, on the one hand . . . on the other hand*, or *somewhat like*.

2. Continue your explanation until your partner says, "I understand." Then your partner should explain one of the other items to you, following the same instructions.

3. You and your partner might like to make up your own exercises on variations of this method of organization. For example, you might want to use an *analogy* (sustained figurative comparison) or you might want to restate your thesis statement in different words. In a short oral presentation to your partner, use either analogy or restatement to organize one of the following broad topics:

- Pope John Paul II
- Vivisection
- The phlogiston theory
- Life is a river

You might want to use a mandala as an organizational tool; see Chapter 25, Exercise Fourteen, and Exercise One above.

EXERCISE NINE
Deductive and Inductive Reasoning

A popular method of presenting an argument involves deductive reasoning: writing a thesis statement and explaining or amplifying it with specific examples. You will also find this method referred to as "general-to-particular order." It is the method most commonly used to organize argumentative paragraphs and essays (Chapter 5).

You might also want to use inductive reasoning (also referred to as "particular-to-general order") in which a general conclusion is drawn from particular examples. Because you must keep your reader in suspense by withholding your conclusion until close to the end of your essay, you might not want to use inductive reasoning for an entire piece of writing, but you could certainly use induction to organize one or more paragraphs in an essay.

1. The following questions will lead to inductive reasoning because they require a definite answer:

- Should we stop nuclear stockpiling?
- Will I go to college next term?
- Are you going to get married?
- Is there a link between humans and monkeys?

Choose one of the questions and present your answer to your partner. However, if you provide a definite answer immediately (for example, to the first question you could answer yes), there would be no discussion, no presentation, and consequently no paragraph. Your task will be to see how long you can withhold your definite answer by using one or more of the tactics related to inductive reasoning:

- *Partial answers.* We should stop stockpiling cruise missiles for submarines, but not other weapons.
- *Possible answers.* We could ask the United Nations to supervise the disposal of present nuclear stockpiles.
- *Negative answers.* If we don't stop, sooner or later some terrorist group will steal our bombs and use them to blackmail us.
- *Comparisons.* Stockpiling nuclear weapons is like playing Russian roulette.
- *Inductive reasoning should conclude with your complete answer.* We should stop nuclear stockpiling before it's too late.

Reverse the exercise by having your partner choose a question and present his or her answer inductively.

2. The more your question suggests your answer, the more you will use deductive reasoning. Deduction is far more common as a method of organization than induction. The following questions will lead to deductive reasoning:

- Should we stop nuclear stockpiling now before it's too late?
- In order to obtain my law degree, should I continue at the university next term?
- Should people marry when they are young or wait until they are more mature?
- What links humans and monkeys?

Choose one of the questions and present your answer to your partner. Your task will be to see how fully you can answer the question through use of deductive reasoning: stating your thesis early, providing several instances which support it, and concluding by restating your thesis.

Reverse the exercise by having your partner choose a question and present his or her answer deductively.

3. You may word your beginning so as to provide a method of organization that requires both induction and deduction. The following statements will encourage inductive reasoning to be included within a basically deductive organization:

- We need to devise some methods of stopping nuclear stockpiling before it's too late.
- If I don't continue at the university next term, I will not obtain my law degree.
- There are advantages and disadvantages to marrying early.
- On the one hand, the links between humans and monkeys are apparent; on the other hand, humans and monkeys are light-years apart.

If you wish to use a graphic with inductive or deductive reasoning, refer to the flowcharts in Chapter 9. Before you do so, however, discuss with your partner the following graphics that illustrate deductive and inductive reasoning.

DEDUCTIVE REASONING: RESULTS TO REASONS, EFFECTS TO CAUSES, GENERAL STATEMENT TO PARTICULAR STATEMENT

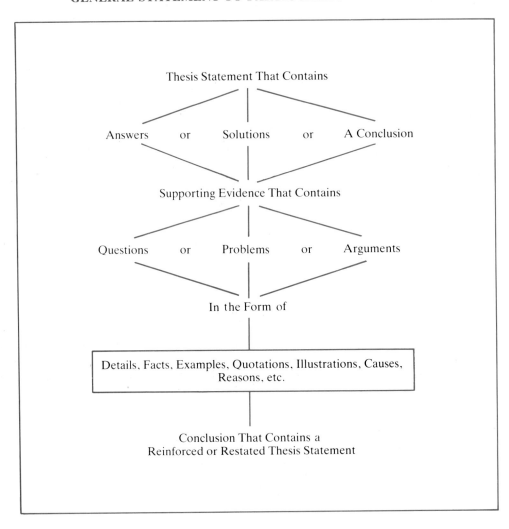

INDUCTIVE REASONING: REASONS TO RESULTS, CAUSES TO EFFECTS, PARTICULAR STATEMENT TO GENERAL STATEMENT

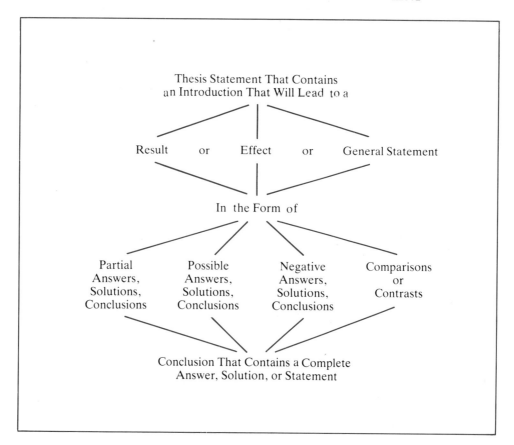

EXERCISE TEN
Development: Supporting Evidence/Methods of Organization

Each of the following pieces of writing has been developed using one main type of supporting evidence and has been organized in one specific manner. The heading on the left of each paragraph indicates the type of supporting evidence; the one on the right, the method of organization.

With your partner, find examples within each piece that illustrate both the type of supporting evidence and the method of organization. In addition, find the topic sentence in each of the paragraphs.

Facts   **Climactic Order**

In 1981 Jimmy Connors was an also-ran in the rich, fiercely competitive world of men's tennis. At age 29, not having won a major tournament since the 1978 U.S.

Open, he had been overshadowed first by Björn Borg and later by John McEnroe. He was known as much for his temper as for his tennis, as petulant as McEnroe when officials' calls went against him. Then, in 1982, a miracle happened. With Borg absent, Connors met McEnroe at Wimbledon and, in a grueling match, defeated him to win there for the first time since 1974. Two months later, at the U.S. Open, after McEnroe had been eliminated, Connors met Czechoslovakian Ivan Lendl and defeated him in four sets to win his fourth U.S. Open championship. Once again, Jimmy Connors was on top of the tennis world.

Definitions   **Chronological Order**

Calling the dog "man's best friend" has become a cliché, but what have dogs done for mankind to deserve the title? The question can be simply, though perhaps flippantly, answered: What haven't they done? From the earliest times, man and dog have been companions on the hunt, with the dog tracking the game and the hunter dispatching it. When hunters became farmers and herders, dogs became guardians of property and livestock. Some became beasts of burden, essential to travel and transport where other pack animals could not work. In the cities and towns of our society, though they still function as guardians and have recently become assistants to the blind and deaf, the dog's role as worker has been largely replaced by that of companion. And the unquestioning companionship and warmth that a dog provides make it indeed worthy to be called "man's best friend."

Examples   **Inductive Reasoning**

What does being "grown-up" mean? It does not just mean the legal entitlement to enter a bar and drink yourself into a stupor, or the right to mark an *X* on a ballot anywhere you choose. Nor is it the right to sign legal contracts for lifetimes of dance lessons and sets of encyclopedias. And it is certainly not simply being able to quit school and get a job. When you leave your family home and find a place of your own, you are generally considered grown-up, but leaving home is only one criterion for adulthood. Regardless of your chronological age, being grown-up means accepting responsibility for your actions and taking the time and effort to make wise decisions about yourself and your life.

Examples   **Deductive Reasoning**

What does being "grown-up" mean? The legal age varies from state to state, but when you reach the official age of twenty-one, you are generally considered to be an adult. In North American society, obtaining a driver's license or being allowed by law to enter a bar or sign a contract are also considered signs that you are an adult. And certainly one of the ultimate indications that you have reached independence is moving into your own apartment. But even if you are over twenty-one, drive a car, go to bars, and live alone, you may not be completely grown-up. Regardless of your age, being grown-up means accepting responsibility for your actions and taking the time and effort to make wise decisions about yourself and your life.

Quoted Material and Details Spatial Order

Stephen King's description of CIA agent John Rainbird in *Firestarter* makes him seem like the most frightening character in the novel. "As big as life and twice as ugly . . . he stood two inches shy of seven feet tall, and he wore his glossy hair drawn back and tied in a curt ponytail. Ten years before, a Claymore had blown up in his face during his second tour of Vietnam, and now his countenance was a horror show of scar tissue with runneled flesh. His left eye was gone. There was nothing where it had been but a ravine. He would not have plastic surgery or an artificial eye because, he said, when he got to the happy hunting ground beyond, he would be asked to show his battle scars." But as an agent, Rainbird, despite his terrifying appearance, is both efficient and successful.

Details Comparison

The masks worn by the goaltenders in the National Hockey League bear a striking resemblance to those worn by Indian medicine men on the Canadian West Coast. A recent cross-country exhibit that showed both types of masks side-by-side made their similarities in design and purpose apparent. The Indian masks were decorated with personal and clan totems; the goalies' masks bear the crest of their team. Their purposes, too, are similar: to protect the wearer from evil spirits (or opponents' pucks) and make the wearer seem terrifying, with an almost supernatural ability. The goalie's mask, like the shaman's, is an element in a ritual: the ritual of a North American sport.

Questions General to Particular

Does your life seem empty? Do you wonder whether, in the bustle of modern living, you have simply been passed by? Do days and evenings stretch ahead of you with no prospect of any meaningful activity to fill them? If you can answer yes to any or all of these questions, why not take a giant step towards self-fulfillment by offering your services as a volunteer to a local service agency? In addition to helping others, you may discover talents and abilities you never knew you had. Isn't there someone in your community who could use your help?

Illustration through Narration Effect and Cause

One of the most common fears is fear of the dark; it usually stems from a childhood incident. My fear started when I was five years old. My brother Bill was two years older, and since no other children lived in our neighborhood, we played together a great deal. One summer afternoon we were playing hide-and-seek, one of our favorite games. Instead of hiding among the raspberry bushes as I usually did, I decided to hide in the old root cellar near the house. I pushed open the heavy door and heard it slam behind me as I ran down the stairs. I found myself in absolute darkness, and I heard what I thought were thousands of mice scrambling around me. I became more and more frightened. Crying, I crawled back up the stairs, only to discover that I couldn't open the door. I banged on it and yelled "Help! Get me out!"

as loudly as I could. Finally Bill heard me and ran to get my mother, who opened the door and rescued me. Almost anyone who fears the dark can relate a similar story.

Examples   **Cause and Effect**

Imagine that a nuclear weapon has been detonated in your area. Can you picture the devastation? Thousands of people have died immediately from the heat and intense vibration of the explosion. Thousands more will die within a few days from either injuries sustained in the blast or from the fires and explosions that follow it. But these quick deaths are only the beginning. Lethal radiation, spread by wind currents, will poison air, water, and soil many miles from ground zero (the site of the blast); and the contamination will last for months, perhaps years. Radiation sickness and cancer will cause slow, agonizing deaths for decades after the initial explosion. Is anything worth the danger of nuclear weapons?

Details   **Sequential Order**

A hard- or soft-cooked (*never* boiled) egg is a healthful, delicious breakfast that anyone can make. Place a fresh egg in a saucepan. Add enough cold water just to cover it and set it over your heat source. Bring the water to a boil, cover the saucepan, remove it from the heat, and let the egg continue to cook in the water until it is done as you like. If you like your egg yolk soft, three to five minutes is long enough; if you like it hard, leave your egg in the pan for up to ten minutes. Crack the shell, add butter and salt to taste, and you have an egg-citing meal.

Examples   **Analogy**

Richard Schickel in his *Time* review of *The History of the World—Part I* gives his opinion succinctly: "If history, as they say, is a pack of tricks the living play on the dead, then Mel Brooks, who should be good at this game, is playing with a very thin deck. In his recreation of four epochs (prehistory, the Roman Empire, the Spanish Inquisition, and the French Revolution), he uses only two cards: cruelty and scatology. They are not aces. They are not even jokers."

Details   **Contrast**

LONDON—Ticket prices, production quality, and depth of cast are among the major differences between Broadway and this city's West End theater scene. Though prices are rising, the best seats in London still cost less than twenty dollars, meaning one can see about twice the number of shows for the same amount of money. But sharp eyes will spot the differences in quality those extra Broadway dollars guarantee. London sets are definitely more flimsy than their American cousins. Costumes seem less coordinated, more likely to have come from the trunk rather than the seamstress. Lighting instruments are fewer by half than the Broadway standard. But nobody seems to mind. Business is brisk. The theatres themselves, about forty of them mostly built around the turn of the century by the same handful of architects, are inviting, exciting, and professionally run. Since each house maintains a full-time technical staff, instead of hiring for each show as on Broadway, they rarely stay dark for long. In this capital city, center of all English arts production, the talent pool makes it easy to pull a revival together quickly, making the West End one of the world's greatest museums of theatrical styles.

Reasons   Cause and Effect

More and more people are discovering the physical and psychological benefits of exercise. The heart of a person who exercises regularly pumps blood more powerfully through the body. The lungs are able to take in more air and process it more efficiently. Regularly used muscles maintain their tone and increase their strength and endurance. Improved blood flow makes skin and hair look and feel better. In addition, a healthy body is better able to withstand the stress of daily living, and its owner is therefore less susceptible to physical and mental illnesses. In short, getting into fitness is a "step in the right direction."

Illustration through Description   Familiar to Unfamiliar

Almost everyone has seen a pig, but very few people have seen one of the pig's distant relatives, the collared peccary. The peccary's short, squat body and stubby legs resemble a pig's, and its snout is somewhat piglike; but the resemblance ends there. Instead of the smooth pink, white, or mottled skin of the domestic pig, the peccary is covered with short, grayish, bristly hair; a ring of lighter-colored hair around the neck gives the collared peccary its name. In the wild, the collared peccary ranges from the southern United States through South America. It is mainly vegetarian, though it will eat grubs and even snakes, since it is apparently immune to rattlesnake venom. Like the pig, the peccary is hunted for its meat and hide. Despite its usefulness, though, its appearance makes it an animal that only its mother could love.

Quoted Material   Climactic Order

Nobody seems to agree on the definition, the nature, or the cause of alcoholism. "Drunkenness is nothing but a condition of insanity, purposefully assumed," says the Roman philosopher Seneca. Aristophanes states that drinkers "are rich and successful and win lawsuits and are happy and help their friends." Oliver Goldsmith points out that "good liquor . . . gives genius a better discerning," while Lord Byron labels drinking "a mere pause from thinking." Many literary figures have condemned alcoholism, few more strongly than Victor Hugo in *Les Miserables*, in which he describes "the four descending degrees of drunkenness: the first, that which enlivens; the second, that which irritates; the third, that which stupefies; finally, the last, that which brutalizes."

EXERCISE ELEVEN
Combinations of Methods

Up to now you have been working with only one method of organization at a time. Most writers use combinations of supporting evidence and methods of organization.

Find several paragraphs similar in length to the one below. Ask your partner to read and analyze them with you. Determine what methods of organization were used to create the product; in other words, say something about *each* sentence and its function in the paragraph, as in the following example.

I believe that the invention for which the twentieth century will be remembered in history will not be the motion picture or the television set, or even the silicon chip. (*This introduces the paragraph and builds up to the thesis by saying what the writer believes will* not *be true.*) It will be the atomic bomb. (*topic statement*) This diabolical device, though it is so simple to construct that an intelligent high-school student can build one, is capable of destroying the earth and everything on it in a matter of seconds. (*An illustration and an effect*) Its main ingredient, plutonium or enriched uranium, is supposedly under strict supervision of the countries who possess a supply. (*A fact*) But enough of the stuff to make several hundred bombs the size of the one that destroyed Hiroshima has "disappeared" from storage facilities or while in transit. (*A fact*) A number of films—*In Like Flint, Thunderball,* and *Superman I,* to name three—have been based on someone's building or stealing an atomic bomb and holding the world for ransom. (*Details and effect*) With the possibility of total destruction at a mad person's whim staring us in the face, I can only hope that there will be someone around a millennium hence to remember the twentieth century. (*Conclusion provides a link to the beginning.*)

SUMMARY

Once you have learned to organize your writing, unifying it should pose no difficulty. You should be able to see which pieces of evidence support your thesis statement and which are irrelevant or illogical.

Drafting your piece of writing is a natural, easy, logical outcome of all the work you have done in collecting, listing, organizing, and unifying your supporting evidence. Do you see how easy it will now be to draft an essay?

30

Coherence

INTRODUCTION

When your writing is coherent, your reader cannot help but understand what you are saying; everything is tied together clearly and logically. To keep your writing flowing and to help your readers follow your ideas, concentrate on these four points:

1. Use some logical method of organization (dealt with in Chapters 7 to 10 and 29).
2. Structure your sentences in such a way that the sequence in which they are arranged links them to each other (dealt with in Chapter 35 and most of the Third Workshop Section).
3. Use transitional devices to connect sentences and paragraphs.
4. Repeat a key word or phrase to remind your reader of the important points of your essay.

EXERCISE ONE
Transitions

Transitions show relationships between thoughts and give a sense of direction and continuity to your writing. They assist your reader in moving not only from detail to detail within a single sentence but also from sentence to sentence and paragraph to paragraph. Like road markers, transitions inform your readers that one part or stage of the discussion has ended; transitions also give them a hint of what connection the next phase of thought has with the just-completed phase. Transitions are a vital factor in coherence.

The following list contains some useful transitional expressions and conjunctions. As you and your partner read the list, notice the specific reasons for introducing certain words into your sentences. When you compose, keep this list handy.

Addition	in addition, in addition to, additionally, another, besides, moreover, further, furthermore, equally important, much more interesting, of even greater appeal, more specifically, accordingly, in fact, likewise, next, too, then, and, both, both . . . and, not only . . . but (also), first, second, in the third place (do not use *firstly, secondly, thirdly*)
Comparison	similarly, likewise, in like manner, by comparison, compared to, vis-à-vis, just as surely, in the same way, not only . . . but (also), both . . . and, either . . . or
Contrast	but, however, yet, still, nevertheless, on the one hand, on the other hand, for all of that, on the contrary, notwithstanding, in contrast, in contrast to, rather, neither . . . nor, although, though, in spite of, whereas
Emphasis	in fact, indeed, in truth, in any event, certainly, definitely, emphatically, unquestionably, undoubtedly, without a doubt, undeniably, without reservation, naturally, obviously, decidedly, markedly, notably, not only . . . but (also), both . . . and
Example	for example, for instance, in this case, in another case, on this occasion, in this situation, as proof, as evidence, such as, take the case of, proof of this, evidence of this, thus
Exception	yet, still, however, nevertheless, in spite of, despite, once in a while, sometimes, nonetheless, though, although
Place	near, beyond, opposite to, adjacent to, at the same place, here, there, from, over, in the middle, around, in front of, in the distance, farther, here and there, above, below, at the right, between, in the foreground, on this side, beside, next to, at the back of, behind
Purpose	to this end, with this object, for this purpose, in order that, in this way, since, so that, on that account, in case, with a view to, for the same reason, in the event that
Repetition	in other words, that is to say, as I have said, again, once again, to reiterate
Result	accordingly, thus, consequently, hence, therefore, thereupon, inevitably, under these conditions, as a result, as a consequence, consequently, because, because of, so that, not only . . . but (also), so as, since

Sequence	first, second, third, A, B, C, 1, 2, 3, next, then, at the outset, following this, at this time, now, at this point, after, afterwards, after this, subsequently, lastly, finally, consequently, before this, previously, preceding this, simultaneously, concurrently, meanwhile
Summary	in brief, on the whole, in sum, to sum up, to conclude, hence, for this reason, in short, in summary, in conclusion, ultimately
Time	at once, immediately, at length, in the meantime, meanwhile, at the same time, in the end, in the interim, then, soon, not long after, at length, at last, finally, some time ago, later, afterwards, presently, from this time on, from time to time, after, before, until, at present, all of a sudden, instantly, at this instant, suddenly, now, without delay, in the first place, forthwith, quickly, at this point, a few minutes later, formerly, yesterday, later in the day, since then, when, whenever, next, as, once, since, occasionally, henceforth, thereupon, sometimes, in a moment, shortly, whereupon, previously, currently

1. The following examples illustrate how a transition placed at the beginning of a new sentence or paragraph not only shows a step forward in the thought but also relates the new material to what precedes it.

- *However*, Woodrow Wilson's desire for United States membership in the League of Nations was not supported by the Senate. (The transitional expression *however* shows that the new paragraph will present material in contrast with that in the preceding paragraph.)
- *Consequently*, when he ran for president, Andrew Jackson could already claim a popular reputation as a man of action. (The transition shows that the sentence is a result of statements previously made.)

With your partner, decide what the following transitions indicate.

- *In addition*, Theodore Roosevelt was a Phi Beta Kappa scholar.
- *In fact*, Thomas Jefferson was *also* an inventor, an architect, and a scientist.
- *Finally*, Lyndon Johnson was elected to the presidency in his own right.

2. Transitional words and phrases may be placed anywhere within sentences to add variety to your sentences. Independently of your partner, move the above transitions elsewhere in their sentences—for example:

- Woodrow Wilson's desire for United States membership in the League of Nations, *however*, was not supported by the Senate. (Note that you need to use commas around the transitional word.)

Compare the effectiveness of your sentences.

3. Reread the example sentences above. Which transitional words from the master list could you substitute for the ones that have been used? As long as the meaning of the sentence does not change, you can easily change the transitional words.

EXERCISE TWO
Experimenting with Transition

1. Examine the following sentences with your partner:

Weak Transition

John Adams and John Quincy Adams were father and son, and they were presidents of the United States.
Stronger Transition

John Adams and John Quincy Adams were father and son; both were presidents of the United States.

Weak Transition

Richard Nixon resigned from office, so Vice-President Gerald Ford became president.
Stronger Transition

Richard Nixon resigned from office; consequently, Vice-President Gerald Ford became president.
Note: Punctuation marks, especially semicolons, can also be effective transitional devices. Would deleting *consequently* and the comma change the transition? Is the semicolon alone as effective?

No Transition

Ulysses S. Grant was skillful as a general. He was not skillful as a politician. He was better able to lead the Union Army than effectively govern the country as president.
Subordination Added

Since Ulysses S. Grant was more skillful as a general rather than as a politician, he was better able to lead the Union Army than to govern the country effectively as president.

No Transition

Dwight Eisenhower built an illustrious, world famous army career. He might have retired among his past military glories. Many other victorious commanders retired among their past military glories. He accepted and won the new challenge of becoming president.
Subordination and Transition Added

Dwight Eisenhower built an illustrious, world famous army career. Because of this, like many other victorious commanders, he might have retired among his past military glories. Instead, he accepted and won the new challenge of becoming president.

Notice the different effect created by changing or adding a transitional device in the following sentences:

No Transition

After serving one term, Grover Cleveland lost the presidency to Benjamin Harrison in 1888. He ran again in 1892 and was able to defeat Harrison.
Transition of Contrast Added

After serving one term, Grover Cleveland lost the presidency to Benjamin Harrison in 1888, yet he ran again in 1892 and was able to defeat Harrison.
Transition of Sequence Added

After serving one term, Grover Cleveland lost the presidency to Benjamin Harrison in 1888; subsequently, he ran again in 1892 and was able to defeat Harrison.

No Transition

James A. Garfield is virtually unknown to most Americans as a president. He had actively served only four months in office when an assassin shot him.
Transition of Emphasis Added

James A. Garfield is virtually unknown to most Americans as a president; indeed, he had actively served only four months in office when an assassin shot him.
Transition of Result Added

James A. Garfield had actively served only four months in office when an assassin shot him; as a result, he is virtually unknown to most Americans as a president. (What effect does reversing the sentence order have on the transition?)

> When you use transitional expressions, be sure that you convey your exact meaning to the reader.

EXERCISE THREE
Key Words

One method of achieving coherence is to repeat your subject's name throughout your writing. Your reader will thus be kept constantly aware of your subject. But repetition for its own sake, without a specific (usually ironic) purpose, can be boring. You might find it a good idea to use replacement nouns or pronouns instead. You might, for example, in a paragraph discussing Ronald Reagan, refer to him as "the President" or "the Chief Executive," as well as use pronouns such as "he," "his," "himself."

Prepare a one-minute talk for your partner on one of the following topics. As you talk, your partner should record your use of key words.

a. The President of the United States **c.** Mother Teresa

b. Your favorite TV personality **d.** The oldest person you know

EXERCISE FOUR
Sentence Work

1. Independently of your partner, choose a reason for joining each of the following sets of sentences. Then use an appropriate transition.

a. Harry Truman won the 1948 presidential election. Most of the country's newspapers confidently predicted he would lose to Thomas Dewey.

b. Before America entered World War II, President Franklin Roosevelt proposed to help the Allies against the Axis powers. He asked Congress to support his lend-lease program in early 1941.

c. James Madison's presidency was eventful. The War of 1812 and the British raid on Washington, D.C., occurred during his term in office.

d. Gerald Ford was the last president to direct any American activity in the Vietnam conflict. Presidents before him oversaw at least some amount of financial or armed involvement there. They were Presidents Nixon, Johnson, Kennedy, Eisenhower, and Truman.

e. George Washington was the first president of the United States. He is called the father of our country. Most Americans know this.

f. Ronald Reagan was the first person from the entertainment world to become president. He was the oldest person to become president.

g. Four presidents were assassinated while in office. They were Lincoln, Garfield, McKinley, and Kennedy. Attempts were made against the lives of Presidents Jackson, Theodore Roosevelt, Truman, Ford, and Reagan.

h. Franklin Delano Roosevelt holds the record for serving the longest term in office. He was president for 12 years and 39 days. William Henry Harrison holds the record for serving the shortest term in office. He was president for 32 days.

i. From 1789 to 1984 forty American men have served in the office of the presidency. Americans are still waiting for a female president. Other countries have female leaders.

Compare your use of transition with your partner's. Then both of you compare your answers with those suggested following Chapter 33.

2. The following sentences support the thesis statement "Each presidency is a unique mixture of power, personality, and circumstance." Rearrange the supporting evidence in a logical order, making sure that *every* sentence is relevant to the claim. Change some key words to pronouns and use a few transitional devices. Compare your paragraph with your partner's. Have you both produced coherent paragraphs? See the Suggested Answers (following Chapter 33) for another treatment.

- The nature of the times and circumstances will certainly affect a presidency.
- Every president will represent that mixture in his own way.
- Andrew Jackson distinguished himself by his strong personality and the ability to effectively promote his policies.

- Each presidency is a unique mixture of power, personality, and circumstance.
- A president's power may dramatically increase during economic depression, periods of social unrest, and wartime.
- Each presidency is inevitably unique.
- Theodore Roosevelt distinguished himself by his strong personality and the ability to effectively promote his policies.
- The chief executive's powers have actually changed little since George Washington's inauguration in 1789.
- The presidents have all varied in political shrewdness, dedication, energy, imagination, communication skills, and other qualities.
- A president's power may decline during periods of peace.
- Each president has used the chief executive's powers somewhat differently.

EXERCISE FIVE
Three Key Words

Beginning a paper with three key words can also give it coherence. Read this paragraph, paying attention to the linking lines.

The Inner City

Stinking, deceiving, threatening, the city lies in wait for its unwary victims. Faceless fetid masses are moving to humorless destinations in pursuit of nameless desires. Gutters carry both the filth of the day and the dregs of the night. Neon signs entice like sweet-singing sirens, inviting the foolish to part with the fruit of their labors. Hucksters share street corners with pimps and harlots, coloring the air with dark shades of danger. Strangers are not subjects of interest but the harbingers of fear. Murderers and cutthroats linger on the edge of obscurity, waiting to become all too conspicuous. Such is life in the inner city.

Study the lines that tie particular words to the first three words. Do you see how the words that have been connected give the paragraph coherence? Can you draw further lines? (*Note:* The writer has used no other transitional devices, yet the paragraph is coherent.)

Besides key words, what type of supporting evidence (facts, details, reasons, and so on) and which method of organization (comparison, cause/effect, analogy, and so on) have been used?

For your partner, write a paragraph beginning with three key words: for example, "Pale, nervous, and uncomfortable"; "Exhausting, challenging, but rewarding"; "Slippery, juicy, and tasty." Give the paragraph to your partner, and ask him or her to draw lines similar to those in the above paragraph *and to point out the details of your organization*.

31

Self-Editing, Peer-Editing, and Instructor-Editing

INTRODUCTION

Revision is an ongoing process for every writer. For many it is standard practice to have a number of editors and several rewrites. A note on the front page of James A. Michener's *The Covenant* reads:

> Working together for two years, we [Michener and his editor, Errol L. Uys] read the finished manuscript together seven times, twice aloud, a most demanding task. I thank him for his assistance.

To those who read *The Independent Writer*, student Mike Jutras writes a letter to encourage peer-editing. Read his letter in the products of Chapter 18.

This textbook has gone through several drafts. Every section has been revised, reformed, refined, and reshaped because the author clarified his thoughts while developing the manuscript and listened to comments from fellow teachers, editors, consultants, and students using pilot editions of the textbook. The result of their interest and concern is *The Independent Writer*.

In this chapter you will learn a few strategies on how to edit not only your own writing but also that of your peers. Before you start looking at the detailed suggestions, however, you should realize that there is no precise list of questions which you can apply to everything you are asked to edit. Editing is an inexact and subjective science. Some writers do not want their work tampered with; "Make only suggestions," they say. Other writers prefer that their editors rewrite their work in order to bring out their points more clearly. Your task as editor will be to maintain the writer's uniqueness while at the same time making sure that the reader will comprehend the message. Editor Brian Vachon says, "I rearrange a writer's words while trying not to clutter up his ideas. It's difficult work but it's also immensely satisfying." Doubtless, your work as an editor of others will result in your becoming a better writer.

Essentially, an editor makes a draft more readable by paring down, building up, moving things around, improving grammar, quickening the pace, clarifying confusions, and correcting inaccuracies. Every draft of everything you write will benefit from a second pair of eyes before you present it to your intended reader. If this paragraph sounds a little overwhelming or if you say, "I don't feel capable of helping because I am not confident enough," remember this: the least you can do for a writer after reading his or her draft is to say, "I love it," or "I don't understand what your point is."

Peer-editing is just another form of brainstorming; therefore, approach the editing process in the same creative way you approach your prewriting and drafting processes.

EXERCISE ONE
Revising Your Own Work

This textbook advocates that when you have completed your final draft, you should ask your peer-editors and instructor-editor for their opinions before you submit your paper to its intended reader. Often, though, you will not have the time or opportunity for editorial assistance. At other times, you may not want to have your writing edited; you may want to give it directly to your intended reader without anyone else's seeing it.

When you have completed your final draft, but *before* you give it to your editors or intended reader, you should examine your content, organization, style, and mechanics. Using the suggestions in the following four charts, judge your work as *superior*, *average*, or *unsatisfactory*. Afterwards, if you are not satisfied with your paper, you should try to revise it to the standard you desire.

CONTENT

Content involves the limited topic (subject, main idea, thesis) of the paper and its development.

Superior

1. The central idea is worthwhile: fresh, true, specific, and clear. The writer has expressed the central idea in a thesis or topic statement accurately and interestingly.
2. The idea is suitable for the length of the paper. The writer has developed it perfectly.
3. The writer has presented all the evidence fully, through high-quality facts, reasons, details, examples, and so on.

Average

1. The central idea is apparent but unoriginal. The thesis or topic statement is clear but not interesting.
2. The development relies on common, everyday details.

3. The development is often incomplete or repetitious and includes unimportant, obvious, or irrelevant support.
4. There may be some inconsistencies in the logical development of the limited topic.

Unsatisfactory

1. The central idea is either nonexistent or totally unimportant and trite. The writer may or may not have expressed the central idea in a thesis or topic statement.
2. If there is a worthwhile idea, the writer provides no specific support of the thesis statement.
3. The development of a reasonable idea is confused and worthless.
4. The thesis statement and its development are inappropriate for the length of the assignment: the idea is either underdeveloped or overly repetitious.

Note: If your content falls into the "unsatisfactory" category, you may be totally unaware of your writing problems. On the other hand, if you thought the above four points applied to your writing, you would not want to give it to your editors, let alone your intended reader, until you found something worthwhile to write about.

How would you judge your content: superior, average, or unsatisfactory?

ORGANIZATION

Organization involves the flow of a paper's development, the linking of each sentence within a paragraph, and the logical progression from one paragraph to the next (See Chapters 28 to 30).

Superior

1. The writer has developed the central idea clearly and logically. It is obvious that the writer has used a process of writing and has considered the writing variables. The reader moves effortlessly from one section of the paper to the next.
2. The development has a specific, definite method of organization: comparison, cause/effect, spatial, chronological, climactic, and so on. The writer has given each piece of supporting evidence just the right emphasis and attention. Furthermore, the supporting evidence is in exactly the right places in the paper.
3. There is nothing irrelevant in the paper.

Average

1. The paper apparently has an organizational plan, but at times it loses its focus.

2. There is something wrong with the emphasis or order of some of the points; the writer over- or under-stresses them, or positions them incorrectly.
3. The writer may miss certain transitions or use painfully predictable ones (for example, first, second, third, fourth, finally).

Unsatisfactory

1. There is no clear organization.
2. The supporting evidence is either sketchy or redundant.
3. The paragraphs are not unified or coherent; transitions are insufficient or confusing.
4. Often, a writer introduces a new idea in a paragraph before fully developing the previous one.

How would you judge your organization: superior, average, or unsatisfactory?

STYLE

Style involves not only the mode of expression but its effectiveness and appropriateness for each particular piece of writing (See Chapter 34).

Superior

1. The readers are always kept on track because the point of view is consistent.
2. Sentence variety is apparent throughout. The mode of expression is as interesting as the thought it contains.
3. The word choice is clear and accurate, always appropriately linking the writer and the subject to the reader.
4. The level of language is consistent.
5. The writer often uses effective figurative language.
6. The beginning and ending of the piece seems just right.

Average

1. The sentence structure is correct but often lacks variety and emphasis. Some sentences may be wordy; others too short.
2. The writer often uses generalized rather than specific words; they are correct but not always apt.
3. Sometimes the writer mixes levels of language.
4. If the writer uses figurative comparisons, they are sometimes strained, mixed, ineffective, or inappropriate.

Unsatisfactory

1. Sentences are confusing and monotonous.
2. Sentences lack emphasis, often because the writer uses weak verbs and overuses pronouns such as *it*, *this*, and *which*.

3. The writer's word choice is limited and often ineffective or inappropriate.
4. Slang expressions, colloquialisms, and triteness fill the paper.
5. The writing is often unidiomatic, using non-English expressions or fracturing idioms.
6. The point of view shifts constantly.

How would you judge your style: superior, average, or unsatisfactory?

MECHANICS

Mechanics deals with the nitty-gritty of writing: spelling, punctuation, grammar, and so on (See the Fourth Workshop Section).

Superior

1. Grammar, punctuation, and spelling are generally accurate.
2. The paper is usually free of small mechanical errors, such as the misuse of apostrophes and hyphens, numbers, capitalization, and so on.
3. The writer punctuates sentences correctly and shows an understanding of the more complex punctuation marks: semicolons, parentheses, dashes, as well as double and single quotation marks.
4. The writing contains no serious sentence errors such as fragment faults, dangling modifiers, run-on sentences, and so on.
5. The writing contains various methods of emphasis.

Average

1. Occasional mechanical errors creep into the writing.
2. The writing is often correct and careful; but to avoid making mechanical mistakes, the writer overuses some words for fear of misspelling or misusing new ones, uses only commas and periods for fear of misusing semicolons, or composes simple sentences for fear of creating misplaced modifiers. (In other words, your instructor may classify your mechanics as "average," even when everything is correct, because you have not used a full complement of various punctuation marks. To become a superior writer, you must take chances and learn from your mistakes.)

Unsatisfactory

1. Because mechanical errors abound, a reader often makes no sense of sentences. The writer has not come to terms with his or her writing problems, does not know why he or she makes mistakes, and does not know how to correct them. The writer continues to shift tenses in mid-sentence, to run sentences together, and to let fragments stand as complete thoughts.
2. Punctuation marks are absent or incorrect.

3. Spelling errors are frequent.
4. Many pronoun references are wrong.

How would you judge your mechanics: superior, average, or unsatisfactory?

EXERCISE TWO
Revising the Writing of Your Peers

Peer-editing is so beneficial to the revision process that you and your peers should attempt to offer each other suggestions on every assignment. Even professional writers require editors, who serve as an important part of their writing process. So, how can you, a student writer, possibly ignore the benefits of peer-editing? With your partner, discuss—at some length—the following material.

Student peer-editing works for a variety of reasons:

- The student writer takes responsibility for learning.
- Students seem to accept peer criticism more readily than criticism from an instructor.
- Immediate personal commentary speeds revision and, therefore, speeds the entire writing process.
- A group of peers provides several different audience members for student writers to consider, cutting down on the possibility of their writing exclusively for instructors.
- Students have a great influence on other students. If peers apply positive pressure, students have unlimited possibilities for improvement.
- Peer-editing serves as an intermediate step between teacher dependence and independence. Through peer assistance the student moves towards becoming an independent writer.

Once you and your peers become comfortable with editing each other's work, you will probably find that you will ask them for their comments before submitting anything you write to your intended reader.

What follows are some specific guidelines and suggestions for handling peer-editing sessions.

1. Every writer appreciates praise, so begin by pointing out the things that work well. Here are a few questions you might respond to after you have read one of your peers' papers:

- Which senses were stimulated?
- What part created the strongest impression?
- What part was the most genuine?
- Where did the paper divulge the most about the writer?
- What overall emotion will the intended audience be left with?

2. During a peer-editing session, make sure that you and your peers comment on the writing variables. You should routinely ask questions like the following:

- Is the limited topic worthwhile?
- Is the limited topic narrow enough or is it too broad to suit the length of the paper?
- Is the limited topic clearly stated in the form of a thesis or topic statement?
- Is the writer's point of view or attitude toward the topic clear?
- Does the material fulfill its purpose: to persuade, to inform, to entertain, and so on?
- Is the material suitable in content, level of language, and sentence length for its intended audience?
- Would the piece of writing be better in another format?
- Has the writer's and audience's situation been fully realized? Does the piece of writing reflect the writer's consideration of situation?
- Is the choice of the writer's voice appropriate? Should the writer have used a persona instead?

3. You should make suggestions about what to delete, add, substitute, or move; this applies to words, sentences, or paragraphs. In this part of the editing process you should consider the effectiveness of each sentence. If you write directly on the author's paper, get into the habit of using the proofreaders' and editorial symbols on the back inside cover of this text. Using these symbols will save you a great deal of time.

The more familiar you become with the Workshop sections of this textbook, the more suggestions for revision you will be able to share during peer-editing sessions. Some of the most recent research refers to this step in the writing process as "reformation," where you, as editor, should encourage the writer to "re-form" what he or she has written.

In essence, a worthwhile peer-editing session should give you an impression of the effect that your writing will have on the intended audience and provide ideas and suggestions on how to sharpen that effect.

4. A successful peer-editing session requires honesty and courage; you must be truthful, and the writer must be willing to accept your criticism. Thoughtfulness and thoroughness are also essential. When something is unsatisfactory, you should tactfully say so, pointing out what is wrong and making suggestions to improve the piece of writing.

5. Peer-editing takes time. It is very easy to say that everything someone writes is wonderful. This kind of statement saves a lot of talk, prevents any anxiety, and perhaps wins an immediate friend. Such a statement, however, does not help a writer. Treat your peer-editing sessions as an essential part of the writing process, and be prepared to spend time talking about a paper's thesis statement, organization, sentence variety, and word choice. If you, as a peer-editor, feel that something in the paper is not working, even *if you do not know exactly what is wrong or how to fix it,* you should say so. When you say, "I'm having a problem with this part," a worthwhile discussion is bound to follow. Your comments and suggestions will probably be tentative at first, but as you continue, you will find the words to express your confusion with the paper you are editing. When you are involved in a peer-editing session, you are involved in both a learning and a teaching experience. When the members of your group learn to share knowledge with each other, you will all learn to write better.

6. All of the assignments in *The Independent Writer* have specific suggestions for peer-editing sessions. If you are involved in peer-editing with more than two people, make sure one of you takes on the duties of leader for that particular session. The leader is responsible for keeping the discussion going and asking the questions contained in the Revising Process in each assignment. Your first attempts at editing may not be too successful, but research has shown that you can learn from your peers (often more effectively than from anyone else).

EXERCISE THREE
Help for Your Editors

From time to time you might like to try one or both of the following suggestions during your revising sessions with your peers and your instructor. Both have proved highly beneficial to the writing process, resulting in a most satisfactory product.

Statement of Writing Variables

If your instructor does not ask you to list your writing variables, you could provide a statement of them for your editors. Include the following:

a. Who you are; whether you are writing in your own voice or role-playing (using a persona); why you chose your persona

b. Who your audience is; what your relationship is to him, her, or them; how familiar your audience is with your topic; any information about the audience that you think would affect your approach to the topic; whether your audience is real or imagined

c. What your purpose is for writing; how other variables influence your purpose; whether you are writing for a real-life or a made-up reason

d. What your limited topic, thesis, or message is; what your thesis or topic statement is; what kind of development you are employing to support your thesis

e. What the situation is for you (the writer) and your audience; whether the situation is real or contrived for this assignment; how the situation affects the writing

f. What your format is; whether the piece is complete as is or is part of a larger work

g. Where or for whom you intend to publish, post, or present your piece; whether you really intend to present it to its intended reader or whether you are using the assignment merely as an exercise.

SELF-EVALUATION OF A PAPER

Attach to your paper a note that gives your own evaluation of it so that your editors can read what you think about your paper. Respond to one or more of the following questions:

a. How long did it take you to write the paper?

b. What part of the writing process did you find easiest?

c. What part of the writing process did you find most difficult?

d. What do you consider the strongest point in your paper?

e. What do you consider the weakest aspect of your paper?

f. What do you like best in your paper?

g. What do you like least in your paper?

h. What do you consider is your strongest rhetorical tactic: sentence structure, diction, comparisons, and so on?

i. What parts of your paper do you think need revision?

j. What would you like your editors to help you with?

EXERCISE FOUR
Different Peer-Editing Sessions

To make all your peer-editing sessions profitable, you and your peers can choose from a variety of editing methods. No matter what kind of peer-editing session you employ, you—as editor—should consider everything that you have read in the previous exercises in this chapter as well as the specific editing suggestions found in each of the assignments in the first twenty-three chapters of *The Independent Writer*.

For Pairs of Students

Silent Reading

a. Exchange papers with your partner.

b. As you read, prepare yourself to talk about what has been written, beginning with the strengths of the piece of writing, but not ignoring the weaknesses.

c. Write directly on the piece of writing or make comments on separate paper.

d. Do not talk until both papers have been read; then discuss one paper at a time, using any of the suggestions above.

Read Aloud

a. Read your paper aloud. Your partner should be able to see what you are reading. This way he or she can hear your inflections while seeing your written words. Often your partner will see what you do not see. A writer often reads what he or she *thinks* is there, not what really *is* there.

b. Your partner should not interrupt your reading but, at the end, may ask you to reread the paper so that he or she can then interrupt in order to ask questions or make a particular point.

c. A discussion, following the suggestions above, should follow.

d. Repeat the procedure with your partner's paper.

For a Three-Member Peer Group

Numbers and Letters

a. Exchange papers.

b. Every time you see something that you would like to comment on, place a number in the margin near it.

c. Then on a separate piece of paper place the number and your favorable or unfavorable comment. For example:

1. opening is very good

2. should appeal to the sense of smell

3. grammatical mistake

d. Then pass the piece of writing, with the numbers on it, to the next person to read. (*Do not* pass your comments. All the next person sees is the piece of writing with a series of numbers in the margin.)

e. The next person should repeat the same process, except he or she should use letters instead of numbers. For example:

A. opening suspenseful

B. a run-on sentence

C. good image—I could really see it!

f. When the piece of writing has been seen twice, the owner should receive it with the two comment sheets.

g. Up to now, there should have been no talking, only reading and writing numbers/letters with comments. As you read, if any comments confuse you, ask your peers for clarification. This is the time to talk about your writing.

Read Aloud

a. Read your paper to the others in your group. No one should interrupt the reading, but one person should sit so that he or she sees your paper. This way he or she can get a better understanding of what your purpose is by being able to hear you at the same time as seeing what you have written. The other person should take notes.

b. A discussion should follow the reading, beginning with the notetaker's comments. Start with praise.

c. When the group is satisfied that everything was said that should have been said, the next person reads his or her paper aloud, and the editing continues in the same way.

Duplicate

a. Give each member of your group a copy of your piece. Comments can be written directly on the paper or on a separate piece of paper.

b. It is possible, using this method, for papers to be taken home in order to have more time to prepare for extensive editing. Thus, class time can be spent on discussion rather than reading.

c. This method is ideal for longer essays and reports. It is also a more realistic approach when only one member of a group has something to be edited. In this case, the duplicated essays can be given out the day before the peer-editing session.

For a Peer Group of Three or More

A Take-Home

a. Duplicate your paper and give a copy to the other members of your peer group to take home.

b. At home, they should write comments on your paper.

c. In class the *next* day, you read your paper aloud to your peer group. They may follow with their duplicated copy.

d. Using their comments, they should discuss how they felt, both as readers of and listeners to your paper. The discussion that follows can deal with ways you can improve your written paper.

e. Your peers then give you their copy of your draft with their written suggestions.

f. You can incorporate into your final copy what you have heard in the discussion and what you read on copies of your draft.

Fours and Twos

a. Divide your peer group into two pairs; then have each pair use any of the above methods to bring each paper up to a level that satisfies both writer and editor.

b. Then the pairs exchange papers. Each pair works together on the papers of the other pair. When the written critiques are complete, the papers are returned to their authors, and the critiques are discussed.

c. The discussion that follows will be quite different because both you and your partner will be able to talk about your paper. Remember, your partner helped you bring your paper up to a standard that satisfied him or her.

d. You should then revise *with* your partner, using or dismissing the suggestions made by the other pair in your peer group.

EXERCISE FIVE
Follow-Up to a Peer-Editing Session

Once you have had your paper peer-edited, you should prepare to write your final draft, using or rejecting the suggestions you have received from your group. In some cases, your peers may suggest that you revise (reform) your paper completely and show them another draft at a later date. If they are willing to edit your revision, you should certainly stick with them.

Occasionally, your writing instructor may suggest that, for certain assignments, the revising process should end with you and your peer group. It is not necessary that your instructor-editor see *everything* you write. Your instructor may devise different methods so that you receive credit for doing the assignment; your peers, for example, could let your instructor know when they think your piece of writing is ready for its intended reader. If this method of revision is used for a particular assignment, you should polish it and send it to its intended audience.

For most of your assignments, however, you will show your latest revised draft to your instructor-editor, who should seldom be your intended reader. This one-to-one session will help you polish your writing for its intended audience. Remember, you should write for a real audience and for a real purpose. Even if both are imaginary, make them sound *real*. Writing something just for the sake of writing usually produces bad results.

After you have had your paper edited by your instructor, you really should share his or her comments and suggestions *with* your peer-editors. Through this sharing experience, you not only will be reinforcing what your instructor has told you but will be helping your peers improve their editing process.

Are you becoming aware that it takes time to produce good writing? If a professional writer spends hours on revision and reformation, it is almost impossible for you, as a beginning writer, to dash off a high-quality, 1000-word essay the evening before it is due. Both you and your intended audience would suffer.

EXERCISE SIX
Publishing

Discuss the following information with your partner:

Like professional writers who desire to have what they write published, you should publish your final product too. As part of your writing process, the word "publish" simply means presenting your paper to its intended audience. After you have spent so much time prewriting, drafting, and revising your paper, you should certainly publish it instead of shoving it into your notebook.

In most cases, publishing will merely entail your giving or sending your product directly to your reader; for example, you will give your piece of writing to your family, peers, co-workers, employer, or professors, or you will send it to newspapers, officials, future employers, or people who live far from you. In most cases, your writing process will be complete when your product leaves your hands. Sometimes you will get a reaction from your reader: thanking you for the information, agreeing or disagreeing with your point of view, asking for you to make an appointment, and so on. When you receive a reader's response, you find out exactly what your reader thinks of your product.

You should always remember that your writing is an extension of you; it represents you. You, therefore, want to make sure that your final product represents you favorably.

Even though your editors (both your peers and your instructor) may give you a great deal of help, offer various suggestions, and even re-edit several of your drafts so that you can finally produce a perfect paper, there comes a time when you must take full responsibility for it. The ultimate choice of accepting or rejecting editors' suggestions will always rest with the writers. As a result, writers will always be responsible for their products. Therefore, just before you send your piece of writing to its audience, you must check for final mechanical errors: misspellings, omitted punctuation marks, lack of agreement, and so on. (Such errors often occur if you type your paper or have it typed. Final proofreading is your responsibility so that you present a polished product to your reader.)

Drawing by Ziegler; © 1978 The New Yorker Magazine, Inc.

32

"Unwriting"—Paraphrase, Précis, Summary, Outline

INTRODUCTION

As a student, you have probably had to take notes during lectures, condense essays, boil down chapters of textbooks, or rewrite complicated passages. In most cases, you were the audience, and the purpose for condensing was to make reviewing faster and easier. In doing these tasks, you reversed the writing process. Rather than building a piece of writing from limited topic to finished product, you reduced a finished product to its main idea. This process can be called "unwriting." In this chapter you will examine several forms of unwriting: the *paraphrase*, *précis*, *summary*, and *outline*. As well, you will learn how to locate thesis or topic statements and main ideas.

This chapter on unwriting, however, has another important purpose. It is placed after the important chapter on revising to show you how to use unwriting as an editing process. If, when you are self-editing or editing someone else's paper, you are having difficulty with the piece of writing, you might try to unwrite all or a portion of the paper in the form of a paraphrase, précis, summary, outline, or main idea. The piece of unwriting will often point out something that is missing in the original piece of writing: a step in a set of directions, a cause of an effect, or a piece of argument that was unexpressed. The process of unwriting can show a writer what needs to be included in a final draft.

EXERCISE ONE
Getting Familiar with Unwriting

1. Tell your partner a story, anecdote, joke, personal experience, or anything else that you can think of. Your partner should listen and enjoy without interrupting. (This is difficult for most listeners, but your story will be easier to paraphrase if its continuity is not broken.)

2. When you have finished, your partner should retell in his or her own words what you have said. This repeated story in your partner's words is a *paraphrase* of your original words.

3. Now ask your partner to retell the story, condensing it to half its original length. He or she must decide what to include and what to omit. The main idea and only the most important parts of the development should remain. This condensation is a *précis* of the original. (By the way, in the précis you can use your original words or the words of your partner's paraphrase.)

4. Then ask your partner to tell you about the story in even fewer words. He or she must mention the main point of the story and, very briefly, what happened. This is a *summary*. (It, too, can be in your words or your partner's words.)

5. Next, ask your partner to tell you the story in point form, using numbers: first, second, third, and so on. This is an *outline*.

6. Finally, your partner should state the main point of your story. This is the *main idea* and can be expressed as a *thesis statement*.

EXERCISE TWO
Unwrite a Short Story

1. With your partner, read Kate Chopin's "The Story of an Hour" (see the Appendix). After reading the selection, discuss with your partner anything that you do not understand.

2. Look up unfamiliar words or metaphors and allusions. Study the structure of the story, the length and types of sentences that the author has used, what sort of transitions are made, and how the story as a whole fits together. (This advice applies to anything you want to unwrite.)

3. Jot down all the things that you think are important. Include each idea only once, although the author may mention it several times.

4. In your own words restate each point, changing its order if you feel it necessary. Remember you are the audience, and the purpose for your unwriting is to make the original clearer and more concise for you.

5. Work together with your partner to collectively write a paraphrase, précis (in the author's or your own words), summary (in the words of either), outline, and main idea.

EXERCISE THREE
Unwriting Difficult or Archaic Literature

You may often find that you are obliged to read something that contains difficult or archaic words, phrases, and allusions. If you unwrite it, suddenly it makes much more sense.

Take turns with your partner in paraphrasing Orlando's wooing of Rosalind (she is disguised as a young man who has agreed to teach Orlando the ways of a proper lover) from Shakespeare's *As You Like It*. Where does Rosalind remind the audience that she is a girl? (For this exercise, it would help if you had a partner of the opposite sex.)

ROSALIND:	Come, woo me, woo me; for now I am in a holiday humor, and like enough to consent. What would you say to me now, and I were your very very Rosalind?
ORLANDO:	I would kiss before I spoke.
ROSALIND:	Nay, you were better speak first, and when you were gravell'd for lack of matter, you might take occasion to kiss. Very good orators when they are out, they will spit, and for lovers lacking (God warn us!) matter, the cleanliest shift is to kiss.
ORLANDO:	How if the kiss be denied?
ROSALIND:	Then she puts you to entreaty, and there begins new matter.
ORLANDO:	Who could be out, being before his belov'd mistress?
ROSALIND:	Marry, that should you if I were your mistress, or I should think my honesty ranker than my wit.
ORLANDO:	What, of my suit?
ROSALIND:	Not out of your apparel, and yet out of your suit. Am not I your Rosalind?
ORLANDO:	I take some joy to say you are, because I would be talking to her.
ROSALIND:	Well, in her person, I say I will not have you.
ORLANDO:	Then in mine own person, I die.

The importance of paraphrasing pieces of literature will become evident when you write literary essays. If you come across a difficult patch of writing in any short story, novel, poem, or play that you are studying, talk through a paraphrase with someone until you completely understand what you are reading.

EXERCISE FOUR
Unwriting an Essay

1. Find a somewhat difficult piece of writing of no more than 300 words from the editorial pages of a newspaper or a magazine.
2. Read the article aloud to your partner. Your partner may make notes but may not interrupt you or look at what you are reading.
3. When you finish, ask your partner to tell you what the article is about. Remember, whether the paraphrase is shorter or longer than the original, it should be easier to understand.
4. When your partner finishes the paraphrase, discuss whether he or she omitted or failed to clarify any important points.
5. Repeat the exercise, with your partner reading his or her article to you.

EXERCISE FIVE
An English Proficiency Test

In many universities and colleges, students are expected to take a written test before they receive their degree or diploma. Often, as part of the test, they are required to write a précis. The original material is usually about 600 words long; students are required to write a précis of approximately 300 words.

While working with the piece of writing in this exercise, imagine that your audience is a university evaluation committee. The members want to see how well you read as well as how well you write.

1. *Before* you write a précis of this challenging excerpt from "Of Two Minds" by G. B. Sinclair, both you and your partner should write a separate paraphrase, following the instructions outlined in Exercise Two.

> We have long known that in typical right-handed people the left hemisphere is essential to language. The right hemisphere was considered a mute and somewhat stupid understudy of the left. This idea was invalidated, however, by Roger Sperry and a group of Cal Tech researchers who, since the early 1960s, have been testing commissurotomy patients. (Commissurotomy, a form of surgery once used in the treatment of severe epilepsy, involves cutting the bundles of fibres connecting the brain's hemispheres. The two hemispheres can then be observed independently.) The Cal Tech research shows that each hemisphere has its own functions. The verbal left hemisphere analyzes, abstracts, marks time, and deals sequentially with rational propositions. The spatial right hemisphere synthesizes, intuits, and deals with metaphor. It responds with feeling, and processes information in its own cognitive style. The two hemispheres possess separate memory banks and personality traits. The left side is more intellectual, realistic, and optimistic in outlook; the right is more negative, emotional, artistic. In computer terms, the left hemisphere works on the digital principle, the right on an analogue model.

2. Now write your précis, in paragraph form. You can either condense the original to the one third or one half of its length by using the author's language, or you can condense it using your own words (that is, you can condense a paraphrase). Both kinds of précis should include the thesis statement and some of the development from the original.

3. When both you and your partner have completed your paraphrase and précis (giving them suitable titles), compare them to see how similar they are. If you are having difficulty, turn to the Suggested Answers (following Chapter 33) to see a sample paraphrase and précis of the above article.

EXERCISE SIX
Using All the Steps of Unwriting

1. For this unwriting exercise, write a paraphrase, précis (first in the author's language, then in your own words), summary, outline, and thesis statement for the following excerpt. In addition, choose a graphic (ladders, mandala, pigeonholes, flowchart) to illustrate the content and organization of the excerpt.

The Practical Writer

From time to time most educated people are called upon to act as writers. They might not think of themselves as such as they dash off a personal note or dictate a memo, but that is what they are. They are practicing a difficult and demanding craft, and facing its inborn challenge. This is to find the right words and to put them in the right order so that the thoughts they represent can be understood.

Some writers deliberately muddy the meaning of their words, if indeed they meant anything to begin with. When most people write, however, it is to get a message across. This is especially so in business and institutions, where written words carry much of the load of communications. The written traffic of any well-ordered organization is thick and varied—letters, memos, reports, policy statements, manuals, sales literature, and what-have-you. The purpose of it all is to use words in a way that serves the organization's aims.

Unfortunately, written communications often fail to accomplish this purpose. Some organizational writing gives rise to confusion, inefficiency, and ill will. This is almost always because the intended message did not get through to the receiving end. Why? Because the message was inadequately prepared.

An irresistible comparison arises between writing and another craft which most people have to practice sometimes, namely cooking. In both fields there is a wide range of competence, from the great chefs and authors to the occasional practitioners who must do the job whether they like it or not. In both, care in preparation is of the essence. Shakespeare wrote that it is an ill cook who does not lick his own fingers; it is an ill writer who does not work at it hard enough to be reasonably satisfied with the results.

Unlike bachelor cooks, however, casual writers are rarely the sole consumers of their own offerings. Reclusive philosophers and schoolgirls keeping diaries are about the only writers whose work is not intended for other eyes. If a piece of writing turns out to be an indigestible half-baked mess, those on the receiving end are usually the ones to suffer. This might be all right in literature, because the reader of a bad book can always toss it aside. But in organizations, where written communications command attention, it is up to the recipient of a sloppy writing job to figure out what it means.

The reader is thus put in the position of doing the thinking the writer failed to do. To make others do your work for you is, of course, an uncivil act. In a recent magazine advertisement on the printed word, one of a commendable series published by International Paper Company, novelist Kurt Vonnegut touched on the social aspect of writing: "Why should you examine your writing style with the idea of improving it? Do so as a mark of respect for your readers. If you scribble your thoughts any which way, your readers will surely feel that you care nothing for them."

In the working world, bad writing is not only bad manners, it is bad business. The victim of an incomprehensible letter will at best be annoyed and at worst decide that people who can't say what they mean aren't worth doing business with. Write a sloppy letter, and it might rebound on you when the recipient calls for clarification.

Where one carefully worded letter would have sufficed, you might have to write two or more.

Muddled messages can cause havoc within an organization. Instructions that are misunderstood can set people off in the wrong directions or put them to work in vain. Written policies that are open to misinterpretation can throw sand in the gears of an entire operation. Ill-considered language in communications with employees can torpedo morale.

2. Compare your pieces of unwriting with those of your partner. If you do not agree on the essentials, go back to some of the directions in the various exercises. If you remain confused, look at the paraphrase, précis, summary, outline, main idea, and graphic of this excerpt in the Suggested Answers (following Chapter 33).

EXERCISE SEVEN
On Your Own

Ask your partner to find you a fairly difficult piece of prose of approximately 600 words, for which you are to write a paraphrase, précis, summary, and outline. When you have completed them, give them to your partner, who will use the principles of unwriting to evaluate your work.

EXERCISE EIGHT
Revising by Unwriting

If you ever feel that an essay you have written is incomplete, you should make an outline in short sentences of *exactly* what your essay contains. In this way, you can often see what your essay is lacking.

Making an outline may also be the very thing you should do *during* the drafting process if you are stuck on part of the development.

You can, however, use the principles of unwriting to help you revise one of your completed drafts. Choose a partner for this exercise who is unfamiliar with your writing.

1. Read the draft to your partner.

2. When you finish, ask your partner to paraphrase, in his or her own words, what the essay is about.

3. By listening to your partner, you will hear what your intended reader will get from your paper. Are you satisfied with your partner's paraphrase? If not, who is at fault—you, because your paper does not include what you thought was in it or your partner, because he or she did not listen to your reading with complete concentration? At any rate, you should discuss the results of the unwriting exercise until you know what you should add, alter, move, or perhaps eliminate.

4. You can vary this exercise by asking your partner to present a précis or summary of your essay. Or you might ask your partner to present an outline and the main idea (thesis statement or topic sentences). If your partner has done a fine job, you should be able to note any deficiencies in your paper and, as a result, revise it with confidence.

EXERCISE NINE
Unwriting and Graphics

For a variation of Exercise Eight, have your partner read your essay and then draw a graphic of its organization and content. By *seeing* the essentials of your essay on a single ladder, double ladder, pigeonholes, flowchart, or mandala, you will readily see that you may need to include more supporting evidence or that your method of organization is illogical or that items are out of order. By completing the graphic that your partner has drawn, you will be able to revise your paper more easily.

EXERCISE TEN
The 25-Word Summary

Whoever said, "If you can't put your idea on the back of a matchbook cover, you haven't got an idea," made a worthwhile point. In this exercise, you are to ask your partner for an essay or short story. Your task is to summarize the selection in *exactly* twenty-five words, not one word more or less. Whether a word is one letter or twenty letters, consider it as one word. (The author's name and the title of the selection, which you should include in your summary, will not, however, count towards the twenty-five words.)

If, in your early draft, you have two or three words too many, you must eliminate them; a 25-word summary is not the place for repetitions, passive voice, weak verbs (*be, seems, says, has, shows, appears, feels*), ineffective adjectives and adverbs, prepositional phrases, and dependent clauses. If you have two or three words too few in your early draft, add words to give a deeper, richer meaning to your summary. Try to write your 25-word summary in a single sentence.

The benefits of writing a 25-word summary are many:

- Practicing unwriting
- Ensuring that you understand the meaning of a selection
- Choosing exact, powerful words
- Improving your vocabulary
- Appreciating sentence-combining patterns
- Using precise punctuation (especially the semicolon) to add focus

Before you write your summary, read the following two 25-word summaries of the excerpt in Exercise Six. Which does a better job of summarizing "The Practical Writer"?

["The Practical Writer"] points out the importance of business writing, illustrating that writers must compose carefully so that their recipients do not have to ask for further clarification.

[The author of "The Practical Writer"] contends that business people must write clearly and coherently to avoid extra work by recipients of communications, to show courtesy, and to lessen internal conflicts.

Word Processors and the Writing Process

INTRODUCTION

Nothing in recent times has made the writing process easier than the invention of word-processing systems. Prolific writers who own a word-processing system, or a computer with word-processing capabilities, even go so far as to say that word processing is the most important discovery of the twentieth century. It literally frees the writer from the horrendous task of retyping drafts.

If you wonder what difference a word processor can make to your writing, think about your revising process. After completing the prewriting process and several drafts, you write your essay. You take it through a peer-editing session and revise it so many times that you never want to see your essay again. Now you are ready to give a clean copy to your instructor for a final editing session. Just before you submit it, you notice that you left out a word in the second line. What do you do? Insert the word and mess up the page or ignore it and hope your instructor will not detect the omission?

With a word processor, you simply insert the disk on which your essay is stored into your machine, call up the offending page on the screen, insert the word in an instant, push a print key, and within seconds you will have a new, correct copy.

Even if your instructor suggests that you make some structural changes to one of your paragraphs and then move it to another position in your essay, you will be able to do so in a matter of a few seconds, on a word processor. Word processing is revolutionizing the writing process.

If you have access to a word-processing system, you are encouraged to use *The Independent Writer* in conjunction with it. Look around your campus. Maybe there are word-processing systems available for student use connected with the various departments or with the library.

Because there are many texts, manuals, and classes available to teach you how to use a word processor, the following suggestions focus on how you can get the most out of your writing process by using a word processor, no matter what experience you have had with computers. Build on these suggestions as you become more and more familiar with word-processing systems, even if you do not know how to type or if you have been using your own personal word processor for years.

Doing the following exercises will vary depending on your experience with word-processing systems. If you own a word processor or have access to one, you are encouraged to implement any of the suggestions and make them part of your writing process; if you have no experience whatsoever with word-processing equipment, simply read over the exercises with your partner and comment on the wonderful features that modern technology is offering to make your writing process more efficient.

EXERCISE ONE
Prewriting Process

Nothing gets lost in the word processor's memory; everything stays on the disk. Depending on the word-processing system you are using, a single disk can hold up to two hundred pages of information. It also can provide a printout of the contents of the disk. Think of the possibilities of storing all your prewriting ideas!

By storing a skeletal outline of all your brainstorming techniques in the word processor's memory, you will be able to recall the one you want in order to flesh out a topic. At the touch of a button, for example, you can call "Aristotle's Topics" to the screen. Because you will have already stored all of the leading questions in your computer's memory, you only have to consider answering the ones that appear on the screen; thus, you have saved yourself the time of typing the same brainstorming questions every time you prewrite.

If, after you answer all the questions, you do not have enough material for your topic, you can call another brainstorming technique to the screen—for example, Pentad Cluster, Newspaper Reporter's Questions, Seven Controlling Questions, and so on. In addition, you might bring particular graphics to the screen (mandalas, ladders, pigeonholes), so that you can list your supporting evidence.

If you ever do not have enough information by storming your own brain and you do not want to engage in a brainstorming session with others, you can, with a telephone modem linked to a library source, request information in any topic. In a few minutes, that information will be "dumped" on your disk for you to read at your leisure.

You can continue to come up with a workable limited topic and a thesis statement. Then you can call up to the screen a list of writing variables, record the pertinent details next to each one of them, and print the results of your prewriting process so that you have it available during your drafting process. Knowing that you can return to any aspect of prewriting to make necessary additions, changes, or omissions will give you additional security during your drafting process.

EXERCISE TWO
Drafting Process

One of the advantages of drafting on a word processor is that you can draft as many times as you like without losing any of your attempted drafts. You can start in the middle of your essay without leaving spaces to fill in later. When you are ready to write your introduction, all you need to do is take your cursor to the beginning and start to type. The introduction will appear on the screen *before* the middle section. Later, you can take your cursor to the end to write your conclusion.

Also, you can write without worrying about making errors. As you read over your draft on the screen, you can make corrections, add details, delete unnecessary details, change wording, and move entire sentences and paragraphs. At the same time, you can work through any of the chapters of the text in order to sharpen the style and organization, sentence structure, and mechanics of your paper. For example, if you used the AAA/BBB method of comparison/contrast (Chapter 8) to develop your essay, you can duplicate your entire essay and then move sentences and paragraphs within the duplicated copy to see what the effect would be if you were to use the ABABAB method. If you do not like the effect, you can delete the entire copy and return to the original. You can also use your word processor to record and file all of your research material (Chapter 39) to help you write your research papers. You can recall onto the screen any of the quotations that you stored on the disk. Later, you will be able to recall all of the sources in alphabetical order so that you can list all your cited references in the correct order.

Just before you print a hard copy of your essay, you can check on a number of mechanics. Depending on the capabilities of your word-processing program, you can do a spelling check (some systems have a built-in 50,000-word memory and will highlight words that are not spelled according to its memory bank), a punctuation and capitalization check (some of the latest systems will highlight irregularities), a synonym check (some systems have a built-in thesaurus that provides five or six alternative words for you to use in place of your original word choices), and a consistency check (some systems will highlight when your subject and verb do not agree or when you shift point of view in tense, voice, and person). Who knows what new capabilities will be on the market in the next few years? As you can see, a word processor will help you become an independent writer. You still need to take your paper through peer- and instructor-editing sessions because word processors cannot check your organization, style, sentence quality, or thought processes. Even though you and your word processor can come up with a neat and, oftentimes, accurate piece of writing, you should not underestimate the benefits that you gain from having your paper edited by others before you present it to your intended audience.

EXERCISE THREE
Revising Process

Rather than discourage your editors from finding fault with your writing because you cannot bear to rewrite your essay, you will encourage them to look more carefully at your overall organization, thankful that if they suggest a massive restructuring to improve the clarity or style of your paper, it will not mean hours of retyping.

You can encourage your peers to use the editing procedures outlined in Chapter 31, and you can present each one of your peers with a clean copy, as it only takes moments to print duplicates. Furthermore, you can present your peer-editors with a list of specific questions about your essay that you wish them to answer. You can make up the questions from those in the Revising Process of each assignment as well as particular ones that are peculiar to your piece of writing. In addition, you can present them with copies of your brainstorming ideas as well as a complete rundown of your writing variables. In this way, they will be able to place themselves in the position of your intended audience. By providing them with plenty of material to help them edit, you will receive more helpful criticism from them.

Once you address all of your peers' comments, you will recall your essay to the screen of your word processor to make the necessary changes, corrections, additions, or deletions. If your peers wish to see your paper again because you intend to change it substantially, you can easily provide copies and repeat the entire peer-editing process.

Once you and your peers are satisfied with your paper, you can submit a clean, professional-looking copy to your instructor-editor for a final editing session. Again, you will not be uptight about suggestions that could require a massive overhaul of your paper. With a word processor, you will be able to attend to most of your instructor's suggestions in a matter of minutes. Even if you have to rewrite your essay several times for your instructor, you will finally go along with the statement that "Writing is rewriting"—only now it's more enjoyable to rewrite on your word processor.

Suggested Answers to the First Workshop Section

CHAPTER 30
Exercise Four

1.a. Harry Truman won the 1948 presidential election, although most of the country's newspapers confidently predicted he would lose to Thomas Dewey.

b. Before America entered World War II, President Franklin Roosevelt proposed to help the Allies against the Axis powers; accordingly, he asked Congress to support his lend-lease program in early 1941.

c. James Madison's presidency was eventful; in fact, the War of 1812 and the British raid on Washington, D.C., occurred during his term in office.

d. Gerald Ford was the last president to direct any American activity in the Vietnam conflict, but others before him—Nixon, Johnson, Kennedy, Eisenhower, and Truman—oversaw at least some amount of financial or armed involvement there.

e. George Washington was the first president of the United States; hence, he is called the father of our country by most Americans.

f. Ronald Reagan was both the first person from the entertainment world and the oldest person to become president.

g. Attempts were made against the lives of Presidents Jackson, Theodore Roosevelt, Truman, Ford, and Reagan; however, Presidents Lincoln, Garfield, McKinley, and Kennedy were assassinated.

h. Because he was president for 12 years and 39 days, Franklin Delano Roosevelt holds the record for serving the longest term in office; because William Henry Harrison served only 32 days, he holds the record for serving the shortest term.

i. After having forty male presidents from 1789 to 1984, Americans are still waiting to be like other countries: to have a female president.

2. Each presidency is a unique mixture of power, personality, and circumstance. This is to say that every president will represent that mixture in his own way. For instance, the chief executive's powers have actually changed little since George Washington's inauguration in 1789, but each president has used these powers somewhat differently. In addition, they have all varied in political shrewdness, dedication, energy, imagination, communication skills, and other qualities. Both Andrew Jackson and Theodore Roosevelt, for example, can be distinguished from many other presidents by their strong personalities and the ability to effectively promote their policies. Equally important, the nature of the times and circumstances will certainly affect a presidency. A president's power, on the one hand, may decline during periods of peace; his power, on the other hand, may dramatically increase during economic depression, periods of social unrest, and wartime. In short, each presidency is inevitably unique.

CHAPTER 32
Exercise Five

Paraphrase of Excerpt from ''Of Two Minds''

Left vs. Right

It was thought that, in most right-handed people, the right half of the brain had little to do. But new research at Cal Tech has shown this is not so. By studying patients who have had the halves of their brains separated by surgery, scientist Roger Sperry has determined what each side of the brain does. The work of the left side has to do with words: it breaks down and processes thoughts step by step. The work of the right side has to do with imagination: its thought processes are not as rational but deal more with feeling and intuition. Both halves can and do work separately. We could say that the left side of the brain thinks and the right side feels.

Précis in Writer's Own Words

From ''Of Two Minds''

We have long known that in typical right-handed people the left hemisphere is essential to language; the right hemisphere was considered mute and somewhat stupid. But Roger Sperry and a group of Cal Tech researchers have invalidated that idea. Testing patients who have had surgery to cut the fibres connecting the brain's hemispheres, the researchers have shown that each hemisphere has its own functions. The left side is intellectual and optimistic; the right, artistic and negative.

Précis of the Paraphrase

Left Brain vs. Right Brain

New research at Cal Tech has shown that the old idea of the right half of the brain's having little to do is wrong. By studying people who have had the halves of their brains separated by surgery, the researchers have discovered that the two hemispheres work differently. The left half is the thinking half, working step by step; the right half is the feeling half, working intuitively.

Exercise Six

Paraphrase of ''The Practical Writer''

Writing Is Your Business

Writing, even if it is only a memo or a letter, is a task that everyone occasionally has to do. The job of any writer—and it is a difficult one—is to say clearly what he or she wants to say.

In the business world, where so much writing must be done, the ability to organize thoughts on paper is essential. For their own benefit and that of the firms they represent, most people try to communicate clearly. But if not enough attention is paid to preparing a message, communication can break down. Writing, like cooking, must be done conscientiously, regardless of the writer's skill and level of ability.

Writers have a duty to consider how their work will be understood by their readers. Kurt Vonnegut suggests that common courtesy is reason enough to write with care and consideration, but there are sound business reasons as well: conveying a message clearly the first time makes it unnecessary to write further letters for clarification and ensures that directions to other people within a firm can be carried out promptly and satisfactorily without confusion and bad feeling.

Précis in the Writer's Own Words

From "The Practical Writer"

The challenge facing the average educated person who has to write is to find the right words and put them in the right order. In business, a writer must use words in a way that represents the organization's aims. Unfortunately, an inadequately prepared message can fail to accomplish that purpose. In writing, as in cooking, care in preparation is of the essence for both professionals and occasional practitioners, because a badly constructed piece of writing, like a half-baked recipe, can cause suffering for whoever must digest it. As well, bad writing can show a lack of respect for readers, can make several letters necessary where one should have sufficed, and can cause havoc within an organization.

Précis of the Paraphrase

Writing Is Your Business

Almost everyone must write once in a while and must make sure that what is to be said is said clearly. In business, where so much communication is written, clarity is especially important; if the message is carelessly written, there can be a breakdown in communication. Common courtesy is one good reason for writing clearly, but there are sound business reasons as well: a good letter makes further clarification unnecessary, and well-written memos and internal instructions can prevent problems within an organization.

Summary

From "The Practical Writer"

The challenge a writer in the business world faces is to express ideas clearly and coherently to serve the organization's aims. Written communications often fail because they are inadequately prepared, and the recipients are forced to do the work the writer neglected. Poor writing shows lack of respect for the recipient, makes more work necessary in order to clarify the original message, and can create ill-feeling within an organization.

Outline

From ''The Practical Writer''

1. In business, writing is the main form of communication.
2. The purpose of business writing is to use words to fulfill the organization's aims.
3. Many letters fail to do this because they are inadequately prepared.
4. The recipient must do the work the writer failed to do.
5. If the recipient must ask for clarification, extra work that should not have been necessary must be done.
6. Within an organization, poor communication can be disastrous.

Thesis Statement

Businesspeople who do not take the time to write carefully can cause problems both inside and outside their organization.

Graphic

Although you could use a mandala and a double ladder to illustrate the excerpt, a flowchart would perhaps do the best job. Study the cause/effect flowchart on page 384, noting that it demonstrates the content and organization of the excerpt.

(If you do not understand the usefulness of the cause/effect flowchart, see Chapter 9.)

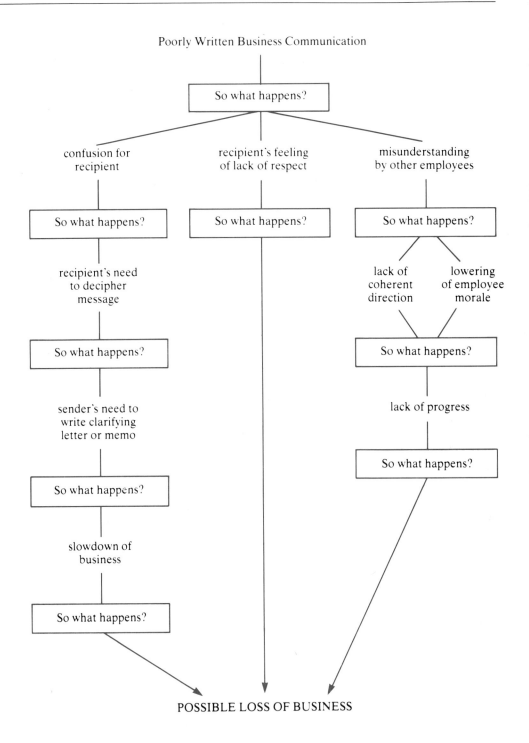

SECOND WORKSHOP SECTION

Style

ABOUT THE SECOND WORKSHOP SECTION

In this section you will find exercises and Special Writing Assignments to help you refine particular aspects of your writing. At times you may need to refer to a dictionary, thesaurus, or handbook. Perhaps your writing instructor will recommend specific reference books so that you and your classmates will be using the same authorities.

You can apply each chapter to any writing you are doing. If you are writing, for example, an exposition and are worrying about your sentence variety, look at Chapter 35; if you are writing a letter and want to include a figurative comparison, look at Chapter 36.

If you take a few moments to discover what the Second Workshop Section contains, you can use it to fulfill your needs. If you cannot decide which chapter to begin with, do the first few. Later, your instructor-editor or your peers may suggest that you should work on a particular chapter to sharpen an aspect of your writing.

How to do a Workshop Chapter

Each chapter in this workshop section is designed so that you work with one other person: a fellow student at school or a friend or relative at home. (Although you can get some benefit from working alone, you really need someone to talk to, to check with, and to ask and answer questions.) Each workshop chapter begins with an introduction, then offers specific projects for you to refine an aspect of writing.

- *Exercises.* Whenever practical, talk through the exercises with your partner rather than write them out; you will be able to do many more exercises this way.
- *Special Writing Assignments.* The chapters culminate in a writing project you can do *for* your partner. It is possible for you to do it for your instructor-editor as well.

Sometimes you should do an entire chapter; sometimes not. Sometimes you may start at the beginning of a chapter; sometimes in the middle. If only one partner needs to do a chapter, the other should act as an adviser and help his or her partner. (*By teaching your partner, you can learn new things yourself.*) The important thing to remember when you work in the Second Workshop Section is that it should fulfill *your* writing needs.

34

Techniques of Style

INTRODUCTION

"Proper words in proper places make a true definition of style."
—*Jonathan Swift*

You have probably heard or read discussions of the style of particular writers; for example, the style is Shakespearean, Shavian, or Hemingwayesque. You may have gathered from these discussions that only professional writers were capable of creating a distinctive, personal style. But you write, just as you walk, talk, or eat, in a way that is uniquely yours. This chapter is designed to help you to acknowledge and develop your writing style and adapt it to suit everything you write.

As you work on the exercises in this workshop, consider how the following affect style:

- Standard or nonstandard vocabulary
- Positive or negative slant
- Short, direct sentences (under ten words); long, contrived ones (over thirty words); or a combination of short, long, and medium-length sentences
- Specific, concrete words or subtle, abstract ones
- Rhetorical devices
- Figurative comparisons, even lengthy analogies, or no imagery
- The writer's own voice or a persona
- A tone that is sincere and direct, genuinely humorous, or ironically comic
- An overall cautious or aggressive attitude towards the topic (and audience)

Some of the factors that affect style, such as slant and word usage, are dealt with elsewhere in *The Independent Writer*; refer to the index for further information.

EXERCISE ONE
Your Background

Among other things, your background has a definite influence on your writing style. Style is influenced by your age, education, experiences, sex, travel, amount or kind of reading, interests, opportunities, and so on. You should not think of your writing style as better or worse than someone else's style; it's just different.

1. With your partner, discuss the various events in your life that have affected the way you presently write.

2. How would you describe your writing style? In what ways is it similar to your personality? In what ways is it different? What would you like to change about your writing style? About your personality? What would you like to add to your writing style? To your personality? What would you like to eliminate from your writing style? From your personality?

EXERCISE TWO
Your Personal Style

1. With your partner, discuss each other's clothes in detail. Try to determine how your clothing contributes to your overall image. Be honest and specific. What words would you use to describe the particular style of each article you are examining? Use these words to help your discussion:

aggressive	up-to-date	stylish	professional
beautiful	unassuming	elegant	functional
ornamental	cautious	fashionable	different
loud	inappropriate	gaudy	flashy
silly	sensible	conservative	eccentric
sloppy	cool	odd	careless
old-fashioned	workable	solemn	

When you have finished discussing each article of clothing, decide on one word that sums up the overall image of your clothes (for example, "Overall, my clothes are *functional*.").

3. Now choose the word that best describes the opposite effect of your image (for example, *flashy*).

4. Does anything that you are wearing seem not to fit in with the rest of your clothes? What is inappropriate about the article? For example, a pair of black patent-leather shoes would not seem appropriate if you were in gym shorts and a T-shirt.

5. Continue the exercise by choosing words to describe your hair, your makeup or colognes, your voice, and other personal characteristics.

6. You might like to continue this exercise by discussing other things that reflect your style. Use specific details to support each descriptive word; for example, you might describe your favorite music or the appearance of your bedroom and how they reflect (or do not reflect) the real you.

EXERCISE THREE
Observing Style

Now that you have discussed your and your partner's styles, consider the styles around you.

1. Working together, you and your partner determine who in the classroom usually dresses most cautiously and who usually dresses most aggressively. Support your choices by specific examples. For instance, "Joe is the most cautious dresser because he always wears blue jeans, a blue T-shirt, blue running shoes, and blue socks."
2. Who in the room has the most cautious hairstyle? The most aggressive? Support your choices by specific details.

EXERCISE FOUR
Your Audience and Your Style

Observing the style of others can be of value to you in developing your own writing style. When you write, you must take into consideration the style of your reader. The more you know about your audience, the more skillful you can be in making your writing style appropriate for your reader. If you write with no particular audience in mind or if you write for "anybody who wants to read it," you will find it extremely difficult to create a distinctive style. Think for a moment about how your style would be affected if you were explaining Columbus's discovery of America to your history instructor and to your ten-year-old nephew.

The Independent Writer was written for many different readers, each with a common interest. Do you feel that it talks directly to you? What aspects of its style give you this feeling?

1. Assume that you have just broken up with someone you have gone out with for the past two years and you want to write to someone else to explain your feelings. Even a cursory glance at the following list of people will tell you that you would not say the same things, in the same way, to each of them:

- A close friend of the same sex (1)
- A close friend of the opposite sex (2)
- A friend of the person you have broken up with (3)
- One of your parents (4)
- One of the parents of the person you broke up with (5)
- A minister (6)
- Your English instructor (7)
- Your counselor (8)
- A child under six who knows you very well (9)
- An agent for a computer dating service who has asked you why you broke up (10)

2. Begin explaining your long (sad or happy) story to your partner. You will probably have to make up a number of details, names, places, and so forth to make your story appear truthful. This oral exercise should last for at least ten minutes.

Whenever your partner feels like it, he or she should interrupt with one of the numbers from the list. When you hear the number, you must immediately assume that you are speaking with that person; thus, you should change your entire style *as* you continue your story. You must sound totally honest with this person. Then, after a few minutes, your partner should say another number. Try not to miss a beat; simply *continue* your story, without going back to the beginning, for your *new* audience. If there is a lull in your story, your partner can ask you a question as though he or she were the person you are talking to.

3. When your story is finished, discuss with your partner the stylistic changes that you made. Were they correct? Appropriate? Effective? In what ways were they inappropriate? Your partner should point out specific examples where your style was inconsistent with your audience, purpose, and situation.

4. Now let your partner do the exercise. You may choose a new topic or use the following idea: your partner must assume that he or she is living in an apartment and wants to persuade his or her next-door neighbors not to be so noisy. As he or she is explaining the situation and the need for peace and quiet, call out one of the following numbers and then assume the role of the corresponding audience:

- Your next-door neighbor (1)
- The building manager (2)
- Another neighbor (3)
- A member of your family who lives with you (4)
- A member of your family who does not live with you (5)
- A police officer whom you have telephoned (6)

After your partner has finished, discuss the different styles and tones of voice that your partner used to show how the different audiences affected him or her.

EXERCISE FIVE
Tone and Style

Some writing is objective in tone; some is subjective. A completely objective piece of writing tries to be informative, factual, and impersonal. It does not show a writer's feelings, personality, or judgments; as far as possible, the writer tries to stay out of the writing. A totally subjective piece, however, presents the writer's feelings. Such a piece is not primarily informative. Rather, it tries to affect the reader's attitude towards the topic.

1. Discuss the different tones in these selections. How does each affect your thinking? How do you react to such writing?

Kiss Me Kate

For one of its summer season productions, the Brewster Little Theatre is presenting *Kiss Me Kate*, an adaptation of Shakespeare's *The Taming of the Shrew* with music and lyrics by Cole Porter. It stars both new and veteran actors and actresses. Why not spend a pleasant, tuneful evening in Brewster Park's exceptional new theatre? (Gnu Tral)

Theatre in the Dark

The Brewster Little Theatre production of *Kiss Me Kate* is terrible. From the moment the tinny orchestra squeaks up the overture to the resounding thuds of a disorganized chorus line landing heavily in less than graceful descents upon the stage, this wonderful Cole Porter musical receives continual savage mauling at the hands of inept players. Properly done, *Kiss Me Kate* is a zippy, wild, and crazy extravaganza of wonderful sights, sounds, and laughs. Done by the Theatre in Brewster Park, it stinks. ... (B.Y. Assd)

Don't Kiss Off Park's Show

There's a big surprise in store these nights for anyone wandering by Brewster Park. The Brewster Little Theatre's current production of *Kiss Me Kate* is a show that holds its own, even by professional standards. It features leading players who actually can sing and act well. The sets and costumes are colorful and well constructed. The orchestra members all manage to play in the same key at the same time. The sound system doesn't turn everything into garbled squawks and chorus members do not indulge in the amateurish histrionics that often have afflicted past Brewster shows. (I.M. Fort)

Discuss the following questions with your partner until you agree on the answers.

a. Which piece has the most objective tone; that is, it is the most factual and impersonal?

b. The other two have a subjective tone. Which of these tries more to affect your feelings? Give examples.

c. Which piece is the most condescending? Give examples.

d. What kind of writer wrote each? List at least three characteristics of each one.

2. Think of something you have recently seen: a show, an event, an accident. Using first an objective tone and then a subjective tone, *tell* your partner about it. Your partner should then point out the differences in tone between your two explanations. When you are finished discussing your two recountings, reverse roles and let your partner try the exercise.

EXERCISE SIX
Persona

The complexities of point of view also affect writing style. Most of what you will write will be from your own personal point of view. When you write in this way, you reveal yourself to your reader whether you want to or not. Just as the clothes you wear tell onlookers about you, the words and sentences you use tell readers about you.

It is possible, however, for you to assume that you are someone else and to write with a different personality, or *persona*, in order to fulfill some purpose for a particular piece of writing. You may have already had a similar experience. For example, have you ever phoned a friend and pretended to be someone else? Have you ever talked to someone about a personal problem and pretended that it was somebody else's problem? Discuss with your partner your past experiences with persona.

1. With your partner, read the following pieces by Ring Lardner, noting carefully his use of personae:

    a.   Years ago, Jim used to travel for a canned goods concern over in Carterville. They sold canned goods. Jim had the whole northern half of the State and was on the road for five days out of every week. He'd drop in here Saturdays and tell his experiences for that week. It was rich.

I guess he paid more attention to playin' jokes than makin' sales. Finally the concern let him out and he come right home here and told everybody he'd been fired instead of sayin' he'd resigned like most fellas would of.

It was a Saturday and the shop was full and Jim got up out of that chair and says, "Gentlemen, I got an important announcement to make. I been fired from my job."

Well, they asked him if he was in earnest and he said he was and nobody could think of nothin' to say till Jim finally broke the ice himself. He says, "I been sellin' canned goods and now I'm canned goods myself."

You see, the concern he'd been workin' for was a factory that made canned goods. Over in Carterville. And now Jim said he was canned himself. He was certainly a card!

Jim had a great trick that he used to play w'ile he was travelin'. For instance, he'd be ridin' on a train and they'd come to some little town like, well, like, we'll say, like Benton. Jim would look out the train window and read the signs on the stores.

For instance, they'd be a sign, "Henry Smith, Dry Goods." Well, Jim would write down the name and the name of the town and when he got to wherever he was goin' he'd mail back a postal card to Henry Smith at Benton and not sign no name to it, but he'd write on the card, well, somethin' like "Ask your wife about that book agent that spent the afternoon last week," or "Ask your Missus who kept her from gettin' lonesome the last time you was in Carterville." And he'd sign the card, "A Friend."

Of course, he never knew what really come of none of these jokes, but he could picture what *probably* happened and that was enough. (from "Haircut")

    b.   Conrad Green woke up depressed and, for a moment, could not think why. Then he remembered. Herman Plant was dead; Herman Plant, who had been his confidential secretary ever since he had begun producing; who had been much more than a secretary—his champion, votary, shield, bodyguard, tool, occasional lackey, and the butt of his heavy jokes and nasty temper. For forty-five dollars a week.

Herman Plant was dead, and this Lewis, recommended by Ezra Peebles, a fellow entrepreneur, had not, yesterday, made a good first impression. Lewis was apparently impervious to hints. You had to tell him things right out, and when he did understand he looked at you as if you were a boob. And insisted on a salary of sixty dollars right at the start. Perhaps Peebles, who, Green knew, hated him almost enough to make it fifty-fifty, was doing him another dirty trick dressed up as a favor.

After ten o'clock, and still Green had not had enough sleep. It had been nearly three when his young wife and he had left the Bryant-Walkers'. Mrs. Green, the former Marjorie Manning of the Vanities chorus, had driven home to Long Island, while he had stayed in the rooms he always kept at the Ambassador.

Marjorie had wanted to leave a good deal earlier; through no lack of effort on her part she had been almost entirely ignored by her aristocratic host and hostess and most of the guests. She had confided to her husband more than once that she was sick of the whole such-and-such bunch of so-and-so's. As far as she was concerned, they could all go to hell and stay there! But Green had been rushed by the pretty and stage-struck Joyce Brainard, wife of the international polo star, and had successfully combated his own wife's importunities till the Brainards themselves had gone.

Yes, he could have used a little more sleep, but the memory of the party cheered him. Mrs. Brainard, excited by his theatrical aura and several highballs, had been almost affectionate. She had promised to come to his office some time and talk over a stage career which both knew was impossible so long as Brainard lived. But, best of all, Mr. and Mrs. Green would be listed in the papers as among those present at the Bryant-Walkers', along with the Vanderbecks, the Suttons, and the Schuylers, and that would just about be the death of Peebles and other social sycophants of "show business." He would order all the papers now and look for his name. No; he was late and must get to his office. No telling what a mess things were in without Herman Plant. And, by the way, he mustn't forget Plant's funeral this afternoon.

He bathed, telephoned for his breakfast, and his favorite barber, dressed in a symphony of purple and gray, and set out for Broadway, pretending not to hear the "There's Conrad Green!" spoken in awed tones by two flappers and a Westchester realtor whom he passed en route.

Green let himself into his private office, an office of luxurious, exotic furnishings, its walls adorned with expensive landscapes and a Zuloaga portrait of his wife. He took off his twenty-five dollar velour hat, approved of himself in the large mirror, sat down at his desk, and rang for Miss Jackson.

"All the morning papers," he ordered, "and tell Lewis to come in." (from "A Day with Conrad Green")

c.   Al: Here I am back with the White Sox again and it seems too good to be true because just like I told you they are all tickled to death to see me. Kid Gleason is here in charge of the 2d team and when he seen me come into the hotel he jumped up and hit me in the stumach but he acts like that whenever he feels good so I could not get sore at him though he had no right to hit me in the stumach. If he had of did it in earnest I would of walloped him in the jaw.

He says Well if here ain't the old lady killer. He ment Al that I am strong with the girls but I am all threw with them now but he don't know nothing about the troubles I had. He says Are you in shape? And I told him Yes I am. He says Yes you look in shape like a barrel. I says They is not no fat on me and if I am a little bit bigger than last year it is because my mussels is bigger. He says Yes your stumach mussels is emense and you must of gave them plenty of exercise. Wait till Bodie sees you and he will want to stick round you all the time because you make him look like a broom straw or something. I let him kid me along because what is the use of getting mad at him? And besides he is all O.K. even if he is a little rough.

I says to him A little work will fix me up all O.K. and he says You bet you are going to get some work because I am going to see to it myself. I says You will have to hurry because you will be going up to Frisco in a few days and I am going to stay here and join the 1st club. Then he says You are not going to do no such a thing. You are going right along with me. I knowed he was kidding me then because Callahan would not never leave me with the 2d team no more after what I done for him last year and besides most of the stars generally always goes with the 1st team on the training trip.

Well I seen all the rest of the boys that is here with the 2d team and they all acted like as if they was glad to see me and why should not they be when they know that me being here with the White Sox and not with Detroit means that Callahan won't have to do no worrying about his pitching staff? But they is four or 5 young recrut pitchers with the team here and I bet they is not so glad to see me because what chance have they got?

If I was Comiskey and Callahan I would not spend no money on new pitchers because with me and 1 or 2 of the other boys we got the best pitching staff in the league. And instead of spending the money for new pitching recruts I would put it all in a lump and buy Ty Cobb or Sam Crawford off of Detroit or somebody else who can hit and Cobb and Crawford is both real hitters Al even if I did make them look like suckers. Who wouldn't?

Well Al to-morrow A.M. I am going out and work a little and in the P.M. I will watch the game between we and the Venice Club but I won't pitch none because Gleason would not dare take no chances of me hurting my arm. I will write to you in a few days from here because no matter what Gleason says I am going to stick here with the 1st team because I know Callahan will want me along with him for a attraction.   Your pal, Jack. (from "You Know Me Al")

2. It's hard to believe that these pieces were written by the same writer, but indeed they were. You can soon figure out, by looking at the pieces, that Lardner is most accomplished. Discuss the following questions until you and your partner agree on the answers.

   a. What can you deduce about the identity of each persona? What sort of person is each?

   b. Which excerpt is written most personally?

   c. For what purpose has Lardner assumed each persona?

   d. How do the differences in sentence structure, word choice, and so on, reflect the purpose of each piece?

   e. Which persona do you think fulfills its purpose most effectively? Why?

   f. If you had a chance to read one of the entire selections from which these excerpts were taken, which one would it be? Why?

3. Tell your partner what you felt after watching a recent movie, TV show, or sports event. Then restate your opinion, assuming the persona of someone of the opposite sex who did not like what he or she saw. Restate your opinion a third time, assuming the persona of a visitor from another planet who is bewildered by the antics of human beings.

By assuming a persona, you will be able to use irony. Furthermore, your audience will often forget that the opinions expressed in the piece are yours rather than the persona's. (See Chapter 38.)

4. In *Myron* Gore Vidal assumes two personae, that of Myra Breckenridge and that of her alter ego, Myron. In *The Adventures of Huckleberry Finn* Mark Twain assumes the persona of young Huck Finn. Can you think of other writers who use personae? Name the work and the persona.

EXERCISE SEVEN
Analyzing Style

With your partner, list at least five specific characteristics of the style of each of the following selections. Use the items in the introduction to this chapter to get you thinking. Then choose one word to describe the overall style of each selection. Discuss the comments or questions that follow each selection until you and your partner agree on the style of the writing.

A Letter

by Christopher Dafoe

To Mr. George Orwell,
Phil's Doss House,
Camberwell.

Dear Mr. Orwell,

This is to let you know that everyone here at Ladybug Books just *loves Animal Farm*. We were surprised when your agent sent us the ms, but surprise turned to joy when we began to read!

We specialize in publishing books about animals with human attributes—you may have seen our *Teddy Hippo's Holiday* and *Animals on Parade*—and *Animal Farm* fits us like a glove. We are eager to publish!

We *would* like one or two changes. Could you make the pigs nicer and perhaps soften the character of Napoleon slightly? We like all our stories to be realistic, but some, I fear, are more realistic than others.

Parts of your story fall into the latter category. Perhaps it would be nice if the piggies gave a picnic for the horses or if one of the pigs fell in love with a cow.

Do what you think is best, Mr. Orwell, and send back the ms as soon as possible.

Yours faithfully,
Emma Chowder,
Editor,
Ladybug Books

This remarkable example of the use of a persona for a satiric purpose contains allusions to the characters and the prose of George Orwell. The address may be an allusion to one of Orwell's books, *Down and Out in Paris and London*. (A doss house is the British equivalent of a flophouse.) The thesis is developed through concrete examples. Clearly, Ms. Chowder has not understood *Animal Farm's* message. However, if a reader of this letter has not read *Animal Farm*, he or she will not appreciate the satire either. The aggressive tone of the piece is illustrated by its exclamation points and italics.

A Return to Traditional Values

from a free pamphlet

The young people of the 60s who opened the doors to the sexual revolution are becoming more open to traditional values. A recent survey by the American Council of Life Insurance and the Health Insurance Association of America shows that:

- 93% believe the value of traditional family ties should be more strongly stressed.
- 87% would like to see more respect for authority.
- 70% oppose wider acceptance of marijuana.
- 63% say only economic necessity should lead a mother of preschoolers to work outside the home.
- 52% would not welcome more sexual freedom.
- 51% believe strict, old-fashioned upbringing and discipline are still the best way to raise children.

a. This is a straightforward passage. Give some examples that are straightforward.

b. What do you think its purpose is? Do you agree with all of its points?

c. Does it contain any irony?

d. For what audience do you think it is meant?

Super-Text

The Muse Software Super-Text package, for Apple II or Apple II Plus systems, has two distinctive features. It includes a built-in, 15-digit, four-function, floating-point calculator with scientific notation. The calculator lets you do automatic column totals within text. Also, the Autolink feature allows file chaining, across up to 12 drives, during both editing and printing. Muse recommends the separately available Dan Paymar lowercase kit to allow your Apple to do word processing in uppercase and lowercase characters. Cursor control commands let you send the cursor to the middle of the screen, to the beginning or end of text, or to the last change made. Super-Text also has a one-key abbreviation for the often-used word "the." Its formatter allows both page numbering and chapter-relative page numbering.

This passage is part of an advertising pamphlet of a few years ago. How can you tell? In common with most advertising, it is positively slanted, and its thesis is developed by concrete examples. It is written for a special, very narrow audience with an interest in word processing. Thus, it is so technically oriented that the average person would not understand it. It uses a formal vocabulary with a large number of compound and jargon words. The sentences are medium to long, and the tone of the passage is impersonal.

1 Corinthians 13

Though I speak with the tongues of men and of angels, and have not charity, I am become as sounding brass, or a tinkling cymbal.

And though I have the gift of prophecy, and understand all mysteries, and all knowledge; and though I have all faith, so that I could remove mountains, and have not charity, I am nothing.

And though I bestow all my goods to feed the poor, and though I give my body to be burned, and have not charity, it profiteth me nothing.

Charity suffereth long, and is kind; charity envieth not; charity vaunteth not itself, is not puffed up;

Doth not behave itself unseemly, seeketh not her own, is not easily provoked, thinketh no evil;

Rejoiceth not in iniquity, but rejoiceth in the truth;

Beareth all things, believeth all things, hopeth all things, endureth all things.

Charity never faileth: but whether there be prophecies, they shall fail; whether there be tongues, they shall cease; whether there be knowledge, it shall vanish away.

For we know in part, and we prophesy in part.

But when that which is perfect is come, then that which is in part shall be done away.

When I was a child, I spake as a child, I understood as a child, I thought as a child: but when I became a man, I put away childish things.

For now we see through a glass, darkly; but then face to face: now I know in part; but then shall I know even as also I am known.

And now abideth faith, hope, charity, these three; but the greatest of these is charity.

a. This is one of the best known of biblical passages. There are many versions of the Bible (King James, Jerusalem, Good News, and so on); can you identify the version used for this excerpt?

b. What do you find the most difficult and most impressive about this passage?

c. Why do so many of the verses use parallel structure?

d. Read the passage aloud. What feeling does it evoke?

e. Find a modern version of 1 Corinthians 13 and compare them. In what ways are they similar? Different? How does a different audience affect the style?

EXERCISE EIGHT
Style in Comics

In this exercise you and your partner will have opportunities to write in a style suitable for a cartoon or comic strip.

1. At home you and your partner should each find a cartoon from a newspaper or magazine that is a few weeks old. Cut off the caption and bring the cartoon and the separated caption to class. Here is an example:

HERMAN

2. Exchange only the cartoons with your partner. Then each of you compose a suitable caption for each other's cartoon. Remember to take into account the style of the drawing so that your caption will be consistent with it.

3. Discuss with your partner the appropriateness of your caption.

4. After your discussion, compare your version with the original. Were the styles of your caption and that of the cartoonist similar? What word would you use to describe the overall style of the original cartoon? The original caption for the Herman cartoon shown here was "Simpson, bring me an order of onion rings and move that candle further down the table." Regular Herman readers would find this caption totally in keeping with Unger's style. If you are unfamiliar with Herman, how appropriate do you find the caption?

5. Repeat this exercise with comic strips. Cut out the original dialogue and make up one of your own to complement the graphic style of the cartoonist.

EXERCISE NINE
Style in Newspapers

In this exercise you and your partner will have opportunities to emulate an existing style by providing appropriate headlines.

1. At home each of you cut out articles on a similar topic from two newspapers. One article should have a headline that you think is sensationally misleading; the other, one that is completely factual. Remove the headlines from the articles; then exchange only the articles with your partner. After reading each article, each of you should provide a headline that suits its style.

2. Compare the headlines with the originals. How similar were they? What purpose did the original headline serve? Did yours fulfill the same purpose? Although all newspaper articles are titled, did you know that the original writer does not usually provide the headline? Do you know who makes up the titles? Do you know why?

3. Discuss in detail each of your articles with your partner. Use the points listed at the beginning of this chapter to help you discover the stylistic differences between the articles. You might talk about the choice of words, the slant, the length of sentences, the imagery, and so on. You might both like to practice on the following articles and the accompanying questions before you work on the articles that you have found. After you have read each article compose a suitable headline that complements its style.

Example One

VATICAN CITY—Pope John Paul II was shot three times in the abdomen today by a man believed to be a Turkish fugitive who had vowed to kill him.

The attack came as the pontiff rode into St. Peter's Square for a general audience before an estimated 15,000 people.

Vatican radio said no vital organ was struck; two bullets were removed and surgery was continuing to remove the third.

Example Two

A raw-edged day yesterday, all murky and dreary, as the bright colors of life ran together and made another puddle of gun-metal grey.

The madmen of the world have augmented the shooting of presidents in the U.S. and each other in Ireland and have taken their guns into the Vatican to shoot holy men. The gentle Pope John Paul II, the reaching-out, touching-hands spiritual father of the world's Catholics, is proved to have earthly guts, mortal enough to bleed, tough enough to absorb bullets from a gun wielded by yet another mind-bent assassin. (by Denny Boyd)

Example Three

He was an intense, youngish man with his left hand jammed into the pocket of his beige jacket, and when he presented his ticket to the forward section of a sunlit St. Peter's Square to attend Pope John Paul II's weekly audience from close up the guard didn't even look twice. He soon wished that he had. In a blurred moment of ferocity, Mehmet Ali Agca, a Turkish terrorist whose road to Rome began 18 months ago when he made up his mind to slay the pontiff, abruptly struck at the object of his obsession . . . with a burst of fire from a nine-mm Browning pistol. The slim, unblinking gunman's bullets failed to kill the most popular Pope in modern times. But he may well have torn the heart out of John Paul's remarkable papacy by permanently damaging his rugged constitution. (by Peter Lewis)

Answer the following questions with your partner so that you both are in agreement.

  a. Which of the three articles is the easiest to read? Why?
  b. Which one mixes levels of vocabulary? Provide examples.
  c. Which one would have appeared on the front page of a newspaper? State why you chose the article you did.
  d. Which one contains the longest sentence?
  e. Which is developed in the most specific, concrete way?
  f. Which is developed in the most subtle, abstract way?
  g. Which piece is designed to appeal to the reader's emotions?
  h. Which one contains satire? Provide an example.
  i. Which uses the most inventive adjectives? Provide two or three examples.
  j. Which contains figurative language? Provide examples.
  k. Which writer is closest to the reader?
  l. Which is the most subjective (personal)? Objective (impersonal)?
  m. Which is the most aggressive? Cautious? Provide examples.
  n. What word would you use to describe the overall style of each article? Use the list of words in Exercise Eleven.

When you finish your discussion, turn to the Suggested Answers (following Chapter 40) to see other responses.

EXERCISE TEN
Rhetorical Devices and Style

Rhetorical devices are techniques that you can use to create a certain stylistic characteristic. When used with discretion, rhetorical devices can help achieve your purpose—that is, to emphasize, to shock, to add humor, to draw attention to word choice, to create suspense, and so on.

The list of rhetorical devices illustrated in this exercise are not exhaustive; many others are dealt with in other parts of *The Independent Writer*. (See the Index for other references.) Follow these instructions for each example:

* Read through each rhetorical device with your partner.
* Discuss what purpose it serves.
* Take turns thinking up a new example of each rhetorical device before you go on to the next one.

1. Use a *rhetorical question* when you want to ask a question to which the answer is implied.

> Can all the hype of Hollywood be taken seriously? Can the hype makers themselves take their products seriously?

2. Use *abnormal word order* when you want to vary and emphasize an idea.

Normal Word Order: Subject, then Verb

> *Heaven's Gate*, a monumental failure that lost millions of dollars, was publicized and republicized as a masterpiece misunderstood by the public.

Abnormal Word Order: Verb, then Subject

> Publicized and republicized as a masterpiece misunderstood by the public was *Heaven's Gate*, a monumental failure that lost millions of dollars.

Normal Word Order: Adjectives, then Noun

> Talented and innovative *Heaven's Gate* director Michael Cimino was expected by United Artists to reproduce the success of his brilliant 1978 film, *The Deer Hunter*.

Abnormal Word Order: Noun, then Adjectives

> *Heaven's Gate* director Michael Cimino—talented and innovative—was expected by United Artists to reproduce the success of his brilliant 1978 film, *The Deer Hunter*.

3. Use *repetition* when you want to emphasize the importance of a particular fact.

> In the two *Godfather* films, Al Pacino portrayed strong-willed Michael Corleone, a son and then himself the Godfather of the strong Corleone family.

4. Use *climactic parallelism* when you wish to present several facts in order of importance.

Margot Kidder will not be remembered for her scatterbrained roles, her schizophrenic portrayals, or even for her unorthodox behavior; she'll be remembered as the woman who stole Superman's virginity.

5. *Balance* one part of a sentence with another part when you have the opportunity to parallel your ideas in two or more equal word groups.

After Barbra Streisand became a star in a New York musical, she became a star in Hollywood movies.

6. Use *opposites* when you want to make a balanced sentence memorable.

Death brought James Dean's fine acting career to a premature close, but memorable film performances will always keep him alive.

7. Use *reversals* (*chiasmus*) when you want to make a balanced sentence even more memorable.

It is just as hard to take the hope out of comedy's promise to cure all ills as it is to take the healthy comedy out of venerable funnyman Bob Hope.

8. Use a *periodic sentence* when you wish to withhold the most important part of the sentence until the period.

One of the highlights of *Little Big Man*, a successful film that dealt with the story of Custer's Last Stand as told by a 122-year-old survivor, was the portrayal of Old Lodge Skins by actor Chief Dan George.

EXERCISE ELEVEN
Your Writing Style

If you have completed the previous ten exercises in this chapter, you understand that everyone has a style in what he or she does. You should also know the importance of acquiring a writing style in order to fulfill the requirements of all the writing you do. In this exercise you can take the opportunity to analyze your writing style.
1. To prove that you have style, work with your partner to apply the fundamentals listed in the introduction of this chapter to your last completed writing assignment. As you discuss each idea presented in the piece, find specific details to support your statements. End the exercise by using one of these terms to describe your style:

cautious	breezy	stiff	dignified
ironic	uneven	slangy	eloquent
distinguished	aggressive	didactic	journalistic
objective	straightforward	confusing	formal
easy-to-read	technical	mixed	comic
impressive	informative	colloquial	direct
moving	conversational	abstract	
down-to-earth	familiar	vigorous	

Make sure that you and your partner have found specific details to support the term that you both have chosen to describe your style.

2. Now reverse the exercise by analyzing your partner's latest piece of writing.

Special Writing Assignment

Using at least two or three of the ideas in this chapter, write a piece with a distinctive style. When you finish, ask your partner to evaluate your piece to see if it has a consistent style. Also, ask your partner to comment on the quality of any special technique you included; for example, you might ask your partner to consider your use of persona, sentence length, rhetorical devices, ironic tone, and analogy. Here is what one student wrote.

Gamblers Are Wild Cards

by Charlene Little, student

Since the day this casino opened, my buddies and I have been standin' here in the front parlor greetin' visitors with our rigid-arm salutes. Don't let all my chrome and red paint fool ya. Tarnation! It's tough bein' a slot machine in one o' the wildest casinos in Vegas. My life's real tough! If my luck changes, the head honcho will cart me off to the back lounge so this ol' soldier can have a rest. It's probably not in the cards though. I'm goin' to be at the mercy of these tourists forever. From the heap o' trouble they give me (and they give me plenty), seems to me the varmits shuffle themselves into three types. I don't know which bunch is the worst!

First comes the big boisterous yahoos who always wear cowboy hats decorated with lots o' feathers. Look the guys in the eye and you know they've been hitten the firewater. They're the "Boppers." As soon as the silver dollar goes into my slot, they're boppin' me on the head while my eyes are still spinnin'. Talk about a headache! That bunch don't last long. They're too interested in makin' noise and jawin' with the ladies.

The ones that can really fool ya are the sweet lil ol' ladies in their "Sunday-go-to-meetin's." Those gals have the patience of saints an' the stamina of long-distance runners. I'm still amazed that they can stand in one spot for a coupla hours, pop in their silver, and pull on my arm 'til it's numb. Only Wayne Newton's dinner show can pull 'em away. Praise the Lord! If it weren't for Mr. Newton, this buckaroo'd never git a rest.

I must be gettin' soft in the head (it's all that boppin') cuz my favorite patrons are the tour-packaged honeymooners. Steppin' off the bus lookin' like a fresh pair o' dice on a high roll, imagining that I'm the Mother Lode, they're always hopin' to strike it rich. Of all my customers, their tug on my arm feels friendly, like a handshake.

A one-armed bandit is what they call me. Yessiree! But with a poundin' headache, triple vision, and people feedin' me constantly, I'm beginnin' to feel almost human.

ANALYSIS

1. The student writer of the above piece wanted her partner to consider her complex use of persona: the narrator is a "western" slot machine; her visitors are cards. Do you think she achieved her aim?

2. How has Little organized her essay?

3. When your partner is editing your piece, ask for suggestions for additional stylistic characteristics. Try to work them into your piece with your partner.

35

Controlling Your Sentences

INTRODUCTION

In this chapter you will have the opportunity to study the infinite variety of sentence structures with your workshop partner, asking questions, testing emphasis, and clearing up problems. Two other parts of *The Independent Writer* deal with sentence structure: all of the Third Workshop Section encourages you to work alone on sentence-combining techniques, and Chapter 56 of the Fourth Workshop Section offers suggestions for you to correct errors in sentence structure. (If, while you and your partner are working through this chapter, you think you have written a sentence that is not correct, you might refer to Chapter 56.)

EXERCISE ONE
Simple to Complex

Every sentence contains one basic idea, but some sentences decorate their basic idea with many additional words, making the sentence more complex.

Simple Idea

Sports interest people.

Complex

Major-league or minor-league, amateur or professional, sports of all kinds interest people in America and throughout the world.

1. Do you see the simple idea, "Sports interest people," within the complex idea?
2. You and your partner work *separately* to convert these simple ideas into complex ones.

    a. College sports are popular.

    b. Students win athletic scholarships.

    c. People watch sports on TV.

    d. Athletes become wealthy.

    e. Men and women participate.

3. Compare your complex sentences. Chances are that, if you worked separately, none of them are identical. Already you are noticing the possibilities of sentence variety.

EXERCISE TWO
Complex to Simple

    The reverse process is just as easy to apply. To be able to isolate the kernel parts of a complex idea is useful when you practice sentence combining.

Complex Idea

The English game of rounders was the ancestor of America's national sport of baseball.

By taking every important word, you can put the kernel parts into simple sentences.

Kernel Parts

    There was a game.

    It was an English game.

    The name of the game was rounders.

    There is a game.

    It is a national sport.

    It is an American sport.

    The name of the game is baseball.

    Rounders was the ancestor of baseball.

1. Working *separately* from your partner, break these sentences into their kernel parts.

    a. The first recorded baseball game took place in Hoboken, New Jersey, on June 19, 1846.

    b. In 1876, the National League was founded to make baseball a popular sport, free from gambling.

    c. During his twenty-three-year playing career, Ty Cobb produced more than four thousand hits.

    d. Many people do not know that Babe Ruth started his remarkable baseball career as a pitcher.

    e. Jackie Robinson, major-league's first black player, helped the Brooklyn Dodgers win six National League pennants.

2. Compare your kernel parts with your partner's. They should be nearly the same. Sentence variety does not occur in the kernel, but in the ways you combine several kernels.

EXERCISE THREE
Sentence Variety

Notice how to vary one sentence.

The agile basketball player leaped into the air and slammed the ball through the hoop to win the game.

The key words are: *agile, basketball, player, leaped, air, slammed, ball, hoop, win,* and *game.* The other words show how the key words are held together: *the, into, the, and, the, through, the, to,* and *the.*

Kernel Parts

There is a player.

She is agile.

She plays basketball.

The player leaped.

She leaped into the air.

The player slammed the ball.

It slammed through the hoop.

The game was won.

Read the different ways of combining these eight kernels:

a. After the agile basketball player leaped into the air, she slammed the ball through the hoop to win the game.

b. Leaping into the air, the agile basketball player slammed the ball through the hoop to win the game.

c. The agile basketball player, who leaped into the air, slammed the ball through the hoop to win the game.

d. The agile basketball player, after leaping into the air, slammed the ball through the hoop to win the game.

e. To win the game, the agile basketball player leaped into the air and slammed the ball through the hoop.

f. Winning the game, the agile basketball player leaped into the air and slammed the ball through the hoop.

g. The agile basketball player, after leaping into the air, slammed the winning ball through the hoop.

h. The agile basketball player leaped into the air, slammed the ball through the hoop, and won the game.

Can you or your partner provide more combinations? You must use all the kernels. See how many ways you and your partner can combine the following sentences.

1. Two sentences:

As a player, Bill Russell starred both in college and with the Boston Celtics.

He became the first black coach in the National Basketball Association.

2. Three sentences:

Bill Bradley was a college star at Princeton.

He signed a lucrative contract with the New York Knicks.

He is now the senior senator from New Jersey.

3. Four sentences:

Lew Alcindor played for the UCLA Bruins.

He helped them win three NCAA titles.

He changed his name to Kareem Abdul-Jabbar.

He stars for the Los Angeles Lakers.

EXERCISE FOUR
Combining

Because there are so many ways of combining sentences, you will need to determine which combination serves your *purpose*, or which is the most emphatic.

If you are ever dissatisfied with the way you have written one of your sentences, just rearrange the most important words in the manner you think might have the greatest impact on your *audience*. The places for key words are at the beginning and end of sentences. Why?

1. Working *separately*, you and your partner combine each group of kernel ideas into a single sentence in at least three different ways.

a. Wimbledon is the best-known tennis facility in the world.
To win there is to gain fame and prestige.
Its official name is the "All-England Lawn Tennis and Croquet Club."
It is located just outside London.

b. Björn Borg is a handsome Swede.
He won five Wimbledon men's championships.
He won them consecutively.
No one else has won as many.

c. John McEnroe is an American tennis star.
He, too, is a Wimbledon champion.
He plays both singles and doubles.
He is notorious for his arguments with officials.

d. Jimmy Connors won the 1982 Wimbledon and the 1982 U.S. Open men's championships.
He also won at Wimbledon in 1974 and at the U.S. Open in 1974, 1976, and 1978.
Like McEnroe, he used to be known for his unsportsmanlike behavior.
Like McEnroe, he is left-handed.

e. Martina Navratilova was born in Czechoslovakia.
She is now an American citizen.
She is left-handed.
In 1984, Navratilova won the most coveted prize in tennis: the Grand Slam.

2. From each group select the sentence you feel creates the greatest impact. Then compare the sentence with your partner's and determine between you which (yours or your partner's) is more emphatic.

EXERCISE FIVE
Subtracting

So far you have had practice in combining and rearranging in order to create emphatic sentences. By *subtracting* certain unnecessary words, you can give even more emphasis and variety to sentences, as the following example shows:

- The United States Olympic hockey team, which was led by a young player named Mike Eruzione, won the gold medal in the Winter Olympics of 1980 as they played before an enthusiastic crowd of people who were rooting for the Americans in Lake Placid, New York.

- The United States Olympic hockey team, led by young Mike Eruzione, won the gold medal in the 1980 Winter Olympics before an enthusiastic pro-American crowd in Lake Placid, New York.

Working *with* your partner, subtract the unnecessary words from these sentences.

a. The Indianapolis Motor Speedway, which has been given the affectionate nickname of "the Brickyard" (because when the surface was originally built, it was paved with bricks), has been the site of both great triumph and great tragedy.

b. In the history of the race called the Kentucky Derby, a race which has been run for more than one hundred years, only two young female horses, or fillies, whose names were Regret and Genuine Risk, have been winners.

c. Every year from 1980 to 1982, an excellent skier named Phil Mahre, who comes from Yakima, Washington, won the World Cup in Alpine skiing; it is even more remarkable that he has a twin brother whose name is Steve and who skis almost as well as he does.

d. The Silver Broom, a trophy that is awarded to the team of male curlers that wins the championship in the world of curling, is the prize that is competed for by curlers who come from Scotland, Sweden, Canada, the U.S., and other countries.

e. Richard Petty was a champion stock-car driver, and he had a father, whose name was Lee Petty, who was a NASCAR champion.

EXERCISE SIX
Expanding

When you write, you should also be prepared to *expand* your ideas. When you revise your sentences, pose and answer the questions *who, what, where, when, why,* and *how.* In this way, you may discover something you can add to improve the clarity of your writing. For example, in the sentence "Mark Moseley kicked a field goal," this procedure would work as follows:

Key Idea	Kicking a field goal
WHO	Mark Moseley of the Washington Redskins
WHAT	(Already indicated)
WHEN	In the last minute of the game
WHERE	From the twenty-five yard line
WHY	To win the 1983 NFC championship
HOW	Nervously

The following are some ways of combining these data:

a. Mark Moseley of the Washington Redskins nervously kicked a field goal from the twenty-five yard line in the last minute of the game to win the 1983 NFC championship.

b. In the last minute of the game, Mark Moseley of the Washington Redskins nervously kicked a field goal from the twenty-five yard line to win the 1983 NFC championship.

c. To win the 1983 NFC championship in the last minute of the game, Mark Moseley of the Washington Redskins nervously kicked a field goal from the twenty-five yard line.

1. Which of these sentences is the most emphatic? Why?

2. You and your partner work *separately* to expand each of the following kernel ideas into a full sentence. Then, by combining, rearranging, subtracting, and expanding, present to each other the one sentence that you consider the most emphatic. Discuss the effectiveness of each choice.

a. Playing high-school football

b. Playing on artificial turf

c. Seeing the Super Bowl

d. Meeting your favorite player

e. Watching your favorite football team (in person or on TV)

EXERCISE SEVEN
Rearranging and Subtracting

1. Using rearrangement and subtraction, combine the following sentences into one complete paragraph, consisting of a number of single sentences. You and your partner should work *separately*, making sure your sentences are varied. Use some short sentences and some long ones. Put key words first in some, last in others. Make sure, though, that your whole paragraph flows logically.

> In 1920, the National Football League was founded.
>
> At that time running was the most important part of every game.
>
> Early football stars were men who could run well.
>
> They included Jim Thorpe and Harold "Red" Grange. Grange was called "the Galloping Ghost."
>
> In early football, passing was thought to be something that only sissies did.
>
> They passed because they were afraid to run.
>
> Several things happened to make passing more important.
>
> The ball was made slimmer.
>
> It then became easier to throw.
>
> A receiver named Don Hutson demonstrated faking and finesse.
>
> A quarterback named Sammy Baugh showed the difference an accurate passer could make to a game.
>
> Nowadays it is almost impossible for a team to be successful without an accurate passer and excellent receivers.
>
> But crowds still love a good runner.
>
> The 1984 Super Bowl will be remembered for Raiders running back Marcus Allen's 191-yard performance.

2. When you both finish, compare the variety of your sentences and the emphasis of your paragraphs.

EXERCISE EIGHT
Types of Sentences

All of the sentences used in Exercises One to Seven have made statements. These *declarative sentences* are the most common in English. There are three other types, however, that can add variety to your writing: *questions*, *exclamations*, and *commands*. The following is an example of what can be achieved without using a declarative sentence.

> Is Wayne Gretzky really the greatest hockey player of all time, as some fans and hockey commentators claim? Not so fast! What about the great Maurice Richard, who led Les Canadiens to one Stanley Cup after another? What about the elegant Bobby Orr, the greatest of modern defensemen, or the fast-skating "Golden Jet," Bobby Hull? What about the ageless wonder Gordie Howe,

knocking about in the corners with players less than half his age? And don't forget Phil Esposito! With all those players and more to choose from, can you still say that Gretzky is the greatest? You bet you can!

Notice the punctuation of each of the sentences. Which are questions? Exclamations? Commands?

Although you should not overuse these three kinds of sentences in your writing, try to write a paragraph where you do not use a single declarative sentence. When you are finished, ask your partner to check that you have not used any declarative sentences, as well as to see that your paragraph holds together.

EXERCISE NINE
Minor Sentences (or Rhetorical Fragments)

From your early writing days, you learned that a sentence is a group of words with a subject and a verb. If you forgot the subject or the verb, you were told your sentence was incomplete. You had written a sentence fragment, and that was taboo. You were told, "A sentence must contain at least one complete thought." So, through your schooling you avoided anything resembling a fragment, and spent those years perfecting whole sentences. Complete thoughts.

But writers do use nonsentence fragments in order to communicate. (Which sentence in the last paragraph is a rhetorical fragment? Did it communicate something to you? Also, did you spot the interrogative fragments in the paragraph about the "greatest hockey player of all time"? You can easily supply the missing parts of these *minor sentences* from the context, so that you do not misunderstand the content.)

1. Perhaps the following paragraph uses the rhetorical fragment excessively. (In fact, your instructor-editor may not approve of this paragraph at all.) But how does the style of the writing relate to its topic? Do the fragments communicate complete thoughts?

Flashing arms. Flailing legs. Pumping hearts. Bobbing heads. Up and down the pool. Butterfly. Breast stroke. Freestyle. Arms up, arms down. The end at last! The gold medal! Competitive swimmers train day after day for years to achieve just one moment of glory. Some never make it.

For another look at minor sentences, read "Snow," in Chapter 2.

2. Write a short piece where you use at least one minor sentence. Exchange it with your partner and discuss whether you have written a rhetorical fragment that works or a fragment fault that needs revision. See Chapter 56 for help in correcting sentence fragments.

Special Writing Assignment

On a topic that you think will please your partner, write a paragraph in which you use various kinds of sentences, including minor sentences. Ask your partner to discuss the effectiveness of your sentence variety.

Here is a sample piece:

Has this workshop whetted your appetite? If so, you should plan to spend time learning the finer details of sentence variety in the various chapters in the Third Workshop Section of *The Independent Writer*. In that section you can work alone. At your own pace. In school. At home. Anywhere. Any time. Start right away! By the time you have mastered the entire section, perhaps you will have acquired the habits of good writing. And, once acquired, the habit will be yours for life.

36

Figurative Language and Allusions

INTRODUCTION

You use comparisons to relate something that may be unfamiliar to your readers with something with which they are familiar. When you use figurative comparisons and allusions, you encourage your readers to look at your subject in a new way. A successful metaphorical comparison is daring, leaving your readers in awe of the person who thought of it.

Before you begin this chapter, you should realize that, theoretically, anything can be compared with anything else. You should also realize, though, that not all comparisons succeed. Elsewhere in *The Independent Writer* you are often encouraged to write an Absurd Analogy as part of a brainstorming method (see Chapter 25).

EXERCISE ONE
Comparing

A comparison can be either literal or figurative. "She looks like her sister" is a literal, or factual, comparison. "She looks like a million bucks" is a figurative comparison. (If taken literally, the latter expression does not make much sense!) A comparison can also allude or refer to someone or something: "She looks like Venus."

1. Write three literal comparisons based on the appearance of a friend of yours. Your responses must be real. Use someone or something who actually looks like your friend.

Bob looks like his uncle.

2. Now create three figurative comparisons. Your comparisons must be imaginative. Think of at least one aspect of your friend's appearance that you can compare with a similar aspect of something or someone else.

Bob looks like every girl's dream.

3. Now create three allusions. Your responses must be references to something or someone specific. Compare at least one aspect of your friend's appearance to that of a character from mythology, literature, history, legend, and so on.

Bob looks like Michelangelo's David.

4. Check your responses with your partner to verify that you have made literal comparisons, figurative comparisons, and allusions.

EXERCISE TWO
Kinds of Figurative Comparisons

You can make several different kinds of figurative comparisons. Some of these are defined below, with examples.

1. A *simile* is a figurative comparison that uses "like" or "as":

- Bill is built like a brick wall.
- Bill's temper is as hot as molten lava.

2. A *metaphor* is a figurative comparison that states or implies that one thing *is* something else:

- Bill is a brick wall.
- Bill scorches everyone with his temper. (*Scorches* implies that he has a hot temper.)

3. *Personification* gives inanimate objects life:

- The waves caressed Bill as he floated on his back.

4. An *allegory* gives life to an abstract quality or condition, for example, death, love, hunger, friendship. You would usually capitalize a word when you use it allegorically:

- In the medieval play *The Summoning of Everyman*, Death tells Everyman that it is his turn to be called to judgment.

5. An *allusion* makes a comparison by reference:

- Bill thinks of himself as an Apollo, probably because he is built like a spaceship.

6. *Metonymy* substitutes one thing for another with which it has a close relationship:

- The kettle boiled. (Actually the water boiled.)
- Perry Mason now sells real estate, and Ben Cartwright sells dog food. (Raymond Burr and Lorne Greene portrayed Mason and Cartwright on television for years.)

7. *Synecdoche* substitutes a part of something for the whole:

- After a particularly moving soliloquy, Bill loves to get a big hand.

8. An *apostrophe* is an address to a thing or person who is not present:

- Critics! Where were you when I had the audience in the palm of my hand?

9. *Paradox (paradoxical statement)* is a seeming contradiction:

- After years of hard work, Dustin Hoffman became an overnight success in *The Graduate*.

10. An *oxymoron* combines contradictory or incongruous terms:

- I can still hear the mute cry of Jane Wyman in *Johnny Belinda* as she had to endure the living hell of a rape.

11. An *analogy* keeps up a figurative comparison for an extended length of time: sometimes a paragraph, sometimes an entire essay, or even an entire book. Barbara McDaniel's description of the writing process is an example:

> When writers actually begin putting words in sequence on paper, they are obviously in the second stage of the writing process, i.e., writing in the narrow sense of the word. The writing stages might be compared to the gears of a car; this one would be the normal "drive" position, with first and second gear the prewriting stage, and high gear, reverse, and idle for revising. There can be shifts up and down from the "writing" stage, but it is better not to spend too much time with either other stage, when writing, for the sake of keeping up momentum. Editors can help students discover the conditions that help them stay "in gear" to get the first draft done as expeditiously as possible; examining the habits of professional writers can prove enlightening.

Make up sentences about a friend, using one of the figurative comparisons above in each sentence. After you have written your sentences, discuss them with your partner to ensure that your use of each type of comparison is correct. If you are having difficulty with this exercise, go on to the next one and come back to this one later.

EXERCISE THREE
Creating Metaphors

Worn-out figurative comparisons are often referred to as *dead metaphors*, or *clichés*. Our language is filled with such clichés as *out of the frying pan into the fire, like a bolt from the blue, teeth like pearls, red as a rose, tired to death,* and so on.

With your partner write out ten clichés. Rewrite them in order to breathe new life into as many of these dead metaphors as possible. Prepare to be a bit silly. Think of them in a literal way and use puns whenever you can. Here are some examples based on the preceding dead metaphors:

- The sausage was out of the frying pan and into Friar Tuck.
- While playing with his meccano set, Bill took a nut from the red pile and a bolt from the blue.
- Her teeth were like pearls, and her face was like the rest of the oyster.

- Henrietta, voting Communist at her first political rally, rose as a Red.
- Burt was tired to death at the rubber factory.

Share with your friends the new metaphors that gave you the biggest chuckle.

EXERCISE FOUR
Three Rules

Once you begin to think metaphorically, your writing can improve tremendously. Here are three rules, with examples, to help you write original figurative comparisons.

Rule One

While the two things compared are usually quite different, in order for the comparison to work they must have at least one thing in common:

The floor of Mary's room was flooded with dust, dolls, and old newspapers. (The floor of Mary's overcrowded room is being compared to a flood tide: both overflow.)

Rule Two

Your comparison should be able to do in reality what you want it to do figuratively. In other words, your metaphor must make complete sense, or it will be strained. Why does the following metaphor not work?

Hal's words were like darts as they squashed into my brain. (Darts pierce; they do not squash. If the writer wanted to keep *darts*, what should he or she change *squashed* to?)

Rule Three

You should not begin with one comparison and end with another. Why would a mixed metaphor such as this be confusing?

The principal told Tom that it was time to turn the other cheek and face the music.

Can you see that the meanings of "turn the other cheek" and "face the music" are not compatible? How would you repair this mixed metaphor?

1. Keeping in mind the three rules above, write figurative comparisons in which you compare the following:

- Your main mode of transportation to an animal's movement
- A person you know to an insect
- Some aspect of weather to an animal

2. Working with the following examples, substitute new figurative comparisons for the words in italics. As you do so, test each one according to the three rules above:

- Working on her term paper, she was *busy as a beaver*.
- The chairman of the board *met his Waterloo* on the night he presented his proposal for the merger.
- The array of spring flowers on the hillsides made me appreciate once more *Mother Nature's* handiwork.

Try not to read the sentences below until you have compared your answers with your partner's. Then discuss both of yours in relation to these. Are yours more original?

- Working on her term paper, she was *busy as a politician during an election campaign*.
- The chairman of the board *met his Watergate* on the night he presented the proposal for the merger.
- The array of spring flowers on the hillsides made me appreciate once more the handiwork of *that celestial, omnipresent craftswoman*.

3. Now exchange with your partner three sentences containing dead metaphors. Each of you must substitute three original, figurative comparisons for the clichés. Evaluate your creations by applying the three rules outlined above.

EXERCISE FIVE
Visual Comparisons

Figurative comparisons do not have to be expressed in words. Cartoonists are fond of making comparisons on editorial pages or in comic strips. For example, a cartoonist may convey the stupidity of a particular politician by putting his or her head on a donkey's body or allude to a similarity between a modern person and some historical character by putting his or her face on the silhouette of Napoleon or Marie Antoinette. Such cartoons can be both funny and satiric.

1. Find five visual figurative comparisons from your local newspaper or any magazines you have around the house. Bring them to class to share with your partner and see if he or she recognizes the two things that are being compared.

2. Do you see what two things are being compared in the cartoon on the opposite page? (If not, turn to the Suggested Answers following Chapter 40.)

EXERCISE SIX
Allusions

Writers who use allusions can save themselves dozens of words. When they see a similarity between their subject and something else that they know well and expect their readers to understand, they will unhesitatingly link them together. Thus, they

unite their topic and situation in the allusion and so help their audience to appreciate their purpose.

Readers will not fully appreciate a particular allusion unless they are familiar with the specific reference. Let us hope that, as you work through the following exercise, you will not find yourself like Paul on the road to Damascus, blind and uncomprehending.

1. Find five *written* figurative comparisons in your local newspaper or in magazines and bring them to class to share with your partner. See if he or she recognizes the two things that are being compared.

2. The following are a few titles of articles in recent newspapers and magazines. Can you tell what the author is alluding to? For example, "The Night Stuff" refers to Tom Wolfe's *The Right Stuff*.

    a. "Encounter of a Chilly Kind"

    b "Terms of Disparagement"

    c. "Play It Again, Pam"

    d. "The Saucer's Apprentice"

    e. "The Bungle Book"

    f. "Mopey Dick"

    g. "To Censor or Not to Censor"

(If you cannot solve some of these, turn to the Suggested Answers following Chapter 40.)

3. The following are taken from a single edition of *Time*. As you examine each, note the allusion (in italics). Make a record of those references you definitely understand, those you could make a reasonable guess at, and those that pass you by.

Discuss with your partner the full significance of each allusion that you recognize. A few of the excerpts are from letters to the editor; most are from the various columns; all are written in hopes that the general public will understand what has been written. You can certainly see that *Time* expects its readers to have had many varied experiences in order to appreciate the many allusions.

   a. *Here we go again*: another four years of our national *soap opera*, with Reagan playing the lead role. But how will the script end, *with a whimper or a bang*? (three different allusions)

   b. *The greatest minds of the 12th century* ran the Mondale-Ferraro campaign.

   c. *Like children, Americans follow the merry tunes of Reagan, happy to fall in line behind his winning personality* . . . .

   d. It does not follow that the belief in a literal *Armageddon* has to be linked with a reckless willingness to enter a nuclear war.

   e. A U.S. astronaut, looking like a modern *knight-errant* in shining space suit, sallies forth into the darkness, powered by a *Buck Rogers* backpack called an MMU. (two allusions)

   f. It was designed to demonstrate that the U.S. is once again roving the high frontier and showing plenty of *the right stuff*.

   g. Other critics fear that Reagan's *Stars Wars* plan will turn space into an *apocalyptic* war zone.

   h. [Joe] Allen's *pas de deux* with the satellite was a slow, surreal dance of weightlessness.

   i. It was like *Moses* bringing back *the tablets* for review. (one connected allusion)

   j. The incident illustrated the troubles faced by Americans and Lebanese, worried about another possible *kamikaze* assault in Beirut.

   k. *Soup kitchens* expect to take in more hungry this year than ever before.

   l. The parched, scabrous earth was *pockmarked* with *foxholes* in which hundreds upon hundreds of [Ethiopian] families crouched for shelter against the chill mountain wind.

   m. Five middle-level agency officials, targeted to be disciplined for their part in drafting the contentious primer, said they were being used as *scapegoats*.

   n. In fact, *crying wolf* has some practical benefits for the Sandinistas.

   o. Like drug addicts, *Valley Girls*, cripples, and others she portrays, [Whoopi] Goldberg is no stranger to life's vicissitudes.

   p. A native New Yorker, she [Whoopi Goldberg] performed in small theaters on both coasts before being *Great-White-Wayed* . . . .

   q. Men have long envied his ability to complete a pass, but even though the enduringly eligible bachelor has finally been sacked, Joe Namath, 41, still managed to honeymoon in the *fast lane*.

r. ... the bravura of (Obi-Wan) [Peter] O'Toole [in *Supergirl*], shameless and affecting as he just about *tears a planet to tatters* ....

s. I probably prefer to travel with my *chimeras*, and leave the baby behind. (Excerpted from a review of *Journey to Kars* by Philip Glazebrook)

t. ... from the failure of the *Edsel* to the follies of *Watergate*. (two allusions)

u. Soviet strategists once trained dogs, in *Pavlovian tradition*, to associate food with the bottoms of tanks.

v. First Class passengers deserve better than First—*Maharajah* Class! (Taken from an advertisement)

(If you cannot solve all of them, turn to the Suggested Answers following Chapter 40.)

EXERCISE SEVEN
How Much Do You Know?

Did you find the preceding exercise difficult? If you did, it may indicate that you do not read enough. The main reason why allusions escape readers is that the readers are not well informed.

Most professional writers know something of the classics, the Bible, world religions, world history, the arts, sports, and so on. When they write, it is perfectly natural for them to call on their knowledge in order to sharpen a particular comparison. They delight in comparing literarily instead of literally.

If you want to understand and appreciate a particular reference, you can ask a friend who is better read than you for an explanation, or you can tackle a secondary source (a dictionary, encyclopedia, or other reference work) in which the allusion may be identified.

The best solution, though, is to start to fill in the gaps in your own knowledge by reading the classics, listening to news programs and documentaries, reading newspapers and periodicals, and listening to well-informed people. In other words, absorb as much as you can from your surroundings.

1. Below are several questions that you and your partner can ask each other. They are designed to allow you to determine your knowledge in a number of fields. If you are unable to supply at least one or two correct answers to each set of questions, you should start to fill your spare time with some necessary reading.

a. What was the tragic flaw (the quality in their natures that destroyed them) of each of the following: Othello, King Lear, Romeo, Juliet, Hamlet, Macbeth, Oedipus, Ajax, Antony, Cleopatra, Brutus, Willy Loman, Antigone?

b. What adjective best describes each character: Falstaff, Gertrude, Polonius, Puck, Bottom, Uncle Tom, Christian (of *Pilgrim's Progress*), Helen, Stanley Kowalski, Big Daddy, Big Brother, Peter Pan, Scarlett O'Hara, the Great Gatsby?

c. For what quality is each political figure known: Mussolini, Hitler, Alexander the Great, Chamberlain, Nixon, John A. Macdonald, Charles II, Elizabeth I,

Napoleon, Pericles, Idi Amin, Eleanor Roosevelt, Ayatollah Khomeni, Indira Gandhi?

d. What sort of philosophy would you associate with each of these people: Sartre, Jung, Freud, Plato, Karl Marx, Mahatma Gandhi, Zeno, Socrates, St. Augustine, Confucius, Martin Luther King, Mother Theresa, Malcolm X, Mother Seton?

e. What do you think of in connection with each of these Biblical characters: Adam, Eve, David, Goliath, Ruth, Jacob, Bathsheba, Shadrach, Joshua, Salome?

f. What is the essence of each of these places: Paradise, Shangri-La, Club Med, Valhalla, Elysian Fields, River Styx, Davy Jones' Locker, limbo, the end of the rainbow, Abraham's bosom?

g. For what is each of these gods and goddesses famous: Zeus, Odin, Neptune, Saturn, Hebe, Shiva, Astarte, Bacchus, Athena, Yama, Glooscap, Aphrodite, Isis? (And in what religions would you find each of these messengers of the gods: Cupid, Mercury, Iris, Gabriel, Yamapurusha?)

h. What is the allusion in each of these titles: *Poseidon Adventure, Blue Collar, And Justice for All, Armageddon, The Secret of NIMH, Author! Author!, Poltergeist, As for Me and My House, Fortune and Men's Eyes, They Shoot Horses Don't They?, E.T.?*

i. With what do you associate each of these names: Horatio Alger, Rockefeller, Machiavelli, Rothschild, Keynes, Cyrus Eaton, John Bull, Uncle Sam, Robespierre, John Q. Public, Newton, Darwin, John Doe, de Sade, Lucrezia Borgia?

j. Which movie star is known by each of these nicknames: the Duke, the Sweater Girl, Ski Nose, Schnozzola, the Great Profile, America's Sweetheart, the Great Lover, the King, the Groaner, Mr. Top Hat, the Little Tramp, Swivel Hips?

k. What kind of writing would you expect from allusions to: Hemingway, Joyce, Woolf, Dickinson, Whitman, Byron, Shaw, Rabelais, Henry James, Jane Austen, Chekhov, Ibsen, Mary Shelley, Percy Bysshe Shelley?

l. What is the main characteristic of each of these artists: Picasso, Rubens, Renoir, Raphael, Modigliani, El Greco, Rembrandt, Tom Thomson, Alex Colville, Audubon?

m. Who do you think of when you hear these lines: "Here's Johnny!," "Old soldiers never die, they just fade away," "The Watergate scandal," "I cannot tell a lie," "Love means never having to say you're sorry," "Never was so much owed by so many to so few," "The state has no place in the bedrooms of the nation"?

2. Make up your own list of famous people or things that stand for something a great many people know about and test them on your partner. Here are two to get you started:

- What do these famous women represent: Florence Nightingale, . . . ?
- What sport do you think of when you hear these names: Joe Louis, . . . ?

Special Writing Assignment

Write a short piece in which you use an analogy (sustaining the image throughout).

---

1. Choose one of the epigrams below and extend the comparison. For example, with Oscar Wilde's epigram "Illusions are like umbrellas; you no sooner get them than you lose them," you would write about illusions in terms of getting and losing umbrellas. The best way to start to write an analogy is to make two columns. Label your subject in the first column and the thing you are comparing in the second. Then write down *everything* you can think of pertaining to the thing you are comparing.

Example:

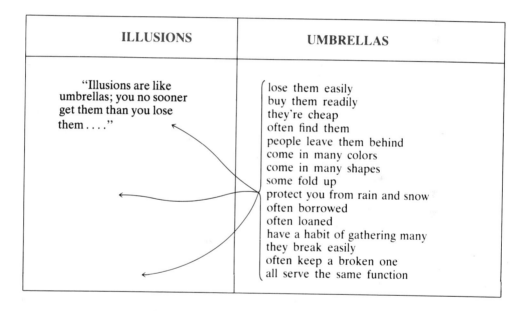

ILLUSIONS	UMBRELLAS
"Illusions are like umbrellas; you no sooner get them than you lose them . . . ."	lose them easily buy them readily they're cheap often find them people leave them behind come in many colors come in many shapes some fold up protect you from rain and snow often borrowed often loaned have a habit of gathering many they break easily often keep a broken one all serve the same function

To write your comparison in the first column, choose appropriate items from the second column. Make sure that whatever you use applies to both *illusions* and *umbrellas*. For example, you would be able to use "lose them easily," but not "protect you from rain and snow."

Make sure that you introduce your analogy in a topic sentence, but note that topic sentences do not have to be the first sentence in paragraphs (see Chapter 27). From then on you should illustrate your subject (illusions) in terms of the figurative comparison (umbrellas) without mentioning the comparison (umbrellas) again. If you attempt to prove in your analogy, you will create a false one; for example, had Wilde written, "Because illusions are like umbrellas, you should understand that as soon as you get one you will lose it," he would have produced a false analogy. (See the analogies at the end of this chapter.)

2. Apply the above techniques to one of the following epigrams and then have your partner check your analogy against the above suggestions and those in Exercise Four.

- "Happiness is a butterfly." (Hawthorne)
- "[Life] is a tale told by an idiot." (Shakespeare)
- "A man's home is his castle." (Anonymous)
- "All the world's a stage." (Shakespeare)
- "Memory is the diary that we all carry about with us." (Wilde)
- "Our little life is rounded with a sleep." (Shakespeare)

Before you write your analogy, read these student products. Test the figurative comparisons and discuss their effectiveness with your partner.

Love and War

by Herb Wendland, student

Being the first time out for all of us, we were naturally scared, but some strange force made us go on. Upon landing in the designated area, I immediately began to sum up the tactical situation. By now the outfit and I were fighting mad, ready to go. When we began our assault we met slight resistance, but things got progressively worse as we worked our way up the canal. My buddies began to drop all around me. Exhausted and demoralized, I thought it would be a miracle if even one of us got to the objective. As it turned out, I was the one; out of an original company of over three hundred million. I burst into the enclosure and fertilized the egg.

Bad Writing is a Disease

by Robin Gilmore, student

Looking at a list of things that can go wrong with your writing is a little like looking at a list of all the diseases that can kill you. You can die of bulimia, cerebro-vascular stroke, Reye's syndrome, atherosclerosis, herpes simplex, coronary thrombosis, Hodgkin's disease, and a host of other unpleasant diseases. Your writing can also "die" from one of a long list of diseases. Some beginning writers can be almost as frightened to find out that they have writing problems as they might be if they found out that they had an incurable disease.

Editors have been known to put the fear of death into a beginning writer. They may say gravely, "Your writing is suffering from *ambiguity*," or they may nod in agreement and in unison whisper, "*Redundancy*!" You take your dying paper home and try to save it from a disease you have never heard of. After hours of rewriting, you think that you have revived it, so you submit your paper for a second opinion. When you see it a week later, you barely recognize it. Red blotches cover its poor body. There is a huge "V" in its midsection; "*ROS*" on every long sentence; and "*AWK*" scattered over its margins. You limp home, wondering if you can ever revive your bloodied piece of writing.

But do not despair when you see writing terms or symbols on your work. They are part of your editors' efforts to help you become a better writer.

Hard Labor

by Jan Lenington, student

With sweat pouring off her brow, she moaned and writhed in anguish. I checked the calendar and then my watch: I knew the time had come.

"This is the most painful experience a woman could have," she groaned.

"Keep pushing," I said, patting her hand in encouragement. Pulling at her hair, she screamed, obviously in agony. I looked at my watch again and warned, "Your time is almost up; it's due very shortly."

"Don't ever do it, Jan," she exclaimed, dashing out the door. "Don't ever take Buchanan's English class," she called back, her completed composition in hand.

Summer Daydreams

by Pedro Brantuas, student

I long for those summer days when my favorite guy puts his arms around my slender body and takes me to the beach. I am filled with happiness just to see his wonderful physique nearby to protect my fragile body. No one dares to touch me because they know I belong to "HIM!" I love the way he plays with me, throwing me in the water, laying me in the sand and never on the rocks. It's all so exciting! But most of all I love it when he rides me and controls my every move. It's sheer ecstasy being a surfboard.

37

Slant

INTRODUCTION

The term *slant* describes the way in which writers may, consciously or unconsciously, convey attitudes or feelings to the reader. As a result of their purpose or attitude, their material may have a *positive* (honorific) or *negative* (pejorative) slant.

EXERCISE ONE
Word Choice

1. In order for you to appreciate how your word choice changes, recall the last time you were out alone with someone. Think about what kind of time you had. Write down about ten key words that you would use to describe the time you had. Use words that you feel comfortable with (*the pits, great, foolish, terrific, boring, OK, grateful,* and so on). For this exercise to work, you must be totally honest in your word choice.

2. Now imagine telling the person you were out with about the time you had. (Your audience, purpose, and situation have changed.) Write down about ten words that you would use. Which of the words you used in No. 1 would you not use now? What words would you use instead? What new words might you add to the list? (If, for example, you had used *terrible* to describe the occasion, you might not want to say that word directly to the person. You might use *not bad* instead.) How many of the original ten words would remain unchanged?

3. Next, imagine telling your best friend of the same sex (new audience) in the place where you usually see each other most often (new situation) about the time you had. Which of the words you used above would you not use now? What words would you use instead? What new words might you use? How many of the ten original words would remain unchanged?

4. Next, imagine telling one of your parents (new audience) about the time you had. Which words from the previous lists would you not use? What words would you use instead? What new words might you use? How many of the original ten words would remain unchanged?

5. To end this exercise, tell your partner (new audience) in the classroom (new situation) about the time you had. How many of the original ten words would you not use?

"GUNBOAT DIPLOMACY"

"POPULAR LIBERATION FORCE"

EXERCISE TWO
Your Attitude

Your description of a subject is affected by your attitude towards it.
1. With your partner, choose a subject (an activity, a person, or a location) that one of you likes and one dislikes.
2. Each of you write (for three minutes) a description of your subject. Do not state how you feel about your subject, but merely describe it.
3. Compare your descriptions. Discuss the differences in word choices, facts, and so on.

EXERCISE THREE
Thinking Slant

1. Think about your best friend and someone you do not like. What fifteen words would you use to describe each of them (*beautiful*, *dishonest*, *popular*, *unkind*, *weepy*)?

2. Now think of these people in figurative terms and complete the following similies:

- My best friend is like a . . . .
- The person I don't care for is like a . . . .

(You might choose nouns like *kitten, black widow spider, oak tree, sausage, overripe banana.* You cannot use a "human" word like *man, lady, child.*)

3. You can classify many of your responses in Nos. 1 and 2 as positive or negative. Words that are positive support your subject (*beautiful, popular, kitten, oak tree*); words that are negative oppose your subject (*dishonest, unkind, weepy, black widow spider, sausage, overripe banana*). Of the words you used, which would you consider positive, and which negative? Are there any that do not seem to fit into either category? Are there any that might be either positive or negative depending on the context?

Writers use words either for their dictionary meaning or for their appeal to the reader's emotions. Words that have only a dictionary meaning are termed *denotative*; words that also have emotional appeal are *connotative*. Denotative words have no slant; connotative words have either *positive slant* or *negative slant*.

EXERCISE FOUR
Slant in Advertising

We are inundated by examples of both negative and positive slant in newspapers, magazines, and direct mail, and on radio, television, and billboards. Advertisers want us to buy their products; politicians urge us to support their platforms; government agencies encourage us to stop smoking and drinking and to start exercising.

Most advertisements have a positive slant. Why? Where would negative slant be used? The following are some advertising words that have a positive slant: *whiter, pretty, smooth, free, healthful, drowsy, wholesome, your home, ours*; the following words have a negative slant: *Brand X, harsh, ugly, sick, dreary, stuffed-up, your house, theirs.*

1. Find at least ten advertisements in the print media and arrange them in two piles depending on whether they contain a positive or negative slant. Look at the names of the products as well; for example, Quik, Dynamo, Magic Touch.

2. Exchange advertisements with your partner to see if you can find the negative and positive slant in each other's examples. Discuss your findings.

EXERCISE FIVE
Indicating Slant

There are four ways to indicate slant:

- **Words.** Words with positive connotations will cause your reader to feel good about your subject and possibly about you; words with negative connotations will cause your reader to react against your subject and possibly against you as well.

- **Comparisons.** If you compare your subject literally or figuratively with something pleasant, your reader will approve of your subject; if you use unpleasant comparisons, your reader will know that you disapprove of your subject.
- **Details.** You can influence your reader by the specific details you choose to include or omit. Favorable details support your point of view; unfavorable ones oppose it.
- **Denotation.** You might use a more subtle fourth way to slant your writing or speech. In this method you would try to use the denotative aspect of words in order to avoid being honorific or pejorative; thus, your writing or speech would be slanted by what you do *not* say. For example, after you have watched a friend's embarrassingly inept performance, you might comment in a neutral way—"It was interesting"—rather than being negative and risk losing a friend. You might use a similar low-key approach rather than be positive when commenting on the performance of someone you do not admire, even though he or she has given a beautifully detailed performance.

1. Which of the following sentences use words with positive connotations, which use words with negative connotations, and which use words with no particular slant?

- The food in your restaurant is tantalizingly delicious.
- Your café chow is all right; it fills you up.
- The menu in your establishment offers a variety of choices.
- His scrawl is impossible!
- His penmanship is illegible.
- His writing is different.
- The breakup of AT&T caused confusion.
- The divestiture of AT&T created uncertainty.

2. Which of the following are positive comparisons and which are negative comparisons? Which are neutral (no slant)?

- He's a living doll!
- He's like a Barbie doll. He's *Ken*!
- He's so good looking he doesn't look real.
- She chews her gum as if she were enjoying it.
- She munches gum like a cow chewing her cud.
- She chews gum as if it were not there.

3. Which of the following details are positive and which are negative?

- The timber lay in straight piles, the odor of pine filling the air.
- The trees were laid in straight lines, the smell of pine sap all over the place.
- He woke in the usual way, picked the grit out of his eyes, coughed up a hunk of phlegm, and staggered to the toilet.
- He awoke in his normal manner, removed the sleep from his eyes, cleared his throat, and walked into the bathroom.

4. You can place most words on a continuum from positive to negative slant. Although each of the following means *night*, notice the subtle difference between each.

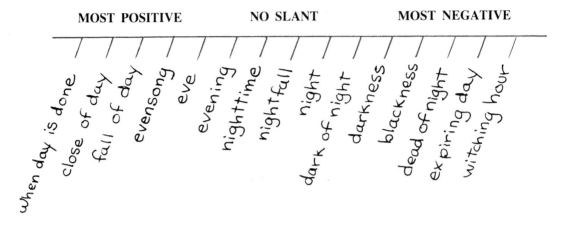

MOST POSITIVE   NO SLANT   MOST NEGATIVE

when day is done / close of day / fall of day / evensong / eve / evening / nighttime / nightfall / night / dark of night / darkness / blackness / dead of night / expiring day / witching hour

You and your partner make a similar continuum for *job*, *bed*, and *die*.

A KNAVE, A RASCAL, AN EATER OF BROKEN MEATS; A BASE, PROUD, SHALLOW, BEGGARLY, THREE-SUITED, HUNDRED-POUND, FILTHY, WORSTED-STOCKING KNAVE; A LILY-LIVER'D, ACTION-TAKING KNAVE; A WHORESON, GLASS-GAZING, SUPERSERVICEABLE, FINICAL ROGUE; ONE-TRUNK-INHERITING SLAVE; ONE THAT WOULDST BE A BAWD, IN WAY OF GOOD SERVICE, AND ART NOTHING BUT THE COMPOSITION OF A KNAVE, BEGGAR, COWARD, PANDAR, AND THE SON AND HEIR OF A MONGREL BITCH: ONE WHOM I WILL BEAT INTO CLAMOROUS WHINING IF THOU DENIEST THE LEAST SYLLABLE OF THY ADDITION.

5. Name one way in which you spend your free time (for example, reading romantic novels). Now write five positive words that you would use to describe this free-time activity in order to convince someone to spend time doing it (for example, "thrilling").

Use one literal and one figurative comparison to describe the pleasantness of your activity (for example, "like seeing a movie," "like being on the moon").

Write down two favorable details to describe your activity (for example, "makes me feel special").

6. Taking turns with your partner, assume that each of you wants the other to stop his or her activity. Write down five negative words to describe the activity (for example, "time-wasting"). Then use unpleasant comparisons to describe the activity (for example, "like sticking your head in a garbage can"). Finally, write two unfavorable details to describe the activity (for example, "It makes you ignore real life.").

EXERCISE SIX
Word Levels

Words can have no slant, a positive slant, or a negative slant. They can also be classified according to levels—standard and nonstandard—and according to whether they are formal, informal, colloquial, or slang. In some cases—as in the following alternatives for the neutral word *lawyer*—you may find many choices in some categories and few or none in others:

| | STANDARD | | NONSTANDARD | |
	Formal	Informal	Colloquial	Slang
Positive	advocate	attorney counselor	legal eagle friend at court	mouthpiece
Negative	pettifogger	latrine lawyer	shyster	ambulance chaser

Just a cursory look at the above chart indicates that there are many degrees of slant to describe one thing. This fact makes your search for the right word a challenge, a goal, a frustration, a joy, a nightmare, a quest for a light at the end of the tunnel.

1. Where, in the table above, would you place the following: solicitor, pleader, proctor, procurator, *amicus curiae*, deputy, intercessor, legalist, Philadelphia lawyer? You should notice that the negative formal form is often used for an ironic purpose. What is ironic about *pettifogger*?

2. Draw five tables similar to the above sample. Choose five of the words from the following list and try to fill in a word for each space. Check with a recent thesaurus or dictionary to verify the level of diction of particular words—especially nonstandard ones. (*Cop*, for example, is now accepted as a standard word, whereas in older dictionaries it is classified as nonstandard.)

> police officer, doctor, anti-feminist, abortion, husband, daughter, child, fat, homosexual, toilet, demonstration, vomit, gun, father, television set, psychiatrist, caucasian, girlfriend, boyfriend, apartment, lie down, afraid, leg, teenager, party, pimple, angry with, sad, song, dishes, die.

See how many spaces you can fill by using your own name—for example, John, Johnny, Johnny-O, boyo!, John Boy, Jack, Jackie, Jojo, J.

Remember that because a word is placed in a particular space, it does not mean that it must forever remain there; for example, if an angry client charges into his lawyer's office, and yells, "See here, counselor!", the word *counselor* suddenly has a negative slant. So, when you work on this exercise, do so with words that *you* would use in situations that *you* would consider normal for *you*.

3. When you have filled as many blanks as you can, go over your five lists with your partner. It might be an amusing as well as a useful exercise for you both to choose at least one similar word, work on it separately, and then compare your responses.

EXERCISE SEVEN
Slant and Style

Slant contributes heavily to style. If you wish to be direct in your approach to your subject, you must use straightforward words; if you wish to be ironic, you should use more contrived words.

The same word can sometimes be used positively and sometimes negatively, as in the following examples:

- When the *sophisticated* lady entered the room, all the men flocked to her. (Positive)
- She looked at the men with an air of *sophisticated* indifference. (Negative)

1. Use the following words in both positive and negative ways: *naive, good, green, bean pole, skeleton, beak, intelligent.*

2. Notice the slant in this long sentence. How does the slant help you to determine that the tone is ironic?

My mangy, oversexed, underslung, disobedient, unintelligent, beer-guzzling, floor-dirtying mutt is the least satisfactory pet I've ever had the misfortune to own, but when he looks trustingly at me with his bleary, nearsighted eyes, I can't help but love him.

Rewrite the sentence, using straightforward words so that the tone is direct.
3. Write two sentences to describe a pet, a friend, or an acquaintance. Make one sentence ironic and the other direct. With your partner, discuss the effectiveness of your sentences.

EXERCISE EIGHT
Propaganda

Writing for propaganda purposes usually requires an excellent appreciation of slant. Notice the use of negative and positive slant in these sentences:

In nations enslaved by the Red Menace, arrogant, all-powerful tyrants dominate the family. In our homeland, however, family love and unity are encouraged to exist as the normal foundation on which individual happiness and democratic freedom can be strongly built.

Can you find examples of both positive and negative slant in these sentences? The slant has been carefully chosen to appeal to the reader's emotions.

Be careful with this kind of writing. Although there will always be a use for propaganda, an intelligent reader soon realizes that propaganda arouses the emotions but provides little information. The following sentence is a rewrite of the propaganda piece. Notice that it contains information with no emotional slant.

The principal difference between a family in the United States and one in a Communist country is that we emphasize the family unit in our democracy, whereas the Communists subordinate the family to the good of the state.

1. Write a short piece of propaganda telling why your college or university is better or worse than another. Make sure you appeal to the emotions of your reader by using negative and positive slant.

2. Rewrite your piece of propaganda so that it contains no emotional slant.

3. Discuss both of your pieces of writing with your partner.

EXERCISE NINE
Use Slant in Your Writing

Before you use slant in what you write from now on, ask yourself: Do I want positive or negative slant in my writing? Or do I want a mixture of positive and negative slant because I have two points of view and want to support one thing and reject another? Do I wish to use a direct or an ironic tone? Always remember your writing variables when you are making these decisions. Because slant can greatly influence readers, you are cautioned not to name call. Because you should always focus on word choice when you write, you should examine each word in your piece to determine whether it should be removed, changed, or amplified by details or metaphors.

The following pieces were written by student Brian Petty especially for this chapter to show different combinations of slant, level of word choice, and tone. Before you read any of them, read Joe Davis's paragraph at the end of the Introductory Section. Petty took the same portion of the paragraph with its standard/informal/no slant word choice and rewrote it four ways. After you read each version, answer the questions that follow it.

1. Why Not Legalize Heroin? Standard/Informal/No Slant

...Let us compare two types of heroin addicts: street junkies and registered addicts. A junkie "shooting" his own fix runs the risk of overdosing, breaking off a needle in his arm, or catching hepatitis from an unsterilized needle. Under clinical supervision, a registered addict fares better. Because he no longer has the pressure of meeting the drug's high street cost, he can follow a medical plan that could eventually lead to his accepting methadone, a less dangerous substitute, or perhaps kicking the habit altogether....

  a. This is an excerpt from the original paragraph. Are there any words that you believe are slanted?
  b. Do you agree that the level of word choice is standard?
  c. Would you make any changes? Where?

2. Hey Man, Let's Make Smack Legal! Nonstandard/Slang/Positive

...Check out two kinds of hypes: the "do-it-yourself" man, an' the dude who is registered with the Man. The dude who fixes hisself is takin' risks; hittin' too big an' toppin' out, breakin' a spike off in his arm, or goin' yellow from a dirty heater. With the med squad, the registered hype ain't got it so bad. He's got no grief over scrapin' up the bucks for his next ride; he gets his shot from someone who knows what they're doin', an' gets medical help that could mean usin' meth or goin' straight altogether....

  a. Who is the narrator? Support your answer.
  b. Are there any nonslanted or negative words that should be changed to slang and positive?
  c. How does this compare with the original? Is it effective?
  d. Continue the process by writing a few more sentences with nonstandard/slang/positive slant.

3. On Considering Diacetylmorphine Legalization Standard/Formal/Positive

...May we consider two types of diacetylmorphine users: the alleged "street" user and the registered user. The first party runs several risks: administration of a miscalculated dosage, breakage of a hypodermic needle in a blood vessel, and contraction of hepatic disorders because of employing infrequently sterilized implements. The registered user, however, is introduced to a very beneficial environment. He is alleviated of the burden of meeting the overwhelming financial responsibility of heroin addiction by receiving his injections from qualified health-care personnel, and may be placed under clinical supervision which will lead to use of the less hazardous methodone or, in some cases, total reformation. . . .

a. Who is the narrator? Support your answer.

b. Should any words be changed because they are not standard/formal/positive?

c. Continue the process by writing a few more sentences.

4. Should Heroin be Legalized?   Standard/Colloquial/Negative

. . . Check out two kinds of junkies: street dirt bags and registered addicts. The street scum who shoots his fix by himself rides the coattail of death. He might O.D., bust a needle in his arm, or get liver disease from using dirty needles. Now look at the registered addict; he hasn't got so much hassle over getting the piles of money to buy his dope, gets his shot from trained nurses, and could be covered under a medical plan that could get him on Meth. He might even get that monkey off his back once and for all. . . .

a. Who is the narrator? Support your answer.

b. Should any words be changed because they are not standard/colloquial/negative?

c. Continue the process by writing a few more sentences.

**5. Why Should We Legalize
Diacetylmorphine Distribution?**   Standard/Formal/Negative

. . . View, if you will, two factions of heroine abusers: the alleged "street junkie," and the "registered addict." The first party, who administers his own injections, is doing so at considerable risk to himself. He has a great chance of administering too large a dosage, fracturing a needle within his arm, or contracting hepatitis from septic implements of administration. The "registered addict" is exposed to a more beneficial environment. Given heroin freely, he feels no monetary strain of heroin addiction, receives his injections from health-care professionals, and follows a program using methadone—another narcotic—as a substitute. With concentrated effort he moves toward possible remission. . . .

a. Who is the narrator? Do you see any elements of irony in this version? Support your answer.

b. Should any words be changed because they are not standard/formal/negative?

c. Continue the process by writing a few more sentences.

Can you tell that Petty had fun writing these pieces? Although it is nearly impossible to make every word fit a precise level of word choice and degree of slant, he has been able to show you that there are many ways of saying the same thing.

Special Writing Assignment

Find a piece of writing that you have already composed and that has a strong point of view. If you do not have such a piece available, compose or find one. Choose a topic you feel strongly about.

Rewrite this piece in the same ways as Brian Petty has done in Exercise Nine, adding a different form of slant and level of diction for each one. Remember to apply slant to words, comparisons, and details.

Discuss with your partner the effectiveness of your several pieces.

38

Humor and Wit

INTRODUCTION

We never seem to tire of telling and listening to funny stories that we have personally experienced or witnessed. We often remember and retell the best ones over and over. Writing humor can be just as much fun as telling a funny story among friends. In fact, writing about one of the many funny situations you have personally witnessed can be one of the most relaxing of your writing experiences.

It is much more difficult, however, to be witty (cleverly saying exactly the right thing at the right time—puns, double entendres, irony, and so on). There is a vast difference between the genuinely humorous story told in a straightforward manner and the brilliantly witty one told to create a specific effect.

Writing humorous pieces is easy and fun; writing wit requires a special talent and unlimited skill. How many people do you know who are "the life of the party," always able to come up with a witty phrase and get a laugh. Most of us think of something witty to say long after the party is over ("If only I had said . . ."). Beginning writers, therefore, will often avoid introducing elements of wit into their work for fear that their readers will not get their point of wit or be critical of its effect. This chapter is designed not only for you to recognize various humorous and witty techniques used by professional writers, but also for you to include some of these techniques in your own writing. (If you find terms in this chapter with which you are not familiar, turn to the Glossary.)

EXERCISE ONE
The Funny Story

There are few events in the average human life that do not contain at least one humorous occurrence: the graduation ceremony at which the keynote speaker loses his place in his speech, then knocks over his water glass, rendering the rest of the speech illegible; the mystery in the theatre where, at the climactic moment, the gun fails to fire and the actor, pointing the gun at the intended victim, whispers, "Bang!"; the suave man-about-town offering to open a bottle of wine, only to catch his tie between the corkscrew and the cork.

If you want to use this exercise in conjunction with Exercise Two, have a cassette tape recorder handy to record what you and your partner say.

1. Prepare to tell your partner something that recently happened to you. Choose an event that contained something that you considered humorous. If you need to, take a few minutes to jot down details such as time, place, other persons involved, and so on.

2. Relate the incident to your partner.

3. Ask your partner if he or she thought your story was humorous. Was the humor in the story itself, or in the way in which you told it?

4. Reverse the process, with your partner telling you a story.

EXERCISE TWO
Writing the Funny Story

You have probably listened to stand-up comedians who can tell funny stories by the hour. Many times the way in which a story is told has just as much to do with its humor as the story itself. A lifted eyebrow, a knowing wink, a change in intonation—these and other tricks of the storyteller's trade help comedians to leave audiences rolling in the aisles, howling for more.

Unfortunately, you cannot use the tricks of the speaker when you write. In writing a funny story, you must rely on the only tools you have—words, phrases, and clauses. The words you use and the way you arrange them can either make the most solemn event wildly hilarious or make the funniest incident deadly dull.

1. If you recorded Exercise One, replay it and transcribe it verbatim, indicating pauses, hesitations, and other interruptions, such as laughter.

2. Ask your partner to read your transcript silently and let you know the effect. Is the written story as funny as the oral one?

3. Working together, revise your transcript in order to bring out the humor.

4. Give the revision to another person and ask for his or her reaction. What makes it funny, or not funny?

5. After your discussion, you might like to put the piece away for several days. As you go through the rest of this chapter, you will note several techniques to create humor. Just as a stand-up comic has many visual tricks to enhance his act, a writer of humor has a number of tricks as well. When you have completed the entire chapter, you and your partner may like to come back to this exercise and introduce into your story some of the tricks of writing humor that you have learned.

EXERCISE THREE
Humor and Wit

If you have a good memory, telling and writing about a genuinely humorous incident that you witnessed is not an especially difficult writing task. But to develop a serious thesis with a purpose of evoking laughter requires a knowledge of the various methods of developing wit (satire, mock epic, travesty, parody) as well as the specific ways to express your supporting evidence (figurative comparisons, hyperbole, understatement, puns, irony, paradox, wit, aphorism, cacophony, alliteration, double entendre, sarcasm, invective, sardonic humor, various types of logical fallacies, and the use of a persona).

Humor is often unintentional; wit is always intentionally comic. A humorous saying is not cast in the form of a neat or startling epigram; a witty saying is always deliberately constructed. For example, notice the difference between the following two pieces. The first is humorous; the second attempts to be witty as well as humorous:

> My grandmother, a very sophisticated lady, was entertaining her friends at an afternoon bridge party. At its height she excused herself to go to the bathroom. When she had finished, she came downstairs. Her guests became silent as she entered the room to take her place at the card table. They didn't know where to look or what to say, knowing that if they were to look or say anything to each other they would burst out laughing.
>
> Grandmother had brought an entire roll of toilet paper with her. In her haste, she must have caught the end of the toilet paper in her panties, because she had dragged a trail of toilet paper all the way from the bathroom.

* * *

> My grandmother, the Queen of the Nile herself, was holding court at one of her afternoon soirees. Never one to do anything unnoticed, she announced, "Ladies, Mother Nature has called." And off she went, knowing that each of her guests were watching her ascend the staircase as if she were visiting St. Peter himself. After completing her ablutions, she descended the stairs, looking down on her subjects as they looked up at their queen. Eyes lowered and silence fell as Grandmother took her place at the card table. Her guests struggled to control themselves, for they knew that any second they would erupt in gleeful gales of guffaws.
>
> Grandmother had trailed a whole roll of toilet paper with her. Knowing that to be out of the room beyond a couple of minutes would invite unnecessary gossip, Grandmother, in her haste to rejoin the festivities, had caught the end of the toilet paper in her unmentionables. Granny looked as though she was connected to the bathroom by a mile-long, white umbilical cord.

1. What specific attempts at witty humor have been introduced into the second version? Did they improve the story for you?
2. Can you find examples of an allusion, an aphorism, a figurative comparison, an alliteration, a hyperbole, a logical fallacy? (If you are unfamiliar with any of these terms, refer to the Glossary.)
3. Which story do you find more humorous? Why?

EXERCISE FOUR
Methods of Developing Witty Satire

Witty writers seem to be able to take any topic, even an extremely serious one, and amuse their readers by treating it satirically. To satirize is to ridicule a social ill or an aspect of the human condition in order to influence readers to do something about it. Of all the styles of writing, you will perhaps find satire the most difficult, even though satire is easy to talk about and usually easy to see in other people's writing. Before you use satire in any format (from a serious expository essay to a comically friendly letter), you should decide whether the purpose, situation, and topic warrant a satiric treatment and whether your audience would appreciate it.

1. With your partner make a list of five or six things that are wrong with today's society. For example, "People are out of work." Then choose the item from your list that you would find easiest to ridicule. How would you ridicule it? For example, Jonathan Swift wrote his entire fourth book of *Gulliver's Travels* in order to point out that Gulliver would sooner live with horses than with his eighteenth-century fellow human beings (ridiculed as "Yahoos").

2. With your partner make a list of five or six things that are part of the human condition. Try to think of some of those silly things you do that seem serious at the time, but that you laugh about afterwards (for instance, when you are on a date and you spend the whole time worrying about what your partner thinks about you). Choose the item from your list that you would find easiest to ridicule. How would you ridicule it? For example, Woody Allen has made a fortune satirizing himself as a weakling who gets his desires only in fantasy.

EXERCISE FIVE
Sardonic Satire

Many columnists write about society's ills. They often delight in using satire and support their opinions in sardonic (biting, contemptuous, often hilarious) ways.

1. If you were to write a piece of sardonic satire, you should be able to answer the following three questions:

* What exactly do you want changed?
* How would you suggest that it might be changed?
* What techniques would you use to achieve sardonic satire?

Read the following example of sardonic satire, keeping in mind the three questions.

> I have been assured by a very knowing American of my acquaintance in London, that a young healthy child well nursed is at a year old a most delicious, nourishing, and wholesome food, whether stewed, roasted, baked, or boiled, and I make no doubt that it will equally serve in a fricassee, or a ragout.
>
> I do therefore humbly offer it to public consideration, that of the hundred and twenty thousand children already computed, twenty thousand may be reserved for breed, whereof only one fourth part to be males, which is more than we allow to sheep, black-cattle, or swine, and my reason is that these children are seldom the fruits of marriage, a circumstance not much regarded by our savages, therefore one male will be sufficient to serve four females. That the remaining hundred thousand may at a year old be offered in sale to the persons of quality, and fortune, through the kingdom, always advising the mother to let them suck plentifully in the last month, so as to render them plump, and fat for a good table. A child will make two dishes at an entertainment for friends, and when the family dines alone, the fore or hind quarter will make a reasonable dish, and seasoned with a little pepper or salt will be very good boiled on the fourth day, especially in winter. (from Jonathan Swift's "A Modest Proposal")

In his biting satire, Swift suggests that the impoverished Irish of the eighteenth century sell their babies to the wealthy British. The savage piece is obviously not to be taken seriously; rather, Swift wants to make the authorities aware of the situation in Ireland through his "A Modest Proposal for Preventing the Children of Poor People from Being a Burden to Their Parents or the Country." Swift supports his sharp view by employing a style filled with understatement. The contrast between vivid details of life-and-death content and a conversational, matter-of-fact style of understatement produces the sardonic satire. Can you find a few examples of understatement? For example, ". . . it will equally serve in a fricassee, or a ragout."

2. In order to write a piece of sardonic satire, you must understand your topic very well, feel strongly about it, want to bring about change, and have a great deal of courage. If you are not confident in developing a piece of straightforward writing with strong supporting evidence, you will find it difficult to develop a piece of satire; hence, you should not continue in this chapter until you have completed Chapter 34.

3. Find a newspaper column that uses sardonic satire and exchange it for one your partner has found. See if you can find examples of methods of achieving satire in each other's column. Then answer the questions in No. 1 as they apply to each column.

4. Working together with your partner, try to come up with a specific example of supporting evidence that you could drop into one of the columns you have been analyzing. It can be a word, phrase, or complete sentence. In the following example the new piece of understatement in brackets adds to the sardonic satire. Ellipsis marks are used because only a portion of the Swift excerpt is quoted. Note that the words in brackets have been added and are not Swift's.

> ...especially in winter. [For a larger gathering, such as a banquet, five or six children—of both sexes—will make a fine feast. Guests will remember the feast for the rest of their lives.]

5. Test to see that *your* piece of satire does not jar the tone of the original. If you read the column aloud, with your part included, it should read smoothly. Does the one above? Does yours?

EXERCISE SIX
Invective in Satire

Invective consists of harsh, derogatory remarks about someone or something. Invective is sometimes, but not always, humorous; its humor springs from the writer's use of devices such as puns, allusions, hyperbole, understatement, double entendres, and outlandish comparisons, as well as the use of overblown language. The writer of a piece of invective tries to make his or her insults so witty and well contrived that the audience will enjoy reading the piece but still understand the author's angry message.

Reviewers and critics are sometimes satirically unkind. They will often pretend to praise a book, play, or movie, and then they sharply criticize it. The following are some examples of invective:

> John Mason Brown on Tallulah Bankhead as Cleopatra:
> "Tallulah Bankhead barged down the Nile last night as Cleopatra and sank." (Pun)

> Kenneth Tynan on John Neville:
> "Here at last, I felt, was the authentic Richard II, a lithe, sneering fellow who curdled the milk of human kindness even as he dispensed it . . . . My excitement was marred, however, by the fact that the play...was *Henry V.*" (Pun, reversal, metaphor)

Below are three ways in which writers use invective. Instead of encouraging you to write invective, this exercise helps your reading process. As you read each excerpt try to identify invective.

Review

It was a positively awful evening in the theatre. It was not just a night where you wished you were somewhere else—this happens—but, more, it was the sort of night where you wished your nearest and dearest enemy was sitting in your seat. And paying for it, yet! . . . The play—the play, why should I be conned into calling it a play merely because it has the effrontery to totter into a Broadway theatre?—is as mean, small, and nasty as its protagonist . . . . No comment is beneath her but not a single feeling goes felt. This absolutely wretched woman tells us such homilies—but you really had to have been there to have believed it—as: "Life is our only defence against death—I know" and "One life is simply not enough for all lessons one has to learn." Wow, philosophy. And we only paid for entertainment . . . . The playwright—luckily I have now forgotten her name, she was never in movies—seemed so incompetent that one idly wondered whether one should call in the Fire Department. (excerpted from Clive Barnes's review of *A Woman of Independent Means*, from *The New York Post*, 4 May 1984)

Obviously Barnes did not like the play and resorts to witty rather than humorous invective to persuade his readers to avoid the play. Can you find within the excerpt examples of a figurative comparison, hyperbole, understatement, double entendre, and chiasmus?

Prose Fiction

Oh! but he was a tight-fisted hand at the grindstone, Scrooge! a squeezing, wrenching, grasping, scraping, clutching, covetous old sinner! Hard and sharp as flint, from which no steel had ever struck out generous fire; secret, and self-contained, and solitary as an oyster. The cold within him froze his old features, nipped his pointed nose, shriveled his cheek, stiffened his gait; made his eyes red, his thin lips blue; and spoke out shrewdly in his grating voice. (*A Christmas Carol* by Charles Dickens)

In order to make Scrooge into an unsympathetic, yet vivid, character, Dickens uses figurative comparisons, hyperbole, negative slant, and clusters of adjectives to heighten his invective. Find one example of each.

Drama

MACBETH:	. . . thou cream-fac'd loon!
	Where got'st thou that goose look?
SERVANT:	There is ten thousand—
MACBETH:	Geese, villain?
SERVANT:	Soldiers, sir.
MACBETH:	Go prick thy face, and over-red thy fear,
	Thou lily-liver'd boy. What soldiers, patch?
	Death of thy soul! those linen cheeks of thine
	Are counselors to fear. What soldiers, whey face?
SERVANT:	The English force, so please you.
MACBETH:	Take thy face hence. [Exit Servant.]

(*Mac.* 5.3.11-18)

Near the end of his play, Shakespeare, by introducing humorous invective at the expense of the Servant, provides comic relief for the audience before Macbeth's downfall. How many different words does Macbeth use to describe the Servant's pale complexion? (See the cartoon on page 430 for another example of invective.)

1. As a writing exercise, rewrite the above three excerpts, taking out the invective and replacing it with straightforward description. Such an exercise tests both your reading and writing ability. To get you started, here is the first sentence of the Dickens excerpt written in a straightforward style:

> Scrooge was a stingy man who always worked hard.

When you complete each rewrite, you and your partner should decide which is more effective: the satiric or the straightforward piece. Why?

2. Find an example of a piece of fiction or a review in which invective has been used and exchange it with one your partner has brought in. Based on your reading of the piece, answer the following questions:

a. What has displeased the author or critic?

b. Can you see what the writer is trying to say?

c. Do you think the writer is justified in using invective?

d. In what other way could the passage be written?

e. Would it be as effective?

3. If you feel confident, try your hand at writing invective. For practice, add an example of invective to one of the above pieces. Does your insert blend well with the writer's satire? In the following example ellipsis marks are used because only a portion of the Barnes review is quoted. Note that the examples of hyperbole and allusion in brackets have been added and are not Barnes's.

> . . . This absolutely wretched woman [who surely sank many more ships than the most beautiful face could possibly have launched] tells us such homilies . . . .

EXERCISE SEVEN
Parody

If you imitate another writer, you are parodying. You can do this by imitating the writer's style and tone or by using many of the actual words from the original piece.

1. Discuss impressionists with your partner. Do you have a favorite? Rich Little and Debbie Reynolds are popular impressionists who parody well-known celebrities, politicians, and movie stars. What techniques does a parodist use to bring his or her subject to the stage so that the audience recognizes who is being parodied?

2. The following is an example of an original song and a parody that was written as part of an advertising campaign. How does the parody resemble, and differ from, the original?

The Original	The Parody
Oh, say, can you see	Oh, say, won't you flee
By the dawn's early light	From the smog and the haze,
What so proudly we hailed	From the noise and the rush
At the twilight's last gleaming,	Of the urban congestion?
Whose broad stripes and bright stars	Won't you visit our place
Through the perilous fight	For a quiet weekend,
O'er the ramparts we watched	With the fish and the fowl?
Were so gallantly streaming?	What a wholesome suggestion!
And the rocket's red glare,	For a nominal sum
The bombs bursting in air	You can hear the bees hum,
Gave proof through the night	And catch a few bass.
That our flag was still there.	Won't you say that you'll come?
Oh, say, does that star-spangled banner yet wave	Oh, call us toll-free and we'll save you a place,
O'er the land of the free and the home of the brave?	Paradise Lake Resorts—ten miles north of Cape Grace.

Many school songs are parodies. If your school has a school song, write it out and compare it with the original. If your school does not have a school song, write one with your partner, basing it on a well-known tune. Use many of the original words as well as the original tune and rhythm. To make this task easier, write out the original and see which words you need to change to fit your school. Although a parody can contain sardonic and sarcastic satire, keep yours good-natured.

3. The following are three famous and often-parodied quotations from Shakespeare. You and your partner, working separately, should compose a parody of each. In the speech from *As You Like It*, the key words have been italicized and the first line of a parody has been started to help you.

a. from *As You Like It*:

All the world's a *stage*,
And all the men and women merely *players*;
They have their *exits* and their *entrances*,
And one man in his time plays many *parts*,
His acts being *seven stages*.

Begin your parody with:

All the world's a *store*
And all the men and women merely *buyers* . . .

b. from *Macbeth*

Is this a dagger which I see before me,
The handle toward my hand? Come, let me clutch thee:
I have thee not, yet I see thee still.

c. from *The Merchant of Venice*

The quality of mercy is not strain'd,

It droppeth as the gentle rain from Heaven

Upon the place beneath. It is twice bless'd:

It blesseth him that gives and him that takes.

4. Parodies of styles of prose fiction, such as Gothic novels, sea stories, and mysteries, have been popular for many years. James Joyce parodied just about every imaginable style in *Ulysses*. In 1981 Erica Jong, well known for her novels about contemporary women, wrote *Fanny*, using the style and heroine of the eighteenth-century novel *Fanny Hill*.

Like a parody of a poem, a parody of a piece of prose should use the style, sentence structure, and some of the vocabulary of the original, while making clear to the reader what the target is.

In this opening excerpt from a story called "Crime and Punishment," columnist Richard J. Needham uses the ancient form of a fairy tale as a foundation for his parody in which he has an imaginary student named Roman Raskolnikov attend high school in Buffalo. As you read the excerpt, try to find a specific example of an allusion, sarcasm, parallelism, repetition, and hyperbole. Also, notice that a specific example of a pun has been dropped into the excerpt as a piece of supporting evidence. Is it in keeping with the parody style of a fairy tale as well as with Dostoevski's *Crime and Punishment*?

Crime and Punishment

Once upon a time, there was a country whose federal authorities confined their activity to the deportation of industrious Greeks. In this country, there was a state whose politicians hid under the bed at the mention of wine, women, or weed. In this state, there was a city where instead of burying the dead, people elected them to high municipal office. And in this city there was a high school named Jugglemarks C.I., where you might have found a student named Roman Raskolnikov.

Raskolnikov was an agreeable young man who did well in such subjects as elementary mumbling, intermediate profanity and advanced cheating, thus preparing himself for a successful career in the business world or the political world or the academic world or indeed any other world. One day, however, he committed a terrible act in the history classroom. When the teacher, Mr. Forcepump Feedback, read out loud from the textbook that Columbus discovered America in 1493, Raskolnikov shot up his hand. "Sir, shouldn't that be 1492?" [It was immediately clear to everyone that in criticizing the textbook he was Roman too far.] The teacher turned purple with rage, the students green with alarm and embarrassment.

Mr. Feedback cried, "Do you mean to tell me, young man, that you have the insolence to question the holy sacred truth as contained in the holy sacred textbook?"—at which all the students reverently bowed their heads in worship, all save Raskolnikov, who stood his ground. "Perhaps, sir, it is a misprint." Mr. Feedback was furious,

"Raskolnikov, you will report immediately to the office of the vice-principal, Mr. Oliver Cramwell, and tell him of your unspeakable conduct. May Almighty God have mercy upon your soul."

5. Find an example of a parody and exchange it with one your partner has brought in. Try to add one or two examples of your own that support the theme and style of the original parody. Discuss the results with your partner. If you cannot find a parody, locate a copy of the classic parody of the *Iliad*, entitled "The Battle of the Frogs and Mice."

6. If your favorite prose author has an identifiable style, and you believe your reader would appreciate the humor in your parody, why not write a takeoff of the style? For example, as you read the following excerpt, can you tell which famous author the writer is parodying?

> Most people don't like the pedestrian part, and it is best not to look at that if you can help it. But if you can't help seeing them, long-legged and their faces white, and then the shock and the car lifting up a little on one side, then it is best to think of it as something very unimportant but beautiful and necessary artistically. It is unimportant because the people who are pedestrians are not very important. . . . If you drive a car and don't like the pedestrian part, then you are one of two kinds of people. Either you haven't very much vitality and you ought to do something about it, or else you are yellow and there is nothing to be done about it at all. (from Walcott Gibbs's "Death in the Rumbleseat")

If you do not recognize Ernest Hemingway's style in the above parody or if you have never heard of his essays glorifying bullfighting (entitled "Death in the Afternoon"), read the following excerpt from Hemingway's *The Sun Also Rises*, noting similar uses of word choice and sentence structure. For example, note the overuse of *it*, *who*, *and*, *that*, and forms of the verb *be*.

> It was not nice to watch if you cared anything about the person who was doing it. With the bull who could not see the color of the capes or the scarlet flannel of the muleta, Romero had to make the bull consent with his body. He had to get so close that the bull saw his body, and would start for it, and then shift the bull's charge to the flannel and finish out the pass in the classic manner. The Biarritz crowd did not like it. They thought Romero was afraid and that was why he gave that little sidestep each time as he transferred the bull's charge from his own body to the flannel . . . .

EXERCISE EIGHT
Travesty and Mock Epic

A travesty is a popular kind of satire in which you take as your subject some lofty, illustrious, distinguished, outstanding, prominent subject and treat it in trivial, frivolous, or even degrading terms. For example, Monty Python's *Life of Brian* is a travesty on the life of Jesus. Although many people found it highly amusing, *Life of Brian* outraged many religious groups.

The mock epic, or mock heroic, is the opposite of travesty. In the mock epic you take a frivolous or unimportant topic and treat it in a grand manner. One of the best examples of a mock heroic is Alexander Pope's *The Rape of the Lock*, in which Pope mocked the preoccupation of eighteenth-century society with trivialities. Pope treated the unimportant activities of ladies and gentlemen in his society as if they were the grand actions of epic heroes. For you to write or even read a mock-heroic satire, you must be familiar with the epic style. Homer's *Iliad* and *Odyssey* and John Milton's *Paradise Lost* are three well-known epics.

1. With your partner, discuss a travesty that you have seen or read. What lofty subject was satirized? How did you feel about it? (You usually either laugh or become outraged at travesties.)

2. As you and your partner read the following excerpt from a travesty, notice the specific examples of hyperbole, paradox, allusion, jargon, understatement, and non sequitur. Also notice that three additions have been inserted to enhance the travesty. Do they mar its overall style?

Accident Report

Ladies and gentlemen, citizens, comrades, this is a flash report to you from General G. Kolnikov, speaking to you from a bunker deep beneath the very topmost central military headquarters. First of all, I must tell you that our preemptive retaliatory strike against the enemy of all mankind was a smashing success. Large portions of their world have been rendered permanently uninhabitable because of vast clouds dense with radioactivity that, even as I speak, continue to spread far and wide. [Fortunately, our plans for post-holocaust rehabilitation have never included their part of the world—large though it is. After all, would it be civilized for us to help men who are the enemies of men? Well? O.K. So we've been prepared all along to forget about their half of the earth. I mean, who cares, anyway? Their half is the empty part. Ours is the full part. Right? O.K.]

Second, I am delighted to announce that because of our detailed plan for evacuation of the capital's government offices—the really important offices, that is—our leader and most of his helpers were successfully shoved out and are with me in this bunker. We are all very, very safe. [Our families and household pets, I'm sure you'll be pleased to know, are also safe with us—as was planned.] As soon as our instruments sense a decline in the level of radioactivity in the capital, we'll come out. [I did mention, didn't I, that the enemy got in a few—well, quite a few, actually—lucky shots? No?] It may be a long time before it's safe for us to be with you; but when it finally is, we promise to resume leading you in the same direction we took you in the past.

3. Can you insert one or two examples of your own which support the theme and style of the above travesty? Discuss the results with your partner.

4. As you read this excerpt from Henry David Thoreau's *Walden*, you should notice that the story of the battle of the ants is told as if it were an instance of war on the grand scale. The red and black warriors are represented as the natural brothers in arms to the fiercely brave Trojans and Achaeans of Homer's *Iliad*. The main epic feature of this piece is the elevated language and heroic imagery to describe the little great warriors ("It was evident that their battle-cry was Conquer or die," "Or perchance he was some Achilles, who had nourished his wrath apart . . . ."). Can you find other examples? Notice, too, the long, sweeping sentences, with many parenthetical expressions; they are characteristic of Homer's epic style. Also notice that the additional examples of hyperbole and allusion have been dropped into the excerpt and are not the words of Thoreau. Do they mar the overall style of the mock epic?

Walden

    I was witness to events of a less peaceful character. One day when I went out to my wood-pile, or rather my pile of stumps, I observed two large ants, the one red, the other much larger, nearly half an inch long, and black, fiercely contending with one another. Having once got hold they never let go, but struggled and wrestled and rolled on the chips incessantly. Looking farther, I was surprised to find that the chips were covered with such combatants, that it was not a *duellum*, but a *bellum*, a war between two races of ants, the red always pitted against the black, and frequently two red ones to one black. The legions of these Myrmidons covered all the hills and vales in my wood-yard, and the ground was already strewn with the dead and dying, both red and black. It was the only battle which I have ever witnessed, the only battle-field I ever trod while the battle was raging; internecine war; the red republicans on the one hand, and the black imperialists on the other. On every side they were engaged in deadly combat, yet without any noise that I could hear, and human soldiers never fought so resolutely. I watched a couple that were fast locked in each other's embraces, in a little sunny valley amid the chips, now at noon-day prepared to fight till the sun went down, or life went out. The smaller red champion had fastened himself like a vice to his adversary's front, and through all the tumblings on that field for an instant ceased to gnaw at one of his feelers near the root, having already caused the other to go by the board; while the stronger black one dashed him from side to side, and, as I saw on looking nearer, had already divested him of several of his members. They fought with more pertinacity than bull-dogs. Neither manifested the least disposition to retreat. [Neither would consider lest he die in shame, that there was any direction but onward.] It was evident that their battle-cry was Conquer or die. In the meanwhile there came along a single red ant on the hill-side of this valley, evidently full of excitement, who either had despatched his foe, or had not yet taken part in the battle; probably the latter, for he had lost none of his limbs; whose mother had charged him to return with his shield or upon it. Or perchance he was some Achilles, who had nourished his wrath apart, and had now come to avenge or rescue his Patroclus. He saw this unequal combat from afar, — for the blacks were nearly twice the size of the red, — he drew near with rapid pace till he stood on his guard within half an inch of the combatants; then, watching his opportunity, he sprang upon the black warrior, and commenced his operations near the root of his right fore-leg, leaving the foe to select among his own members; and so there were three united for life, as if a new kind of attraction had been invented which put all other locks and cements to shame. I should not have wondered by this time to find that they had their respective musical bands stationed on some eminent chip, and playing their national airs the while, to excite the slow and cheer the dying combatants. I was myself excited somewhat even as if they had been men. The more you think of it, the less the difference. And certainly there is not the fight recorded in Concord history, at least, if in the history of America, that will bear a moment's comparison with this, whether for the numbers engaged in it, or for the patriotism and heroism displayed. For numbers and for carnage it was an Austerlitz or Dresden. Concord Fight! Two killed on the patriots' side, and Luther Blanchard wounded! Why here every ant was a Buttrick, — "Fire! for God's sake fire!" — and thousands shared the fate of Davis and Hosmer. There was not one hireling there. I have no doubt that it was a principle they fought for, as much as our ancestors, and not to avoid a three-penny tax on their tea; and the results of this battle will be as important and memorable to those whom it concerns as those of the battle of Bunker Hill, at least.

I took up the chip on which the three I have particularly described were struggling, carried it into my house, and placed it under a tumbler on my window-sill, in order to see the issue. Holding a microscope to the first-mentioned red ant, I saw that, though he was assiduously gnawing at the near fore-leg of his enemy, having severed his remaining feeler, his own breast was all torn away, exposing what vitals he had there to the jaws of the black warrior, whose breast-plate was apparently too thick for him to pierce; and the dark carbuncles of the sufferer's eyes shone with ferocity such as war only could excite. They struggled half an hour longer under the tumbler, and when I looked again the black soldier had severed the heads of his foes from their bodies, and the still living heads were hanging on either side of him like ghastly trophies at his saddle-bow, still apparently as firmly fastened as ever, and he was endeavoring with feeble struggles, being without feelers and with only the remnant of a leg, and I know not how many other wounds, [for the mighty battle had by now raged long, and every warrior had answered his call to duty again and again] to divest himself of them; which at length, after half an hour more, he accomplished. I raised the glass, and he went off over the window-sill in that crippled state. Whether he finally survived that combat, and spent the remainder of his days in some Hotel des Invalides, I do not know; but I thought that his industry would not be worth much thereafter. I never learned which party was victorious, nor the cause of the war; but I felt for the rest of that day as if I had had my feelings excited and harrowed by witnessing the struggle, the ferocity and carnage, of a human battle before my door.

5. Find an example of a mock epic and exchange it with one your partner has brought in. Try to include one or two examples of your own which support the theme and style of the original mock epic. Discuss the results with your partner.
6. Why not try writing your own travesty or mock epic? You might consider discussing an international conflict as a football game or even a dogfight; on the other hand, you might want to write about a football game as though the fate of the world rested on its outcome. Commentators often treat the World Series, the Super Bowl, and the Olympic Games in this way.

EXERCISE NINE
Persona and Satire

Instead of using their own voice and supporting their satire indirectly, many writers adopt a persona so that they can express themselves more directly. A persona can express itself in ways that a writer would not dare in his or her own voice; thus, a persona can be harsh, crude, sarcastic, and insulting, and can even distort the truth.

The main challenge in using a persona when writing satire is to choose an appropriate persona for the topic. You have probably already encountered the naive narrator in your reading. Mark Twain's Huckleberry Finn, Jonathan Swift's Gulliver, for example, accept unquestioningly whatever anyone tells them and pass the information on to the reader with a minimum of comment. As you read the following excerpt from *Teenage Romance or How to Die of Embarrassment*, notice that Delia Ephron is satirizing the inordinate anxieties of a teenager's going steady. Try to figure out what the teenage narrator (the persona) is like. In the excerpt, find a specific example of hyperbole, understatement, exclamation, allusion, irony, apostrophe, and allegory. You should have a clear understanding of both the persona's and Ephron's attitudes towards the subject of going steady. Who is Ephron's intended audience and what is her purpose? In what way do the drawings by Edward Koren contribute to the satire? As you read, notice that an additional example of irony (not in Ephron's words) has been dropped into the excerpt. Is it in keeping with the persona and satiric style?

How to Go Steady

Dear Diary,
Good news! Judi found out! She asked Wendy to ask Michelle to ask Jennifer to ask Doug if he was interested in me. If he thought I

was cute, etc., etc., etc., and he said—are you ready, diary?—
"Yes!" Naturally Jennifer told him I was interested back. Anyway,
I am going to see him this weekend at the party. Seth's parents are
going away so we are all going over there.

DD,

    I can't believe it—Denise wasn't invited to Seth's and I was. If
she knew, would she be upset! I'd never tell, that's for sure. All week
I was so worried that Denise would ask what I was doing Saturday but
it's already Friday and so far so good. I feel so bad for her. Judi and I
discussed whether we should ask Seth to ask Denise to the party. We
talked to Michelle about it. Michelle says that guys just don't like
Denise, and if she did go she probably wouldn't have a good time, so
it would be better not to. I guess there's nothing I can do.

    Oh Doug, I hope you like me. I can't wait to see you. Time,
please go fast.

DD,

    It's very late—2.30 a.m.!!—but I can't sleep. I had to write. It
was incredible. We talked all night. Doug's really interesting. He
plays the guitar. He's really into it. He especially likes the Grateful
Dead because he says they stand for something. He really respects
them. He says they're not just in it for the money. I felt like we really
communicated.

    I hope he didn't think I was a jerk, or real boring, or anything.
Oh diary, I think something is happening. At last! I thought my
whole life I'd just be guys' friends—always a friend, never a
girlfriend. Do you think Doug could, does he really . . . ? I hope so.
Doug said he'd call this week and maybe we'd go to a concert. He
kissed me—actually we kissed quite a lot. Do you know what he said

after he kissed me the first time? He said, in this really pleased voice, "Allllllllllll right!" We frenched—his tongue is smooth and doesn't have any little bumps or anything. Also he did this weird thing where he ran his tongue across my gums—sounds disgusting? Diary, you are a real prude. I think Doug kisses like a thirty-year-old.

Tonight I shall hug my pillow and pretend that it is Doug and we are locked in a permanent embrace—'til death do us part. [Mrs. Douglas Horowitz. Mrs. Doug Horowitz. Mrs. D. Horowitz. Ms. Joanie Horowitz. Decisions, decisions!] Goodnight, dear diary, dearest diary, sweet dreams.

DD,

This is what I did today—lay on the bed and stared. I'm in a trance. All I can think about is Douglas. I close my eyes and we're kissing again. It feels like we really are, especially in my stomach, isn't that strange? There's this funny feeling like jumps—well, I can't describe it, diary, but you'd know it if you had it. Anyway, I keep imagining that Doug and I are sitting on the bed together, locked in passion, kissing, kissing, kissing, and then we start to fall over, and that's the end of my fantasy, ha ha. I wonder what happens next!!!!!!!!!

You have probably also seen writers use the persona of the smug, self-contented, pretentious narrator who is fully conscious of how he or she is exaggerating for effect. Novelist Philip Roth uses, for the most part, the pretentious persona in the following excerpt. Mr. Shrewd, in spite of his name, represents a persona that is naive in comparison with Tricky. Here Roth is satirizing the wholly self-serving, shamelessly contrived political "answers" that Tricky gives during a press conference held before the 1972 presidential election. As you read, notice the specific examples of irony (Mr. Shrewd's very name is ironic), inflated rhetoric, political jargon, allusion, and analogy. In this excerpt from *Our Gang*, what are the attitudes of the two personae and Roth towards the possible enfranchisement of the unborn? Notice that an additional example of irony has been added to Roth's prose. Is it in keeping with the self-serving, ever-deceiving Tricky?

Our Gang

MR. SHREWD: As you must know, Mr. President, there are those who contend that you are guided in this matter solely by political considerations. Can you comment upon that?

TRICKY: Well, Mr. Shrewd, I suppose that is their cynical way of describing my plan to introduce a proposed constitutional amendment that would extend the vote to the unborn in time for the '72 elections.

MR. SHREWD: I believe that is what they have in mind, sir. They contend that by extending the vote to the unborn you will neutralize the gains that may accrue to the Democratic Party by the voting age having been lowered to eighteen. They say your strategists have concluded that even if you should lose the eighteen-to-twenty-one-year-old vote, you can still win a second term if you are able to carry the South, the state of California, and the embryos and fetuses from coast to coast. Is there any truth to this "political" analysis of your sudden interest in Prenatal Power?

TRICKY: Mr. Shrewd, I'd like to leave that to you—and to our television viewers—to judge, by answering your question in a somewhat personal manner. I assure you I am conversant with the opinions of the experts. Many of them are men whom I respect, and surely they have the right to say whatever they like, though of course one always hopes it will be in the national interest . . . But let me remind you, and all Americans, because this is a fact that seems somehow to have been overlooked in this whole debate: I am no Johnny-come-lately to the problem of the rights of the unborn. The simple fact of the matter, and it is in the record for all to see, is this great republic. My own wife was once unborn. As you may recall, my children were both unborn. [In fact, most Americans—most *good* Americans, that is—were once unborn.]

So when they say that Dixon has turned to the issue of the unborn just for the sake of the votes . . . well, I ask only that you consider this list of the previously unborn with whom I am associated in both public and private life, and decide for yourself. In fact, I think you are going to find, Mr. Shrewd, with each passing day, people around this country coming to realize that in this administration the fetuses and embryos of America have at last found their voice. Miss Charmin', I believe you had your eyebrows raised.

1. Find an example of a piece written in a persona and exchange it with one your partner has brought in. Try to include one or two examples of your own that support the theme and style of the persona. Discuss the results with your partner.

2. Why not try writing your own piece with a persona? You might consider discussing an event that you would find difficult if you were to use your own voice.

Special Writing Assignment

For this special writing assignment you may choose between writing a piece of pure humor or witty humor. To write a piece of pure humor, you must make sure that the story you are telling is genuinely funny. Your task will be to relate the story without using any tricks of wit. To write a piece of witty humor on a serious topic, however, is not easy; but if you investigate your present surroundings, you will probably see something you can satirize for your partner. When your partner has finished reading your piece, discuss the method(s) of satire you used and any satirical points that your partner missed.

A word of caution about satire: you cannot suddenly drop a single example of irony, non sequitur, part of a parody, and so on, into your straightforward, logical prose. Your *entire* piece of writing must contain wit and satire.

If you cannot think of a topic, take a look at how the following two student writers deal with humor and wit: the first tells of a humorous event told humorously; the second tells of a serious event told wittily.

As you read "Group Therapy—Help or Hindrance?" notice how Nancy Fenton finds herself in a situation in which she would love to burst out laughing and yell, "You are all too funny to be real!" Besides telling her story, does Fenton use any rhetorical devices to achieve humor?

Group Therapy—Help or Hindrance?

by Nancy Fenton, student

Having worked for a psychiatrist several years ago, I emphatically believed that being on the receiving end of a group encounter would probably be most offensive to me. I, who had been intensely scrutinized by a psychiatrist before being hired, had always believed that psychiatrists best served the psychotic personality, not those of us with limited neuroses.

With great uncertainty, I timidly entered the office for my first encounter. My eyes immediately locked upon the first person who entered my range of vision. It was my odd, wife-dominated, uncommunicative neighbor of fifteen years. "Flee immediately," my brain signaled. Maurice, my startled neighbor, made furtive motions towards the door, but lowered his eyes and shrugged helplessly, instead of exiting.

At that moment, an extremely tall, gaunt, Lincoln-like gentlemen beckoned the room's other subjects, Maurice, and me, to follow. Hypnotized by this enigmatic spectre, we filed into a back office.

As we seated ourselves, my rehearsed mental oratories for this first session completely escaped me. I remained motionless, unable to emit a sound or sentence. My fellow neurotics also remained wordless. All eyes turned towards our leader who remained expressionless and said nothing.

At this moment, my eyes surveyed the other members of our group: two plumpish, middle-aged women with long-suffering expressions; one pleasant-looking, smiling, youngish man whose eyes darted from client to client; a stern, unattractive, ill-kept man whose eyes never strayed from straight ahead; and a jolly, overweight, attractive man in his thirties. The silence remained unbroken despite much throat clearing, furtive sidelong glances, and body shifting.

With a quick flurry of words, one of the plumpish women expelled a volley of disjointed words. It became clearly apparent that her life was in somewhat of a turmoil, perhaps of her own making. It became further evident that the allotted time for all to share our stories rapidly vanished in her burst of tears. Her marriage, children, and—God forbid—sex life, all became the topic for our immediate inspection.

With time running out, I blocked her next verbal pass by emphatically turning my attention to the jolly, overweight gentleman. "Why are you here?" I demanded, ignoring the penetrating eyes of the psychiatrist who continued to say nothing. "I am here because I desire to be five again, would prefer to be unmarried, and dislike both my children," he grinned. Was he for real—or kidding? It occurred to me at this point that perhaps my relationship problems (my reason for going) were not serious and could be more constructively dealt with in the quiet of my study while composing a self-evaluation survey of the "must haves" and "don't wants" of future involvements.

At the conclusion of the session, my fellow "patients" and I left together. Maurice, without comment or eye elevation, sped off on his bicycle towards home. The others with Cheshire-cat smiles also drove off, leaving me alone with the session's monopolizer. She appeared stimulated by the encounter and fervently desired my phone number because, as she stated, she was badly in need of a mother replacement, having lost her mother some fifteen years previously. This revelation seemed a bit confusing to me as she was perhaps a year or so older than I!

I never went back. Considering the sum total of the psychiatrist's contribution, I could probably do better by myself. Maybe my shingle will read "Counseling, Self-Taught"!

As you read "A Letter to Rocko," notice Mike Rutherford's use of persona as well as his use of several witty techniques to enhance his satirical treatment of the security personnel on his campus.

A Letter to Rocko

by Mike Rutherford, student

Dear Rocko,

As a result of my intelligence-gathering mission of last week, I think that we had better reconsider our planned robbery of State College. Although our plans were well thought out, I do believe we have overlooked an area of strength that the college has: a highly trained police force. Let me brief you on some of my observations.

First off, these officers exhibit an obvious air of camaraderie. Unlike the city cops who often are seen patrolling alone, these officers frequently congregate in groups of two, three, or even four. As these meetings are generally held way-the-heck on the other side of campus, far from the noise and possible interference of the students, I was not able to get close enough to hear exactly what was being said. I was, however, able to observe several of these meetings via my high-powered binoculars. Judging by their smiles, frequent laughter, and backslapping, they were undergoing some form of mutual therapy, probably ordered by their higher-ups to relieve stress. Don't forget, Rocko: "A happy officer is an efficient officer." If this is not enough to cause us to drop our plans, read what I found out next.

I have discovered that these officers are vitally concerned with the important task of gathering intelligence. This is so important to them that it is one of the few times you'll see them alone. Being obviously well trained in police science, they waste little time interrogating the male students; instead, they concentrate on the "weaker sex." I was able to overhear part of one of these sessions, which are usually held in the cafeteria. I was amazed at the cunning of the officer. He managed to extract the name, address, and phone number of his "interviewee" and—mark this man's dedication—made arrangements to continue the session later that evening—*on his own time*! These officers have so refined their intelligence gathering that they have given a rating to each woman on campus based, I suppose, on how much useful information she has. The officers are frequently overheard trading this information: "She's a seven," or "Here comes a real two." One point in our favor, Rocko, is that these officers can't seem to find a "ten" anywhere on campus.

Another strength that I have found is their dogged attention to matters of seemingly questionable importance. As an example, let me point out the officer stationed in the men's locker room. He is seldom seen there when the P.E. students are in class, obviously confident that no one would dare break into the unguarded lockers. As soon as class is dismissed, however, and the men are taking their showers, he snaps into action, stationing himself in the area where the dirty towels are exchanged for clean ones. Using his finely tuned police sense, he ensures that no one gets a clean towel without first handing over a dirty one. With such strict attention being paid to a relatively inexpensive towel, can you imagine how securely they must be guarding the truly valuable things on campus?

Honestly, Rocko, taking into consideration these factors, I do believe we shall drop our plans to rob State College: it's too well guarded!

Your partner in crime,

Bugsy

Research Skills

INTRODUCTION

A library has two kinds of books—the ones you read for enjoyment from cover to cover and the ones you read selectively to locate facts. In this chapter you will concentrate on the latter, the library's reference books.

Before you begin any of the exercises, you should tour your college or public library and note the following areas:

- *The catalog.* Some catalogs are on cards classified by subjects, titles, and authors; some are wholly or partly on microfilm or microfiche; and some are on computers. No matter what system your library uses, you should take the time to learn how to find the call numbers of particular books. These call numbers are based on either the Library of Congress system or the Dewey decimal system. They allow you to locate the section in the library where you can find a particular book.

- *The reference area.* This area, usually conveniently close to the card, microfilm, or computer catalog area, contains important research books—dictionaries, encyclopedias, indexes, concordances, and the like. These reference books are usually not allowed out of the library.

- *The periodical area.* Most well-stocked libraries subscribe to current magazines and newspapers. Back issues are bound yearly in hard covers or put on microfilm. If you suspect that something you are researching is in a magazine, you should look through one of the guides to periodicals under the proper subject area. Well-known periodical indexes such as *Reader's Guide to Periodical Literature*, *New York Times Index*, and *Applied Science and Technology Index* provide easy-to-follow instructions for their use. Ask where the guides to periodicals are kept. A librarian will be happy to introduce you to them.

- *The reserve section.* Most instructors put aside frequently used books in a two-hour or overnight reserve area. Often these books are listed in a special temporary catalog under your instructor's name or the name of the course. Find out if any of your instructors have done this for your courses; it will save you fruitless searches through the stacks of books.

- *The media area.* Many libraries contain collections of tapes, records, slides, and films. You should familiarize yourself with this important area and plan to spend some time there. To sit at a tape recorder with a Mozart concert or a Shakespeare play filling your ears is a wonderful experience. Your media library may have tapes and slides on basic spelling, grammar, biology, or chemistry, which you can use to help clear up a problem. As well, you may be able to borrow a film or a set of slides to help you with a special presentation you have to make for a class.

- *The file drawers.* Often, near the catalog area or in the periodical section, libraries maintain clipping files. These files contain articles and pamphlets on many topics; original clippings may be kept in file drawers or on microfilm.

- *The stacks.* Books are usually stored by call number on rows of shelves, sometimes occupying several floors, to which you may or may not have access. You should note carefully the location of the book in which you are interested. For example, in the Library of Congress classification, *ND* indicates books on art, *PS* books on literature, and so on. You will quickly get to know the whereabouts of books in your particular field. Often there are study areas near the stacks where you can sit and organize your material for research.

- *The librarian.* Unquestionably the librarians are your most important resource. They not only can provide information about the location of a book or the documentation of a fact, but also can offer inspiration in what may seem a fruitless search. Most librarians have a knowledge of and a love for their collections and are only too glad to encourage you to get to know the contents of the library. So if you have not already done so, make yourself known to your local librarians.

EXERCISE ONE
Library Tour

As you and your partner go on your library tour, answer these questions:

1. Does your library use a card, microfiche, or computer catalog?
2. Are the books in the library listed by subject, title, or author?
3. Does the library use call numbers based on the Library of Congress system or the Dewey decimal system?
4. Go to the reference area.
   a. What is the title of the smallest English dictionary? The biggest English dictionary? Besides size, what are the main differences between the two dictionaries? (Compare a single entry; for example, read what each dictionary says about the word *home*.)
   b. Which set of encyclopedias would you find most useful to write a scientific report? Why?
   c. Name one bibliography. What would you use it for?
   d. Look for a concordance. What is it used for? Name another concordance.
   e. What is a variorum? What would you use one for?
   f. Assuming that you were to write several essays, name one specific reference work that you would use for each of the following topics: art history, mythology, American history, a British poet, music, religion, science, mathematics.

g. What would you use a book-review index for? Name one book-review index.

h. What is the name of a world atlas in the reference section?

i. What yearbooks are contained in the reference section?

5. Name two current magazines available in your library.

6. Name one foreign newspaper that the library subscribes to.

7. Look at the library's indexes to periodicals. For the year 1984, how many articles in magazines could you find on the subject of the Mediterranean fruit fly?

8. Have any of your instructors set aside books in the reserve section?

9. If your library has a media area, what audiovisual equipment does it contain?

10. List two entries in the file drawers or on microfilm under the subject of automobile racing?

11. Answer (a) or (b).

a. Under the Library of Congress classification, what types of books are kept in the *F*, *W*, and *Q* sections?

b. Under the Dewey decimal system, what types of books are numbered 800, 300, 600?

12. If your library does not have a book that you want, how could you get it on interlibrary loan from another library?

EXERCISE TWO
Library Search

Plan a library search with your partner. Then decide together the number of questions to ask each other and the time limit for the search.

1. Write the questions on index cards. Each answer must appear in a secondary source (a reference book) or a primary source (a work of literature, a collection of letters, an autobiography, or some other first-person account). Set up a question like this:

> What scene from Mark Twain's childhood did he recreate for the setting of _Huck Finn_ and _Tom Sawyer_?

2. Exchange the cards with your partner and go to the library.

3. For each question, begin at the catalog area. Use the subject catalog to identify titles. Find the title of a book that you believe has the answer and then locate the book in the library.

4. When you find the answer, write it on another index card in the form of either a direct quote from the book, with quotation marks, or a summary of the author's original words. For longer answers, you might use a paraphrase or précis. Make sure that you include the author's name and the number of the page(s) where you found the answer. Thus, your answer to the question above would look like this:

> Twain, pp. 1–4
>
> The setting for parts of Huck Finn and Tom Sawyer was based on his uncle's farm, actually located in Missouri. For the books however, he moved the scene to Arkansas.

5. On another card place the bibliographical information. Set up your card like this:

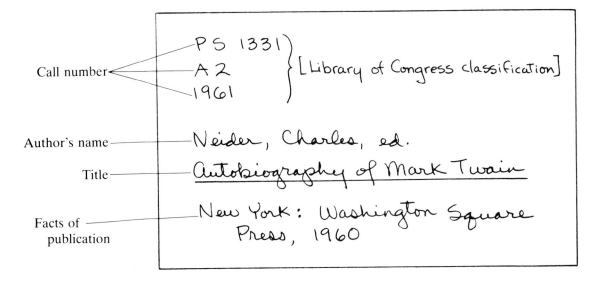

Call number ← PS 1331 / A 2 / 1961 } [Library of Congress classification]

Author's name — Neider, Charles, ed.

Title — Autobiography of Mark Twain

Facts of publication — New York: Washington Square Press, 1960

6. If you have had to use another book to refer you to your answer, you should make up a bibliographic card for that book too.

7. When time expires, exchange cards with your partner. Did you and your partner use the same sources—you in preparing the questions and your partner in finding the answers? Discuss the instances where your sources differed.

8. Here are a few sample questions that you might ask your partner; each is based on a part of *The Independent Writer* and requires a degree of research.

    a. In "Agent Orange" (Appendix B), what exactly is Agent Orange?

    b. Most of Anne Baxter's *Intermission* (Chapter 1) is set in what country?

    c. Who played John Glenn in the film version of Tom Wolfe's *The Right Stuff* (Chapter 58)?

    d. What was F. Scott Fitzgerald's first novel (Chapter 64)?

    e. Who has served the longest as president of the United States (Chapter 30)?

EXERCISE THREE
Researching

    When you must write a research paper or a report, you will need to spend a few hours in the library gathering facts. The following suggestions should make your research easier:

1. Purchase a set of index cards on which to write your notes. Write one note per card so that you can organize them as you wish.

2. If you plan to use any portion of a book, first make up a bibliography card. It should look something like this:

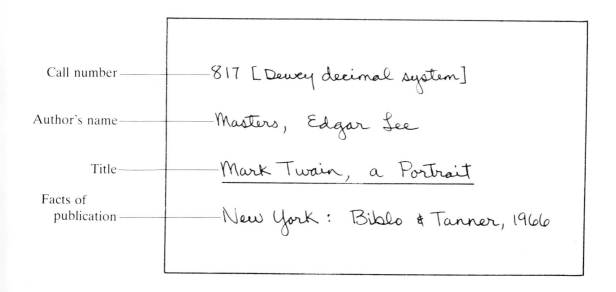

Call number ——— 817 [Dewey decimal system]

Author's name ——— Masters, Edgar Lee

Title ——— Mark Twain, a Portrait

Facts of
publication ——— New York: Biblo & Tanner, 1966

3. At the top of the next card write a subject heading to help you organize and find the card quickly. Identify the source of your quotation by listing the author's last name and the page number on which you found the quotation. When you quote an author's exact words, use quotation marks around them; in this way, you will help yourself avoid unintentional plagiarism. Your card should look like this:

Masters, p. 7   Twain's Life & Haley's Comet

"... born on Nov. 30, 1835. Haley's Comet was at its perihelion on Nov. 16 of that year..... Mark Twain ... accepted the comet as somehow pacing his life and influencing it. In fact, [the comet] reached its perihelion again on Nov. 16, 1910, a few days before Mark Twain's death."

4. Wherever possible, summarize what you read. This way you can select and extract what is important to your purpose. Too many quotations in a research essay or report give your reader the feeling that you have not written it but have merely strung together statements made by others. When you do summarize long portions, you should still identify the source and provide a subject heading:

Masters, pp. 8-9   Twain's Birthplace

Mark Twain was born in a very humble log cabin, which housed his large family in Florida, Missouri. His beginnings have been compared with Lincoln's meager start in life.

5. For practice, you and your partner make up a research essay topic for each other. Go to the appropriate area in your library to do the following things:

   a. Write on an index card one direct quote that you would like to use if you were to write an essay on your partner's topic.

   b. On another index card write out the bibliographical information on the book you used.

   c. Find another book on your topic and write on an index card a summary of something that you would like to use if you were to write the essay. If your summary takes up two or more cards, indicate at the top of each card: "1st of 3," "2nd of 3," and "3rd of 3." This will help keep your cards organized.

   d. On another index card write out the bibliographical information on the book you used for (c).

   e. Give all cards to your partner so that he or she can check the entries against the suggestions in (a) to (d) above.

   f. Here are some general topics if you cannot think of one:

   - Crossbows
   - Solar Heating
   - Daylight Saving Time
   - Anorexia Nervosa
   - The History of U.S. Air Travel

EXERCISE FOUR
Bibliographies

1. New Guidelines of the Modern Language Association (MLA). In 1984, the MLA introduced dramatic changes in writing research papers. The new style has stream-lined the task of giving credit to sources by eliminating traditional footnotes, endnotes, and all that went with them: *ibid.*, *op. cit.*, raised numbers, and so on. If you must use the traditional MLA method for your audience, refer to an MLA handbook published prior to 1984. *The Independent Writer* uses the new MLA guidelines throughout. Unless you have been directed to use a different style manual, you should employ the following MLA guidelines for all of your research essays.

At the end of a research paper, under the title "Works Cited," you place alphabetically only the sources from which you quoted. The best way of understanding how to record the various bibliographic entries is to look at a few examples. With your partner, discuss the commonsense approach of the new MLA guidelines. When you examine each of the following, note the order, spacing, punctuation, capitalization, abbreviations, and other particular conventions.

> ### Typical Entry
>
> Author's last name, First name. <u>Underlined Title</u>. City of publication: Abbreviated publisher, Year of publication.
> (*Note*: You should leave two spaces after each period and indent each additional line five spaces from the left.)

Books

One author

Kluger, Richard. <u>Simple Justice</u>. New York: Knopf, 1975.

Subtitle

Fincher, Ernest B. <u>The Presidency: An American Invention</u>. New York: Abelard-Schuman, 1977.

Two authors

Millet, Nancy C., and Helen J. Throckmorton. <u>How to Read a Short Story</u>. Boston: Ginn, 1969.

Three authors

Young, Richard E., Alton L. Becker, and Kenneth L. Pike. <u>Rhetoric: Discovery and Change</u>. New York: Harcourt, 1970.

More than three authors

Chester, Lewis, et al. <u>An American Melodrama</u>. New York: Viking, 1969.
(*Et al* means "and others"; note that it is not underlined.)

Editor as author

De Bell, Garret, ed. <u>The Environmental Handbook</u>. New York: Ballantine, 1970.

Another edition

Voeks, Virginia. <u>On Becoming an Educated Person</u>. 3rd ed. Philadelphia: Saunders, 1970.

Book with no author

<u>A Manual of Style</u>. 13th ed. Chicago: U of Chicago, 1984.

A work in more than one volume

Sandburg, Carl. <u>Abraham Lincoln</u>. 3 vols. New York: Harcourt, 1969.

Article in a book edited by someone else

Trilling, Diana. "The Image of Women in Contemporary Literature." <u>The Woman in America</u>. Ed. Robert J. Lifton. Boston: Houghton, 1965.

A translation

Dostoevsky, Feodor. Crime and Punishment. Trans. Jessie Coulson. Ed. George
  Gibian. New York: Norton, 1964.

Corporate author

American Red Cross. Standard First Aid and Personal Safety. 2nd ed. Garden City:
  Doubleday, 1979.

Public document

U.S. Bureau of the Census. Pocket Data Book: U.S.A. 1984. Washington: U.S.
  Government Printing Office, 1984.

Magazines and Newspapers

Signed magazine article

Bradlee, Benjamin. "He Had That Special Grace." Newsweek 2 Dec. 1963: 38.

Unsigned magazine article

"A Whale of a Failure." Time 13 July 1970: 44–45.

Signed newspaper article

Sperling, Godfrey. "Campus Warning for Nixon." The Christian Science Monitor
  1 July 1970: 1.

Unsigned newspaper article

"Kansas City Will Sell Its Old Parking Meters." Los Angeles Times 23 Apr. 1975,
  sec. IV: 1.

Book review

Wolfe, Alan. "Turning Economics to Dust." Rev. of Free to Choose: A Personal
  Statement, by Milton and Rose Friedman. Saturday Review 2 Feb. 1980:
  35–36.

Encyclopedias, Dictionaries, and Almanacs

Signed article

Ryther, John H. "Marine Biology." World Book Encyclopedia. 1976 ed.

Unsigned article

"Country Music." Encyclopedia Americana. 1975 ed.

Dictionary entry

"Bedbug." Webster's New World Dictionary of the American Language. 2nd
  College Edition. 1982.

Almanac entry

"Pulitzer Prizes in Journalism, Letters, and Music." <u>World Almanac and Book of Facts</u>. 1979 ed. 409–14.

Pamphlets

<u>Academic Freedom and Civil Liberties of Students in Colleges and Universities</u>. New York: American Civil Liberties Union, 1970.

Letters

To the editor

Eddy, Mary. Letter. <u>New York Times</u>. 2 Aug. 1985.

Published

Wolfe, Juan. Letter to John Charles. 22 June 1832. John Charles Papers. Southwest Museum Library, Los Angeles.

Personal

Corry, Betty. Letter to the author. 31 Dec. 1985.

Nonprint Sources

Motion picture

<u>Indiana Jones and the Temple of Doom</u>. Dir. Steven Spielberg. Paramount. 1984.

Television or radio program

"Nancy Astor" part 7. <u>Masterpiece Theatre.</u> PBS. WNET, New York. 27 May 1984.

White, Jim. <u>At Your Service</u>. KMOX. St. Louis. 13 Mar. 1981.

Stage play

<u>Cats</u>. By Andrew Lloyd Webber. Based on T. S. Eliot's <u>Old Possum's Book of Practical Cats</u>. Dir. Trevor Nunn. New London Theatre, London. 11 May 1981.

Recording

Newhart, Bob. "Merchandising the Wright Brothers." <u>The Button-Down Mind of Bob Newhart</u>. Warner Bros., WS 137, 1960.

Computer software

Oogle, Boris. <u>Fun with Numbers</u>. Computer software. Krell Software, 1985.

Lecture

Axelrod, Rise. "Who Did What with Whom." MLA Convention. Chicago, 30 Dec. 1977.

Recorded interview

Gordon, Suzanne. Interview. All Things Considered. Natl. Public Radio. WNYC, New York. 1 June 1983.

Personal interview

Nought, John. Personal interview. 12 May 1985.

2. *Guidelines of the American Psychological Association (APA).* If you need to become familiar with alternate styles of research, spend a few minutes noting the characteristics of the APA style. (See the list of other style books and manuals in Suggestions for Further Study at the end of the textbook.) The APA and new MLA styles are now quite similar. When you write a research paper for one of your social or behavioral science courses, you will probably use the term "References" or "References Cited" as a title of your sources. Also, you will place the date of publication in parentheses after the author's name and use an initial for the author's first name. To be on the safe side, you should ask your science professors which style they want you to use.

Following are three examples using the APA style. Each title comes from the above MLA examples. You and your partner convert some of the other examples as though you were preparing them for the *reference* page at the end of a science research paper. If you run into difficulties, see the latest *APA Publication Manual* or your school's APA style sheet.

One author

Kluger, R. (1975). Simple Justice. New York: Knopf.

Two authors

Millet, N. & Throckmorton, H. (1969). How to Read a Short Story. Boston: Ginn.

Signed newspaper article

Sperling, G. (1970). "Campus Warning for Nixon." The Christian Science Monitor, 1 July: 1.

3. Final words on listing your bibliographies:

- Sort through your bibliographic index cards and keep only those works you have used in your essay.
- Arrange the cards alphabetically by author's last name or by title if there is no author.
- Prepare the list of "Works Cited" or "References" for the end of your paper.
- Ensure that you copy complete details (author, title, place of publication,

publisher, and year of publication). Page numbers are not necessary unless you have used only one article from an anthology.

- In the MLA style, the first line of each entry is flush with the left margin; indent subsequent lines five spaces. The APA style is similar except that you should indent subsequent lines three spaces.

- In the MLA style, if you use more than one work by the same author, list the works alphabetically by title. Give the author's name with the first title, but substitute three unspaced hyphens and a period for the name in subsequent entries. In the APA style, list the works in order of publication date, the earliest first, and repeat the author's name for each entry.

MLA style

Emig, Janet. <u>The Composing Process of Twelfth Graders</u>. NCTE Research Report, no. 13. Urbana, Ill. NCTE, 1971.

---. "Hand, Eye, Brain: Some 'Basics' in the Writing Process." <u>Research on Composing: Points of Departure</u>. Ed. Charles R. Cooper and Lee Odell. Urbana, Ill. NCTE, 1978.

APA style

Emig, J. (1971). <u>The Composing Process of Twelfth Graders</u>. NCTE Research Report, no. 13. Urbana, Ill. NCTE.

Emig, J. (1978). "Hand, Eye, Brain: Some 'Basics' in the Writing Process." <u>Research on Composing: Points of Departure</u>. Ed. Charles R. Cooper and Lee Odell. Urbana, Ill. NCTE.

EXERCISE FIVE
Citations

This exercise gives you and your partner an opportunity to practice using the MLA method of citing your sources within the body of your research essays. In the future, the only times you will need to use footnotes are to add additional information or to provide definitions of something contained in your essay.

MLA suggests that after you have presented a direct quotation or a paraphrase in your essay, you should include an extremely brief parenthetical citation that refers the reader to a list of the works cited at the end of the paper. In other words, you need to provide all the details of your sources only once.

In order to learn the main rules of employing parenthetical citations, instead of using obsolete footnotes or endnotes, talk through the following points carefully with your partner.

Original Sources

Assume that you are going to write a research paper on the mysteries of the brain and that you have collected the following ten quotations from various sources. Each quotation includes full bibliographic details; these details *do not* represent a method of citation. Later, when you study several parenthetical citations, you will be able to note which details from the original material were included and which were left out.

a. "The difference between the life of a skin-clad hunter leaving a cave with a spear over his shoulder to hunt mammoth, and a smartly dressed executive driving along a motorway in New York, London or Tokyo, to consult his computer print-out, is not due to any further physical development of body or brain during the long period that separates them, but to a completely new evolutionary factor." (David Attenborough, *Life on Earth*, William Collins Sons & Co., Ltd., London, 1979, page 302)

b. ". . . the storage capacity of your grapefruit-sized brain is staggering—conservatively estimated at ten billion units of information." (Wayne W. Dyer, *Pulling Your Own Strings*, Harper and Row Publishers, Inc., New York, 1978, page 13.)

c. "All the thoughts in your head that contribute to your thinking of yourself as a loser are easier to send away when you think of them as choices. Once you take responsibility for your losing thoughts, you can make the choice to convert them to winning thoughts. If you play a tennis match against a strong opponent and emerge defeated, you are a loser only if you think that way. Actually, every single defeat you experience is something which builds character and improves your ability. You could leave the match saying to yourself that you learned some things today, that you know what shots you have to work on, that you had a really terrific experience, playing against such excellent competition." (Wayne W. Dyer, *The Sky's the Limit*, published by Pocket Books, New York, 1980, page 337.)

d. "In human beings it is a 1.3-kg (3-lb) mass of pinkish-gray tissue composed of about 10 billion nerve cells, each linked to another and together responsible for the control of all mental functions." ("Brain," *Funk & Wagnalls New Encyclopedia*, Volume 4, page 294, Funk & Wagnalls, Inc., 1983)

e. "In general, the greater the brain weight, the longer the life span. The higher the ratio of brain to body weight, the longer the species' average life span." (Durk Pearson and Sandy Shaw, *Life Extension: A Practical Scientific Approach*, Warner Books, New York, 1982, page 143.)

f. "John F. Kennedy attracted and sought out men and women of ideas; intellectuals and academics now entered government in unprecedented numbers." (John M. Blum, Edmund S. Morgan, Willie Lee Rose, Arthur M. Schlesinger, Jr., Kenneth M. Stampp, and C. Vann Woodward, *The National Experience*, Fifth Edition, Harcourt Brace Jovanovich, Inc., New York, 1981, page 810.)

g. The eight-part PBS documentary examines the mysteries of the human mind. The first part, "The Enlightened Machine," reviews the theories of several nineteenth-century thinkers in brain science and examines sophisticated tools available to modern medical detectives, such as the CAT scan, which can penetrate the skull to X-ray tissue. The second part, "Vision and Movement," explores how the brain perceives and interprets what the eyes see. ("The

Enlightened Machine'' and ''Vision and Movement'' from the series *The Brain*, PBS, WGBH, Boston, Oct. 10 and 17, 1984.)

h. "What time the promise after curse was said:
'Thy seed shall bruise his head.'

Poor Memory's brain is wild,
As moonstruck by that flaming atmosphere
When she was born; her deep eyes shine and shone
With light that conquereth sun
And stars to wanner paleness, year by year."
(Elizabeth Barrett Browning, "Memory and Hope," lines 7 and 8 from the first stanza and the entire second stanza, *Poems of Elizabeth Barrett Browning*, P. F. Collier & Son, New York, 1902, page 362.)

i. "Canst thou not minister to a mind diseas'd,
Pluck from the memory a rooted sorrow,
Raze out the written troubles of the brain,
And with some sweet oblivious antidote
Cleanse the stuff'd bosom of that perilous stuff
Which weighs upon the heart?"
(William Shakespeare, *Macbeth*, Act V, Scene 3, Lines 40 to 45.)

j. "For God hath not given us the spirit of fear; but of power, and of love, and of a sound mind."
(*Bible*, 2 Timothy, Chapter 1, Verse 7.)

The MLA Method of Citing Your Sources

So that you understand the main features of quoting from and giving credit to your sources using the MLA style, read and discuss the various main features. If you wish more specific details, you should refer to the *MLA Handbook for Writers of Research Papers*, by Joseph Gibaldi and Walter S. Achtert, published by The Modern Language Association of America, New York, 1984 or *Writing the Research Paper: A Handbook*, by Anthony Winkler and Jo Ray McCuen, published by Harcourt Brace Jovanovich, San Diego, 1985.

Quoting Prose Carefully

Notice the different ways in which careful writers might use parts of the above sources within their own prose.

a. Within the parenthetical citation you should include the author's last name and the page number of the material used from the source, *with no punctuation to separate them*. Notice also that the final punctuation mark for your sentence comes *after* the parenthetical citation.

It is believed that the difference between primitive and modern humans "is not due to any further physical development of body or brain during the long period that separates them" (Attenborough 302).

b. If you mention the author's name within your own prose, you need only place the page number in parentheses. As a general rule, you do not have to mention any information within your parenthetical citation that you have already mentioned within your own prose.

> David Attenborough believes that the difference between primitive and modern humans "is not due to any further physical development of body or brain during the long period that separates them" (302).

c. If you are using two books by the same author, you should include a shortened but easily understood form of the title *with a comma separating author and title but no punctuation separating title and page number.*

> In the "storage capacity of your grapefruit-sized brain" (Dyer, Pulling 13), you have many negative thoughts, which are "easier to send away when you think of them as choices" (Dyer, Sky's 337).

d. In the next two examples, notice what happens when you include the author's name or both the author's name and the title in your own prose.

> Wayne Dyer states that in the "storage capacity of your grapefuit-sized brain" (Pulling 13) you have many negative thoughts, which are "easier to send away when you think of them as choices" (Sky's 337).

> In Pulling Your Own Strings, Wayne Dyer says that we have an estimated ten billion units of information in our "grapefruit-sized brain" (13). In The Sky's the Limit, he tells us that it is easy to get rid of negative thoughts when we "think of them as choices" (337).

e. If you quote from a book by two authors, place both their last names in the parenthetical citation. Of course, if you mention the authors within your own prose, you would only have to provide the page number in parentheses.

> It is accepted that "the greater the brain weight, the longer the life span" (Pearson and Shaw 143).

f. If you quote from a book by three or more authors, you may place all of their last names in the parenthetical citation or you may use only the first author's last name plus *et al.* The convention you use must correspond to the way you list the book in your bibliography. Do not underline *et al.*

> Because John F. Kennedy sought the best brains in the country, "intellectuals and academics now entered government in unprecedented numbers" (Blum et al. 810).

> According to Blum et al., the best brains in the country, "intellectuals and academics" (810), entered Kennedy's government in "unprecedented numbers" (810).

g. If no author is mentioned in the work, use a shortened version of the title. You will need to do this when you cite from dictionaries, encyclopedias, handbooks, magazines, newspapers, and so on. When a source is arranged alphabetically—as in dictionaries and encyclopedias—you do not provide page numbers in your parenthetical citations.

It is hard to believe that each nerve cell in the brain is "linked" to one of the other ten billion brain cells and that, together, they are "responsible for the control of all mental functions" ("Brain").

Note: If you use two or more dictionaries or encyclopedias for information, you would have to include an abbreviated title of your main source—for example ("Brain," Funk)—so the reader would know which dictionary or encyclopedia you quoted from.

h. If you are quoting from a television or radio program, film, lecture, or interview, you may include as many details as possible within your own prose, thus eliminating the need for a parenthetical citation.

As illustrated clearly in the first part of the PBS documentary, The Brain, doctors now use a "CAT scan, which can penetrate the skull to X-ray tissue."

As illustrated clearly in the PBS documentary, The Brain, doctors now use a "CAT scan, which can penetrate the skull to X-ray tissue" ("Enlightened Machine").

Note: You must provide the title of the individual part because The Brain is an eight-part series.

Some Useful Conventions for Quoting Prose

a. Sometimes you may wish to paraphrase one of your authorities. In such a case, you do not have to use quotation marks; however, you should give credit in a parenthetical citation.

Dyer claims that you can turn any defeat into a victory by simply dismissing thoughts of losing from your brain (Sky's 337).

b. If you wish to cite two authorities for the same researched material, include them both in parentheses, separated by a semicolon.

A single human brain contains ten billion pieces of information (Dyer, Pulling 13; "Brain").

c. If you wish to refer to an entire work, rather than a specific passage, you should not provide a page number in the parentheses.

Wayne Dyer encourages his reader to develop positive thoughts and ignore negative thoughts (Sky's).

d. To make a quotation fit smoothly into your own prose, you might need to add a word or words within the quotation. You must, however, place brackets around any words that are not part of the quotation. (See Chapter 62 for more details on brackets.)

In the 1960s, both "intellectuals and academics now entered [the Kennedy] government in unprecedented numbers" (Blum et al. 810).

e. To make a quotation fit smoothly into your own prose, you might need to delete a word or words within the quotation. You must, however, place ellipsis points (three dots) in place of the word(s) you have deleted. (See Chapter 62 for more details on ellipsis points.)

> Blum et al. claim that because Kennedy sought out the best brains, "intellectuals and academics...entered government in unprecedented numbers" (810).

What word has been omitted from the original source?

f. When you include prose quotations of four or more typed lines, indent from the left margin *ten* spaces, double-space, and omit the quotation marks. Note that the parenthetical citation appears *after* the final punctuation mark.

> Dyer illustrates how to turn losing thoughts to winning thoughts:
>> If you play a tennis match against a strong opponent and emerge defeated, you are a loser only if you think that way . . . . You could leave the match saying to yourself that you learned some things today, that you know what shots you have to work on, that you had a really terrific experience playing against such excellent competition. (Sky's 337)

What do the ellipsis points indicate in the above quotation?

Quoting Poetry, Drama and Sacred Works

When you refer to poetry, drama, and sacred works, you can include quotations as you would prose, or you can set them apart if you wish to draw attention to the quotation.

a. When you quote a single line or part of a line of poetry, you use the same rules as you use for prose.

> Poets often write about a troubled brain; for example, Elizabeth Barrett Browning says, "Poor Memory's brain is wild" ("Memory and Hope").

When you refer to a short poem, you do not have to provide a page or line number.

b. Use a single slash (with a space on either side) when you wish to incorporate into your own prose any consecutive words from a poem that do not appear on the same line.

> Writing of a troubled brain, Browning states that it "is wild, / As moonstruck by that flaming atmosphere / When she was born" ("Memory and Hope").

c. Use a double slash when you wish to incorporate into your own prose any consecutive words that do not appear in the same stanza.

> In "Memory and Hope," Browning talks in allegory of the brain's power to look back (Memory) or look forward (Hope). She also includes negative thoughts with " 'Thy seed shall bruise his head.' // Poor Memory's brain is wild."

Notice that the single quotation marks indicate a quotation within a quotation. See the quotation in the Original Sources above.

d. Use neither slashes nor quotation marks when you indent the lines of a quotation and set it up as the original. Note also that the lines appear *exactly* as they appear in the poem.

In "Memory and Hope," Browning describes Memory's brain in allegorical terms:

> her deep eyes shine and shone
> With light that conquereth sun
> And stars to wanner paleness, year by year.

e. When you quote from a play, you should generally refer the reader to the act, scene, and line of your quotation. Use Arabic numbers throughout. In addition, use periods to separate the numbers.

> Dyer's philosophy could certainly be based on Macbeth's lines: "Pluck from the memory a rooted sorrow, / Raze out the written troubles of the brain" (<u>Mac</u>. 5.3.41–42).

f. When you quote from sacred writings, you should indicate the book, chapter, and verse in parentheses.

> Ever since biblical times, we have esteemed "a sound mind" (2 Tim.1.7).

Quoting Carelessly

a. The following is an example of gross plagiarism. After reading Wayne Dyer's theories, the writer, instead of quoting him, uses his idea and claims it as his own.

> I have come to the conclusion that you can easily send away loser thoughts when you think of them as choices; for example, you can convert losing a tennis match to winner thoughts.

b. The following is an example of a slight case of plagiarism, but it is plagiarism nonetheless. The writer has tried to compose an original sentence by borrowing ideas from two original quotations.

> A human brain is no bigger than a large orange, but it contains approximately ten billion nerve cells.

For more on the subject, read the product on plagiarism in Chapter 10.

Preparing a Bibliography of Works Cited

Independent of your partner, prepare a bibliography of the ten original sources from which the above quotations were taken. Make sure that you record the works alphabetically. Use the heading "Works Cited."

Afterwards, compare your bibliographies, noting any discrepancies. When you are both in agreement, compare your bibliographies with the Suggested Answers following Chapter 40.

The APA Method of Citing Your Sources

Once you are familiar with the MLA method of parenthetical citation, learning the APA method will be easy. The only significant difference is that you include the year of publication in an APA parenthetical citation. As in the MLA method, if any element is mentioned in the text, you do not need to repeat it in the parenthetical citation.

The following four quotations have been taken from the MLA examples above. With your partner, discuss the significant differences between the two methods of citation, noting the placement of commas.

> It is believed that the differences between primitive and modern humans "is not due to any further physical development of body or brain during the long period that separates them" (Attenborough, 1979, p. 302).

> In the "storage capacity of your grapefruit-sized brain" (Dyer, Pulling, 1978, p. 13), you have many negative thoughts. They are "easier to send away when you think of them as choices (Dyer, Sky's, 1980, p. 337).

> Wayne Dyer states that in the "storage capacity of your grapefruit-sized brain" (Pulling, 1978, p. 13), you have many negative thoughts. They are "easier to send away when you think of them as choices" (Sky's, 1980, p. 337).

> In Pulling Your Own Strings, Wayne Dyer says that we have an estimated ten billion units of information in our "grapefruit-sized brain" (1978, p. 13). In The Sky's the Limit, he tells us how to get rid of negative thoughts. They are "easier to send away when you think of them as choices" (1980, p. 337).

With your partner, convert a few of the other MLA citations to the APA method. Then, convert your "Works Cited" to "References" for the APA style. Afterwards, compare your bibliographies, noting any discrepancies. When you are both in agreement, compare your bibliographies with the Suggested Answers following Chapter 40.

Special Writing Assignment

Before you write a long research report, you should write one or two short ones in order to ensure that you understand the MLA or APA guidelines. Try to find, among the following suggestions, one or two subjects that might interest you. Plan to write these short, 250-word reports for your partner.

A Word

From the approximately 800,000 English words, choose one that you are not familiar with. This will force you to do research. If you cannot find a word, choose one of the following: *Lilliputian, hedonist, bowdlerize, googol, sandwich, America, tote, whiskey, masochist, cocaine.*

- Discover the complete derivation of the word.
- Find out when it came into use. (The *Oxford English Dictionary* gives this information.)
- Discover whether its meaning has changed through the ages.
- Give today's meaning.
- Use the word in one of your sentences.

A Well-Known Saying

Choose a saying or cliché that you often use, for example, "a stitch in time saves nine" or "early to bed, early to rise . . . ." If you cannot think of a saying, you might use one of these: "sticks and stones may break my bones," "putting the cart before the horse," "wearing one's heart on one's sleeve."

Take this opportunity to research the origin of the saying. Books such as *Bartlett's Familiar Quotations*, *Brewer's Dictionary of Phrase and Fable*, and the *Oxford English Dictionary* contain useful information on sources.

An Allusion

Have you ever wondered for whom or what a particular object was named? Often the name of an object contains a special reference or allusion. Think of one you would like to research. If you cannot think of a name to research, use one of these: *New York steak*, *Caesarian birth*, *Dutch treat*, *Scotch tape*, *reds* (for communists), *pandemonium*, *AWOL*, *Valentine*, *Best Boy* (in film credits). Use the *Oxford English Dictionary* or an encyclopedia to help you.

A Thing or a Fact

Choose something small enough to be handled in 250 words. Here are some things to research if you cannot think of a topic yourself: *artificial turf*, *the American $2.00 bill*, *the discovery of penicillin*, *the Parsons table*.

- If it was invented, explain when, by whom, why, and how. Has the original use changed through the ages? How is it used today?
- If it's a fact, explain when was it discovered, by whom, and so forth.

1. You must be thorough in your knowledge of your subject; therefore, your research must be complete. Whatever your topic, your partner should feel satisfied that he or she has *all* the facts. If your partner has a single relevant question, you have not been thorough enough in your research.

2. Make a working outline based on your research. The outline should consist of your topic, thesis, several subtopics, and supporting facts. Before you do this, you should use a few of your favorite brainstorming methods to gather supporting evidence. A research report is like any other piece of writing in that it needs a lot of the author's point of view. Stringing one quotation after another results in a bored reader. All of your quotations should support your thesis statement.

The following is a working outline for the report on *serendipity* found in the Products section:

Origin of the Word "Serendipity"

Thesis Statement: The word "serendipity" has an intriguing past.

   I. Source
     A. Persian fairy tale "The Travels and Adventures of the Princes of Serendip"
     B. Horace Walpole first used—1754

II. Former meaning
III. Characteristics of Word
   A. Corruption of Sanskrit "Sinhaladvipa"
   B. Also spelled Sarendip and Serendib
   C. Arabic name for Sri Lanka
IV. Present meaning

When you have completed your short research report, ask your partner to read it and then answer the following questions:

a. Is your research thorough? Have you left any questions un-answered? Are there areas where the research is insufficient?

b. Are there any signs of plagiarism?

c. Have you used a consistent style—informal/formal, MLA/APA?

d. Have you blended the quoted material and your prose smoothly?

e. Is the use of scholarly techniques correct? Have you punctuated quotations correctly? Have you set up and punctuated all your references to your sources correctly?

Read the following products. The first illustrates MLA techniques; the second APA.

Serendipity

by Charles Nelson, student

While reading through some reference material to select a topic for this research paper, I ran across a new word that diverted my attention, aroused my curiosity, and impelled me to look into its meaning. To my surprise, I found an old fable behind its meaning; to my relief, I found a topic for my English assignment. The word "serendipity" has an intriguing past. Using an old Persian fairy tale, "The Travels and Adventures of the Princes of Serendip," as a source of inspiration for the modern meaning of this very expressive word, Horace Walpole employed it for the first time in 1754. Discovering things by chance and sagacity while looking for something else was the ability the princes had. For instance:

> . . . one of them discovered that a mule blind of the right eye had travelled the same road lately . . . because the grass was eaten only on the left side, where it was worse than on the right.
>
> (Toynbee 3: 203–4)

No longer used, the word "Serendip" has three characteristics: it is a corruption of the Sanskrit "Sinhaladvipa," it is also spelled Sarendip and Serendib, and it is the Arabic name for Sri Lanka.

Today, the definition of "serendipity" is "the faculty of making happy and unexpected discoveries by accident" (Van Loon 64).

Strange—I did not originally intend to write on serendipity. Yet the element of serendipity seems to have worked in this particular instance.

Works Cited

Toynbee, Mrs. Paget, ed. Letters of Horace Walpole. 16 vols. Oxford: Clarendon, 1903–1905.

Van Loon, Hendrik Willem. The Arts. New York: Simon and Schuster, 1973.

Oh No

by Bob Janowicz, student

After three years of exhaustive research, the time has come for me to shed light on a subject completely misunderstood. "Disband all rumors and feast on the truth about the most fascinating, newly discovered species, the Ono Bird" (Sparrow, 1976, p. 28).

This beautiful creature, class Aves, is found only in the deepest, darkest jungles of Borasia. Creation smiled upon my co-discoverer, Dr. Bo, and myself, on that eventful day, May 15, 1972: the day our eyes first beheld the secret bird. In Landing the Ono Bird, Thomas recorded the incident accurately: "The plumage radiated crimson red: wings speckled with scarlet: the downy soft underbelly toned with carmine mesmerized me" (1976, p. 44).

Our round-the-clock vigilance enabled us to ascertain detailed information about the bird, whose overall length seldom exceeds forty-five centimeters. Its needle-pointed beak, two and a half centimeters long, is the tool by which the bird selects and ingests its food. With many possible foods available, the Ono Bird has developed a taste for only Tree Salamander eyes. Poorly coordinated in flight, the bird uses its large, powerful claws to dash along tree branches, pinning its victims by the neck. With the Salamander paralyzed, the bird easily pecks the eyes out and sucks the nutrients from them.

Before sunset the Ono Bird gathers fresh Sial Fern fronds and weaves an ornate mat "ingeniously hung between two branches, forming a hammock on which the bird blissfully sleeps" (Ho & Janowicz, 1975, p. 201).

Undoubtedly the most interesting feature of the bird is its call. Owing to its extremely soft underbelly, and to its uncoordinated flight, it feels excruciating pain each time it lands. The bird's name is derived from its call resounding through the forest as it comes in for a landing, "Oh no! Oh no! Oh no!"

References

Ho, B. & Janowicz, B.   (1975).   Birds Eye.   New York: Fox Publishers.

Sparrow, J.   (1976).   "Stalking the Ono Bird."   Owl Magazine, Jan.: 28–33.

Thomas, P.   (1976).   Landing the Ono Bird.   Djakarta: Eagle Press.

40

The Reading Process

INTRODUCTION

What does "reading" mean to you? Is it something you do—reluctantly—to fulfill work or classroom commitments? Is it something you do on a plane or bus to pass the time? Or is it something you look forward to and make time for in your schedule? Whatever the circumstances under which you read, examining and, if necessary, improving your reading process will have a beneficial effect on the way you write.

As a student, much of what you write will be about what you read. Your instructors will require you to write reviews, reports, summaries, examinations, analyses, creative pieces, and literary essays. In order to write clearly, coherently, and interestingly about anything you read, especially literature, you must let the work move you and, if possible, become passionately involved with it.

Think about a few of your first meetings with friends and acquaintances and how they have changed your life. Were any of them like Howard Town's when he met Jacqueline Valentine, a famous artist's model of the 1940s?

> She was Venus with arms, Eve smothered in applesauce, Helen of the modelling stand. . . . She changed me, led me to opera, candlelight, science fiction, food with garlic (which I now hate) and the boggy edges of whatever maturity I have acquired.

When you read, open yourself to the possibility of experiencing something new or of being reminded of something you have forgotten. Ask yourself some of the same questions that you may ask yourself when you plan to cultivate a friendship: What kind of a relationship can I expect to have? Will I become involved? What is preventing me from having a relationship? What is my reaction when I see others enjoying (or not enjoying) the relationship? Why do I feel the way I do? Allow yourself to feel sad, happy, angry, contented, afraid, or whatever emotion a piece of literature awakens in you.

The first time you read a piece of literature, do so without stopping. Do not analyze it; just let its plot, characters, or mood sweep you along. When you have finished, sit for a while and think about the work as a whole and how it has affected you. Ask yourself what you have learned, or what you have experienced in a new way:

you may have gained a deeper understanding of some aspect of the human condition—for example, the fickleness of fate, honesty, duty versus love, people's inhumanity to each other, death, trust, and so on.

But reading need not be a solitary affair. You need to talk about literature in order to increase your enjoyment. By talking, reacting, and responding to a literary work with others, you will be able to reflect on and write with greater confidence about the larger issues that literature offers. Accordingly, you should attempt to talk through all of the exercises in this workshop with at least two or three other people. If possible, plan to do the exercises with your peer group. Make sure that each member of the group has a chance to speak, respond, suggest, or share ideas. Listening to others discuss their reading process may improve yours.

As you work through the exercises, open yourself to what literary scholar John Dixon calls the "luxury of being wrong." In taking every opportunity to confirm your ideas, you may often ask silly questions and offer sillier answers. But remember, the silliest question is the one that you do not ask. Talk to your peers about what you consider relevant and immediate. React and respond openly. Talking and sharing most often leads to greater knowledge.

This chapter will help you approach your reading with more confidence, so that you will be able to produce a piece of writing in which you give your responses and reactions to an uninformed reader. Afterwards, you should gain enough confidence so that you will be able to share your ideas in a literary essay for an informed reader (Chapter 13).

As a bonus, the study of good writing will improve your own writing. Consequently, by improving your reading process, you will improve your writing process.

EXERCISE ONE
Examine Your Reading Process

Just as you should consider all the writing variables that make up your writing process, you should consider all the reading variables that you use (or do not use) during your reading process. By talking with your peers about how you read, you may discover that your reading skills need improving.

In a discussion with your peers, respond honestly to the following questions:
1. Do you consider yourself a good or bad reader? Why?
2. Where do you read most comfortably: at a desk, with others, in bed, around a pool, or in some other place? Why?
3. When do you do your best reading: in the morning, at midnight, or at some other time? Why?
4. What kind of reading do you like best? Least? Why?
5. Do you read because you have to or because you want to? How is your reading time divided between pleasure reading and compulsory reading?
6. How do you read most often? Depending on the material, you may use any or all of the following reading methods:

    a. registering groups of words at a glance

    b. reading each word to yourself as though reading aloud

    c. moving your tongue silently

    d. moving your lips

    e. reading aloud

7. What factors from your background—for instance, the age at which you began to read, the attitude to reading in your home, the availability of reading material—have influenced your present reading habits?

8. What could you now do in order to improve your reading process? (Take a reading comprehension course, read more slowly, take a speed-reading course, read aloud, read more often, and so on.)

    In your journal, reflect on what you have learned from participating in this exercise. How would you compare your reading process with that of your peers? What strategies might you follow to make your reading process more enjoyable and profitable?

EXERCISE TWO
Examine What You Read

    For one week you and the other members of your peer group should keep a list of everything you read. At the end of the week share your list and your responses to the following questions with your group.

1. What types of reading material do you all have in common?

2. What type of material does each person read?

3. What proportion of each person's reading was done for pleasure?

4. Did others in your group suggest material you would like to read?

    Afterwards, in your journal, reflect on the quantity and quality of the reading material within your peer group. What bearing do you think this reading material has on the quality of writing among your peers?

EXERCISE THREE
Kinds of Reading

    How does your reading process vary, depending on the material you read? How does your purpose for reading each of the following affect the way you read it?

- Phone book
- Examination paper
- Legal document
- Pleasure reading
- Recipe
- Store catalog
- Comic strip
- Assigned Novel
- Textbook

Share your answers with your peers.

    In your journal write about how your reading process differs for each kind of reading that you do.

EXERCISE FOUR
Reading Textbooks and Other Nonfiction

You read textbooks and other nonfiction works (autobiographies and biographies, reference books, newspapers, magazines) mainly to discover information, either to satisfy your own curiosity or to fulfill the requirements of an assignment. This is not to say, however, that you cannot read nonfiction for enjoyment; some people make nonfiction the majority of their reading, even reading encyclopedias and dictionaries for fun.

But certainly the most important nonfiction you read as a student will be textbooks, and the more effectively and skillfully you can extract from them the information you need, the better equipped you will be for success in your studies. Here are some strategies to help you discover what textbooks can offer you:

Get the Complete Picture

If you are using a text for only one or two pieces of information, you may not find this step necessary. However, you ought to make yourself as familiar as you can with all the features of the main texts in your courses. (As *The Independent Writer* is designed to be the main text for a writing course, you might want to follow the steps outlined here, using it as a model.)

Almost all textbooks have a table of contents, outlining what sort of information the text contains. The table of contents lists main chapter headings, and subheadings if applicable, to let you know what each chapter contains. The table of contents will also list other material in the book (preface, appendixes, glossary, bibliography, index).

Turn to the Table of Contents in *The Independent Writer*. How many chapters does it contain? How many appendixes? Is there a glossary, bibliography, and index? What sort of material do you find in a preface? In a glossary? In a bibliography? In an index?

Zero In

By consulting the table of contents, as well as the index and glossary (if applicable), you will discover where to seek the information you need. You should have no trouble consulting a single page to find out what you need to know, but if you must read several pages or chapters, you need to locate and extract necessary information. This is where a reading strategy, such as SQ3R, can be useful.

SQ3R

You may already be familiar with the reading process called SQ3R (Survey, Question, Read, Recite, Review). It was especially developed to help students gain the greatest possible benefit from reading textbooks. Here is a brief summary of the technique:

   a. *Survey*: Read only the title and headings or subheadings of a chapter, as well as the opening and closing paragraphs. Note whether the chapter or section contains pictures, diagrams, or other illustrative material.

b. *Question*: Compose questions based on the title and main headings. For example, this chapter is titled "The Reading Process." You might ask, "What does the reading process mean? How is *reading* a process?" Also, question the author's use of material: "What is he or she trying to say? How? Why?"

c. *Read*: Here you do your main reading of the chapter or section, discovering the details of its contents and what useful information it contains. Use the questions you have already composed as a starting point, reading carefully the passages that contain the answers to those questions and omitting or reading quickly those that do not. If you find some essential passages difficult to understand, reread them slowly, ask your workshop partner for help, or try to paraphrase them (Chapter 32).

d. *Recite*: Reciting (talking or writing about what you have read) reinforces your grasp of the information you have gained and helps you remember it. Writing in your journal and talking to your workshop partner are invaluable aids in your reciting process; work with either or both to make the information you have read truly yours.

e. *Review*: You will usually review textbook material in preparation for a test; however, you should also try to review it throughout the term so that you are fully acquainted with it and do not need to "cram" the night before a test. Review may be accomplished by doing the following:

- Quickly rereading the material, along with your questions and answers and any journal entries
- Discussing it with your workshop partner or a friend
- Writing a 25-word summary of particular passages (Chapter 32)
- Making up possible exam questions about the material (or having your partner do so) and answering them (Chapter 20).

Here are some questions about *The Independent Writer* that you might answer to test your knowledge of SQ3R:

- What is the significance of the cover design?
- What is the main point of the Note to Students? Summarize it in twenty-five words. Should the Note to Instructor be read by students? Why?
- How many sections does *The Independent Writer* have? What is the main feature and purpose of each section?
- What are the differences among the four workshop sections?
- In which section are there examples of fiction?
- In what way will you find the Glossary useful?
- How is the Index organized? Is there cross-referencing?
- What is the point and use of the Acknowledgments for the reader?
- Where and why are Suggested Answers provided in the text?
- If you want to study another textbook for further information on a particular subject that is giving you trouble (for example, *sentence combining*), where would you look in *The Independent Writer*?

- Where are all the games in the textbook listed together?
- Locate the Progress Chart. How has it been designed so that you can locate it quickly, without referring to page numbers? What is the purpose of the Progress Chart?
- Why do you think the text contains cartoons?
- Notice that the text is printed in two colors. Why?
- Look at the top of any page. What information will you find there to let you know where you are in the textbook?

Reading Other Nonfiction

Depending on your reason for reading them, you may or may not need to use a close-reading technique such as SQ3R for other nonfiction works. You should use the principles of SQ3R when you read encyclopedias, scientific and technical journals, and other sources you are consulting for information. However, for pleasure reading of a biography or "how-to" book, or for casual perusal of a newspaper or magazine, you probably do not need to read with such attention to detail.

EXERCISE FIVE
Good Literature

During your high-school years your teachers probably encouraged you to read "good literature" or "the classics." Perhaps you wondered what makes a hundred-year-old novel qualify as good literature while the latest best-seller does not. Quite simply, a classic piece of fiction is part of our literary heritage; it continues to be relevant because it can give a reader a fresh view of the human condition that a mass-market thriller or romantic novel cannot.

Take a few minutes to share ideas with your peers about good literature. Which books (stories, poems, plays) do you consider so important that everyone should read them? Why should everyone read them? Which pieces of good literature do you think you should read at the next opportunity? Make a list of ten books that you intend to read soon.

For many people, best-sellers fill a need for reading material to pass the time, while soaking up the sun on a vacation, for instance. But as you read one, be critical. Is the book so poorly written that you waste your time in reading it? Do not hesitate to discard any book in which the writing lacks quality.

In your journal reflect on your attitude towards reading good literature.

EXERCISE SIX
Good Literature or Bad?

Each member of your peer group should plan to bring two very short excerpts to the next class: one that is an example of good literature and one of bad. Share them and discuss the quality of the pieces of writing. Why is each either memorable or a waste of time?

Which of the following pieces by Mark Twain is an example of good literature and which of bad literature?

Pretty soon a spider went crawling up my shoulder, and I flipped it off and it lit in the candle; and before I could budge it was all shriveled up. I didn't need anybody to tell me that that was an awful bad sign and would fetch me some bad luck, so I was scared and most shook the clothes off of me. I got up and turned around in my tracks three times and crossed my breast every time; and then I tied up a little lock of my hair with a thread to keep witches away. But I hadn't no confidence. You do that when you've lost a horseshoe that you've found, instead of nailing it up over the door, but I hadn't ever heard anybody say it was any way to keep off bad luck when you'd killed a spider.

It was a crisp and spicy New England morning in early October. The lilacs and laburnums, lit with the glory fires of autumn, hung burning and flashing in the brilliant air, a bridge provided by kind Nature for the wingless wild things that have their home in the treetops and would visit together. The larch and the pomegranate flung their purple and yellow flames in broad splashes along the slanted westward sweep of the woodland; and the sensuous fragrance of innumerable deciduous flowers rose upon the atmosphere in a swoon of incense. Far in the empty sky, a solitary pharynx slept among the empyrean on motionless wing. And everywhere brooded stillness, serenity, and the peace of God.

EXERCISE SEVEN
Text and Subtext

We all have a tendency to put something of ourselves into a piece of literature. But you must be careful that you do not put into a story something that the author has not written or intended. This is known as *reading into a story*, and although it may be enjoyable, it is discouraged when you are interpreting literature. What you should do is to go beyond the words of the literary work to see what is implied. This is often referred to as *reading between the lines*, and it is encouraged. Read what the author has written and try to deduce what he or she is implying.

To become aware of the differences in what people see in a work, look at this drawing. Do you see a young, beautiful woman or an old, ugly hag? If you see the young woman, she is the *text* of the drawing, while the old hag is the *subtext*. However, if you see the old hag, she is the text, and the young woman is the subtext.

Sometimes when you read, you comprehend immediately, instantly recognizing and enjoying both text and subtext. Sometimes, however, you only perceive the text and are unaware of the subtext. By listening to the interpretations of others, you will often discover the significance of the subtext and thus enjoy the literary work on another level. In fact, the subtext will often become more important to you than the main text. When you return to the drawing will you see the hag or the young woman, since you now know that *both* are there?

In your journal write about your tactics for discovering subtext.

EXERCISE EIGHT
Reading Prose Fiction

With your peers, find a short story from Appendix B to read. Use the following reading process:

1. One member should read the story aloud to the others, or the members of the group should take turns reading aloud. Read strictly for enjoyment, allowing the voice of the narrator to take over your consciousness.

2. Appoint a leader who will be responsible for seeing that everyone has an opportunity to share his or her responses.

3. After the oral reading, each member should make some kind of statement. You might share your feelings about how a particular part of the story made an impression on you or affected you in some way. Each speaker may build on what a previous speaker has said or introduce a new subject. More suggestions, topics, strategies, and questions to invite peer responses appear below.

4. If there is a lull in the responses, each member should read a portion of the selection aloud and make a comment on it.

5. After approximately fifteen minutes, someone should read the selection orally again while the others reflect on what has been shared.

6. In your journal write about your reflections on the story.

Suggestions, Topics, Strategies, and Questions

As you read fiction, remember that writers are on your side. They do not want you to be confused; in fact, they expect you to understand what they have written.

Good writers, in order not to be misconstrued, deliberately leave clues, signs, comments, descriptions, and details to point you in the direction of understanding. They use every focusing technique possible to make sure you understand significant points. As you reread any parts that moved you, intrigued you, or even confused you, begin checking to see if the author has used some focusing technique to steer you in the right direction. Imagine that you are putting a jigsaw puzzle together: all the pieces are in front of you, ready to be interlocked. A full and satisfying interpretation of a literary work should resemble the completed picture of a jigsaw puzzle in which all the pieces fit together.

Use any of the following items to help you fully enjoy literature:

1. Before you meet any of the characters in a story, you meet the narrator. The narrator may be the author, one of the characters, or an unidentified person. When interpreting a piece of prose, you should ask, "Who is the narrator? Is he or she to be trusted?" If the narrator is one of the characters in the story, he or she may be biased for or against particular characters; for example, the narrator may be in love with the heroine or may be the hero's enemy.

How does the author reveal the character of the narrator? In some stories the answer to this question becomes very important. Think how you might misinterpret an entire story if you accepted a narrator's ironic tone at face value.

2. The story may be told in the first person by the narrator, and therefore from a *limited* point of view. It can also be told in the third person, by an unidentified narrator, from an *omniscient* point of view. Some modern novels are told from both the first- and third-person points of view; this shifting of point of view requires care on the reader's part to determine the identity of the narrator of a given passage.

3. Differentiate between the author's point of view and a character's point of view. Realize that a character's lines (especially those of a narrating character) may not be the author's opinion, just as a narrating author may not approve of a character's point of view. Consciously separate the viewpoint of the author from that of his or her characters.

4. The situation of a story consists of the external and the internal factors that affect the main character. The external factors include the other characters and the setting. The internal factors include the ways in which the main character deals with conflict and the *archetypal* experience he or she is undergoing. Is the main character in the selection coming of age, losing innocence, becoming disillusioned, questing, taking a journey, losing paradise, being reborn, escaping from something or someplace or someone, or sacrificing something?

5. In nearly every story there is at least one specific conflict. The hero or heroine is in conflict with individuals, society, the environment, or himself or herself. This "specific conflict" should be obvious to you as you go through the story. Generally you will find yourself empathizing with the main character and, in some stories, *living* the character, because you have been able to relate completely to him or her. With which character do you most empathize? Why?

6. Once you have dealt with the specific conflicts, you should stand back from the story to see what the larger conflict is. For instance, if the story is about a boy who finds out several things about himself during a day's outing, the specific conflict would be between the boy and the incidents that take place during the day. In addition, his experiences and inner conflicts represent those of every young person. Authors will often use a specific conflict in their prose to make their readers think about these larger, *archetypal* conflicts. Identify the archetypal conflict involved in the story you are reading: the battle of the sexes (man and woman have been in conflict from the beginning); the generation gap (children and parents have never seemed to see eye to eye); love (lovers nearly always have to go through the steeplechase of boy meets girl, boy loses girl, boy gets girl); race (whites against black, yellows against reds, Martians against people from Earth); religion (believers against nonbelievers, or one person or group against a supernatural being.).

7. Characters as well can be archetypal. Does the story contain any characters to which you can give these titles: struggling student, whiz kid, frustrated lover, Cinderella, frustrated artist, separated lover, martyr, scapegoat, wise old man, apprentice, nature boy, innocent, stranger, devil, victim, Mother Earth, seductress, seducer, magician, healer, leader, follower, savior, and so on? The character does not have to be the same age or sex as the archetypal character; for example, Piggy in *Lord of the Flies* is an archetypal wise old man; Oliver in *Oliver Twist* is an archetypal Cinderella.

8. An author often will structure a story in a significant way; for example, the structure will parallel the events of the protagonist on a real or figurative journey. During the journey, the hero or heroine learns several things about himself or herself. Does the story you are reading involve any kind of journey—for example, a journey through life from birth to death, a circular journey that brings the protagonist back to where he or she began, a dead-end journey, a journey of self-discovery?

9. Sometimes a protagonist may be involved in a series of climactic events, the author describing each in progressively more detail. Does the protagonist in the story move up or down in fortune? Are there other characters with whom the protagonist's fortunes are contrasted? Does the author use a crisscross structure in which two characters meet—one on the way up, the other on the way down?

10. Does the author build events by using flashbacks or flash-forwards towards the protagonist's victory or defeat?

11. The author may be retelling from his or her point of view an older or familiar story (a tale, myth, legend, fable) in a modern setting. In order for you to appreciate the modern version fully, you really should know the original. If you find one clear reference to a myth or legend, you may discover that the story is a retelling of the original.

12. Consider whether the story contains symbols. A symbol often has a cluster of associations, and these associations can provide a clue to the story's deeper meaning. The title of a work is often symbolic; its significance becomes clear as you read the story.

13. You should be aware that the author manipulates literary elements in developing his or her theme or general idea. The theme is seldom stated explicitly; you must discover it from the experiences of the characters in the story. Can you express the theme of the work as a generalization about life; for example, "Our attempts to find a lifelong mate are futile," or "Life is unpredictable"?

14. Some writers hide themselves behind one or more philosophies: capitalist, Marxist, Freudian, Jungian, existentialist, Christian, atheist, sexist, liberationist, and so on. Often, a reader with strong philosophical leanings of his or her own will interpret a story along one or more of these lines. Thus, if you find that you are opposed to the philosophies in the story you are reading, spend a little time studying the author's philosophies as well as evaluating your own. When you are interpreting a story, you should not impose your own standards on it.

15. What impact has the author's style made on you? Consider the use of imagery and how the author sustains it, the dialogue and how realistic or revealing it is, the descriptions and how they contribute to the mood, the author's use of coincidence and how sentences and situations are contrived, the characterizations and the techniques used in their presentation, the degree of realism that the author has established and how this realism is supported (particularly useful in works of science fiction), the vocabulary and how it contributes to an understanding of the story, the themes and the techniques that you might recognize from other works by the same author.

16. Have you ever had to endure a truth about yourself in the same way as one of the characters in the work—for example, that you are not Olympic material, that you will never be rich and famous, that you have fallen in (or out of) love? How does the character in the story react to his or her situation? Was the character's decision right or wrong? Why? How would you have reacted if you were in the character's place?

17. Some stories live for centuries, while the appeal of others quickly fades. Do you think that the story you and your peers are talking about will be popular in twenty years? Why?

18. Every human being shares a literary inheritance. Appreciating this fact can help you to relate to particular situations, incidents, and characters in the stories you read. Sometimes you can recognize yourself participating in an archetypal situation. Other times you can recognize yourself (or part of yourself) as an archetypal character. Discuss the archetypal situations and characters that you may see in the literary work and how you relate to them.

EXERCISE NINE
Reading Poetry

With your peers, choose a poem from Appendix B. Follow the reading process outlined in the six points at the beginning of Exercise Eight. In addition, focus on the following strategies that should make the poem come alive for you.

Suggestions, Topics, Strategies, and Questions

A good poem is inexhaustible. Like a good piece of music, it will bring enjoyment no matter how frequently you read and reread it.

A poem should not *mean*; it should *be*. Rather than trying to figure out the hidden meanings in a poem, you should concentrate on how it affects you. What you should plan to do when you meet a poem is to allow the sounds and images of the poem to work within you so that you will be left with an overall impression or emotion.

Poetry is meant to be heard; often, it is set to music. The same students who say they never read poetry, or even that they hate poetry, often spend hours listening to their favorite hit records—all poems set to music. Share your favorite song with your peers. Explain why it is your favorite (for example, because of the words, images, sounds, rhythm, and so on).

Like a song, a poem is not *in* the reader or *in* the text, but is constantly being recreated by the collaboration of both. When you read poetry, you should concentrate on the language of the poem in order to illuminate the text, rather than analyzing the structure of the poem.

The following questions will help you appreciate a poem:

1. What is your immediate response to the poem you are reading—for example, does the poem make you feel happy, sad, confused, concerned, hopeful?

2. How has the poem's effect been accomplished—for example, through language, imagery, sound, symbols, rhythm, rhyme?

3. Which words or images create favorable impressions? Which create unfavorable impressions? Which are ambiguous?

4. How does the poet show that he or she is communicating as one human being to another?

5. How has the poem been designed so that you can enjoy it—for example, by how it appears on the page, its rhyme, its meter?

You will find other strategies to use in approaching many poems throughout Exercise Eight.

EXERCISE TEN
Reading Drama

Because plays and scripts are meant to be performed rather than studied in a classroom, the process of reading drama is probably the most difficult kind of fiction-reading you will ever do. As you read a piece of drama (one-act or full-length play, film or TV script), you must visualize the entire production, often with very little help from the playwright.

To make the reading process easier, you should improvise a production of a script through a play reading. With your peers, choose one of the plays in Appendix B. Assign parts within your peer group and conduct a play reading. You might use the following four lines to audition each other for the parts. Read the lines by accenting the italicized words. Who, in your group, can give four distinctly different meanings to the four lines? That person should take the leading role.

Get me out.

Get *me* out.

Get me *out.*

Get me out.

Through an oral reading, you will learn the importance of accenting words and phrases; hence, you will understand more clearly what each character is really saying. Once you have read the play, follow the reading process outlined in points one to six at the beginning of Exercise Eight. In addition, focus on the following strategies, which should help the play come alive for you.

Suggestions, Topics, Strategies, and Questions

Drama is the oldest form of literature; the father of drama was surely the prehistoric man who, on returning from a hunt, acted out the details of the hunt for those who did not accompany him. Thus began theatre: the interaction of an actor with an audience. Since then, theatre has been irrevocably linked to religion:

> The theatrical profession may protest as much as it likes, the theologians may protest, and the majority of those who see our plays would probably be amazed to hear it, but the theatre is a religious institution devoted entirely to the exaltation of the spirit of man. It is an attempt to prove that man has a dignity and a destiny, that his life is worth living, that he is not purely animal and without purpose. There is no doubt in my mind that our theatre, instead of being, as the evangelical ministers used to believe, the gateway to hell, is as much of a worship as the theatre of the Greeks and has exactly the same meaning in our lives. (Maxwell Anderson, Preface to *Candle in the Wind*)

In what way does the play that you have just read conform to Anderson's thesis?

As you talk about the play, imagine yourself having to act in or direct the play. Actors and directors must find deeper meanings within the plays they work on.

1. Why do theatre enthusiasts see the same play several times? The answer is simple: to appreciate a different interpretation. They will compare Laurence Olivier's Hamlet and John Gielgud's Hamlet. In 1980, the Stratford Festival in Canada alternated three actors in the role of Richard II; many people attended the play three times to compare the three interpretations. Have you ever seen a TV and a movie version of the same story? Which interpretation did you prefer? Why?

2. A playwright introduces scenes in a play for specific reasons (objectives). Divide the play that you are studying into French scenes (a division of a play indicated by the entrance or exit of a character). Study each French scene until you know why the playwright included it. Some objectives may be simple (just to introduce a new character) or very complex (to foreshadow an intended murder or to create suspense by prolonging the climax). Unless the play is a very poor drama, there should be at least one objective for each French scene.

3. Besides objectives relating to plot, you should know each character's objectives. First, establish each character's overall objective for being in the play. Then, discover why each character is in each French scene. Sometimes, objectives change; for example, have you ever come into a room for a glass of water (your main objective) and had the phone ring? Your main objective changes but is not necessarily forgotten. Apply this simple analysis to each of the characters in a play you are studying. Actors who do not know their objectives give only superficial performances; writers who do not know each character's objectives write superficial essays.

4. To prepare an analysis of the characters in a play is usually much more difficult than for characters in a short story or novel. The main reason for this is that the reader of a play is often given only the dialogue, without explanations of why and how it should be delivered.

There are several ways to analyze a character in a play:

a. Pay attention to what the playwright says about the character: in a foreword, explanation, stage direction, and so on. Take what the playwright says as true.

b. Study what the character says; however, not all of the lines may be true to character. The character could be deliberately lying in order to deceive another character.

c. When the character talks directly to an audience, take what he or she says as true.

d. Note particularly what a character does. Actions are usually a better indicator of character than words.

e. Test what another character says *to* the character you are analyzing. By putting the facts of the previous three analyses together, you can often determine whether what is said during a conversation is to be taken as true.

f. Pay particular attention to what another character says *about* the character you are analyzing. Generally you should consider these lines as true, because the playwright is using this method in order to provide the audience with a necessary detail of characterization.

Character analysis is not always so cut and dried as the above points indicate, but reviewing each point will help.

5. A superb actor can inject ironic humor into a line of tragedy or a touching note of sadness into a blatantly comic soliloquy and make the words sound as though the playwright had intended them to be read that way. Therefore, as you are discussing characterization, stretch your imagination. As long as your interpretation is based on the text, you should share it with your peers.

6. Make up a list of questions like the following that you can ask about the character you are analyzing. You must find textual evidence to prove each answer.

* How old is the character?
* Is he or she basically honest or dishonest?
* Is he or she considerate of others or self-centered?
* Is he or she selfish? Ambitious or lazy? A bully? Cruel? Mentally sound?
* Is the character the protagonist? Antagonist? A supporter of one or the other? A neutral character?

7. Try to relate the character to someone you know by answering questions like the following:

- Is there anyone like him or her among your friends? Acquaintances? Relatives?
- What similar qualities does the character have to someone you know?
- In what way(s) are you (are you not) like the character?
- What qualities do the character and a particular animal share? If you were to act the role of the character, how could you bring out the animal image?
- Whom would you cast in the part? Why?

8. Every play, even a modern one, has a history. Some scripts have been adapted from short stories or novels. Study the original source. Some plays have been reviewed after performances on Broadway or in London's West End. Study the reviews. Some plays have been talked about in essays. Look them up in periodicals. Some were written or set hundreds of years ago. Study the times in which the story takes place: the political environment, foibles of the day, moral problems, religion, styles of dress, and so on.

9. You should also get to know as much as you can about the playwright. What else has he or she written? Is the play that you are studying typical of the playwright? Why was the play written?

10. Find a line that causes you some difficulty. Why do you think the playwright wants the character to say that particular line the way it appears?

11. In what ways is a particular piece of dialogue real or artificial? For example, in real life you may not speak in full sentences or use a sustained metaphor.

12. Imagine that you are a producer with a lot of money and want to put the play on the stage, on the movie screen, or on television. Visualize how an ideal, full-scale production of the play should look. Share your thoughts about the set, lighting, and costume designs. Be prepared to give reasons for your choices.

13. Besides the preceding points, you might also consider the ones outlined for prose fiction throughout Exercise Eight above.

EXERCISE ELEVEN
Visualizing Literature

By making all or a part of a literary work visual, you can often discover a significant aspect of its overall theme. If your peer group is going to work on any of the following suggestions, first work independently; then share your visual creations with each other in order to discuss the significance of their similarities and differences.

1. Rewrite a poem (or a portion of it) as a concrete poem by changing the position of the words on the page to form an appropriate shape. In your discussions see if your peers recognize the significance of the shape of your concrete poem. Does it emphasize a special feeling, a new meaning, a symbol, or something else?

2. Rewrite a sentence or two from a short story or play as a "found poem" (see Chapter 24). You may combine the sentences, leave words out, and arrange the words on the page in concrete fashion. In your discussions see if your peers recognize the reasons why you wrote the found poem.

3. Design a book jacket for a story that you are reading. In your discussions talk about the significance of each person's design. Which were similar? Which was unique?

4. Draw a set design for a play that you are reading. In your discussions note the differences in each other's designs. Discuss the reasons for any significant differences.

5. When you think of the structure of a literary work, think of the events of the entire plot in terms of a diagram or a graph. This often points out significant structural features.

EXERCISE TWELVE
Writing for the Uninformed

This exercise is an important step in preparing to write a literary essay for an informed reader (Chapter 13). By writing a literary essay for an uninformed reader first, you will be able to bridge the transition to the formal paper more easily. You may benefit from working through this exercise several times before you write the assignment described in Chapter 13.

1. Choose a short selection that no one in your group knows, either from Appendix B or from another text. The selection may be a short story, poem, or one-act play.

2. Read the selection silently.

3. When you have finished, make a list to describe the feelings that the selection aroused in you—for example, loneliness, melancholy, sadness, joy.

4. Then write down a few observations about the piece—for example:

- The description seemed realistic.
- I could hear the poet's voice speaking to me.
- The first two lines reminded me of my childhood.

5. Make up four or five questions to discover a narrow topic that you would ask a class if you were planning to teach the literary work—for example:

- What is the writer's main concern?
- How is the first half of the poem like the second half?
- What is the point of view of the narrator?
- What impression or emotion are you left with?

6. Share these questions with one member of your group, allowing him or her to choose one. Become the teacher and answer the question orally. Your peer should then offer an evaluation of your answer. Afterwards, choose one of your peer's questions and continue the exercise.

7. You may carry this exercise a step further and write your answer for your peer.

8. Finally, you could make up a few questions or topics based on the literary work that would be suitable for an informed reader or examiner. You may be able to use one of these questions to write a literary essay.

9. In your journal, write about your reactions to the approach to literature described above.

Game: Play Doctor

One member of the group becomes a psychologist, another a character from a story, play, or narrative poem, and the other members become observers. The "character" visits the "psychologist" and asks for advice.

Both should look for insights into the "character's" psyche, motivations, or anything that occurs to them.

When the interview is over, the "observers" should comment on the effectiveness of the "character's" explanation of his or her problem and the "psychologist's" solution.

Repeat the game, changing roles.

Special Writing Assignment

Ask your workshop partner to give you a topic based on a piece of literature that is causing him or her trouble. The topic should be one that will benefit your partner's understanding or appreciation of the work; thus, make sure that your partner presents a useful topic so that you can write for him or her as though writing for an uninformed reader.

Spend a few minutes finding out exactly what your partner is looking for in your essay. Ask him or her questions so that you know exactly why you are writing.

List your writing variables before you write your first draft.

When you have presented your essay, find out from your partner if you have cleared up the problem, provided a worthwhile interpretation, or helped your partner to a greater appreciation of the literary work.

Read the following product written by a student for his partner.

Insight into Insight

by *James Deacon, student*

Ferlinghetti's poem, "The pennycandystore beyond the El," is a compassionate account of a young man's first awareness of love. Ferlinghetti gives us this account not only from the boy's point of view, but with his own more seasoned reflection.

The first half of the poem introduces the reader to the boy's childhood paradise, the candy store. A world of tangible delights, the store is portrayed as a magic place—the "jellybeans glowed" and

> A cat upon the counter moved among
> the licorice sticks
> and tootsie rolls
> and Oh Boy Gum

The boy could reach out and touch these treats, inhibited only by his tempter, the watchful cat.

Where the candies are tangible in the first half of the poem, the love object of the second half, the girl, is "unreal." She represents an attraction the boy does not understand in the same way he understands the candy. Indeed, she has a physical attraction that doesn't escape his notice—her "rainy" hair and her "breathless" breasts are images impressed on his mind. But the qualities indicated by "rainy" and "breathless" are more than physical, or the boy would have ignored this intruder into wonderland. He is every bit as intrigued by her as by the candy.

In the final line of the poem Ferlinghetti gives us the benefit of his hindsight. He can now see the beauty of his childhood in all its simplicity: he can see that the innocent event in the candy store marks the beginning of his adulthood, and he says "Too soon! too soon!" Childhood, in Ferlinghetti's view, is a time of our lives too lightly thrown aside.

Suggested Answers to the Second Workshop Section

CHAPTER 34
Exercise Nine

    a. One—simple vocabulary, straightforward style—"just the facts"

    b. Three—"blurred moment of ferocity," "torn the heart out"

    c. One—same answer as (a).

    d. Three—"In a blurred moment . . . Browning pistol."

    e. One

    f. Two

    g. Two

    h. Two—"the shooting of presidents in the U.S. and each other in Ireland"

    i. Two—"raw-edged," "gun-metal," "touching-hands spiritual"

    j. Two and Three—"the bright colors of life ran together," "he may well have torn the heart out of Jean Paul's remarkable papacy"

    k. Two

    l. Two, One

    m. Two—aggressive: "the madmen of the world," "another mind-bent assassin"
One—cautious: "a man believed to be a Turkish fugitive," "no vital organ was struck"

    n. One—Straightforward
Two—moving
Three—journalistic

CHAPTER 36
Exercise Six

The reference at the beginning of this exercise alludes to the Bible story about Paul's blindness. Once he comprehended, he was cured of his blindness, changed his name from Saul to Paul, and became the most famous of the early Christian missionaries.

Exercise Six

2. a. "Encounter of a Chilly Kind" to *Close Encounters of the Third Kind*

   b. "Terms of Disparagement" to *Terms of Endearment*

   c. "Play It Again, Pam" to *Play It Again, Sam*

   d. "The Saucer's Apprentice" to *The Sorcerer's Apprentice*

   e. "The Bungle Book" to *The Jungle Book*

   f. "Mopey Dick" to *Moby Dick*

   g. "To Censor or Not to Censor" to "to be or not to be"

Exercise Six

3. a. *Here we go again* was the catch phrase that Ronald Reagan used in both the 1980 and 1984 presidential campaigns.
   Soap opera is a daily, melodramatic story with a continuing plot line.
   With a whimper or a bang is a play on "This is the way the world ends / Not with a bang but a whimper" from T.S. Eliot's "The Waste Land." All allusions indicate a dissatisfaction with the reelection of President Reagan.

   b. *The greatest minds of the 12th century* refers to the fact that there were no great minds in the twelfth century; hence, the sentence is an understatement for satiric purposes.

   c. *Like children, Americans follow the merry tunes of Reagan, happy to fall in line behind his winning personality* . . . refers to the Pied Piper—thus indicating the winning charm of President Reagan.

   d. *Armageddon* refers to the final and conclusive battle between the forces of good and evil, as outlined in the book of Revelation from the Bible; thus, the writer does not wish us to bring about Armageddon ourselves.

   e. *Knight-errant* refers to one of King Arthur's knights who used to go about (sally) in shining armor searching for adventure.
   Buck Rogers refers to the fictional, futuristic space hero. Both allusions indicate that our astronauts are exploring unknown territory.

   f. *The right stuff* refers to Tom Wolfe's book and movie by the same name. In his story, he explains that the astronauts must be made of the "right stuff" in order to be successful.

g. *Star Wars* refers to the space film by the same name, in which the Death Star (an orbiting war machine) blew up Princess Leia's planet.
Apocalyptic refers to the Apocalypse, a cosmic cataclysm in which, according to the biblical book of Revelation, God destroys the ruling powers of evil and raises the righteous to life in a messianic kingdom. The critics, thus, disagree with any plan to introduce weapons into space.

h. *Pas de deux* is a ballet for two; Allen and his satellite, both in a weightless state, appeared to be dancing gracefully.

i. *Moses'* bringing back *the tablets* refers to the two stone tablets on which were written the ten commandments; since the contents were considered God's word, review of them by humans might seem inappropriate.

j. *Kamikaze* refers to a member of a Japanese air attack corps assigned to make a suicidal crash on a target; thus, the Americans and Lebanese do not want another similar "truck" assault in Beirut.

k. *Soup kitchens* were set up during the Depression of the 1930s; the term is used to emphasize that history is repeating itself.

l. *Pockmarked* refers to the holes on the skin caused by smallpox, chicken pox, or measles.
Foxholes refer to the craters caused by bombs and shells. Both allusions refer to the fact that the Ethiopian feeding camp looks like a war zone.

m. A *scapegoat* is a sacrificial animal; thus the five middle-level agency officials felt that they were taking the blame for others' mistakes.

n. *Crying wolf* refers to the fable of the boy who repeatedly frightened people by screaming that a wolf was coming. Eventually no one paid attention to him, even when a wolf really did come onto the scene. The Sandinistas' crying wolf draws international attention away from their stranglehold on power in Nicaragua.

o. *Valley Girls* refers to a California group that introduced among other things, a new level of diction—"gag me with a spoon," "totally awesome," and the like. Whoopi Goldberg portrays a large range of characters.

p. The *Great-White Way* is Broadway, New York, where all the theatre lights make the street look white. Whoopi Goldberg has now played in a Broadway theatre.

q. Living in the *fast lane* is living at top speed as on the fast lane of a freeway; Joe Namath concluded several business deals during his honeymoon.

r. *Tears a planet to tatters* refers to an actor's "tearing a passion to tatters" in Shakespeare's *Hamlet*; obviously, Peter O'Toole, according to *Time's* critic, indulges in "shameless and affecting" overacting in *Supergirl*.

s. A *chimera* is a fabulous mythological Greek monster, but today it refers to an illusory fancy, a wild, incongruous scheme; Glazebrook obviously prefers to travel alone instead of taking his family with him.

t. If writers wish to refer to utter failures, they can allude to either the *Edsel*, a well-known Ford car of the 1950s that failed to become popular, or *Watergate*, a complete fiasco filled with deceit and intrigue and leading eventually to President Nixon's resignation.

u. *Pavlovian tradition* refers to Ivan Pavlov's work with dogs in developing his theories about conditioned reflexes. The allusion simply refers to the fact that Soviet strategists trained dogs in the manner of Pavlov.

v. A *Maharajah* is a fabulously wealthy Indian prince; thus the airline advertisement considers the Maharajah service better than "First Class."

Note: If you would like to see the allusions in context, see *Time*, 26 November 1984.

CHAPTER 39
Exercise Five

The following is an example of how you would set up a bibliography according to the MLA guide.

Works Cited

Attenborough, David   Life on Earth.   London: Collins, 1979.
Bible.   2 Tim.
Blum, John M., et al.   The National Experience.   5th ed.   New York: Harcourt, 1981.
"Brain." Funk & Wagnalls New Encyclopedia. 1983 ed.
Browning, Elizabeth Barrett.   "Memory and Hope."   Poems of Elizabeth Barrett Browning.   New York: Collier, 1902.
Dyer, Wayne W.   Pulling Your Own Strings.   New York: Harper, 1978.
---.   The Sky's the Limit.   New York: Pocket, 1980.
"The Enlightened Machine."   The Brain.   PBS.   WGBH, Boston.   10 Oct. 1984.
Pearson, Durk, and Sandy Shaw.   Life Extension: A Practical Scientific Approach.   New York: Warner, 1982.
Shakespeare, William.   Macbeth.
"Vision and Movement."   The Brain.   PBS.   WGBH, Boston.   17 Oct. 1984.

The following is an example of how you would set up a bibliography according to the APA guide.

References

Attenborough, D.   (1979).   Life on Earth   London: Collins.
Bible.   2 Tim.

Blum, J. M., et al.   (1981).   The National Experience.   5th ed.   New York: Harcourt.

"Brain."   Funk & Wagnalls New Encyclopedia.   1983 ed.

Browning, E. B.   (1902).   "Memory and Hope."   Poems of Elizabeth Barrett Browning.   New York: Collier.

Dyer, W. W.   (1978).   Pulling Your Own Strings.   New York: Harper.

Dyer, W. W.   (1980).   The Sky's the Limit.   New York: Pocket.

"The Enlightened Machine."   (1984).   The Brain.   PBS.   WGBH, Boston.   10 Oct.

Pearson, D. & Shaw. S.   (1982).   Life Extension: A Practical Scientific Approach.   New York: Warner.

Shakespeare, W.   Macbeth.

"Vision and Movement."   (1984).   The Brain.   PBS.   WGBH, Boston.   17 Oct.

THIRD WORKSHOP SECTION

Sentence Combining and Variety

ABOUT THE THIRD WORKSHOP SECTION

Professional writers bring variety to their work by using combinations of different word groups: independent clauses, dependent clauses, prepositional phrases, verbal phrases, absolute phrases, adjective clusters, adverb clusters, appositives, and emphatic words, phrases, and interjections. The chapters in this section are designed to help you master these word groups, so that you can express yourself with clarity, emphasis, and variety.

The chapters in this section have been designed for individualized instruction. You can work through this section alone and at your own pace. When you work on a chapter by yourself, and there is something you do not understand, there are four things you should do before you ask your instructor for help:

1. Reread the section of the chapter slowly, noting every word, every example. You may have missed something significant.

2. Go to one of the many available grammar handbooks and look up the problem. Another author may have presented the problem from a different point of view.

3. Ask your workshop partner to help you. If your partner is able to supply a satisfactory answer to your question, he or she will have gained something too.

4. You should note that suggested answers are given for all sentence work at the end of this workshop section. Do not worry if your response differs from any one in the Suggested Answers following Chapter 55. The English language is in constant flux: "formal" spelling changes, "bad" grammar becomes acceptable, and "correct" punctuation seems superfluous. The answers given are correct but are not necessarily the *only* answers.

If you have tried all the above suggestions and still cannot understand a point, *then* ask your writing instructor for assistance. You must remember, though, that your instructor is the editor for the entire class; conducting one-to-one conferencing sessions is time-consuming.

To ensure that you truly understand and appreciate the writing techniques discussed in each chapter, begin to use them in your own writing. Read this sample journal entry that a student completed after studying Chapter 41.

The Writing Juggler

Using eight different word groups in sentences is like juggling eight balls at the same time. No one would be very impressed if a juggler used only three balls in his act; a reader is not impressed if a writer uses only independent clauses, dependent clauses, and prepositional phrases in his sentences. But the writer who can throw an absolute, appositive, or verbal phrase into his writing can please his reader just as an expert juggler can thrill his audience.

You will never be able to master the use of the thousands of English words, but you can master the use of the few word groups and learn how to combine them in every possible way. Good luck.

Learning the Basic Terminology

INTRODUCTION

Why do I have to know about nouns and verbs?

Why should I have to know what a dangling modifier is?

Why should I know the difference between a clause and a phrase?

Students have been asking these questions for years. The simple answer to each one is that knowledge of terms will be useful when you and your readers discuss, edit, and improve your drafts. In other words, you and your readers need a common language.

If you spend a little time becoming familiar with some basic writing terms, you will be able to enjoy and appreciate both this workshop section and the comments of those who read your work. But, remember, the purpose of this chapter is to make you a more concise and emphatic writer, not an expert grammarian.

EXPLANATION

Many freshman students have difficulty recognizing much of English grammar terminology. To determine whether or not you know basic English grammar, do the following three-part quiz. The answers to the quiz appear in the Suggested Answers following Chapter 55. From the results of your quiz, you will be able to determine if you need to work through the rest of this chapter.

First Quiz (value: 25 points)

Identify the underlined word or words as main subject, main predicate, direct object, indirect object, complement, or object of preposition.

a. "Thriller" skyrocketed Michael Jackson to fame and fortune.

507

    b. Most <u>Americans</u> <u>know</u> <u>that he won an unprecedented</u> <u>number</u> of <u>awards</u>.

    c. <u>Most</u> of America knows that he <u>won</u> an unprecedented <u>number</u> of <u>awards</u>.

    d. <u>Jackson</u> is a <u>star</u> of <u>stage</u>, video, and <u>film</u>.

    e. <u>Organizations</u> and <u>individuals</u> <u>must send</u> <u>him</u> so much <u>mail</u> that <u>he</u> <u>could</u> not possibly <u>answer</u> <u>it</u> all <u>himself</u>.

Second Quiz (value: 7 points)

    Identify the underlined words as prepositional phrases, absolute phrases, or one of the three verbal phrases (participial, gerundial, infinitive).

    a. Fans, <u>screaming his name</u> and <u>buying his records by the millions</u>, ensure his popularity.

    b. <u>Their enthusiasm unlimited</u>, some <u>of his fans</u> follow him wherever he happens <u>to be living or performing</u>.

    c. Hey, <u>creating superstars like Michael Jackson</u> is not just an American phenomenon; other countries enjoy <u>creating superstars too</u>.

Third Quiz (value 18 points)

    Identify the following words by their part of speech: noun, pronoun, verb, adjective, adverb, preposition, conjunction, and interjection. The words are taken from the sentences in the Second Quiz.

    a. fans, and, by, millions, ensure.

    b. enthusiasm, some, him, be, or.

    c. hey, like, not, an, American, other, enjoy, too.

Correct your own quiz and, depending on your score, determine how you should complete the rest of this chapter.

Over 45 points: Go to another chapter.

35–45:	Do any sentence work activity that looks unfamiliar.
25–35:	Read the chapter slowly, then do all of the sentence work.
15–25:	Do the chapter with someone, discussing each item thoroughly before you proceed to the next item. After you do the sentence work, give it to your partner to correct. Go over any item that you get wrong.
5–15:	Plan a crash program where you work with additional written material (titles of other texts appear in Appendix D) and visual material (your learning center may have videos and slide presentations to help you). When you feel more confident, work through the chapter with a partner.
Under 5:	See your instructor.

The rest of this chapter is organized so that you will meet the important grammatical terms often; by seeing and using these terms, you will soon make them part of your vocabulary. You should become familiar with the tools of your trade—grammatical terms are a writer's tools.

A. Clauses

There are two kinds of clauses: independent and dependent. Both contain subjects and predicates (verbs):

1. An *independent clause* may stand alone as a grammatically complete sentence. It is a word group with at least one subject, either understood or expressed, and one verb.

Because a single *verb* may convey a complete thought, it can be an independent clause.

Sing. Dance. Compose.

These are all complete sentences with *you* as an understood subject—[You] sing. [You] dance. [You] compose.

Similarly, the following are independent clauses:

SUBJECT	VERB
Michael Jackson	entertains.
Fans	cheer.
He	will be remembered.

Notice that the last sentence has a verb phrase, *will be remembered*, made up of the helping or auxiliary verbs *will be* plus the main verb *remembered*.

To add more information for the reader, a writer may compound either the subject or the verb.

SUBJECT	VERB
Women, men, and children	marvel and applaud.
His family	supports and encourages.
Jackson and talent	are linked.

Writers also enrich their main subjects and verbs by adding any number of clauses, phrases, and single words. Each of these additions has a particular relationship with the main subjects and verbs: some modify or describe; some complete the sense of the sentence. But no matter how long an independent clause is, it can be divided into two sections: the *complete subject* and the *complete predicate*. All words that are associated with the main subject are known as the *complete subject*, just as all words associated with the verb are the *complete predicate*. In the examples below, the main subjects and main verbs are in italics. Notice that the sentences would make no sense without the main subject and the main verb, although they make a certain amount of sense without one or two of the other words.

COMPLETE SUBJECT	COMPLETE PREDICATE
Nearly every *American*	*knows* about Michael Jackson.
Michael	*was born* in Gary, Indiana, on August 19, 1958.
He	*is* the seventh of Joseph and Katherine Jackson's nine children.
Jackson	now *lives* in Encino, California, with some of his family.
Awards	*are* always *being presented* to him.
Many of his adoring fans	*follow* him everywhere.

Can you determine which words in the above examples *modify* the subject or the verb and which words *complete the sense* of the sentence? In the first sentence, for example, *Nearly every* modifies *American* and *about Michael Jackson* completes the sense of *Nearly every American knows*. Try to determine what work the other words are doing in the sentences.

A single word or group of words that completes the sense of a sentence has one of four definite connections with the main verb.

- A *direct object* of the verb answers the question "What" or "Who".

COMPLETE SUBJECT	COMPLETE PREDICATE	
	Verb	Direct Object
Joe Jackson	*encouraged*	his sons.
Michael	*overshadowed*	his brothers.
The Jackson 5	*entertained*	school children.
They	*performed*	their own music.

- An *indirect object* of the verb answers the question "To what? or To whom?"

COMPLETE SUBJECT	COMPLETE PREDICATE		
	Verb	Indirect Object	Direct Object
Motown Records	*offered*	The Jackson 5	a contract.
The Jackson 5	*gave*	Motown	hit records.
Epic Records	*offered*	them	opportunities.

- *Modifiers* simply describe the subject or verb, rather than completing the sense of the sentence.

COMPLETE SUBJECT		COMPLETE PREDICATE	
	Modifiers	**Verb**	**Modifiers**
Jermaine Jackson		*stayed*	with Motown.
Randy	then	*was introduced*	into the group.
The new *group*		*was known*	as the Jacksons.
The *Jacksons*	never really	*suffered.*	

Depending on how they are used, verbs are transitive or intransitive. *Transitive verbs* take objects; *intransitive verbs* take modifiers. Can you tell which is which in the following examples—two are transitive; two are intransitive?

COMPLETE SUBJECT	COMPLETE PREDICATE
The *Jacksons*	*recorded* under the Epic label.
They	*recorded* the hit song albums *Destiny* and *Triumph.*
Michael	*sang* alone on *Off the Wall.*
He	*sang* solos.

- Transitive and intransitive verbs contain some kind of action. If a verb has no action, it is known as a linking verb (*be, seem, appear*). It requires a *complement* rather than an object. Without the complement, a linking verb makes no sense (*Michael is*). Notice that the complements answer the question *what* or *who*, or that they modify the subject. Complements are called *Predicate Nouns* or *Predicate Adjectives*.

COMPLETE SUBJECT		COMPLETE PREDICATE	
	Verb	**Complement**	
		Predicate Noun or Predicate Adjective	
Michael Jackson	*became*	a sensation.	(sensational)
He	*is*	an enigma.	(enigmatic)

To Sum Up

The *subject* does the action or has the experience.
The *verb* reveals what the action or the experience is.
The *direct object* says who or what received the action.
The *indirect object* is associated with the direct object and answers the questions "To what?" "To whom?" "With what?" "In what?" and so on.
Modifiers describe (they are discussed more fully below).
The *complement* completes the thought expressed by a linking verb.

All the main subjects, objects, and predicate nouns that have been used so far in the sample sentences have been *nouns* (names of persons, animals, plants, places, things, substances, qualities, ideas, or states of being) or *pronouns* (words that take the place of nouns).

From the examples above, find other nouns besides *Michael Jackson*, *fans*, *women*, *men*, and *talent*. Also, find pronouns such as *he* and *them*.

Throughout the chapters in this section, there are similar questions for you to answer. If you cannot answer one, get into the habit of rereading the material until you understand it. If you are absolutely stumped, ask someone for help. Do not continue the chapter if there is something you do not understand; otherwise, you will only compound your confusion.

2. A *dependent clause*, which also contains a complete subject and complete predicate, cannot stand alone as a sentence. It *depends* on something else to make complete sense. The following are examples of dependent clauses:

- when he had plastic surgery on his nose
- because his voice is so high
- whoever talks about Michael

The following are independent clauses. They can stand alone. They are both acceptable sentences.

- Michael's movie career began with *The Wiz*.
- His movie career reinforced his childlike qualities.

These two independent clauses can be combined by making the first one dependent on the second. The underlined section of the new sentence is the dependent clause.

- His movie career, which began with *The Wiz*, reinforced Michael's childlike qualities.

The same sentence combining technique is used in the following two examples:

From
On the set of *The Wiz*, he became attached to his Scarecrow character.
He was reluctant to become himself at the end of a day's shooting.

To
On the set of *The Wiz*, he became so attached to his Scarecrow character that he was reluctant to become himself at the end of a day's shooting.

From
He had to wear painful makeup every day for seven months.
His skin became blotchy.
His eyes grew red and sore.

To
Because he had to wear painful makeup every day for seven months, his skin became blotchy and his eyes grew red and sore.

These sentences are divided into separate word groups below so that you can see the function of each part. Each clause is presented separately: the main subject and the main verb of the independent clauses are in bold type; the main subject and main verb of the dependent clauses are in italics.

Notice that a dependent clause is part of either the complete subject or the complete predicate, depending on how it relates to each. Notice as well that each dependent clause either modifies or completes the sense of the independent clause. In other words, it can be a modifier, a subject, an object, or a complement.

COMPLETE SUBJECT	COMPLETE PREDICATE
a. His movie **career**, which began with *The Wiz*,	**enhanced** Michael's childlike qualities.
His movie **career**	**enhanced** Michael's childlike qualities.
which	*began* with *The Wiz*
b. On the set of *The Wiz*, **he**	**became** so attached to his Scarecrow character that he was reluctant to become himself at the end of a day's shooting.
On the set of *The Wiz*, **he**	**became** so attached to his Scarecrow character
that *he*	*was* reluctant to become himself at the end of a day's shooting.
c. his **skin**	**became** blotchy
and his **eyes**	**grew** red and sore [Because *he had* to wear painful makeup every day for seven months]
his **skin**	**became** blotchy
and his **eyes**	**grew** red and sore
Because *he*	*had* to wear painful makeup every day for seven months

The first dependent clause is "which began with *The Wiz*." What are the two other dependent clauses?

Notice that all the independent clauses are able to stand alone as sentences, while the dependent clauses are unable to stand alone as sentences. Furthermore, notice that all of the dependent clauses modify; indeed, they could be dropped from the sentences and the sentences would still make sense.

Here are a few sentences that have more than one dependent clause. You will notice that some of the verbs in the independent clauses need a dependent clause to make complete sense.

From

Fans noticed his appearance.
They assumed incorrectly.
He was not on drugs.

To

Fans who noticed his appearance incorrectly assumed he was on drugs.

COMPLETE SUBJECT	COMPLETE PREDICATE
Fans	incorrectly **assumed**
who	*noticed* his appearance
[that] *he*	*was* on drugs

From

Nothing could be further from the truth
Michael makes two claims.
He has never even tried marijuana.
He hates the word "high."

To

Nothing could be further from the truth because Michael claims that he has never even tried marijuana and hates the word "high."

COMPLETE SUBJECT	COMPLETE PREDICATE
Nothing	**could be** further from the truth
because *Michael*	*claims*
that *he*	*has* never even *tried* marijuana and *hates* the word "high"

From

I want to feel free with my mind sometimes.
I go walk the beach.
I read a beautiful book.
I write a song.

To

If I want to feel free with my mind, I will go walk the beach, read a beautiful book, or write a song. (Michael Jackson)

COMPLETE SUBJECT	COMPLETE PREDICATE
If *I*	*want* to feel free with my mind
I	**will go walk** the beach, **read** a beautiful book, or **write** a song

From

Few people realize things about Michael Jackson.
He is a devout and practicing Jehovah's Witness.
He is a strict vegetarian.
He does not even touch alcohol.

To

What few people realize is that Michael Jackson is a devout and practicing Jehovah's Witness and a strict vegetarian who does not even touch alcohol.

COMPLETE SUBJECT	COMPLETE PREDICATE
What few people realize	**is** that Michael Jackson is a devout and practicing Jehovah's Witness and a strict vegetarian
who	*does* not even *touch* alcohol.
What few *people*	*realize*
that *Michael Jackson*	*is* a devout and practicing Jehovah's Witness and a strict vegetarian

In the last example, the main subject of the verb "is" is an entire dependent clause. Can you distinguish the independent from the dependent clause? To show that you understand clauses, write a sentence that contains both an independent and a dependent clause. If you are unsure about your sentence, ask your workshop partner for an opinion.

B. Modifiers

Although you have already seen several modifiers in the previous section of this chapter, now is the time to examine them in more detail. Both independent and dependent clauses can contain modifiers to enrich the nouns, pronouns, and verbs. Modifiers are either single *adjectives* or *adverbs* or groups of words functioning as adjectives or adverbs.

1. Adjectives (which include the articles *a*, *an*, and *the*) describe nouns or pronouns. Which nouns or pronouns are being modified by the italicized adjectives?

- "Michael is one of *the last living* innocents who is in *complete* control of *his* life. I've never seen anybody like Michael. He's *an emotional star* child." [Steven Spielberg]
- "He's *two* people. He's either *the oldest, wisest,* most *mature, calm, peaceful* individual in *the* world, or else he's *an innocent* child—completely *sophisticated* or in *a fairy* tale." (Lynn Goldsmith, freelance photographer)
- Jackson's *commanding* presence on *many* videos turns *mean* anger into *good, clean, exhausting* exercise instead of *pointless* violence.

2. Adverbs (which explain *where, when, why,* or *how*) describe verbs, adjectives, or other adverbs. Which words do the italicized adverbs modify?

- Katherine Jackson *very often* says that one of her boys might be a *little more* talented, but that does *not* make him *better*.
- Michael is *extremely* reclusive; some say *too* reclusive, except on stage.

- *Sensationally* and *unbelievably*, Michael choreographs one hit video album after another.

    Add adjectives and adverbs to these sentences. Then ask someone to edit your sentences to see that you have used both adjectives and adverbs.

- His zoo includes fawns, a llama, a boa constrictor, swans, and peacocks.
- He loves Disneyland.
- He and his brothers make commercials.
- He got hurt.
- He wins awards.

C. Phrases

The difference between phrases and clauses is that phrases do not have both complete subjects and complete predicates; therefore, a phrase can never stand alone as a sentence. There are three different kinds of phrases; all can be used within independent or dependent clauses.

1. *Prepositional Phrases.* A *prepositional phrase* begins with a *preposition* and modifies words in exactly the same way as adjectives and adverbs. The following prepositional phrases do not contain subjects or verbs: *in Jackson's honor, of his many talents, because of his family.*

In order to make your writing more concise and emphatic, you can combine sentences by making one or more of either the independent or dependent clauses into *prepositional phrases.*

From

Michael made the solo album *Thriller.*
It was released in 1982.
It broke all records.
It was still No. 1 over two years after its release.

To

Michael's solo album *Thriller*, released in 1982, broke all records and was in No. 1 position for over two years. (three prepositional phrases)

From

Thriller fostered Jackson's three big videos.
Michael, a beautiful girl, and a private detective are featured in "Billie Jean."
Michael turns a mean gang into a magical gang in "Beat it."
In "Thriller" he is a shy young teenager who becomes the worst fiend of his—and his girlfriend's—nightmares.

To

Thriller fostered Jackson's three big videos: "Billie Jean" about Michael, a beautiful girl, and a private detective; "Beat it" about Michael's turning a mean gang into a magical gang; and "Thriller" about a shy young teenager who transforms himself into the worst fiend of his—and his girlfriend's—nightmares. (six prepositional phrases)

Now write a sentence that contains at least two prepositional phrases. Make sure your phrases begin with prepositions like these:

about	because of	down	near	regarding	up
above	before	during	notwithstanding	save	upon
across	behind	except	of	since	with
after	below	excepting	off	through	within
against	beneath	for	on	throughout	with
along	beside	from	on account of	till	respect
alongside	besides	in	onto	to	to
amid	between	in front of	out	toward	without
amidst	beyond	inside	out of	under	
among	by	in spite of	outside	underneath	
around	concerning	into	over	until	
at	despite	like	per	unto	

2. *Verbal Phrases.* The second kind of phrase is one that has a *verbal* (form of the verb) in it. Because it does not contain a complete verb or a subject, it is dependent on something else in the sentence to make complete sense. The following are verbal phrases: *evoking admiration, inspired by playwright J. M. Barrie, to fulfill God's purpose.*

Notice how sentences can be combined by using *verbal phrases.* In the sample sentences the *verbal phrases* are in italics. The *verbal* itself is in bold type.

From

Dancers Gene Kelly, Fred Astaire, and Bob Fosse admire Jackson's talents.
They offered warm words of praise in *Time* magazine's cover story on Michael Jackson.

To

Admiring *Jackson's talents*, dancers Gene Kelly, Fred Astaire, and Bob Fosse offered warm words of praise in *Time* magazine's cover story on Michael Jackson.

From

Jackson says he's color-blind.
He means that one day he strongly suspects every color will live together as one family.

To

"I happen ***to be*** *color-blind.* One day I strongly suspect every color ***to live*** *as one family*." [Jackson]

From

When you move your body, it is art.
When you dance, it shows your emotions through bodily movement.

To

Moving *your body* is an art. ***Dancing*** is really ***showing*** *your emotions through bodily movement.* [Jackson]

Being able to use phrases like these in your writing is absolutely essential if you want to become a skilled writer. Now write a sentence that contains a *verbal phrase*. If you are not sure that your sentence is correct, ask one of your workshop partners for an opinion.

3. *Absolute Phrases.* The third kind of phrase is one that has a *verbal* and a *subject*, but it cannot stand alone because it does not contain a complete verb. Like the others, this kind of phrase is dependent on something else in the sentence to make sense. This kind of phrase is known as an *absolute phrase* and acts as a modifier in the same way an adjective does. The following are examples of absolute phrases: *well-wishers lining the entrance of the hospital, an adoring fan staking out the gates of his Encino house, the president honoring him.*

Notice how sentences can be combined by using an absolute phrase.

From
His uniqueness has always been apparent.
Jackson became a trend setter.

To
His uniqueness being always apparent, Jackson became a trend setter.

In the example above, *uniqueness* is the subject and *being* is the verbal in the absolute phrase. The entire phrase describes *Jackson.* The verbal *being* is almost always omitted from absolutes.
His uniqueness always apparent, Jackson became a trend setter.

Which version of the absolute phrase above do you like better? Why?

From
His records and videos sold by the millions.
Jackson soon became a multimillionaire.

To
His records and videos having sold by the millions, Jackson soon became a multimillionaire.

In the above combination, you would not drop the verbal *having sold* because the sentence would not make sense without it.

4. One interesting method of using phrases is to place a complete dependent clause within a phrase. Being able to do this will enrich your writing immeasurably. Your sentence structure will thus become varied, concise, and emphatic.

Notice how the following sentences have been combined. The *phrases* are underlined and the dependent clause within the phrase is in italics.

From
Jackson dances and sings.
Absorbing magnetism surrounds him.
Jackson reminds you of how graceful the human body can be.

To
Dancing and singing with the absorbing magnetism *that surrounds him,* Jackson reminds you *of how graceful the human body can be.*

From

Some do not wish to buy records.

They want to hear how exciting or how soothing a singer's voice can be.

They should listen to Jackson on the radio.

To

For those *who do not wish to buy records* to hear *how exciting or how soothing a singer's voice can be*, they should listen to Jackson on the radio.

From

The 1984 reunion tour caught the imagination of the entire media.

The tour marked the first time in eight years that all six Jackson brothers had performed together.

To

The 1984 reunion tour, marking the first time in eight years *that all six Jackson brothers had performed together*, caught the imagination of the entire media.

D. Conjunctions and Interjections

So far you have seen six of the eight parts of speech: noun, pronoun, verb, adjective, adverb, and preposition. Now look at the last two parts of speech: conjunctions and interjections.

1. *Conjunctions*, such as *and, neither . . . nor, because, nevertheless*, join single words or word groups, or even paragraphs. Note how the conjunctions *not only . . . but also* combine the two clauses in the following:

From

Michael wants to play Peter Pan in the movie.

Steven Spielberg (of *ET* fame) wants to direct him.

To

Not only does Michael want to play Peter Pan in the movie, *but* Steven Spielberg (of *ET* fame) *also* wants to direct him.

See if you can identify what is being joined by the italicized conjunctions in the following two examples.

From

Elvis had his gilded belt.

Elton had his spectacular spectacles.

Michael has a glittering glove.

It is made of twelve hundred round Austrian-crystal rhinestones, each individually sewn on cotton fabric.

To

Elvis had his gilded belt, Elton his spectacular spectacles, *and now* Michael has a glittering glove that is made of twelve hundred round Austrian-crystal rhinestones, each individually sewn on cotton fabric.

From
It should be obvious to everyone by now.
Any one of Jackson's accomplishments is only the tip of the iceberg.
Each is just the beginning of an era in rock history.
Twenty years from now, this era will be described by people.
It will be referred to as the Michael Jackson era.

To
It should be obvious to everyone by now that any one of Jackson's accomplishments is only the tip of the iceberg, just the beginning of an era in rock history that twenty years from now will be described *and* referred to as the Michael Jackson era.

Now write a sentence using a conjunction. Ask a partner to edit it.

2. The eighth and final part of speech is the *interjection*, which is an exclamation. An interjection has little or no grammatical function.

People who see Michael Jackson for the first time often say, "*Wow*, I wasn't expecting that!"

SUMMARY

In this chapter you have seen only a few of the hundreds of grammatical terms. They are the ones that are used frequently in *The Independent Writer* to help you become a better writer.

You can divide sentences into *independent* and *dependent* clauses, each of which must contain a *main subject* and a *main verb*. All other words in the clauses modify or complete the sense of either the main subject (making up the *complete subject*) or the main verb (making up the *complete predicate*). Clauses can be constructed by using eight different parts of speech: *noun, pronoun, verb, adjective, adverb, preposition, conjunction,* and *interjection*. Clauses may also contain three different kinds of phrases: *prepositional, verbal,* and *absolute*. Moveover, to make writing richer and more interesting to read, *dependent clauses* can be made a part of any of the three kinds of phrases.

Your grammar lesson is over. In future chapters in this section you will find various refinements of the grammatical points that you have learned in this chapter.

Now see how much you remember by testing yourself with the Sentence Work.

SENTENCE WORK

The purpose of these exercises is to see if you can identify your tools. Later chapters deal with sentence combining. Compare your answers with those in the Suggested Answers following Chapter 55. *Suggestion*: Do not look at the Suggested Answers until you have written out all of your answers.

1. Divide the following sentences into complete subjects and complete predicates.
   a. Cesar Chavez is a Chicano who has guided the United Farm Workers movement.

    b. Chavez, who was himself a farm worker, organized the struggle for better pay.

    c. He led the famous Delano grape pickers' strike, which was a success.

    d. Mohandas Gandhi, who was called Mahatma, which means "great soul," inspired the people of India, who wanted independence from Britain.

    e. Those who favor nonviolent resistance to authority still use Gandhi's methods today.

    f. While Winston Churchill was a war correspondent during the Boer War, the South African government considered him so dangerous that it put a price on his head.

2. In the preceding sentences, separate the independent clauses from the dependent clauses.

3. Identify the words in italics as independent clauses or dependent clauses.

    a. *The young Shoshone Sacagawea proved herself invaluable* while acting as interpreter for the Lewis and Clark expedition.

    b. The Israeli commandos *who raided Entebbe airport in Uganda in 1976* became heroes overnight.

    c. *Before Franklin D. Roosevelt became our country's thirty-second president,* he had established a record of social reform as governor of New York.

    d. *President Roosevelt initiated many national social-reform programs.*

    e. After Roosevelt urged that they do so, *Congress passed the Social Security Act in 1935.*

    f. *The Peace Corps is full of unsung heroes.*

    g. Peace Corps volunteers serve with the sort of unselfishness *that most of us associate with heroism.*

    h. Thousands of American men and women have volunteered to work in developing nations, *where they have helped build schools, roads, and hospitals.*

4. Identify the words in italics as one of the eight parts of speech: noun, pronoun, verb, adjective, adverb, preposition, conjunction, or interjection.

    a. Americans won the pole vault *competition* in *every* Olympic Games *between* 1896 and 1968. *Amazing!*

    b. Florence Nightingale both *revolutionized* the *nursing* profession *and* revealed the *inhuman conditions* faced by British soldiers in the Crimea.

    c. The Apache chief Geronimo tried to prevent *his* people *from* being confined on *reservations.*

    d. Dr. Martin Luther King *definitely gave* black Americans *inspiration* in their fight for *civil* rights.

    e. *Surely it* is Martin Luther King *who heads* the list of *great American* black heroes.

5. Identify the words in italics as *phrases* or *clauses*.

    a. Yuri Gagarin was a hero *of the Russian people* and to millions of others as well.

    b. His 1961 orbit of the earth was the first *by a human being*.

    c. After his death, *his birthplace was renamed* in his honor.

    d. Gagarin's fame is naturally greater in Russia than in the West, *where Neil Armstrong is remembered* as the first American who walked on the moon.

    e. Amelia Earhart, *born in Atchison, Kansas, in 1897*, was one of America's first record-breaking pilots.

    f. *Accompanied by two men*, she was the first woman *to fly across the Atlantic*. (two word groups)

    g. *Having completed a long list of recognized flying achievements*, Earhart has earned a secure place in the history of aviation.

    h. Dr. Frederick Banting's discovery of insulin allowed millions *to live more productive lives*.

    i. In his work, Banting removed the pancreases of dogs *to test the dogs' reactions*.

    j. *Jonas Salk proved his dedication to the search for a polio vaccine* by experimenting for years before *success finally came*. (two word groups)

    k. *Salk's testing the vaccine on himself* demonstrated both confidence and courage.

    l. Eleanor Roosevelt was one of the most influential women in American politics, *encouraging thousands of women* to support her husband's New Deal.

    m. *During the 1984 presidential election*, Geraldine Ferraro, a well-respected Congresswoman from Queens, New York, became a national celebrity *as Walter Mondale's running mate*. (two word groups)

    n. Ralph Nader has worked to make both consumers and business people more aware *of consumers' rights*.

    o. *Because he exposed their practices in his book, Unsafe at Any Speed*, General Motors, as well as other American automakers, became his implacable foes.

    p. Nader has been in the news less often in recent years; however, he and the public-interest research groups *he has inspired* continue to battle on behalf of the consumer.

    q. *Though she was born in Poland*, Marie Curie performed her Nobel-Prize-winning scientific experiments in Paris.

    r. The unauthenticated story of Betsy Ross and her work on the first American flag was that in June 1776, before the adoption of the Declaration of Independence, George Washington, Robert Morris, and George Ross, *representing a committee of the congress*, came to her upholstery shop in Arch street, Philadelphia, showed her a rough draft of a flag with stars and stripes, and asked if she could make a flag. *She did*. (two word groups)

s. One of the foremost social reformers *of her time*, Jane Addams founded the first American settlement house *to offer a variety of services to the urban poor.* (two word groups)

t. *What became of Henry Hudson,* / *who discovered Hudson Bay and tried to find the Northwest Passage*, has never been determined. (two word groups)

PARAGRAPH WORK

Rewrite the following paragraph so that you change the carpentry analogy to another figurative comparison.

Substitute the italicized key words *carpenter's helper, hammer, saw, carpenter, criss-cross on the end, middle-sized square head, Phillips screwdriver, Robertson screwdriver* for ones of another trade, profession, hobby, or interest that you know something about.

If you were to choose a medical analogy, the first three words you might use would be *nurse, scalpel,* and *stethoscope.* If you were to choose a sewing analogy, you might use *tailor, needle,* and *thimble.*

This, more than any of the other chapters in *The Independent Writer*, is your tool kit. In the same way as a *carpenter's helper* needs to know the difference between a *hammer* and a *saw*, you need to know the difference between a subject and a verb when your editor refers to one or the other. What a waste of time it would be if a *carpenter* had to ask, "Give me the one with the kind of funny *criss-cross on the end*," or "I want the one with the *middle-sized square head*." All he should need to say is "Give me a *Phillips screwdriver*," or "I want the *Robertson screwdriver*." When one of your editors says, "I think you should have used a phrase instead of a clause," you have to know what he or she is talking about. Words and word groups are a writer's tools. Learn to identify them.

Now choose your own analogy and complete the paragraph. If you need further assistance, turn to the Suggested Answers following Chapter 55.

42

A Look at Sentence Patterns

INTRODUCTION

This chapter presents an overall view of the word groups used to create the sentence patterns that writers have at their disposal. A knowledge of all the patterns will make you more aware of the various choices you can make. If you become a little confused during this chapter, do not worry; these patterns are discussed separately and in more detail in subsequent chapters. (Chapter references are given in parentheses after each sentence pattern is introduced.)

EXPLANATION

1. The most common word group is the simple, single, independent clause or *simple sentence* (Chapter 43):

The native Americans' exact origins are uncertain.

2. If you combine two or more independent clauses, the new sentence pattern is called a *compound sentence* (Chapter 44). Notice that the italicized independent clauses in the following are joined by the conjunctions *and* and *but*.

From

Some native Americans have brown skin.
Some tribes have skin with a reddish tinge.
Some are whiter than the so-called whites.
The term "Red Indian" or "redskin" is a misnomer.

To

Some native Americans have brown skin, *some have skin with a reddish tinge*, and *some are whiter than the so-called whites*, but *the term "Red Indian" or "redskin" is a misnomer.*

3. If an independent clause is combined with one or more dependent clauses, the new sentence pattern is called a *complex sentence* (Chapter 45). The dependent clauses are italicized.

From

Native Americans have inhabited this continent from prehistoric times.
Native Americans are divided into a great many tribes.

To

Native Americans, *who are divided into a great many tribes*, have inhabited this continent from prehistoric times.

From

The ancestors of a great number of native Americans came to North America via the Bering Straits.
Most scholars are still searching for the origins of the Aztecs, Incas, and Anasazi.

To

Although the ancestors of a great number of native Americans came to North America via the Bering Straits, most scholars are still searching for the origins of the Aztecs, Incas, and Anasazi.

4. If you add one or more dependent clauses to two or more independent clauses, you will have created a *compound-complex sentence* pattern (Chapter 46). The dependent clause in the combined sentence below is italicized. Do you see the independent clauses?

From

Crazy Horse tried to obtain fresh supplies for his warriors after the Battle of Little Big Horn.
He was being relentlessly pursued by Colonel Nelson A. Miles and his forces.
Crazy Horse followed the advice of Red Cloud and surrendered.

To

Crazy Horse tried to obtain fresh supplies for his warriors after the Battle of Little Big Horn, but *since he was being relentlessly pursued by Colonel Nelson A. Miles and his forces*, he followed the advice of Red Cloud and surrendered.

Note: All the other word groups that will be introduced can be added to any of the above sentence patterns to enrich them. In order for you to see the function of each word group clearly, however, each has been added to an independent clause.

5. By adding a *prepositional phrase*, you can elaborate on a particular point and thus create a new sentence pattern (Chapter 47).

From

Chief Dan George spoke a famous lament.
His subject was the forgotten native Americans.

To

In his famous lament, Chief Dan George spoke *of the forgotten native Americans*.

From

The Battle of Little Big Horn was over.
Canada was Sitting Bull's destination.
He took his followers confidently to Canada because he heard that Queen Victoria was merciful.

To
With confidence in Queen Victoria's mercy, Sitting Bull took his followers *to Canada after the Battle of Little Big Horn*.

Read the preceding sentences without the italicized prepositional phrases to see what details have been added to the independent clauses.

6. The addition of a *verbal phrase* creates a new sentence pattern as well (Chapter 48). Notice how verbal phrases affect the independent clauses in the following examples. The verbal phrases are italicized.

From
Many native Americans live in harmony with the earth.
They respect the wildlife.
They love the land and the things that grow on it.

To
Tutored by their respect for wildlife and their love of the land and growing things, many native Americans live in harmony with the earth.

OR

To show their respect for wildlife and their love for the land and growing things, many native Americans live in harmony with the earth.

OR

Many native Americans live in harmony with the earth, while *showing respect for wildlife and love for the land and growing things*.

7. Professional writers often use the sentence pattern that includes an *absolute phrase* (Chapter 49). Notice how extra detail is added by the italicized absolute phrase.

From
Beatian Yazz is one of the great Navajo painters.
His talents have been acknowledged by all.

To
Beatian Yazz, *his talents acknowledged by all*, is one of the great Navajo painters.

8. You can create an interesting sentence pattern if you use two adjacent word groups (a) that refer to the same thing and (b) that can be substituted for each other (Chapter 50). Notice that the subject of the following sentence and the italicized word group *refer* to the same place and can be *substituted* for each other. The italicized word group is called an *appositive*.

From
Wounded Knee has gained infamy as the site of the massacre of many native Americans.
Wounded Knee is a town in South Dakota.

To
Wounded Knee, *a town in South Dakota*, has gained infamy as the site of the massacre of many native Americans.

Notice that you could leave either *Wounded Knee* or *a town in South Dakota* out of the sentence and it would make sense. This feature is characteristic of appositives.

9. You can develop a useful sentence pattern by *clustering* a few adjectives, adverbs, or other parts of speech somewhere in the sentence (Chapter 51). The adjective cluster in the following example is italicized.

From

Joseph Brant was an important leader of the Mohawks.
He was brave as well as controversial.
He was well educated.

To

Well-educated, controversial, and brave, Joseph Brant was an important leader of the Mohawks.

You can develop another pattern by clustering adverbs:

From

Buffy Sainte-Marie combines folk-rock and native-American rhythms smoothly.
She seems quite sure of herself.
The overall effect is pleasing.

To

Buffy Sainte-Marie—*smoothly, surely, and pleasingly*—combines folk-rock and native-American rhythms.

10. Finally, you can create an effective sentence pattern by the use of an *emphatic word or phrase* (Chapter 52).

From

The Northwest Coast art of totem-pole carving has come back to life.
This kind of carving is gaining new popularity.

To

Revived, the Northwest Coast art of totem-pole carving is gaining new popularity.

From

The native American has much to teach the world.
That is certain.

To

Indeed, the native American has much to teach the world.

As you work through the other chapters in this workshop section, you will see that you can place all the word groups before, after, or in the middle of independent or dependent clauses to give variety to your writing. The word groups are few, but the combinations are limitless.

SENTENCE WORK

Your purpose in this exercise is to identify word groups; later, you will be writing combined sentences.

Examine each of the italicized word groups and match each sentence pattern with the models in the Explanation section of this chapter. Then identify the sentence pattern by the numbers 1 to 10.

Example:

Geronimo, *a Chiricahua Apache*, was one of the most daring native American leaders.

Answer:

This sentence follows the same sentence pattern as Number 8.

   a. The Navaho now claim *as their present homeland* a large area *of the Southwest*.

   b. The Iroquois, *many terrorizing the Hurons and other nearby tribes*, were feared and hated.

   c. *Diseased, debilitated, and decimated*, the Great Plains native Americans finally surrendered in the 1870s.

   d. *Northwest Coast native Americans are renowned fishermen.*

   e. Nootka canoes, *constructed from a single hollow log*, could withstand the rough Pacific Ocean.

   f. "Firewater," *raw or adulterated alcohol*, was made readily available by invading white men and helped to destroy native American societies.

   g. *Fortunately*, some tribes now manage their reservation resources profitably.

   h. *Starring as the wise Tonto in* The Lone Ranger *TV Series* was Jay Silverheels's claim to fame.

   i. *The powerful Five Nations confederacy consisted of the Mohawk, Oneida, Onondaga, Cayuga, and Seneca tribes;* however, *few full-blooded members of these tribes survive today.*

   j. Chief Dan George said [*that*] *the next hundred years shall be "the greatest in the proud history of our tribes and nations"*; native Americans and nonnative Americans hope his prophecy comes true.

   k. In the 1970s a number of militant and well-publicized protest actions were led by the American Indian Movement (AIM), *which was organized to expose through direct confrontation the abuses of racism.*

PARAGRAPH WORK

Complete the paragraph below by combining each group of sentences in brackets into a single sentence.

Example:

[A very important factor in the survival of native-American tribes was their constant discipline in certain arts. They participated in war and physical training.]

Satisfactory Combining:

A very important factor in the survival of native-American tribes was their constant discipline in the arts of war and physical training.

[In most regions native-American boys were taught to swim in the icy waters. The boys were approaching adolescence. The time was midwinter.] [All were taught the meaning of pain at an early age. Their elders deliberately decided this.] [The lads were switched. They were from the Northwest Coast. They emerged from icy ocean waters.] [Coals glowed. Iroquoian lads were taught the feel of them on bare skin.] [The warrior-designate of the Great Plains faced the ordeal of the Sun Dance. He did so by his own will. It was the way by which his manhood might be proved.] [The warriors danced. They took part in religious ceremonies. They feasted. The Sun Dance involved three or four days of these activities.] [With some tribes, a feature of the Sun Dance was the supreme test of the young warrior's endurance. It was done to see how much pain he could stand.] [The pectoral muscles were slit. The slitting created bridges of muscle. Lengths of thong were run through them.] [The free ends were tied to the center-post of the Sun Lodge. The warrior danced. He pulled against the thongs. He did this until he either broke the muscle bridges or fainted with pain and exhaustion.] [Alternately, the shoulder muscles were slit. The thongs were tied to a buffalo skull. He had to jerk the skull across the prairie. He did this until the thongs broke the muscle bridge.]

43

Simple Sentences

INTRODUCTION

A simple sentence contains *only one* independent clause. The simple sentence can be a most useful writing tool. In this chapter you will look at the ways to bring variety to the simple sentence.

EXPLANATION

Examine these simple sentences.

1. Simple sentence with *you* as an understood subject:

   Rejoice!

2. Simple sentence with a single subject and a single verb (or verb phrase):

   The *eagle comes. It is soaring* through the heavens.

3. Simple sentence with descriptive words:

   Its *long, curved* talons seize its prey.

4. Simple sentence with a compound subject:

   The eagle's *feathers* and *talons* are powerful fetishes among all native Americans.

5. Simple sentence with a compound verb:

   They *coveted, wore, traded,* and *bequeathed* eagle feathers.

6. Simple sentence with a compound subject and a compound verb:

   The United States' *Great Seal* and *currency portray* and *commemorate* the North American bald eagle.

7. Simple sentence with an appositive:

   A powerful, keen-sighted, long-lived bird, the North American bald eagle symbolizes the United States.

8. Simple sentence with a prepositional phrase:

Legends *of the eagle* abound *among native American tribes throughout the United States*. (three prepositional phrases)

9. Simple sentences with different verbal phrases:

Celebrated as Creator, the eagle is honored by the Achomawi native Americans.

To make the mountains, Eagle scratched up ridges of earth and rock.

By *rooting some down and pin feathers in the ground*, Eagle made the bushes and forests.

10. Simple sentence with an absolute phrase:

Its habitat slowly diminishing, the bald eagle is an endangered species in all states except Alaska.

11. Simple sentence with a single emphatic word:

Happily, forty thousand bald eagles thrive throughout Alaska.

12. You can join two or more simple sentences to make a single, more detailed simple sentence. As long as you add only single words or phrases to the independent clause, you will still have a simple sentence. The subjects and verbs in the following combined sentences are italicized.

From
The bald eagle is not really bald.
Its head is covered with white feathers.

To
Not really bald, the bald eagle's *head is covered* with white feathers.

From
Eagle families nest in the same place year after year.
These nests are called eyries.
An old eyrie could measure ten feet across and twenty feet deep.
It could weigh as much as two tons.

To
An eagle's *nest*, called an eyrie, *will be used* by generations of birds and *could measure* ten feet across and twenty feet deep and *weigh* as much as two tons.

From
The eagle is an exceptional bird.
This fact is beyond doubt.

To
Undoubtedly, the *eagle is* an exceptional bird.

From
The eagle preys upon fish and rabbits.
It may also kill squirrels and birds.

To
The *eagle preys* upon fish, rabbits, squirrels, and birds.

From
A mother eagle will teach her young how to soar.
She pushes them out of their nest.
She saves them just before they crash to the ground.
She returns them to the nest.
She repeats the whole process.

To
A mother *eagle will teach* her young how to soar by pushing them out of their nest, saving them just before they crash to the ground, returning them to the nest, and repeating the whole process.

SENTENCE WORK

Combine each of the following groups of simple sentences into a single, more detailed simple sentence. Vary the methods of sentence combining by varying the different patterns outlined above.

Example:
The eagle is the subject of much folklore.
Eagles are reputed to see their prey at a distance of one thousand miles.
The eagle is said to brighten its eyes with wild lettuce.

Incorrect Answer—because the sentence has two clauses (one independent, the other dependent):
The subject of much folklore, *eagles are reputed* to see their prey at a distance of one thousand miles because *they brighten* their eyes with wild lettuce.

Correct Answer—because the sentence has only one independent clause:
The subject of much folklore, *eagles are reputed* to brighten their eyes with wild lettuce in order to see their prey at a distance of one thousand miles.

1. According to legend, the feathers of the eagle are powerful.
   An eagle's feathers will devour the feathers of other birds.

2. The Iroquois hold an eagle dance.
   The dance celebrates the eagle and the hunt.
   The dancer hops from side to side.
   The hopping represents the eagle's approach to its meat.

3. Between 1795 and 1933, the United States minted a gold coin worth ten dollars.
   The coin was stamped with an eagle on the reverse side.
   The coin was popularly called an eagle.

4. Eagle feathers were very valuable among prairie tribes.
   They were the medium of exchange.
   Two to four eagle feathers were rated equal to a horse.

5. The Fraternal Order of Eagles is famous.
   It has over a million members in 1,900 aeries.
   There are Eagle aeries in the United States, Canada, and the Philippines.

6. The Fraternal Order of Eagles helps people.
   It supports cancer research.
   It supports heart research.
   It aids retarded children and the elderly.
   It has a motto.
   The motto is "Eagles are people helping people."

7. In native-American legend, also, the eagle is a helper.
   It gambled with Fire Owner to win fire for the Karok tribe.
   It carries the Arapahoe ghost dancer to the Messiah.

8. The eagle is a majestic bird.
   Part of its majesty stems from its large size.
   The bald eagle may measure from thirty to thirty-five inches from bill to the tip
   of the tail.
   Its wingspan may be seven feet.

9. Walt Whitman wrote a poem about eagles.
   It celebrates their mating ritual.
   The poem is called "The Dalliance of the Eagles."

10. The mating season is in early spring.
    Pairs of eagles engage in intense nest building.
    They also repair nests.

11. An eagle appears to have a favorite stunt.
    It spots a protruding branch from a tree.
    It soars at the dead branch.
    It seizes it in those razor-sharp, inward-curving talons.
    It snaps the branch loose.

12. Even more spectacular is its mating ritual.
    The pair soar out on thermal currents far above the earth.

13. One of them rolls over.
    It continues to soar upside down.
    Its legs are extended.

14. The mate soars above it.
    The talons of the two lock together.

15. They set their wings.
    They intertwine their feet.
    The pair pinwheel over and over.
    They tumble earthward in a wild, cartwheeling ecstasy.

16. The results of all this connubial recklessness are fairly modest.
    The female eagle produces two or three white eggs.
    They are not much larger than chicken eggs.

17. In 1973, George Laycock detailed the great birds' life and perilous decline.
    The book is called *Autumn of the Eagle.*
    In 1982, John Belushi drew attention to the extinction of the bald eagle in a film.
    The film is called *Continental Divide.*

PARAGRAPH WORK

Fill in the blanks in the paragraphs below so that each sentence remains a simple sentence and the paragraphs remain unified and coherent. Use the following information for your simple sentences. The first one is done for you. Before you check the Suggested Answers, make sure that every sentence is still a simple sentence. Underline the subject(s) and verb(s) in each sentence.

- Eagles soar.
- Some people loathed eagles.
- Our ancestors thought a thread connected earth and the place of spirits.
- Eagles were important to the ancient Greeks.
- Delphi indicated the center of the world.
- The earthly and divine touched above Delphi.
- Eagles carried dead pharaohs' spirits into the heavens.
- Romans marched behind the eagle banner.
- The character of the eagle was considered sacred by many native American tribes.

A (soaring) eagle is an ideal symbol for America. People from other times, however, have made the eagle an important part of their culture too. Human attitudes toward eagles have always vacillated between reverence and (   ). For our remote ancestors, the wheeling freedom of the giant birds was a (   ) between earth and the supreme place of spirits. The ancient Greeks believed in the (   ). Eagles were released by Zeus and met above Delphi, (   ). There (   ).

Eagles released at the burials of Egyptian pharaohs were thought to carry (   ). The legions of Rome welded together an empire marching (   ). The Iroquois peace dance, Pueblo rain rituals, Northwest totemic art—all acknowledged the (   ) of the "king of birds."

44

Compound Sentences

INTRODUCTION

In this chapter you will examine ways to combine simple sentences. When you have two or more simple sentences on similar topics with thoughts of equal importance, you should try blending them into one sentence. This method of sentence combining is known as *coordination*, and the type of sentence produced is a *compound sentence*.

EXPLANATION

You can combine simple sentences in five ways.
1. Using only a semicolon:

From
The first permanent English settlement in America was at Jamestown, Virginia. It was founded in 1607.

To
The first permanent English settlement in America was at Jamestown, Virginia; it was founded in 1607.

Many inexperienced writers are reluctant to use semicolons because they are afraid of making a punctuation mistake. Before you use a semicolon, make sure your two independent clauses are equally important and are closely related. Had you joined the two simple sentences above with a comma, you would have created a *comma splice*; had you joined them without a punctuation mark, you would have produced a *run-on sentence*. Avoid both the comma splice and the run-on sentence either by leaving the simple sentences as they are or by joining them with a semicolon. (Both run-on sentences and comma splices are discussed in detail in Chapter 56.)
2. Using a colon:

From
For a variety of reasons, the early New England colonists were able to succeed in America.

They possessed the support of strong religious convictions.
They created generally effective local governments.
They drew from apparently endless reserves of determination.

To

For a variety of reasons, the early New England colonists were able to succeed in America: they possessed the support of strong religious convictions, they created generally effective local governments, and they drew from apparently endless reserves of determination.

You can use a colon when one or more independent clauses explain another independent clause. Note that the three final clauses in the above example are a more detailed explanation of the first clause. Because of this fact, a colon is used rather than a semicolon.

Now omit the last two *theys* from the above example sentence. What is the effect? Notice the effect of rewriting the sentence with a coordinating conjunction:

> The early New England colonists were able to succeed in America, for they possessed the support of strong religious convictions, created generally effective local governments, and drew from apparently endless reserves of determination.

If you were to use conjunctive adverbs in the last three clauses, you would make the sentence clearer:

> For a variety of reasons, the early New England colonists were able to succeed in America: notably, they possessed the support of strong religious convictions; also, they created generally effective local governments; finally, they drew from apparently endless reserves of determination.

Even though these sentences are very long, they are still easy to understand. Why? Which of the different versions do you like best? Why?

3. Using a coordinating conjunction. Coordinating conjunctions include *and, but, for, so, nor, or, yet.*

From

The French and Spanish were the most active early explorers of North America east of the Mississippi.
The English established the greatest number of successful colonies there.

To

The French and Spanish were the most active early explorers of North America east of the Mississippi, but the English established the greatest number of successful colonies there.

You use a comma before *but* because the two simple sentences have different subjects, and a coordinating conjunction joins them.

If the simple sentences to be combined are short and very close together in content, you do not need to use a comma:

From

European explorers sought the West Indies.
They found America.

To

European explorers sought the West Indies but they found America.

4. Using correlative conjunctions. Refer to this list of correlative conjunctions when you need to stress the equality of both parts of your sentences: *both . . . and, either . . . or, so . . . as, neither . . . nor, not only . . . but (also), whether . . . or.*

Note: Correlative conjunctions come in pairs. You should use both parts and not mix them—for example, *either . . . nor* would be incorrect usage.

From

English colonists came to America seeking political and religious freedom.
Some also came to make fortunes.

To

Not only did English colonists come to America seeking political and religious freedom, but some also came to make fortunes.

By using correlative conjunctions, you stress the equality of the two parts of your sentence.

5. Using a conjunctive adverb. Here are some frequently used conjunctive adverbs:

accordingly	furthermore	moreover	similarly
additionally	however	namely	still
also	hence	nevertheless	then
anyway	in fact	no	therefore
at any rate	in other words	nonetheless	thus
besides	in short	notably	yes
consequently	indeed	on the contrary	yet
especially	likewise	on the other hand	

From

The Plymouth colonists were not entirely alone in their new world.
Within months of arriving, they were befriended by helpful native Americans.

To

The Plymouth colonists were not entirely alone in their new world; indeed, within months of arriving, they were befriended by helpful native Americans.

OR

The Plymouth colonists were not entirely alone in their new world; within months of arriving, they were, indeed, befriended by helpful native Americans.

Notice how the punctuation marks change when the conjunctive adverb *indeed* is moved. The semicolon and comma are the traditional way to separate the conjunctive adverb from the rest of the sentence. The modern trend, though, is to omit the comma unless its absence would impair the clarity of the sentence.

Both examples above illustrate sentence combining through coordination. Chapter 45 deals with combining independent and dependent clauses by subordination, but it is a good idea at this point for you to examine the difference between coordination and subordination.

In reading the following sentence, notice particularly the use of the subordinating conjunction *because*, which joins the two clauses.

The Plymouth colonists were not entirely alone in their new world, because within months of arriving, they were befriended by helpful native Americans.

Do you see that you cannot move *because* anywhere else in the sentence? This proves that you are not coordinating one element with another; you are subordinating one element to the other. Knowing this difference helps you to punctuate correctly. Remember the following rules:

- Never put a semicolon before a subordinating conjunction.
- Never surround a subordinating conjunction with commas.

Now go back and examine the punctuation in the two sentences in which the conjunctive adverb *indeed* was used.

SENTENCE WORK

Combine each of the groups of simple sentences in *three* different *coordinating* ways. Be careful not to use *subordination*. If you do, although your sentences may be good ones, you will not be gaining practice in using coordination. When you combine your sentences, try to vary your technique so that you practice using all five ways of coordination.

1. Norsemen are believed to have established the earliest European settlement in North America around 1000 A.D.
   They abandoned it after some fifty years of occupation.
2. During the seventeenth century, North America was colonized by religious refugees.
   It was exploited then by commercial adventurers as well.
3. By the middle of the eighteenth century, the English at home were pleased with the growing prosperity of their American colonies.
   At the same time, they were becoming alarmed by the frequent instances of rebellion against their authority.
4. The English antagonized the American colonists in several ways.
   They tried to manage all colonial trade for the benefit of England.
   They subjected the colonists to an unrepresentative bureaucracy.
   They imposed unpopular taxes on a number of products imported into the colonies.
5. During the American Revolution, most colonists fought for independence.
   Some supported the English side.

PARAGRAPH WORK

Write a short paragraph on your personal heritage. Include two compound sentences that use two of the following transitional devices to join your independent clauses.

, and	, but	, for	, yet
;	:	; however,	; moreover,
both . . . and	not only . . . but also	neither . . . nor	either . . . or

Ask your workshop partner to read your paragraph to see whether it contains two compound sentences.

Complex Sentences

INTRODUCTION

If you want to combine important and less important ideas in the same sentence, you can put the less important ideas into dependent clauses. This technique is called *subordination*, and a sentence that has one or more dependent clauses combined with a single independent clause is called a *complex sentence*.

EXPLANATION

A dependent clause is a group of words, containing a subject and a verb, that depends on some other word or words in another clause for its meaning. It is always joined to the other clause by a special connecting word, either a *relative pronoun* or a *subordinating conjunction*.

Relative Pronouns
  that, who, whom, where, what, which, whoever, whichever
Subordinating Conjunctions (with the relation that they indicate)
Time: as, as long as, as soon as, often, before, since, until, when, while
Reason or cause: as, because, inasmuch as, since, why, although, though, if, unless, whether . . . or
Purpose: in order that, so, that, lest
Comparison: than

There are three ways to subordinate through sentence combining. In each of the following examples the dependent clauses are italicized.
1. Treat the dependent clause as if it were a single adjective. An *adjective clause* modifies a noun or pronoun.

From
The modern Olympics have attracted some of America's finest athletes.
The modern Olympics were established in 1896.

To

The modern Olympics, *which were established in 1896*, have attracted some of America's finest athletes.

The dependent clause modifies the noun *Olympics*. Note that it has commas around it because it is not essential to the sentence; if it were left out, the sentence would still make sense.

From

Americans have gained fame at the Olympics.
American Olympic champions include Debbie Armstrong, Scott Hamilton, Mary Lou Retton, Evelyn Ashford, and Carl Lewis.

To

Americans *who have gained fame at the Olympics* include Debbie Armstrong, Scott Hamilton, Mary Lou Retton, Evelyn Ashford, and Carl Lewis.

Which noun does the dependent clause modify? Because it is essential to the sentence, no commas are required. To see if a dependent clause is essential, leave it out and read the rest of the sentence. If it does not make sense, the dependent clause is essential to the sentence; thus, no commas should be used. Does "Americans include Debbie Armstrong, Scott Hamilton, Mary Lou Retton, Evelyn Ashford, and Carl Lewis" need something for it to make complete sense?

From

His name was Phil Mahre.
He was an exceptionally talented skier.
He competed very successfully at the 1984 Winter Olympics.
His home is White Pass, Washington.

To

The exceptionally talented skier *who competed so successfully at the 1984 Winter Olympics* was Phil Mahre, *whose home is White Pass, Washington.*

Why does the first dependent clause not have commas around it while the second one is set off from the rest of the sentence by a comma? Note that all the dependent clauses have been placed as near as possible to the nouns they modify. This is essential when you subordinate with clauses that function as adjectives. Why? If you cannot answer this question, try to move the dependent clauses elsewhere in their sentences. Do they make sense?

2. Treat the dependent clause as if it were a single adverb. An *adverb clause* modifies a verb, adjective, or other adverb.

From

Many tourists will go to Calgary in 1988 to see the Winter Olympics.
The city's best-known tourist attraction is the annual Stampede.

To

Although most tourists will go to Calgary in 1988 to see the Winter Olympics, the city's best-known tourist attraction is the annual Stampede.

The italicized dependent clause works quite differently from those in Number 1. You can move it to other positions in the sentence. Try to move it to see the effect.

Wherever you move it, remember to set it off from the independent clause with commas.

Another feature of this kind of dependent clause is that you may be able to reverse the emphasis in the sentences by subordinating the independent clause and making the dependent clause your main one.

> *Although the city's best-known tourist attraction is the annual Stampede*, most tourists will go to Calgary in 1988 to see the Winter Olympics.

When you use this technique, *you* must decide which idea to subordinate. If you make errors when you subordinate, refer to Chapter 56.

From

The world's enduring ideological conflicts are very powerful.
Nothing is really safe from the pernicious effects of these conflicts.
The modern Olympic Games have been as much a political confrontation as an athletic competition.

To

Because the world's enduring ideological conflicts are very powerful and *because nothing is really safe from the pernicious effects of these conflicts*, the modern Olympic Games have been as much a political confrontation as an athletic competition.

Could you move the two dependent clauses to other positions? Is it necessary to repeat the subordinating conjunction *because*? What word do both the dependent clauses modify?

3. Treat the dependent clause as if it were a noun or pronoun. (Remember that a noun or pronoun can do many things in a sentence, so a clause that functions as a noun or pronoun is extremely versatile.) Such a dependent clause is often referred to as a *noun clause*.

From

The 1980 and 1984 Summer Olympics were boycotted by many countries.
The boycott caused those games to be less successful than those of previous years.

To

The boycott of the 1980 and 1984 Summer Olympics by many countries was *what caused those games to be less successful than those of previous years.*

Notice that in the dependent clause the subject is *what* and the verb is *caused*. You can find subjects and verbs in all clauses. If you were to rewrite this sentence without a dependent clause, you would write something like this:

> The boycott of the 1980 and 1984 Summer Olympics by many countries caused those games to be less successful than those of previous years.

Now the sentence is a simple sentence with only one subject, *boycott*, and one verb, *caused*.

From

A person may wish to compete in the Olympics.
He or she must possess physical skill, mental determination, and an athletic spirit.

To

Whoever wishes to compete in the Olympics must possess physical skill, mental determination, and an athletic spirit.

The italicized dependent clause functions as the subject of the verb *must possess* in the same way that the pronoun *you* would. The dependent clause begins with the relative pronoun *whoever*.

From

The International Olympic Committee requires one thing of athletes.
Competing athletes must be true amateurs.

To

The International Olympic Committee requires *that competing athletes be true amateurs.*

What single noun or pronoun could replace the dependent clause?

From

The title "greatest swimmer of all time" must go to someone.
That person would have to beat Mark Spitz's record of seven Olympic gold medals.

To

The title "greatest swimmer of all time" must go to *whoever beats Mark Spitz's record of seven Olympic gold medals.*

Name the subject and verb in the italicized dependent clause. Do you see that the noun clause is the object of the preposition *to*?

SENTENCE WORK

Although there are a number of ways to combine sentences, in this exercise you should do so by producing (a) one single independent clause and (b) one or more dependent clauses. Your dependent clauses should begin with either a relative pronoun or a subordinating conjunction. Think your sentences through carefully so you do not have any faulty subordination. If one of your sentences does not make complete sense, rewrite it. After completing each of your sentences, identify the kind of dependent clause(s) that you used: adjective, adverb, or noun.

1. Evelyn Ashford continues to win sprint races.
   Injuries have often prevented her from consistently competing in top form.

2. Baseball is supposedly America's very own national game.
   The Summer Olympics demonstration tournament showed that many countries from around the globe have strong baseball teams.
   These teams seem dedicated to making "our" game the world's.

3. The Soviet Union was boycotted as host of the 1980 Olympic Games.
   They decided to boycott the U.S.-hosted 1984 Games.
   This led some people to demand something.
   The Olympics should no longer be held in some countries.
   Those countries tend to provoke gestures of protest from political adversaries.

4. Nadia Comaneci is a gymnast from Romania.
   She scored a perfect ten during the 1976 Olympics in Montreal.

5. Native American Jim Thorpe's Olympic decathlon and pentathlon gold medals were withdrawn.

He had committed a minor infraction of the rules governing athletes' amateur status.

The medals were returned to his family seventy years later, in 1982.

6. The regular breaking of Olympic records makes a strong suggestion.
   It suggests that the final limits of athletic achievement cannot be determined.
   It suggests that men and women would have to end athletic competition to finally determine the limits.

7. Windgliding on sailboards is not widely recognized as a competitive sport.
   It was premiered in the 1984 Summer Games as a sailing event.
   It attracted both curious and enthusiastic spectators.

8. Anyone can examine the list of sites for the modern Olympics.
   Something will be noticed.
   The U.S. has had the honor of hosting the Summer Games three times and the Winter Games three times.

PARAGRAPH WORK

Convert the independent clauses in parentheses to dependent clauses. *Note:* Punctuation has not been included; therefore, you must decide whether to insert commas to separate the dependent clauses from the independent clauses. Here is an example:

From

The modern Olympic Games (the modern Olympic Games began less than one hundred years ago) are in their infancy compared with the life span of the ancient Olympics.

To

The modern Olympic Games, which began less than one hundred years ago, are in their infancy compared with the life span of the ancient Olympics.

The ancient Olympic Games (the ancient Olympic Games only slightly resemble the modern ones) probably began nearly three thousand years ago (three thousand years ago was the time runners gathered to race at Olympia). (Some historians believe this: the games were held as much as centuries earlier) no certain date for an earlier starting point has been established. These early games were actually held to celebrate the festival of Herakles (Herakles was a god) (Herakles raised the infant Zeus). The Eleans (the Eleans lived on the plains of Olympia) originated this festival (this festival eventually became the occasion for all of the Greek city-states to meet in athletic competition). (Lambs, wine, and grain were sacrificed to Zeus on the first day of competition) it seems that the games had as much religious significance (the games had as much athletic excitement). In any case, the games (the games drew spectators) (the spectators lived in all regions of the Mediterranean) evidently were immensely popular (the games were staged some 320 times over a period of about 1200 years).

Athletes took solemn oaths (the games started after the oaths) (the oaths the athletes took said they would compete as honest sportsmen). The contests (all agreed) had to be impartially judged (impartially judged contests ensured something) (well-deserved glory was granted to a champion) (a champion demonstrated superiority in fair competition) (winners were crowned with wreaths of "sacred" olive). Apparently the respect for and dedication to these competitions in running, discus throwing, javelin throwing, jumping, boxing, and wrestling were strong enough to keep the ancient Olympic Games vital from 776 B.C. to A.D. 394 (this makes them one of our most long-lasting institutions). Perhaps the modern Olympics have begun a new tradition (this will prove equally durable).

46

Compound-Complex Sentences

INTRODUCTION

This chapter is a combination of the previous two chapters (44 and 45). If you are not familiar with them, you really should not continue with this chapter. If you have completed them, however, you will find this one quite easy.

If you write a sentence containing at least two independent clauses and at least one dependent clause, you will have a *compound-complex sentence*. This kind of sentence is very useful when you wish to include a great deal of information within a single sentence.

EXPLANATION

1. When you create a compound-complex sentence, you must make sure to punctuate it carefully so that your reader will not become confused. What you must do, which can be a bit complicated at first, is to follow the rules for both compound and complex sentences. So, as you go through this chapter, pay particular attention to the punctuation. Notice the various parts of the following compound-complex sentences.

From
The history of American blacks is filled with distinguished achievements.
Much of this history was widely ignored until the 1960s.
The civil rights movement focused attention on the rightful place of blacks in our society.

To
The history of American blacks is filled with distinguished achievements, but *much of this history was widely ignored until the 1960s*, when the civil rights movement focused attention on the rightful place of blacks in our society.

The two independent clauses are italicized. What are the subject and verb of each of them? What coordinating conjunction joins them? What is the dependent clause? What are its subject and verb? What subordinating conjunction joins it to the other clauses?

So that you can clearly see the different kinds of sentences that went into the previous compound-complex sentence, notice the effect created when the sentences are combined separately. What is absent from each?

Compound Sentence

The history of American blacks is filled with distinguished achievements, but much of this history was widely ignored until the 1960s.

Complex Sentence

Much of this history was widely ignored until the 1960s, when the civil rights movement focused attention on the rightful place of blacks in our society.

The compound sentence has two independent clauses; the complex sentence has one independent and one dependent clause.

2. Now examine how the following sentences have been combined to make a compound-complex sentence.

From

Paul Laurence Dunbar was the first nationally recognized black American poet.
There were earlier black poets.
Their published work gained less fame.

To

Paul Laurence Dunbar was the first nationally recognized black American poet, but there were earlier black poets whose work gained less fame.

In what other way could you combine the above sentences so that you would still have a compound-complex sentence?

Can you separate the four clauses in each of the two combined sentences below? There are two dependent and two independent clauses in each case. Pick out the subject and verb in each clause.

From

Admiral Peary was the leader of the 1909 expedition that discovered the North Pole.
Matthew Alexander Henson was the black expedition member who actually first set foot there.

To

Admiral Peary was the leader of the 1909 expedition that discovered the North Pole, yet *Matthew Alexander Henson was the black expedition member* who actually first set foot there.

From

Harriet Tubman worked with the so-called Underground Railroad.
The Underground Railroad brought thousands of slaves to freedom before the Civil War.
In her work she constantly risked her own freedom.
She was herself an escaped slave.

To
Harriet Tubman worked with the so-called Underground Railroad, which brought thousands of slaves to freedom before the Civil War, and *in her work she constantly risked her own freedom*, because she was herself an escaped slave.

Besides having two independent clauses, the following sentence has a long dependent clause. In order for the various parts of the dependent clause to be clear to the reader, they are arranged in a logical order. Can you think of a better order?

From
Blacks have always appeared in television shows, but their status has changed since the 1950s.
Amos 'N' Andy represented blacks as buffoons in the 1950s.
In the 1960s, Bill Cosby was a legitimate co-star on *I Spy*.
In the 1970s, a number of shows starring blacks became successful.
In the 1980s, some of the most popular shows are made up of only black actors.

To
Blacks have always appeared in television shows, but *their status has changed since the 1950s* when *Amos 'N' Andy* represented blacks as buffoons, to the 1960s when Bill Cosby was a legitimate co-star on *I Spy*, to the 1970s when a number of shows starring blacks became successful, to the 1980s when some of the most popular shows are made up of black actors.

SENTENCE WORK

Combine the sentences in each of the following groups to create a compound-complex sentence. Make sure each sentence has at least two independent clauses and one dependent clause. Watch your punctuation.

1. Duke Ellington wrote numerous immensely popular jazz compositions.
   These compositions have been played and recorded frequently.
   We have come to recognize them as jazz standards.

2. Vanessa Williams was indeed the first black to become Miss America.
   She was also the first black given the chance to prove she deserved that title.
   This has made her experience a test as well as an honor.

3. Jesse Jackson was the first black to mount a serious national campaign for the Democratic presidential nomination.
   He did not win.
   His efforts helped open the political process for minority participation at the highest level.

4. Eddie Murphy became one of the most popular members of the *Saturday Night Live* television show.
   He is only in his early twenties.
   A bright comedy star was born.

5. Martin Luther King, Jr. first rose to national prominence in 1955 as a leader of the Montgomery, Alabama, public transportation boycott.

He began leading his nonviolent crusade for black civil rights.
He pursued his crusade tirelessly until his assassination in 1968.

PARAGRAPH WORK

Fill in the blanks with an independent clause or a dependent clause so that each sentence is compound-complex. Check carefully that each has two independent clauses and at least one dependent clause. To help you fill in the blanks, use the material from these simple sentences:

King was a devout pacifist.

His greatest triumph of nonviolent protest came during a massive demonstration in Washington, D.C., on August 28, 1963.

His "I have a dream" speech is recognized as the greatest oration of the civil rights movement.

Martin Luther King, Jr., [who . . .], was convinced of the need for a broad civil rights movement based on a philosophy of determined pacifism; therefore, he organized the nonviolent Southern Christian Leadership Conference to head this movement in 1957. With the SCLC behind him, King peacefully led numerous demonstrations throughout the South, where he focused the movement's efforts; [but . . .]. Two hundred fifty thousand Americans gathered in the nation's capital that day, and they heard King give his stunning "I have a dream" speech, [which . . .].

Prepositional Phrases

INTRODUCTION

In this chapter you will examine ways to pare down a dependent or an independent clause into a *prepositional phrase*. This is another one of the various ways to combine sentences. *Warning*: Stringing together too many prepositional phrases will produce tedious writing and a confused and bored reader.

EXPLANATION

A prepositional phrase always begins with a preposition. Whether it is short or long, a prepositional phrase functions as a single adjective or adverb. In the following combined sentence, the prepositional phrase is italicized:

From
John F. Kennedy was a United States president.
He was vigorous and determined.

To
John F. Kennedy was a United States president *of vigor and determination*.

The italicized phrase acts as an adjective and modifies *president*.

Prepositional phrases follow the principles of subordination in exactly the same way as do dependent clauses. Like dependent clauses, prepositional phrases can be essential or nonessential to a sentence. Remember, essential phrases are not separated by commas, whereas nonessential ones often are.

Notice how concise the following combined sentences are because of the use of prepositional phrases:

From
Kennedy's family was large and close-knit.
His parents, brothers, and sisters supported and advanced his political aspirations.

To

With a large and close-knit family, Kennedy had his political aspirations supported and advanced *by his parents, brothers, and sisters.*

From

Winning the presidency did not begin Kennedy's political career.
He was first a congressman and then a senator.

To

Before winning the presidency, Kennedy was first a congressman and then a senator.

From

He was a World War II naval officer.
The Pacific is where he served.

To

During World War II, he was a naval officer *in the Pacific.*

Where else could you move any of the above prepositional phrases? Can you make any of the sentences more emphatic by relocating the phrases? As you read other combined sentences, try to move the phrases into various positions.

If you find that you can get rid of a clause by using a prepositional phrase and still *keep the original sense*, then do so. Notice the following pairs of sentences. Decide which is more effective.

From

Kennedy was an avid reader, and he had a special interest in history and biography.

To

Kennedy was an avid reader, *with a special interest / in history and biography.* (*Note*: two prepositional phrases)

From

When he was a boy, he learned to love the sea as he spent time sailing off the coast of Massachusetts.

To

During his boyhood, he learned to love the sea *while spending time sailing / off the coast / of Massachusetts.* (four phrases)

From

He met Jacqueline Bouvier when he was in Washington, and they were married on September 12, 1953.

To

In Washington, he met Jacqueline Bouvier, *to whom he was married / on September 12, 1953.* (three phrases)

Notice that the prepositional phrases in the last example have been separated from the rest of the sentence by commas. Why?

A prepositional phrase may contain a dependent clause or a verbal phrase. Which one of the sentences above contains a dependent clause? Which a verbal phrase?

Including clauses and verbal phrases in your prepositional phrases will give your writing variety and will allow you to use the various word groups in endless combinations.

SENTENCE WORK

Use prepositional phrases to join or pare down these sentences. Then underline all of the prepositional phrases.

1. Kennedy served in the United States Navy, where he was a torpedo boat commander.

2. Kennedy wrote a book called *Profiles in Courage*.
   It won nationwide acclaim.
   It was awarded the Pulitzer Prize in 1957.

3. Kennedy became a congressman in 1947.
   It was the first time he was elected to public office, and he represented Massachusetts.

4. In 1960, when he was forty-three, he defeated Richard Nixon and became president.

5. Kennedy gave a brilliant speech on Inauguration Day.
   He was able to inspire Americans with a sense of hope and purpose for the country's future.

6. Kennedy, who was from the liberal wing of the Democratic party, proposed sweeping new civil rights legislation, an increase in Social Security benefits, and medical care for the elderly when he became president.

7. While he was president, Kennedy became widely known because he was witty and intelligent.

8. After John F. Kennedy was assassinated, his death was deeply mourned throughout the entire country, which recognized a great and tragic loss.

PARAGRAPH WORK

Write a paragraph about some aspect of John F. Kennedy's life or how he changed American thinking. Underline every prepositional phrase you use, trying to include both short and long phrases in emphatic positions. (When you finish, ask your workshop partner to suggest possible ways of creating more prepositional phrases within your paragraph or repositioning a prepositional phrase to gain greater emphasis.) Here are two possible beginnings for your paragraph work:

Of all the problems Kennedy faced during his presidency, the Cuban Missile Crisis of 1962 was among the most challenging. . . .

or

"Ask not what your country can do for you, but what you can do for your country" will be remembered as a cry / for a change / in values / from the "gimme-gimme" mentality / of the 1950s. . . .

48

Verbal Phrases

INTRODUCTION

The verbal phrase is a useful word group to use in combining sentences. Mastering the varied uses of the verbal phrase will be well worth your efforts, since a verbal phrase allows you to be brief and emphatic. In this chapter you will examine ways to pare down a dependent clause, or even an independent clause, into a verbal phrase.

EXPLANATION

1. A *verbal* has the qualities of a verb in all respects except one: a verbal cannot stand alone as a sentence.

Verb

Seek. Discover. Establish. (*You* is the understood subject of each verb.)

Verbal

Seeking. To discover. Having established. (Adding *you* would not make sense.)

Like a verb, a verbal can take modifiers (single words, phrases, or clauses), and in some cases it can even have a subject. A verbal and its related words are called a *verbal phrase*, but even a verbal phrase cannot stand alone. It always requires a word in the rest of the sentence to complete its sense. All the following verbal phrases are fragments:

- Seeking a route to the riches of the Indies
- To discover the fabled El Dorado and the fountain of eternal youth
- Having established themselves in North and South America by the sixteenth century

For a verbal phrase to make sense it requires other words—for example:

- *Seeking a route to the riches of the Indies* drove the early Spanish explorers across the Atlantic to the New World.
- *To discover the fabled El Dorado and the fountain of eternal youth* was the Spanish explorers' great ambition.

- *Having established themselves in North and South America by the sixteenth century*, the Spanish people can rightfully be called the first Europeans to have settled in the New World.

Read over the following verbal phrases:

- Often referred to as Hispanics
- To sail around the Cape of Good Hope
- Having searched in vain for the fountain of youth
- Fighting off English privateers such as Sir Francis Drake
- While marching through the jungles of Peru

They, too, require other words to complete their sense—for example:

- *Often referred to as Hispanics*, Mexican Americans, Cuban Americans, Puerto Ricans, and all other Spanish-speaking people make up the second largest minority group in the United States.

Add words to the other four verbal phrases above so that you make sense of them. The words can come *before* or *after* the verbal phrase.

2. When a verbal or verbal phrase is within a complete sentence, it *always* relates to a word in the rest of the sentence. It may function as an adjective or adverb and modify, or it may function as a noun and connect itself to a verb or a preposition. The verbal, then, is extremely versatile.

3. Verbals can modify in the same way as do adjectives. The verbals in the following sentences are called *participles*. You can use them in sentence combining as follows:

From
The Spanish conquistadors marched through Central and South America.
They encountered the Incas, Aztecs, and other native peoples.
They conquered them.
They brought them the benefits of civilization.
They taught them the elements of Christianity.

To
Conquering, civilizing, and *Christianizing,* the Spanish conquistadors marched through Central and South America, encountering the Incas, Aztecs, and other native peoples.

From
The Spanish ruled over the Aztec empire in Mexico by the mid-sixteenth century.
By this time the Aztec empire was weakened.
The Spanish also established a settlement in Santa Fe, New Mexico.
This settlement thrived.
The Pilgrims did not land at Plymouth Rock for another seventy years.

To
By the mid-sixteenth century, the Spanish not only ruled over the *weakened* Aztec empire in Mexico, but also established a *thriving* settlement in Santa Fe, New Mexico; the Pilgrims did not land at Plymouth Rock for another seventy years.

From

The native Americans had been weakened by battles with the Spanish settlers.
They suffered from the white settlers' diseases.
They were exploited by the Spanish.
They still managed to drive the settlers out of Arizona and Texas in the early 1700s.
The Spanish had been living there for a century.

To

Though *weakened*, *diseased*, and *exploited*, native Americans in the early 1700s still managed to drive Spanish settlers, who had lived there for a century, out of Arizona and Texas.

The verbals known as *infinitives* can also modify.

From

Spain conquered the New World easily.
Spain ruled the New World with difficulty.

To

Spain found the New World easy *to conquer*, but difficult *to rule*.

From

The conquistadors introduced a new way of living for the native Americans.
They could not accept this new way easily.

To

The way of living introduced by the conquistadors was not easy for the native Americans *to accept*.

4. Verbal phrases can modify in the same way as do adjective phrases. The verbal phrases used in combining the following sentences are called *participial phrases*.

From

People from the American South moved to Texas in large numbers in the 1820s.
They abandoned their plantations.
They were lured by promises of abundant, fertile land.

To

Abandoning their plantations and *lured by promises of abundant, fertile land*, southerners moved to Texas in large numbers in the 1820s.

From

Distrust between Mexicans and Texans caused numerous boundary clashes after Mexico's conquest of the Alamo.
This distrust was based on political and cultural differences.

To

Distrust between Mexicans and Texans, *based on political and cultural differences*, caused numerous boundary clashes after Mexico's conquest of the Alamo.

From

Many Mexicans expressed uneasiness when half their territory was ceded to the United States.
They were angered by Mexico's loss of the lands where their ancestors had settled centuries before.
They were overwhelmed by Americans in search of gold.

To
Angered by Mexico's loss of the lands where their ancestors had settled centuries before and *overwhelmed by Americans in search of gold*, many Mexicans expressed uneasiness when the United States ceded half their territory.

The verbal phrases used in combining the following sentences are called *infinitive phrases*. Note that the first infinitive phrase functions as an adverb, while the second functions as an adjective.

From
Woodrow Wilson sent American troops into Mexico in 1916.
He thought Pancho Villa's raids into the United States should stop.

To
Woodrow Wilson sent American troops into Mexico in 1916 *to stop Pancho Villa's raids into the United States.*

From
Since the 1920s, Mexicans have thought of the United States.
They have wanted better jobs there.
They have wanted higher wages there.

To
Since the 1920s, Mexicans have thought of the United States as the place *to find better jobs and higher wages.*

EXERCISE ONE

Which word do each of the italicized verbal phrases in the combined sentences in Numbers 3 and 4 above modify? If you have trouble with any of them, look at the Suggested Answers following Chapter 55.

5. When you use a verbal or verbal phrase that modifies, you must make sure that it comes next to the word that it describes and that it is set off by commas. If it does not come near the word it describes, it will probably confuse the reader. Such a verbal or verbal phrase is called a *misplaced modifier*. If it appears in a sentence where there is no word for it to modify, it is called a *dangling modifier*. If you regularly make these errors when using verbals, refer to Chapter 56.

Look over the following pairs of sentences. The first sentence contains a well-positioned dependent clause; the second a well-positioned verbal phrase. Find the words they modify.

   a. *Because they share a border with Mexico*, California and Texas have the largest Mexican-American, or Chicano, populations in the United States.

   Sharing a border with Mexico, California and Texas have the largest Mexican-American, or Chicano, populations in the United States.

   b. Many Chicanos work as migrant farm laborers, *who enable farmers all over the country to harvest crops efficiently*.

   Many Chicanos work as migrant farm laborers, *enabling farmers all over the country to harvest crops efficiently*.

c. *When he attempted to organize farm workers in California*, Cesar Chavez gained nationwide attention *when he persuaded many Americans / that they should boycott California grapes.*

Attempting to organize farm workers in California and *persuading many Americans / to boycott California grapes*, Cesar Chavez gained nationwide attention.

Rewrite the following sentences by changing the dependent clauses to more emphatic verbal phrases:

a. *Because they have gained political power*, Mexican-Americans such as San Antonio Mayor Henry Cisneros are finally being listened to by Anglos.

b. *Since he has pitched brilliantly for the Los Angeles Dodgers*, Fernando Valenzuela has become a sports hero to his fellow Chicanos.

When you compose your verbal phrases, compare them with the two in the Suggested Answers following Chapter 55.

EXERCISE TWO

Tighten or combine the following sentences by using verbals or verbal phrases that modify. Hints are given after each item. You are to begin each verbal phrase with the word(s) in parentheses. Make sure you place each verbal or verbal phrase near the word it describes and set each apart from the rest of the sentence by using commas.

a. After he had sailed with Columbus in 1493, Ponce de Leon returned to the Caribbean in 1508 and claimed Puerto Rico for Spain. (Having sailed, claiming)

b. Puerto Rico was ceded to the United States by Spain in 1898 and became a self-governing commonwealth in 1952. (Ceded)

c. Puerto Ricans have enjoyed the opportunity of unrestricted immigration to the United States mainland, and thousands have come in hopes that they will find a better life. (Having enjoyed, hoping, to find)

d. Leonard Bernstein updated the *Romeo and Juliet* story to contemporary New York in *West Side Story*.
He portrayed the dreams of young Puerto Rican immigrants. (portraying)

e Some Puerto Ricans, who favor statehood or even independence for the commonwealth, have formed political parties; others, unfortunately, have chosen violent means of demanding change. (favoring, to demand)

Before you continue with the next portion of this chapter, make sure you have combined or tightened the above sentences correctly. Check your responses with the ones in the Suggested Answers following Chapter 55.

6. Verbals and verbal phrases can also function as nouns. Verbals that end in *ing* and function as nouns are called *gerunds*. Here are some examples of how you might use gerunds:

From,
Columbus's first voyage to the New World resulted in the discovery of Cuba. He also claimed Cuba for Spain.

To
Columbus's first voyage to the New World resulted in the *discovering* and *claiming* of Cuba for Spain.

From
Columbus made four voyages across the Atlantic.
He devoted his life to that of an explorer.

To
Exploring was Columbus's life—he made four voyages across the Atlantic.

Verbal phrases that contain a gerund and function as nouns are called *gerundial phrases*. Here are some examples:

From
Cubans suffered under Spanish rule.
This prompted American intervention in 1898.

To
The suffering of the Cubans under Spanish rule prompted American intervention in 1898.

From
Teddy Roosevelt was the commander of the Rough Riders.
They stormed Cuba's San Juan Hill.
Roosevelt was also to become a president.

To
Commanding the Rough Riders and *storming Cuba's San Juan Hill* were two of the early exploits of future President Teddy Roosevelt.

From
Franklin D. Roosevelt declared a "Good Neighbor" policy toward Latin America.
He eased relations with Cuba and other Latin American countries.

To
By *declaring his "Good Neighbor" policy toward Latin America*, Franklin D. Roosevelt eased relations with Cuba and other Latin American countries.

Note that the *infinitive* is the most versatile of the verbals. It can function as an adjective, an adverb, or a noun:

- Americans in the 1940s and 1950s considered Havana's nightclubs excellent places *to celebrate*. (adjective)
- Many Americans found the Bay of Pigs invasion impossible *to defend*. (adverb)
- According to President Kennedy, the Soviet Union's purpose in sending missiles to Cuba in 1962 was *to intimidate* and *to provoke*. (nouns)

The *infinitive phrases* in the following examples function as nouns:

From
If people wanted to escape from Fidel Castro's Cuba, they had to travel across the open ocean in a small boat and risked sinking or capture by the Cuban navy.

To
To escape from Fidel Castro's Cuba was *to travel across the open ocean in a small boat* and *to risk sinking or capture by the Cuban navy*.

From

When driving through some parts of Miami, you might think you are in Havana.

To

To drive through some parts of Miami is *to think you are in Havana.*

Did you notice that the italicized verbals and verbal phrases in the examples above generally have no commas to set them off from the rest of the sentence? The reason for this is that they do not modify; they function as nouns. Both infinitives (functioning as nouns) and gerunds are directly connected to either the verb or a preposition. Because you would not put a comma before or after *is* in the sentence "Miami is like Havana," you should not put a comma before or after *is* in the sentence *"To drive through some parts of Miami* is *to think you are in Havana."*

7. When you compose sentences with verbals or verbal phrases that function as nouns, you will seldom make the mistake of misplacing them or letting them dangle. There is, however, one instance where this might happen. When a gerund phrase immediately follows a preposition, the entire phrase functions just as a modifier does. Therefore, it needs to be near the word it modifies. If there is no word for it to modify, it can easily dangle.

A dangling phrase occurs most often when the verb is in the passive voice. Using active voice, therefore, will make dangling phrases less likely. If you regularly make such errors, refer to Chapter 56.

In the following examples, note two things: the gerundial phrases are part of a prepositional phrase and the prepositional phrase modifies a word in the rest of the sentence. Find the word each prepositional phrase modifies.

- By *allowing the entry of the so-called Marielitos*, President Carter greatly increased the Cuban-American population.

- In *agreeing in 1984 to take back some of the Marielitos*, Fidel Castro might have been indicating a desire for friendlier Cuban-American relations.

EXERCISE THREE

Combine, tighten, or change each of the following items by using a verbal or verbal phrase so that it functions as a noun. Watch your punctuation. (Words are provided in parentheses to get you started.)

a. When they look to the United States as a refuge from political and economic turmoil in their homelands, Central Americans follow a centuries-old tradition. (In looking to the United States)

b. Because some immigrants know little or no English, this means that they must attend special schools to become fluent. (Some immigrants' knowing)

c. Since they have been exposed to Hispanic-American culture, many high-school students have decided to study Spanish as their second language. (Through being exposed)

d. When students examine the Hispanic culture, they learn that it is the second oldest in the United States. (In examining)

e. America has focused on the British literary tradition.
   The result of this has been that we have nearly ignored such Spanish writers as García Lorca and Lope de Vega. (America's having focused . . . has resulted in our ignoring)

f. It is a fact that no comprehensive collection of Hispanic literature exists at the moment.
   This is unfortunate for all students. (The fact of no . . . literature's existing)

Do not continue with this chapter until you have checked your answers with the suggested ones following Chapter 55.

8. Using a verbal phrase correctly can add distinction to your writing style; using one incorrectly shows you in poor light. In order to appreciate verbals and their functions so that you do not make errors, spend a few minutes examining the differences between these pairs of sentences. The first verbal phrase in each pair is a participial phrase (functioning as an adjective, modifying a noun, requiring commas); the second in each pair is a gerundial phrase (functioning as a noun, connecting directly to a verb, requiring no commas).

Participial Verbal Phrase

Hispanic-American singers and musicians, *sharing their unique talents with audiences throughout the world*, are performers of whom we can all be proud.

Gerundial Verbal Phrase

Hispanic-American singers' and musicians' sharing of their unique talents with audiences throughout the world makes them performers of whom we can all be proud.

Participial Verbal Phrase

José Feliciano, *performing such hits as "Light My Fire" and "Malagueña,"* has had his records become million sellers.

Gerundial Verbal Phrase

José Feliciano's performing of such hits as "Light My Fire" and "Malagueña" has made his records million sellers.

Participial Verbal Phrase

Dynamic Rita Moreno, *having won an Oscar, a Tony, a Grammy, and an Emmy*, is probably best known as a performer on TV's *The Electric Company*.

Gerundial Verbal Phrase

Dynamic Rita Moreno's winning of an Oscar, a Tony, a Grammy, and an Emmy has not overshadowed what is probably her best-known role, as a performer on TV's *The Electric Company*.

EXERCISE FOUR

Combine these sentences in two ways: first by using a participial phrase, then by using a gerundial phrase. Watch your punctuation. When you finish, compare your sentences with those provided in the Suggested Answers following Chapter 55.

   a. Lee Trevino won the U.S., British, and Canadian Open golf championships in a row.

     This feat brought "Super Mex" to the attention of thousands of golf fans.

   b. Anthony Quinn has portrayed Greeks, Italians, native Americans, and many other nationalities.

     He is proud of his Hispanic ancestry.

   c. The members of the popular Puerto Rican singing group Menudo reach the age of sixteen.

     At this time they must leave the group.

PARAGRAPH WORK

Rewrite this short paragraph, making it more concise and emphatic by using verbals and verbal phrases.

Many Americans who live in areas with sizable Hispanic populations realize that there are hundreds of Spanish-speaking media in our country. Others are less exposed, and they have not yet discovered how widespread the Spanish influence is. Only two TV network situation comedies, *Chico and the Man*, which was cut short by the tragic death of its star, Freddie Prinze, and *AKA Pablo*, which was conceived by innovative producer Norman Lear, have featured Hispanic stars. We look forward to future opportunities so that we can learn more about Hispanic culture.

49

Absolute Phrases

INTRODUCTION

In this chapter you will examine ways to add a descriptive or narrative detail to a sentence by introducing an *absolute phrase*. Used regularly by professional writers, the absolute phrase is often shunned by beginning writers. But once you have mastered the absolute phrase, your writing will take on a new and interesting dimension.

EXPLANATION

1. You should learn the several ways of constructing absolute phrases so that you will be able to use them with confidence and purpose. First, examine the following sentences. The absolute phrases are underlined. Notice that (a) they add details to a word in the rest of the sentence, and (b) they are always set off from the rest of the sentence by commas.

- Many of the most successful films in recent years have been science fiction, *Star Wars, Return of the Jedi, E.T., the Extra-Terrestrial,* and the *Star Trek* films being some of the best known.
- His bullwhip cracking in the air, his distinctive hat pulled down low, Harrison Ford has become one of the screen's most popular heroes as Indiana Jones.
- The Marx brothers, their comedy routines and imaginative shenanigans world famous, made their best films in the 1930s.

Now take a look at each absolute phrase so you can recognize one when you see it. First of all, it has a subject. The subjects in the absolute phrases above are all the movie names in the first sentence, *bullwhip* and *hat* in the second, and *routines* and *shenanigans* in the third.

Absolute phrases do not have full verbs; that is why they are phrases, not clauses. Some have verbals; some have none. The verbals in the absolute phrases in the first two sentences above are *being, cracking* and *pulled.* The absolute phrase in the third sentence above has no verbal.

By supplying a verb or part of a verb to each absolute phrase, you could easily compose a full independent clause—for example:

* *Star Wars*, *Return of the Jedi*, *E.T.*, *the Extra-Terrestrial*, and the *Star Trek* films *are* some of the best known.
* His bullwhip *cracked* in the air.
* His distinctive hat *was pulled* down low.
* Their comedy routines and imaginative shenanigans *were* world famous.

You can create an absolute phrase by reversing the procedure: in some cases, remove the verb from an independent clause; in other cases, change the verb to a verbal. Once you have created an absolute phrase, you can place it in the sentence so that it adds a descriptive or narrative detail to a noun you want to modify. Absolute phrases, therefore, function exactly as adjectives.

2. Notice how to combine sentences by using absolute phrases:

From

The film *Kramer vs. Kramer* established Meryl Streep as an outstanding dramatic actress.
She has gone on to play dramatic roles in such films as *The French Lieutenant's Woman*, *Sophie's Choice*, and *Silkwood*.

To

The film *Kramer vs. Kramer* having established her as an outstanding dramatic actress, Meryl Streep has gone on to play dramatic roles in such films as *The French Lieutenant's Woman*, *Sophie's Choice*, and *Silkwood*.

From

John Travolta has been unable to top his success in *Saturday Night Fever*.
His dancing, macho image is well known.

To

John Travolta, his dancing, macho image well known, has been unable to top his success in *Saturday Night Fever*.

How have the above two absolute phrases been created? What verbs have been deleted or changed?

3. Now examine how to tighten longer sentences by changing dependent clauses to absolute phrases.

From

Sylvester Stallone, after his *Rocky* films had become smash hits, has been able to pursue an active writing and directing career, which has had its ups and downs.

To

Sylvester Stallone, his *Rocky* films having become smash hits, has been able to pursue an active writing and directing career, which has had its ups and downs.

Tightened Further by Removing the Verbal

Sylvester Stallone, his *Rocky* films smash hits, has been able to pursue an active writing and directing career, which has had its ups and downs.

4. By including several absolute phrases in a single sentence, you can be more concise than you would be if you include the details in several sentences or clauses. In the following example, note as well the effect created by moving a cluster of absolute phrases.

At the Beginning
Their eyes shining, their hearts palpitating, their voices screaming his name, fans all over the world worshipped American singer and movie star Elvis Presley.

At the End
Fans all over the world worshipped American singer and movie star Elvis Presley, *their eyes shining, their hearts palpitating, their voices screaming his name.*

For practice in making up some absolute phrases, continue the sentence about Elvis by filling in the blanks:

... their voices screaming his name, their arms _____ , their ears _____ , their stomachs _____ , their psyches _____ , their toenails _____ .

Do you see that you can create absolute phrases by subdividing the subject, in this case *fans*, into an infinite number of parts?

5. Besides adding several absolute phrases to a sentence, you will be able to add other word groups as well. Such is the flexibility of absolute phrases.

From
Doug Henning, indeed, performs remarkable feats of magic.
He skillfully makes tigers and elephants disappear.
He astounds theatre, nightclub, and television audiences.
He is also thrilling movie fans.

To
Astounding theatre, nightclub, and television audiences as well as thrilling movie fans, Doug Henning, *his skill making tigers and elephants disappear,* indeed, performs remarkable feats of magic. (Which of the italicized phrases is an absolute phrase? Which is a participial phrase?)

From
Paul Newman is familiar to millions.
He has sparkling blue eyes.
He has a shining, white-toothed smile.
He is an all-American guy.

To
An all-American guy, Paul Newman, *his blue eyes sparkling, his white-toothed smile shining,* is familiar to millions. (Which of the italicized word groups is not an absolute phrase?)

6. Besides merely adding details, absolute phrases can suggest relationships of cause and effect:

From
William Shatner was the logical choice to play Captain Kirk in *Star Trek—The Motion Picture.*
The television show of *Star Trek* has been syndicated all over the world.
William Shatner's face and exploits are known to thousands of devoted "Trekkies."

To

Because his television show has been syndicated all over the world and *because his face and exploits are known to thousands of devoted "Trekkies,"* William Shatner was the logical choice to play Captain Kirk in *Star Trek—The Motion Picture.* (A natural cause-and-effect relationship is created using dependent clauses.)

Notice, however, the conciseness of the cause-and-effect relationship when absolute phrases are used:

His television show syndicated all over the world, his face and exploits known to thousands of devoted "Trekkies," William Shatner was the logical choice to play Captain Kirk in *Star Trek—The Motion Picture.*

SENTENCE WORK

Tighten or combine these sentences by using absolute phrases.

1. Once they have made small fortunes and their "greatness" has been established with one hit film, some actors and actresses will find it impossible ever to recapture their first success.

2. Ronald Reagan has gained one of the world's highest offices—president of the United States.
   His career as an actor began in the 1930s.

3. Bruce Lee was the hero of several martial-arts movies.
   His face seldom wore a smile.
   His hands and feet were always flying.

4. Katharine Hepburn has received more Academy Award nominations and Oscars than any other actor.
   Her most recent award-winning performance was in the popular *On Golden Pond.*

5. Woody Allen is finding it difficult to satisfy his audiences while still pursuing his artistic goals.
   His serious films have been rejected by many fans of his comedies.
   His most recent works have done only moderately well at the box office.

6. Brooke Shields' name has become synonymous with "star" after only a few movie roles.
   She has gained her greatest fame as a successful fashion model.

7. Robert Redford's career has spanned more than two decades.
   His numerous roles have shown him to be an accomplished actor.
   His talent as a director has been acknowledged with an Oscar for *Ordinary People.*
   He is one of the most talented and popular men working in films today.

PARAGRAPH WORK

Using at least three absolute phrases, write a short paragraph about an American entertainer who has become an international star. Ask your partner to check to see that you have written absolute phrases.

50

Appositives

INTRODUCTION

If you would like to provide details in a single sentence *without* using adjectives, phrases, or clauses, consider using an *appositive*, the word group discussed in this chapter. Appositives have four significant characteristics:

- They are usually found next to the word to which they refer.
- They are always separated from the word by punctuation marks.
- They can usually be easily substituted for the word to which they refer.
- They can be left out without changing the meaning of the sentence.

EXPLANATION

1. An appositive is an extremely useful word group for emphasizing or tightening a part of a sentence.

Single Sentences
Sandra Day O'Connor was born in El Paso, Texas.
She is the first woman to become a justice of the United States Supreme Court.

Satisfactory Sentence Combining
Sandra Day O'Connor, who is the first woman to become a justice of the United States Supreme Court, was born in El Paso, Texas.

Tighter Sentence Combining
Sandra Day O'Connor, the first woman to become a justice of the United States Supreme Court, was born in El Paso, Texas.

Notice how this last sentence follows each of the four characteristics outlined in the Introduction:

- The appositive "the first woman to become a justice of the United States Supreme Court" comes next to the words it refers to, "Sandra Day O'Connor."
- The appositive is separated from the rest of the sentence by commas.

- The sentence would read just as well if written:

  The first woman to become a justice of the United States Supreme Court, Sandra Day O'Connor, was born in El Paso, Texas.

- The sentence without the appositive makes sense:

  Sandra Day O'Connor was born in El Paso, Texas.

- It would also make sense to use the appositive as the subject:

  The first woman to become a justice of the United States Supreme Court was born in El Paso, Texas.

  Try to apply these four characteristics to the following two italicized appositives:

- The president of the United States, *Ronald Reagan*, appointed a woman, *Jeane Kirkpatrick*, as United States Ambassador to the United Nations.

- Virginia Woolf, *one of the great novelists of the twentieth century*, committed suicide.

2. You may use appositives in various ways. Notice the effect of the italicized appositives in the following examples.

a. Place an appositive first:

A truly great operatic artist, Leontyne Price was the first black female singer to have a leading role in a Metropolitan Opera premiere.

b. For a particularly strong effect, place an appositive at the end of a sentence:

Margaret Thatcher, who as prime minister of Britain is known for her no-nonsense attitude, has gained a stern nickname—*the Iron Maiden*.

The dash, a stronger form of punctuation, seems more appropriate here than a comma.

c. Make the appositive longer than the main sentence:

A world-famous film star and singer who has won numerous awards, Barbra Streisand began her career on Broadway.

d. Make your appositive negative:

Not the sort of person who hides or denies her past, former First Lady Betty Ford has publicized her successful fight against alcoholism in an effort to help other alcoholics.

e. Use effective repetition to connect an appositive:

Shirley Chisholm was elected to Congress in 1968, *the first black Congresswoman in U.S. history*.

f. Introduce appositives by connecting words like *for example, in other words, mainly, including, particularly, namely, such as*:

Some of the best television news reporters, *such as Judy Woodruff, Connie Chung, and Lesley Stahl*, are women.

g. Note that you could use a list of adjectives in the same way as you would an appositive:

Susan B. Anthony—*courageous, determined, independent*—tirelessly crusaded for women's suffrage.

Why is the italicized word group *not* an appositive? Apply the list of four characteristics in answering this question.

3. There are three ways to set appositives apart from the rest of the sentence: with a comma, a dash, or a colon. The comma is matter-of-fact, the dash emphatic, and the colon formal. Which of these three sentences seems most effective to you?

- Her work among the forgotten people of Calcutta has gained a Nobel Prize and worldwide admiration for a remarkable woman, Mother Teresa.
- Her work among the forgotten people of Calcutta has gained a Nobel Prize and worldwide admiration for a remarkable woman—Mother Teresa.
- Her work among the forgotten people of Calcutta has gained a Nobel Prize and worldwide admiration for a remarkable woman: Mother Teresa.

SENTENCE WORK

Combine or tighten each of the following into a single sentence containing at least one appositive. Underline the appositive in each sentence. Here is an example:

From
Emmeline Pankhurst was a British suffragist.
She went to jail.
She urged women to fight for the right to vote.

To
Emmeline Pankhurst, <u>a British suffragist</u>, went to jail for urging women to fight for the right to vote.

1. Sarah Bernhardt, who was one of the most remarkable actresses who ever lived, toured North America several times in her private railway train.

2. American singers have appeared with opera companies all over the world.
   Some of these singers are Grace Bumbry, Beverly Sills, and Jessye Norman.

3. Indira Gandhi was the prime minister of India.
   She held the same post as her father once did.
   His name was Jawaharlal Nehru and he was the first prime minister of India.
   Her son is now India's prime minister.
   His name is Rajiv Gandhi.
   (See if you can include five appositives in one sentence.)

4. An American woman attended the Cordon Bleu Cooking School in Paris.
   She was instrumental in bringing the art of French cooking to the United States.
   Her name is Julia Child.

5. The women's liberation movement has done much to raise the consciousness of women throughout the world.
   Examples of women who are leaders of the movement are Betty Friedan, Gloria Steinem, and Jane Fonda.

6. She was a hard-working woman.
   She was dedicated to her ambition.

She was determined to become a doctor.
Elizabeth Blackwell became the first female doctor in the United States.

PARAGRAPH WORK

Read the following pairs of sentences, then combine them so that there is an appositive in each sentence. Finally, join the sentences into a unified, coherent paragraph.

Women make up over one half of the human race.
In many countries they have no rights.

Women in the United States can vote, own property, and earn their own living.
Women in the United States are among the most fortunate in the world.

We must fight for equal rights for all women.
We are the people of the United States.

51

Clusters of Words and Phrases

INTRODUCTION

By introducing a cluster of words or phrases to a sentence, you can add information and emphasis. But proceed with caution. Overdoing clusters can be boring, repetitive, and ineffective if used in sentence after sentence.

EXPLANATION

1. *Clusters of Adjectives.* Notice the effect of putting a cluster of adjectives in two different positions:
Before the Noun
Humans have always been tempted by the *mysterious, alluring, and forbidden* prospect of traveling through outer space.
After the Noun
Humans have always been tempted by the prospect—*mysterious, alluring, and forbidden*—of traveling through outer space.

Notice the position and punctuation of these clusters of adjectives:
At the Beginning
Unmanned, small, and primitive, Sputnik was launched by the Soviet Union in 1957.

(The above cluster of adjectives works in the same way as an appositive.)
At the End
In 1957, the Soviet Union launched Sputnik—*unmanned, small, and primitive*.
(Although you could use a comma to separate the cluster from the rest of the sentence, the dash seems more appropriate.)

Can you think of other positions for the adjective cluster in this sentence? Now see how to combine sentences by using adjective clusters.

From
We launched our first successful satellite on July 1, 1958.
It was called Explorer 1.
It was small and unmanned, and its mission had a scientific purpose.

To

We launched Explorer 1, our first successful satellite—*small, unmanned, scientifically oriented*—on July 1, 1958.

From

When astronauts Gagarin, Carpenter, and Glenn made their flights, space travel was unsophisticated, had had little real experimentation, and cost a lot of money. Today, when Voyager is being aimed at the fringes of the solar system, space travel is streamlined, has had extensive experimentation, and costs an enormous amount of money.

To

When astronauts Gagarin, Carpenter, and Glenn made their flights, space travel was *unsophisticated, untried, and expensive*. Today, when Voyager is being aimed at the fringes of the solar system, space travel is *streamlined, well planned, and very expensive*.

2. *Clusters of Phrases That Function as Adjectives.* A blend of adjectives, participial phrases, absolute phrases, and prepositional phrases can add an effective touch to a long sentence. Arrange all phrase clusters in some kind of order (climactic, spatial, structural, importance, and so on), but aim for parallelism as well as order:

From

The seven original American astronauts were the folk heroes of the 1960s. Their dedication was much praised. Everyone cheered them for achieving great things.

To

Chosen for their courage, praised for their dedication, cheered for their achievements, the seven original American astronauts were the folk heroes of the 1960s. (Here, the cluster of participial phrases acts as an adjective cluster.)

From

The astronauts rode the early rockets through space. They had the courage of combat pilots. Their dedication was that of scientists.

To

With the courage of combat pilots and [with] the dedication of scientists, the astronauts rode the early rockets through space. (Here two prepositional adjective phrases are clustered.)

From

Several chimpanzees also become successful astronauts. Their training was as strenuous as a human's. Everything they did was conditioned by rewards and punishments.

To

Their training as strenuous as a human's, their every action conditioned by rewards and punishments, several chimpanzees also became successful astronauts. (The absolute phrase cluster acts in the same way as an adjective cluster.)

From

American space flights contrast with the secret flights of the Soviet Union.

The American flights have been broadcast from lift-off to splashdown.
Therefore, most of the world shared them.

To
American space flights, *broadcast from lift-off to splashdown* and so *shared with most of the world*, contrast with the secret flights of the Soviet Union.
(Notice the pair of participles and prepositional phrases that form the cluster.)

3. *Clusters of Adverbs.* Like adjectives, clusters of adverbs can be placed before or after the word they modify. Use adverb clusters appropriately, economically, and judiciously.

From
On May 25, 1961, President John F. Kennedy committed our nation to landing a man on the moon and returning him safely to earth.
This commitment was firm and without equivocation.
It was a wise commitment.

To
On May 25, 1961, President John F. Kennedy *firmly, unequivocally, and wisely* committed our nation to landing a man on the moon and returning him safely to earth.
(Can you place the cluster of adverbs in other positions in this sentence?)

Notice the effect of placing the adverb cluster at the beginning and end of the sentence in this example:

At the Beginning
Stoutly, unhesitatingly, and loyally, Congress rallied to support the moon-shot endeavor.

At the End
Congress rallied to support the moon-shot endeavor, *stoutly, unhesitatingly, and loyally.*
(Can you place the cluster of adverbs in other positions in this sentence?)

Generally you should use commas or dashes to set off a cluster of adverbs that disturbs the normal flow of your sentence:

After Kennedy presented the idea—*intelligently, clearly, passionately*—the nation became enthusiastic about sending a man to the moon.
(Where else could you place the cluster? Would you still use dashes around it?)

From
The U.S. aerospace industry was quick to expand to meet the needs of the Apollo moon-shot program.
The industry did this with determination.
It was successful.

To
The U.S. aerospace industry—*quickly, determinedly, successfully*—expanded to meet the needs of the Apollo moon-shot program.

4. *Clusters of Phrases That Function as Adverbs.* Prepositional adverb phrases can be clustered in the same way as single adverbs and can add an effective touch to a long sentence. You should always arrange the adverb phrases in your clusters in some kind of order (climactic, quality, and so on). When you are using phrases, aim for parallelism as well as order.

The following prepositional adverb phrases work on the same principle as adverbs; they modify the verb *was maintaining*.

By venturing into the unknown, by crossing yet another frontier, by accepting the challenge to advance humanity, the United States was maintaining the vigorous spirit that has energized this country since its inception.
(Where else could you place the cluster of prepositional adverb phrases?)
From
The very beginning of the Apollo program held the interest of the scientific community and much of the public.
The periods of intermittent failure and success, and the final triumph held their interest.
To
From the very beginning, through the periods of intermittent failure and success, to the final triumph, the Apollo program held the interest of the scientific community and much of the public.

5. *Clusters of Nouns.* If you understand how to cluster adjectives and adverbs, you will have no trouble clustering nouns.
From
On July 20, 1969, the nation's commitment to the Apollo program was rewarded when Neil A. Armstrong set foot on the moon.
The nation's support was rewarded.
The nation's efforts were rewarded.
To
On July 20, 1969, the nation's *commitment, support, and efforts* were rewarded when Neil A. Armstrong set foot on the moon.
From
Much fame came back to earth with the Apollo 11 astronauts on July 24, 1969.
With them came much glory.
They brought back forty-seven pounds of moon rocks.
To
Much fame, much glory, and forty-seven pounds of moon rocks came back to earth with the Apollo 11 astronauts on July 24, 1969.

6. *Clusters of Verbs.* Clustering verbs is as easy and effective to do as clustering other parts of speech.
From
The space shuttle—the latest United States effort in space flight—has maneuverability that is much like an airplane.
The gliding of the space shuttle and its landing also resemble that of an airplane.
To
The space shuttle—the latest United States effort in space flights—*maneuvers, glides, and lands* much like an airplane.

From

The space shuttle's many flights have given thrills to all who follow them.
The flights create interest for followers.
The flights make a strong impression.

To

The space shuttle's many flights *thrill, interest, and impress* all who follow them.

To add more variety to verb clustering, you might add nouns, adverbs, or phrases to the cluster of verbs. To the above three verbs add words, of your own choice, to enlarge the verb cluster—for example, *thrill the children* . . . .

SENTENCE WORK

Tighten each of the following by using clusters of adjectives, adverbs, verbal phrases, absolute phrases, prepositional phrases, nouns, or verbs.

1. The first men who went into space were, according to popular belief, physically strong, of high IQ, and mentally well balanced.

2. The Viking 1 and 2 spacecrafts were designed to conduct an examination of Mars.
   Mars is a planetary neighbor of Earth.
   The examination was to be detailed.
   It was to continue for a long time.
   It was for scientific purposes.

3. Television programs that are clear have no distortion.
   They are not interrupted by commercials and can be picked up on earth by simple radar dishes aimed at satellites.

4. Satellites can beam American television programs to countries all over the world.
   These broadcasts are entertaining and of a high technical quality, but they are often foreign to many native cultures.

5. It is small and it is devoid of life, but nevertheless the moon casts a spell that has made it the subject of books and the object of dreams.

6. America's female astronauts are now traveling into space.
   They have been chosen for their knowledge.
   They are justly famous for their abilities.
   Their courage has been acclaimed.

7. Voyager II has more than satisfied American scientists.
   Its importance to space exploration is unquestioned.
   It made an astonishingly successful trip to Saturn, and the data it will send back from the outer reaches of the solar system are being eagerly awaited.

8. The space shuttle is an economic means by which satellites can be carried into space.
   The shuttle can be relied on to do this job with efficiency.

9. The space shuttle crews have demonstrated that they are like the skillful Apollo program astronauts.
   And like the astronauts, the crews are dedicated.
   They also perform as professionally as the Apollo astronauts.

10. Some have said that the space shuttle is like a remarkable hybrid that has the propulsion system of a rocket, the gliding ability of an eagle, and when it lands, the appearance of an airliner.

PARAGRAPH WORK

Using the following sentences, fit them into the short paragraph below. Include only clusters of words or phrases in the spaces. When you finish, compare your paragraph with the one in the Suggested Answers following Chapter 55.

- The space shuttle was designed to serve America's scientific interests.
- It was designed to serve the country's commercial interests.
- It was designed to help the military's task of defending the country.
- There were cheers when the first shuttle, Columbia, was launched in 1981.
- There were awed gasps at the launch.
- There was probably even amazement among the hopeful spectators.
- It is a marvel.
- It possesses spectacular qualities.
- Columbia made an elegant landing that was graceful and almost gentle.

Columbia Space Shuttle

The space shuttle is perhaps the most ambitious of America's space efforts, designed to serve the nation (   ). When the first shuttle, Columbia, was launched (   ), a new era in space flight was begun. And when the Columbia—(   )—landed (   ) after her first voyage, that belief in the beginning of a new era was powerfully confirmed.

52

Emphasis

INTRODUCTION

In this chapter you explore the possibilities of paring down a clause or a phrase to a single word. As a writer, you should always be ready to be precise, concise, and emphatic.

EXPLANATION

1. The strongest positions in a sentence are the beginning and the end. To place a single word or a short phrase in either position—especially if it is set apart by a comma or a dash—will make it emphatic.

- Women's literature was not widely recognized as a separate category of American writing *prior to the 1970s.*
- *Then*, the rapid proliferation of distinctly feminist writing drew scholarly attention.
- *As a result*, women's literature can be studied in many American universities today.

2. Single words or short phrases can also be effective in mid-sentence; sometimes they are set off by punctuation, and sometimes not.

- Mark Twain, *undoubtedly*, will endure as one of America's most popular writers.
- Mark Twain will endure *without a doubt* as one of America's most popular writers.

3. An existing single word or phrase can often be repositioned for greater emphasis.

- Both Alice Walker and Beth Henley *recently* won a Pulitzer Prize for their writing.
- *Recently*, both Alice Walker and Beth Henley won a Pulitzer Prize for their writing.

Where else could you place *recently* and *undoubtedly* and *without a doubt* (from Number 2) so that they would be in emphatic positions?

4. Changing the position of an existing word or phrase may not only give it greater emphasis but may also change the meaning of the sentence. For example, move *only* to the position indicated by each asterisk in the following sentence:

- *Only* William Styron * wrote * a novel * about Nat Turner's slave rebellion * .

How does each move change the meaning of the sentence? Which position is the most correct and emphatic?

5. The occasional coined word or phrase, which may or may not be set in quotation marks, can also be emphatic.

- Many novelists would be pleased to have their work praised as "Faulknerian"; thus, they would know that their novels could be judged alongside the great ones of William Faulkner.

- Ernest Hemingway's terse, direct style inspired what many critics have called the "tough guy" school of American writers.

6. When you combine or condense sentences, you may often find that you can substitute a short, emphatic word or phrase for a longer word group.

Complex Sentence
Readers are fortunate that native American writer N. Scott Momaday has preserved Kiowa Indian oral folk tales in his celebrated book, *The Way to Rainy Mountain*.

Single Phrase Emphasis
Fortunately for readers, native American writer N. Scott Momaday has preserved Kiowa Indian oral folk tales in his celebrated book, *The Way to Rainy Mountain*.
(Is *fortunately for readers* in the most emphatic position?)

A Wordy Sentence
One can lament the fact that most contemporary American poetry has few readers.

Single Word Emphasis
Alas, most contemporary American poetry has few readers.
(Is *alas* in the most emphatic position?)

7. You might notice as you revise your writing that you could combine and then pare down several of your sentences to a single, concise, and emphatic sentence.

From
Toni Morrison is black.
Ernest Gaines is black.
Both write novels.

To
Both Toni Morrison and Ernest Gaines are black novelists.

From
James Baldwin grew up in a section of New York City.
Most of the population there was black.

To
James Baldwin grew up in a predominantly black section of New York City.

From
Woody Allen, who is best known as a movie actor and director, is also a writer of short stories.
Moviegoers may be surprised to learn that he is critically acclaimed for his written work.

To
Moviegoers may be surprised to learn that actor-director Woody Allen is also a critically acclaimed short-story writer.

SENTENCE WORK

1. Move the italicized word or phrase to a more emphatic position.
   a. John Updike is, *to say the least*, a prolific novelist, short-story writer, and critic.
   b. Saul Bellow's novels discuss, *with intelligence and humor*, the enduring questions of the human condition.
   c. Of all Norman Mailer's books, *The Deer Park only* has been successfully adapted for the New York stage. (Move *only*.)
   d. Sam Shepard is *finally* having his talent as a playwright widely acknowledged in America.

2. Reduce each sentence or group of sentences into a single sentence that contains at least one emphatic word or phrase.
   a. Maxine Hong Kingston wrote a penetrating memoir of her Chinese-American childhood.
   It was called *The Woman Warrior*.
   b. Sinclair Lewis wrote a novel called *Babbitt*.
   He described in it a type of American who is showy but who has no substance.
   c. In a mystical way, Annie Dillard in *Pilgrim at Tinker Creek* tells of her experiences in Virginia's Blue Ridge Mountains.
   d. Philip Roth is a novelist who has gained great fame.
   e. Poets such as Gary Snyder and Lawrence Ferlinghetti have become respected by many critics; they write and live on the West Coast.
   f. Walt Whitman, Thomas Wolfe, and John Dos Passos are three of the many writers who have tried to communicate how diverse America is.
   g. In a vivid fashion, Henry David Thoreau, in *Walden*, tells of his experiences at Walden Pond.

PARAGRAPH WORK

Write a short paragraph about your favorite American author. Include two sentences where you use a single word or phrase emphatically. When you finish, ask your workshop partner to edit your paragraph.

53

Parallelism

INTRODUCTION

When elements of a clause or sentence function in the same way and also have a similar structure, they are said to be parallel. To master parallel structure is to add strength and control to your writing. Parallelism helps not only to structure ideas but also to clarify the relationships among them. In this chapter you will discover how effective and useful parallel structure can be.

EXPLANATION

1. To include several ideas in a single sentence, use parallelism to express the relationship among them. Even when there are only two elements in a sentence, you can use parallelism.

There may be parallelism between words, phrases, or clauses: noun matched with noun, adjective with adjective, verbal phrase with verbal phrase, and so on. Sometimes the parallelism may be so natural that it requires no effort by the writer and goes almost unnoticed by the reader; at other times, it is elaborate and striking. Study the following examples of parallel structure:

Nouns
Eskimos and *native Americans*, it is believed, came originally from Asia.

Verbs
They *crossed* a land bridge from Siberia and *migrated* through Alaska.

Adjectives
Immigrants to the United States have been compelled to leave their homelands because of *religious*, *political*, and *economic* considerations.

Verbal Phrases (Participial)
Huguenots, *arriving from France* and *settling on Parris Island, South Carolina, in 1562*, were among the earliest European immigrants to America.

Verbal Phrases (Infinitive)
To leave their accustomed lives and *to endure the hardships of a new land* were more than some immigrants could manage.

Verbal Phrases (Gerundial)
According to one woman, *becoming drunkards, deserting their families,* or *committing suicide* proved the only answers for some of her fellow immigrants.

Prepositional Phrases
On foot, on horseback, by boat, and *by wagon,* thousands of new settlers moved into the wilderness.

Dependent Clauses
When their potato crops rotted in the fields and *when their British landlords disposses-sed them,* the Irish flocked to the United States. (The second *when* could be omitted.)

The above sentences contain parallel elements that are all linked by coordinate or correlative conjunctions. Nouns are paralleled by nouns, phrases by phrases, clauses by clauses.

2. If writers join *unlike* elements, their sentences contain faulty parallelism. Faulty parallelism is discussed in detail in Chapter 56.

Examine the following sentences to see what elements are parallel:

- Thousands of Russians *having declined* to support the 1917 October Revolution and *having experienced* a permanent disruption of their way of life, *emigrated from their homeland* and *settled in the United States.*
- Thousands of Russians *declining* to support the 1917 October Revolution and *experiencing* a permanent disruption of their way of life, *emigrated from their homeland* and *settled in the United States.*
- The transcontinental railroads were built principally by hardworking Chinese laborers *who had great stamina* and *who received low wages.*

3. Now notice how to combine sentences by using parallelism:

From
Congress was concerned about the labor shortage caused by the Civil War.
It wanted new workers from overseas.
It passed the Act to Encourage Immigration in 1864.

To
Congress, being concerned about the labor shortage caused by the Civil War and wanting new workers from overseas, passed the Act to Encourage Immigration in 1864.

From
Tens of thousands of Poles have come to the United States.
Many of them settled in New York.
Many others made their homes in Illinois and Pennsylvania.

To
Tens of thousands of Poles have come to the United States, many of them settling in New York, Illinois, and Pennsylvania.

4. The *balanced sentence*, a special kind of parallelism, is discussed briefly in Chapter 44. The balanced sentence gives your writing neatness and precision; it allows no part of the thought to get lost.

a. Examine these two balanced sentences:

- Puritans left England because of religious persecution; Vietnamese left Vietnam because of political persecution.
- Many Mexicans immigrated to the United States after the 1910–20 revolution, and many Cubans after the 1959 revolution.

These sentences have four things in common:

- They are composed of two independent clauses.
- They use parallel structure.
- They rely on identical or closely similar words.
- They have approximately the same number of words in each clause. You should notice, however, that you can omit some words in the second clause.

b. When you write a balanced sentence with similar ideas, make the clauses parallel to each other:

- Some states have been described as melting pots of immigrants; other states have been described as mosaics of immigrants.

Then see if you can take out any unnecessary words. Your sentence will still be balanced:

- Some states have been described as melting pots of immigrants; others, as mosaics.

c. There are two main ways of writing a balanced sentence. To show *similar* relationships between its parts, use a comma plus *and*:

- According to the 1980 census, the largest number of immigrants that have come to the United States have been of German origin, and the second largest, of Italian origin.

Or use a semicolon:

- According to the 1980 census, the largest number of immigrants that have come to the United States have been of German origin; the second largest, of Italian origin.

To show *opposite* relationships between its parts, use a comma plus *but*:

- In the 1940s, Mexicans were encouraged to come to the United States as workers, but in the 1980s, they have been discouraged from coming.

Or use a semicolon:

- In the 1940s, Mexicans were encouraged to come to the United States as workers; in the 1980s, they have been discouraged from coming.

d. After a detailed introduction, use balanced phrases to summarize or illuminate:

- The number of immigrants coming to the United States has varied enormously during past decades: more than 8 million in 1901–1910, fewer than 600,000 in 1931–1940, more than 4 million in 1971–1980.

e. When you want to make a balanced sentence memorable, try using reversals (chiasmus):

- Some people believe that too many people have been admitted to America lately—they want emigration of immigrants rather than immigration of emigrants. (What two words have been reversed?)

f. It is not only possible but effective to balance three ideas:

- If the Hungarians were the political refugees of the 1950s, and the Cubans of the 1960s, the Vietnamese "boat people" were the political refugees of the 1970s.
- Ugandan Asians fled racial injustice; poor Haitians, economic injustice; and Soviet Jews, religious injustice.

What three things are balanced in each of the above sentences?

g. You can balance dependent as well as independent clauses within sentences, but then only part of the sentence will be balanced. After you have written the main part of a sentence, you can balance independent clauses, dependent clauses, or phrases.

Sentence with Balanced Independent Clauses
The earliest British arriving in America came for two principal reasons: many were fleeing religious persecution and others were seeking wealth.

Sentence with Balanced Dependent Clauses
Because unemployment is widespread and because the economy is unsettled, some Americans want to reduce or eliminate immigration.

Sentence with Balanced Phrases
Because of widespread unemployment and (because of) an unsettled economy, some Americans want to reduce or eliminate immigration.

    When you balance portions of a sentence, you should follow the same guidelines as you would for a perfectly balanced sentence. Look over the last three sample sentences. Point out the characteristics of the balanced parts according to point (a) above; notice if the parts are similar or opposite according to point (c).

h. The following examples illustrate how to achieve a balanced sentence by combining separate sentences:

From
The first people to emigrate to Australia were convicts.
Those who first came to the United States were those who disagreed with religious opinions.

To
The first people to emigrate to Australia were convicts; the first to the United States were religious dissenters.

From

When the weather was good, the passage from England to America could be made in twenty days.

It could take more than two months to cross the Atlantic when the sea was stormy.

To

In good weather, the passage from England to America could take twenty days; but in bad weather, it could take more than two months.

From

Many people's lives are in danger in their own countries.

The United States and Canada have always welcomed political refugees.

Many visitors from eastern Europe have sought political asylum in the United States or Canada.

To

Because their lives are in danger in their own countries and because the United States and Canada have always welcomed political refugees, many visitors from eastern Europe have sought political asylum in either the United States or Canada.

SENTENCE WORK

Combine these sentences by using parallelism. Create a balanced sentence where appropriate.

1. Daniel Greysolon Duluth was a French-Canadian immigrant who explored the American wilderness and had a city named after him.
   The same is true of Julien Dubuque.

2. Until about thirty years ago, most immigrants arriving in the United States were of European origin.
   Now the majority of immigrants coming to the United States are from Asia, the West Indies, and Mexico.

3. During the Second World War many Japanese-Americans were sent to internment camps.
   Most of these persons had been born in America.
   A large number of them were second- and third-generation Americans.

4. During 1979 and 1980, individuals took the opportunity to sponsor Vietnamese immigrants.
   Groups also helped them to settle in their new communities.

5. Three large groups of Americans emigrated from the United States.
   Canada accepted them.
   In the eighteenth century, many Loyalists who did not support the American Revolution settled in Canada.
   In the nineteenth century, many black slaves fled to Canada.

In the twentieth century, many American draft resisters moved to Canada instead of fighting in the Vietnam War.

PARAGRAPH WORK

Write a paragraph about someone you know who is an immigrant, explaining some aspect of the difficulties he or she faced in settling in America. Include at least two examples of parallel structure. When you finish, ask your partner to evaluate your paragraph.

54

Loose and Periodic Sentences

INTRODUCTION

Although you will usually use loose sentences in your writing because they correspond closely to normal speech rhythms and patterns, you will, nonetheless, find many opportunities to write a periodic sentence. (You have just read a periodic sentence.)

EXPLANATION

The meaning of a *loose sentence* is disclosed to the reader near the beginning of the sentence; however, in a *periodic sentence* the meaning is not clear until almost at the end of the sentence.

1. Notice the two ways in which you can combine these simple sentences:

Simple Sentences
The most famous chronicler of the Klondike Gold Rush is Robert W. Service.
He wrote most of his best poetry before he ever saw the Klondike.
The gold rush had long since finished when he finally arrived.

Combined as a Loose Sentence
The most famous chronicler of the Klondike Gold Rush is Robert W. Service, although he wrote most of his best poetry before he ever saw the Klondike and although the gold rush had long since finished when he finally arrived.

Combined as a Periodic Sentence
Although he wrote most of his best poetry before he ever saw the Klondike and although the Klondike Gold Rush had long since finished when he finally arrived, its most famous chronicler is Robert W. Service.

Notice that there is built-in suspense in periodic sentences because the topic is withheld until the last moment. In what formats would you most likely include periodic sentences?

2. In order to create a good periodic sentence, you need to know how to subordinate ideas using dependent clauses, prepositional phrases, verbal phrases, and absolute phrases. A periodic sentence should (a) end with what you consider the most important item from an independent clause and (b) begin with all other information in subordinate constructions.

Simple Sentences
John Sutter developed a prosperous ranch on his vast California land grant.
Gold was discovered there in 1848.
This touched off the famous "gold rush."
Prospectors overran Sutter's property.
He was ruined and died in poverty.

Combined as a Periodic Sentence Using Dependent Clauses
Although John Sutter developed a prosperous ranch on his vast California land grant, although gold was discovered there in 1848, which touched off the famous gold rush, although his property was overrun by prospectors, he was ruined and died in poverty.

Combined as a Periodic Sentence Using Participial Phrases
After having developed a prosperous ranch on his vast California land grant, after having discovered gold there in 1848, which touched off the famous gold rush, and after having his property overrun by prospectors, John Sutter was ruined and died in poverty.
  Rewrite this periodic sentence using subordinate constructions in a different way.

3. When you write a periodic sentence, you must decide which piece of information to withhold from your reader by putting it last in the sentence. Read these different versions.

Version making greed and thieving corruption of their fellow prospectors *the final words*
The Alaska and California gold seekers often discovered not only the precious metal but also the greed and thieving corruption of their fellow prospectors.

Version making gold seekers *the final words*
Not only the precious metal but also the greed and thieving corruption of their fellow prospectors was often discovered by the Alaska and California gold seekers.

(Try making *precious metal* the final words.)

4. When you add parallel structure to a periodic sentence, you increase suspense:

Simple Sentences
Jefferson "Soapy" Smith fleeced many unwary goldseekers at his Skagway saloon.
The dance-hall hostesses were experienced.
The shell game was a sure thing.
The dice were controlled.
The card tables had a concealed ace for the dealer.

Combined as a Periodic Sentence Using Parallel Dependent Clauses
Because the dance-hall hostesses were experienced, the shell game a sure thing, the dice controlled, and the card tables equipped with a concealed ace for the dealer, Jefferson "Soapy" Smith fleeced many unwary goldseekers at his Skagway saloon.

Can you think of another way to write a periodic sentence from the last group of simple sentences?

SENTENCE WORK

Convert the following loose sentences into periodic ones and the periodic sentences into loose ones. Underline the main subject and the main verb in each of your sentences.

1. Having exhausted the gold fields of California and seeking new frontiers, to the Kansas Territory on Cherry Creek in 1858 came many of the "Forty-Niners."

2. Prospectors continued to rush to Alaska at the turn of the century, despite many seekers' finding little or no gold on their claims, and despite the fact that fortunes were being made by only the few, because new discoveries were regularly made.

3. Despite the miners' having to pan by hand and use primitive sluicing methods, between 1896 and 1904 in the Klondike, more than $100,000,000 worth of gold was recovered.

4. A new kind of "black gold fever" struck the far North in the early 1970s because of a phenomenal increase in the price of oil and the widespread fear of Western nations' industrial collapse.

5. Although the entire "black gold" drilling operation bears little resemblance to the efforts of the hardy individuals who formerly took riches from beneath the ground, Alaska is once again releasing new wealth to those who have prospected for it.

PARAGRAPH WORK

Write a paragraph about your feelings on wealth, betting, gambling, or gold. Include at least two periodic sentences. When you finish, ask your workshop partner to evaluate your paragraph. Ask if he or she can spot the periodic sentences.

Elliptical Constructions

INTRODUCTION

For compactness, writers use elliptical constructions; that is, constructions where certain unnecessary words have been omitted. This chapter examines a few of the delights, as well as the pitfalls, of using elliptical constructions. (*Note*: This chapter deals with elliptical construction; Chapter 62 deals with the use of ellipsis points.)

EXPLANATION

The following are some examples of legitimate elliptical constructions. The words in parentheses are unnecessary to the meaning of the following sentences. You can legitimately omit them.

Subject and Verb of Dependent Clause Omitted

The Sears Tower, (which is) in Chicago, Illinois, is the world's tallest office building at 1,454 feet.

Second Subject Omitted

With 250 rooms, Biltmore House in Asheville, North Carolina, is the world's largest private house, but (it) is not the most expensive.

Verb Omitted With than

The thirty-million-dollar house of William Randolph Hearst in San Simeon, California, cost twenty-six million dollars more to build than (did) Biltmore House.

1. The following examples illustrate how you can use legitimate elliptical constructions in combining sentences:

Two Sentences

The first man to orbit the earth was a Russian.
The first man to walk on the moon was an American.

Sentence Combining

The first man to orbit the earth was a Russian, but the first man to walk on the moon was an American.

Legitimate Ellipsis

The first man to orbit the earth was a Russian; the first to walk on the moon, an American.

Two Sentences

The world's record as tallest man has been fixed at 8 feet, 11.1 inches by Robert P. Wadlow of Alton, Illinois.

He was called both a freak and a wonder.

Sentence Combining

The world's record as tallest man, who was called both a freak and a wonder, has been fixed at 8 feet, 11.1 inches by Robert P. Wadlow of Alton, Illinois.

Legitimate Ellipsis

The world's record as tallest man, called both freak and wonder, has been fixed at 8 feet, 11.1 inches by Robert P. Wadlow of Alton, Illinois.

2. The following are some examples of illegitimate elliptical constructions. Avoid them in your writing.

a. Include all *necessary* words. The omission of necessary words causes awkwardness or obscurity:

- World's biggest pizza, nine tons, baked Glens Falls, New York.

Do not use this style in your essay writing; reserve it for the telegram you send your great-aunt when you need money or for the recipe for your favorite cookies.

b. Repeat key articles in certain parallel structures:

From

In the 1968 Olympics, the United States set a jumping and running record. (This sentence suggests that one record was set in one event that requires an athlete to first jump and then run.)

To

In the 1968 Olympics, the United States set a jumping and a running record.

If this is still not clear to you, using a correlative conjunction might help:

- In the 1968 Olympics, the United States set *both* a jumping *and* a running record.

c. Repeat certain pronouns for clarity:

From

In the 1936 Olympics, Jesse Owens won the gold medal for his 100-meter dash and long jump. (This sentence suggests that the dash and long jump constitute one event.)

To

In the 1936 Olympics, Jesse Owens won the gold medal for his 100-meter dash and *his* long jump.

You could also use a correlative conjunction here:

- In the 1936 Olympics, Jesse Owens won the gold medal *not only* for his 100-meter dash *but also* for his long jump.

d. Include certain prepositions when the idiom demands it:

From

Australian Ben Carlin has made the only circumnavigation of the globe in a vehicle that could travel in water and land.

To

Australian Ben Carlin has made the only circumnavigation of the globe in a vehicle that could travel in water and *on* land.

Why is the *on* necessary? Revise the following sentence by adding a necessary preposition:

- Other record-setting circumnavigators have traveled, for example, in aircraft and foot.

e. Include certain parts of a verb phrase for clarity:

From

Before the invention of rocket-powered cars, such tremendous land speeds as Stan Barrett's record of 739.666 MPH had not and could not be approached.

To

Before the invention of rocket-powered cars, such tremendous land speeds as Stan Barrett's record 739.666 MPH had not *been* and could not be approached.

From

Englishman Tom Luxton was probably not expected but did play his accordion nonstop for a record eighty-four hours.

To

Englishman Tom Luxton was probably not expected *to play* but did play his accordion nonstop for a record eighty-four hours.

f. Include both verbs when the subject of one part of a sentence is singular and that of another part plural:

From

At 3,150 feet above the ground, the world's highest tightrope walker Steve McPeak was very steady, and his steps very, very careful.

To

At 3,150 feet above the ground, the world's highest tightrope walker Steve McPeak was very steady, and his steps *were* very, very careful.

What is needed before *temporarily* in the following sentence?

- Few world records are permanent, but each temporarily unique.

g. Make sure that you complete the thought when you use *so*, *such*, or *too* for emphasis. (You can use these three words in speech because you can say them with special inflections.)

Incomplete

Orville Wright is so famous.

Complete

Orville Wright is so famous because he made the world's first airplane flight.

or

Orville Wright is famous.

Incomplete

Joan Joyce is such an extraordinary softball pitcher.

Complete

Joan Joyce is such an extraordinary softball pitcher that in one season she was able to strike out seventy-six batters and pitch two perfect games.

Can you write this last sentence in another satisfactory way?

SENTENCE WORK

If one of the following items requires an elliptical construction, provide it; if it needs an extra word, provide it.

1. Human beings have long sought to establish world records in a variety of endeavors, whether these endeavors are considered silly or serious.

2. Competitive athletes, especially if they are competitive athletes like Mary Decker and Evelyn Ashford, run after records with great seriousness.

3. But it seems the competitive bubble gum blowers, car wreckers, pogo stick jumpers, and custard pie throwers have and continue to be ever ready to pursue their world records with a healthy dose of great silliness.

4. But tobacco-spitting champions and world-class hula hoopers do indeed prepare and participate in competitions that are apparently serious enough for the record keepers; in fact, Norris McWhirter's *Guinness Book of World Records* is a work that he has compiled which notes the results of a wide variety of human endeavors, including spitting and hoop spinning.

5. In McWhirter's book, the silly and the serious are so close together.

PARAGRAPH WORK

Write a paragraph in which you describe a record that you would like to break. Include at least three legitimate elliptical constructions. When you finish, ask your workshop partner to evaluate your paragraph for you.

Suggested Answers to the Third Workshop Section

CHAPTER 41
Three-Part Quiz

First Quiz (value: 25 points)

a. main subject ["Thriller"], main predicate [skyrocketed], direct object [Michael Jackson], object of preposition [fame and fortune]

b. main subject [Americans], main predicate [know], direct object [that he won . . . of awards]

c. main subject [Most], main predicate [won], direct object [number], object of preposition [awards]

d. main subject [Jackson], main predicate [is], complement [star], object of preposition [stage, video, and film]

e. main subject [Organizations], main subject [individuals], main predicate [must send], indirect object [him], direct object [mail], main subject [he], auxiliary verb of main predicate [could], main verb of main predicate [answer], direct object [it], indirect object [himself]

Second Quiz (value: 7 points)

a. verbal (participial) phrase [screaming his name], verbal (participial) phrase [buying his . . .]

b. absolute phrase [Their enthusiasm unlimited], prepositional phrase [of his fans], verbal (infinitive) phrase [to be living . . . .]

c. verbal (gerundial) phrase [creating superstars . . .], verbal (gerundial) phrase [creating superstars too]

Third Quiz (value: 18 points)

a. noun [fans], conjunction [and], preposition [by], noun [millions], verb [ensure]

b. noun [enthusiasm], pronoun [some], pronoun [him], verb [be], conjunction [or]

c. interjection [hey], preposition [like], adverb [not], adjective [an], adjective [American], adjective [other], verb [enjoy], adverb [too]

Sentence Work

1. Complete Subject

Complete Predicate

a. Cesar Chavez

is a Chicano who has guided the United Farm Workers movement.

b. Chavez, who was himself a farm worker

organized the struggle for better pay.

c. He

led the famous Delano grape pickers' strike, which was a success.

d. Mohandas Gandhi, who was called Mahatma, which means "great soul,"

inspired the people of India, who wanted independence from Britain.

e. Those who favor nonviolent resistance to authority

still use Gandhi's methods today.

f. the South African government

While Winston Churchill was a war correspondent during the Boer War, considered him so dangerous that it put a price on his head.

2. Independent Clause

Dependent Clause

a. Cesar Chavez is a Chicano

who has guided the United Farm Workers movement

b. Chavez organized the struggle for better pay

who was himself a farm worker

c. He led the famous Delano grape pickers' strike

which was a success

d. Mohandas Gandhi inspired the people of India

who was called Mahatma
which means "great soul"
who wanted independence from Britain

e. Those still use Gandhi's methods today

who favor nonviolent resistance to authority

f. the South African government considered him so dangerous

While Winston Churchill was a war correspondent during the Boer War that it put a price on his head.

3. a. independent clause
b. dependent clause
c. dependent clause
d. independent clause

e. independent clause
f. independent clause
g. dependent clause
h. dependent clause

4. **a.** noun, adjective, preposition, interjection
   b. verb, adjective, conjunction, adjective, noun
   c. adjective, preposition, noun
   d. adverb, verb, noun, adjective
   e. adverb, pronoun, pronoun, verb, adjective, adjective

5. **a.** phrase
   b. phrase
   c. clause
   d. clause
   e. phrase
   f. phrase, phrase
   g. phrase
   h. phrase
   i. phrase
   j. clause, clause
   k. phrase
   l. phrase
   m. phrase, phrase
   n. phrase
   o. clause
   p. clause
   q. clause
   r. phrase, clause
   s. phrase, phrase
   t. clause, clause

Paragraph Work

This, more than any of the other chapters in *The Independent Writer*, is your tool kit. In the same way as a (*caddy*) needs to know the difference between a (*club*) and a (*ball*), you need to know the difference between a subject and a verb when your editor refers to one or the other. What a waste of time it would be if a (*golfer*) had to ask, "Give me the (*club*) with the kind of funny (*thick, wooden head with the number 1 on it*)," or "I want the one with the (*thin, bladelike, straight-faced, iron head*)." All he should need to say is "Give me a (*driver*)," or "I want the (*putter*)." When one of your editors says, "I think you should have used a phrase instead of a clause," you have to know what he or she is talking about. Words and word groups are a writer's tools. Learn to identify them.

CHAPTER 42
Sentence Work

a. 5, **b.** 7, **c.** 9, **d.** 1, **e.** 6, **f.** 8, **g.** 10, **h.** 6, **i.** 2,
j. 4, **k.** 3

Paragraph Work

The word groups that you used may differ from the ones in this paragraph and still be correct. If you are in doubt about the effectiveness of any of your sentences, discuss it with your workshop partner.

In most regions native-American boys, approaching adolescence, were taught to swim in the icy waters of midwinter. At an early age, all were taught the meaning of pain by deliberate decision of their elders. Northwest Coast lads were switched as they emerged from icy ocean waters. Iroquoian lads were taught the feel of glowing coals on bare skin. The warrior-designate of the plains willingly faced the ordeal of the Sun Dance, where his manhood might be proved. The Sun Dance involved three or four days of dancing, religious ceremony, and feasting. With some tribes, a feature of the Sun Dance was a supreme test of the young warrior's endurance and his ability to withstand pain. The pectoral muscles were slit creating bridges of muscle through which lengths of thong were run. The free ends were tied to the center-post of the Sun Lodge and the warrior danced, pulling against the thongs until he either broke the muscle bridges or fainted with pain and exhaustion. Alternately, the shoulder muscles were slit and the thongs were tied to a buffalo skull that he had to jerk across the prairie until the thongs broke the muscle bridge.

CHAPTER 43
Sentence Work

If your responses differ from these, make sure that each of your sentences has only *one independent clause*. If your sentence has more than one clause, it may read perfectly well, but the assignment was to write only simple sentences. To help you check your answers, note that both the main subject and main verb of each sentence are italicized. Some sentences have compound main subjects and main verbs.

1. According to legend, an eagle's own powerful *feathers will devour* the feathers of other birds.

2. An Iroquois *dancer*, holding an eagle dance to celebrate the eagle and the hunt, *will hop* from side to side to represent the eagle's approach to its meat.

3. Between 1795 and 1933, the *United States minted* eagles, ten-dollar gold coins with an eagle stamped on their reverse side.

4. Prairie *tribes*, valuing eagle feathers as a medium of exchange, *rated* two to four feathers equal to a horse.

5. With over a million members in 1,900 aeries in the United States, Canada, and the Philippines, the *Fraternal Order of Eagles is* famous.

6. With the motto "Eagles are people helping people," the *Fraternal Order of Eagles supports* cancer and heart research and *aids* retarded children and the elderly.

7. Gambling with Fire Owner to win fire for the Karok tribe and carrying the Arapahoe ghost dancer to the Messiah, the *eagle is* a helper in native-American legend also.

8. Because of its large size of thirty to thirty-five inches from bill to the tip of the tail and of its seven-foot wingspan, the *eagle is* a majestic bird.

9. Walt Whitman's *poem*, "The Dalliance of the Eagles," *celebrates* their mating ritual.

10. The mating season being in early spring, *pairs* of eagles *engage* in intense nest building and repairing.

11. Appearing to have a favorite stunt, an *eagle spots* a protruding branch from a tree, *soars* at the dead branch, *seizes* it in those razor-sharp, inward-curving talons, and *snaps* the branch loose.

12. Even more spectacular *is* its mating *ritual*, the pair soaring out on thermal currents far above the earth.

13. *One* of them *rolls* over and *soars* upside down with legs extended.

14. The *mate soars* above it, the talons of the two locking together.

15. With wings set and feet intertwined, the *pair pinwheel* over and over, tumbling earthward in a wild, cartwheeling ecstasy.

16. The *results* of all this connubial recklessness *are* fairly modest, two or three white eggs, not much larger than chicken eggs.

17. In 1973, *George Laycock*, in his book called *Autumn of the Eagle*, and in 1982, *John Belushi*, in his film *Continental Divide*, *detailed* the life and possible extinction of the bald eagle.

Paragraph Work

The main subject(s) and the main verb(s) of each sentence are italicized.

A (soaring) *eagle is* an ideal symbol for America. *People* from other times, however, *have made* the eagle an important part of their culture too. Human *attitudes* toward eagles *have* always *vacillated* between reverence and (loathing). For our remote ancestors, the wheeling *freedom* of the giant birds *was* a (connecting thread) between earth and the supreme place of spirits. The ancient *Greeks believed* in the (importance of eagles). *Eagles were released* by Zeus and *met* above Delphi, (indicating the center of the world). There the *earthly* and *divine touched*.

Eagles released at the burials of Egyptian pharaohs *were thought* to carry (the dead rulers' spirits into the heavens). The *legions* of Rome *welded* together an empire marching (behind the eagle banner). The Iroquois peace dance, Pueblo rain rituals, Northwest totemic art—all *acknowledged* the (sacred character) of the "king of birds."

CHAPTER 44
Sentence Work

If any of your three versions are not the same as the ones below, do not be concerned. They may still be correct. Discuss your responses with your partner and check carefully that you have used coordination and not subordination. An answer using subordination would be wrong for this workshop, even if it makes perfect sense.

1. **a.** Norsemen are believed to have established the earliest European settlement in North America around 1000 A.D.; they abandoned it after some fifty years of occupation.

   b. Norsemen are believed to have established the earliest European settlement in North America around 1000 A.D.; however, they abandoned it after some years of occupation.

   c. Norsemen are believed to have established the earliest European settlement in North America around 1000 A.D., but they abandoned it after some fifty years of occupation.

2. **a.** During the seventeenth century, North America was colonized by religious refugees; furthermore, it was exploited then by commercial adventurers as well.

   b. During the seventeenth century, North America was colonized by religious refugees, and it was exploited then by commercial adventurers as well.

   c. Not only was North America colonized during the seventeenth century by religious refugees, but it was also exploited by commercial adventurers as well.

3. **a.** By the middle of the eighteenth century, the English at home were pleased with the growing prosperity of their American colonies; at the same time, they were becoming alarmed by the frequent instances of rebellion against their authority.

   b. By the middle of the eighteenth century, the English at home were pleased with the growing prosperity of their American colonies; at the same time, however, they were becoming alarmed by the frequent instances of rebellion against their authority.

   c. By the middle of the eighteenth century, the English at home were pleased with the growing prosperity of their American colonies, but at the same time, they were becoming alarmed by the frequent instances of rebellion against their authority.

4. **a.** and **b.** The English antagonized the American colonists in several ways: they tried to manage all colonial trade for the benefit of England, [they] subjected the colonists to an unrepresentative bureaucracy, and [they] imposed unpopular taxes on a number of products imported into the colonies.

   c. The English antagonized the American colonists in several ways: first they tried to manage all colonial trade for the benefit of England; then they subjected the colonists to an unrepresentative bureaucracy; finally they imposed unpopular taxes on a number of products imported into the colonies.

5. **a.** During the American Revolution, most colonists fought for independence; still, some supported the English side.

   b. During the American Revolution, most colonists fought for independence, but some supported the English side.

   c. During the American Revolution, most colonists fought for independence; some, on the other hand, supported the English side.

CHAPTER 45
Sentence Work

1. *Even though injuries have often prevented her from consistently competing in top form*, Evelyn Ashford continues to win sprint races. (adverb clause)

2. *Although baseball is supposedly America's very own national game*, the Summer Olympics demonstration tournament showed *that many countries from around the globe have strong baseball teams / that seem dedicated to making "our" game the world's.* (adverb, noun, and adjective clauses)

3. The Soviet Union, *which was boycotted as host of the 1980 Olympics*, decided to boycott the U.S.-hosted 1984 Games, *which led some people to demand / that the Olympics no longer be held in countries / that tend to provoke gestures of protest from political adversaries.* (adjective clause, adjective clause, noun clause, adjective clause)

4. Nadia Comaneci, *who is a gymnast from Romania*, scored a perfect ten during the 1976 Olympics in Montreal. (adjective clause)

5. *After native American Jim Thorpe's Olympic decathlon and pentathlon gold medals were withdrawn / because he had committed a minor infraction of the rules governing athletes' amateur status*, the medals were returned to his family seventy years later, in 1982. (two adverb clauses)

6. The regular breaking of Olympic records strongly suggests *that the final limits of athletic achievement cannot be determined / unless men and women end athletic competition.* (noun clause, adverb clause)

7. *Though windgliding on sailboards is not widely recognized as a competitive sport*, it was premiered in the 1984 Summer Games as a sailing event *that attracted both curious and enthusiastic spectators.* (adverb clause, adjective clause)

8. *Whoever examines the list of sites for the modern Olympics* will notice *that the U.S. has had the honor of hosting the Summer Games three times and the Winter Games three times.* (two noun clauses)

Paragraph Work

The ancient Olympic Games, which only slightly resemble the modern ones, probably began nearly three thousand years ago when runners gathered to race at Olympia. Although some historians believe that they were first held as much as centuries earlier, no certain date for this has been established. These early games were actually held to celebrate the festival of Herakles, who was the god that raised the infant Zeus. The Eleans, who lived on the plains of Olympia, originated this festival that eventually became the occasion for all of the Greek city-states to meet in athletic competition. Because lambs, wine, and grain were sacrificed to Zeus on the first day of competition, it seems that the games had as much religious significance as they had athletic excitement. In any case, the games, which drew spectators who lived in all regions of the Mediterranean world, evidently were immensely popular, since they were staged some 320 times over a period of about 1200 years.

Before the games started, athletes took solemn oaths that said they would compete as honest sportsmen. The contests, as all agreed, had to be impartially judged, which ensured that the winners, who were crowned with "sacred" olive wreaths, could enjoy the well-deserved glory that is granted to a champion who demonstrated his superiority in fair competition. Apparently the respect for and dedication to these competitions in running, discus throwing, javelin throwing, jumping, boxing, and wrestling were strong enough to keep the ancient Olympic Games vital from 776 B.C. to A.D. 394, which makes them one of our most long-lasting institutions. Perhaps the modern Olympics have begun a new tradition that will prove equally durable.

CHAPTER 46
Sentence Work

The independent clauses in the following sentences are italicized. *Note*: There must be at least two in each compound-complex sentence.

1. *Duke Ellington wrote numerous immensely popular jazz compositions* that have been played and recorded frequently; therefore, *we have come to recognize them as jazz standards.*

2. *Vanessa Williams was indeed the first black to become Miss America*; but *she was also the first black given the chance to prove* she deserved that title, which has made her experience a test as well as an honor.

3. *Jesse Jackson was the first black to mount a serious national campaign for the Democratic presidential nomination,* and though he did not win, *his efforts helped open the political process for minority participation at the highest level.*

4. *Eddie Murphy*, who is only in his early twenties, *became one of the most popular members of the Saturday Night Live television show; / in this way, a bright comedy star was born.*

5. *Martin Luther King, Jr.*, who first rose to national prominence in 1955 as a leader of the Montgomery, Alabama, public transportation boycott, *began leading his nonviolent crusade for black civil rights*; / *he pursued his crusade tirelessly until his assassination in 1968.*

Paragraph Work

Martin Luther King, Jr., who was a devout pacifist, was convinced of the need for a broad civil rights movement based on a philosophy of determined pacifism; therefore, he organized the nonviolent Southern Christian Leadership Conference to head this movement in 1957. With the SCLC behind him, King peacefully led numerous demonstrations throughout the South, where he focused the movement's efforts; but his greatest triumph of nonviolent protest came during a massive demonstration in Washington, D.C., on August 28, 1963. Two hundred fifty thousand Americans gathered in the nation's capital that day, and they heard King give his stunning "I have a dream" speech, which is now recognized as the greatest oration of the civil rights movement.

Can you spot the two independent and one or more dependent clauses in each of the compound-complex sentences? The subjects and verbs of each are:

1. Martin Luther King, Jr. was convinced; who was; he organized.
2. King was; he focused; triumph came.
3. Americans gathered; they heard; King give; I have; which is recognized.

CHAPTER 47
Sentence Work

1. Kennedy served <u>in the United States Navy</u> / <u>as a torpedo boat commander</u>.
2. <u>For writing *Profiles in Courage*</u>, Kennedy won nationwide acclaim <u>for his book</u> and was awarded the Pulitzer Prize.
3. Kennedy became a congressman <u>for Massachusetts</u> / <u>for the first time</u> / <u>in 1947</u>.
4. <u>In 1960</u>, / <u>at forty-three</u>, he defeated Richard Nixon <u>for the presidency</u>.
5. <u>On his Inauguration Day</u>, Kennedy gave a brilliant speech and succeeded <u>in inspiring Americans</u> / <u>with a sense</u> / <u>of hope and purpose</u> / <u>for the country's future</u>.
6. Kennedy, <u>of the Democratic party's liberal wing</u>, proposed sweeping new civil rights legislation, increased Social Security benefits, and medical care <u>for the elderly</u> / <u>after becoming president</u>.
7. <u>As president</u>, Kennedy became widely known <u>for his wit and intelligence</u>.
8. <u>After John F. Kennedy's assassination</u>, his death was deeply mourned <u>throughout the entire country</u> / <u>as a great and tragic loss</u>.

CHAPTER 48
Exercise One

Verbals and the words they modify from Number 3:

Verbals	Words They Modify
Conquering, civilizing, Christianizing	conquistadors
weakened	empire
thriving	settlement
weakened, diseased, exploited	native Americans
to conquer	easy
to rule	difficult
to accept	easy

Verbal phrases and the words they modify from Number 4:

Verbal Phrases	**Words They Modify**
abandoning their plantations	southerners
lured by promises of abundant, fertile land	southerners
based on political and cultural differences	distrust
angered by Mexico's loss of the lands where their ancestors had settled centuries before	Mexicans
overwhelmed by Americans in search of gold	Mexicans
to stop Pancho Villa's raids into the United States	sent
to find better jobs and higher wages	place

5. Emphatic verbal phrases:

   a. *Having gained political power*, Mexican-Americans such as San Antonio Mayor Henry Cisneros are finally being listened to by the Anglo community.

   b. *Pitching brilliantly for the Los Angeles Dodgers*, Fernando Valenzuela has become a sports hero to his fellow Chicanos.

Exercise Two

a. *Having sailed with Columbus in 1493*, Ponce de Leon returned to the Caribbean in 1508, *claiming Puerto Rico for Spain*.

b. *Ceded to the United States by Spain in 1898*, Puerto Rico became a self-governing commonwealth in 1952.

c. *Having enjoyed the opportunity of unrestricted immigration to the U.S. mainland*, thousands of Puerto Ricans have come *hoping to find a better life*.

d. Leonard Bernstein updated the *Romeo and Juliet* story to contemporary New York in *West Side Story*, *portraying the dreams of young Puerto Rican immigrants*.

e. Some Puerto Ricans, *favoring statehood or even independence for the commonwealth*, have formed political parties; others, unfortunately, have chosen violent means *to demand change*.

Exercise Three

a. In *looking to the United States as a refuge from political and economic turmoil in their homelands*, Central Americans follow a centuries-old tradition.

b. *Some immigrants' knowing little or no English* means that they must attend special schools to become fluent. (Note the needed apostrophe.)

c. Many high-school students, through *being exposed to Hispanic-American culture*, have decided to study Spanish as their second language.

    d. In *examining the Hispanic culture*, students learn that it is the second oldest of the United States.

    e. *America's having focussed on the British literary tradition* has resulted in *our ignoring such Spanish writers as García Lorca and Lope de Vega.*

    f. The fact of no comprehensive collection of *Hispanic literature's existing at the moment* is unfortunate for all students.

Exercise Four

    a. Lee Trevino, *having won the U.S., British, and Canadian Open golf championships in a row*, brought "Super Mex" to the attention of thousands of golf fans. (participial phrase)

    Lee Trevino's having won the U.S., British, and Canadian Open golf championships in a row brought "Super Mex" to the attention of thousands of golf fans. (gerundial phrase)

    b. Anthony Quinn, *portraying Greeks, Italians, native Americans, and many other nationalities*, is proud of his Hispanic ancestry. (participial phrase)

    Anthony Quinn's portraying of Greeks, Italians, native Americans, and many other nationalities has not diminished his pride in his Hispanic ancestry. (gerundial phrase)

    c. The members of the popular Puerto Rican singing group Menudo, *having reached the age of sixteen*, must leave the group. (participial phrase)

    The members of the popular Puerto Rican singing group Menudo must leave the group after *having reached the age of sixteen*. (gerundial phrase)

Paragraph Work

    Many Americans, living in areas with sizable Hispanic populations, realize that there are hundreds of Spanish-speaking media in our country. Others, less exposed, have yet to discover how widespread the Spanish influence is. Only two TV network situation comedies, *Chico and the Man*, cut short by the tragic death of its star, Freddie Prinze, and *AKA Pablo*, conceived by innovative producer Norman Lear, have featured Hispanic stars. We look forward to future opportunities to learn more about Hispanic culture.

CHAPTER 49
Sentence Work

    1. Their small fortunes made and their "greatness" established with one hit film, some actors and actresses will find it impossible ever to recapture their first success.

2. His career as an actor having begun in the 1930s, Ronald Reagan has gained one of the world's highest offices—president of the United States.

3. Bruce Lee, his face unsmiling, his hands and feet flying, was the hero of several martial-arts movies.

4. Katharine Hepburn, her most recent award-winning performance in the popular *On Golden Pond*, has received more Academy Award nominations and Oscars than any other actor.

5. His serious films rejected by many fans of his comedies and his most recent works doing only moderately well at the box office, Woody Allen is finding it difficult to satisfy his audiences while still pursuing his artistic goals.

6. Brooke Shields, her name synonymous with "star" after only a few movie roles, has gained her greatest fame as a successful fashion model.

7. His career having spanned more than two decades, his numerous roles having shown him to be an accomplished actor, his talent as a director having been acknowledged with an Oscar for *Ordinary People*, Robert Redford is one of the most talented and popular men working in films today.

CHAPTER 50
Sentence Work

Though your appositives may look quite different from the underlined ones, they very well may be excellent. For your sentences that are different, apply the four characteristics in the Introduction to Chapter 50 or discuss your sentences with your workshop partner.

1. Sarah Bernhardt, one of the most remarkable actresses who ever lived, toured North America several times in her private railway train.

2. American singers—for example, Grace Bumbry, Beverly Sills, and Jessye Norman—have appeared with opera companies all over the world.

3. Indira Gandhi, the former prime minister of India, held the same post as her father, Jawaharlal Nehru, the first prime minister of India, and as her son, Rajiv Gandhi, the present prime minister. (Do you see the five appositives in this sentence?)

4. The person instrumental in bringing the art of French cooking to the United States was an American woman who attended the Cordon Bleu Cooking School in Paris: Julia Child.

5. Women such as Betty Friedan, Gloria Steinem, and Jane Fonda, leaders of the women's liberation movement, have done much to raise the consciousness of women throughout the world.

6. A hard-working, dedicated, determined woman, Elizabeth Blackwell became the first female doctor in the United States.

Paragraph Work

Women, <u>over one-half of the human race</u>, have no rights in many countries. Among <u>the most fortunate women in the world</u>, women in the United States can vote, own property, and earn their own living. We, <u>the people of the United States</u>, must fight for equal rights for all women.

CHAPTER 51
Sentence Work

1. The first men who went into space were, according to popular belief, *rugged, intelligent, and stable.*

2. The Viking 1 and 2 spacecrafts were designed to conduct a *detailed, long-term scientific* examination of Earth's planetary neighbor, Mars.

3. Television programs that are *clear, interference-free, and uninterrupted by commercials* can be picked up on earth by simple radar dishes aimed at satellites.

4. Satellites can beam American television programs, *entertaining and technically competent, but culturally alien,* to many countries all over the world.

5. *Small, barren, spellbinding,* the moon has been the subject of books and the object of dreams.

6. *Chosen for their knowledge, renowned for their abilities, and acclaimed for their courage,* America's female astronauts are now traveling into space. (Note the cluster of verbals and prepositional phrases.)

7. *Its importance to space exploration unquestioned, its trip to Saturn an astonishing success, its data from the outer reaches of the solar system eagerly awaited,* Voyager II has more than satisfied American scientists. (Note the cluster of absolute phrases.)

8. *Economically, reliably, and efficiently,* the space shuttle will carry satellites into space.

9. The space shuttle crews have demonstrated the same sort of *skillfulness, dedication, and professionalism* as did the Apollo astronauts.

10. Some have said that the space shuttle—a remarkable hybrid—*blasts off like a rocket, glides like an eagle, and lands like an airliner.* (Note the cluster of verbs and prepositional phrases.)

Paragraph Work

Columbia Space Shuttle

The space shuttle is perhaps the most ambitious of America's space efforts, designed to serve the nation *scientifically, commerically, and militarily.* When the first shuttle, Columbia, was launched *to the cheers, to the awed gasps, to probably even the amazement* of hopeful spectators throughout the country, a new era in space flight was begun. And when the Columbia—*spectacular, beautiful, marvelous*—landed *with elegance, with grace, almost with gentleness* after her first voyage, that belief in the beginning of a new era was powerfully confirmed.

CHAPTER 52
Sentence Work

1. a. *To say the least*, John Updike is a prolific novelist, short-story writer, and critic.
   b. *With intelligence and humor*, Saul Bellow's novels discuss the enduring questions of the human condition.
   c. Of all Norman Mailer's books, *only The Deer Park* has been successfully adapted for the New York stage.
   d. *Finally*, Sam Shepard is having his talent as a playwright widely acknowledged in America.
2. a. Maxine Hong Kingston wrote a penetrating memoir of her Chinese-American childhood, *The Woman Warrior*.
   b. Sinclair Lewis's novel *Babbitt* described a type of American who is *all show and no substance*.
   c. *Mystically*, Annie Dillard, in *Pilgrim at Tinker Creek*, tells of her experiences in Virginia's Blue Ridge Mountains.
   d. Novelist Philip Roth is *renowned*.
   e. *West Coast poets* such as Gary Snyder and Lawrence Ferlinghetti have become respected by many critics.
   f. Walt Whitman, Thomas Wolfe, and John Dos Passos are three of the many writers who have tried to communicate America's *diversity*.
   g. *Vividly*, Henry David Thoreau, in *Walden*, tells of his experiences at Walden Pond.

CHAPTER 53
Sentence Work

1. Both Daniel Greysolon Duluth and Julien Dubuque were French-Canadian immigrants who explored the American wilderness and had cities named after them.
2. Until about thirty years ago, most immigrants arriving in the United States came from Europe; now most come from Asia, the West Indies, and Mexico.
3. During the Second World War, many Japanese-Americans, most of whom had been born in America and a number of whom were second- and third-generation Americans, were sent to internment camps.
4. During 1979 and 1980, individuals and groups took the opportunity to sponsor Vietnamese immigrants and to help them to settle in their new communities.

5. Canada has accepted large numbers of American immigrants: in the eighteenth century, Loyalists who did not support the American Revolution; in the nineteenth century, blacks who did not want to remain slaves; and in the twentieth century, draft resisters who did not want to fight in the Vietnam War.

CHAPTER 54
Sentence Work

1. <u>Many</u> of the "Forty-Niners" <u>came</u> to the Kansas Territory on Cherry Creek in 1858, having exhausted the gold fields of California and seeking new frontiers. (This is a loose sentence.)

2. Despite many seekers' finding little or no gold on their claims, and despite the fact that fortunes were being made by only the few, because new discoveries were regularly made, <u>prospectors</u> <u>continued</u> to rush to Alaska at the turn of the century. (This is a periodic sentence.)

3. <u>Miners</u> <u>recovered</u> more than $100,000,000 worth of gold in the Klondike between 1896 and 1904, despite the miners' having to pan by hand and use primitive sluicing methods. (This is a loose sentence.)

4. Because of the 1970s' phenomenal increase in the price of oil, a new <u>kind</u> of "black gold fever" <u>struck</u> the far North. (This is a periodic sentence.)

5. <u>Alaska</u> <u>is</u> once again <u>releasing</u> new wealth to those who have prospected for it, although the entire "black gold" drilling operation bears little resemblance to the efforts of the hardy individuals who formerly took riches from beneath the ground. (This is a loose sentence.)

CHAPTER 55
Sentence Work

1. Human beings have long sought to establish world records in a variety of endeavors, whether considered silly or serious.

2. Competitive athletes, especially competitive athletes like Mary Decker and Evelyn Ashford, run after records with great seriousness.

3. But it seems the competitive bubble gum blowers, car wreckers, pogo stick jumpers, and custard pie throwers have *been* and continue to be ever ready to pursue their world records with a healthy dose of great silliness.

4. But tobacco-spitting champions and world-class hula hoopers do indeed prepare *for* and participate in competitions apparently serious enough for the record keepers; in fact, Norris McWhirter's *Guinness Book of World Records* notes the results of a wide variety of human endeavors, including spitting and hoop spinning. (Note the three changes to this sentence.)

5. In McWhirter's book, the silly and the serious are so close together that we are made to think that they are equally important.

FOURTH
WORKSHOP
SECTION

Mechanical Conventions

ABOUT THE FOURTH WORKSHOP SECTION

In the Fourth Workshop Section you will find exercises and games to help you eliminate mechanical and technical errors in your writing. At times you may need to refer to a dictionary, thesaurus, or handbook. Perhaps your writing instructor will recommend specific reference books so that you and your classmates will be using the same authorities. See Suggestions for Further Study at the end of this textbook if you need additional help.

The chapters in this section are designed for you and a workshop partner to use together so that you will have someone to talk to, to check with, or to question. A fellow student at school or a friend or relative at home will make an ideal partner for all of the chapters in this section.

Consider, for a moment, your past performance as a writer. For example, perhaps you have come into contact with the rules of the comma by reading many textbooks, doing umpteen exercises, or listening to several lectures. Perhaps you still have difficulty, however, in determining whether or not to use a comma in a particular sentence construction. By working in depth with your partner on the various exercises and games, you can eliminate, once and for all, the errors that have made your writing imprecise, inaccurate, and unemphatic.

The best way to work in the Fourth Workshop Section is to do the quiz at the beginning of each of the chapters. Depending on your results, you can decide if you need to do the whole chapter, to do a part of it, or to ignore it completely.

If you need to work through the chapter, try to find a partner who knows more about the material than you. Although it is not absolutely necessary, a knowledgeable partner—involved in a one-to-one session with you—can speed up the process of your learning how to correct mechanical errors. If, however, your partner needs to do the chapter as well, do not be too concerned. Each of the chapters in the Fourth Workshop Section has all of the answers to the questions asked; as you *both* work through the chapter, one of you will soon discover the solutions to your problems.

You will benefit from each of the exercises if you and your partner role-play. One of you should be the student; the other should play the teacher. Do not be alarmed by being a teacher for a few minutes; people can learn as they teach. Rather than writing out the exercises, whenever possible talk through them with your partner; in that way, you can ask questions immediately, receive instant answers, and complete more exercises. Question your teacher-partner on anything that you do not understand. It will be his or her responsibility to come up with additional information so that you have a satisfactory answer. Sources of further information may include other textbooks, handbooks, handouts from your instructor, filmstrips, videotapes, and so on.

Common Sentence Errors

INTRODUCTION

Have you ever been shocked to hear that you make errors in your sentence construction? When you are by yourself and read over the sentences that you have just composed, they seem to say exactly what you wanted them to communicate. Your readers, however, sometimes receive different messages from your sentences from those you thought you were conveying. One reason for the breakdown in communication could be the result of your making one of the more common sentence errors: using a sentence fragment, a run-on sentence, a comma splice, a misplaced modifier, a dangling modifier, faulty parallel structure, faulty coordination, or faulty subordination.

Can you detect the sentence errors in the following paragraph? If so, write a corrected version *before* you check the Suggested Answers following Chapter 66.

I look over my paragraph and I read what I *think* I have written instead of what I really wrote. For my readers, one sentence may not make much sense, they must wonder what I'm really trying to say. By following a good workshop exercise on how to correct sentence errors, my writing style can become greatly improved. Learning from my instructor, talking with my peers, and working solo, I know I will be able to detect common sentence errors. After months of study when I finish taking this course. I anticipate that I will not make so many sentence errors. In the meantime, because I am never truly confident about my sentence structure, I never really know if I am right or wrong. But now I am determined to learn how to improve my sentences by concentrating on the rest of this chapter, I should improve. I'll give it my best shot at least. I haven't noticed too many errors in sentence structure while reading this paragraph. Therefore, I guess I had better look at the Suggested Answers to find out what sentence errors I need to work on at the end of this section.

If you need to work in this chapter, do the appropriate exercises below *with a partner who does not have problems with sentence structure*. It is important that you put yourself into the hands of your partner. Suggested answers for all of the exercises appear following Chapter 66, but let your partner refer to them rather than doing so yourself.

EXERCISE ONE
Sentence Fragments

The error known as a sentence fragment is sometimes called a nonsentence fragment, fragment fault, or incomplete sentence. In essence, a sentence fragment is a group of words that does not have a main verb or subject and, therefore, does not make complete sense. Do not confuse a sentence fragment with a legitimate fragment, also called a minor sentence (refer to Chapter 35).

If you regularly write sentence fragments, the best way to correct them is to read your work aloud. In addition, insert the punctuation aloud; for example, say the word *period* at the end of your sentences.

1. Here are a few examples of fragment faults. Make corrections and give them to your partner for comments. If you cannot correct any of them, ask your partner to help you.

Fragment Fault
When young and old visit California's Disneyland or Florida's Walt Disney World-Epcot Center. (Expand this sentence by supplying a missing clause or simply eliminate *when*.)

Fragment Fault
Disneyland, the amusement park that transcends all others. (Expand this sentence by supplying the missing verb.)

Fragment Fault
Disney World having many of the same attractions as Disneyland. (Expand by supplying a more complete verb.)

Fragment Fault
Is there a child who doesn't want to go to Disneyland? Adult, too? (Combine these.)

2. Without the aid of suggestions, correct the following sentences for your partner. One is satisfactory the way it stands.

   a. Each day the amusement park opens, the turnstiles record the customers. Automatically. Repeatedly. Rhythmically.

   b. Walt Disney with his daughter at an amusement park when he first dreamed of a park to entertain adults as well as children.

   c. He put substance to his dream by building scaled-down antique railroads. First in his backyard, then at the studio.

   d. Thirty thousand guests celebrating Disneyland's opening in 1955.

3. If you are still having problems, ask your partner to make up more examples. If possible, give your partner some of your old essays so that he or she can find examples of incomplete sentences from your own writing.

EXERCISE TWO
Run-on Sentences and Comma Splices

These two sentence construction errors are often linked, and rightly so. A run-on sentence or a comma splice indicates to your reader that you have treated two or more independent clauses as though you were composing only one. In a run-on sentence, you omit any punctuation between the independent clauses, causing them to run together; in a comma splice error, you separate the independent clauses with only a comma. You correct both errors in the same way: either separate the independent clauses into separate sentences or, if appropriate, compound them by separating them with a semicolon. (Chapter 44 provides many examples of compound sentences.)

1. Here are examples of sentences that run together. After you have corrected them, give them to your partner. If you cannot correct them, ask your partner to help you.

Run-on Sentence
Thousands of people visit Disneyland and Disney World every day that both amusement parks are open they go to be entertained. (Add a semicolon.)

Comma Splice
After visiting Disneyland and Disney World, tourists are surprised to see the same features, Main Street, daily parades, restaurants, shops, and most attractions are identical in both amusement parks. (Make two sentences.)

2. Without the aid of suggestions, correct the following sentences for your partner. One is correct.

  a. In the Haunted Mansion you will see the latest photographic inventions, dancers actually materialize and perform in 3-D as you are whisked past a ballroom.

  b. When you leave the Haunted Mansion, a ghost appears as you prepare to leave your moving seat, you can see one sitting beside you.

  c. Moving from the busy grounds, lining up in front of the Pirates of the Caribbean, and descending into the bowels of the earth, tourists are amazed by the enormity of the presentation.

  d. Just one trip through the Pirates of the Caribbean ride is simply not enough to see everything you need to go through several times.

3. If you are still having problems, ask your partner to make up more examples. If possible, give your partner some of your old essays so that he or she can find examples of run-on sentences or comma splices from your own writing.

EXERCISE THREE
Misplaced or Dangling Modifiers

Whether dealing with single words or groups or words that modify, you should apply the same general rules: for misplaced modifiers, place your modifiers near the word they describe; for dangling modifiers, because there is not a word in the sentence for your modifiers to describe, introduce one.

1. Here are examples of misplaced and dangling modifiers for you to correct. Afterwards, give them to your partner for comments. If you cannot correct any of them, ask your partner to help you.

Several Misplaced Modifiers

Everyone is warned of the potential danger in Space Mountain to heart patients who enters. (Three word groups need to be moved. You might cut a word so that the sentence makes better sense.)

Misplaced Prepositional Phrase

The ride because of its speed takes one's breath away. (Move the phrase "because of its speed" to two different positions. Which is better?)

Misplaced Verbal Phrase

Visitors often head for one of the three popular roller coaster mountains having passed through the front gates. (Instead of having a trailing verbal phrase, place it as an introductory verbal phrase.)

Dangling Prepositional Phrase

Sometimes, in Alpine costume, the face of the Matterhorn is climbed. (Introduce a word for the phrase to modify. Do you notice that you will have to change the verb from passive voice to active voice?)

Dangling Verbals

Screaming, laughing, getting wet, the Matterhorn has become a must-ride attraction. (Introduce a word for the verbals to modify.)

Dangling Verbal Phrase

Getting a glimpse of the sites of the Old West, rugged scenery can be seen whizzing past on the Big Thunder Mountain Railroad. (Introduce a word into the sentence that the phrase can modify. Do you notice that you will have to change the verb from passive voice to active voice?)

    Note: If you have had difficulties in understanding the suggestions to prevent misplaced or dangling modifiers, you might refer to other parts of *The Independent Writer* for more assistance. For example, you will see correctly placed phrases in Chapters 47, 48, and 49; clusters of adjectival and adverbial modifiers in Chapter 51; emphatic words and phrases in Chapter 52; and examples of verbs in the passive voice in Chapter 57.

2. Without the aid of suggestions, correct the following sentences for your partner. One is correct.

    a. The Disneyland Railroad was the first attraction planned by Disney, outlining the perimeter of the park.

    b. Riding the horse-drawn carriages, Main Street can be seen in a slow-paced, relaxing way.

    c. The Monorail, whizzing back from Tomorrowland to the nearby Disneyland Hotel, gives riders a good sense of the size of the park.

    d. Graphics treat passengers on the Peoplemover to an illusion of great speed in "The World of Tron."

3. If you are still having problems, ask your partner to make up more examples. If possible, give your partner some of your old essays so that he or she can find examples of misplaced or dangling modifiers from your own writing.

EXERCISE FOUR
Faulty Parallel Structure

When you present any kind of a list in a sentence, you should attempt to keep all elements of the list in the same form. If you do not, your parallel structure will be faulty. For a positive look at the benefits of using parallel structure, refer to Chapter 53.

1. Here are examples of faulty parallel structure (in italics) for you to correct. Afterwards, give the sentences to your partner for comments. If you cannot correct any of them, ask your partner to help you.

Faulty Parallel Structure

Glittering white horses lend *romance and a nostalgic air* to Cinderella's Golden Carrousel; it was originally built for a Detroit amusement park in 1917. (Make two adjectives.)

Faulty Parallel Structure

With its slender towers, lacy filigree, and because, overall, it's graceful, Disney World's 180-foot high Cinderella Castle towers over Disneyland's Sleeping Beauty Castle by 100 feet. (Make all the word groups phrases or dependent clauses.)

Unbalanced Sentence

Anaheim's recently rebuilt Fantasyland once looked like a cartoon collage; now the Tudor buildings make it resemble a small village. (Change some words in one of the clauses so that it is parallel in structure to the other.)

2. Without the aid of suggestions, correct the following sentences for your partner. One is correct.

a. It's a Small World has mechanical singing dolls, that also dance, from every country imaginable.

b. Rides such as the Jungle Cruise and Pirates of the Caribbean exploit a yearning for visitors to see the exotic, and the Haunted Mansion and 20,000 Leagues Under the Sea confront the unknown.

c. 20,000 Leagues Under the Sea, much like its Anaheim cousin, takes visitors past coral beds, near the lost city of Atlantis, under a polar ice cap, and it travels to the bottom of the sea.

d. Because the citrus groves that originally rimmed the Disneyland site soon gave way to unsightly commercial development and because Disney was concerned about the Florida wildlife, he planned his second Magic Kingdom four miles from the nearest interstate.

3. If you are still having problems, ask your partner to make up more examples. If possible, give your partner some of your old essays so that he or she can find examples of faulty parallel structure from your own writing.

EXERCISE FIVE
Faulty Coordination

Coordinating conjunctions (*and, or, but*) join equals. If you use a coordinating conjunction to join two clauses that are not really equal in ideas, your sentence will be faultily coordinated. For a look at well-coordinated sentences, see Chapter 44.

1. Here are examples of faulty coordination for you to correct. Afterwards, give them to your partner for comments. If you cannot correct any of them, ask your partner to help you.

Faulty Coordination
Disneyland was dismissed at first by architectural circles as vulgar and unprofessional, but Disney World wasn't. (Correct by making both clauses equal in structure and importance.)

Faulty Coordination
Disney was a brilliant animator and an environmentalist too. This is proved by the fact that Disney World's surroundings are wildlife sanctuaries. (Join the sentences and add a correlative conjunction to sharpen the relationship between its parts. See Chapter 44 for a list of correlative conjunctions.)

Faulty Coordination
Epcot Center's most impressive structure hovers on the horizon like a spaceship—and it's even called Spaceship Earth. (Add a conjunctive adverb to sharpen the relationship between the clauses. See Chapter 44 for a list of conjunctive adverbs. Remember to add a semicolon before and a comma after your conjunctive adverb.)

Faulty Coordination
Disney began plans for his Florida park in 1964; he died six months before the first shovelful was dug; Walt Disney World became a reality. (Subordinate two clauses.)

2. Without the aid of suggestions, correct the following sentences for your partner. One is correct.

    a. Epcot seeks to address serious issues, such as transportation, communications, energy, and agriculture, but the Magic Kingdom is just fun.

    b. Disney promised that Epcot would be a community of tomorrow that will never be completed, but will always be introducing and demonstrating new materials and systems.

    c. In Future World, 550 electronically controlled Audio Animatronics figures imitate life with lifelike movements and sounds and really is an example of art imitating life.

    d. Sometimes guests, going from Future World to the World Showcase, walk the mile-long promenade, but sometimes they take the bus.

3. If you are still having problems, ask your partner to make up more examples. If possible, give your partner some of your old essays so that he or she can find examples of faulty coordination from your own writing.

EXERCISE SIX
Faulty Subordination

Much of what you write should be placed in a subordinate position, so that the important points stand out. If, within a single sentence, you place important ideas in phrases or dependent clauses and unimportant ideas in independent clauses, you have subordinated incorrectly. For a look at several examples of correct subordination, see Chapters 45 and 46.

3. Here are examples of faulty subordination for you to correct. Afterwards, give them to your partner for comments. If you cannot correct one or more of them, ask your partner to help you.

Faulty Subordination
A placid, handmade lake is surrounded by the World Showcase, which consists of slightly scaled-down scenes of eight countries and an Independence Hall. (Reverse the emphasis: subordinate the independent clause; emphasize the dependent clause.)

Faulty Subordination
Because Canada's entry to this attraction features a beautiful hotel and a replica of the Rocky Mountains, it is a highlight of the World Showcase. (This sentence is not logical. Remove the subordination and then coordinate the clauses by introducing a correlative conjunction. See Chapter 44 for a list of correlative conjunctions.)

Faulty Subordination
At the World Showcase, because France, of course, contains an Eiffel Tower, a restaurant is operated by three French master chefs. (This sentence is not logical. Remove the faulty subordination, then coordinate the clauses by introducing a conjunctive adverb. See Chapter 44 for a list of conjunctive adverbs. Remember to add a semicolon before and a comma after your conjunctive adverb.)

Faulty Subordination
Troupers of England's Renaissance Street Theatre, who pick reluctant cast members from the audience, entertain the rest. (Use a verbal phrase to make the subordination clear.)

2. Without the aid of suggestions, correct the following sentences for your partner. One is correct.

   a. A little mouse named Mickey made his film debut in *Steamboat Willie*, which tops the bill at the Main Street Theater.

   b. Disney's castles, which were inspired by the architecture of twelfth- and thirteenth-century France and by that of the mad Bavarian King Ludwig at Neuschwanstein, invite visitors to Fantasyland.

   c. If visitors to the Haunted House think the attic is hard to keep dusted, they're right. The park buys and distributes dust by the five-pound bagful.

   d. Visitors have no idea of the flurry of activity going on in the basement thirty feet below the huge promenade deck they walk on.

3. If you are still having problems, ask your partner to make up more examples. If possible, give your partner some of your old essays so that he or she can find examples of faulty subordination from your own writing.

Inconsistency

INTRODUCTION

Even if your writing is unified and coherent, it can still confuse your audience if it is not consistent. For example, you should not shift from one verb tense to another, from the active to the passive voice, from a singular subject to a plural verb, from the third-person point of view to the second-person point of view, from informal to formal word choice, and so on.

The following exercises and games are varied and detailed. They shall involve you and your partner in oral rather than written activities so that you can quickly patch up any one of those inconsistencies that occurs. Because this chapter deals with many types of consistency, one should do only the exercises that really need to be done. (If you have noted five errors in consistency in the paragraph that you have just read, you do not need to do this chapter. Look at the Suggested Answers following Chapter 66 for a rewrite of this paragraph.)

EXERCISE ONE
Verb Tenses

The *tense* of a verb refers to the time in which an action takes place. The verb tense you use tells your reader whether the events you are discussing occur in the present, the past, or the future. Besides these three simple tenses, you may use a number of variations within each tense; for example, you could use the present progressive tense, the past perfect tense, or the conditional future tense. Learning to use the various tenses correctly will always be more important than being able to name the tense you are using; therefore, this exercise uses only the basic terminology.

You do not necessarily have to use the same verb tense throughout a piece of writing; indeed, you might have to change tenses more than once to make your piece coherent. But you should have a good reason for each change of tense and make sure that your reader knows why you have made the change.

With your partner, study the verb *know* by making up sentences in which you use each of the following inflections:

a. *Present tenses*: know, knows, have known, has known, is knowing, am knowing, has been knowing, is being known, do know

b. *Past tenses*: knew, had known, have known, is known, was known, was knowing, has been knowing, have been knowing, had been knowing, was being known, did know

c. *Future tenses*: shall know (use with first-person subjects, otherwise *shall* indicates determination), will know (use with second- or third-person subjects, otherwise *will* indicates determination), shall/will be knowing, shall/will have known, shall/will have been known, shall/will have been knowing (In speech, informal writing, and poetry the contractions *I'll*, *you'll*, *he'll*, *she'll*, and *they'll* indicate either futurity or determination. Traditionally, contractions have no place in formal writing.)

d. *Auxiliaries*: may know (implies permission, doubt, or possibility), might know (implies more doubt than *may*), can know (implies ability), could know (implies less certainty than *can*), should know and would know (expresses futurity from the standpoint of some past time; *should* implies duty, doubt, or hesitancy; *would* implies habitual action, determination, or condition), must know (implies necessity, obligation, or conviction), ought to know (implies duty or obligation more strongly than *should*)

e. *Verbal forms*: to know, to have known, known, knowing, having known, being known, having been known

Game One: A Tense Game

Play an oral game with your partner to reinforce your understanding of tenses. In preparation for the game, you and your partner will each need to draw up a list of verbs with their inflections. Make sure you know the three main inflections of irregular verbs; for example, *begin, began, begun; lie, lay, lain*. A dictionary or grammar handbook will provide you with more examples. Taking turns, give each other a verb. The object of the game is for your opponent to provide a sentence for each inflection of the verb. If a player uses a part of the verb incorrectly and you draw it to his or her attention, he or she loses one point. Continue the game until both players have used a predetermined number of verbs.

> From now on, when you write, consider the advantages of rewriting your work in a different tense. For example, rewriting in the present tense a piece that you originally wrote in the past tense may make it more vital and direct for your reader.

EXERCISE TWO
Active and Passive Voice

Beginning writers often shift between the active and the passive voice because they want to bring variety to their writing, but this shift may confuse the reader.

Remember that in the active voice the subject is the *doer* of an action, while in the passive voice the subject is the *receiver* of an action. Generally, the active voice, because it is direct, is stronger than the passive voice, which is indirect. The passive voice, however, is appropriate and effective in circumstances where you do not want the subject to be the doer of the action—for instance, "I *am expected* to help at my church's thrift sale." It may be inappropriate for you to use the more forthright active voice: "The church expects me to help at the thrift sale." Or there may be no specific doer of an action: "All citizens are encouraged to obey the law."

To ensure that your reader will stay on track, keep the verbs within a single sentence (and perhaps in your entire piece of writing) in the *same* voice.

1. Ask your partner to provide a sentence in the passive voice that you can convert to the active voice. Decide which sentence is better for your purpose. The following is an example:

- Passive: The touchdown *was scored* by the wide receiver. (The *wide receiver* who actually scored the *touchdown* is not the doer of the action.)
- Active: The wide receiver *scored* the touchdown. (The subject *wide receiver* is now doing the scoring.)

After working from passive to active, reverse the procedure, for example:

- Active: The Olympic champion *ran* a wonderful race.
- Passive: A wonderful race *was run* by the Olympic champion.

2. When you are certain of the difference between the active and passive voices, examine a recent piece of your writing. Underline all the verb forms, including auxiliaries. Do you shift from the active to the passive voice within your sentences?

Before you rewrite your piece, examine this excerpt from a piece of student writing:

> ... After three years in Portland, Oregon *was left* behind for the fourth time. I really *liked* living in Oregon but *kept* on leaving to find work as a musician. After Portland, I *traveled* to Lake Tahoe to spend a year working in the many resorts which *were* previously *found* on my last visit there. ... The next two years *were spent* working on the East Coast. All of my experiences *were relished*, and I *wouldn't give* up one of them.

Was left, were found, were spent, and *were relished* are passive. The inconsistencies in voice are confusing. In the first sentence, it appears that Oregon was "three years in Portland." The following version is clear and consistent:

> ... After three years in Portland, I *left* Oregon for the fourth time. I really *liked* living in Oregon but *kept* on leaving to find work as a musician. From Portland, I *traveled* to Lake Tahoe to spend a year working in the many resorts that I *had found* on my last visit there. ... (Continue revising this passage, using active verbs in the last two sentences.)

Game Two: Verb Usage

In preparation for this game on verb usage, you and your partner should prepare a predetermined number of sentences, each with at least one example of a verb used inconsistently. The object of the game is for your opponent to make the verbs consistent in tense and voice. Award one point for each inconsistency identified and corrected. If you present a sentence with two errors and your opponent catches only one of them, you pick up an extra point. (If you find it difficult to make up sentences, look in several different grammar handbooks for sample sentences. See Suggestions for Further Study at the end of this book.)

The following is a sample game: **A** gives **B** the sentence "Wyoming is known for the spectacular scenery of its vast plains and towering mountains, and many vacationers will be attracted there." **B** says that the future tense *will be* should be replaced by the present tense *are*, and receives one point. **B** then gives **A** the sentence "The warm Gulf Stream may raise the ocean temperature to eighty degrees as it would flow past the tip of Florida." **A** says that *would flow* should be *flows* for one point. **B** points out that *can* should be used instead of *may* because no permission is involved; thus, **B** receives an additional point. **A** then gives **B** another sentence, and the game continues until the players have used all the sample sentences.

EXERCISE THREE
Subject/Verb Agreement

Subjects and verbs must be consistent in number with each other. Unknowingly, beginning writers often provide a plural verb for a singular subject, or vice versa. The following suggestions may help you determine whether a subject is singular or plural. Study them with your partner. (When you make up sentences in the following exercise, make sure that *all* your verbs are in the *present tense*.)

1. Nouns that act as collective units take singular verbs:

- Recently, tourists have begun to flock to magnificent Alaska; their *number increases* every year.

If the parts of the collective unit are considered more important than the collective whole, however, the verb must be plural:

- Of all the tourists who visit Hawaii, a *number are* happy simply to lie on the warm beaches for hour after hour.

Concentrating on subject/verb agreement, you and your partner make up sentences with the following subjects: *jury, society, committee, class, audience.*

2. Some plural nouns that are singular in meaning take singular verbs:

- The *economics* of West Virginia largely *depends* on coal mining.

Other plural nouns that are singular in meaning take plural verbs:

- The *odds are* that, if the coal mining industry is in a slump, the entire state suffers.

Many plural nouns, depending on their meaning, can take either singular or plural verbs:

- *Statistics show* that Wisconsin leads the nation in milk and cheese production.
- *Statistics is* a science that many of the Sunbelt states have used to attract new industries.

Concentrating on subject/verb agreement, you and your partner make up sentences with the following subjects: *measles, ethics, pliers, linguistics, barracks, scissors, acoustics.*

3. Always consider quoted literary titles and names of organizations as singular nouns:

- The *United States is* one of the most richly diverse countries in the world.

Concentrating on subject/verb agreement, you and your partner make up sentences with the following subjects: *the House of Representatives, the Florida Keys, The Adventures of Tom Sawyer, San Diego State University.*

4. Compound singular subjects joined by *and* take plural verbs:

- *Iowa and Kansas are* among the country's most agriculturally productive states.

However, coordinate nouns (joined by *and*) that refer to the same person or thing take singular verbs:

- The *development and exploitation* of the Rocky Mountain states' mineral resources *is* actively *pursued* by private industry.

Concentrating on subject/verb agreement, you and your partner make up sentences with the following subjects, treating them respectively with singular and plural verbs: *the President and the Speaker of the House, an officer and a gentleman, the local teacher and minister, strawberries and cream.*

5. Use a singular verb when *every* or *each* precedes two coordinate nouns:

- *Every young man and woman* in New York *knows* that there are numerous opportunities for a higher education throughout the state.

Concentrating on subject/verb agreement, you and your partner make up sentences with the following subjects: *each plant and animal, every nook and cranny.*

6. Singular subjects followed by parenthetical expressions introduced by *with, along with, together with, as well as, like, including, in addition to,* and *no less than* take singular verbs:

- The *Californian,* as well as the Arizonan and New Mexican, *has* good reason to call her state a land of sunshine.

To avoid this rather formal construction you might use *and.* Note that the verb then changes because the number of the subject has changed:

- *The Californian, the Arizonan, and the New Mexican have* good reason to call their states lands of sunshine.

Concentrating on subject/verb agreement, you and your partner make up sentences with the following subjects: *a Georgian, as well as a Vermonter; a person from Illinois, like one from Michigan; a skilled farmer, together with a well-maintained machine; a steel worker, along with a lettuce harvester; an office manager, no less than a secretary.*

7. The constructions *one of those . . . who, one of those . . . which* and *one of those . . . that* take plural verbs:

- Louisiana is one of those *states* that *have* an important seaport.

However, notice the verb number in this sentence:

- Louisiana is one state that *has* an important seaport.

To determine whether the verb in a clause introduced by *who, which,* or *that* should be singular or plural, locate the antecedent of the pronoun. (*Note:* An *antecedent* is the word the pronoun replaces.) In the first example sentence above, the antecedent of *that* is *states,* so you should use a plural verb. In the second sentence, the antecedent is *state,* so you should use a singular verb.

Concentrating on subject/verb agreement, you and your partner make up sentences that begin with the following words:

- Daniel Boone was one of those Americans who . . .
- Chicago is a city which . . .
- Shirley Chisholm is one of those black members of Congress who . . .
- New England is one of those areas that . . .

8. When a compound subject is joined by *or, either . . . or, neither . . . nor, not only . . . but (also),* the verb agrees with the nearest subject:

- Not only *Massachusetts* but also *Maine wishes* to preserve a strong fishing industry. (There are two singular subjects; verb is singular.)
- Neither Ohio's *citizens* nor its *government wants* to allow uncontrolled dumping of pollutants in Lake Erie. (There is a plural subject plus a singular subject; verb is singular.)
- *Minneapolis* or its adjacent *municipalities contain* the head offices of several large American corporations. (There is a singular subject plus a plural subject; verb is plural.)

Concentrating on subject/verb agreement, you and your partner make up sentences with the following subjects:

- Either the South or the Midwest . . .
- Not only Connecticut but also the other New England States . . .
- Neither Nebraska's state legislators nor the governor . . .

9. When the subject of the verb differs in number from the complement, the verb always agrees with the subject rather than the complement. (*Note:* A *complement* follows a verb that has no action; the verb, therefore, needs to be completed.) The following sentence makes no sense without the complement *source:*

- Pittsburgh's *steel mills have been* a steady source of wealth for decades.

Concentrating on subject/verb agreement, you and your partner make up sentences with the following words, noting that you must provide a suitable verb that includes *has* or *have*:

- The women _____ the leaders.
- The book _____ a biography.
- Her tasks _____ a discovery.
- That university _____ his choice.

10. The number of the noun in a prepositional phrase does not affect the number of the verb:

- The *closing* of these mills *puts* thousands of persons, mostly blue-collar workers, out of work.

If you read the sentence *without* the prepositional phrase, you will then have no problem with agreement:

- The *closing puts* thousands of persons, mostly blue-collar workers, out of work.

Concentrating on subject/verb agreement, you and your partner make up sentences with the following subjects: *memory of the events, construction in the factories, excerpts from the book.*

11. *There* and *here* are adverbs, not subjects, and do not affect the number of the verb:

- Here are Southern California's two main industries: sun and fun.

Industries, not *here*, is the subject; therefore, you should use a plural verb. Concentrating on subject/verb agreement, you and your partner make up sentences with the following words, noting that you will have to supply a verb:

- Here _____ the list.
- There _____ the reasons.

12. Indefinite pronouns often cause problems with agreement. Writers can easily lose track of the nouns to which their pronouns refer; thus, they create an inconsistency between the antecedent and the pronoun reference. Because Chapter 60 deals extensively with the problems of pronouns, you should spend some time working on that chapter if you are having trouble with agreement.

EXERCISE FOUR
Consistency in Person

Most of the writing you do as a student is in the third person; that is, you use names of people, places, and things as well as pronouns, such as *he/she, it,* and *they* with their inflections: *him/her, his/hers, himself/herself, its/itself, them/themselves, their,* and so on. Often, you will use the first person (*I*) and its inflections: *my, mine,* and *myself*. Less frequently, you might use the second person (*you*) and its inflections *your*, *yours* and *yourself*.

1. Try explaining something to your partner using different points of view as illustrated below. When you have completed the exercise, try to determine which point of view you found the most comfortable and which the most awkward to use.

a. Start by explaining something to your partner from your point of view. You must use *I*, *me*, *my*, *myself*, and *mine*. Here is an example:

> If I want to see the United States, I think I would go by myself on a train. That way, I could see all the magnificent scenery and would not have to drive. That would suit me perfectly. My family has other ideas, but I prefer mine.

b. Reexplain your subject to your partner from the second-person point of view. Use *you*, *your*, *yours*, *yourself*. For example:

> If you want to see the United States, you should go by yourself on a train. . . .

Notice that other words may need to be changed.

c. Now use the third-person male or female point of view *(he/she, his/her, him/her, himself/herself*:

> If Jorge wants to see the United States, he should go by himself on a train.

d. Now use the impersonal third person (*one, one's, oneself*):

> If one wants to see the United States, one should go by oneself on a train.

e. Use the first- or third-person plural points of view (*we* or *they*):

> If we want to see the United States, we think we would go by ourselves on a train.

f. Exchange roles with your partner and repeat the exercise.

EXERCISE FIVE
Consistency in Diction

Chapters 37 and 64 deal with levels of word choice (diction); however, in this exercise you should note the importance of maintaining a consistent level of diction throughout a single piece of writing. If you start informally, for example, do not shift to formal word choice; if you are using formal language, do not introduce colloquialisms.

Inconsistent use of diction—mixing standard and substandard:

> One of our country's largest, most economically and culturally diverse, and—yessir, folks—most nonstoppably wild and ka-razy greater metropolitan areas is Los Angeles. Besides having other, perhaps more important, features, the Big Orange looks about ripe to explode with juicy fun-in-the-sun spots by the sea. Almost seventy miles of continuous and lovely sand beaches—nearly all of them costing users a big zero and wide open to every single John Q.

Citizen—stretch like a recreational blessing alongside the City of Angels. And in addition to its justly acknowledged recreational wealth, the coast of the kook 'n' cult capital of California protects one of the busiest and largest—I mean big, *really* big, humungous!—commercial ports in the world.

Consistent use of diction:

One of our country's largest, most economically and culturally diverse, and certainly most exciting greater metropolitan areas is Los Angeles. Besides having other, perhaps more important, features, the area is full of spots for the enjoyment of those who love the sun and ocean: almost seventy miles of continuous and lovely sandy beaches—nearly all of them free and accessible to the public—stretch like a recreational blessing alongside the City of Angels. And in addition to its justly acknowledged recreational wealth, the coast of the Los Angeles area protects one of the busiest and largest ports in the world.

The above example demonstrates a consistent use of standard diction. You and your partner should try to rewrite the paragraph so that it demonstrates a consistent use of substandard diction.

Game Three: Diction Consistency

Follow the same rules as in the game 'Verb Usage' described above. If you find it difficult to make up sentences, adjust ones from newspapers, journals, or textbooks by substituting one or more of the words in an original sentence for a word or words of a different level of diction. For example, you could begin with the following excerpt from *Time*: "All too frequently, fledgling African democracies have become hostage to leaders intent solely on gaining and holding power. In the past 25 years, more than 70 leaders in 29 African nations have been deposed by assassination, purges or coups." You could then create inconsistent diction by changing "leaders" to "top dogs" and "assassination" to "being bumped off." When your partner examines your rewrite of the original, he or she will have to indicate that the two changes you made are too informal for the established formal level of diction.

58

Wordiness

INTRODUCTION

A wordy sentence or selection is one that contains unnecessary words or details. But a long selection may not be wordy. If the extra details add meaning, they help you communicate what you want to say; if they do not, they merely confuse your reader. The following four simple rules will help keep you from being snared in words:

1. Use only those words necessary to fulfill your purpose; avoid really superfluous descriptive words and basically roundabout phrases.

2. Use words, when you write, that your audience or your readers are likely to know—that is, words they will understand.

3. Use very precise and solid concrete words for your topic, rather than quite vague and slightly abstract ones.

4. And last but not least, you should definitely work on this chapter if you did not notice an example of wordiness (or verbosity, as it is sometimes called) in each and every one of the foregoing rules. (See the Suggested Answers following Chapter 66.)

EXERCISE ONE
Redundancy

In their belief that the more words they use the clearer their ideas become, beginning writers often inject too many useless words into their sentences. As a consequence, a reader may become confused or exhausted. Notice how the italicized words are unnecessary in the following sentences:

- In much of his prose, Ernest Hemingway *actually* used large numbers of *tremendously* short words to tell his *deeply* exciting stories.

- Hemingway became *very* well known after most of his stories became *really* successful films.

1. Try to use one of these descriptive words in a sentence so that it is not redundant: actually, very, really, tremendously, too, quite, totally, especial, especially, even, important, deeply, completely, positively.

- Because of his numerous articles in popular magazines, Hemingway was *actually* better known to the general public as a big game hunter than as a novelist.

2. Try the same thing with these words: rather, a little, slightly, somewhat, sort of, something like, kind of.
3. Now try the same with these words: simply, generally, basically, always, obviously, particularly, effectively, as far as . . . concerned, incidentally, usually.
4. Have you discovered that you cannot easily justify your use of any of these words? If your writing resembles the following sentence, you and your partner should repeat all three of the above exercises.

- It is *so* easy to use words like these *very* ones that *actually* most people are *quite* unaware that they *usually* use them *a little* here and there.

EXERCISE TWO
Circumlocution

Circumlocution comes from Latin words meaning "to talk around." It involves using many vague and imprecise words instead of a few clear, precise ones.
1. Work with your partner to remove any wordiness from these sentences:

a. The famous writer Ernest Hemingway is one of the best-known American novelists who wrote long works of narrative fiction.

b. He had his life deeply and profoundly affected by the experiences he himself underwent as a volunteer who offered to drive an ambulance in the first one of our globe's two world wars.

c. Using some of his own personal war experiences as his background material, Hemingway wrote the novel *A Farewell to Arms*, which is one of the great war novels of our own century; that is, the twentieth century.

d. He began his writing career as a newspaper writer, and he wrote for the *Kansas City Star* and the *Toronto Star*.

e. He wrote as a foreign correspondent after the First World War, reporting on foreign affairs in Europe before he began his first serious fiction writing.

f. Hemingway practiced his writing in a number of various different forms: he was a journalist, a poet, a short-story writer, a playwright, and a novelist.

2. When you finish, go over the sentences again to see if you can eliminate even more words while retaining the same meaning as the original sentences.

3. When you cannot cut another word, turn to the Suggested Answers following Chapter 66 to compare your sentences with the ones there.

EXERCISE THREE
Monosyllable Power

Are you aware that many of our most important words are monosyllabic? Here are a few: love, live, birth, work, sex, sleep, health, eat, rich, poor, sun, good, God, hope, fun, food.

1. You and your partner add at least ten important monosyllabic words to the list.

2. Read this short paragraph:

In His Time

He learned to write in a time when the world had just felt the blast caused by the Great War. Men were then forced to see that they had been cut loose for good from an old and dead world they had grown up in and had known well. Now they were set down, at the end of this war, in a new kind of world that they had to sense as cold, tough, and sad, but which they had still to learn to face. His well-known prose bears all the marks of a man who tried to face this new world, to learn to live in it with some sort of grace, and to write—in a fine, clean style that was short and to the point—the harsh truth he saw there. His work tells much of what was seen and shared in his time by men, all of whom, it has been said, were "lost." But he wrote for our own time as well and used the words of John Donne to warn that none of us should "send to know for whom the bell tolls; it tolls for thee." That is to say that we, too, have been cut loose for good from an old and dead world that was once safe. He has made his time ours.

Did you notice that each word is monosyllabic? What is the effect? Do you find the writing immature? Why? In what way might writing a monosyllabic paragraph be helpful if you suffer from wordiness?

3. Write a short monosyllabic paragraph about yourself. Give it to your partner to check that you have included no words containing more than one syllable.

EXERCISE FOUR
Rewrite a Paragraph

1. With your partner read and rewrite the grossly overwritten paragraph below, according to the three rules mentioned in the Introduction to this chapter. Start with the title of the paragraph and take out all redundant words and circumlocutions, as well as jargon, dead metaphors, superfluous verbs, passive voice, and unnecessary uses of *be* and *which*. (If you do not understand any of these terms, see the Glossary or Index.)

The Work of Mr. Ernest Hemingway

It is a well-known and unarguable fact that writer Ernest Hemingway's greatness as a novelist and short-story writer rests partly (though not completely) on his ability to accurately depict human beings' experiences in addition to the appearance of the look of physical places. This consummate skill has gained for him his widest popular recognition by the reading public and has earned for him, also, his widest popular praise from that same reading public. And this is understandable and readily comprehended, for he (Ernest Hemingway) is probably unsurpassed, perhaps, in writing exactly what it is that a man *sees* in a wide variety of various experiences. The effects and the results of war are made plain and clear, to be sure, in the novel *A Farewell to Arms* and the novel *For Whom the Bell Tolls*; the sport of bullfighting is described with remarkable and noteworthy truthful fidelity as artful combat in the nonfiction book *Death in the Afternoon* and the fictional novel *The Sun Also Rises*; deep-sea ocean fishing is believably and convincingly presented to readers in the novel *The Old Man and the Sea*; *Green Hills of Africa* comes to life with vivid descriptions and depictions of big game hunting of African animals; and the chilling impression of the nearness of imminent death is exactly and precisely rendered in the short story "The Killers," and the novel *Islands in the Stream*. And Mr. Ernest Hemingway is also unsurpassed besides in describing the rivers and the hills and the jungles and the sea and the mountains and the plains that serve as background to these very human experiences that human beings have. He graphically illustrates for his reader the visual appearance of specific locales (or places): the words of Upper Michigan in "Big Two-Hearted River" (a short story), the snow-covered mountain Kilimanjaro in Africa in "The Snows of Kilimanjaro" (yet another short story), Paris, France, in *A Moveable Feast* (a short autobiographical work about a part of his own life), and Venice, Italy, in *Across the River and into the Trees* (a novel). All of this richly vivid prose writing forms the foundation for and supports the judgment and assessment that Ernest Hemingway—as a writer— is indeed one of literature's greatest and most eminent masters of literary description.

2. When you have tightened the paragraph as much as you can, turn to the Suggested Answers following Chapter 66 to see one possible rewrite.

59

Ineffective Constructions

INTRODUCTION

Many writers do not realize how ineffective some of their sentences are until they discover how bored their readers become with their work. Ineffective sentence constructions, however, are not the same as incorrect ones. In this chapter you will discover how to revise ineffective sentences.

Instead of doing a quiz of unfamiliar material to determine whether or not you should complete this chapter, you should test your latest piece of writing by circling all parts of the verb *be—is, am, are, was, were, being, been*—and bracketing every *which, who, whom, that, there,* and *it.* These words, especially if you have used them excessively, result in ineffective constructions.

Notice how this paragraph from a student's essay on Ibsen's *The Wild Duck* has an excessive use of the verb "be" and "it."

Symbolism in *The Wild Duck*

Ibsen uses the symbol of the wild duck to give force to his theme. The duck, [which] (is) a living, wild creature, and its relationship with other characters and its environment (is) unique. The relationship (is) so intertwined [that] certain events may not (be) occurring within the duck's presence. The symbolism of the duck (is) present throughout the play, and [there] (is) a parallel between the duck's existence and human existence. The duck (is) a wild creature; [it] (is) wild and untouched by humankind. [It] (is) happy in its wild state until [it] (is) shot by a hunter. Its natural instinct, when [it] (was) wounded, [is] to hide so [it] dives into the ocean. But [it] (is) retrieved by the hunter's dog. The duck, [which] (was) still alive, (is) adopted by a family and placed in an artificial environment where [it] exists, but [it] (is) not happy.

If your piece looks like the above one, you should complete all of the following exercises.

EXERCISE ONE
Ineffective Use of Verbs

The various parts of the verb *be* are essential to many sentences, and you do not have to banish them from your writing. Sentences like the following are effective:

- Norman Mailer *is* an essayist and social critic as well as a novelist.
- The American writer *is* a special person, according to Mailer, who *has been* the most reliable interpreter of American culture.

With your partner write a similar sentence in which a form of *be* is essential.

Only when you use the parts of *be* excessively does your writing suffer. In most cases your sentences will be healthier with other, stronger verbs. Note the difference between these two pairs of sentences:

From
Saul Bellow and Norman Mailer are two Americans who are writers of novels. (excessive use of *be*)

To
Saul Bellow and Normal Mailer are two American novelists.

From
Both are writing about the problems and the obsessions of men. (*be* as an auxiliary verb)

To
Both write about the problems and obsessions of men.

Substituting other linking verbs (*feel, become, seem*) for *be* will not make the construction more effective. For example:

- In Saul Bellow's *Humboldt's Gift*, the poet Fleisher is troubled during his wild swings between manic and depressive moods. (ineffective use of *be*)
- In Saul Bellow's *Humboldt's Gift*, the poet Fleisher feels troubled during his wild swings between manic and depressive moods. (ineffective use of linking verb *feels*)
- In Saul Bellow's *Humboldt's Gift* the poet Fleisher suffers during his wild swings between manic and depressive moods. (effective use of *suffers*)

The verbs *do* and *have* often cause the same problems as *be*. *Do* is often unnecessary and can be eliminated, as in the following examples:

From
Many readers do prefer the wide variety of Mailer's work to Bellow's more concentrated efforts.

To
Many readers prefer the wide variety of Mailer's work to Bellow's more concentrated efforts.

You can often substitute a specific verb for *have* by changing a word already in the sentence to a verb, as follows:

From
Mailer's writing has a great deal of criticism of the various uses of power in America.

To

In much of his writing, Mailer criticizes the various uses of power in America.

 If you are interested in eliminating other weak verbs from your writing, you might refer to Chapter 64, Exercise Four.

1. Find a sentence from your work that contains an overuse of the verb *be* and other linking verbs. With your partner, rewrite it in the same way as the sentences above.

2. If you or your partner has used any parts of *do* (*do, did, done, does*) or *have* (*have, has, had*) in your writing, try to substitute specific verbs for them.

EXERCISE TWO
"Bewhichment"

 The use of *which* or other relative pronouns (*who, whom, that*) with the verb *be* can create a strong sentence.

  • Men *who* are stronger than their illusions and *who* triumph by making the best of their circumstances are important characters in some of Bellow's novels.

 Many beginning writers, however, use this type of dependent clause because it's easy to use. Consequently, their writing becomes riddled with *be* and *which*; such writing is not only tedious, it is "bewhiched." "Bewhichment" includes the following constructions: "It was...which is...," "That is...who will be...," and so on. Overuse of the *which* clause is easy to cure—change the clause to a verbal phrase or absolute. Study the following examples:

From

One of Mailer's early novels is *The Deer Park*, which was considered obscene by some readers at the time of its publication and which was banned from some public bookshelves.

To

One of Mailer's early novels is *The Deer Park*, considered obscene by some readers at the time of its publication and banned from some public bookshelves.

 The verbal phrases "considered obscene by some readers" and "banned from some public bookshelves" in the second sentence are more emphatic than the *which* clauses in the first sentence because they are more concise.

From

Bellow, who had already established his reputation as a serious writer in the 1940s, finally won national popularity with his 1953 novel, *The Adventures of Augie March*.

To

Bellow, his reputation as a serious writer already established in the 1940s, finally won national popularity with his 1953 novel, *The Adventures of Augie March*.

 The absolute "his reputation as a serious writer already established in the 1940s" is more emphatic than the *who* clause in the first sentence.

 Find a similar sentence from your own or your partner's work and rewrite it in the same way as the above examples.

Many writers are fond of using *it* and *there*. If you are too, you may find that your sentences contain the patterns "There is...which..." or "It is...that...." These patterns produce verbs in the passive voice rather than the active voice, and the wordier dependent clause rather than the more mature phrases and appositives:

From

There is one of Mailer's novels, *The Naked and the Dead*, that has been made into a successful movie by famed director Raoul Walsh.

To

Famed director Raoul Walsh made one of Mailer's novels, *The Naked and the Dead*, into a successful movie.

From

It is one of Bellow's middle novels, *Henderson the Rain King*, that is regarded most highly by many critics.

To

Many critics regard most highly *Henderson the Rain King*, one of Bellow's middle novels.

Notice that the active voice is stronger than the passive voice in both the above examples. (See Chapter 57, Exercise Two for more details on voice.)

If you or your partner has used an *it* or *there* with a part of the verb *be* in one of your sentences, rewrite it in the same way as the above. For more practice, you and your partner rewrite the following sentences to make them more effective. Do not look at the Suggested Answers following Chapter 66 until you have both worked on each sentence.

a. Norman Mailer himself is the central figure in *The Armies of the Night*, which tells of people who are demonstrating against the war in Vietnam.

b. Bellow has lived in Chicago for much of his life, and there are novels like *Dangling Man*, *Herzog*, and *Humboldt's Gift* that use that city for background.

c. *Of a Fire on the Moon* is a book that has been written by Mailer and that describes the Apollo 11 moon shot.

d. It is notable that both Mailer and Bellow have had their work acclaimed internationally, and it is also notable that they have both received the Pulitzer Prize.

e. Mailer has been fascinated by the life of Marilyn Monroe, who was one of Hollywood's true stars, and in 1973, he published a book about her, which was called *Marilyn*.

f. Critic Diana Trilling says that Bellow's novel *The Victim* is successful on many levels.

g. *King of the Hill* is Mailer's account of one of the championship fights between heavyweights Muhammad Ali and Joe Frazier.

h. The Nobel Prize in literature, which was awarded to him in 1976, has done much to make Saul Bellow better known to more people.

i. Something we can all debate is whether Norman Mailer or Saul Bellow has done more to promote most effectively the fact that a genuine writer is a deliberate and hardworking artist.

j. Lately there has been another "writer," one who apparently thinks that the craft of writing requires no care more painstaking than that demanded by casual howling—he is C. Fred Bush, who is Vice-President George Bush's dog and the author of *C. Fred's Story*.

EXERCISE THREE
Detecting Ineffective Constructions

1. Read the following excerpts, paying particular attention to the verbs and pronouns discussed in this chapter. In fact, it might be helpful if you were to underline every form of *be* (and all other linking verbs), *do*, *have*, as well as *which*, *who*, *that*, *there*, and *it*.

a.   He had had a wife—two wives—and been the object of such death-flavored fantasies himself. Now: the first requirement of stability in a human being was that the said human being should really desire to exist. This is what Spinoza says. It is necessary for happiness (*felicitas*). He can't behave well (*bene agere*), or live well (*bene vivere*), if he himself doesn't want to live. But if it's also natural, as psychology says, to kill mentally (one thought-murder a day keeps the psychiatrist away), then the desire to exist is not steady enough to support a good life. Do I want to exist, or want to die? But at this social moment he couldn't expect to answer such questions, and he swallowed freezing bourbon from the clinking glass instead. The whisky went down, burning pleasurably in his chest like a tangled string of fire. Below he saw the pock-marked beach, and flaming sunset on the water. The ferry was returning. As the sun went down, its wide hull suddenly filled with electric lights. In the calm sky a helicopter steered toward Hyannis Port, where the Kennedys lived. Big doings there, once. The power of nations. What do we know about it? Moses felt a sharp pang at the thought of the late President. (I wonder what I would say to a President in actual conversation.)...(from *Herzog*, by Saul Bellow)

b.   Over the years, a photographer named Clayton had taken photographs of the poor, of the very poor, of Southern Black faces so poor they were tortured by hunger. Remarkable faces looked back at him, the faces of saints and ogres, of emaciated angels and black demons, martyrs, philosophers, mummies and misers, children with the eyes of old vaudeville stars, children with faces like midgets and witches, children with eyes which held the suffering of the lamb. But they were all faces which had gone through some rite of passage, some purification of their good, some definition of their remaining evil—how loyal could evil be to people so poor? Aquarius retreated from these photographs with no unhappy sense of shock—these poor to whom he like every other middle-class mother of a professional gave money from time to time (or to their charities at least) were a people on a plane of subsistence which had tortured their flesh, but delivered some essence of their nature, some delineation which never arrived to the face of men and women who were comfortable. They had survived, they looked indeed as if they had passed under one of the four corners of the winding-sheet of the dead, and so knew more than he would ever know. Yes, remarkable faces looked back at him, more beautiful by far than his face would ever be . . . . (from *Of a Fire on the Moon*, by Norman Mailer)

c.   I quickly explored and found out that the kitchen and laundry room are in the basement. The first floor has a dining room, a living room, a sun porch, a library with books about and by vice presidents—collected by Walter Mondale, forty-second Vice President of the United States of America—and a big entrance hall. On the second floor there are two big, beautiful bedrooms, a family sitting room and George's dressing room-office. George loves his little spot and works there every night with me by his feet and his pet bonefish on the wall. On the third floor there is one gymnasium-size bedroom and two tiny bedrooms where Paula reigns. I sleep there when George and Bar are gone. Bar has her office on the third floor. It's a combination office and exercise room with a stationary bike, a running machine, a typewriter, files and a desk. The walls are covered with pictures. There is one especially good one of me with President and Mrs. Reagan. (from *C. Fred's Story*, by C. Fred)

2. Do you think any of these writers needs to get rid of any excessive use of *be*, *which*, *there*, *it*, and so forth? Try to rewrite some of their sentences. Are your sentences better?

3. Which piece did you find easiest to read? Most difficult? Why?

4. Which book would you like to read in its entirety? Why?

EXERCISE FOUR
Write to Order

Write a piece of approximately 100 words for your partner on a topic you think he or she will enjoy. In this exercise, however, you are not permitted to use any of these words:

it	be	is	am	was	were	being
there	been	are	which	that	who	whom
do	does	done	have	has	had	having
feel	felt	seem	seemed	become	becoming	became

EXERCISE FIVE
Revise Your Ineffective Constructions

1. Now with your partner, go back to the beginning of this chapter and rewrite "Symbolism in *The Wild Duck*." Try to get rid of every form of *be*, *do*, and *have*, as well as every *which*, *who*, *that*, *it*, and *there*. After you have rewritten the paragraph, turn to the Suggested Answers following Chapter 66 to compare your version with another.

2. Now, by yourself, rewrite your own piece of writing that you marked at the beginning of this chapter. Use the ideas in the exercises to increase your writing effectiveness. Ask your partner to read your piece to see if you have succeeded. Has your style changed significantly?

60

Pronoun Weakness

INTRODUCTION

Of the eight parts of speech, the pronoun causes the most confusion and is the most likely to lead to grammatical errors. Before you start this chapter, find out your pronoun power by doing the following quiz.

Do you think there is anything wrong with the italicized pronouns in these sentences? Which pronoun should be used instead? Do not look at the Suggested Answers following Chapter 66 until you have completed the *entire* quiz. The instructions there will let you know if you should do this chapter.

a. There is no difference in height between *her* and *me*.

b. My cousin, *whom* she knows well, works at McDonald's.

c. My brother is meeting *her* at the airport, but doesn't know *who she* is.

d. Every one of the boys has *his* favorite sport.

e. They all have one movie star of *whom* they are fond.

f. We have never been quite so conscious of *who we* are as today.

g. Every night our dog howls *its* head off, and *it's* embarrassing.

h. Consider *yourselves* lucky that all three of you survived the plane crash.

i. Jeff wanted to come with *me* to Miami; *he* and *I* decided to share expenses.

j. Either all or none have *their* climbing equipment in the car.

After you have checked the Suggested Answers, determine whether you should complete this chapter. To have complete pronoun power, you should be familiar with *all* the different kinds of pronouns.

EXERCISE ONE
Recognizing Pronouns

No new pronouns have been introduced into the English language for centuries; in fact, their number is now decreasing. Why, then, are they so troublesome to master? The main reason is that they, like verbs, can be inflected; for example, by inflecting *I*, we get *me, my, myself*; by inflecting *who*, we get *whom, whose, whoever*. Because English speakers are not used to inflection, some have never learned the difference between *Billy and me* and *Billy and I* and could just as easily flip a coin to decide when to use *whom* and when to use *who*. Nonnative speakers, in learning English, catch on quickly, because many are used to inflecting; for example, notice how the most common English word, *the*, is inflected in other languages:

- French: *le, la, l', les*;
- German: *der, das, die*;
- Spanish: *el, la, los, las, lo*;
- Italian: *il, lo, la, l', i, gli, gl, le*.

1. Make up some sentences for your partner that contain an overabundance of nouns. Your partner must substitute a pronoun for as many of the nouns (antecedents) as possible, as in the following example:

From

The agent said to the actor that the agent would be the actor's agent and would make the actor a legend if the actor would sign the agent's contract.

To

The agent said to the actor that *she* would be *his* agent and would make *him* a legend if *he* would sign *her* contract.

2. Repeat the exercise, exchanging roles with your partner.

EXERCISE TWO
Personal Pronouns

1. Use the following chart to clarify any problems you have with inflection. Notice that these pronouns inflect for case (subjective or nominative, objective, and possessive) and for number (singular and plural). (Note that the italicized words in the chart are, in fact, possessive adjectives.)

SUBJECT FORMS			OBJECT FORMS		POSSESSIVE FORMS	
Person	Singular	Plural	Singular	Plural	Singular	Plural
First	I	we	me	us	*my*, mine	*our*, ours
Second	you	you	you	you	*your*, yours	*your*, yours
Third Masculine	he	they	him	them	*his*, his	*their*, theirs
Third Feminine	she	they	her	them	*her*, hers	*their*, theirs
Third Neuter	it	they	it	them	*its*, its	*their*, theirs

2. Answer the following questions with your partner:

a. Which personal pronouns do not have different subject and object forms?

b. Notice that personal possessive forms do not use apostrophes. Also notice that most have two forms: one as a modifier ("This is *your* book.") and the other to stand alone ("This is *yours*."). Make up a few sentences using *their* and *theirs*, *her* and *hers*, *our* and *ours*.

c. Why do *his* and *its* not have two forms? Make up two sentences for *his*: use it first as a modifier and then on its own. Do the same for *its*.
Note: The word *it's* (with the apostrophe) is a contraction for *it is* or *it has* ("*it's* been good" = it has been good), not a possessive form. Make up a few sentences containing *it's*.

3. Once you appreciate the difference between and the significance of the subject and object forms, you will no longer be confused about which personal pronoun to use. Study the following pairs of examples carefully:

a. *Movie stars* come and go.   (subject of verb)
They come and go.   (subject of verb)

b. Fans remember *movie stars*.   (object of verb)
Fans remember *them*.   (object of verb)

c. They write letters to *movie stars*. (object of preposition)
They write letters to *them*.   (object of preposition)

d. It was *Marilyn Monroe* who became a legend.   (complement of linking verb; requires subject form)
It was *she* who became a legend.   (complement of linking verb; requires subject form)

e. This is *Marilyn's*.   (possessive complement)
This is *hers*.   (possessive complement)

f. Handling stardom was *Monroe's* biggest problem.   (possessive noun)
Handling stardom was *her* biggest problem. (possessive adjective)

Problems in using personal pronouns usually occur when they are coupled with nouns or are compounded. If you forget, for a moment, the compound group and use the personal pronoun alone, you will *always* choose the correct form of the pronoun. Here are some examples:

- Joe DiMaggio and she married. (*She* married. NOT *Her* married.)
- The marriage gave Monroe and him more publicity. (The marriage gave *him* more publicity. NOT gave *he*.)
- Publicists wanted interviews with Marilyn and him. (Publicists wanted interviews with *him*. NOT with *he*.)
- It was Arthur Miller and she who next captured the headlines. (It was *she* who next captured the headlines. NOT It was *her*.)

4. Change any incorrect personal pronouns in the following sentences after considering the case of each. Look at the Suggested Answers following Chapter 66 if you have any difficulty.

a. Mae West and W. C. Fields were legends in their own time. Between she and he, they made countless successful films in the thirties.

b. Some of the films took him and her through impossible adventures.

c. The real stars, he and her, demanded top billing in all of their films.

d. Supporting actors were always overshadowed by the real stars, her and he.

e. Us boys are going to see Mae West.

f. She always promised to entertain we boys if we would "come up to see her sometime."

g. It was him who said, "Don't act with kids or animals."

h. She was taller than he.

i. He could drink more than her.

j. They acted as though they were better than us.

THE FAR SIDE By GARY LARSON

"So, then . . . Would that be 'us the people' or 'we the people?' "

Reprinted by permission of Chronicle Features.
San Francisco, California.

Game One: Personal Pronoun Power

Use the game rules outlined in Chapter 64, to play the following game. Prepare for the game by making up sentences similar to those above.

With your partner, take turns presenting your sentences to each other; for example, **A** says to **B** "Give it to George and he before you leave." **B** says "It should be 'to George and *him*'" for one point. **B** then gives **A** "She and her friend came over for a party with my mom and me." The game continues in this way until you present all of the prepared sentences.

EXERCISE THREE
Reflexive Pronouns

Note that the pronouns in the following chart are the only reflexive forms; *hisself*, *theirselves*, and *ourself* do not exist in standard English.

PERSON	SINGULAR	PLURAL
First	myself	ourselves
Second	yourself	yourselves
Third Masculine	himself	themselves
Third Feminine	herself	themselves
Third Neuter	itself	themselves
Third Indefinite	oneself	—

There are two uses for the reflexive pronoun:
  1. To indicate that an action turns back on the subject:

  • Charlie Chaplin directed *himself* in films like *The Gold Rush*.
  Make up a few sentences containing reflexive pronouns used this way.

  2. To indicate emphasis. When used this way, a reflexive pronoun is called an *intensive pronoun*:

  • He *himself* starred in and wrote many silent classics.

  • His movie fans *themselves* made him a legend.
  Make up a few sentences containing intensive pronouns.

EXERCISE FOUR
Relative Pronouns

Notice the limited inflection of relative pronouns:

SUBJECT FORM	OBJECT FORM	POSSESSIVE FORM
who	whom	whose
whoever (whosoever)	whomever (whomsoever)	whosesoever
which	which	whose
that	that	—
as (if *as* can take the place of *that*, it's a relative pronoun.)		

Who refers to persons; *which*, to animals or things; and *that*, to persons, animals, or things.

Relative pronouns introduce dependent clauses and refer to an antecedent in the independent clause:

- Some people *who* have seen Chaplin's earliest films do not care for them.
- Those films, *which* are mostly wild chases, are no longer interesting.
- They do not have the same appeal for us *as* they did for audiences in 1910.
- Mack Sennett, *whose* best-known characters are the Keystone Kops, directed some of Chaplin's early films.

The main difficulty in mastering relative pronouns lies in the confusion of *who* and *whom*. When in doubt substitute *he* for *who* and *him* for *whom*. However, you should be aware that the objective form (*whom, whomever, whomsoever*) is disappearing from our speech, although it is still used in formal, written English. Through usage, *who* is acceptable in the following sentences:

- Who does the Little Tramp remind you of?
- Do you know who you think of, when you hear "Chaplin"?
- Who was he with?
- You may invite who (whoever) you want to go to *Limelight* with you.
- Who (Whoever) shall we invite to see *Monsieur Verdoux*?

Technically, *who* in each instance above is in the objective case, but it looks like a subject. Which pronouns are the true subjects in each of the above sentences?

Whom is still used when it follows a preposition:

- To whom are you sending a photo of Chaplin?
- With whom are you going to see *The Great Dictator*?

The major error is the use of *whom* when *who* is correct. If you break up each clause into its main subject and main verb, you should have no difficulty. For example, the sentence "Who do you think welcomed Chaplin after he left America?" contains "You do think/Who welcomed Chaplin/He left America." Because you would say "He welcomed Chaplin" rather than "Him welcomed Chaplin," you should never write "Whom do you think welcomed Chaplin."

The same is true of the sentence "Chaplin was a man who we all knew would succeed." (Chaplin was a man/We knew/Who would succeed.) You would say "He would succeed" rather than "Him would succeed"; therefore, you should never write "Chaplin was a man whom we all knew would succeed."

With your partner, break these sentences into parts to prove that *who* is correct usage.

- **a.** Chaplin, who Senator Joseph McCarthy thought was guilty of being a Communist, was never proved guilty.
- **b.** Chaplin, the Little Tramp, who you recall stole the hearts of millions, will be remembered longer than Chaplin the person.

EXERCISE FIVE
Demonstrative Pronouns

Demonstrative pronouns have only one simple inflection:

	SINGULAR	PLURAL
	this	these
	that	those

Demonstrative pronouns point out:

- *This* is my favorite film. *These* are my favorite films.
- Give me *that*. Give me *those*.

If they are used to modify, these words become demonstrative adjectives:

- *This* film is my favorite. *These* films are my favorites.
- Give me *that* film. Give me *those* films.

For your partner, make up sentences using *this*, *that*, *these*, and *those*. See if your partner can tell the difference between a demonstrative pronoun and a demonstrative adjective.

Writers often incorrectly use a singular demonstrative with a plural antecedent, or vice versa, as in the following examples:

- This is the kinds of movies I enjoy more than any other.
- These are the kind of movies I enjoy more than any other.

The correct forms are as follows:

- This is the kind of movie I enjoy more than any other.
- These are the kinds of movies I enjoy more than any others.

EXERCISE SIX
Pronouns That Do Not Inflect

What, whatever, and *that* do not have different subjective and objective forms; thus, no matter how you use them, their form does not change:

- *What* goes up must come down. (pronoun in subjective case)
- *What* do you want to see? (pronoun in objective case)

For your partner, make up sentences using *that* and *whatever* in different forms.

EXERCISE SEVEN
Indefinite Pronouns

This large group of pronouns causes problems because some are singular, some plural, and some either singular or plural (depending on usage).

SINGULAR	PLURAL	EITHER SINGULAR OR PLURAL
anyone	both	none
everyone	many	some
no one	several	any
each	few	most
everybody	a few	all
somebody	a number	more
someone	a variety	
either		
neither		
nothing		
anything		
everything		
anybody		
nobody		
something		

These pronouns are called *indefinite* because they do not refer to a specific person or thing and often do not have a definite antecedent.

Knowing to which column in the above chart each of the indefinite pronouns belongs will help you avoid making agreement errors. Singular indefinite pronouns must have singular verbs:

- *Everybody loves* the films of the legendary team of Fred Astaire and Ginger Rogers.

Plural indefinite pronouns must have plural verbs:

- *Many* of his dances and *all* of hers *were* choreographed by Hermes Pan.

Pronouns from the third column are singular or plural depending on their use. Use singular verbs and other pronoun references with these pronouns when they refer to quantity or bulk; use plural verbs and other pronoun references when they refer to units or numbers:

- *All was* harmony when they danced together.
- *All* who watched *were* spellbound by the magic they created.
- *No one moves his* body so suavely as Astaire.
- *None* of his partners matched *themselves* so well to his style as Rogers did.

Using the list of indefinite pronouns, decide with your partner which of the words in parentheses to use. Look at the Suggested Answers following Chapter 66 if you have difficulty.

a. Someone who was very close to Astaire (was, were) his sister and former partner, Adele.

b. Some of the difficulties Rogers had to surmount when dancing (was, were) high-heeled shoes, awkward costumes, and highly polished floors.

c. Nothing (was, were) ever left to chance in the long, elaborate duets.

d. Neither of them (was, were) satisfied with second best.

   e. They were such fine dancers that they rarely refilmed a dance; most (was, were) completed in a single take.

   f. Astaire and Rogers made a number of memorable films; a few (is, are) *Flying Down to Rio, The Gay Divorcée,* and *The Story of Vernon and Irene Castle.*

To add to your mastery of the indefinite pronoun, you should note that eight indefinite pronouns—*anybody, anyone, everybody, everyone, somebody, someone, nobody, no one*—inflect for the possessive case. Like nouns, they use an apostrophe plus *s* to denote possession (anybody's script, someone's script, no one's script).

If you add *else* to any of these eight pronouns, you would add the *s* to the *else* rather than the pronoun (anybody else's script).

The versatile indefinite pronoun may also have modifiers. Generally, however, modifiers *follow* indefinite pronouns, as in the following examples:

   • Something *extraordinary* lights up the screen when Astaire and Rogers dance.
   • Nothing *stagy or overblown* appears in their numbers.
   • Each *of their dances* is a masterpiece of timing and skill.
   • Everyone *who enjoys movie musicals* has a favorite Astaire/Rogers film.

If you are having problems with pronoun subject and verb agreement, try reading the above sentences *without* their modifiers:

   • Something lights up the screen when Astaire and Rogers dance.
   • Nothing appears in their numbers.
   • Each is a masterpiece of timing and skill.
   • Everyone has a favorite Astaire/Rogers film.

The correct number of the verb quickly becomes apparent. You would never say "each are" or "everyone have."

Finally, many indefinite pronouns can lose their identity and become adjectives. Determine whether the italicized words function as indefinite pronouns or adjectives in the following sentences:

   • *Most* of their fans will see their films again and again.
   • *Most* fans will see their films again and again.
   • Only *a few* of the trivia fans remember the plots of the films.
   • Only *a few* trivia fans remember the plots of the films.

Game Two: Indefinite Pronoun Power

   Use the same instructions as for Game One. This game might be played as follows:

   A gives **B** "Some of the boys walks to school." **B** says "It should be 'Some of the boys *walk* to school'" for one point. Then **B** gives **A** "Not every one of the fans of television's *Star Trek* enjoys the movie version." The game continues in this way until you use all the sample sentences.

EXERCISE EIGHT
Ambiguity

When you use the full complement of pronouns and possessive adjectives, you can inadvertently create confusion for your reader if he or she does not know the exact antecedent of each pronoun. Such an error is called *ambiguity* or *faulty pronoun reference*.

A pronoun (or a possessive adjective) by itself is meaningless. Only when it refers to its antecedent does a pronoun have meaning. For example, in the sentences "Movie fans can create legends; they can also destroy them. Each fan has at least one favorite star. Who is yours?" the pronoun *they* refers to *fans* and *them* to *legends*. The indefinite adjective *each* refers to *fan*. The pronoun *who* refers to *star* in the previous sentence, and the pronoun *yours* refers to the reader. In the following sentence, however, the pronoun reference is ambiguous:

- John Wayne made films and legends for almost fifty years, which include *Stagecoach*, *The Alamo*, and *True Grit*.

Do you see that *which* could refer to *films* or *legends*?

You can correct this ambiguity in three ways:

a. By *placing the pronoun close to its antecedent*: John Wayne made films, which include *Stagecoach*, *The Alamo*, and *True Grit*, and legends for almost fifty years.

b. By *recasting the sentence*: The legendary John Wayne made films for almost fifty years; they include *Stagecoach*, *The Alamo*, and *True Grit*.

c. By *repeating the antecedent rather than using the pronoun*: John Wayne made films and legends for almost fifty years; the films include *Stagecoach*, *The Alamo*, and *True Grit*.

With your partner, read and discuss the following specific ideas for achieving accurate pronoun references:

1. Place your pronoun carefully so it does not refer to more than one antecedent.

Ambiguous
The daughter of Judy Garland who stars on stage and screen is Liza Minnelli.

Accurate
Liza Minnelli, who stars on stage and screen, is the daughter of Judy Garland.

2. Do not use pronouns to stand for ideas. If a pronoun has an implied, rather than a clearly stated, antecedent; your reader will not be certain of what you mean. Always use a specific noun reference rather than a vague pronoun reference.

Ambiguous
Clark Gable, as Rhett Butler, told Scarlett O'Hara, "Frankly, my dear, I don't give a damn"; this offended many religious groups.

Accurate
Clark Gable, as Rhett Butler, told Scarlett O'Hara, "Frankly, my dear, I don't give a damn"; his statement offended many religious groups.

Ambiguous

Though cynical politicians said it couldn't be done, James Stewart in *Mr. Smith Goes to Washington* portrayed a small-town character who triumphed over the city slickers.

Accurate

Though cynical politicians said he couldn't succeed, the small-town character portrayed by James Stewart in *Mr. Smith Goes to Washington* triumphed over the city slickers.

Ambiguous

Greta Garbo had a reputation as a recluse, which made her portrayals of beautiful, lonely women more poignant.

Accurate

Greta Garbo's reputation as a recluse made her portrayals of beautiful, lonely women more poignant.

Game Three: Ambiguity

In this game you and your partner take turns repairing sentences that contain ambiguous pronoun references.

The game might proceed as follows: **A** gives **B** "I was late for class, which made my instructor angry." **B** replies "I was late for class, so my instructor was angry" for one point. Then **B** gives **A** "My mother gave my aunt a box of chocolates; at her party, she ate them all." **A** corrects the sentence, and the game continues.

61

Misspelling

INTRODUCTION

The latest word-processing systems have a built-in 50,000-word spelling memory. This means that when you complete an essay on the machine, all you have to do is push the "spell" key and the machine will check for misspellings. The machine, however, does not correct your spelling; it just brings to your attention words that do not agree with its memory. You must correct the misspelled words yourself. A remarkable invention, the spelling memory not only saves valuable time but reduces spelling to a mechanical chore, its rightful place in the writing process.

It may be a long time, however, before you have a word processor sitting on your desk. In the meantime, remember the adage "From your spelling you will be judged."

To determine whether or not you need to do this chapter, find the ten misspelled words in the following list and correct them:

accelerator	accomodate	acknowledgment	adolescence	analysis
arctic	argument	attendence	beneficial	broccoli
calendar	changeable	committee	complexion	concede
conqueror	conscientious	contagious	debatable	defendant
definate	develop	discernible	echoes	ecstasy
embarrassment	environment	exaggerate	existence	experience
fascinate	February	fourty	government	grammar
grievance	guerilla	guidance	hemorrhage	hygiene
hypocrisy	idiosyncrasy	incidentally	independent	indispensable
irony	irreplaceable	irresistible	jeopardy	jewelry
judicial	knowledgeable	library	lieutenent	loneliness
maintenance	maneuver	medicine	medieval	metaphor
miscellaneous	mischievious	mortgage	necessary	neice
noticeable	occasion	occurrence	omission	parallel
perceive	perseverance	picnicked	playwright	pneumonia

preceed	preference	prejudice	privilege	procedure
psychology	questionnaire	queue	recede	receive
reconnaissance	repentance	resistance	rheumatism	rhythm
ricochet	roommate	sacrilege	schedule	scissors
seize	seperate	sergeant	siege	sieve
smorgasborg	sophomore	stupefy	subtlety	subtly
supersede	surprise	susceptible	thinness	thorough
tragedy	truly	unnecessary	usable	vacuum
valuable	vengeance	veterinarian	Wednesday	yacht

Turn to the Suggested Answers following Chapter 66 to find the ten misspelled words. How did you do?

FOUND AND CORRECTED ALL TEN:	Bravo! Go to another chapter.
FOUND AND CORRECTED 6–9:	Give this chapter some attention.
FOUND AND CORRECTED 3–5:	Read this chapter carefully, occasionally working with your workshop partner.
FOUND AND CORRECTED 0–2:	Work through the entire chapter with your partner.

Spelling is the bane of many a student. No matter how wonderful the topic, how honorable the purpose, or how necessary the situation, readers are prone to discount a piece of writing if the writer cannot spell. The only safe rule about spelling remains: when in doubt, check the dictionary, where every word is spelled correctly. As well, never put yourself in the position where you do not use a word because you cannot spell it. Always have a dictionary handy when you write.

You can play the games in this chapter anywhere, at any time. So if you have a couple of minutes to spare, play a spelling game.

EXERCISE ONE
The Rules

There are rules in spelling that can be learned; it's the exceptions to these rules that confuse poor spellers.

Rule One
One-syllable words *usually* double the final consonant when a suffix beginning with a vowel is added (knit, knitting; swim, swimming).

Rule Two
Words of two or more syllables *usually* double the final consonant when a suffix beginning with a vowel is added to an accented final syllable (prefer, preferred; cancel, cancelled).

Rule Three
Words that end with a doubled consonant *usually* keep both consonants when a suffix is added (stuff, stuffing; embarrass, embarrassed).

Rule Four
When the same consonant ends the prefix and begins the root word, both consonants are kept (natural, unnatural; spell, misspell).

Rule Five
Similarly, when the same consonant ends the root word and begins the suffix, both consonants are kept (accidental, accidentally; mean, meanness).

Rule Six
Words that end with a silent *e usually* drop the *e* before a suffix beginning with a vowel (provoke, provoking; elate, elated).

Rule Seven
The final *e* in a root word is *usually* kept before a suffix beginning with a consonant (elope, elopement; plate, plateful).

Rule Eight
A final silent *e* preceded by *c* or *g* is kept before a suffix beginning with *a* or *o* (enforce, enforceable; courage, courageous).

Rule Nine
Words that end in *y* preceded by a consonant *usually* change the *y* to *i* before a suffix (merry, merriment; happy, happiness).

Rule Ten
Words that end in *y* preceded by a vowel *usually* keep the *y* before a suffix (dismay, dismaying; enjoy, enjoyed).

Rule Eleven
Words ending in *c* add *k* before adding suffixes that start with *e*, *i*, or *y* (mimic, mimicking; traffic, trafficker).

Rule Twelve
The *ei* or *ie* rule needs special attention.

   a. *Usually e* follows *i* (believe, thieves).

   b. However, *i* follows *e* after *c* and whenever it is pronounced like a long *a* (deceive, weight).

Rule Thirteen
Learning four words will make the *ceed/cede* rule easy:

   a. *Supersede* is the only English word that ends in *sede*.

   b. *Exceed, proceed,* and *succeed* are the only English words that end in *ceed*.

   c. All other words having the same sound end in *cede* (precede, intercede).

Rule Fourteen
If you cannot remember whether a word should end with *er* or *or*, remember this: if you can put a *shun* sound (*tion* or *sion*) on the word, add *or*; if not, add *er* (dictator, editor, processor, developer).

Rule Fifteen
There are some words that you just have to learn how to spell. They follow no rules (conscious, necessary, rhythm, psychology, conscientious).

Rule Sixteen

There are many rules for spelling plurals:

a. Nouns *usually* form plurals by adding an *s* to the singular (tree, trees; student, students).

b. If the plural will make another syllable, *es* should be added (dish, dishes; fox, foxes).

c. Nouns ending in *o* preceded by a vowel form plurals by adding *s* (stereo, stereos; studio, studios).

d. Nouns ending in *o* preceded by a consonant form plurals by adding *s* or sometimes *es* (soprano, sopranos; hero, heroes).

e. Nouns ending in *f* or *fe usually* change the *f* to *ve* and add *s* (shelf, shelves, wife, wives).

f. Nouns ending in *y* preceded by a consonant change the *y* to *i* and add *es* (city, cities; flunky, flunkies).

g. Nouns ending in *y* preceded by a vowel add *s* to form plurals (donkey, donkeys; toy, toys).

h. Nouns borrowed from other languages may retain their original plurals or may use the same forms as similar English words (radius, radii; formula, formulae or formulas).

i. Compound nouns form plurals by making the most important part of the word plural (mothers-in-law, lieutenant-governors).

j. Several nouns have their own unique way of forming plurals (die, dice; ox, oxen; crisis, crises). If you are in doubt, check the dictionary.

Game One: Rules or Exceptions

For this and subsequent spelling games, follow the general game rules outlined in Exercise Seventeen, Chapter 64.

You do not need to memorize the spelling rules to play these games, but have them handy and consult them when you need to. Game One might proceed as follows:

A says "*Picknicker* is spelled correctly. Which rule does it follow, or is it an exception to a rule?" **B** says "*Picknicker* follows Rule Eleven" for one point. Then **B** says "*Gaseous* is spelled correctly. Which rule does it follow, or is it an exception to a rule?" **A** says "*Gaseous* is an exception to Rule One" for one point and then says "*Heartily* is spelled correctly. Which rule does it follow, or is it an exception to a rule?" The game continues in this manner.

Game Two: Plurals

This game might proceed as follows:

A says "Spell the plural of *governor general.* Which rule should you follow?" **B** spells *governors general* for two points and says "It follows Rule 16(i)" for one point.

Then **B** says "Spell the plural of *solo*. Which rule should you follow?" The game continues in this way.

Game Three: Frequently Misspelled Words

You and your partner can each make up (or find) a short list of frequently misspelled words and plan to dictate them to each other at predetermined intervals (each week or every two weeks).

Decide if you want the words to come as a surprise or whether to exchange them the week before you dictate them. Also, decide on scoring procedures and misspelling penalties.

BY JOVE, SMEDLEY! IT IS A SPELLING ERROR!

EXERCISE TWO
Pronounce When in Doubt

In English, many words have letters that do not make any sound (*knife*), that have one sound for two letters (*written*), or that sound nothing like what you would expect (*phlegm*). Herein lies the speller's dilemma. If you know how to pronounce a word correctly, however, you stand a better chance of spelling the word correctly. If you come across a word that you regularly misspell, check your dictionary to see how it is pronounced. For example, *pronunciation* is pronounced prə nun′ sē ā′ shən; hence, you would not put an *o* before the *u*, as you would in *pronounce.*

If you do not understand how to interpret pronunciation marks, check the pronunciation key at the front or back of your dictionary.

Game Four: Pronunciation Only

This game might proceed as follows:

A gives **B** a piece of paper with the word *ptomaine* written on it. **B** pronounces it "tō′ mān" for one point, then gives **A** the word *Puccini.* The game continues in this manner.

Game Five: The Silent Letter

This game might proceed as follows:

A says "What is the silent letter in *ghastly*?" **B** answers "The *h*" for one point, then spells it for two points. **B** then says "What is the silent letter in *cape*?" and the game continues.

Game Six: Double or One?

This game is played as in the following example:

A says "Do you double the *t* in *writing* or is there only one?" **B** says "Only one" for one point, then spells it for two points. **B** then says "Do you double the *m* in *accommodation*?" **A** continues.

Game Seven: Sounds Unfamiliar

This game might proceed as follows:

A says "Spell *phlegm.* Hint: the *f* sound is spelled *ph.*" **B** spells "p-h-l-e-g-m" for two points. If he or she spells it wrong the first time, he or she could try again for one point. Then **B** says "Spell *cough.* Hint: the *f* sound is spelled *gh.*" **A** continues.

Game Eight: Homonyms

Many students make unconscious errors with homonyms (words that sound the same but are spelled differently). The only solution to this problem is always to be aware of which word you want to use. If it is a homonym and you are unsure of the correct spelling, consult your dictionary. This homonym game might proceed as follows:

A says "Spell the homonym for *r-e-d*." (Do not pronounce the word.) **B** says "*R-e-d* is pronounced *red*" for one point and says "Its homonym is *r-e-a-d*" for two points. Then **B** says "Spell the homonym for *a-t-e*." **A** continues.

EXERCISE THREE
Mnemonics

One way to learn how to spell difficult words is to link them to something else. Such a memory-association technique is called *mnemonics* (pronounced ni mon'iks) from the Greek word that means "to remember."

1. The following are some examples of mnemonics using *sight* spelling techniques:

- *Sergeant* equals *serge* plus *ant*.
- There is *sin* in *business*.
- We get to the *cemetery* with *es* (ease).

2. Many words are spelled exactly as they sound. Break these words into syllables, carefully pronouncing each syllable. The word is written exactly as you say it. The following are some examples of mnemonics using *sound* spelling techniques:

- tem per a ture
- part ner
- gov ern ment
- trag e dy

Game Nine: Mnemonics

This game might proceed as follows:

A says "A sight mnemonic for *develop* is to *lop* off the final *e*. Spell *develop*." **A** spells "*d-e-v-e-l-o-p*" for two points, then says "Break *superintendent* into syllables before you spell it." **B** says "*Su per in ten dent*" for one point and spells it for two. Then **B** says "Break *criticism* into syllables before you spell it." **A** continues the game.

EXERCISE FOUR
British vs. American

You may not be aware of the fact, but many words are spelled differently in the United States than in Great Britain and Canada. Ever since Noah Webster published his dictionary, American custom has been to use *-or* instead of the British *-our* and to discontinue doubling many final consonants before adding suffixes. If you have trouble with spelling and you occasionally read books and magazines published in

Great Britain and Canada, you might be confused when you see words like *honour*, *travelling*, *judgement* instead of *honor*, *traveling*, *judgment*, and so on.

With your partner, decide which word in the following pairs uses an acceptable American or British spelling. There may be some words that are unacceptable altogether. Dictionaries cite the accepted American spelling first; therefore, if you run into difficulties in this exercise, refer to a dictionary.

kilometer/kilometre	metre/meter
color/colour	fulfil/fulfill
analyse/analyze	alright/all right
donut/doughnut	realise/realize
counselor/counsellor	centre/center
thru/through	tonite/tonight

"No, No! How many times do I have to tell you?
It's ⌒ before ⌒ except after ⧓ !"

62

Incorrect Punctuation

INTRODUCTION

Writers use punctuation marks for the purpose of communicating their thoughts more clearly to their audience. Punctuation is discussed throughout *The Independent Writer*, but in this chapter you and your partner can take the opportunity to observe the main functions of all the end and internal punctuation marks.

One way to determine whether you have punctuated correctly is to read your paper aloud. If you pause or change pitch or tone as you read, you should probably insert a punctuation mark. But do not punctuate without a sound reason. The adage "When in doubt, leave it out" should be your guide as you learn how to punctuate properly.

Test yourself to determine whether you need to do this chapter. If the following passage needs punctuation, fill in the blanks with the appropriate marks. Note the following three hints: (1) Morrow did not include the words "in 1984" in his original article; the author of *The Independent Writer* added the words, (2) In reality, Jackson said a number of other words between "am" and "somebody," (3) Where two spaces are provided, you may be expected to place two punctuation marks; for example, .‟ or‟ ?.

> In his essay ___ The Powers of Racial Example ___ ___ which appeared in *Time* ___ Lance Morrow wrote ___ ___ What is unfolding now ___ in 1984 ___ may be thought of in years to come as the Jesse Jackson era for black America ___ ___ For years ___ Jackson has stood in front of audiences of both young and old ___ and led them in psychological cheers ___ ___ I am ___ somebody ___ ___ It may be many years before the U.S. elects a black president ___ or ___ for that matter ___ an Hispanic-American president ___ But is it not now thinkable for a black child to entertain a fantasy that used to be advertised as every white boy's dream ___ that he might grow up to be president ___ Jesse Jackson is a ___ first ___ in American history ___ others will be routine ___

656

Check your answers in the Suggested Answers following Chapter 66. If you have made any errors, you should do the appropriate exercises.

EXERCISE ONE
End Punctuation

Use one of the following three punctuation marks at the end of every sentence: period, question mark, or exclamation point.

1. Use a *period* at the end of a statement or a command:

- No army can withstand the strength of an idea whose time has come. (Victor Hugo)
- In time of peace prepare for war. (ancient Roman saying)

2. Use a *question mark* at the end of a question:

- Is there anyone so wise as to learn by the experience of others? (Voltaire) However, use a period at the end of an indirect question:
- I had rather men should ask why *no* statue had been erected in my honor than why one has. (Marcus Cato, "The Censor")

3. Use an *exclamation point* at the end of an exclamation or an emotional command:

- History is bunk! (Henry Ford)
- A horse! a horse! my kingdom for a horse! (Shakespeare)

Note: A single exclamation point suffices.

Game One: End Punctuation

The object of the following game is to see who can use more punctuation marks correctly—you or your partner. Repeat the game as often as you need to.

a. Each of you find a newspaper or magazine article in which all three kinds of end punctuation are used.

b. Paint out a predetermined number of end punctuation marks. Keep a record of which marks you painted out.

c. Exchange articles, supply end punctuation marks, return the articles, correct them, and compare scores.

EXERCISE TWO
The Comma

Of all the internal punctuation marks, the *comma* is the most common. It is the least emphatic way of indicating that the reader should pause. There are a great number of uses of the comma, but the following seven are perhaps the most important. Discuss each one with your partner.

1. When the subjects of two independent clauses joined by a coordinating conjunction (*and, but, or, for, so, yet*) are the same, you generally do not use a comma:

- I have made mistakes but I have never made the mistake of claiming that I never made one. (James Gordon Bennett)

When the second subject is dropped, you still do not use a comma:

- I have made mistakes but have never made the mistake of claiming that I never made one.

Sometimes you use a comma to emphasize a contrast:

- Literature may be light as a cobweb, but it must be fastened down to life at the four corners. (Nellie McClung)

When the subjects of the two clauses are not the same, however, you generally use a comma before the coordinating conjunction:

- I respect faith, but doubt is what gets you an education. (Wilson Mizner)

Because the following two independent clauses are short and closely related, the comma is not necessary, even though the subjects are different:

- Man proposes and God disposes. (Ariosto)

2. Using a comma to separate *all* parts of a series of three or more single words, phrases, or clauses poses a real problem for beginning writers. Even though many professional writers drop the comma before the coordinating conjunction, you will never be wrong if you use one:

- I have nothing to offer but blood, toil, tears, and sweat. (Churchill)

You definitely need the commas when there is no coordinating conjunction:

- He came, he saw, he concurred. (Clyde Gilmour)
- Concentration is the secret of strength in politics, in war, in trade; in short, in all management of human affairs. (Emerson)

3. Use a comma if two or more adjectives modify a noun individually:

- A moral, sensible, and well-bred man / will not affront me, and no other can. (Cowper)

Note: the slash (/) is used to denote the end of a line of poetry. The slash is discussed in detail in Chapters 39 and 63.

Use a comma if *and* would work in the same position.

- A moral *and* sensible *and* well-bred man / will not affront me, and no other can.

4. Use a comma to set off a long dependent clause or phrase when you wish to emphasize it:

- At the beginning: *If you would know and not be known*, live in a city. (Charles C. Colton)

- Internal: Live, *if you would know and not be known*, in a city.
- At the end: Live in a city, *if you would know and not be known.*

5. Use a comma to set off absolutes, no matter where they appear in the sentence:

- To go into teaching was a matter of sheer necessity, *my education fitting me for nothing except to pass it on to the other people.* (Stephen Leacock)

6. Use a comma when a clause or phrase breaks the continuity of the sentence by offering additional but incidental information:

- Nonessential clause: If you play to win, *as I do*, the game never ends. (Stan Mikita)
- Nonessential phrase: There are people who, *like new songs*, are in vogue only for a time. (La Rochefoucauld)

Hint: If the sentence makes complete sense *without* the clause or phrase, it is nonessential; hence, commas are required. Without their nonessential elements, the above sentences make sense:

- If you play to win, the game never ends.
- There are people who are in vogue only for a time.

Notice, though, that you should not use commas around essential clauses and phrases. They are necessary to the independent clause, which makes no sense without them.

- Essential clause: He *who never leaves his country* is full of prejudices. (Carlo Goldoni)
- Essential phrase: One of the first and most important things for a critic to learn is how *to sleep undetected at the theatre.* (William Archer)

Note: Read the above sentences without their essential elements. Do they make complete sense?

7. Use commas to set off parenthetical expressions and mild interjections, appositives, or adjective and adverb clusters. (Note that none of these is essential to the sense of the sentence.)

- Parenthetical expression: We are here to add what we can to, *not to get what we can from*, life. (Sir William Osler)
- Mild interjection: *Oh*, a man's got to die of something! (Adam Shortt)
- Appositive: The middle of the road is all of the usable surface. The extremes, *right and left*, are in the gutters. (Dwight D. Eisenhower)
- Adjective cluster: *Dissolute, damned and despairful, crippled and palsied and slain*, this is the Will of the Yukon,—Lo, how she makes it plain! (Robert W. Service)

The preceding are only a few of the many comma rules that exist. When you look at all of the examples one at a time, they make sense. But if you use several rules in a single sentence, you could eventually use so many commas that they would strangle your sentence. Every comma in the following sentence can be justified, but which ones should be omitted?

Use commas sparingly, but, to avoid misreading, you must, occasionally, include one.

Game Two: Commas Galore

Play the following game, using the same rules as in Game One, or you and your partner can present each other with one prepared sentence at a time, saying "For one point, add a comma, omit a comma, or leave it the way it is." For example:

A presents **B** with "My brother asked me to buy him a bag of potato chips (,) when I went to the store." **B** answers "The comma should be deleted" and earns one point. **B** then presents **A** with "What is the difference between a cat and a comma? The answer is ( ) that a cat has claws at the end of his paws (,) but a comma is a pause at the end of a clause." The game continues.

EXERCISE THREE
Dashes and Parentheses

1. Review Item 7 in the last section on the comma before you proceed. If the parenthetical expression, interjection, or appositive is a strong interruption, you might use a pair of *dashes* instead of commas:

- Strong parenthetical expression: The answer for all our national problems—the answer for all the problems of the world—comes to a single word. That word is "Education." (Lyndon B. Johnson)
- Strong interjection: When a young man in Manhattan writes a letter to his girl in Brooklyn, the love message gets blown to her through a pneumatic tube—pfft—just like that. (E. B. White)
- Strong Appositive:
  Man—whose heaven-erected face
  The smiles of love adorn—
  Man's inhumanity to man
  Makes countless thousands mourn! (Robert Burns)

2. If the parenthetical expression, interjection, or appositive is quite remote, you might use *parentheses*:

- Remote parenthetical expression: These two, I imagine, could tell a long tale if they would (perhaps they would be glad to if they could), having watched so many, for so long, struggling in the fishhooks, the barbed wire of this avenue. (James Baldwin)
- Remote interjection: I'm not sure that you have the poetic control (yet!) which one needs if one is going to write free verse. (Lyn Coffin)

- Remote appositive: Such a computer, which has been called STAR (self-testing and repairing computer), is on the threshold of development. (Carl Sagan)

3. You might find occasion to use a *single* dash in your writing. Single dashes are appropriate in the following instances:

    a. To stress a word or phrase at the end of a sentence:
- Man is the only animal that blushes—or needs to. (Mark Twain)

    b. To set off a summary or a conclusion to an involved sentence:
- No great literature or art is possible without a great people, a people ripened by experience, stirred by curiosity, and alive to wonder—a people with the daring capacity to expect the wonderful and then attempt to realize it. (Lorne Pierce)

    c. To indicate an interruption in dialogue:
- "Really, now you ask me," said Alice, very much confused, I don't think—" "Then you shouldn't talk," said the Hatter. (Lewis Carroll)

Think, however, before you use a single dash. A comma, colon, semicolon, or even a period may be better. Overuse of the single dash can take away emphasis from your writing.

When typing, use two hyphens (--) to indicate a dash; when handwriting, use a line that is longer than a hyphen.

Game Three: Interruptions

Follow the rules in Game One to play this game. Find sentences that have interruptions, paint out the punctuation marks, and see if your partner knows whether to fill the spaces with commas, dashes, or parentheses.

EXERCISE FOUR
Semicolons

The semicolon is perhaps the most incorrectly used punctuation mark. Most people know that its function is somewhere between that of a comma and a period; however, its actual purpose in writing so bewilders beginners that they will write strings of simple sentences or join all of their sentences with conjunctions, rather than take a chance and use a semicolon.

The most important purpose of the semicolon is to separate elements of equal and substantial rank. The examples below will help you to understand when to use the semicolon.

1. Use a semicolon to join independent clauses:

- Nothing is so dangerous as an ignorant friend; a wise enemy is worth more. (La Fontaine)

You have already seen that if independent clauses are joined by a coordinating conjunction, you usually place a comma before the conjunction when the subjects of the two clauses are not the same:

- Nothing is so dangerous as an ignorant friend, yet a wise enemy is worth more.

For emphasis, some writers use a semicolon instead of a comma before a coordinating conjunction:

- To err is human; but to wear out the eraser before you wear out the pencil is taking too many liberties. (A. B. Yates)

If you were to hand in a sentence like the above one, an editor might circle the semicolon, and write the comment "You *must* use a comma." If this happens to you, you should mention that you were using the semicolon for emphasis and then discuss the effect of using a comma.

The semicolon in the Yates sentence works, but the semicolon in the following one does not:

- Religion is a disease; but it is a noble disease. (Heraclitus)

Why is the semicolon wrong in this sentence? Can you see why the two semicolons are correctly used in the following sentence?

- It is true that you may fool all of the people some of the time; you can even fool some of the people all of the time; but you can't fool all of the people all of the time. (Abraham Lincoln)

2. Use a semicolon when you use a conjunctive adverb (see Chapter 44), such as *therefore*, *nevertheless*, *hence*, *however*, *moreover*, and so on, to join two clauses. You should precede the conjunctive adverb with a semicolon and follow it with a comma.

- Thought makes the whole dignity of man; therefore, endeavor to think well. That is the only morality. (Blaise Pascal)

Notice the punctuation when the conjunctive adverb moves within the clause:

- Thought makes the whole dignity of man; endeavor, therefore, to think well.

With your partner, rewrite the sentence in a different way, moving the *therefore*. Remember to retain the semicolon.

3. Use a semicolon when you use specifying words, such as *for example*, *that is*, and *namely*. (Note that you should use these English words instead of the abbreviations of their Latin equivalents—*e.g.*, *i.e.*, and *viz.*).

- Woody Allen is well known for his humorous self-mockery; for instance, he once said of his life, "Most of the time I don't have much fun. The rest of the time I don't have any fun at all."
- Philosopher Marshall McLuhan originated one of the most popular phrases of the 1960s; namely, "The medium is the message."

4. Use a semicolon to separate a longer series that contains commas.

- The photograph pictured a tall, gray-haired, dark-eyed woman; a red-haired, green-eyed, bespectacled girl; and a long-tailed, long-eared, black-and-white dog.

Without the semicolons the reader will confuse the commas that separate each item in the series with the commas that are *within* each part of the series. For example, can you make sense of the following sentence?

- The photograph pictured a tall, gray-haired, dark-eyed woman, a red-haired, green-eyed, bespectacled girl, and a long-tailed, long-eared, black-and-white dog.

Game Four: Semicolon Confidence

Play the following game using the same rules as in Game One. To make the game more difficult, but more helpful, find sentences that have long dependent clauses with either commas or semicolons joining them. The game might proceed as follows:

A presents **B** with "I don't care what happens (;) I'm going skydiving this weekend." **B** says "The semicolon is correct" for one point. Then **B** presents **A** with "If women had been running the world back when the wheel was invented (;) they would have invented the pill instead." (Doris Anderson) The game continues in this way.

EXERCISE FIVE
Colons

You probably use a colon after the salutation in your business letters (*Dear Editor*: or *Dear Board Member*:) and in separating hours from minutes when you write *12:45*, but you can use the colon to serve other purposes in your writing as well.
1. Use a colon between two clauses in a sentence when your second clause is a more detailed explanation of your first:

- It might be appropriate at this point to note the difference between the colon and the semicolon: a semicolon indicates to your readers that they are at a stop sign; a colon tells them that they are at a green light.
- Never use a semicolon as a colon: its effect is exactly opposite. (Sheridan Baker)

Discuss with your partner the use of the colons in the two preceding sentences. In the following sentence the second clause merely provides a more detailed explanation of the first part of the sentence:

- Mankind are very odd creatures: one half censure what they practice, the other half practice what they censure. (Benjamin Franklin)

In the following sentence, however, the first part serves as an introduction to the second:

- One merit of poetry that few persons will deny: it says more and in fewer words than prose. (Voltaire)

2. Use a colon to separate a list from the rest of the sentence or to introduce a formal statement, extract, or speech in a dialogue:

- The four elements of news are: love, money, conquest, disaster. (Gordon Sinclair)
- In our country we have these three unspeakably precious things: freedom of speech, freedom of conscience, and the prudence never to practice either. (Mark Twain)

3. Use a colon to add a dramatic touch to a sentence before you introduce a single word or phrase:

- The cynic puts all human actions into two classes: openly bad and secretly bad. (Henry Ward Beecher)

Game Five: Colon Accuracy

Play a game based on the use of colons, following the same rules as those outlined in Game Four.

EXERCISE SIX
Brackets

Use *brackets*, [ ], not to be confused with parentheses, ( ), when you wish to include something that is not in a quotation.

1. If you use a quotation that does not completely fit into your own prose so that you have to introduce a word to make it fit, you must put brackets around that word to tell the reader that *you* added it.

- I have the happiness to know that [democracy] is a rising, and not a setting sun. (Benjamin Franklin)

2. Use [sic] when you quote correctly something that might be thought to be incorrect.

- There's no tyranny on airth [sic] equal to the tyranny of a majority. (T. C. Haliburton)

EXERCISE SEVEN
Ellipses

Use *ellipsis points* (three dots) within quotations to indicate an omission. (Some writers prefer to leave spaces between the dots; however, some typewriters and computers include three closely arranged dots on a single key.)

1. If you wish to omit one or more words from a quotation, use ellipsis points in place of what you omit:

- "I decline to accept the end of men . . . I believe that man will not merely endure; he will prevail." (William Faulkner)

2. Sometimes you may introduce ellipsis points when you omit words at the end of a sentence that can easily be supplied by your reader.

- He prayed, "Our Father, who art in . . ."

3. Ellipses are a versatile punctuation mark in that they can indicate a passage of time and events that a reader probably knows. As you read the following example, can you fill in the events at each set of ellipsis points?

- The journey of American blacks has been a series of epic passages: the "Middle Passage" from Africa . . . the long passage through slavery to the Emancipation Proclamation . . . the false dawn of Reconstruction . . . the terrorist Klan era with its night-riding death squads . . . the passage north to South Side Chicago and Detroit and Harlem . . . then *Brown vs Topeka* and desegregation and the Martin Luther King era and the Great Society. (Lance Morrow)

4. Fiction writers use ellipsis points to indicate pauses, as well as to heighten suspense:

- Jack could be behind a chair or couch . . . maybe behind the registration desk . . . waiting for her to come down . . . (Stephen King)

Use this kind of ellipses judiciously; overuse ruins the effect.

5. At times, you may include a period with ellipsis points; hence, you use four dots. Notice the two uses of ellipsis points in the following:

- Clearly, Charlie Wales remains a tissue of contradictions: "He woke up feeling happy . . . . He made plans . . . for Honoria and himself, but suddenly he grew sad, remembering all the plans he and Helen had made."

To find out what has been omitted, compare the quoted material above with the following original quotation:

- He woke up feeling happy. The door of the world was open again. He made plans, vistas, futures for Honoria and himself, but suddenly he grew sad, remembering all the plans he and Helen had made. She had not planned to die. (F. Scott Fitzgerald, "Babylon Revisited")

EXERCISE EIGHT
Quotation Marks

Quotation marks have many uses. Discuss with your partner the differences between each of the following uses of quotation marks.

1. When you introduce dialogue or a short quotation into a passage, use *double* quotation marks:

- A man said to the Universe:
  "Sir, I exist!"

"However," replied the Universe,
"The fact has not created in me
A sense of obligation." (Stephen Crane)

- On how many people's libraries, as on bottles from the druggist, one might write: "For External Use Only." (Alphonse Daudet)
- "Know Thyself"? If I knew myself, I'd run away. (Goethe)
- Did George Washington really say "I cannot tell a lie"?
- What is the meaning of the question "For what is a man profited, if he shall gain the whole world, and lose his own soul?"?
- I knew what to think of his boast "I'm money-motivated": he's greedy.
- The judge said, "I'd like you to spend a little time in a correctional therapeutic community"; however, the criminal heard, "You're going to prison."

Do not let the exact position of closing quotation marks confuse you. The following points will help you decide where to place them.

a. Place closing quotation marks *after* periods and commas. From the above quotations, you and your partner find all the places where a closing quotation mark comes after a period or comma.

b. Place closing quotation marks *before* colons and semicolons. Find two illustrations from the above sentences.

c. Place closing quotation marks *before* or *after* question marks and exclamation points, depending on whether they are punctuating only the quotation or the entire sentence. Find all the examples and discuss the reason for the position of the question marks and exclamation points.

2. When you introduce dialogue within dialogue or a quotation within a quotation, you use *single* quotation marks:

- "We wake, if we ever wake at all, to mystery, rumors or death, beauty, violence ... 'Seems like we're just set down here,' a woman said to me recently, 'and don't nobody know why.'" (Annie Dillard)
- "He remembered poor Julian and his romantic awe of [the rich] and how he had started a story once that began, 'The rich are very different from you and me,' and how someone had said to Julian, 'Yes, they have more money.'" (Ernest Hemingway)

From the above two examples, what do the ellipsis points and brackets indicate?
3. Use double quotation marks to enclose terms or expressions that seem out of harmony with the general tone of the writing:

- When the halfback came off the field after his touchdown, his teammates gave him "the high five."

Do not overuse quotation marks for this purpose. Why?
4. Use double quotation marks to enclose a word or phrase that you are using in a special sense.

- One of our defects as a nation is a tendency to use what have been called "weasel words." (Theodore Roosevelt)

You could also use underlining in place of double quotation marks here.

5. Use double quotation marks to enclose titles of poems, stories, chapters, essays, or articles appearing in a larger work.

- T. S. Eliot's long poem "The Waste Land" appears in F. O. Matthiessen's edition of *The Oxford Book of American Verse*.

6. When dialogue extends over several paragraphs, use one set of double quotation marks only at the beginning of each of a set of paragraphs (rather than at the end of each). This usage makes clear that, until the closing quotation marks appear, the original speaker is still speaking.

Game Six: Quotation Marks

Follow the same rules as in Game One and play a game based on the use of quotation marks. Find examples of double and single quotation marks that involve other punctuation marks. Correctly ordering the quotation marks with the other punctuation marks will earn a player one point.

63

Word-Punctuation and Convention Errors

INTRODUCTION

Well-trained writers, when they think of punctuation, consider not only internal and end punctuation within sentences and paragraphs, but also punctuation for and within words. Word punctuation involves the hyphen, the apostrophe, and capital letters. In this chapter you will also be able to examine certain writing conventions: abbreviations, the slash, underlining, and citing numbers.

Some word punctuation is necessary; some is added by the writer for the purpose of bringing a word or words to the audience's attention.

In the following quiz, all of the word punctuation and conventions are correct. Read the sentences, carefully noting the use of hyphens, apostrophes, capital letters, underlining, and number citations. If you are in doubt about any of them, do the appropriate exercises.

- It's difficult for non-rock fans to tell the difference between one band's music and another's.
- Paul Dean of Loverboy has what one interviewer described as "a calm, I've-been-through-this-before manner."
- After twenty years, the Beatles are as popular as ever. The death of John Lennon dashed fans' hopes of there ever being a reunion of the Beatles.
- Duran Duran's popular single, "Reflex," is one cut on the album <u>Seven and the Ragged Tiger</u>.

EXERCISE ONE
Hyphen

The *hyphen* is essentially a combining mark. If you trace the derivation of many compound English words, you will find that at one time they were two words, then they became hyphenated words, and finally compound words. When you come to such a word in your writing, consult a current dictionary to see if the word is indeed two words, a hyphenated word, or a compound word.

Note the following ways in which you can use hyphens. Practice the rules in the ways suggested for each.

1. Use a hyphen with two words acting as one adjective:

- Many American musical groups began playing together in high school; some of these high-school bands stayed together for years.

Note that *high-school* is considered a single word describing *bands*, while *high* modifies the noun *school*. Make up sentences using *rainy* and *day* as separate and hyphenated words.

2. Use a hyphen with a very long phrase used as a single adjective:

- David Lee Roth of Van Halen has what one writer called "a frenetic, don't-stop-now approach to daily living."

Note that the hyphenated word modifies *approach*. Make up a sentence using a long phrase made up of hyphenated words.

3. Use a hyphen to separate a prefix from a capitalized word:

- Since its very beginning, rock music has been praised as distinctly American by some and condemned as distinctly un-American by others.

Make up a sentence with *ex* and *President* as well as *neo* and *Nazi*.

4. Use a hyphen with a compound adjective and noun containing *self*:

- The last thing any band needs is a self-conscious lead singer.

Make up a sentence with *self* and an adjective or noun.

5. Use a hyphen in a compound noun consisting of a verb and a preposition. However, in some words the hyphen is no longer used. Check the dictionary if you are in doubt.

- The problem many musicians have is in recording a follow-up to a hit single.

Using a hyphen, make up a sentence with *send* and *off*.

6. Use a hyphen in fractions and in compound numbers under one hundred used as adjectives. Note that *one-third* is an adjective while *two-thirds* is a noun.

- Thirty-three-and-one-third RPM is the standard turntable speed for a standard album; more than two thirds of many record collections are albums.

7. Adverbs modifying adjectives do not take hyphens. The only exception is *well*, which is hyphenated when it precedes the noun (the adjective position) but not when it follows the noun (the predicate position).

- A well-respected and much honored American named Peter Goldmark invented the long-playing record. This fact is not well known or fully appreciated.

Note that the first *well* is an adverb modifying *respected*. (It is the only adverb to take a hyphen.) *Much* is also an adverb, but it does not take a hyphen to connect it to *honored*. *Long* and *playing* act as a compound adjective modifying *record*. The second *well* is in the predicate position; hence, it is not joined by a hyphen to *known*. *Fully* is an adverb and is not joined to *appreciated* with a hyphen. (Maybe you should go over that one more time.)

Apply the same rules for *better* and *best*, the comparative and superlative degrees of *well*:

- In the 1960s, the Supremes were dominated by the better-known Diana Ross, who today is best known as a superstar soloist.

Make up sentences in which *well* is combined with different adjectives both in the adjective and predicate positions.

8. Use a hyphen with the prefix *re* when it denotes repetition or to avoid confusion between words—for example, between *recreation* and *re-creation*. Here is another example:

- Musicians frequently do not re-sign with the same recording company after an unsuccessful record; instead, they resign.

Make up sentences using *reform* and *re-form*.

9. To divide a word that does not fit at the end of a line, place the hyphen between syllables or between double letters. The hyphen is always placed *after* the final syllable on the first line.

- In the last few years rock musicians have found that they can increase their popularity and boost record sales by performing their songs on imaginative videos. The better and more imaginative the video, the greater the benefits for the musicians who produce it.

Where would you place a hyphen if these words did not fit at the end of the line: *rock*, *musicians*, *popularity*, *imaginative*, *videos*, *more*, *benefits*? (Which of these words would you not be able to hyphenate? Why?)

Play the following games with your partner, using the same rules outlined in Chapter 64, Exercise Seventeen.

Game One: Hyphen I

A says "In the sentence 'I am well respected around town,' is *well respected* two words, a hyphenated word, or a compound word?" **B** answers "*Well respected* is not hyphenated" for one point. Then **B** asks "In the sentence 'He has a pet inchworm,' is *inchworm* two words, a hyphenated word, or a compound word?" Continue the game. If each of you prepare a list of words prior to the game, you will speed it up.

Game Two: Hyphen II

Present a written sentence to your partner in which you have the same word group twice. In one place, the word group should have a hyphen; in the other, it should not. Your partner should try to figure out which word group needs a hyphen and why.

For example, **A** presents the sentence "For a band to become well known, it should play concerts with well known bands." **B** says "The second *well-known* should be hyphenated because it acts as a single adjective, modifying *bands*" for one point. Then **B** presents the sentence "She gave him a come up and see me sometime look, then murmured Mae West's phrase, 'Why don't you come up and see me sometime?'"

Continue the game. You will be able to play more quickly if you prepare sentences in advance.

EXERCISE TWO
Apostrophe

The *apostrophe* is a mark of omission. You should be aware that some universities and instructors do not sanction contractions; therefore, you are advised to check the rules of your audience before you use *aren't* for *are not*, *don't* for *do not*, *I'd* for *I would*, and so on.

Read the following sentences, noting particularly which letters have been omitted and replaced by apostrophes:

- *Rock 'N' Soul, Part I* was a hit album for Daryl Hall and John Oates.
- Rock performers can become successful simply because they're wildly bizarre on stage; it helps, though, if they've got musical talent as well.

The apostrophe is also used to show possession. The following are some rules for its use in this way:

1. For most inanimate objects, use an *of* phrase rather than an apostrophe:

- Most musicians are concerned about the quality of their instruments.

It would be wrong to say "Most musicians are concerned about their instruments' quality."

2. Use an apostrophe in everyday references to time and measurement:

- a month's holiday, their money's value, seven days' grace.

3. For most other nouns, use apostrophes to show possession as follows:

   a. Both singular and plural nouns that do not end in *s* take an apostrophe plus an *s*:
   - man's voice, the child's singing, his daughter-in-law's band, the ox's lowing.
   - men's voices, the children's singing, his daughters-in-law's band, the oxen's lowing.

   b. Singular nouns that end in *s* take an apostrophe plus an *s*:
   - the bus's interior, James's piano, the actress's singing.

   c. But plural nouns ending in *s* add only an apostrophe:
   - the buses' interiors, the Jameses' pianos, the actresses' singing.

   d. If two or more people possess something jointly, only the last person in the list needs an apostrophe:
   - Frank and Dave's band; Joe and his father's company; Susan, Rachel, and Sheila's accompanist.

If you were to write "Frank's and Dave's band," your reader may wonder whether you mean that each has a band. It would be better to indicate this to the reader by writing "Frank's and Dave's bands." Rewrite the other two items so that Joe and his father have separate companies and the three musicians have separate accompanists.

Note the difference in meaning among the following:

- Paul McCartney's music, John Lennon's music, Lennon's and McCartney's music, Lennon and McCartney's music, The Beatles' music.

Which two possessives are plural?

4. Very few pronouns take apostrophes to show possession.

   a. Personal pronouns never use apostrophes to show possession:

   - my voice; its bark; your clothing; our band; The record is theirs, not ours.

If you ever see or use an apostrophe with a personal pronoun, it signifies a contraction, *not* possession:

- He's playing. = He is playing.
- It's howling. = It is howling.

   b. Relative pronouns follow the same rule as personal pronouns; they never use apostrophes to show possession. Note the differences in the following sentences:

   - Whose band is this? (possession)
   - Who's playing in the band? (contraction for *who is*)

   c. Indefinite pronouns take apostrophes exactly as if they were nouns:

   - one's home, somebody's microphone, the other's decision.

However, you can use an indefinite pronoun with a contraction, so use apostrophes with care. Note the following examples:

- Someone's crying. = *Someone is* crying.
- Someone's crying disturbed us. = The crying *of some person* disturbed us.

   d. If you are still having trouble with the use of apostrophes with pronouns, read Chapter 60.

5. If you want to show possession using one or more nouns and a personal pronoun, you must use an apostrophe with the nouns and the possessive form of the pronouns.

   - Frank's and my band, your and your sister's dresses, the boys' and my time.
   - Doug and the Slugs' first album has been their most successful so far.

6. *No* parts of speech other than nouns and indefinite pronouns use the apostrophe to show possession; therefore, an apostrophe used correctly in other parts of speech indicates a contraction, not possession.

   - he's (he is), there's (there is), it's (it is)

Thus, there is no such word as *its'*. As well, *make's* is incorrect in "My guitar *make's* a good sound" because verbs cannot show possession and there is no such expression as *make is*.

7. Some writers use apostrophes to indicate plurals of numbers and letters, for example, *100's, B's, 1980's*. But to avoid confusion with the apostrophes used to indicate possession or contractions, many writers use *100s, Bs, 1980s*.

Notice how the use of the apostrophe avoids any misreading in this sentence:

- The 1970's trend in music seems to be lasting into the 1980s.

Game Three: Apostrophes

Play the following game to help you learn when to use the apostrophe. To start, **A** hands **B** a piece of paper with the sentence "Simon's and Garfunkel's immensely popular music was heard in concert once again when they reunited in 1983 for a tour." Then **A** says "Is there any mistake in the use of the apostrophe?" **B** says "*Simon's* should be *Simon*" for one point, then presents **A** with "Donna Summers hit song's are recognized for having excellent arrangements." **A** replies "*Summers* should be *Summer's* and *song's* should be *songs* for two points." Then **A** presents "Its difficult to discover exactly how young Americans' tastes in music differ from young Western Europeans'." Continue the game in this way.

EXERCISE THREE
Capitalization

Capitalization helps the reader to know when a new sentence begins. Words within a sentence can also begin with capital letters. An initial capital letter indicates that a word is a proper noun or adjective. You and your partner read these sentences, paying particular attention to the capitalization.

- Phil Spector has been recognized for over two decades as one of America's most successful rock music producers. (The proper nouns require capital letters.)
- Many of America's most talented rock musicians have come from the South. (Capitalizing *South* makes it a specific geographical area.)
- To tell the truth, American rock music got its real start with the classic film *The Blackboard Jungle*, which featured a song titled "Rock Around the Clock" by Bill Haley and the Comets. (The proper adjective *American* requires a capital letter. Important words in titles are also capitalized.)

EXERCISE FOUR
Abbreviations

Abbreviations are perfectly appropriate in certain situations and formats: condensing material, writing a memo, or writing a personal letter. The following points will help you use abbreviations correctly.

Most of the time you should not use abbreviations in formal writing; you should write *and so forth* rather than *etc.* and *for example* rather than *e.g.* Such abbreviations are acceptable, however, in footnotes and in parenthetical statements.

1. You may use certain conventional abbreviations (Mr., Mrs., Ms., Dr., Jr., A.D., B.C., M.D., et al.) even in formal contexts. Note, however, the correct way to use an abbreviation:

- *You would write*: I visited Dr. Jones yesterday.
- *You would not write*: I visited my Dr. yesterday.

Make up correct sentences using *St.* and *saint* as well as *Rev.* and *reverend*.
2. Some commonly used abbreviations do not require periods: CBS, TNT, NAACP, NATO, OPEC, SOS, OED (*Oxford English Dictionary*), and so on. Checking an up-to-date dictionary will help you to determine if an abbreviation requires periods. Some abbreviations without periods are pronounced as words (NATO, OPEC, Snafu, scuba, radar) and are referred to as *acronyms*. Make up a sentence using an acronym.

EXERCISE FIVE
Underlining

Underlining is a punctuation device that calls attention to a word or words. When you handwrite or type, underline the words you wish to emphasize. When they are set in type (in a printed book, for example), they are set in *italic type*.
1. You should not underline titles of cuts from an album; you would place them within quotation marks.

- "Beat It," a song from Michael Jackson's album Thriller, was used in a nationwide campaign against drunk driving.

2. You should underline a non-English word that has not been assimilated into English.

- In one of his early hit songs, Stevie Wonder effectively used the French expression Ma Cherie Amour, which means "My Dearest Love."

3. Underline titles of complete works or publications: books, all theatrical works, newspapers, periodicals, television programs, names of artistic works. But put quotation marks around parts of published works: essays, poems, short stories, songs, chapter titles, lecture or speech titles, episodes within a larger work.

- Sound Effects is a book by Simon Frith about rock music's influence on youth.

4. Underline to indicate the importance of a word, letter, or number. Do not, however, overuse this method of gaining an emphatic effect.

- Groups such as the Rolling Stones make millions during their North American tours.

EXERCISE SIX
The Slash

The *slash* was once little used, but, in informal writing at least, it has made a comeback.

1. You can use the slash to replace one or more other words.

    a. In technical writing it can replace *per*: "The band will receive $50/night."

    b. Between two dates, it means *up to and including*: "Each member made $5000 from 1978/1981."

2. The expression *and/or*, in which the slash denotes *or*, has become popular. Usually, however, you will be clearer if you use either *and* or *or*. Discuss with your partner the meanings of the following sentences:

- The band leader said men and/or women should apply.
- The band leader said men and women should apply.
- The band leader said men or women should apply.
- The band leader said men/women should apply.

    The following sentence was taken from a band's advertisement: "The BBs can play jazz and/or rock and classical music and/or show tunes." What sort of songs do you think they play?

3. For another use of the slash, see Chapter 39.

EXERCISE SEVEN
Citing Numbers

    Depending on how much technical writing you do, you may or may not include numbers within the text of a piece of writing. The conventions professional writers follow in writing numbers have changed within the last few years, so the information included here may differ from what you have previously learned. If so, you may have to consult with your instructor or other potential audience to see which convention he or she wants you to follow.

1. Write out in full all numbers from one through ninety-nine:

- The four young men known as the Beatles created a musical revolution.

2. If any number under ninety-nine is part of a compound adjective or noun, use arabic numerals:

- The odds are probably greater than 100,000-to-1 that any adolescent rocker who knows a few chord changes will become a star!

3. Write out larger numbers when they appear at the beginning of a sentence; use arabic numerals when they appear within sentences:

- The sale of 1,000,000 copies of a hit single in the United States earns a singer a gold record.
- One million in sales of an album earns a platinum record.

4. Spell out fractions wherever they appear in a sentence:

- Record sales in the United States have exceeded two and three-quarter billion dollars.

5. When citing a number of less than one in decimal form, write a zero before the decimal point to avoid misreading:

- One half of one percent is written in decimal form as 0.5.

Game Four: Mixed Bag

Make up a predetermined number of sentences with up to three word-punctuation or writing-convention mistakes in each sentence. Then use them to play the following game with your partner:

A gives **B** the sentence "Willie Nelsons broad success with such albums as "Always on My Mind" and singles like "To All the Girls I've Loved Before" demonstrates that nonrock musicians can appeal to rock audiences." **B** says "*Nelsons* should be *Nelson's*, *Always on My Mind* should be underlined, and *nonrock* should have a hyphen. Everything else looks right." **B** earns three points. **B** then gives **A** "A 'New Wave' supposedly swept americas rockmusic scene in the late 1970's." **A** says "*americas* should have a capital and an apostrophe (*America's*), *rockmusic* should be *rock music*, and I don't see any more." **B** points out that *1970's* does not show possession and therefore should not have an apostrophe and that *rock music* should by hyphenated. Thus, **A** gets two points; **B** gets two. **A** gives **B** "English rock musicians, who's so called 'invasion' of America began in the 1960's, have had a strong influence on the direction of Rock-n-Roll and sold 1,000,000's of records."

Continue the game in this way. Play the game again if you forget any of the word-punctuation or writing-convention rules.

64

Misusage and Weak Vocabulary

INTRODUCTION

In America, television and radio influence word usage and vocabulary more than does any other aspect of society. Millions of people hear Mr. T, the Fonz, the Ricker, and other characters and imitate their ways of speaking; thus, almost instantly, a new usage is born. "Where's the beef?" swept the nation after if was introduced in a TV commercial. Columnists, cartoonists, politicians, and the general public made it part of their vocabulary.

From watching TV, reading, and talking with others, you as a speaker of American English become familiar with acceptable words and forms. You may change these words and forms when you discover that people around you have found new ones, or when you join another group with different patterns.

When you write, you consider not only what your friends accept in speech but also the fact that written communication is more formal than the spoken word. For instance, while you may say "Can you loan me five dollars 'til payday?" you are likely to write something more formal, such as "May I borrow five dollars until payday?"

Many people associate word usage with grammar: correct grammar is good usage; bad grammar is poor usage. This opinion fails to consider that English is a living, changing language. Certainly correct grammar is useful as a basis for correct usage, but in some circumstances, correct grammar can produce poor usage. (Can you think of a situation where fastidiously correct grammar would be incorrect usage?) The point of linking grammar and usage is that the words you use and the way in which you use them will change; if you are a careful writer, you should consider what your audience will accept as correct usage and what is appropriate to the time and place in which you are writing.

Standard usage involves a remarkably small number of words. Of the approximately 800,000 words in the English language, the average American high-school graduate *uses* not many more than 2,000 words in conversation, about 4,000 in written communication, and recognizes approximately 6,000 in reading. But all of us combine the words we use in a vast number of inventive and ever-changing combinations to suit our various audiences.

Reprinted with permission — *Vancouver* magazine.

Emerson, Vancouver Magazine.

Besides this chapter, other parts of *The Independent Writer* deal with usage. You should refer to the index for a complete cross-reference to word usage and vocabulary.

There are approximately thirty errors in standard usage in the following paragraph. Locate each error and change it to acceptable usage. Then rewrite the entire paragraph to eliminate wordiness. If your rewrite does not resemble the one in the Suggested Answers following Chapter 66, you should continue with this chapter.

A great amount of people are enthused about acid-rock music, but for me personally, it is a symbol of my aggravation. From the time the instrumentalists start to play, I hear only the loud, constant continual throb from their loudspeakers, due to the fact that they have been turned up to the extreme. Doubtlessly, acid rock certainly effects me on three different counts. First, it gives me a headache. Secondly, it causes a pain in my guts to form. And last but not least, my eyes start to really hurt too. I feel like alot of acid-rock fans can take acception to my averse criticism, but, hopefully, they gotta understand implicitly that there are many alternate forms to music, viz. each form differs with another. They may have to always play their acid rock, as long as I can have my country and western.

EXERCISE ONE
Classifying Words

You can classify words into two main categories: standard and nonstandard. You can further divide standard English into formal and informal diction and nonstandard English into colloquial and slang.

STANDARD		NONSTANDARD	
Formal	**Informal**	**Colloquial**	**Slang**
automobile	car	auto	wheels
lady	woman	gal	fox

1. See if you or your partner can come up with a formal, colloquial, and slang equivalent for each of the following informal words: house, man, student, dentist, sofa, library.

2. You might find it useful to discuss with your partner under what circumstances you would choose each of the words in parentheses to complete the following sentences:

- A woman is (underweight, skinny, a bean pole, a willow, a slip of a thing, skin and bones, a shadow, a scrag, a spindleshanks, a barebones, slender, svelte, slight, slim, a string bean, delicate, gaunt, lean, emaciated, lanky, scrawny, wizened, a scarecrow, anorexic).

- A racehorse runs (ploddingly, proudly, smartly, gingerly, ridiculously, haltingly, exhaustedly, pokily, enthusiastically, intrepidly, awkwardly, hesitatingly, consistently, sleepily, mechanically, courageously, redoubtably, amok, inexhaustibly).

- A boy (walks, stumbles, trips, strides, plods, glides, sidles, strolls, tramps, stalks, flits, moves, struts, wanders, saunters, marches, steps, paddles).

- A child (cries, screams, sobs, yowls, yelps, screeches, weeps, bawls, whoops, bellows, shrieks, pules).

Which of the verbs in the last two sentences would you use in a formal research essay, which in an argumentative essay, and which in a conversation with a friend? **3.** You and your partner should separately write three drafts of the following sentence, using the words in parentheses. Think about levels of word choice and slant (Chapter 37) before you write. (Normally you should avoid mixing word levels.) Also, consider the writing variables. Write the first draft to a friend of both you and the deceased. Write the second draft for a cheap pocketbook thriller. Write the third draft for the deceased's pastor.

> When (Aunt Emily, Auntie Em, my old lady's sis) (died, passed away, kicked the bucket, went to her maker, didn't wake up, croaked, bought the farm, cashed in her chips) (last evening, last night, sometime yesterday, at 8:30 last night, at nightfall, at evening's close), she (bequeathed, left, willed, handed out, passed on, handed down) (all her wealth, a bundle, all that lovely green stuff, her loot, her assets, her property, her money, all her worldly goods) to (charity, the needy, charity cases, the down-and-outs, paupers, indigents, the unfortunates of the world, a bunch of do-gooders, the screwballs of the world) and not to (me, I, myself, yours truly, the writer of this sentence, old Numero Uno).

After you have written the three drafts of the sentence, you and your partner should compare your sentences and discuss the type of audience who would appreciate each sentence. You should also discuss the type of person who would have written each version.

EXERCISE TWO
Abstract/Concrete Words

A concrete word names a specific idea; an abstract word names a general idea. The more abstract the topic, the more concrete your language should be; however, when you deal with a clear, concrete topic, you can use abstract words and figurative language to enrich your treatment of it. In other words, do not use only abstract language to write about an abstract topic.

1. With your partner, rewrite the following paragraph so that you either cut any vague abstract words or change them for precise, concrete ones. The first sentence has been rewritten for you. Both of you should be in complete agreement with the revision of the rest of the paragraph.

> In the case of Wayne Gretzky, the degree of his ability to play hockey forces one to think of him as an outstanding hockey player. He possesses character traits that give him the status of a hero among his young fans. He has a friendly and positive attitude, which increases his popularity to an unprecedented degree. Many observers try to bestow on him some kind of title to indicate the extent of his talent.

By ridding the first sentence of the abstract words, you can produce a sentence something like this:

Wayne Gretzky plays outstanding hockey.

2. Find other examples of overly abstract writing (either from your own writing or from that of others). Work with your partner to rid the pieces of unnecessary abstractions.

EXERCISE THREE
Redundancy

Redundancy refers to the repetition of the same idea, where the repetition does not add anything to a reader's understanding of the idea. Other types of wordiness are dealt with in Chapter 58.

1. With your partner, rewrite the following paragraph so that you eliminate any redundancies. The first sentence has been rewritten for you; both of you should be in complete agreement with the revision of the rest of the paragraph.

> Eudora Welty's several devoted readers are many in number. She has demonstrated in writing that she is a female literary genius of great psychologically descriptive talent who has a great skill in writing about what the inner lives of people appear like to a careful observer. Although this skill is not absolutely unique (Katherine Anne Porter was another female writer who also possessed it), Welty is able to get herself inside of characters and show what the psychological interiors of their lives look like.

By ridding the first sentence of redundancy, you can produce a sentence something like this:

> Eudora Welty's devoted readers are many.

2. Find other examples of redundant writing (either from your own writing or from that of others). Work with your partner to rid the pieces of unnecessary words.

EXERCISE FOUR
Vivid Verbs

To discover one difference between experienced and inexperienced writers, examine the verbs they use. Inexperienced writers overuse linking verbs (Chapter 59) as well as *go, come, say, walk, run, think, know, get, fix,* and the like. Although indispensable in our language, such verbs often fail to provide a precise image. With your partner, substitute the italicized verbs in the following paragraph for more vivid ones. To make the sentences more vital, think of a vivid verb rather than one that requires an adverb. The first sentence has been rewritten for you; you should be in complete agreement with your partner concerning the revision of the rest of the paragraph.

When novelist William Faulkner *went* to Stockholm, Sweden, in 1950 to *get* the Nobel Prize in literature, he *was* able to *make* a speech that *is* among the most moving assessments of the human condition. He *said* that he *knew* men and women *were* not simply biological creatures but that they *were*, most importantly, spiritual creatures. He also *said* that he would not *go* along with the notions of people who *thought* that mankind must soon *come* to an end. He *said* that he *thought* that a human would not merely *be* someone who endures, but that he or she would *be* someone who prevails. Do you *think* that what Faulkner *says is* true?

By changing some of the verbs and introducing adverbs in the first sentence, you might produce a strong sentence, such as the following:

When novelist William Faulkner *proudly went* to Stockholm, Sweden, in 1950 to *gratefully receive* the Nobel Prize in literature, he *confidently gave* a speech that *stands securely* among the most moving assessments of the human condition.

However, if you were to avoid adverbs and concentrate on more vivid verbs, you could produce something like this:

When novelist William Faulkner *traveled* to Stockholm, Sweden, in 1950 to *accept* the Nobel Prize in literature, he *strode* to the stage to *deliver* a speech that *ranks* among the most moving assessments of the human condition.

Find other examples of writing containing dull verbs (either from your own writing or from that of others). Work with your partner to replace the dull verbs with vivid ones.

EXERCISE FIVE
Lively Adjectives and Adverbs

You should not use adjectives and adverbs in place of vivid verbs; however, when you do use them, fresh and lively adjectives and adverbs can contribute to a vigorous diction. Avoid "dead" adjectives, such as *nice, pretty, awful, terrific, horrible, dumb, mean, big, little*, and so on. In addition, avoid overusing adverbs such as *rather, quite, so, very, extremely, somewhat*, and so on. Rewrite the following paragraph by eliminating dead adjectives and adverbs, using vivid verbs, and introducing lively adjectives or adverbs. The first sentence has been rewritten for you; you should be in complete agreement with your partner concerning the revision of the rest of the paragraph.

F. Scott Fitzgerald is usually judged, along with William Faulkner and Ernest Hemingway, as one of the really classic American fiction writers of the twentieth century. And he was indeed a terrific writer, who produced some extremely good novels and short stories.

But his private life, after years of very big success, turned out in some respects to be pretty awful. His quite brilliant wife, Zelda, suffered a horrible nervous breakdown, and Scott, whose very great popularity had sort of declined gradually after the 1920s, had to provide for her care by working extremely hard as a Hollywood screenwriter. (Some of the projects he worked on in the movie industry were so dumb in comparison to his penetrating, really insightful fiction.) He died rather young, but a forty-four-year life span was quite long enough for him to have written some very good novels and short stories. *The Great Gatsby*, though somewhat short, is one of the really terrific works of literature that deals with the American Dream—a very important theme. His novel *Tender Is the Night* is also quite good. And a number of his short stories—"Winter Dreams," "Babylon Revisited," and "The Rich Boy," for instance—are awfully nice. A lot of people said that Scott himself was an awfully nice man.

By eliminating the dead adjectives and adverbs from the first two sentences, you might produce something like this:

F. Scott Fitzgerald is usually judged, along with William Faulkner and Ernest Hemingway, as one of the genuinely classic American fiction writers of the twentieth century. And he was indeed a wonderfully gifted writer, who produced some superb novels and short stories.

Find other examples of writing that contain dead adjectives and adverbs (either from your own writing or from that of others). Work with your partner to replace them with vivid ones.

EXERCISE SIX
Clichés

The cliché is a trite, hackneyed, or stereotyped word or phrase that has become stale from overuse. Many dead metaphors (Chapter 36) are clichés. Revise the following paragraph by substituting fresh images for the clichés. The first sentence has been rewritten for you; you and your partner should be in complete agreement with the revision of the rest of the paragraph.

Right from the start, believe it or not, Theodore Roosevelt looked like one slick dude who was headed straight for the big time. Let's face it, he *did* become an outstanding statesman, a distinguished scholar, an avid reader, and, last but not least, one of our country's best presidents. Busy as a bee, Roosevelt accomplished much during his two terms. First and foremost, perhaps, he made our country a better place to live in by helping to establish our system of national parks, thus ensuring that nature's glory would be accessible for future generations. (It goes without saying that the national parks, even those off the beaten path, are places where a good time can be had by all.) And to all intents and purposes Roosevelt beefed up the armed forces, an action, it stands to reason, that helped protect our cherished freedoms. In the last analysis (some would say beyond a shadow of a doubt), however, his work to bring about the construction of the Panama Canal was probably one of the wonders of the modern world. We can all thank our lucky stars that Roosevelt burned the midnight oil to get the job done. Thanks, Teddy, we needed that.

By eliminating all of the clichés from the first sentence and using fresh images, you might end up with something like this:

Even as a young man, Theodore Roosevelt impressed others as a person destined for greatness.

Find other examples of writing containing clichés (either from your own writing or from that of others). Work with your partner to eliminate them.

EXERCISE SEVEN
Idioms

Often, particular combinations of words no longer make literal sense, but we continue to use them nonetheless. These combinations of words are known as *idioms*.
People rarely question common idiomatic expressions; they simply use them. But when you hear nonnative speakers of English misusing them, you become aware that idioms are illogical. A Scandinavian, for example, might say to a girl "May I follow you home?" instead of using the idiom "May I walk you home?" Non-American English speakers have their own idioms. For example, an Englishwoman might ask you whether you want her to "knock you up" when she means to "awaken you." To "pig out" in Australia means "to die"; in the United States it means "to overeat."
1. Discuss with your partner the illogicality of these common idioms:

How do you do?	Shoot the breeze!
Look up a word.	Shoot! I lost the game!
Kiss and make up.	We're late; let's hustle.
Spend a penny.	Hang it all, I'm mad!
Taking a spin.	Talking up a storm.
Draw a bath.	I nearly died laughing.

2. Each of you think of five similar idiomatic expressions, then discuss the illogicality of each of them.

EXERCISE EIGHT
Fractured Idioms

Some English scholars call mixed-up combinations of words *fractured idioms*, although technically the problem is improper word usage. At any rate, you should not use expressions such as "the solution to the question" for "the solution to the problem," "the remainder of their dinner" for "the rest of their dinner," "the consensus of opinion" for "consensus," or "less calories" for "fewer calories."

You may wonder why you have to use only accepted combinations of words in academic writing. The simple answer is that much of your writing will be read by informed people. Your incorrect usage will give the impression that you are uninformed. Sometimes your word usage may even cost you a job or prevent you from being considered for a promotion.

In order to master standard word usage, you should read and listen to informed people, such as professional writers, who are the leaders in the use of language. To keep up with current usage, you should listen to news broadcasts, watch documentaries, and pay attention to popular speakers. Occasionally even informed speakers or writers may use words improperly, but you are generally in good company when you follow their example.

1. Make up some sentences using these words: *accept, except, all right, among, between, amount of, number of, as, like, because of, due to, can, may, compare to, compare with, lie, lay, sit, set.* If you are having difficulty in determining the exact meaning of these words in order to use them properly, you might refer to a current book of usage. (See the Suggestions for Further Study at the end of this book.)

2. Discuss the correctness of your word usage with your partner.

3. Some pairs of words, such as the following, at one time had different meanings, but now are used interchangeably: *til, until; though, although.* However, some words retain their subtle differences, and only when you have taken the time to discover their exact meanings will you be able to use them correctly. With your partner, find pairs of words that are often incorrectly used interchangeably; then determine their exact meanings and when to use each. Start with the following pairs or groups: *famous, infamous; reaction, response; fewer, less; admission, admittance; childish, childlike; insure, ensure; uninterested, disinterested; annoy, aggravate, irritate; continuously, continually; among, between.*

4. Rewrite the following paragraph, correcting any fractured idioms that you see. The first sentence has been rewritten for you. You and your partner should be in complete agreement with the revision of the rest of the paragraph.

Emily Dickinson's life was different than that of most poets. She got born and raised in Amherst, Massachusetts. Compared to men at her social class, she was only formerly educated a little farther than one year in Mount Holyoke Female Seminary, an academic locale she attended between 1847 to 1848. She published, synonymously for the most part, only a short amount of her poems (seven from an approximate total of 1,775) in her life span. She was disinterested with the public life of a man of letters. On the contrary, she preferred, instead, to set at her desk in her room and struggle among the twin demands of a very private exterior life and the life of artfulness. But now she is a notorious woman. Her infamous works—almost all of them—are far and widely inspected for their linguistic and rhythmic cleverness. (Even her childish poetry is admirable.) Hopefully, if you have not read any of Dickinson's astounding work, you may; you shall find her more enjoyable than any other poetesses you personally know.

The first sentence would be idiomatically correct if you were to write something like this:

Emily Dickinson's life was different from that of most poets.

5. Find other examples of fractured idioms (either from your own writing or from that of others.) Work with your partner to correct them.

EXERCISE NINE
Slang

When you are with your friends, you likely use words and expressions that people of another generation, or from another country, would not understand. These colorful slang expressions are quite appropriate in casual conversation but are usually considered out of place in written communication.

1. With your partner, decide what group of people would use (or have used) the following slang:

   a. got my head on straight, relating, tripping out, Mary Jane

   b. goldbrick, re-upping, snafu, AWOL

   c. doing an all-nighter, pulling a B, hitting the books, prof

   d. gross me out the door, gag me with a spoon, tubular

If you are having difficulty, turn to the Suggested Answers following Chapter 66.

2. With your partner, share some slang expressions that you use when you are in the company of friends. Does you partner understand the slang expressions?

EXERCISE TEN
Jargon

There are special words that people use in various professional situations. Language that is used in a special sense (by and for members of a particular profession or group) is called *jargon*. The following is an example of sports jargon: "Williams takes the ball in back court. The Sonics run it up the floor on a fast break. Sikma dekes around the guard, skyhooks the ball, and stuffs it!" Do you know what sport is being talked about? Defend your answer by explaining to your partner the meaning of the jargon used.

One of the dangers of using jargon of any kind in your writing is that you may not be understood. Jargon has a purpose in sports and in technical reports, but in ordinary writing, jargon may confuse your reader. So reserve technical language for technical uses.

There is an increasing tendency to use scientific and technological jargon words in ordinary speech and writing—for example, *input, overview, interface, feedback, conceptualize, mechanizing, dehumanizing* (and other words ending in "-ize"), and words ending in "-wise" such as *computerwise*. Jargon used in this way can make writing not only wordy and pretentious, but also confusing.

1. List five examples of jargon that you would use legitimately in one of your specialized subjects: chemistry, psychology, data processing, education, and so on. See if your partner can understand what the words mean.

2. Can you tell what facts are hidden in the following illegitimate use of jargon?

The unanticipated rebound in consumer spending in the third quarter of 1979, which more than regained the ground lost in the second quarter's decline, has combined with the shift in monetary policy announced in early October to change significantly the configuration of economic activity during 1980, although the full-year results will not differ greatly from the forecast issued in September as part of the long-range-plan background material.

Try to rewrite this sentence into a much shorter sentence. Remove the confusing jargon. Then turn to the Suggested Answers following Chapter 66 to see one version.

Game One: Name that _____!

Describe for your partner a portion of a game, sport, or activity without naming it. Make sure that you use specialized jargon to describe the event. The object of the game is to see how long it takes your partner to name the game, sport, or activity. In playing the game, say as many specialized words (slang or jargon) related to a single subject (game, sport, activity, and so on) as you can before your partner determines the subject you are referring to. You must start with "Name that . . ."

For example, **A** says to **B** "Name that game!", and gives the word *dibs*. **B** does not know the game, so **A** receives one point. **A** gives the words *cat's eye*. **B** still does not know the game. **A** has now earned two points. **A** says *steelie*. **B** says "The game is marbles." It is now **B**'s turn.

B says to **A** "Name that country!", and gives **A** the word *outback*. **A** does not know the country, so **B** receives one point. **B** says *bloke*. **A** says "The country is Australia." **A** continues the game.

A says "Name that activity!" and gives **B** the word *julienne*. The game continues in this way until one player accumulates a predetermined number of points and thus wins the game. Continue the game in this way.

EXERCISE ELEVEN
Vocabulary Fun

1. *Coined Words.* Words are continually being coined. For example, these blended (portmanteau) words caught on after someone joined parts of two words: *chuckle* plus *snort* equals *chortle*, *breakfast* plus *lunch* equals *brunch*. What two words have been blended to produce *smog, flurry, squelch, motel, flare, glimmer, smash, broil,* and *riffle*?

With your partner, read the following excerpt, noting the portmanteau words. What is the meaning of each?

> "You seem very clever at explaining words, sir," said Alice. "Would you kindly tell me the meaning of the poem called 'Jabber-wocky'?"
>
> "Let's hear it," said Humpty Dumpty. "I can explain all the poems that ever were invented—and a good many that haven't been invented just yet."
>
> This sounded very hopeful, so Alice repeated the first verse:
>
> > "Twas brillig, and the slithy toves
> > Did gyre and gimble in the wabe:
> > All mimsy were the borogoves,
> > And the mome raths outgrabe."
>
> "That's enough to begin with," Humpty Dumpty interrupted: "There are plenty of hard words there. 'Brillig' means four o'clock in the afternoon—the time when you begin *broiling* things for dinner."
>
> "That'll do very well," said Alice: "and 'slithy'?"
>
> "Well, 'slithy' means 'lithe' and 'slimy.' 'Lithe' is the same as *active*. You see it's like a portmanteau—there are two meanings packed up into one word." (Lewis Carroll, *Alice Through the Looking Glass*)

Advertisers are fond of coining words for their new or improved products. By using a new word, they hope that their product name will remain in the minds of their audience. For instance, a canner called a combination of apple and apricot juice "Apple-Cot juice." Another advertiser, wanting to suggest that his gum contained aspirin, called it "Aspergum."

a. What two words are blended to form *participaction, McNuggets, scrumpdillyi-cious, gynormous, guesstimate, sniglet*?

b. You and your partner each choose five types of products (soft drinks, tooth-paste, shoes, and so on). Each of you should try to coin a word to describe a new product of each type. For example, for a new soft drink product you might come up with "Orancola."

2. *"Tom Swifties."* In the 1930s and 1940s, Tom Swift was the hero of a series of books written for boys. One feature of these books was the way in which the author used descriptive words: Tom and the other characters always said things *quietly*, *abruptly*, or *emphatically*. "Tom Swifties" use this feature and carry it one step further: they show a punning relationship between the descriptive word and the quotation. Here are a few examples:

- "Move to the back of the boat," ordered Tom *sternly*.
- "I do know a lot, don't I?" asked Betty *smartly*.
- "Have you seen that famous triumphal monument in Paris?" asked Bill *archly*.
- "I have to use my hands because it's pitch dark here," explained Bob *feelingly*.
- "I should have stayed away from the poison ivy!" cried Barbara *rashly*.

You and your partner make up three "Tom Swifties" for each other.

3. *Malapropisms*. In a wonderful play, *The Rivals*, by Richard Sheridan, the character of Mrs. Malaprop appears. In this scene with Anthony Absolute, Mrs. Malaprop shows him what she likes to do best—talk. Examine her choice of words.

MRS. MALAPROP: Fy, fy, Sir Anthony, you surely speak laconically.

ABSOLUTE: Why, Mrs. Malaprop, in moderation now, what would you have a woman know?

MRS. MALAPROP: Observe me, Sir Anthony. I would by no means wish a daughter of mine to be a progeny of learning; I don't think so much learning becomes a young woman; for instance, I would never let her meddle with Greek, or Hebrew, or algebra, or simony, or fluxions, or paradoxes, or such inflammatory branches of learning—neither would it be necessary for her to handle any of your mathematical, astronomical, diabolical instruments.—But, Sir Anthony, I would send her, at nine years old, to a boarding-school, in order to learn a little ingenuity and artifice. Then, sir, she should have a supercilious knowledge in accounts;—and as she grew up, I would have her instructed in geometry, that she might know something of the contagious countries;—but above all, Sir Anthony, she should be mistress of orthodoxy, that she might not mis-spell, and mispronounce words so shamefully as girls usually do; and likewise that she might reprehend the true meaning of what she is saying. This, Sir Anthony, is what I would have a woman know;—and I don't think there is a superstitious article in it.

Even if you do not know everything that Mrs. Malaprop is saying, you can enjoy the fact that she misuses words shamelessly. With your partner, try to figure out what she "would have a woman know." Use a dictionary to help you out.

Comedian Norm Crosby knowingly uses malapropisms. Some poor speakers unknowingly confuse, for example, *except* for *accept*, *progeny* for *prodigy*, and mix-up dozens of other words that sound almost the same. What they must do is to note carefully the difference in the pronunciations of the pair. What words do you mix up? Share them with your partner.

4. *Purple Prose.* This was coined to describe high-flown language that can disguise and even distort true meaning. Euphemisms, euphuisms, neologisms, inflated titles, and expressions that incorporate technical jargon are some of the sorts of language that can obscure, rather than clarify, what you want to say.

Find a few examples of precise, powerful, and simple statements. Rewrite these lines so that you disguise their meaning, then present them, with their sources, to your partner to see if he or she can discover the originals. For example, the following have been rewritten from original statements (the first one provides the original for you):

- The query I raise is whether to remain in this corporeal state or to depart from it. (Shakespeare) To be or not to be, that is the question.
- Donate us the implements and we shall finalize the situation. (Churchill)
- To inflict a fatal injury on a human person is proscribed. (Bible)
- Motorized modules will be provided with an exclusive thoroughfare during active arrival and departure periods. (city planner)
- He expired in indigent circumstances. (on a tombstone)
- This means of ingress and egress is alarmed through the full rotation of the earth upon its axis. (sign on a door in New York City)

5. *Words with Double Meanings.* Some English words have changed their meaning over the centuries. For example, when Shakespeare used "presently," he meant "immediately"; when we use "presently," we mean "in a while." Many words, however, have changed their meanings during your lifetime—or, for example, *choice, gay, groove, sauce, high, speed, streak.* Discuss the double meanings of each of them (and other modern words) with your partner.

EXERCISE TWELVE
Grammar vs. Usage

Coming out of a movie theatre after a double feature, a woman turned to her husband and asked, "Which film did you like best?" Her husband, an English professor, retorted, "Better." End of conversation.

This story reflects the current struggle between grammar and usage. Not so long ago, good grammar and good usage were considered synonymous both in speech and in writing. Nowadays, however, few people concern themselves with whether their speech is grammatically correct, especially when they are speaking with people they know well.

Writing, though, is more permanent, and less personal and immediate, than speech. When you write, you may be recording a document to be read and reread by someone you will never meet in a place and time you will never see. You cannot take the easy way out, as you can in speech, of saying what is almost right and letting your listener deduce what you mean. To make yourself clear in writing, you should follow grammatically correct forms much more closely than you do in speech.

Since this textbook deals with writing from a positive approach, it does not contain long lists of rules such as "Never end a sentence with a preposition," "Do not use an adjective in place of an adverb," or "Never split an infinitive." However, it does advise you to make yourself familiar with both basic grammar and current usage. In that way, you will know what rules you may choose to break. (See Suggestions for Further Study at the end of this text for the titles of some books dealing with grammar and usage.)

Advertisers often break the rules of grammar in order to achieve emphasis or make their slogans memorable. Often, an entire country adopts the mistake and it becomes common usage.

With your partner, examine the following pieces of advertising (the names of the products have been changed), and try to figure out what is grammatically wrong with them. Reword them so that they are grammatically correct. Are the slogans more effective when they are correct?

- A Stinton tastes good like a cigarette should.
- Late beer has one-third less calories than our regular beer.
- Aticin relieves your headaches fast.
- Families using Prest have fewer cavities than families using any leading toothpaste.

EXERCISE THIRTEEN
Multiple Meanings

Some words are extremely versatile. You can use them in many different ways in a sentence: as nouns, verbs, adjectives, or other parts of speech (Chapter 41).
1. Compete with your partner to see who can use each of the following words in more ways in a single sentence: *eye, fire, bill, strike, leg*. Here are examples using *watch* and *set*:

- The sailor on the dog*watch watch*ed his *watch* and his *watch*dog.
- As the sun *set*, her *set* purpose was to *set* out a *set* of dishes in a *set* pattern.

2. With your partner, compose three examples in which a sentence can be misread. If you cannot think of a key word, use one of the following: *plane, serve, pole, shoot, stand*. For example:

- "She gave her dog biscuits" can mean (a) She gave biscuits to her dog, or (b) She gave dog biscuits to a female person.
- "Baby swallows fly" can mean (a) An infant swallows an insect, or (b) The babies of the swallow family are able to fly.

3. The meanings of many English words can vary according to their context. Compete with your partner to see who can write more sentences using the following words as nouns with different meanings: *rest, pitch, beat*. When you finish, look up the words in a good dictionary (OED) to see which meanings you both missed. The following examples using *set* are provided to help you get started:

- The band played a twenty-minute *set*.

- John and Roger played a *set* of tennis.
- My sister received a *set* of dishes as a wedding gift.
- Bill went to the dentist for a new *set* of teeth.
- I could tell by the *set* of his shoulders that he had bad news.
- We spent all weekend building the *set* for *Romeo and Juliet*.
- Before you go boating, check the *set* of your sails.

4. Repeat the previous activity using the same three words (*rest*, *pitch*, *beat*) as verbs. Here are some examples using *set*:

- He *set* the new plants in his garden.
- Mary *set* the table.
- The jelly will *set* in ten minutes.
- The crew *set* the stage an hour ago.
- My brother and his friends *set* sail for Hawaii yesterday.
- I *set* my alarm for 7 A.M.
- The sun *set* at nine o'clock last night.
- He *set* fire to his business to collect the insurance.

EXERCISE FOURTEEN
Synonyms

"The difference between the right word and the almost right word," Mark Twain wrote, "is the difference between lightning and the lightning bug." When you write, you want to find the word that says exactly what you want to say. If you have the almost right word, you can consult a thesaurus to find synonyms (words that mean approximately the same thing) for it.

Although a thesaurus does not provide definitions, it will let you see several words that differ only in shades of meaning. You might discover words with a positive or negative slant; these are useful in argumentative writing. You might find formal words to use for a satiric purpose or for a learned audience. You will certainly discover the infinite richness of the English language.

1. With your partner, discuss the different shades of meaning among the words in each of the following groups:

a. When is money a payment, an allowance, an offering, a bribe, a gift, a remuneration, a dividend, an honorarium, a tax, a payoff, a stipend, a salary, a grant, earnings, winnings?

b. When is a forest a woods, timber, a jungle, a woodland, a grove, a thicket, scrubland?

c. When is a sofa a chesterfield, a couch, a settee, a lounge, a davenport, a hide-a-bed, a loveseat, a settle?

2. Continue this exercise by playing a synonym game with your partner. Alternate saying synonyms to each other. The one who cannot provide a synonym loses.

3. You and your partner each find a paragraph written by a professional writer. Underline a predetermined number of key words. Exchange paragraphs. The object of the exercise is to see if you can replace the underlined words with other equally suitable words that mean nearly the same thing.

EXERCISE FIFTEEN
The Word and the Poet

You may have heard of poets who will jot down dozens of words to fit into a single position in a poem. After much agonizing, they finally decide on one word that fits both the subject and the rhythm. The process is rather like that used in filming a movie. For one scene that the audience sees, perhaps as many as fifty scenes wind up on the editor's floor.

1. You and your partner fill in each blank in the following verses with a word that fits the sonnet's rhythm, meter, tone, rhyme scheme, purpose, and meaning.

The Mowing
by Charles G. D. Roberts

This is the _____ of high midsummer's heat.
   The rasping vibrant clamour soars and _____
   O'er all the meadowy range of shadeless hills,
As if a _____ of giant cicadae beat

The cymbals of their wings with _____ feet,
   Or brazen grasshoppers with triumphing note
   From the long swath proclaimed the fate that _____
The clover and timothy-tops and meadowsweet.

The _____ knives glide on; the green swath lies.
   And all noon long the sun, with _____ ray,
   Seals up each cordial essence in its cell,
That in the _____ stalls, some winter's day,
   The spirit of June, here prisoned by his _____,
   May cheer the herds with _____ memories.

Find the poem in your library and check to see if your word choices match the poet's.

2. Each of you find a poem. Duplicate it but leave a few key words out. Exchange duplicated poems with your partner and try to fill in the blanks in the poem you have been given with appropriate vocabulary. Afterwards, discuss the choices.

EXERCISE SIXTEEN
The Word and the Prose Writer

A poet has a much more difficult task with vocabulary than does a prose writer. However, prose writers must also take into account the connotative and denotative meanings of the words they use, the positive and negative slant of their words, the level and appropriateness of the words, and the effect they wish to achieve by their word choice. A thesaurus and a dictionary will help you find words, but if you do not take into account the *full* meanings of the words you choose, your audience may misinterpret your meaning.

1. You and your partner try to supply a suitable word for the missing words in this piece of prose:

> And I remember that we went singing carols once, a night or two before Christmas Eve, when there wasn't the _____ of a moon to light the secret, white-flying streets. At the end of the long road was a drive that led to a large house, and we _____ up the darkness of the drive that night, each one of us afraid, each one holding a stone in his hand in case, and all of us too _____ to say a word. The wind made through the drive-trees noises of old and unpleasant and maybe web-footed men _____ in caves.
>
> We reached the back _____ of the house.
>
> "What shall we give them?" Dan _____.
>
> "'Hark the Herald'? 'Christmas comes but Once a Year'?"
>
> "No," Jack _____: "We'll sing 'Good King Wenceslas.' I'll count three."
>
> One, two, three, and we began to sing, our voices _____ and seemingly distant in the snow-felted darkness round the house that was occupied by nobody we knew.
>
> We stood close together, near the _____ door.
>
> Good King Wenceslas looked out
> On the Feast of Stephen.
>
> And then a small, dry voice, like the voice of someone who has not spoken for a long time, suddenly joined our singing: a _____, _____ voice from the other side of the door: a _____, _____ voice through the key hole. And when we stopped running we were outside *our* house; the front room was lovely and _____; the gramaphone was playing; we saw the red and white balloons hanging from the gas-bracket; uncles and aunts sat by the fire; I thought I smelt our supper being _____ in the kitchen. Everything was _____ again, and Christmas _____ through all the familiar town.
>
> "Perhaps it was a ghost," Jim said.
>
> "Perhaps it was _____," Dan said, who was always reading.
>
> "Let's go in and see if there's any jelly left," Jack _____. And we did that.

If you would like to see the author's original word choices, see Dylan Thomas's "Quite Early One Morning."

2. Find a short piece of prose and prepare a similar exercise for your partner. After you have completed each other's exercise, discuss your vocabulary choices. Then, for interest, compare your choices with the author's.

EXERCISE SEVENTEEN
Building a Larger Vocabulary

There are many ways to build your vocabulary; the next few two-way games will give you practice. Decide with your partner, before you play, what the specific rules will be, and how you will keep score. Use the games that you enjoy most to build an extensive vocabulary.

Scoring and General Rules

1. Take turns providing one answer at a time. The one who cannot come up with a correct response loses. Or write your responses separately on a piece of paper. The one who has the greater number of correct responses wins.
2. Because the object of the games is to improve your vocabulary, it is assumed that you know the meanings of the words you use in the game. You may bluff and use a word whose meaning you are not sure of. However, if your partner challenges a word you must explain its meaning. Check the meaning in a dictionary. If, on the challenge, you are right, you gain a point; if you are wrong, you lose one.
3. You can use reference books (dictionaries and thesauri) during the game only in the event of a challenge. You can, of course, use them before and after games to prepare for the next game.
4. To make each game fair, take turns in choosing which game to play and which word to use to begin each game.

Game Two: Roots

A root (or stem) is the part of a word that contains the core of meaning: *aster* (meaning "star") is the root of such words as *aster*isk, *astr*onomy (Notice the *e* has been dropped. Can you think why?), and dis*aster*.

Rules: Alternate with your partner in choosing a root and giving its meaning. Then proceed as in the sample game that follows, using either of the methods of scoring outlined above. **A** begins the game by saying the root word *fin* (meaning "boundary"). Then **A** says "Finish"; **B** says "Finite"; **A** says "Infinity"; **B** says "Definite." If **A** cannot think of another word with *fin* in it, the score is tied unless **B** can come up with a word.

To use the second method of scoring, you can independently write down all of the words that have *fin* in them. Whoever produces the higher number of correct responses wins.

To get you started, here are some roots that you might use: *chronos* (meaning "time"), *therme* ("heat"), *algia* ("sickness"), *phonos* ("sound"), *equ* ("equal," "just"), *voc, vok* ("to call") *trans* ("across").

Game Three: Prefixes

Rules: The rules are exactly as in Game Two except that the parts of the word you are allowed to use must be prefixes. For example, if you use the prefix *ab* which means "from" or "away from," you might suggest *abnormal, abduct,* and *absent.*

Here are a few prefixes to get you started: *ambi* ("both"), *ante* ("before"), *bi* ("two," "twice"), *bene* ("good" or "well"), *circum* ("around") *tele* ("far off"), *epi* ("upon"), *dia* ("through"), *peri* ("around").

Game Four: Suffixes

Rules: The rules are exactly the same as in Game Two except that you use suffixes. For example, if you use the suffix *dom* meaning "condition," you might suggest *freedom* and *wisdom.*

Here are a few suffixes to get you started: *fold* ("number" or "quantity"), *less* ("lacking" or "wanting"), *ward* ("in the direction of"), *wise* ("way" or "manner").

Game Five: Plurals

Rules: Take turns with your partner in giving each other singular nouns, for which the other must then furnish the plural. For example, **A** gives "datum"; **B** answers "data," and then gives "formula"; **A** answers "formulas (or formulae)," and then gives "mongoose"; and so on.

Here is a list to get you started: *deer, Siamese, agendum, city, alumnus, alumna, buffalo, census, basis.* (If you want to include a spelling challenge in your rules, this would be an appropriate place. In other words, ask your partner to spell the word correctly for an additional point. If he or she cannot, and you spell it correctly, you get the point.) You can also reverse this game by providing the plural and requiring the singular form.

EXERCISE EIGHTEEN
Word Calendar

If you really want to build your vocabulary, you and your partner can make word calendars for each other. Learning a new word each day can be a painless way of building your vocabulary.

For example, prepare a list of words for each day in a month. Exchange the list with your partner. Each list should look something like this:

October 1   jocular

2   myriad

3   perspicuous

4   anomaly

5   clandestine

If you already know the meaning of the word that your partner has chosen, you can have that day off. If you are unfamiliar with the word, look up its meaning and try to use it throughout the day. See if the adage "Use a word ten times and it's yours" is true. Arrange a periodic check to see if your partner has mastered the words.

65

Fallacies

INTRODUCTION

You have perhaps been warned, and rightly so, against using fallacies. The term *logical fallacy* or *false logic* refers to any of the various types of erroneous reasoning that render arguments logically unsound. They mislead a reader through trickery and deception.

But logical fallacies exist, and many writers use them in creatively satiric ways. A knowledge of fallacies will ensure the recognition of unsound reasoning in what you read, as well as the ability to use them for specific reasons.

If, as you do the following quiz, you cannot find a fallacy in each sentence, you should continue working in this chapter. Although it's not as important, see if you can identify each fallacy by name—for example, non sequitur, sweeping generalization, begging the question, and so on. Check your answers in the Suggested Answers following Chapter 66.

1. You support the Republican party; therefore, your opinion is worthwhile.
2. Nine out of ten people in Somewhere, U.S.A., support gun-control laws; more people in the U.S. support gun-control laws than oppose them.
3. All politicians are human beings; a saint is a human being; therefore, all politicians are saints.
4. I'd appreciate your vote; I've been out of work six months and really need this job.
5. No wonder the leader of the other party likes bananas; he looks like a monkey.
6. Hitler, Mussolini, and J. Watt Furr are three of the best-known leaders of the twentieth century.
7. Everybody in Texas supports the idea of Texas separating from the rest of the United States.
8. America's most powerful politicians eat spinach; you should eat spinach too.
9. If you vote for my opponent, taxes are sure to increase.

10. I won every primary election I've entered since January, so this must be my lucky year; I'm sure to win the general election in November.

11. A good man serves others; politicians who play tennis serve others; therefore, politicians who play tennis are good men.

12. Why wait for November 1988? Do it now.

13. I won't do this question because it's number 13. Everyone knows 13 is unlucky, so I'm sure to get it wrong.

EXERCISE ONE
Classification of Logical Fallacy

An argument may be fallacious in matter (misstating facts), in wording (playing with words), or in the process of inference (shifting the focus away from the real issue).

You and your partner examine each set of sentences, noting the particular logical fallacy and its specific name. Discuss what makes each an example of false logic. If you get stuck, turn to the Suggested Answers following Chapter 66.

1. Misstatements of fact:
   a. *False emphasis*: The Goodtimes party vows to reduce inflation by at least 10 percent.
   b. *Accent*: J. Watt Furr is a devoted husband, father, and congressman.
   c. *Misuse of statistics*: Since J. Watt Furr has been president, old-age pensions have doubled; therefore, pensioners are twice as well-off now as they were five years ago.
   d. *Sweeping generalization*: Everyone who meets Furr likes him.

2. Playing with words:
   a. *Double meaning or equivocation*: Because J. Watt Furr believes in freedom of speech, he never charges a fee for his public lectures.
   b. *Pejorative association*: The leader of the Goodtimes party, J. Watt Furr, accuses the opposition leader of attending the same gatherings as suspected organized-crime bosses.
   c. *Taking figurative language literally*: To her astonishment, when she told J. Watt Furr to "jump on the bandwagon" for income-tax reform, he asked her where he could catch it.

3. Shifting away from the real issue:
   a. *Misdirection*: When he stands up in the Senate, he has *such* a winning smile.
   b. *Begging the question*: J. Watt Furr is a hard-working politician; therefore, he deserves your vote.
   c. *Appeal to sympathy*: J. Watt Furr needs a job; therefore you should vote for him.

d. *Appeal to individual or ad hominem*: J. Watt Furr is supported by the Chamber of Commerce; consequently, he must be a better candidate than his opponent.

e. *Threat or ad baculum*: If you don't vote for Furr, your taxes will double next year.

f. *Bandwagon or ad populum*: The Gallup poll says 75 percent of those polled support Furr. Join the crowd; they must be right.

g. *Non sequitur*: Furr will make a fine president; he attended the University of Albuquerque.

h. *Post hoc, ergo propter hoc*: J. Watt Furr delivered his speech against inflation last week; this week the inflation rate is down 2 percent; Furr's speech must have caused the inflation rate to drop.

i. *False analogy*: J. Watt Furr would make a fine president; after all, he has run a successful fertilizer business for years.

j. *Undistributed middle*: On the campaign trail Furr caught a cold. He said, "I must have gotten my feet wet."

k. *Ridicule*: Furr said of his opponent, "If he had a brain, it would be lonely."

l. *False assumption*: Furr and his opponent were to speak at a gathering. Only Furr turned up so he said to the crowd, "A bird in the hand is worth two in the bush. And I will tell you why. . . ."

EXERCISE TWO
False Advertising

Both you and your partner bring three or four examples of false advertising to your next class. Exchange them and prepare to point out all of the logical fallacies in each one. If you cannot find one in print, write out one that you saw on television (or make up one).

Can you find an example of something fallacious in every one of the following sentences?

There's no sale like it! Woodrot Furniture's semiannual sale offers the discriminating shopper the buys of a lifetime. Genuine hardwood veneer dining room sets are on sale for as low as $10.00 off the list price (plus what we have to give to Uncle Sam). You'll be sorry if you miss this opportunity to save a bundle on furniture. We offer easy credit terms too! See Woodrot Furniture today—have a better life tomorrow.

EXERCISE THREE
Illogical Argument

Independently, you and your partner find or make up a piece of illogical argument. Exchange and pick out the false logic and identify each by name. Then discuss the illogical argumentation of each example.

Before you work on your own, use the following paragraph for practice. Locate each example of false logic, identify each by name, and discuss with your partner the overall illogical argument.

Need a Psychiatrist?

Everyone needs a psychiatrist to live a full, complete life. If you don't have a psychiatrist, it's like not knowing what's in a book before you read it. Psychiatrists help you know yourself better in the same way you read a book to know a story better. With a psychiatrist, you will also be able to spend an interesting hour once a week, talking about yourself. Where else could you spend an exciting time with your very own shrink? Everyone likes to talk about himself or herself. There are many different psychiatric clinics throughout America, proving that America is basically a country that believes in psychiatry. Because these clinics were built by deeply dedicated Americans, it stands to reason that only good can come from attending one. So if you don't already go to a psychiatrist, you had better hurry before you end up in a looney bin.

© 1956 Used by permission of Selby Kelly, Executrix.

66

Sexist Writing

INTRODUCTION

During the last few years, many people have pointed out that sexist writing not only demeans women, but also makes a piece of writing inexact, unclear, and unconvincing. On the other hand, nonsexist writing is both courteous and correct.

To see whether you are sexist or nonsexist in your writing, read the following sentences. Find the one that is clearly nonsexist and rewrite the others so that they, too, are nonsexist. Then check your answers with those in the Suggested Answers following this chapter.

1. The television show, *The Living Planet*, demonstrates clearly that man has been on the earth for thousands of years.

2. When Neil Armstrong stepped on the moon's surface, he said, "That's one small step for a man, one giant leap for mankind."

3. The Girl Scouts should be congratulated for manning the exhibit at the World's Fair.

4. In his manuscript the author pointed out that only one manager manufactured dresses from man-made materials.

5. Is it true that Frenchmen drink a lot of wine?

6. All American children know something about George Washington, the Father of our country; the authors of the United States Constitution, the Founding Fathers; and the people who came over on the *Mayflower*, the Pilgrim Fathers.

7. The college catalog stated: "The student nurse will gain much knowledge and experience by taking on extra practical sessions in the nearby hospital when she completes her classwork."

8. The peacock, its tail fanned majestically, stood at the entrance of the zoo.

9. When I came home on British Airways, I sat directly opposite two Englishmen and their wives.

10. I think Joanna will make the best woman doctor in the world.

11. While Peter worked in the yard, Maria stayed inside to fix dinner.

12. Mr. James Baxter and Mrs. Ann Carter are my favorite teachers; but if I had to choose one, I'd choose Baxter over Mrs. Carter.

13. After cracking a bottle of champagne on her stern, Bill took his boat out on her maiden voyage.

14. Leading suffragettes in America included Elizabeth Cady Stanton, Lucretia Mott, Susan B. Anthony, Lucy Stone, Ida B. Wells, Anna Howard Shaw, Mary Church Terrel, Carrie Chapman Catt, and Alice Paul.

15. Emily Dickinson has always been my favorite poet.

Most people who discriminate against women in speech and writing do so unconsciously. If after you have checked your answers with those in the Suggested Answers, you determine that your writing is sexist, you might want to examine your fundamental beliefs about men and women. For example, do you believe that there is "man's work" and "woman's work"? Is a woman's place really in the home? Do you think one sex is superior? If you have answered yes to these questions, this chapter might prompt you to change your attitudes—the first step along the road to developing a nonsexist writing style.

EXERCISE ONE
Man

The generic term *man* has been used in two ways: to refer to an adult male human being and as a synonym for "human being." To be accurate and nonsexist, you should use the following words only when you refer to an adult male: *male*; *men*; words beginning with *man*, such as *mankind* and *manpower*; words ending with *man*, such as *spokesman* and *tradesman*; and some words containing *man*, such as *sportsmanship* and *workmanlike.*.

Obviously, when you use *man* and related words to refer to both women and men, you are being sexist. With your partner, study the ways of changing sexist writing to nonsexist. Also notice how much more precise the rewrites are.

Sexist
Since the beginning of time man has toiled. (The generic term implies that there were no women or children.)

Nonsexist
Since the beginning of time people (human beings) have toiled.

Sexist
The average man on the street often looks preoccupied. (Women and children are also average.)

Nonsexist
The average person on the street often looks preoccupied.

Sexist
If we think our forefathers had to work hard, we should stop for a moment and think about the life-styles of ancient man. (*Forefathers* is just another substitute for the generic *man*.)

Nonsexist
If we think our ancestors (forebears) had to work hard, we should stop for a moment and think about the life-styles of primitive societies (primitive men and women).

Sexist
One ward in a hospital that is manned all the time is the emergency ward. (The verb *man* is sexist.)

Nonsexist
One ward in a hospital that is staffed (covered) all the time is the emergency ward.

Sexist
Each day in front of the manpower office the line of people looking for work seems to get longer. (Avoid using the generic *man*, both by itself and in compounds, because it is no longer accurate.)

Nonsexist
Each day in front of the employment office the line of people looking for work seems to get longer.

Sexist
She wore a beautiful man-made bracelet. (Products are made by both men and women.)

Nonsexist
She wore a beautiful handmade bracelet.

Sexist
Martha, the chairman of the Student Council, conducted a lively meeting. (If you know the sex of the person in charge, use *chairman* or *chairwoman* as appropriate. If you do not, use *chairperson*, *chair*, or consider recasting the sentence.)

Nonsexist
Martha chaired a lively Student Council meeting.

Sexist
Do Irishmen really have fiery tempers? I don't believe it! (Combining the generic *men* and a nationality ignores women.)

Nonsexist
Do the Irish really have fiery tempers? I don't believe it!

Sexist
CCTV advertised for a new weatherman for their popular morning show. (Since women also report the weather, the generic *man* should go.)

Nonsexist
CCTV advertised for a new weather reporter (person) for their popular morning show.

Sexist
Our team lost the meet but got a special sportsmanship award. (Although not blatantly sexist, *sportsmanship* nonetheless contains the generic *man*.)

Nonsexist
Our team lost the meet but got a special award to acknowledge our high ideals of fair play. (Do you think the wordiness is justified? You must determine whether your

audience's situation warrants such a treatment in order to avoid possible sexist writing.)

Do not apply any of the above suggestions to words that clearly have nothing to do with sex: *man*ager and *man*ufacturing. Think of three more words that contain *man* in the same way.

EXERCISE TWO

Woman

Many writers, in trying to be nonsexist, use *woman* incorrectly. Indeed, when they use *woman* in some sentences, they demean women. The use of *girl* and *lady* also causes problems for writers.

Note carefully the difference between the following sexist and nonsexist examples. In many cases, you can detect sexist writing if you substitute female terms for male terms.

Sexist
Since the beginning of time man, with his helpmate woman, has toiled. (*Helpmate* places women in a subordinate position to men.)

Nonsexist
Since the beginning of time men and women have toiled.

Sexist
During the interview, Congresswoman Black demonstrated her womanly ways with the rude reporter. (Unless it is imperative that the sex of the member of congress be stated, do not refer to it. Do not use *womanly* to denote behavior. Would you say "...demonstrated his manly ways to the rude reporter"?)

Nonsexist
During the interview, Senator (Representative) Black treated the rude reporter graciously.

Sexist
An employer to his associate: "I'll get my girl to bring us some coffee." (Calling a woman a *girl* is demeaning.)

Nonsexist
An employer to his associate: "I'll ask my secretary (Mrs. Johns) to bring us some coffee."

Sexist
A lady teacher was named president of the PTA. *or* A woman teacher was named president of the PTA. (Both *lady* and *woman* are nouns, not adjectives. If you need to identify the sex of the teacher, use *female*; if not, leave out the reference altogether.)

Nonsexist
A female teacher was named president of the PTA. *or* Martha Thompson was named president of the PTA. (better)

Sexist
Three young female persons were arrested for shoplifting. (The word *person* sounds forced; adding adjectives *male* or *female* to *person* creates wordiness.)

Nonsexist
Three young women were arrested for shoplifting.

Sexist
Most ads on TV use words and terms that even a housewife can understand. (Implies that a woman who works at home lacks intelligence.)

Nonsexist
Most ads on TV use words and terms that an average viewer (householder) can understand.

Sexist
If you have a working mother, I bet you receive a better allowance than if your mother is just a housewife. (Implies that a woman does not work in a house.)

Nonsexist
If your mother works outside the home, I bet you receive a better allowance than if your mother works only in your home.

Sexist
I pronounce them man and wife. (*Man* and *wife* are not parallel terms, whereas *man* and *woman* and *husband* and *wife* are.)

Nonsexist
I pronounce them husband and wife.

With the impact of the women's movement, overt sexism is becoming rare. Subtle sexism, however, is still present in speech and writing all around us—difficult to detect and therefore hard to eradicate.

If you wonder whether what you say or write could be subtly sexist, ask yourself, Would I say or write the same thing in the same way if my audience were male? For instance, you might have said to a female friend, "You play pretty good basketball ... for a girl," and meant it as a compliment. But would you say to a male friend, "You play pretty good basketball ... for a boy"? Probably not. And if you did, your friend would probably think you were insulting him rather than praising him. Why not just compliment your friends on their ability and leave their sex out of the discussion? Thus, you will be on your way to developing a nonsexist speaking and writing style.

Sexist
I was hit by a careless woman driver. (Would you say "careless man driver"?)

Nonsexist
I was hit by a careless driver.

Subtle Sexist Writing
Mother Teresa not only helps to feed and house the needy but also serves to represent the highest ideals of a woman. (Even though Mother Teresa herself would humbly suggest that she helps and serves humanity, the writer of this sentence, in trying to be complimentary, indicates that a woman's main purpose is to help and serve.)

Nonsexist
A remarkable world citizen, Mother Teresa feeds and houses the needy.

Subtle Sexist Writing
Headline in recent newspaper: "Mother of 6 appointed School Board Superinten-

dent." (The fact that a mother has six children is immaterial. Would the newspaper print "Father of six"?)

Nonsexist
Headline in recent newspaper: "Juanita Gomez appointed School Board Superintendent." *or* "Leading educator appointed School Board Superintendent."

Subtle Sexist Writing
Mrs. Fritz Gobbeiling has just published her second novel. (Most married women, even though they take their husbands' last names, retain their own first names.)

Nonsexist
Freda Gobbeiling has just published her second novel.

Subtle Sexist Writing
Headline in recent magazine: "Ohio Granny, 72, drives her own van to California." (Would you consider "Ohio Grandpa, 72, drives his own van"?)

Nonsexist
Headline in recent magazine: "Elderly Ohioan drives her own van to California."

Sexist
Dr. Rudi Schwartz and his wife Ramona practice medicine in the same clinic. (Mentioning Ramona only as Dr. Rudi Schwartz's wife implies that her status does not equal his.)

Nonsexist
(Drs.) Ramona and Rudi Schwartz practice medicine in the same clinic. (Why *not* put the woman first?)

Sexist
In their meetings John Smith and Ms. Juli Henle always agree to disagree. (*John Smith* and *Ms. Juli Henle* are not parallel terms.)

Nonsexist
In their meetings Smith and Henle (John Smith and Juli Henle) always agree to disagree.

Sexist
If you do not know the name of the person you are writing to, use "Dear Sir" or "Gentlemen." (Although it's much better to find the name of the person to whom you are writing, when you cannot, you should not assume the person is male.)

Nonsexist
If you do not know the name of the person you are writing to, use "Dear Madam or Sir (Sir or Madam)."

EXERCISE THREE
He or She

How many times have you heard sentences like the following?

- Everyone should do his best.

- If a child misses school, he must bring a note to his teacher.
- Because every newborn baby looks cute, I always want to cuddle him.

In the above sentences the generic *he, his,* and *him* obviously refer to both sexes.

As you have already noted in Exercises One and Two, you can easily avoid the generic *man* by using *woman* and *female* accurately and correctly and thus produce nonsexist writing. On the other hand, use of the generic *he, his,* and *him* is so widespread and proves so difficult to eliminate from both speech and writing that even those who conscientiously want to rid their writing of sexist overtones often find themselves backed into a corner of indecision. Some writers alternate between *he* and *she* but, as a result, confuse their readers. Some use only *she, her,* and *hers* but, as a result, produce sexist writing by excluding male references. A few writers have tried to introduce new pronouns (*hir, per, tey, hesh*) to refer to both men and women, but none of these terms have caught on. The following exercise does not totally solve the problem, but it does provide several realistic alternatives for you to consider to avoid the generic *he.*

Sexist
If someone wishes to succeed in school, he should do his best every time he attempts a new project.

Made Nonsexist but Cumbersome
If someone wishes to succeed in school, he or she should do his or her best every time he or she attempts a new project. (Writers also use *she or he, he/she,* or even the elliptical *s/he* in order to avoid using the generic *he.* What method is used throughout *The Independent Writer?*)

If the combination method of *he or she* is used throughout an entire passage, however, a writer can often bog down in an excess of pronouns. Note the alternative methods below:

Made Nonsexist but Ungrammatical
If someone wishes to succeed in school, they should do their best every time they attempt a new project.

Made Nonsexist by Making the Subject Plural
If students wish to succeed in school, they should do their best every time they attempt new projects.

Made Nonsexist by Changing Point of View
If you wish to succeed in school, you should do your best every time you attempt a new project. *or* If I wish to succeed in school, I will have to do my best every time I attempt a new project.

Made Nonsexist by Avoiding Pronouns Altogether
In order to succeed in school, a student should work to capacity on every new project.

Note ways to eliminate the generic *his* from the following sentence:

Sexist
A conscientious company president should know what is happening in all parts of his organization.

Made Nonsexist but Cumbersome
A conscientious company president should know what is happening in all parts of his or her organization.

Made Nonsexist but Ungrammatical
A conscientious company president should know what is happening in all parts of their organization.

Made Nonsexist by Making the Subject Plural
Conscientious company presidents should know what is happening in all parts of their organization.

Made Nonsexist by Changing Point of View
As a conscientious company president, you should know what is happening in all parts of your organization. *or* As a conscientious company president, I should know what is happening in all parts of my organization.

Made Nonsexist by Avoiding Pronouns Altogether
A conscientious company president should know what is happening in all parts of the organization.

In your writing and speech, you should also avoid obvious sexist references to inanimate objects—for example:

- Of your boat: "Isn't she a beauty?"

- At the garage: "Fill'er up!"

- To natural phenomena: Will man destroy the earth or will he restore her? Only time in his wisdom will tell.

With your partner, rewrite the above examples, using either the nonsexist *it* reference or eliminating the pronoun altogether. Read the following example first:

Sexist
When the child found the bird he put her in a little box.

Nonsexist
The child found a bird and put it in a little box.

SENTENCE WORK

In all of your writing and speech, you should pay particular attention to your audience's situation. Will he or she be offended by the generic *he*? By the ungrammatical pronoun reference (*someone...they*)? By the cumbersome *he/she*? Would it be better to make everything plural? Change the point of view? Avoid the pronoun altogether? Invent a new term (*hir*)?

Rewrite the following sentences for your instructor, but first determine your instructor's situation. When you finish, find out if you were correct.

1. The teacher announced to her class, "Tomorrow everyone will have to write a letter to his Congressman."

2. It's enough to drive anyone out of their senses. (George Bernard Shaw)

3. The college catalog stated: "Every student kindergarten teacher must complete a one-month practice-teaching assignment before receiving her certificate.

4. I shouldn't like to punish anyone, even if they'd done me wrong. (George Eliot)

5. The rooster, its crowing echoing across the farmyard, stood proudly on the fence.

6. Nothing is more thrilling to a sailor than taking his boat out on her maiden voyage.

7. And how easy the way a man or woman would come in here, glance around, find smiles and pleasant looks waiting for them, then wave and sit down by themselves. (Doris Lessing)

EXERCISE FOUR
Feminine and Masculine Words

After years of established usage, many "feminine" words are being dropped from our vocabulary because they are deemed sexist: poetess, heroine, actress, usherette, blonde, coed, sculptress, waitress, maiden, mistress, and many other words that end in *ine*, *ette*, and *ess*. Note the following examples:

Sexist
While she was waiting for her chance to become a Hollywood actress, Dorrie worked as a stewardess for Air Am.

Nonsexist
While she was waiting for her chance to become a Hollywood actor, Dorrie worked as a flight attendant for Air Am.

Sexist
As she cooked in her cute kitchenette, the coed read a book on women's lib.

Nonsexist
As she cooked in her neat kitchen, the student read a book on women's liberation (feminism *or* the women's movement).

Sexist
The divorcee was asked to write her maiden name on the application form.

Nonsexist
The divorced woman was asked to write her birth name (former name) on the application form.

In addition, many masculine occupational titles are being dropped, because women are employed in these jobs as well—for example, busboy, paperboy, salesman, cameraman, airline steward, and so on. In order to avoid confusion and ambiguity, writers have come up with new nonsexist words, as illustrated in the following examples:

Sexist
What would an office be without its office boy?

Nonsexist
What would an office be without its office helper?

Sexist
On the set, Betti-Lee was the number one cameraman.

Nonsexist
On the set, Betti-Lee was the number one camera operator.

Sexist
The junior executives were all waiting to see which one of them would be chosen for advancement.

Nonsexist
The executive trainees were all waiting to see which one of them would be chosen for advancement.

From time to time when you use a singular nonsexist title, you may run into difficulties when using an antecedent. For example:

- The camera operator will have to check his light meter carefully.

Because there is only one camera operator and his or her sex is unknown, you should not use the generic *his*. Instead of making everything in the sentence plural, you might employ the passive voice. For example:

- The light meter must be carefully checked by the camera operator.

Sexist
A hard-working, experienced real-estate agent justifiably earns her large commission.

Nonsexist Using Passive Voice
A large commission is justifiably earned by a hard-working, experienced real-estate agent.

Game One: Alternative Words

You and your partner make up a list of at least ten words or terms that could be construed as sexist, for example: hat-check girl, brunette, longshoreman, sculptress.

Exchange your lists and provide a suitable nonsexist alternative for each: hat-check attendant, brunet, stevedore, sculptor. The winner is the one who provides the most nonsexist responses.

SENTENCE WORK

Rewrite the following, removing any sexist writing.

1. Many ladies in the nineteenth century served their fellowman; for example, Ms. Susan B. Anthony, a well-known American suffragette, was a true heroine who showed many progressives the need for political reforms.

2. During both of his terms in office, President Reagan usually took his wife with him wherever he went. Nancy's womanly charms and even her serious interruptions into some of the President's interviews demonstrated that the First Lady and her man were a loving pair.

3. Deirdre, a stunning coed in my science class, actually receives the best grades.

4. Because many working mothers drop off their children before they go to work,

schools must provide extra supervision. To keep order, lady teachers must come earlier to school to assist with little girls' needs and men teachers to make sure little boys keep out of mischief.

5. While Hurricane Hilda tore up palm trees off the Mexican coast and screamed with delight as she impaled several pleasure boats on jagged rocks, Tornado Tom flattened shacks in Central America and, as it gained strength, ripped off several roofs from substantial buildings.

6. After running unsuccessfully as the first woman vice-president, Geraldine Ferraro served as a perfect mother figure in a diet-soft-drink ad.

7. A salesman or saleslady should take a course on public relations before he or she meets persons who may want to buy what he or she is going to sell, whether it be man-made or machine-made.

8. Now that we have sent man into space, it's just a matter of time before a child will want to go—of course, with his favorite pet.

EXERCISE FIVE
Stay Aware

It is extremely easy to fall into the trap of sexist language, but if you become more aware of your word choice, your writing and speech will be not only nonsexist but much more accurate.

Spend a little time questioning what you hear or read and note the existence of sexist or nonsexist language. You will notice that people are often unaware that they are being sexist. Independent of your partner, gather a few current examples of sexist writing: newspapers, magazines, speeches, cartoons, advertisements, TV programs, films, and so on. Exchange your items with your partner. The object of the exercise is to point out the sexist words, terms, or attitudes and then make a suggestion on how they would be made nonsexist and more accurate.

Note the following examples:

- Political quotation: "If I didn't run as President, I'd be diminished as a man."

- Cartoon:

Adam®   **by Brian Basset**

You and your partner should examine the original quotations in Chapter 62; many of them are sexist. Together, rewrite them so that they are nonsexist.

If you find that you are still not very aware of what comprises sexist writing, turn to the Suggestions for Further Study.

Suggested Answers to the Fourth Workshop Section

CHAPTER 56
Quiz

Each sentence in the quiz has an error of syntax. Compare the corrected version with yours; then read the simplified explanation of each error. If you wish more details about any error, work through the particular exercise in Chapter 56 that discusses it.

(1) When I look over my paragraph, I must read what I *think* I have written instead of what I really wrote. (2) For my readers, one sentence may not make much sense; they must wonder what I'm really trying to say. (3) By following a good workshop exercise on how to correct sentence errors, I can greatly improve my writing style. (4) Learning from my instructor, talking with my peers, and working by myself, I know I will be able to detect common sentence errors. (5 and 6) After months of study when I finish taking this course, I anticipate that I will not make so many sentence errors. (7) In the meantime, because I never really know if I am right or wrong, I am never truly confident about my sentence structure. (8) But now I am determined to learn how to improve my sentences; by concentrating on the rest of this chapter, I should improve. (9) At least, I'll give it my best shot. (10) While reading this paragraph, I haven't noticed too many errors in sentence structure. (11) Therefore, I guess I had better look at the Suggested Answers at the end of this section to find out what sentence errors I need to work on.

Details of sentence errors:

1. Faulty coordination: Readers expect that "and" will join items of equality. The two clauses in (1) are not equal; therefore, subordinate one of them.

2. Comma splice: Readers never expect that a mere comma joins two independent clauses; therefore, they misread the sentence. By using a semicolon or period, you will not confuse your readers.

3. Dangling modifier: Readers think that "my writing style" is doing the "following." Because there is no word in the sentence that is "doing the following," you should introduce one. "I" can follow.

4. Faulty parallel structure: After the first two word groups, readers expect the third one to have exactly the same structure: a verbal plus a prepositional phrase. When you introduce another structure, you break down your reader's confidence.

5. and **6.** Sentence fragment: Readers can make no sense from a fragment, and neither can writers if they take the word group out of context and read it aloud. By joining (5) and (6), you will not confuse your readers.

7. Faulty subordination: When the wrong clause is subordinated, readers are confused because the sentence, as a whole, is illogical.

8. Run-on sentence: Readers always misread sentences that run together without any punctuation mark. Two independent clauses must be separated by a strong punctuation mark—such as a period or semicolon.

9. **10,** and **11.** Misplaced modifiers: Readers never get your exact meaning if you place word groups too far away from the words they modify. In each of the last three sentences, the following word groups are ambiguously placed: "at least," "while reading this paragraph," and "at the end of this section."

ATTENTION: Only your partner should look at the following suggested answers. It will make your partner's job of helping you improve your sentence structure *if you resist even a peek at what follows.*

To Your Workshop Partner:

Use the following suggested answers as you see fit; however, instead of giving the entire answer of any one sentence to your "student," try to share only a little information on how he or she may correct the sentence. It will be more beneficial to your student if he or she can provide a correction with only slight suggestions from you.

Exercise One

1. When young and old visit California's Disneyland or Florida's Walt Disney World-Epcot Center, *they are in for a thrill of a lifetime.* (The sentence will be correct if it is expanded by supplying any subject and verb.)

   Disneyland is the amusement park that transcends all others. (As long as the verb makes sense, let it stand.)

   Disney World has many of the same attractions as Disneyland. (No other change will do.)

   Is there a child or adult who doesn't want to go to Disneyland? (Make sure to combine the sentences.)

2. **a.** Correct as it stands even with the three minor sentences

    b. Walt Disney was with his daughter at an amusement park when he first dreamed of a park to entertain adults as well as children.

    c. He put substance to his dream by building scaled-down antique railroads, first in his backyard, then at the studio.

    d. Thirty thousand guests celebrated Disneyland's opening in 1955.

Exercise Two

1. Thousands of people visit Disneyland and Disney World every day that both amusement parks are open; they go to be entertained. (Point out the two different independent parts of the sentence that are separated by the semicolon. Both could stand alone as independent sentences. *Note*: You cannot place the semicolon any other place in the sentence for it to make complete sense.)

After visiting Disneyland and Disney World, tourists are surprised to see the same features. Main Street, daily parades, restaurants, shops, and most attractions are identical in both amusement parks. (Experiment with a semicolon instead of a period. Perhaps a colon would even be better. Explain why.)

2. a. In the Haunted House you will see the latest photographic inventions: dancers actually materialize and perform in 3-D as you are whisked past a ballroom.

    b. When you leave the Haunted House, a ghost appears; as you prepare to leave your moving seat, you can see one sitting beside you.

    c. Correct

    d. Just one trip through the Pirates of the Caribbean ride is simply not enough; to see everything, you need to go through several times.

Exercise Three

1. Everyone who enters Space Mountain is warned of the potential danger to heart patients. (Keep the student moving the word groups around until everything makes perfect sense.)

Because of its speed, the ride takes one's breath away. *or* The ride takes one's breath away because of its speed. (Discuss the more emphatic position.)

After passing through the front gates, visitors often head for one of the three popular roller coaster mountains. (Point out that it's more emphatic to place the phrase first.)

Sometimes students from nearby colleges, in Alpine costume, climb the face of the Matterhorn. (Make sure the student introduces a subject that makes sense. Talk about the fact that the passive "is climbed" is weaker than the active "climb.")

Screaming, laughing, getting wet, thousands of guests have made the Matterhorn a must-ride attraction. (Make sure the student introduces a subject that can scream, laugh, and get wet. Also point out the difference between the active and passive verbs.)

Getting a glimpse of the sites of the Old West, passengers on the Big Thunder Mountain Railroad can see rugged scenery whiz past. (Make sure the student introduces a subject that can "get a glimpse." Comment on voice of verbs also.)

2. **a.** Outlining the perimeter of the park, the Disneyland Railroad was the first attraction planned by Disney.

   b. Riding the horse-drawn carriages is a slow-paced, relaxing way to see Main Street.

   c. Correct

   d. Graphics in "The World of Tron" treat passengers on the Peoplemover to an illusion of great speed.

Exercise Four

1. Glittering white horses lend *a romantic and nostalgic air* to Cinderella's Golden Carrousel; it was originally built for a Detroit amusement park in 1917. (Point out that "romance" is a noun and "nostalgic" is an adjective. Try to get the student to use *romance* and *nostalgia*.)

   With its slender towers, lacy filigree, and overall grace, Disney World's 180-foot high Cinderella Castle towers over Disneyland's Sleeping Beauty Castle by 100 feet. (Have the student start with "Because it has slender towers" to see if he or she can make the other two elements parallel as dependent clauses.)

   Anaheim's recently rebuilt Fantasyland once looked like a cartoon collage; it now resembles a small Tudor village. (Point out the balancing of the words that follow *once* and *now*.)

2. **a.** It's a Small World has mechanical singing and dancing dolls from every country imaginable.

   b. Rides such as the Jungle Cruise and Pirates of the Caribbean exploit a yearning for visitors to see the exotic, while the Haunted Mansion and 20,000 Leagues Under the Sea satisfy an urge for them to confront the unknown.

   c. 20,000 Leagues Under the Sea, much like its Anaheim cousin, takes visitors past coral beds, near the lost city of Atlantis, under a polar ice cap, and to the bottom of the sea.

   d. Correct

Exercise Five

1. Architectural circles at first dismissed Disneyland as vulgar and unprofessional, but Disney World faced no such criticism. (Point out how both clauses are balanced in structure and importance.)

Much of the land surrounding Disney World is reserved as a wildlife sanctuary, proving that Disney was not just a brilliant animator but an environmentalist as well. (There are many ways to join these sentences. Make sure that the student uses a correlative conjunction and sharpens the relationship between its parts.)

Epcot Center's most impressive structure hovers on the horizon like a spaceship; accordingly, this huge sphere is called Spaceship Earth. (Experiment by adding other conjunctive adverbs in order to sharpen the relationship between the clauses. Note that the weak pronoun reference has been changed from *it* to *this huge sphere*.)

Although Disney began plans for his Florida park in 1964 and died six months before the first shovelful was dug, Walt Disney World, nonetheless, became a reality. (If the student has not come up with a similar response, have him or her point out the most important clause in order to subordinate the other two. *Note: Nonetheless* makes the sentence more emphatic.)

2. **a.** Unlike the Magic Kingdom, Epcot seeks to address serious issues, such as transportation, communications, energy, and agriculture.

   b. Correct

   c. In Future World, 550 electronically controlled Audio Animatronics figures imitate life with lifelike movements and sounds; decidedly, this is an example of art imitating life.

   d. Sometimes guests going from Future World to the World Showcase walk the mile-long promenade; other times they take the bus.

Exercise Six

1. The World Showcase, which surrounds a placid, handmade lake, consists of slightly scaled-down scenes of eight countries and an "Independence Hall." (Point out that by reversing the subordination, the student makes sense of the sentence.)

   Canada's entry to this attraction, which features both a beautiful hotel and a replica of the Rocky Mountains, is a highlight of World Showcase. (Point out the logic in this sentence as compared with the illogic of the one that was faulty.)

   At the World Showcase, France's entry, of course, contains an Eiffel Tower; additionally, three French master chefs operate a restaurant. (Point out the logic in this sentence as compared with the illogic of the one that was faulty.)

   To entertain crowds, troupers of England's Renaissance Street Theatre pick reluctant cast members from the audience. (Point out the clarity in this sentence as compared with the confusion of the one that was faulty.)

2. **a.** *Steamboat Willie*, in which a little mouse named Mickey made his film debut, tops the bill at the Main Street Theater.

   b. Correct

c. Visitors to the Haunted Mansion think the attic is hard to keep dusted; in fact, the park buys and distributes dust by the five-pound bagful.

d. Walking on a huge promenade deck, visitors have no idea of the flurry of activity going on in the basement, thirty feet below.

CHAPTER 57
Quiz

In the second paragraph of the Introduction, the errors in consistency are as follows:

- "They shall" indicates determination not future tense.
- "patched up" is too colloquial for the established level of diction.
- The singular verb "occurs" does not agree with the plural "inconsistencies."
- "one" is a shift from the established "you" subject.
- The passive voice of "need to be done" is inconsistent with the active "deals" and "should do."

A rewrite of the second paragraph:

The following exercises and games are varied and detailed. They *will* involve you and your partner in oral rather than written activities so that you can quickly *correct* any one of those inconsistencies that *occur*. Because this chapter deals with many types of consistency, *you* should do only the exercises that *you really need to do*.

CHAPTER 58
Quiz

If you eliminated the wordiness from the four rules in the Introduction, you might have come up with something like this:

1. Use only those words necessary to fulfill your purpose; avoid superfluous descriptive words and roundabout phrases.

2. Use words that your audience is likely to know.

3. Use precise and concrete words for your topic, rather than vague and abstract ones.

4. If you did not notice examples of wordiness, do the chapter.

Exercise Two

a. Ernest Hemingway is one of America's best-known novelists.

b. He was deeply affected by his experiences as a volunteer ambulance driver in the First World War.

   c. Using some of his war experiences, Hemingway wrote one of the great twentieth-century war novels, *A Farewell to Arms*.

   d. He began his writing career as a newspaperman, writing for the *Kansas City Star* and the *Toronto Star*.

   e. He was a correspondent in Europe after the First World War before he began serious fiction writing.

   f. Hemingway was a journalist, a poet, a short-story writer, and a novelist.

Exercise Four

Hemingway's Work

Hemingway's greatness as a writer rests partly on his ability to depict accurately both human experience and places. This consummate skill has gained him his widest popular recognition and praise. And this is understandable, for he is probably unsurpassed in writing exactly what a man *sees* in a wide variety of experiences. He makes the effects of war stunningly forceful in *A Farewell to Arms* and *For Whom the Bell Tolls*; he describes bullfighting with remarkable fidelity as artful combat in *Death in the Afternoon* and *The Sun Also Rises*; he presents deep-sea fishing as a great battle in *The Old Man and the Sea*; he describes big game hunting in *Green Hills of Africa*; and he chillingly annotates imminent death in "The Killers" and *Islands in the Stream*. And he is unsurpassed in describing the rivers, hills, jungles, sea, mountains, and plains that serve as background to these human experiences. He graphically illustrates the appearance of specific locales: the woods of Upper Michigan in "Big Two-Hearted River," a mountain in Africa in "The Snows of Kilimanjaro," Paris in *A Moveable Feast*, and Venice in *Across the River and into the Trees*. All of this richly vivid writing supports the judgment that Ernest Hemingway is indeed one of literature's greatest masters of description.

(If you detect any wordiness in the above suggested answer, try cutting it.)

CHAPTER 59
Exercise Two

   a. Norman Mailer, himself a central figure in *The Armies of the Night*, tells of people demonstrating against the war in Vietnam.

   b. Bellow, having lived in Chicago for much of his life, used that city for background in *Dangling Man, Herzog*, and *Humboldt's Gift*.

   c. In *Of a Fire on the Moon*, Mailer describes the Apollo 11 moon shot.

   d. Both Mailer and Bellow have had their work acclaimed internationally and have received Pulitzer Prizes.

   e. Fascinated by the life of Hollywood super-star Marilyn Monroe, Mailer published *Marilyn* in 1973.

   f. Critic Diana Trilling says that Bellow's novel *The Victim* succeeds on many levels.

g. In *King of the Hill*, Mailer accounts one of the championship fights between heavyweights Muhammad Ali and Joe Frazier.

h. After receiving the Nobel Prize in literature in 1976, Saul Bellow became better known to more people.

i. People debate whether Norman Mailer or Saul Bellow has done more to demonstrate the deliberate and hardworking craft of writing.

j. C. Fred Bush, Vice-President George Bush's dog and author of *C. Fred's Story*, has lately demonstrated that the craft of writing requires no care more painstaking than that demanded by casual howling.

Exercise Five

Symbolism in *The Wild Duck*

Ibsen uses the symbol of the wild duck to give force to his theme. The duck, as a living, wild creature, relates uniquely with the other characters in the play as well as with its environment. Because of this intertwined relationship, certain events may not occur within the duck's presence. The duck's existence parallels humanity's throughout the play. As a wild creature, the duck lives happily until shot by a hunter. Following its natural instinct, the duck dives into the ocean to hide, but the hunter's dog finds the bird. Still alive, the duck, adopted by a family and placed in an artificial environment, carries on an unhappy existence.

CHAPTER 60
Quiz

All of the pronouns in the quiz are correctly used. If you thought more than three pronouns were used incorrectly, you should continue with this chapter.

Exercise Two

4. a. between her and him

b. Correct

c. he and she

d. her and him

e. We boys

f. us boys

g. he

h. Correct

i. she

j. we

Exercise Seven

a. was

b. were

c. was

d. was

e. were

f. are

CHAPTER 61
Quiz

accommodate	attendance	definite	forty	lieutenant
mischievous	niece	precede	separate	smorgasbord

CHAPTER 62
Quiz

In his essay "The Powers of Racial Example," which appeared in *Time*, Lance Morrow wrote: "What is unfolding now [in 1984] may be thought of in years to come as the Jesse Jackson era for black America." For years, Jackson has stood in front of audiences of both young and old and led them in psychological cheers: "I am . . . somebody!" It may be many years before the U.S. elects a black president—or, for that matter, an Hispanic-American president. But is it not now thinkable for a black child to entertain a fantasy that used to be advertised as every white boy's dream: that he might grow up to be president? Jesse Jackson is a "first" in American history; others will be routine.

CHAPTER 64
Quiz

Incorrect Usage	Correct Usage
amount	number
enthused	show enthusiasm for
personally	(redundant with "me")
aggravation	irritation *or* annoyance
instrumentalists	band
continual	continuous
constant	(redundant with "continuous")
due to	because of
the fact that	(unnecessary)
extreme	limit
doubtlessly	doubtless *or* without doubt
effects	affects
on	in
counts	ways
secondly	second (you would not say "eleventhly" or "twelfthly")
guts	stomach

last but not least	(cliché for "last")
too	(redundant)
like	that
alot	a lot
can	will
acception	exception
averse	adverse
hopefully	I hope
gotta	have to
implicitly	explicitly
alternate	alternative
forms on music	forms of music
viz.	namely
differs with	differs from
They may have	They can have
to always play	always to play (Generally you should not split an infinitive "play" and its sign "to." Notice, however, that "to really hurt" is accepted usage in the third sentence in the rewrite below.)

Rewrite of Quiz

Many people are enthusiastic about acid-rock music, but it annoys me. From the time the band starts to play, I hear only the loud, continuous throb from their loudspeakers because they have been turned up to their limit. Without doubt, acid rock affects me in three different ways: my head, stomach, and eyes start to really hurt. Acid-rock fans may take exception to my adverse criticism, but I hope that they will understand explicitly that there are alternative forms of music; namely, each form differs from another. They can play their acid rock, as long as I can play my country and western.

Exercise Nine

1. **a.** hippie slang
   b. military slang
   c. college slang
   d. San Fernando Valley slang

Exercise Ten

2. More spending from July to September 1979 (making up for a loss from April to June) has combined with October's change in policy to make a difference in 1980 spending, though the full-year's pattern will show no real difference from September's forecast. (42-word sentence)

CHAPTER 65
Quiz

1. Appeal to individual or ad hominem: Other people, besides supporters of the Republican party, have worthwhile opinions.
2. Misuse of statistics: In some places in the United States no one may support gun control. Statistics from one small faction cannot be used to represent the consensus of the whole group.
3. Non sequitur: The conclusion in the last clause does not reasonably follow the first two statements.
4. Appeal to sympathy: Because you *need* does not mean you deserve a job. Maybe you have to get the job the old-fashioned way, "Earn it!"
5. Ridicule: Such a low form of argumentation implies that you have nothing of value to say.
6. Pejorative association: Placing an unknown with the known implies that they are all the same; in this case the slant is negative.
7. Sweeping generalization: It is simply not true that *everybody* supports the idea.
8. Bandwagon or ad populum: Eating spinach will not make you a powerful politician or as strong as Popeye.
9. Threat or ad baculum: Threats are not sound logic.
10. False assumption: Previous success does not mean continued success.
11. Double meaning or equivocation: *Serve* is used in two different senses.
12. Accent: There is no sound reason for doing anything now. Why not wait?
13. Post hoc: Thirteen may be lucky for some.

Exercise One

1. a. How it proposes to do this is not stated.
   b. The fact that he may also be a convicted thief (or whatever) is not mentioned.
   c. The fallacy consists of ignoring the decrease in purchasing power of the dollar in five years.
   d. But how many have met Furr?
2. a. Here *freedom* has been wrongly linked with getting something for nothing.

    b. The association implies that the opposition leader is dishonest.

    c. This implies that Furr is not too bright.

3. a. But what does he say?

    b. This unsound argument implies that a hard worker must for that reason alone be the best man for the job.

    c. Appeals to emotions rather than to impartial reasoning.

    d. This appeals to the individual rather than to impartial reasoning.

    e. Instead of a sound argument, this logical fallacy emphasizes force, sympathy, expense, and so on.

    f. It does not say how many were polled. But it does make the uncareful listener or reader want to join a winner.

    g. The second clause has nothing to do with the first clause.

    h. Post hoc, a form of non sequitur, says that one action was the logical outcome of another; this may not be so. (The Latin phrase means "after this; therefore, because of this.")

    i. You should use an analogy to *illustrate*, not *prove*. False analogies, like this one, try to prove one thing is something else. It is an unfounded assumption that if something resembles something else in some aspects, it will resemble it in other aspects.

    j. Because we know or believe that wet feet result in colds, we often accept fallacies like this. But notice that there may have been many other reasons why Furr caught a cold.

    k. Such a low form of argument may receive a laugh, but it has no place in solid argumentation.

    l. Proverbs or sayings should not be accepted uncritically. They often lead to error.

CHAPTER 66
Quiz

1. The television show, *The Living Planet*, demonstrates clearly that human beings have been on the earth for thousands of years. (The generic *man* is considered sexist.)

2. When Neil Armstrong stepped on the moon's surface, he said, "That's one small step for a man, one giant leap for humanity." (Apologies to Armstrong, but *humanity* is both precise and nonsexist.)

3. The Girl Scouts should be congratulated for running the exhibit at the World's Fair. (Employing *man* as a verb can often sound sexist.)

4. In his manuscript the author pointed out that only one manager manufactured dresses from synthetic (handmade) materials. (The materials can just as easily be made by women.)

5. Is it true that the French drink a lot of wine? (French women may also drink wine.)

6. All American children know something about George Washington, the Father of our country; the authors of the United States Constitution, the Founding Fathers; and the people who came over on the *Mayflower*, the Pilgrims. (The Pilgrims were comprised of fathers, mothers, and children, whereas the authors of the Constitution were all men.)

7. The college catalog stated: "Student nurses will gain much knowledge and experience by taking on extra practical sessions in the nearby hospital when they complete their classwork." (Both men and women become nurses.)

8. The peacock, his tail fanned majestically, stood at the entrance of the zoo. (The sex of a peacock is definitely male, so do not use the neutral *it*, just as a baby is never an *it*.)

9. When I came home on British Airways, I sat directly opposite two English couples. (*Man* and *wife* are not parallel; you may use *husbands* and *wives* instead of *couples*.)

10. I think Joanna will make the best doctor in the world. (Although *woman* is not needed, you might use the adjective *female* before *doctor*, but *female* is redundant when you already know the doctor's sex.)

11. While Peter worked in the yard, Maria made dinner inside. (*Worked* and *fixed* are not equal; *worked* and *made* are; so are *tinkered* and *fixed*.)

12. Mr. James Baxter and Mrs. Ann Carter are my favorite teachers; but if I had to choose one, I'd choose Baxter over Carter. (If you drop the title for the man, you should do the same for the woman.)

13. After cracking a bottle of champagne on its stern, Bill took his boat out on its first voyage. (Do not refer to inanimate objects as male or female.)

14. Leading suffragists in America included Elizabeth Cady Stanton, Lucretia Mott, Susan B. Anthony, Lucy Stone, Ida B. Wells, Anna Howard Shaw, Mary Church Terrel, Carrie Chapman Catt, and Alice Paul. (Generally, do not use *ette* endings.)

15. The sentence is nonsexist. Had you changed *poet* to *poetess*, you would have made it sexist.

Sentence Work

1. Many women in the nineteenth century served their fellow citizens; for example, Susan B. Anthony, a well-known American suffragist, was a true hero who showed many progressives the need for political reforms.

2. During both of his terms in office, President Reagan usually traveled with his wife wherever he went. Nancy Reagan's graciousness and serious contributions during some of the President's interviews demonstrated that the First Lady and her husband were a loving pair.

3. Deirdre, a student in my science class, receives the best grades.

4. Because many working parents drop off their children before they go to work, schools must provide extra supervision. To keep order, teachers must come earlier to school to assist with students' needs and ensure proper discipline.

5. While Hurricane Hilda tore up palm trees off the Mexican coast and screamed as it impaled several pleasure boats on jagged rocks, Tornado Tom flattened shacks in Central America and, as it gained strength, ripped off several roofs from substantial buildings.

6. After running unsuccessfully as vice-president, Geraldine Ferraro agreed to make a diet-soft-drink ad.

7. Sales agents should take a course on public relations before they meet potential customers who may want to buy what they are going to sell, whether it be handmade or machine-made.

8. Now that we have sent men and women into space, it's just a matter of time before a child will want to go—of course, with his or her favorite pet. (*or* before children will want to go—of course, with their favorite pets.)

APPENDIXES

A

Special-Interest Programs

To help you decide which assignments from the Assignment Section to complete, decide to which one of the following Special-Interest Groups you belong.

Academic	*Goal*: counselor, lawyer, librarian, minister, psychologist, social worker, teacher, and other jobs requiring a university degree
Commercial	*Goal*: accountant, banker, bookkeeper, computer operator, computer programmer, investment broker, real-estate agent, receptionist, secretary, travel agent, and other business-oriented jobs
Arts	*Goal*: actor, announcer, dancer, designer, journalist, motion picture producer or director, musician, painter, press agent, sculptor, writer, and other creative jobs
Specific Training	*Goal*: athlete, driver, farmer, fire fighter, fisherman, flight attendant, police officer, rancher, sailor, salesperson, soldier, telephone operator, foodserver, and similar jobs requiring specific training
Science	*Goal*: biologist, chemist, dentist, dietitian, doctor, nurse, optometrist, pharmacist, physical therapist, physicist, radiologist, respiratory therapist, veterinarian, and other science-related jobs
Technical/ Vocational	*Goal*: carpenter, chef, contractor, electrician, hairdresser, mechanic, plumber, and other jobs requiring a specific diploma

Listed below are a number of chapters corresponding to each of the above Special-Interest Groups (ACA, COM, ART, STR, SCI, and T&V). You should begin with the Introductory Section of this text and complete as many of the chapters *in the order listed below* as your instructor thinks necessary. You will also notice that additional programs for more specific interest groups are included—for example:

- for independent study, if you do not attend a regular class (IND)

- for literature-oriented students (LIT)

- for a general well-rounded program when an entire class works together or for a writing course by correspondence (GEN)
- for basic writers who are experiencing a number of difficulties (BAS)
- for new Americans where English is a second language (ESL)

NOTE: If you are in a basic English or ESL program, be prepared to move to your special-interest program when your instructor indicates that you no longer have difficulties.

Specialized-Writing Programs

A C A	C O M	A R T	S T R	S C I	T & V	I N D	L I T	G E N	B A S	E S L
3	16	2	15A	2	15A	18A	1	1	15A	18A
4	18B	1	1	23A	16	18B	4	3	16	15A
7	2	4	2	3	1	16	11B	4	21	16
8	3	11A	3	6	2	15A	12	5	1	19A
9	15A	12	15B	23B	3	1	13	6	3	19B
10	15B	13	16	14A	12	4	21	12	18A	1
5	19A	5	18A	12	15B	2	18C	13	18B	2
18C	19B	6	18B	20	17A	3	13	2	18C	3
6	7	18C	19A	7	17B	5	2	14A	20	21
13	5	18A	19B	9	18B	6	14A	15B	19A	22
2	6	18B	5	10	19A	11A	15B	18B	19B	23
14A	18C	20	6	11B	19B	18C	13	18C	2	4
20	17A	21	18C	5	20	19A	5	20	7	6
21	17B	14B	20	15B	22	19B	10	21	8	5

Writing across the Curriculum

Instead of the above programs, you may use the Assignment Section to assist you in your writing for all of your college courses. Depending on your interests or needs, you should begin such an interdisciplinary writing program with Chapter 21, "Writing for the Humanities" (Parts A to F), Chapter 22, "Writing for the Social Sciences" (Parts A to E), or Chapter 23, "Writing for the Natural Sciences" (Parts A and B). Within each of these three chapters, you will be encouraged to work on other assignment chapters.

Literature Selections

INTRODUCTION

Use the short stories, poems, and plays that appear in this appendix in conjunction with Chapter 13, "Literary Essay," and Chapter 40, "The Reading Process." Use any of the accompanying suggested essay topics and questions as a basis for your writing.

Short Stories

The Story of an Hour

by Kate Chopin

Knowing that Mrs. Mallard was afflicted with a heart trouble, great care was taken to break to her as gently as possible the news of her husband's death.

It was her sister Josephine who told her, in broken sentences, veiled hints that revealed in half concealing. Her husband's friend Richards was there, too, near her. It was he who had been in the newspaper office when intelligence of the railroad disaster was received, with Brently Mallard's name leading the list of "killed." He had only taken the time to assure himself of its truth by a second telegram, and had hastened to forestall any less careful, less tender friend in bearing the sad message.

She did not hear the story as many women have heard the same, with a paralyzed inability to accept its significance. She wept at once, with sudden, wild abandonment, in her sister's arms. When the storm of grief had spent itself she went away to her room alone. She would have no one follow her.

There stood, facing the open window, a comfortable, roomy armchair. Into this she sank, pressed down by a physical exhaustion that haunted her body and seemed to reach into her soul.

She could see in the open square before her house the tops of trees that were all aquiver with the new spring life. The delicious breath of rain was in the air. In the street below a peddler was crying his wares. The notes of a distant song which someone was singing reached her faintly, and countless sparrows were twittering in the eaves.

There were patches of blue sky showing here and there through the clouds that had met and piled above the other in the west facing her window.

She sat with her head thrown back upon the cushion of the chair quite motionless, except when a sob came up into her throat and shook her, as a child who has cried itself to sleep continues to sob in its dreams.

She was young, with a fair, calm face, whose lines bespoke repression and even a certain strength. But now there was a dull stare in her eyes, whose gaze was fixed away off yonder on one of those patches of blue sky. It was not a glance of reflection, but rather indicated a suspension of intelligent thought.

There was something coming to her and she was waiting for it, fearfully. What was it? She did not know; it was too subtle and elusive to name. But she felt it, creeping out of the sky, reaching toward her through the sounds, the scents, the color that filled the air.

Now her bosom rose and fell tumultuously. She was beginning to recognize this thing that was approaching to possess her, and she was striving to beat it back with her will—as powerless as her two white slender hands would have been.

When she abandoned herself a little whispered word escaped her slightly parted lips. She said it over and over under her breath: "Free, free, free!" The vacant stare and the look of terror that had followed it went from her eyes. They stayed keen and bright. Her pulses beat fast, and the coursing blood warmed and relaxed every inch of her body.

She did not stop to ask if it were not a monstrous joy that held her. A clear and exalted perception enabled her to dismiss the suggestion as trivial.

She knew that she would weep again when she saw the kind, tender hands folded in death; the face that had never looked save with love upon her, fixed and gray and dead. But she saw beyond that bitter moment a long procession of years to come that would belong to her absolutely. And she opened and spread her arms out to them in welcome.

There would be no one to live for during those coming years; she would live for herself. There would be no powerful will bending her in that blind persistence with which men and women believe they have a right to impose a private will upon a fellow-creature. A kind intention or a cruel intention made the act seem no less a crime as she looked upon it in that brief moment of illumination.

And yet she had loved him—sometimes. Often she had not. What did it matter! What could love, the unsolved mystery, count for in face of this possession of self-assertion which she suddenly recognized as the strongest impulse of her being.

"Free! Body and soul free!" she kept whispering.

Josephine was kneeling before the closed door with her lips to the keyhole, imploring for admission. "Louise, open the door! I beg; open the door—you will make yourself ill. What are you doing, Louise? For heaven's sake open the door."

"Go away. I am not making myself ill." No; she was drinking in a very elixir of life through that open window.

Her fancy was running riot along those days ahead of her. Spring days, and summer days, and all sorts of days that would be her own. She breathed a quick prayer that life might be long. It was only yesterday she had thought with a shudder that life might be long.

She arose at length and opened the door to her sister's importunities. There was a feverish triumph in her eyes, and she carried herself unwittingly like a goddess of Victory. She clasped her sister's waist, and together they descended the stairs. Richards stood waiting for them at the bottom.

Someone was opening the front door with a latchkey. It was Brently Mallard who entered, a little travel-stained, composedly carrying his grip-sack and umbrella. He had been far from the scene of accident, and did not even know there had been one. He stood amazed at Josephine's piercing cry; at Richards' quick motion to screen him from the view of his wife.

But Richards was too late.

When the doctors came they said she had died of heart disease—of joy that kills.

Story of the Bad Little Boy

by Mark Twain

Once there was a bad little boy whose name was Jim—though, if you will notice, you will find that bad little boys are nearly always called James in your Sunday-school books. It was strange, but still it was true that this one was called Jim.

He didn't have any sick mother either—a sick mother who was pious and had the consumption, and would be glad to lie down in the grave and be at rest but for the strong love she bore her boy, and the anxiety she felt that the world might be harsh and cold towards him when she was gone. Most bad boys in the Sunday-books are named

James, and have sick mothers, who teach them to say, "Now, I lay me down," etc., and sing them to sleep with sweet, plaintive voices, and then kiss them good-night, and kneel down by the bedside and weep. But it was different with this fellow. He was named Jim, and there wasn't anything the matter with his mother—no consumption, nor anything of that kind. She was rather stout than otherwise, and she was not pious; moreover, she was not anxious on Jim's account. She said if he were to break his neck it wouldn't be much loss. She always spanked Jim to sleep, and she never kissed him good-night; on the contrary, she boxed his ears when she was ready to leave him.

Once this little bad boy stole the key of the pantry, and slipped in there and helped himself to some jam, and filled up the vessel with tar, so that his mother would never know; but all at once a terrible feeling didn't come over him, and something didn't seem to whisper to him, "Is it right to disobey my mother? Isn't it sinful to do this? Where do bad little boys go who gobble up their good kind mother's jam?" and then he didn't kneel down all alone and promise never to be wicked any more, and rise up with a light, happy heart, and go and tell his mother all about it, and beg her forgiveness, and be blessed by her with tears of pride and thankfulness in her eyes. No; that is just the way with all other bad boys in the books; but it happened otherwise with Jim, strangely enough. He ate that jam, and said it was bully, in his sinful, vulgar way; and he put in the tar, and said that was bully also, and laughed, and observed "that the old woman would get up and snort" when she found it out; and when she did find it out, he denied knowing anything about it, and she whipped him severely, and he did the crying himself. Everything about this boy was curious—everything turned out differently with him from the way it does to the bad Jameses in the books.

Once he climbed up in Farmer Acorn's apple-tree to steal, and the limb didn't break, and he didn't fall and break his arm, and get torn by the farmer's great dog, and then languish on a sick bed for weeks, and repent and become good. Oh! no; he stole as many apples as he wanted and came down all right; and he was all ready for the dog too, and knocked him endways with a brick when he came to tear him. It was very strange—nothing like it ever happened in those mild little books with marbled backs, and with pictures in them of men with swallow-tailed coats and bell-crowned hats, and pantaloons that are short in the legs, and women with the waists of their dresses under their arms, and no hoops on. Nothing like it in any of the Sunday-school books.

Once he stole the teacher's pen-knife, and, when he was afraid it would be found out and he would get whipped, he slipped it into George Wilson's cap—poor Widow Wilson's son, the moral boy, the good little boy of the village, who always obeyed his mother, and never told an untruth, and was fond of his lessons, and infatuated with Sunday-school. And when the knife dropped from the cap, and poor George hung his head and blushed, as if in conscious guilt, and the grieved teacher charged the theft upon him, and was just in the very act of bringing the switch down upon his trembling shoulders, a white-haired, improbable justice of the peace did not suddenly appear in their midst, and strike an attitude and say, "Spare this noble boy—there stands the cowering culprit! I was passing the school-door at recess, and unseen myself, I saw the theft committed!" And then Jim didn't get whaled, and the venerable judge didn't read the tearful school a homily, and take George by the hand and say such a boy deserved to be exalted, and then tell him to come and make his home with him, and sweep out the office, and make fires, and run errands, and chop wood, and study law, and help his wife do household labors, and have all the balance of the time to play, and get forty cents a month, and be happy. No, it would have happened that way in the books, but it didn't happen that way to Jim. No meddling old clam of a justice dropped in to make trouble, and so the model boy George got thrashed, and Jim was glad of it because, you know, Jim hated moral boys. Jim said he was "down on them milksops." Such was the coarse language of this bad, neglected boy.

But the strangest thing that ever happened to Jim was the time he went boating on Sunday, and didn't get drowned, and that other time that he got caught out in the storm when he was fishing on Sunday, and didn't get struck by lightning. Why, you might look, and look, all through the Sunday-school books from now till next Christmas, and you would never come across anything like this. Oh no; you would find that all the bad boys who go boating on Sunday invariably get drowned; and all the bad boys who get caught out in storms when they are fishing on Sunday infallibly get struck by lightning. Boats with bad boys in them always upset on Sunday, and it always storms when bad boys go fishing on the Sabbath. How this Jim ever escaped is a mystery to me.

This Jim bore a charmed life—that must have been the way of it. Nothing could hurt him. He even gave the elephant in the menagerie a plug of tobacco, and the elephant didn't knock the top of his head off with his trunk. He browsed around the cupboard after essence of peppermint, and didn't make a mistake and drink *aqua fortis*. He stole his father's gun and went hunting on the Sabbath, and didn't shoot three or four of his fingers off. He struck his little sister on the temple with his fist when he was angry, and she didn't linger in pain through long summer days, and die with sweet words of forgiveness upon her lips that redoubled the anguish of his breaking heart. No, she got over it. He ran off and went to sea at last, and didn't come back and find himself sad and alone in the world, his loved ones sleeping in the quiet churchyard, and the vine-embowered home of his boyhood tumbled down and gone to decay. Ah! no; he came home as drunk as a piper, and got into the station-house the first thing.

And he grew up and married, and raised a large family, and brained them all with an axe one night, and got wealthy by all manner of cheating and rascality; and now he is the infernalist wickedest scoundrel in his native village, and is universally respected, and belongs to the Legislature.

So you can see there never was a bad James in the Sunday-school books that had such a streak of luck as this sinful Jim with the charmed life.

Californian, December 23, 1865; 1867, 1875

Killing Time

by Lorraine Aho, student

Amy sat curled up at one end of the L-shaped couch, reading. Across the room an unwatched television was on for the noise. When the car pulled into the driveway, Amy glanced at her watch, registered 2:30 A.M., then went back to her book. She didn't look up as the car door slammed and footsteps scuffed up the porch steps. A key searched for its place in the lock and the door swung open.

Dan lurched into the room, bringing with him the smell of the barroom he had just left. He stood unsteadily for a moment, waiting for acknowledgment from Amy. Amy read.

"Hey, what's there to eat?" he slurred.

Amy glanced up. "The kitchen closed at eight," she said, and looked back down at her book.

"Goddammit," Dan muttered as he crossed the room and sat at the other end of the couch. He muttered a few obscenities and mumbled about being hungry and having a wife who didn't care. Amy turned another page. She knew from experience that by the time she had something ready to eat, Dan would be passed out.

"Why didn't you eat some jerky or pickled eggs before you left the bar?" she said without looking up, and was rewarded with a glare.

Dan fumbled with a crushed pack of cigarettes and got one into his mouth. He leaned forward to reach the lighter, lit his cigarette on the third attempt, and sank back on the couch. His elbow rested on the arm of the couch, holding the cigarette up.

Dan's eyes slowly closed and his head fell back. The hand that held the cigarette flopped backwards and the cigarette coal pushed into the cushion.

The smell of something burning caught Amy's attention. She looked up, sniffing. She saw the smoke curling up from the cushion next to Dan. His hand still held the cigarette on the smouldering couch.

Amy didn't move. Someday if he doesn't kill all of us, he'll at least kill himself, she thought. She sat, watching the black mark get larger, the smoke get thicker. He could die right now. I could just go to bed and he would die. No one would be surprised. I wouldn't have to worry anymore about his driving drunk and maybe killing some-one—maybe killing us by setting the house on fire. Smoke inhala-tion. The kids will be hurt by the smoke. I could close their bedroom door. It might still hurt them. Vinnie might be okay, but the baby pro-bably wouldn't be. I could open their windows and then close their door. No, that would look suspicious. It's too cold at night to have their windows open. The smoke is thicker. You son-of-a-bitch! Why couldn't you do this in summer when the windows would all be open! It would be so easy for him to be dead. It would be so easy. All I have to do is go to bed. My babies. I can't take a chance on harming my babies. The only way I can protect them would make it look suspicious. I want him dead! I really want him dead. NO! I can't let him die. I just want him gone. Death would be faster and easier, but I can't let him die. Just his being gone is what I want.

Amy leaped up and shook Dan. "Wake up! Wake up!" Dan opened his eyes and tried to focus on Amy. She ran into the kitchen, filled a pan with water, and ran back to pour it on the smouldering cushion. Dan still sat on the couch, not comprehending what was happening. Amy pulled the cushion from behind him and rushed it out the back door. She threw it on the patio floor and doused it with the hose. Then she stood there for a long time, looking down at the damaged cushion.

She finally turned and went back inside. Dan was lying across the couch, sound asleep, unaware. I really can't go on, Amy thought, looking down at him. I almost let you die. I was truly considering murder. You've turned me into someone I don't know and I don't like. I won't. I won't be that person. Sleep. This is the last night you'll spend in this house. In the morning you're gone.

She walked into the bedroom. She pulled a suitcase down from the storage space above the closet and began filling it with Dan's clothes. He'll be grateful I saved his life, she thought. She giggled. He'll thank me for not killing him. She burst out laughing. She sat on the edge of the bed and laughed so hard she cried.

SUGGESTED TOPICS

1. What universal (or archetypal) conflict does the specific conflict in one of the stories represent?

2. What similar archetypal characters or situations are involved in two of the stories?

Explain how the authors have treated them: similarly or differently? Which treatment do you find more effective?

3. Point out how and why one of the authors uses irony.

4. "The Story of an Hour," written in 1894, has also been published under the title, "The Dream of an Hour." Compare and contrast these two titles. Point out the significance of each title. Indicate which title you prefer. Why?

5. Relate the content of "The Story of an Hour" to the time in which it was written and to society's attitude towards women at that time. To answer this completely, you will have to do some research.

6. Using examples from "Story of the Bad Little Boy," discuss Mark Twain's mastery of storytelling. Note that originally the story would have been read aloud.

7. Compare the bad little boy with any other Mark Twain character with which you are familiar.

8. In "Killing Time," why did Amy decide not to kill Dan?

9. There are many similarities and differences between "Killing Time" and "The Story of an Hour." Explore one or two aspects thoroughly—for example: the women's attitudes towards death, the lack of honesty in each relationship, each woman's "happiness" at the thought of her husband's death, the similar situations despite differences in setting and era, how one woman has control of the episode and the other has none.

10. Compare and contrast Aho's treatment of Dan with Twain's treatment of the bad little boy.

11. In an essay on characterization, point out ways in which the heroes/heroines of all three stories are alike/different. Who are the victims? Who are the victors?

12. "The Story of an Hour" has been made into an hour-long television production entitled, "The Joy that Kills" (American Playhouse, PBS). If you are able to see the production, compare and contrast it with the short story.

Poetry

When I Heard the Learn'd Astronomer

by Walt Whitman

When I heard the learn'd astronomer,
When the proofs, the figures, were ranged in columns before me,
When I was shown the charts and diagrams, to add, divide, and
    measure them,
When I sitting heard the astronomer where he lectured with much
    applause in the lecture-room,
How soon unaccountable I became tired and sick,
Till rising and gliding out I wander'd off by myself,
In the mystical moist night-air, and from time to time,
Look'd up in perfect silence at the stars.

Because I Could Not Stop for Death

by Emily Dickinson

Because I could not stop for Death,
He kindly stopped for me;
The carriage held but just ourselves
And Immortality.

We slowly drove, he knew no haste,
And I had put away
My labor, and my leisure too,
For his civility.

We passed the school where children played,
Their lessons scarcely done;
We passed the fields of gazing grain,
We passed the setting sun.

We paused before a house that seemed
A swelling on the ground;
The roof was scarcely visible,
The cornice but a mound.

Since then 'tis centuries; but each
Feels shorter than the day
I first surmised the horses' heads
Were toward eternity.

From *The Tempest*

(Act IV, Scene 1, lines 148–158)
by William Shakespeare

Our revels now are ended. These our actors
As I foretold you, were all spirits, and
Are melted into air, into thin air;
And like the baseless fabric of this vision,
The cloud-capp'd towers, the gorgeous palaces,
The solemn temples, the great globe itself,
Yea, all which it inherit, shall dissolve,
And like this insubstantial pageant faded,
Leave not a rack behind. We are such stuff
As dreams are made on; and our little life
Is rounded with a sleep.

The Tiger

by William Blake

Tiger! Tiger! burning bright,
In the forests of the night,

What immortal hand or eye
Could frame thy fearful symmetry?

In what distant deeps or skies
Burnt the fire of thine eyes?
On what wings dare he aspire?
What the hand dare seize the fire?

And what shoulder and what art
Could twist the sinews of thy heart?
And when thy heart began to beat,
What dread hand? and what dread feet?

What the hammer? what the chain?
In what furnace was thy brain?
What the anvil? what dread grasp
Dare its deadly terrors clasp?

When the stars threw down their spears,
And watered heaven with their tears,
Did he smile his work to see?
Did he who made the lamb make thee?

Tiger! Tiger! burning bright
In the forests of the night,
What immortal hand or eye
Dare frame thy fearful symmetry?

The pennycandystore beyond the El

by Lawrence Ferlinghetti

The pennycandystore beyond the El
is where I first
                    fell in love
                              with unreality
Jellybeans glowed in the semi-gloom
of that september afternoon
A cat upon the counter moved among
          the licorice sticks
          and tootsie rolls
          and Oh Boy Gum

Outside the leaves were falling as they died

A wind had blown away the sun

A girl ran in
Her hair was rainy
Her breasts were breathless in the little room

Outside the leaves were falling
          and they cried
                    Too soon! too soon!

Agent Orange

by Elizabeth Brewster
(For Jeff and Peter)

Did not know
back in the summer of 1966
that trees twenty miles or so from Fredericton
where I was living
(a sister's family lived nearer)
were being sprayed with a defoliant
Agent Orange
to test it for use in the Vietnam War.

> Wrote in my diary the 12th of June:
> Sunned in back yard.
> Foliage in the trees
> thick and summery.
> The dandelions are almost gone
> except for the white, feathery heads,
> the "old men" we used to call them.
> Strawberry blossoms thick
> under the trees.
> The lilac is already past its prime,
> withered and faded.

The Vietnam veterans now claim
that Agent Orange causes
cancer, skin disorders, birth defects
and other miscellaneous afflictions
often not recognized for years to come.

> On Sunday June 19th, noted:
> The Gammon children brought me
> a single lady's slipper
> which they had picked
> near their cottage at Grand Lake,
> a beautiful little flower.
> They might have picked more, they said,
> but their father told them
> the flowers were rare
> and must be preserved.

One of those boys had amused his mother
when he had told her he was afraid
he might be drafted when he grew up
for military service in the American army.

Maybe he wasn't so far wrong after all.

All through July
and part of August
complained of being tired,
having a sore throat,
sore neck, sore ear,
sore ankle,
a weight on my chest.

It's something going the rounds.
the doctor said,
doesn't seem to yield to treatment
though I felt better
when I took the bus down to Saint John.
Was it the salt air, I wondered,
that helped me to breathe?

Of course I can't know
if the friends, children of friends
who have had cancer since
were at all affected by Agent Orange.

But poisons travel
more readily than truth
even in a time that prides itself
on rapid communication.

How can any of us know
we won't be casualties of wars
we had no intention of fighting?

One optimistic note:
Evergreens don't appear
to be harmed by Agent Orange.

Hope you are an evergreen

Ozymandias

by Percy Bysshe Shelley

I met a traveler from an antique land
Who said: Two vast and trunkless legs of stone
Stand in the desert...Near them, on the sand,
Half sunk, a shattered visage lies, whose frown,
And wrinkled lip, and sneer of cold command,
Tell that its sculptor well those passions read
Which yet survive, stamped on these lifeless things,
The hand that mocked them, and the heart that fed:
And on the pedestal these words appear:

"My name is Ozymandias, king of kings:
Look on my works, ye Mighty, and despair!"
Nothing beside remains. Round the decay
Of that colossal wreck, boundless and bare
The lone and level sands stretch far away.

No Comment

by Laura DeBoer, student

Go out to dinner.
How about a dance?
Never stop to think of the world's circumstance.
Buy you a beer.
How 'bout a smoke?
Always the bartender to tell you a joke.
Go see a movie.
Watch some T.V.
Never stop to think of what life could be.
Tennis tomorrow?
How about lunch?
"See you at twelve, love you a bunch."
Always a friend to give you some toot.
Love California, ain't it a hoot?
When you go home and get in your bed
You deal with the nightmares that come from your head.
People starving in India,
Dying in Lebanon,
Wino you kicked in the street.
Newspaper headlines, that's all they are.
Grab some more food.
How 'bout one more drink?
Anything, *anything*, so you don't have to think.
Go out to dinner.
How about a dance?
Never stop to think of the world's circumstance.

SUGGESTED TOPICS

1. Discuss the portrayal of the lover and the beloved in one or two poems. Mention why you chose the poem(s).

2. Using two of the poems for your examples, contrast a highly structured verse form with a free verse form. Indicate which you prefer. Why?

3. Discuss the way in which the rhythm or the shape of one of the poems contributes to its theme.

4. Discuss the double irony in "Ozymandias": Ozymandias' belief that he was creating an enduring work and yet his unintentional words are true.

5. What effect does the punctuation and grammar of "The pennycandystore beyond the El" have on the way you approach it?

6. Compare the excerpt from *The Tempest* with "Because I Could Not Stop for Death" in order to show how each poet demonstrates an awareness of the fragility of life.

7. Compare the way in which two of the poems deal with immortality.

8. Write an essay entitled "Grave Imagery." Use at least two of the poems to illustrate your thesis.

9. Choose one of the poems above and discuss its benevolent or malevolent view of nature.

10. Examine the structure of "Agent Orange" and point out how the structure affects the message that the poem conveys.

11. Write an essay entitled "Poetic Words," in which you point out the importance of how an exact word evokes a perfect and complete image. Use as many of the poems in this section as you need.

12. In an essay entitled "Styles of Poetry," support your thesis by referring to at least three poems from this section.

13. Poets say that sound is the vehicle to open yourself to accepting a poem's image; after doing this, you can think about content. Discuss the sounds that you find in three poems from this section. How do the sounds affect you emotionally as well as physically? How do they affect the content (meaning) of the poems?

14. Compare "No Comment" by student writer Laura DeBoer with any of the professional poems. Choose any two or three aspects to compare the poems—for example: rhyme scheme, rhythm, conflict, archetype, and structure.

Plays

The Victim

by Betty Keller

CAST: one man, one woman

TIME: *the present*

SCENE: *South America, where the kidnap of foreign businessmen for ransom is no longer headline-making.*

> *A bare room, with one wooden chair* DRC,* *a door* ULC, *a window* UL; *through the window a desolate mountain landscape.*

CHARACTERS:

THE VICTIM: *in his forties; his business suit and shirt indicate a certain prosperity. His clothing is now a little rumpled, the knees of his*

---

* Stage directions: D = downstage (near audience); U = upstage (away from audience); R = right; L = left; C = center.

pants dirty, his tie loosened. His shoes are very dusty. He is blindfolded tightly with a white rag; his right hand is bleeding from a cut across the knuckles.

THE ABDUCTOR: *in her early thirties; dressed in wind-breaker, jeans and boots. She carries an army rifle. The actress must not play her as a toughie, or as a caricature of a women's libber; she is simply carrying out an assignment. Neither her femaleness nor his maleness are factors in her reactions to him; ultimately it is her compassion for him as a victimized human being that is his salvation.*

(At rise, the stage is empty. The door ULC opens and the VICTIM is pushed into the room, followed by the ABDUCTOR.)

VICTIM: Easy now, fella, easy! Just remember I can't see!
(The ABDUCTOR shoves him forcibly with the gunbutt. He crashes into a wall, clutching at it to avoid falling. His automatic response is to remove his blindfold. He stops with one hand on the rag, sensing that there is a reaction behind him. There is; the abductor has raised the gunbutt to club him.)

VICTIM: No! It's okay, fella, I won't touch the blindfold. *(He lowers his hand and begins to massage his wound gently.)* I remembered. I won't do it again . . . Am I allowed to sit down? . . . I'm very tired. . . . *(The ABDUCTOR lowers her rifle.)* I'm not used to all this walking. Fact is, I don't walk at all if I can help it. Would you believe I don't even play golf? . . . *(His monologue peters out; he turns his head in the direction he imagines his guard to be.)* Can I sit down . . . please? *(There is silence while the ABDUCTOR studies him.)* Just here with my back against the wall . . . for support. . . . Surely it can't hurt if . . . *(With the gunbutt she shoves him roughly in the direction of the chair. He does not quite achieve its position, but realizing that there must be some reason for the push, he gropes around with his feet and kicks the chair. It topples over. He gropes now with his hands, finds the chair, rights it, and sits down facing downstage.)* Thanks . . . thanks a lot. *(He leans forward, his elbows on his knees, hands dangling between his knees, head drooping. A moment passes, a new thought strikes the VICTIM and he raises his head.)* Hey, are we alone? Just the two of us? . . . You're not supposed to answer me, are you? I just meant . . . *(She becomes tense; there is a pause, then he relaxes somewhat.)* No, there's no one else, is there? You can feel it when someone's watching you . . . sort of sense it, can't you? . . . Yeah. . . . *(His head droops again. She relaxes a little, moves DL, sits on the floor facing DR; the VICTIM again raises his head and turns in her direction).* Are you sitting on the floor? . . . This must be the only chair. Hey, does that mean I'm considered company? (*He laughs drily. The* ABDUCTOR *takes a cloth from her pocket, begins to polish her gun.*) Ah, you guys must get kinda tired too . . . even if you're used to the life. (*He starts to droop again; then raises his hands towards his face. The polishing ceases.*) It's all right. I'm just going to rest my head in my hands, see. I'm not going to touch the blindfold. Just going to hold my . . . (*She rises to her feet.*) All right! It's okay, I won't! I'll keep my hands down. . . . I'll rest my head here on the back of the chair, okay? (*He waits, senses there is no opposition, and adjusts his position to rest his head. After a moment she sits again, and resumes polishing.*) What I said just now . . . about being alone . . . was just because I wondered if someone was going to interrogate me . . . or something. . . . I wasn't thinking about escape. . . . I don't even know where I am anyhow. Oh sure, we're up in the hills! I thought we'd never stop climbing. (*massaging his thigh muscles*) I really am out of condition, I guess, but . . . God, I'm beat! (*There is a long pause while he rolls his head wearily back and forth on the chairback.*) This is the first time I've been into the hills in your country, you know. Marian and I were always going to take a vacation at Lake Juerna but we never managed it. . . . Marian's my wife . . . but you know that, I guess. (*The* ABDUCTOR *is quite relaxed now; obviously the pattern of the encounter is settling into familiar lines.*) Funny, you read about these things happening but it always happens to the important guys . . . and I'M not important! That's why I kept asking if you'd got the right man. . . . Remember in the truck I said . . . (*He sits up; the lack of a reply has become annoying.*) Well, dammit, I'm not IMPORTANT enough! I know you guys have made a mistake! I'm just Joe Nobody at Tanasco Oil . . . damn near a clerk! . . . Well, a little more than that . . . but a cost accountant for chrisake! . . . . You might as well have taken the doorman! And my COUNTRY won't pay the kind of money you guys ask. For a company president or an ambassador maybe, but a cost accountant! (*leaning back*) Just ask my wife how low and despicable a cost accountant is! She'll tell you . . . boy, she'll really tell you. (*attempting a friendly sociable air*) Hey, do you have a wife? I'll bet you haven't in this kind of racket. No wife's going to put up with the hours you guys must keep . . . but the pay's all right, eh? . . . Or maybe the organization takes all the loot and you guys just do the dirty work! (*becoming rather loud and overhearty*) As they say, let's hear it for idealism! Everything for the cause, eh? Let's clean up on the bad guys so us good guys can make it! (*She is faintly amused. His mood changes again, he sighs, rests his head on the chairback. The* ABDUCTOR *takes out a package of cigarettes, lights up. This business is complete at ". . . stupid thing to say."*) I've never felt anything about my job. . . . It's just a job. . . . Marian

says I haven't any drive ... no guts, she says. ... She's right
.... She is really right! Mel Falhurst, he started with Tanasco
the same time I did; he's way up there, three secre-
taries. ... Mel's her shining example. ... Why can't you get
ahead like Mel? she says. Why don't you get a fat expense
account like Mel's? ... Y'know, sometimes I wonder if there
isn't something going on there ... Marian and good old. ... No,
that's a stupid thing to say. (*He sits up.*) Hey, what about a
cigarette for me, too? ... I haven't had one since breakfast and
you guys cleaned out my pockets ... please?
(*The* ABDUCTOR *studies him for a moment, decides he is now
relatively harmless, and relents. She rises, tucks her rifle under
one arm, and approaches him with the pack extended. She
touches his hand with the pack. He gropes for it, grabbing her
hand. He takes a cigarette, still holding her hand and the pack.
Suddenly his hand moves up to her wrist, and then he becomes
quite still.*)

VICTIM (*exploding*): You're not a man! You're a girl, for chrisake!
Just a girl!
(*Alarmed and angry, she pulls away, backing off to* DR. *He raises
a hand to his blindfold.*)

ABDUCTOR: Stop, or I'll have to shoot you.

VICTIM (*amused*): Oka-a-ay, baby, I believe you! I'll behave! (*He
stands up.*) But listen, honey, can't we be a little friendlier?

ABDUCTOR: Sit down! (*She replaces the cigarette pack in her pocket.*)

VICTIM (*waving his cigarette*): Come on now, how about a light for
this thing, honey?

ABDUCTOR: SIT DOWN!

VICTIM (*moving towards her voice*): Ah, come on now...
(*She hits him in the stomach with the riflebutt. He falls backwards, toppling the chair, his cigarette flying. He groans, arms
across his stomach, rolling on the floor. She walks to the window
and looks out. Gradually he becomes capable of speech again.*)

VICTIM: What'd you do that for? I'm defenceless, dammit! ... You've
got the gun! (*He sits up.*) Listen, I know we can come to some
kind of agreement. ... Hey? ... I mean, there must be things
you'd like to have for yourself, right? I bet you'd like some
fancy clothes, eh? ... perfume, jewelry? (*He feels for the chair;
she kicks it out of his reach.*) Come on now, don't be like that!
I'm trying to help you. (*She laughs harshly.*) All right, so I'm
trying to help myself, too. ... But look, this is no life for a
girl. ... You're probably just doing this cause there's no other
way of making it in this country. But listen, I've got an idea.
You get what you want out of it and I get what I want. (*She
watches him suspiciously.*) That guy I was talking about, Mel
Falhurst, now he's worth a fortune, and the company would

really pay to get him back. You'll never get a nickel from them for me, but with Mel the sky's the limit! And I'll help you get him.... I'm not asking for a share of the loot...that's all yours...all you have to do is make sure he doesn't come back! (*She smiles at him with pity, shaking her head.*) Well, how about it?...Come on...Baby, it's a good deal! I cut out all the risks, and you get all the dough. (*She starts to laugh.*) Now don't be a dummy, this'll give you everything you've ever...

Sound Effect: Helicopter engine fading in.

VICTIM: What's that? It sound like an engine?

(*The* ABDUCTOR *goes to the window* UL.)

VICTIM: That's a helicopter!...that's right isn't it? (*The* ABDUCTOR *ignores him. The noise indicates that the helicopter has landed close by. The* ABDUCTOR *leaves through the door* ULC *under cover of the engine noise.*)

VICTIM (*shouting above the engine sounds*): Is this the big brass arriving? Are you taking me somewhere else?...Is someone else here?...For chrisake, what's happening?

(*The* ABDUCTOR *returns with a photo in her hand, comes close to the* VICTIM *and studies him. She puts the photo in her pocket, releases the safety catch on the rifle, and points it at his head. Slowly she lowers the gun again, returns to the door, closes it, then raises the rifle and shoots just behind the* VICTIM. *He leaps to his feet, terrified, clawing at his blindfold. She clubs him on the back of the head with the riflebutt. He slumps to the floor. She walks back to the door, then turns to look back at him. After a moment, she returns to him, bends down to check his pulse. Then she takes out her cigarettes and matches and places them in his outstretched limp hand. After a moment she rises again and exits without looking back.*)

Sound Effect: Helicopter engine increases, then fades in the distance.

So Far Untitled

by Michelle Briseño, student

SCENE: *An empty stage. Curtain is pulled to allow the writer, Julie, to walk to the front of the stage. She will then address the audience and continue the rest of the script, with the characters planted in the audience.*

CHARACTERS:

JULIE: *The young writer, in her early twenties, wearing a baggy sweatshirt and a pair of jeans.*

CORA: *An old woman, gaudily dressed, conservative thoughts.*

ROBERT: *A college student, wears glasses, athletic type.*

TOM: *A construction worker, hardworking, dressed in levis and work boots.*

MAGGIE: *A housewife, early forties.*

DIRECTOR: *Man, middle thirties, well dressed, very business-like.*

(Julie walks across the stage; stops in middle to address the audience.)

JULIE: Hello. This isn't easy to tell you, but there isn't going to be a play tonight after all. I'm sorry for the inconvenience.

CORA: What?

JULIE: I said there isn't going to be a play tonight. It has been canceled. I wasn't able to finish the last act—that's why I've been chosen to break the news to you.

TOM: Hey, what in the hell is going on here? I paid good, hard-earned money to come see this thing. I thought it would be worth the bucks to support a community event. Boy, was I dumb.

ROBERT: Yeah, I agree. Are we going to get our money back? Why wasn't something mentioned earlier? I could have gone to the spa.

JULIE: Hey, I'm really sorry! I didn't realize until the last minute that the last act wasn't going to come together. I typed pages and pages of dialogue, but I couldn't make anything of it. I bet there must be some way that you can receive free passes to another event or something.

CORA: This isn't fair. How can you people inform the public that there is going to be a special production and then cancel? I don't know about the other people here, but it was very difficult for me to get here. It cost me three dollars to ride in a taxi, because I'm afraid to walk alone at night.

MAGGIE: And I'm keeping my children up past their bedtimes for nothing?

JULIE: I'm very sorry, but my God, my mind went blank! I was under so much pressure to finish this play that I lost it. My boss has been keeping me after hours so he can do bookwork—so I really haven't had the time I need to devote to writing this play.

ROBERT: Hey, we all have problems. I read on the back of tonight's brochure that you're an English major taking English 249a. I took that same course, and I didn't think it was so tough. All playwrights and writers have to keep to a deadline. You're just making excuses.

JULIE: You've got to be kidding. We may have taken the same class, but did you have Ms. Sullivan for your professor? She expects high-quality work, not just touchy-feely, let's-love-everybody poetry. It's hard work, and I didn't have enough time. I'm sorry.

MAGGIE: I'm glad that I listened to my father and got married to my husband, Joe, instead of running off to school in Arizona. Now I have three lovely children. Maybe school really isn't your thing, dear.

JULIE: Yes, it is my thing. I love English. I had thousands of ideas for this play. It really excited me to have such an opportunity.

TOM: A lot of good that is going to do us now. I work real hard laying bricks all day, and my boss is going to lay me off pretty soon. According to my finances, I'm already not supposed to be able to eat! Don't you people ever think about reality? Why don't you write about that? Shit! I can't believe that I'm still here.

JULIE: Excuse me, dear Sir, but I also work—six nights a week cooking for other people and washing their goddamn dishes. Do you think I enjoy slopping about in other people's food and working for men that think I'm stupid—just someone to make advances on? They are always directing some sort of sexual innuendo at me. Talk about verbal rape! They make me feel cheap.

CORA: Young lady, how dare you speak to us like that! There are children present. Why don't you just put your boss in his proper place?

MAGGIE: That's right. I'm trying to set a good example for my children. Have some decency! If you work for a man who abuses you, then you deserve it. If anyone ever tried to take advantage of me, I'd quit first thing!

TOM: Hey lady, how in the hell can you expect her to just up and quit? It's damn hard to find a decent job nowadays. Man, if I had it to do over again, I would have stuck it out in school. I would have made a damn good math professor—instead of having to grub around like a dog!

ROBERT: Hey, have you tried talking to your boss? Maybe he doesn't know that he is offending you.

MAGGIE: Once some man kept making eyes at me in the supermarket. I told my husband, and he punched that awful lecher in the parking lot. Maybe you could get somebody to talk to your boss for you.

JULIE: I think we're really off the subject here. I mean . . . I really don't feel like having my personal life argued over.

CORA: Sorry, I'm sure we didn't mean to embarrass you.

ROBERT: By the way, what was the play supposed to have been about?

TOM: Yeah. Since we paid, we might as well hear the general outline. Jesus! Look at all of these people looking at us!

MAGGIE: Oh, there's Claire. She still owes me money from last month's bake sale. Once in awhile our bridge club holds a sale, and . . .

JULIE: The general plot is how a ticket sales agent and a play director sell tickets to a play that doesn't exist. They arrange a fire backstage to delay the opening of the play, and in the meantime they collect the money from the advance ticket sales and skip town.

TOM: That's a bit unbelievable don't you think?

MAGGIE: Well, it really is just a story. I mean, anything can happen on T.V. can't it?

ROBERT: How are they supposed to get away with it?

JULIE: I don't know. I never resolved it. However, I do want them to get away with it, because they are so desperate for money . . .

MAGGIE: How can you sympathize with criminals? They deserve to be punished. I never stole a thing in my life. My father taught me morals. If I ever caught my children . . .

TOM: Lady, this isn't Sunday school. It's just a play plot.

MAGGIE: Well, excuse me, Mr. . . . .

ROBERT: God, all those people lost their money. I'd be pissed if that happened to me.

CORA: Who's that?

(*Director enters*)

DIRECTOR: What's going on here, Julie? I told you to inform them that there wouldn't be a play—not to hold a gab session!

JULIE: I'm sorry. I was just trying to apologize to them for the cancelation.

DIRECTOR: You've already caused enough trouble. Christ! Hasn't anybody left yet?

CORA: Sir! You shouldn't take the Lord's name in vain. Some people find it very offensive.

TOM: Since we already shelled out our dough, we wanted to hear about what we were supposed to see. We should get something for our money.

DIRECTOR: Well, I'm afraid we're going to have to call it a night. Come along, Julie.

JULIE: I really don't feel right about this. I mean . . .

DIRECTOR: I said come on. Can't you keep to a simple schedule? Procrastination kills all great plots. (*exits*)

JULIE: I know damn it! That's why I'm not a writer . . . Good night ladies and gentlemen, I have nothing more to say. (*exits*)

SUGGESTED TOPICS

1. Discuss the effect in "The Victim" of concealing from the Victim that the Abductor is female.

2. Compare the use of soliloquy in "The Victim" and "So Far Untitled." What is your opinion about the use of soliloquies in plays?

3. Discuss the various conflicts in either play. Which do you relate to more?

4. Compare and contrast Julie and the Victim.

5. In what way is "So Far Untitled" a gimmick or an excuse for getting the characters together? Will the audience feel satisfied at the end of the performance? Justify your answer in such a way that you bring out the significant meaning that the playwright wants to convey to the audience.

6. Compare the play of the student playwright with that of the professional playwright from two or three aspects—for example: characterization, dialogue, suspense, conflict, and theatricality.

GENERAL ESSAY TOPICS

1. What parallels do you see between "No Comment" and "Killing Time"?

2. Write an essay entitled "Prejudice in Literature." Use a short story, poem, and play from this section to support your thesis.

3. Choose a short story, poem, and play that have similar archetypal characters, conflicts, or situations. Compare and contrast the authors' treatments of the archetypes.

4. Which selection most affected you? How will your life be changed because of this selection? Which selection meant nothing to you? Why has it no bearing on your life? Respond to these four questions in a single essay.

5. Some objects in the selections in this section hold particular significance for readers. Choose one symbol each from a short story, poem, and play and discuss its significance.

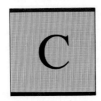

Progress Chart

BACKGROUND

So that you will be able to tell, at a glance, how you are progressing through *The Independent Writer*, you are encouraged to fill in the accompanying Progress Chart each day.

Each assignment and workshop exercise in the textbook has been included in the chart. You should fill in the first of the three boxes beside each item when you complete it. If you must redo the item, fill in the second or the third box beside it.

Although you can complete the Progress Chart in many different ways, the following are some possibilities:

Introductory Section
☑ ☐ ☐   = you are working on the Introductory Section.

Introductory Section
■ ☐ ☐   = you have completed the Introductory Section.

Introductory Section
■ ■ ☐   = you have completed the Introductory Section for the second time.

Introductory Section
■ ■ ■   = you have completed the Introductory Section for the third time.

Sexist Writing
Three: He or She
■ ☑ ☐   = you are working on Exercise Three for the second time. You are asking your workshop partner to give you extra help.

Incorrect Punctuation
Two: Commas
■ ■ ☑   = you are working on Exercise Two for the third time. You are asking your instructor to give you extra help.

Introductory Section
☐ ☐ ☐

Assignment Section

1. **Narrative Paragraph**
☐ ☐ ☐
2. **Descriptive Paragraph**
☐ ☐ ☐
3. **Expository Paragraph**
☐ ☐ ☐
4. **Narrative Essay**
☐ ☐ ☐
5. **Argumentative Essay**
☐ ☐ ☐
6. **Informative Essay**
☐ ☐ ☐
7. **Classification and Division**
☐ ☐ ☐
8. **Comparison and Contrast**
☐ ☐ ☐
9. **Cause and Effect**
☐ ☐ ☐
10. **Definition**
☐ ☐ ☐
11. **A. Autobiography**
☐ ☐ ☐
11. **B. Biography**
☐ ☐ ☐
12. **Review**
☐ ☐ ☐
13. **Literary Essay**
☐ ☐ ☐
14. **A. Research Report**
☐ ☐ ☐
14. **B. Feature Article**
☐ ☐ ☐
15. **A. Instructions**
☐ ☐ ☐
15. **B. Process Analysis**
☐ ☐ ☐
16. **Memo**
☐ ☐ ☐
17. **A. Proposal**
☐ ☐ ☐

17. **B. Report**
☐ ☐ ☐
18. **A. Personal Letter**
☐ ☐ ☐
18. **B. Business Letter**
☐ ☐ ☐
18. **C. Letter to the Editor**
☐ ☐ ☐
19. **A. Full Résumé**
☐ ☐ ☐
19. **B. Partial Résumé and Cover Letter**
☐ ☐ ☐
20. **Exam Essay**
☐ ☐ ☐
21. **A. Humanities Term Paper**
☐ ☐ ☐
21. **B. Humanities Research Paper**
☐ ☐ ☐
21. **C. Analysis Paper**
☐ ☐ ☐
21. **D. Researched Literary Essay**
☐ ☐ ☐
21. **E. Critique**
☐ ☐ ☐
21. **F. Contemplative Paper**
☐ ☐ ☐
22. **A. Critique**
☐ ☐ ☐
22. **B. Process Analysis Paper**
☐ ☐ ☐
22. **C. Social Science Research Paper**
☐ ☐ ☐
22. **D. Social Science Term Paper**
☐ ☐ ☐
22. **E. Case Study**
☐ ☐ ☐
23. **A. Laboratory Report**
☐ ☐ ☐
23. **B. Scientific Review Paper**
☐ ☐ ☐

First Workshop Section

24. **Journal Writing**
☐ ☐ ☐
25. **Brainstorming**
One: Think/Write
☐ ☐ ☐
Two: Talk/Write
☐ ☐ ☐
Three: See/Write
☐ ☐ ☐
Four: Experience/Write
☐ ☐ ☐
Five: Read/Write
☐ ☐ ☐
Six: Assign/Write
☐ ☐ ☐
Seven: Write/Write
☐ ☐ ☐
Eight: Free Association Cluster
☐ ☐ ☐
Nine: Absurd Analogies
☐ ☐ ☐
Ten: Random Lists
☐ ☐ ☐
Eleven: Senses Cluster
☐ ☐ ☐
Twelve: Positive/Negative/Neutral Pigeonholes
☐ ☐ ☐
Thirteen: Positive Cluster
☐ ☐ ☐
Fourteen: Negative Mandala
☐ ☐ ☐
Fifteen: Pentad Cluster
☐ ☐ ☐
Sixteen: Pentad Connection
☐ ☐ ☐
Seventeen: Four-Faces-of-Knowledge Cluster
☐ ☐ ☐
Eighteen: Pro/Con Ladder
☐ ☐ ☐

Nineteen: Aristotle's Topics
☐ ☐ ☐

Twenty: Newspaper
Reporter's Questions
☐ ☐ ☐

Twenty-one: Seven
Controlling Questions
☐ ☐ ☐

Twenty-two: Flowchart
☐ ☐ ☐

Twenty-three: Brainstorming
across the Curriculum
☐ ☐ ☐

26. Notetaking
One: Unwriting
☐ ☐ ☐

Two: Visualize Your Notes
☐ ☐ ☐

Three: Write Yourself a Note
☐ ☐ ☐

Four: Predict the Content
☐ ☐ ☐

Five: Draw Relationships
☐ ☐ ☐

**27. Thesis and Topic
Statements**
One: Why Write a Thesis
Statement?
☐ ☐ ☐

Two: How to Limit Your
Topic
☐ ☐ ☐

Three: Composing Thesis and
Topic Statements
☐ ☐ ☐

Four: Placement of Topic
Statements
☐ ☐ ☐

Five: Discovering and
Evaluating Thesis
☐ ☐ ☐

Six: Making Up Thesis and
Topic Statements
☐ ☐ ☐

Seven: Test Your Ability
☐ ☐ ☐

**28. Beginnings, Middles, and
Endings**
One: Beginnings
☐ ☐ ☐

Two: Middles
☐ ☐ ☐

Three: Endings
☐ ☐ ☐

Four: Titles
☐ ☐ ☐

Five: Narration and
Description
☐ ☐ ☐

29. Unity
One: Visual Organization
☐ ☐ ☐

Two: Comparison and
Contrast
☐ ☐ ☐

Three: Cause and Effect
☐ ☐ ☐

Four: Sequential Order
☐ ☐ ☐

Five: Spatial Order
☐ ☐ ☐

Six: Chronological Order
☐ ☐ ☐

Seven: Climactic Order
☐ ☐ ☐

Eight: Familiar to Unfamiliar
☐ ☐ ☐

Nine: Deductive and
Inductive
☐ ☐ ☐

Ten: Development
☐ ☐ ☐

Eleven: Combination of
Methods
☐ ☐ ☐

30. Coherence
One: Transitions
☐ ☐ ☐

Two: Experimenting
☐ ☐ ☐

Three: Key Words
☐ ☐ ☐

Four: Sentence Work
☐ ☐ ☐

Five: Three Key Words
☐ ☐ ☐

**31. Self-Editing, Peer-Editing,
and Instructor-Editing**
One: Revising Your Own
Work
☐ ☐ ☐

Two: Revising the Writing of
Your Peers
☐ ☐ ☐

Three: Help for Your Editors
☐ ☐ ☐

Four: Different Peer-Editing
Sessions
☐ ☐ ☐

Five: Follow-up
☐ ☐ ☐

Six: Publishing
☐ ☐ ☐

32. Unwriting
One: Getting Familiar
☐ ☐ ☐

Two: Short Story
☐ ☐ ☐

Three: Difficult or Archaic
☐ ☐ ☐

Four: Unwriting an Essay
☐ ☐ ☐

Five: English Proficiency Test
☐ ☐ ☐

Six: Using All the Steps
☐ ☐ ☐

Seven: On Your Own
☐ ☐ ☐

Eight: Revising by Unwriting
☐ ☐ ☐

Nine: Graphics
☐ ☐ ☐

Ten: 25-word Summary
☐ ☐ ☐

33. Word Processors
One: Prewriting
☐ ☐ ☐
Two: Drafting
☐ ☐ ☐
Three: Revising
☐ ☐ ☐

Second Workshop Section

34. Techniques of Style
One: Your Background
☐ ☐ ☐
Two: Your Personal Style
☐ ☐ ☐
Three: Observing Style
☐ ☐ ☐
Four: Your Audience
☐ ☐ ☐
Five: Tone
☐ ☐ ☐
Six: Persona
☐ ☐ ☐
Seven: Analyzing Style
☐ ☐ ☐
Eight: Comics
☐ ☐ ☐
Nine: Newspapers
☐ ☐ ☐
Ten: Rhetorical Devices
☐ ☐ ☐
Eleven: Your Writing Style
☐ ☐ ☐
Special Writing Assignment 34
☐ ☐ ☐

35. Controlling Your Sentences
One: Simple to Complex
☐ ☐ ☐
Two: Complex to Simple
☐ ☐ ☐
Three: Sentence Variety
☐ ☐ ☐

Four: Combining
☐ ☐ ☐
Five: Subtracting
☐ ☐ ☐
Six: Expanding
☐ ☐ ☐
Seven: Rearranging
☐ ☐ ☐
Eight: Types of Sentences
☐ ☐ ☐
Nine: Minor Sentences
☐ ☐ ☐
Special Writing Assignment 35
☐ ☐ ☐

36. Figurative Language
One: Comparing
☐ ☐ ☐
Two: Kinds of Figurative Comparisons
☐ ☐ ☐
Three: Creating Metaphors
☐ ☐ ☐
Four: Three Rules
☐ ☐ ☐
Five: Visual Comparisons
☐ ☐ ☐
Six: Allusions
☐ ☐ ☐
Seven: How Much Do You Know?
☐ ☐ ☐
Special Writing Assignment 36
☐ ☐ ☐

37. Slant
One: Word Choice
☐ ☐ ☐
Two: Your Attitude
☐ ☐ ☐
Three: Thinking Slant
☐ ☐ ☐
Four: Advertising
☐ ☐ ☐
Five: Indicating Slant
☐ ☐ ☐
Six: Word Levels
☐ ☐ ☐

Seven: Slant and Style
☐ ☐ ☐
Eight: Propaganda
☐ ☐ ☐
Nine: Use Slant
☐ ☐ ☐
Special Writing Assignment 37
☐ ☐ ☐

38. Humor and Wit
One: Funny Story
☐ ☐ ☐
Two: Writing the Funny Story
☐ ☐ ☐
Three: Humor and Wit
☐ ☐ ☐
Four: Witty Satire
☐ ☐ ☐
Five: Sardonic Satire
☐ ☐ ☐
Six: Invective
☐ ☐ ☐
Seven: Parody
☐ ☐ ☐
Eight: Travesty and Mock Epic
☐ ☐ ☐
Nine: Persona and Satire
☐ ☐ ☐
Special Writing Assignment 38
☐ ☐ ☐

39. Research Skills
One: Library Tour
☐ ☐ ☐
Two: Library Search
☐ ☐ ☐
Three: Researching
☐ ☐ ☐
Four: Bibliographies
☐ ☐ ☐
Five: Citations
☐ ☐ ☐
Special Writing Assignment 39
☐ ☐ ☐

40. Reading Process
One: Examine Your Reading
☐ ☐ ☐

Three: Mnemonics
☐ ☐ ☐
Four: British vs. American
☐ ☐ ☐

62. Incorrect Punctuation
One: End Punctuation
☐ ☐ ☐
Two: Commas
☐ ☐ ☐
Three: Dashes and Parentheses
☐ ☐ ☐
Four: Semicolons
☐ ☐ ☐
Five: Colons
☐ ☐ ☐
Six: Brackets
☐ ☐ ☐
Seven: Ellipses
☐ ☐ ☐
Eight: Quotation Marks
☐ ☐ ☐

63. Word-Punctuation and Convention Errors
One: Hyphen
☐ ☐ ☐
Two: Apostrophe
☐ ☐ ☐
Three: Capitalization
☐ ☐ ☐
Four: Abbreviations
☐ ☐ ☐

Five: Underlining
☐ ☐ ☐
Six: Slash
☐ ☐ ☐
Seven: Citing Numbers
☐ ☐ ☐

64. Misusage and Weak Vocabulary
One: Classifying Words
☐ ☐ ☐
Two: Abstract/Concrete Words
☐ ☐ ☐
Three: Redundancy
☐ ☐ ☐
Four: Vivid Verbs
☐ ☐ ☐
Five: Lively Adjectives and Adverbs
☐ ☐ ☐
Six: Clichés
☐ ☐ ☐
Seven: Idioms
☐ ☐ ☐
Eight: Fractured Idioms
☐ ☐ ☐
Nine: Slang
☐ ☐ ☐
Ten: Jargon
☐ ☐ ☐
Eleven: Vocabulary Fun
☐ ☐ ☐
Twelve: Grammar vs. Usage
☐ ☐ ☐

Thirteen: Multiple Meanings
☐ ☐ ☐
Fourteen: Synonyms
☐ ☐ ☐
Fifteen: Word and the Poet
☐ ☐ ☐
Sixteen: Word and the Prose Writer
☐ ☐ ☐
Seventeen: Larger Vocabulary
☐ ☐ ☐
Eighteen: Word Calendar
☐ ☐ ☐

65. Fallacies
One: Classification
☐ ☐ ☐
Two: False Advertising
☐ ☐ ☐
Three: Illogical Argument
☐ ☐ ☐

66. Sexist Writing
One: Man
☐ ☐ ☐
Two: Woman
☐ ☐ ☐
Three: He or She
☐ ☐ ☐
Four: Feminine and Masculine Words
☐ ☐ ☐
Five: Stay Aware
☐ ☐ ☐

Dates To Remember

Suggestions for Further Study

Although it is intended that you will use *The Independent Writer* for all of your present and future writing needs, you may, from time to time, have occasion to refer to other books for additional help. A number of resources have been listed here for that purpose, arranged according to the following broad subjects: Style, Sentence Combining, Usage and Vocabulary, Basic Grammar, Spelling, Business Writing, Research Reports, Literary Essays, English as a Second Language, and Nonsexist Writing.

You should have these three essential texts available when you write:

1. an up-to-date dictionary, such as:

Webster's Ninth New Collegiate Dictionary. Springfield Mass.: Merriam-Webster, 1983.

2. a thesaurus, such as:

Roget, Peter M. *Roget's International Thesaurus*. 4th ed. New York: Crowell, 1977.

3. a book of quotations, such as:

Bartlett, John. *Bartlett's Familiar Quotations*. Rev. ed. Boston: Little, 1980.

STYLE

Baker, Sheridan. *The Practical Stylist*. New York: Harper, 1982.

Gibaldi, Joseph and Walter S. Achtert, *MLA Handbook for Writers of Research Papers*. New York: MLA, 1984.

McCrimmon, James M. *Writing with a Purpose*. 8th ed. Boston: Houghton, 1984.

Strunk, William and White, E.B. *The Elements of Style*. 3d ed. New York: Macmillan, 1979.

Weathers, Winston and Winchester, Otis. *The New Strategy of Style*. 2d ed. New York: McGraw, 1978.

SENTENCE COMBINING

Daiker, Donald A. et al. *The Writer's Options: Combining to Composing*. 2d ed. New York: Harper, 1982.

O'Hare, Frank. *Sentence Craft*. Lexington, Mass.: Ginn, 1975.

Strong, William. *Sentence Combining: A Composing Book*. New York: Random, 1983.

USAGE AND VOCABULARY

Bernstein, Theodore M. *The Careful Writer: A Modern Guide to English Usage*. New York: Atheneum, 1965.

Brewer, E. Cobham. *Brewer's Dictionary of Phrase and Fable*. Revised by Ivor H. Evans. London: Cassell, 1982.

Davis, Nancy B. *Vocabulary Improvement*. 3d ed. New York: McGraw, 1978.

Feinstein, George W. *Programmed College Vocabulary 3600*. 2d ed. Englewood Cliffs, N.J.: Prentice, 1979.

Fowler, Henry W. *A Dictionary of Modern English Usage*. 2d ed. Revised by Sir Ernest Gowers. Oxford: Clarendon, 1983.

Partridge, Eric. *Usage & Abusage: A Guide to Good English*. New York: Penguin, 1982.

Safire, William. *On Language*. New York: Avon, 1981.

BASIC GRAMMAR

Baldauf, Richard B. *A Handy Guide to Grammar and Punctuation*. Reading, Mass.: Addison-Wesley, 1973.

Blumenthal, Joseph C. *English 3200*. 3d ed. New York: Harcourt, 1981.

Emery, Donald W. et al. *Handbook of English Fundamentals*. New York: Macmillan, 1978.

Feinstein, George W. *Programmed Writing Skills*. Englewood Cliffs, N.J.: Prentice, 1976.

Glazier, Teresa F. *The Least You Should Know About English Basic Writing Skills*. New York: Holt, 1983.

Hodges, John C. et al. *Harbrace College Handbook*. 10th ed. San Diego: Harcourt, 1986.

Loewe, Ralph E. *The Writing Clinic*. 3d ed. Englewood Cliffs, N.J.: Prentice, 1983.

Perrin, Porter G. *Reference Handbook of Grammar & Usage*. New York: Morrow, 1972.

SPELLING

Learning Technology Inc. *Basic Spelling Skills*. 2d ed. Edited by Alton L. Raygor. New York: McGraw, 1979.

McClelland, Lorraine et al. *English Sounds and Spelling*. Englewood Cliffs, N. J.: Prentice, 1979.

Mersand, Joseph and Griffith, Francis. *Spelling Your Way to Success*. Rev. ed. Woodbury, N.Y.: Barron's Educational Series, 1982.

BUSINESS WRITING

Ehrlich, Eugene and Murphy, Daniel. *The Art of Technical Writing*. New York: Crowell, 1964.

Fear, David E. *Technical Writing*. 2d ed. New York: Random, 1978.

Federal Electric Corporation. *How to Write Effective Reports*. Reading, Mass.: Addison-Wesley, 1965.

Kolin, Philip C. *Successful Writing at Work*. Lexington, Mass.: Heath, 1982.

Shurter, Robert L. et al. *Business Research & Report Writing*. New York: McGraw, 1965.

RESEARCH REPORTS

Gibaldi, Joseph and Achtert, Walter S. *MLA Handbook for Writers of Research Papers*. New York: MLA, 1984.

Sears, Donald A. *Harbrace Guide to the Library and the Research Paper*. San Diego: Harcourt, 1984.

LITERARY ESSAYS

General

Barnet, Sylvan. *A Short Guide to Writing About Literature*. 4th ed. Boston: Little, 1979.

Beckson, Karl and Ganz, Arthur. *Literary Terms: A Dictionary*. Rev. ed. New York: Farrar, 1975.

Bryfonski, Dedria, ed. *Contemporary Issues Criticism: Excerpts from Criticism of Contemporary Writings*. Contemporary Issues Criticism Series. Detroit: Gale Research, 1982–.

Cohen, B. Bernard. *Writing About Literature*. Rev. ed. Glenview, Ill.: Scott, 1973.

Griffith, Kelley. *Writing Essays About Literature*, 2d ed. New York: Harcourt, 1985.

Gunton, Sharon, ed. *Contemporary Literary Criticism*. Contemporary Literary Criticism Series. Detroit: Gale Research, 1973–.

Hall, Sharon K., ed. *Twentieth Century Literary Criticism*. Twentieth Century Literary Criticism Series. Detroit: Gale Research, 1978–.

Hogins, J. Burl and Bryant, Gerald A. *Reading for Insight*. Beverly Hills, Calif.: Glencoe, 1970.

McGuire, Richard L. *Passionate Attention: An Introduction to Literary Study*. New York: Norton, 1973.

Perrine, Laurence. *Literature: Structure, Sound, and Sense*. 4th ed. San Diego: Harcourt, 1983.

Roberts, Edgar V. *Writing Themes About Literature.* 5th ed. Englewood Cliffs, N.J.: Prentice, 1983.

Roberts, Edgar V. *Writing Themes About Literature.* Brief ed. Englewood Cliffs, N.J.: Prentice, 1982.

Rohrberger, Mary and Woods, Samuel H. *Reading and Writing About Literature.* New York: Random, 1971.

Sutton, Walter and Foster, Richard, eds. *Modern Criticism: Theory and Practice.* New York: Irvington, 1983.

Short Stories

Magill, Frank N. *Critical Survey of Short Fiction.* Englewood Cliffs, N.J.: Salem, 1981.

Walker, Warren S. *Twentieth Century Short Story Explication.* 3d ed. Hamden, Conn.: Shoe String, 1977.

Novels

Abernethy, Peter et al. *English Novel Explication: Supplement One to 1975.* Hamden, Conn.: Shoe String, 1976.

Gerstenberger, Donna and Hendrick, George. *The American Novel: 1789–1959.* Athens, Ohio: Swallow, 1961.

Palmer, Helen H. and Dyson, Anne J. *English Novel Explication: Criticisms to 1972.* Hamden, Conn.: Shoe String, 1973.

Vinson, James, ed. *Contemporary Novelists of the English Language.* New York: St. Martin's, 1982.

Poetry

Altenbernd, Lynn and Lewis, Leslie L. *A Handbook for the Study of Poetry.* Rev. ed. New York: Macmillan, 1966.

Beacham, Walton. *The Meaning of Poetry.* Boston: Allyn, 1974.

Cline, Gloria S. and Baker, Jeffrey A. *An Index to Criticisms of British and American Poetry.* Metuchen, N.J.: Scarecrow, 1973.

Martinez, Nancy C. and Kuntz, Joseph M. *Poetry Explication: A Checklist of Interpretation Since 1925 of British and American Poems Past and Present.* Boston: Hall, 1980.

Smith, William J. *Granger's Index to Poetry.* 7th ed. New York: Columbia University, 1982.

Drama

Amberg, George, ed. *The New York Times Film Reviews 1913–1970.* New York: Times Books, 1972.

Bowles, Stephen E., ed. *Index to Critical Film Reviews in British and American Periodicals.* New York: Burt Franklin, 1975.

Charney, Maurice. *How to Read Shakespeare.* New York: McGraw, 1971.

Coleman, Arthur and Tyler, Gary R. *Drama Criticism.* Athens, Ohio: Swallow, 1970.

Eddeman, Floyd E. *American Drama Criticism: Interpretations 1890–1977*. 2d ed. Hamden, Conn.: Shoe String, 1979.

Halliwell, Leslie. *Halliwell's Film Guide*. 4th ed. New York: Scribner, 1983.

Hayman, Ronald. *How to Read a Play*. New York: Grove, 1977.

Heinzkill, Richard. *Film Criticism: An Index to Critics' Anthologies*. Metuchen, N.J.: Scarecrow, 1975.

Magill, Frank N., ed. *Magill's Survey of Cinema*. 6 vols. Englewood Cliffs, N.J.: Salem, 1981.

Reaske, Christopher R. *How to Analyze Drama*. New York: Monarch, 1966.

Salem, James M. *A Guide to Critical Reviews*. 4 pts. New York: Scarecrow, 1973–1984.

Tennyson, G.B. *An Introduction to Drama*. New York: Holt, 1967.

ENGLISH AS A SECOND LANGUAGE

Costinett, Sandra. *Advanced Readings and Conversations*. Silver Springs, Md.: Institute of Modern Languages, 1973.

Croft, Kenneth. *Reading and Word Study: For Students of English as a Second Language*. Englewood Cliffs, N.J.: Prentice, 1969.

Croft, Kenneth and Brown, Billye W. *Science Readings: for Students of English as a Second Language*. New York: McGraw, 1968.

Frank, Marcella. *Modern English: Exercises for Non-Native Speakers*. Englewood Cliffs, N.J.: Prentice, 1972.

Glass, Elliot S. and Arcario, Paul J. *Speak Freely*. San Diego: Harcourt, 1985.

McCallum, George P. *Idiom Drills: For Students of English as a Second Language*, 2d ed. New York: Harper, 1983.

Maclin, Alice. *Reference Guide to English: A Handbook of English as a Second Language*. New York: Holt, 1981.

NONSEXIST WRITING

Henley, Nancy et al. *Language and Sex II*. Rowley, Mass.: Newbury House, Fall 1980.

Miller, Casey and Swift, Kate. *The Handbook of Nonsexist Writing*. New York: Barnes & Noble, 1980.

Miller, Casey and Swift, Kate. *Words and Women*. Garden City, N.Y.: Anchor Press/Doubleday, 1977.

Glossary

INTRODUCTION

This glossary contains grammatical and literary terms that you may find useful during your drafting and revising processes. Chapter references are provided so that you can find examples and further information. If a word or phrase within a definition appears in **bold** type, you will also find a definition of that word or phrase in the glossary.

absolute a word or phrase that modifies the entire sentence in which it appears, rather than modifying a particular word: "*Without a doubt*, the U.S. is a vast country"; "*Yes*, I have visited Texas."

absolute phrase one containing a **subject** and either a **verbal** and its **modifiers** or no **verb**; it functions as an **adjective**. (Chapter 49)

abstract words those that refer to qualities or states of being which cannot be perceived by the senses—for example, *hatred, boring*. See also **concrete words**.

accent a **logical fallacy** that emphasizes one fact while de-emphasizing another that may be equally important: "This complete toy is only $19.95 (*batteries not included*)." (Chapter 65)

active voice see **voice**.

ad baculum a **logical fallacy** in which a stated or implied threat is used: "Failing to vote for this candidate could mean that nuclear war will occur within five years." (Chapter 65)

ad hominem a **logical fallacy** that argues against the character of an opponent instead of against the point at issue: "How can you believe what he says about disarmament? Everyone knows he's a Communist." (Chapter 65)

adjective a word, **phrase** or **clause** that modifies a **noun** or **pronoun** (Chapter 41)

adverb a word, **phrase**, or **clause** that modifies a **verb**, **adjective**, or adverb. (Chapter 41)

agreement the concept by which a **verb** is either singular or plural, depending on its **subject**; also, the concept by which a **pronoun** has the same person, number, and gender as the **noun** to which it refers. (Chapters 57, 60)

allegory a **metaphor** in which an abstract or nonliving quality is given life: "Because I could not stop for *Death* / He kindly stopped for me." (Dickinson)

alliteration a type of **rhyme** in which two or more words contain the same initial consonant sounds: "The *cloud-capp'd* towers, the *gorgeous* palaces / The solemn temples, the *great globe* itself." (Shakespeare)

allusion a reference within a work to a well-known person, thing, or event (Chapter 36): "*Tootsie Rolls* / and Oh Boy Gum" (Ferlinghetti)

ambiguity (also called *equivocation*) using the same word in two or more different meanings. Sometimes ambiguity or equivocation is used deliberately as a **logical fallacy**. (Chapter 65)

analogy a sustained comparison of two things which have some features in common: "These our actors... were all spirits, and / Are melted into air, into thin air." (Shakespeare)

antagonist the character opposed to the **protagonist**.

antecedent a preceding **noun** or **pronoun** to which a pronoun refers. (Chapter 60)

anticlimax the resolution of the **subplot**, or the solution of minor problems, which comes when a reader is expecting something more important.

antonym a word having the opposite meaning to another word; for instance, *down* is the antonym of *up*.

APA American Psychological Association style. (Chapter 39)

aphorism a concise, memorable statement. (Chapter 34)

appositive a word or **phrase** which identifies, and can replace, a preceding **noun** or **pronoun**. (Chapter 50)

archetype a character (archetypal character) or situation (archetypal situation) which occurs frequently in literature and which fits a pattern of human experience. (Chapter 40)

argument the presentation of ideas in order to persuade or convince a reader. (Chapter 5)

articles the words *a* or *an* (indefinite article) or *the* (definite article); they function as **adjectives**.

aside a line in a play that is said directly to the audience, but is not meant to be heard by other characters on stage.

assonance a type of **rhyme** in which identical vowels occur but the consonants preceding and following the vowels are different: "In what distant deeps or skies / Burnt the fire of thine eyes?" (Blake)

association a **logical fallacy** which implies that something is to be admired or despised by mentioning it along with other things which have either a positive or negative **connotation** for the audience: "Hitler, Mussolini, and our candidate are three of the great politicians of our time."

atmosphere the physical reaction created by the description of the setting of a piece of writing. See also **mood**.

audience the intended reader or readers of a piece of writing. See also **writing variables**. (Introductory Section)

auxiliary verb one such as *may, can, might,* or *should* as well as *be, do,* or *have*, which joins with the main **verb** to form a **verb phrase**: "I *should* learn the names of all of the U.S. presidents"; "*Do* you know where Poughkeepsie is?"

balanced sentence one in which each part has a similar pattern. (Chapter 53): "Marilyn Horne is a mezzo-soprano; Beverly Sills, a coloratura soprano.

begging the question a **logical fallacy** which states as true the proposition that is to be proved, usually by expressing it in another way: "Our candidate is the best for the job because he is the most capable person available." (Chapter 65)

bibliography a list of books and other references used in preparing an **essay**, thesis, or other scholarly piece of writing. (Chapter 39)

blank verse poetry written in unrhymed iambic pentameter. Shakespeare wrote much of his work in blank verse. See also **meter**.

brainstorming various methods and techniques of inventing ideas and supporting evidence. (Chapter 25)

cacophony the deliberate use of particular words to create an unpleasant sound: "The *buzz*-saw *snarled*" (Robert Frost)

caesura a pause or break in a line of poetry: "he might be drafted|when he grew up / for

military service|in the American army."
(Brewster)

case the **inflection** of **nouns** and **pronouns** that shows their relationship to other words in a **sentence**. The three cases used in English are: nominative or subjective, used for the **subject** or **complement** of a **sentence** or for an **appositive**; objective, used for the direct or indirect **object** of a **verb** or a **verbal** or the **object of a preposition**; and possessive, used to show to whom or what an **object** belongs. (Chapter 60)

clause a group of words containing a **subject** and a **verb**, which can either function by itself as a **sentence** (independent or main clause) or depends on an independent clause in order to make complete sense (dependent or subordinate clause). (Chapter 45)

cliché a **figurative expression** that has lost its effect through overuse. (Chapter 36)

climax the highest point of the **rising action** of a work of fiction.

coherence the logical arrangement of **sentences** in a **paragraph**, or of paragraphs in a longer work, so that the work as a whole is unified. (Chapter 30)

colloquial language **diction** used mainly in speech and occasionally in informal writing.

comedy a drama in which the **protagonist** is in the same or a better position at the end of the play than at the beginning.

comic irony see **dramatic irony**.

comma splice the error in which a comma is used instead of a period or semicolon. See **run-on sentence**. (Chapter 56)

complement a **noun**, **pronoun**, or **adjective** which follows a **linking verb** and completes its meaning. (Chapter 41)

complete predicate the **verb** (predicate) of a **sentence** with its **modifiers**, **objects**, and **complements**. (Chapter 41)

complete subject the **subject** of a **sentence**, with its **modifiers**. (Chapter 41)

complex sentence one in which an independent **clause** is joined to one or more dependent **clauses** by **subordination**. (Chapter 45)

compound sentence one in which two or more independent **clauses** are joined by **coordination**. (Chapter 44)

compound-complex sentence one in which two or more independent **clauses** are joined with one or more dependent **clauses**. (Chapter 46)

concrete words those referring to things or states which directly appeal to the senses, such as *horse, blue*. See also **abstract words**.

conflict the struggle of the **protagonist** of a work against a person or thing, against his/her environment, or against himself/herself.

conjunctive adverb one which is used with a semicolon to join two or more independent **clauses**. Unlike other adverbs, it modifies the entire **clause** in which it appears. Some conjunctive adverbs are *however, still,* and *nevertheless*. (Chapter 44)

connotation the ideas or impressions connected with a word in addition to its dictionary meaning. See also **denotation**. (Chapter 37)

consonance a type of **rhyme** in which identical consonants are followed and preceded by different vowels: "Lately things don't *seem* the *same*." (Jimi Hendrix)

content the information contained in a piece of writing. The worth of your **topic** or **thesis** determines the merit of your content. (Chapter 3 and Introductory Section)

coordinating conjunction one which joins two words, **phrases**, or **clauses** of equal importance. Some coordinating conjunctions are *and, but,* and *yet*. (Chapters 41, 44)

coordination the combination of two or more words, **phrases**, or **clauses** which have the same function within a **sentence**, usually involving a **coordinating conjunction**. (Chapter 44)

correlative conjunction a pair of words which join words, **phrases**, or **clauses** of equal importance. Some correlative conjunctions are: *both...and, not only...but [also],* and *either...or*. (Chapter 44)

couplet two lines of rhyming **verse**: "Now it

looks as though they're here to *stay*, / Oh, I believe in *yesterday*." (Lennon/McCartney)

crisis the point in the **plot** at which the action that brings on the **climax** takes place.

dangling modifier one with no specific word to modify in the **sentence** in which it appears. (Chapter 56)

dead metaphor one which, through overuse, is no longer thought of as a **figurative expression**.

deduction the process of reasoning in which a conclusion is followed by the evidence that supports it. See also **induction**. (Chapter 29)

denotation the dictionary meaning of a word. See also **connotation**. (Chapter 37)

dénouement the point during a story or play at which all loose ends are tied up and all questions answered.

description a piece of writing which depicts a person, place, or object. (Chapter 2)

deus ex machina a new character or incident created by a playwright or author specifically to resolve the plot (literally "god from the machine"). The use of a *deus ex machina* usually connotes an unsatisfying ending.

diction choice of words which contribute to a desired writing **style**. (Chapters 37, 64)

direct object see **object**.

direct question one which is asked in question form: "Who was Franklin Pierce?" See also **indirect question**.

drafting process the part of the **writing process** during which a writer composes one or more preliminary drafts of a piece. (Introductory Section)

dramatic irony an occasion in a tragedy when the full significance of something a character says is unknown to him/her, but is known to another character or to the audience. In a comedy this is called **comic irony**.

elision the omission of part of a word in order to make a line of verse read more smoothly. There are several types of elision: dropping of a syllable (*'gainst* for *against*); omitting within a word (*o'er* for *over*); omitting at the end of a word (*ope* for *open*).

elliptical construction one in which some words are omitted from a sentence, but in which the missing words are understood. (Chapter 55)

equivocation (see **ambiguity**).

essay a short **nonfiction** work dealing with one theme or subject.

essential modifier (also called a *restrictive modifier*) one which identifies the word being modified: "The mountain *which was named for the McLoughlins* is located in Southern Oregon." (Chapter 62)

euphemism an expression used in place of one a writer believes an **audience** may find offensive: "Pianist Glenn Gould *passed away* [instead of *died*] in 1982."

euphony the deliberate use of particular words to create a pleasant sound: "... our little life / Is rounded with a sleep." (Shakespeare)

exposition denotes a piece of **nonfiction** writing which explains an idea or presents an opinion.

fallacy see **logical fallacy**.

falling action the part of a play that follows the climax. See also **rising action**.

false analogy a **logical fallacy** stating that two things are alike in all respects when they are actually alike in only a few, or proving that two dissimilar things are alike: "Our candidate is like Winston Churchill; he is bald and smokes cigars." (Chapter 65)

false cause (or *post hoc, ergo propter hoc*) a **logical fallacy** stating that because one event followed another, the first event had to be the cause of the second: "Our candidate spent two years in college; he must be a man of culture and refinement." (Chapter 65)

false generalization a **logical fallacy** that assumes that something is true in all cases when it is true only in a few particular cases: "Everyone who votes for our candidate is in favor of capital punishment." (Chapter 65)

false logic see **logical fallacy**.

faulty coordination two or more unequal elements, that are joined as if equal. (Chapter 56)

faulty parallelism one or more elements in a sentence that do not have the same structure (Chapter 56)

faulty subordination emphasizing the wrong element in a sentence (Chapter 56)

fiction a piece of writing based on its author's imagination rather than on fact. See also **nonfiction**.

figurative expression one in which two objects or concepts which are usually not considered alike are compared. See also **allegory**, **metaphor**, **metonymy**, **personification**, **simile**, and **synecdoche**. (Chapter 36)

figure of speech see **figurative expression**.

flashback the description of events that took place before the major **plot** of the story or narrative.

flash-forward the description of a future event that is set within the major **plot** of the story or narrative.

foot a method of measuring **verse** by finding patterns of stressed and unstressed syllables. See also **meter**.

foreshadowing the insertion of hints throughout a story which indicate how it will end.

formal diction language used in scholarly reports, government documents, and other formal pieces of writing.

format the form in which a piece of writing will be presented to its **audience**—for example, as a **paragraph**, **essay**, or letter. See also **writing variables**. (Introductory Section)

fractured idiom one which does not follow the conventions of English idiomatic usage. (Chapter 64)

fragment see **sentence fragment**.

free verse **verse** written in irregular forms. (See "The pennycandystore beyond the El" in Appendix B.)

French scene the division of a play that occurs when a character enters or exits.

gender the designation of words as masculine, feminine, or neuter. In English, gender is used mainly in some **pronouns** and **adjectives**: "*She* and *her* mother flew to Grand Rapids; *he* stayed home."

gerund (also called a *verbal noun*) a verbal which functions as a **noun**. Gerunds end in *ing* (Chapter 48): "*Seeing* is *believing*."

gerundial phrase one which consists of a **gerund** and its **modifiers**, and functions in the same way as a **gerund** (Chapter 48): "*Seeing Niagara Falls* is *believing in the majesty of Nature*."

grammar the rules and constructions of a language.

hero *or* **heroine** the central character in a work of fiction.

homonyms words that are pronounced alike but spelled differently, such as *male* and *mail*.

honorific slant *see* **slant**.

humor speech or writing that describes a comic situation or character only in order to provoke laughter. (Chapter 38)

hyperbole a **figurative expression** in which exaggeration is used for effect. (Chapter 36)

idiom a common expression whose meaning as a whole is different from that of the words comprising it (Chapter 64): "Jackie was *in the chips* after she won the state lottery."

image the description in words of something perceived by one or more of the five senses.

imagery descriptive poetic language used repeatedly throughout a work. **Metaphor**, **simile**, **personification**, and so on are types of imagery.

independent clause see **clause**.

indirect object see **object**.

indirect question one which is asked without using the question form: "Susan wanted to know who Franklin Pierce was." See also **direct question**.

induction the process of reasoning in which a conclusion is drawn from a number of different facts. See also **deduction**. (Chapter 29)

infinitive   a **verbal**, usually preceded by *to (to see)* which can function as a **noun**, **adjective**, or **adverb**. (Chapter 48)

infinitive phrase   one which consists of an **infinitive** and its **modifiers**, and functions in the same way as an **infinitive** (Chapter 48): "It was impossible *to see the Statue of Liberty clearly.*"

inflection   a change in all or part of a word to indicate a change in its function. For instance, *she* becomes *her*, *tall* becomes *taller*, *climb* becomes *climbed*.

informal diction   language used both in speech and in personal and most academic writing.

interjection   a **part of speech** which has no grammatical function in a **sentence**, but is inserted to indicate a speaker's strong feeling or to attract attention. (Chapter 41)

intransitive verb   one which does not take an **object** or **complement**. (Chapter 41)

invective   harsh and abusive writing. (Chapter 38)

irony   the use of words in a way that expresses their opposite meaning. (Chapter 38)

jargon   language used among members of a particular profession or group, such as scientists or sports fans. (Chapter 64)

linking verb   one which needs a **noun**, **pronoun**, or **adjective** to complete its meaning. Some linking verbs are *be, seem, feel, taste, appear*. (Chapter 41)

logic   the use of the principles of reasoning to draw conclusions from facts.

logical fallacy   an error in reasoning in which the principles of **logic** are ignored or misused. See also **accent, ad baculum, ad hominem, ambiguity, association, begging the question, false analogy, false cause, false generalization**, and **non sequitur**. (Chapter 65)

loose sentence   one in which the **main clause** is completed before the end. The majority of English sentences are loose sentences. (Chapter 54)

main claim   see **thesis statement**.

main clause   see **clause**.

mechanics   spelling, punctuation, and other aspects of a piece of writing dealt with during the **polishing process**. (Fourth Workshop Section)

metaphor   a figurative comparison that describes one object as being another: "Tiger! Tiger! *burning bright* / In the *forests of the night.*" (Blake)

meter   the recurrent patterns of a piece of poetry. Lines of verse are measured in *feet* according to the number and kind of stressed(´) and unstressed (˘) syllables in each line. The feet most often used in English are:
iamb: most common meter in English poetry (*dĕfénd*)
trochee: very common in English verse (*púrplĕ*)
spondee: (*lífetíme*)
pyrrhic: (*mŭrmŭr*)
anapest: (*pĕrsĕvére*)
dactyl: (*hésĭtăte*)
By counting the number of feet in each line of poetry, you can classify the line length (or meter): monometer (1), dimeter (2), trimeter (3), tetrameter (4), pentameter (5), hexameter or alexandrine (6), heptameter (7), octometer (8). See also **scansion**.

metonymy   a figurative comparison in which an object is used to stand for something closely related to it: "What immortal *hand* or *eye* / Could frame thy fearful symmetry?" (Blake). See also **synecdoche**.

minor sentence   (also called rhetorical fragment) a **sentence fragment** which is understood as containing a complete thought (Chapter 35): "What is the capital of New Mexico? *Santa Fe.*"

misplaced modifier   one which is not located near the word it modifies. (Chapter 56)

mixed metaphor   one in which two **images** are confused: "You can lead a dead horse to water, but you can't make him drink."

MLA   Modern Language Association style. (Chapter 39)

modifier   an **adjective**, **adverb**, **phrase**, or **clause** which describes or limits another part of a **sentence**. See also **adjective, adverb**,

dangling modifier, and **misplaced modifier**. (Chapters 41, 56)

mood   the emotional tone of a piece of literature. See also **atmosphere**.

myth   a story of unknown origin, often involving supernatural elements, in which an attempt is made to explain a fundamental belief; for example, all peoples have an explanation of how men and women were created.

narrator   the teller of a story. The narrator can be the author, one of the characters, or an unidentified person.

narration   a piece of writing which tells a story. (Chapters 1, 4)

nonessential modifier   (also called a **nonrestrictive modifier**) one which gives further information about, but does not identify, the word being modified; it is usually set off from the rest of the sentence by commas: "Mount St. Helens, *which erupted in 1980*, is located in Washington State."

nonfiction   a piece of writing based entirely on fact. See also **fiction**.

nonrestrictive modifier   see **nonessential modifier**.

nonsentence fragment   see **minor sentence**.

non sequitur   a **logical fallacy** consisting of an **argument** whose conclusion does not necessarily follow from what precedes it: "Our candidate for mayor speaks three languages; he can count on the support of new American voters." (Chapter 65)

noun   a word which names a person, place, thing, or condition, and functions as the **subject**, **object**, or **complement** of a sentence. (Chapter 41)

object   a **noun** or **pronoun** that receives the action of a **verb**, either directly (**direct object**) or in association with the direct object (**indirect object**). (Chapter 41)

object of a preposition   a **noun**, **pronoun**, **verbal**, or **clause** which follows a **preposition** and completes the **prepositional phrase**: "The population of *the U.S.* is over *250 million*"; "Give the book to *whoever wants it*."

onomatopoeia   the use of words whose meaning is suggested by the way they sound: *shrieks*, *babble*, *tinkle*.

outline   a brief plan indicating the arrangement of ideas which are or will be contained in a written work. (Chapters 29, 32, 39)

paradox   a statement that seems to contain a contradiction (Chapter 34): "It was the best of times; it was the worst of times." (Dickens)

paragraph   a unit containing one or more sentences which relate to one **topic sentence**. The first line of a paragraph is usually indented. (Chapter 27)

parallelism   the arrangement of words, **phrases**, **clauses**, or **sentences** so that they are similar in structure and appearance. See also **balanced sentence**. (Chapter 53)

paraphrase   a restatement of a piece of writing in one's own words. (Chapter 32)

parenthetical citation   citing references within a research essay as opposed to using footnotes and endnotes. (Chapter 39)

parody   a humorous imitation of a certain writing style. (Chapter 38)

part of speech   the grammatical category into which a particular word fits according to its function in a sentence. See also **adjective**, **adverb**, **article**, **conjunction**, **interjection**, **noun**, **preposition**, **pronoun**, **verb**. (Chapter 41)

participle   a **verbal** which functions as an **adjective**. (Chapter 48) There are three commonly used participles: past participle ("*Exhausted*, Jesse Owens crossed the finish line"), perfect participle ("*Having finished*, he awaited the results of the race"), and present participle ("*Smiling*, he accepted the gold medal for the United States")

participial phrase   one which consists of a **participle** and its **modifiers**, and functions in the same way as a **participle** (Chapter 48): "*Exhausted by his efforts*, Jesse Owens crossed the finish line"; "*Having finished his run in record time*, he awaited the results of the race"; "*Smiling broadly*, he accepted the gold medal for the U.S."

passive voice see **voice**.

past participle see **participle**.

pejorative slant see **slant**.

persona an identity assumed by a writer to achieve a particular result through a piece of writing. See also **writing variables**. (Chapters 34, 38, Introductory Section)

personification a figurative expression in which an inanimate object is given human characteristics: "When the stars *threw* down their spears, / And *watered* heaven with their *tears*" (Blake)

phrase a group of words that does not contain either a **subject** or a full **verb**, and that functions as a single **part of speech**. See also **absolute phrase, gerundial phrase, infinitive phrase, participal phrase, prepositional phrase**. (Chapters 47, 48, 49)

plagiarism the use of another writer's words or ideas without crediting them to him/her. (Chapter 39)

plot the sequence of events which make up the action of a story.

point of view the perspective from which an author chooses to tell a story. It can be *omniscient*, so that the **narrator** knows what all the characters are doing, saying, and thinking, as well as all external circumstances affecting the **plot**, or it can be *limited*, so that the narrator tells the story from one character's viewpoint as he/she hears or sees it.

post hoc, ergo propter hoc see **false cause**.

précis the condensation of a piece of writing to about one half its length, using either one's own words or those of the original writer. (Chapter 32)

predicate see **verb**.

preposition a word linking the **noun, pronoun, verbal**, or **clause** that follows it to another word in the **sentence**. See also **object of preposition**. (Chapter 41)

prepositional phrase one consisting of a **preposition**, its **object**, and **modifiers** of the object. (Chapter 47)

present participle see **participle**.

prewriting process the part of the **writing process** in which ideas for a piece of writing are generated or invented. (Introductory Section)

pronoun a word which refers to and replaces a **noun**. (Chapters 57, 60)

protagonist the leading character in a literary work. See also **antagonist**.

punctuation mark one used in writing to assist in the reading of a piece and to make its meaning clear, such as a period, question mark, exclamation mark, comma, semicolon, colon, dash, parenthesis, bracket, ellipsis points, slash, or quotation mark. (Chapter 62)

purpose the reason a piece of writing is composed. See also **writing variables**.

References the title of a **bibliography** for a research essay, following the **APA** style. (Chapter 39)

revising a part of the **writing process** in which a piece of writing is corrected and improved.

resolution the portion of a story in which the problems posed in other parts of the work are solved.

restrictive modifier see **essential modifier**.

rhetoric the study and practice of the effective use of language.

rhetorical device a word, **phrase**, or **clause** used for a special literary purpose. See also **figurative expression** and **trope**. (Chapter 64)

rhetorical fragment see **minor sentence**.

rhyme or **rime** the similarity of sound patterns occurring at the end of lines (end or terminal rhyme) or within a line (internal rhyme). Terminal rhyme: "*Yesterday* / All my troubles seemed so far *away*" (Lennon/McCartney); internal rhyme: "Now *only lowly* creatures find you home" (Jon Furberg)

Rhymes may be perfect (complete or true rhyme), or may have similar, but not identical, sound patterns (imperfect, partial, or slant rhyme). True rhyme: "In what distant deeps or *skies* / Burnt the fire of thine *eyes*?" (Blake); slant rhyme: "What immortal hand or *eye* / Could frame thy fearful *symmetry*?" (Blake)

rhyme scheme the pattern in which the rhymes of the final words of each line of a poem occur. Each rhyme is usually assigned a letter, starting with *a*; for example, the rhyme scheme of the first verse of Blake's "The Tiger" is *aabb*, that of the second verse is *ccdd*, and so on.

rhythm the regular beat or pulse of poetry or music. See also **meter**.

rising action the part of a plot which occurs before the **climax**.

run-on sentence one which contains two or more independent **clauses** joined either without any punctuation, or with only a comma (also called **comma splice**).

sarcasm a form of **wit**, usually verbal, in which the speaker means the opposite to what he/she says. (Chapter 38)

sardonic humor that using bitter or scornful language. (Chapter 38)

satire a form of **wit** in which persons or institutions are ridiculed in order to convey to an audience the necessity for change. Satire is achieved through the use of **invective, irony, parody, sarcasm,** and **sardonic humor.** (Chapter 38)

scansion the division of lines of poetry into **feet** in order to determine the **meter** of a poem. See **meter** for scansion marks. A line of iambic pentameter would be scanned in this way:

ăre mél/tĕd ĭn/tŏ aír/intó/thĭn aír/ (Shakespeare)

sentence a group of words containing a **complete subject** and a **complete predicate**, beginning with a capital letter and ending with a period if it is a statement or command, an exclamation mark if it expresses strong emotion, or a question mark if it asks a question. See also **minor sentence, simple sentence, complex sentence, compound sentence, com-**

pound-complex sentence. (Chapters 35, 43–46)

sentence fragment a group of words punctuated as a **sentence**, but which does not contain both a **complete subject** and a **complete predicate**, or expresses a complete thought. See also **minor sentence.** (Chapter 56)

setting the time (both the era of history and the time of day) and the geographical location of a piece of literature.

simile a **figurative expression** which states that one object is like another: "My Luve is like a red, red rose" (Robert Burns); "I am become as sounding brass" (1 Corinthians 13).

simple sentence a group of words containing only one independent clause.

situation the physical conditions, including the **setting, mood,** and **atmosphere,** which are present in the exposition of a work; also, the circumstances of a writer or a reader, which will affect the way in which a piece of writing is written and read. See also **writing variables.** (Introductory Section)

slang informal **diction** used mainly in speech. (Chapter 64)

slant the choice of words made by a writer in order to achieve a favorable (positive or **honorific slant**) or unfavorable (negative or **pejorative slant**) reaction from a reader to an idea. (Chapter 37)

soliloquy a speech in a play during which a character speaks his/her inner thoughts to the **audience**.

split infinitive one in which *to* is separated from the rest of the infinitive by at least one word: *to suddenly laugh.*

stanza a distinct group of lines in a poem.

stereotype an unoriginal character or **situation**.

style the choice and arrangement of words in a piece of writing as they reflect the personality of the writer. (Chapter 34)

subheading a title that appears below a main title in research reports (Chapters 17, 22, 23)

subject the word/words in a **sentence** that indicate who or what performed the action of the **verb**. The subject with its **modifiers** is called the **complete subject**. (Chapter 41)

subordinate clause   see **clause**.

subordination   the act of making one part of a **sentence** less important than another. (Chapter 35)

subplot   a less important story contained within a work. The **anticlimax** often resolves the subplot.

suspense   the anticipation of the outcome of a story which an author creates in an **audience**.

symbol   a person or object which represents both itself and a larger idea.

synecdoche   a **figurative expression** in which a part of an object signifies the entire object, or vice versa: "And what *shoulder* and what *art* / Could twist the *sinews* of thy heart?" (Blake). See also **metonymy**.

synonym   a word with a similar meaning to another word; for example, *scarlet* is a synonym for *red*.

syntax   the way in which words are arranged into **sentences**.

tense   the expression by a **verb** of the time in which an action takes place. The three main verb tenses in English are present (*begins*), past (*began*), and future (*will begin*). (Chapter 57)

theme   the main idea of a literary work.

thesis statement   the main claim of an essay. (Chapter 27)

tone   the writer's attitude toward a work and its **audience**, conveyed by the way the work is written: if the tone is direct, the audience should take what the writer says at face value; if the tone is ironic, the audience should take the opposite meaning from what is written.

topic   the subject of a piece of writing. See also **thesis statement**, **topic sentence**, and **writing variables**. (Chapter 27)

topic sentence   the main claim of a paragraph (Chapter 27)

tragedy   a drama in which the **protagonist** is in a lower position at the end of the play than at the beginning.

transitional device   a word or **phrase** which links one part of a work to another. (Chapter 30)

transitive verb   one which takes an **object**. (Chapter 41)

trope   a **rhetorical device**, such as **metaphor** or **irony**, in which words are used in other than their literal meaning.

verb   the word in a **sentence** which describes an action or state of being of the **subject**, or which connects it to the **object** or **complement**. See also **complete predicate** and **linking verb**. (Chapter 41)

verbal   a form of a **verb** which functions not only as a verb but also as another **part of speech**, such as a **noun** or **adjective**. See also **gerund**, **infinitive**, **participle**. (Chapter 48)

verse   a single line of poetry; also used to refer to poetry in general.

voice   the form of a verb which indicates whether the **subject** performs (active voice) or receives (passive voice) the action (Chapter 57). Active: "The American people *elect* the government"; passive: "The government *is elected* by the American people."

word punctuation   certain **punctuation marks** used within words in order to assist in the reading of a piece and to make its meaning clear. Word-punctuation marks commonly used in English are the apostrophe, the hyphen, the capital letter, underlining or italics, and the period in abbreviations. (Chapter 63)

Works Cited   title of a **bibliography** for a research essay, following the **MLA** style (Chapter 39)

writing process   the stages (**prewriting, drafting**, and **revising**) in which a piece of writing is composed.

writing variables   the circumstances affecting the composition of any piece of writing. See also **audience, format, purpose, situation, topic, voice**. (Introductory Section)

Copyrights and Acknowledgments

Index

intensive, 641
noninflecting, 643
personal, 638–41
possessive, 638–39
reflexive, 641
relative, 540, 641
Proofreaders' symbols, inside back
cover
Propaganda, 432–33
Proposal, 186–96
Protagonist, 491
Prove in exam question, 225
Publishing (a piece of writing),
366–67
Punctuation, 656–67
end, 657
internal, 657–67
word, 668–76
Purple prose, 690
Purpose, 9 and *passim*

Question
as a beginning, 325
mark, 657
Quotation
as a beginning, 325
marks, 665–67
researching, 463–64
Quoting
drama, 476
poetry, 475–76
prose, 472–75
sacred works, 476

Random lists (brainstorming
technique), 289
Read/write (brainstorming
technique), 285
Reading process, 482–99
and Pentad Connection, 294–96
Real audience. *See* Audience
Reasoning, inductive and deductive,
338–41
Redundancy, 625–26, 681
Reference page in research report,
465, 469–70, 477
References in laboratory report,
257–58
Reflexive pronoun. *See* Pronoun
Relate in exam question, 225
Relative pronoun. *See* Pronoun
Repetition (rhetorical device), 401
Report, 188–96
laboratory, 253–54
research, 152–67

Reporter's questions (brainstorming
technique), 299–303
Research, 459–81
Research paper
humanities, 231
social sciences, 244
Research report, 152–67
formal, 152–67
informal (feature article), 153–67
Results in laboratory report, 257
Résumé, 211–19
full, 211–13, 217
partial, 213–16, 219
Reversals (rhetorical device), 402,
582
Review, 135–40
paper, scientific, 254
Review in exam question, 225
Revising, 3, 11 and *passim*
Rhetorical
devices and style, 401–402
fragments. *See* Sentence, minor
question, 401
Ridicule (logical fallacy), 700
Roots, 695, 696
Run-on sentence. *See* Sentence

Satire, 439–58
and invective, 442–43
and parody, 443–47
and persona, 451–55
sardonic, 440
Science paper. *See* Essay
Scientific review paper, 254–70
Secondary sources, 145
See/write (brainstorming technique),
284–85
Semicolon, 535, 537, 661–63
vs. colon, 663
Senses cluster (brainstorming
technique), 289–90
Sentence
balanced, 581–83
complex, 524–25, 540–45
compound, 524, 535–39
compound–complex, 525, 546–49
declarative, 428
errors, 609–15
fragment, 610
loose, 585–87
minor, 412
patterns, 524–29
periodic, 402, 585–87
run-on, 535, 611
simple, 524, 530–34
variety, 407–13

Sequential order. *See* Order
Seven controlling questions
(brainstorming technique),
303–304
Sexist writing, 702–13
Short story
different from narrative essay,
52–53
reading, 489–92
Sic, 664
Simile, 415
Simple sentence. *See* Sentence
Single quotation marks, 666
Situation, 10–11 and *passim*
archetypal, 490–91
audience's, 10, 11
in literature, 490–91
writer's, 10, 11
Slang. *See* Word level
Slant, 426–36
negative (pejorative), 426
positive (honorific), 426
and style, 432
using, 433–35
Slash, 475–76, 674–75
double, 475
Social sciences, writing for the,
243–52
Sources
primary, 145
secondary, 145
Sources, citing
APA style, 476–77
MLA style, 470–76
Spatial order. *See* Order
Special-interest programs, 730
Specialized-writing programs, 731
Specific conflict. *See* Conflict
Spelling, 648–55
American vs. British, 654–55
frequently misspelled words,
648–49
and pronunciation, 652–54
rules, 649–51
SQ3R, 485–87
Strained metaphor. *See* Metaphor
Structure
basic essay, 66
basic paragraph, 43–44
parallel. *See* Parallelism
Style, 387–403
and audience, 389–90
and background, 387–88
in comics, 398–99
evaluation, 358–59
in newspapers, 399–400

PROOFREADERS' SYMBOLS

(numbers in parentheses indicate chapters in which the topic is discussed)

Symbol	Meaning	Example	Correction
ℐ	delete, take out	in in the car	in the car
∧	insert	This∧my best writing.	This is my best writing.
#	insert space	picture#frame	picture frame
⋏	insert a comma (62)	A polished∧publishable	A polished, publishable
∨	insert an apostrophe (63)	teacher's guide	teacher's guide
∨∨	insert quotation mark (62)	"Out! he shouted	"Out!" he shouted
⊙	insert period	⊙ Mr∧ Saul Bellow	Mr. Saul Bellow
⊼	insert hyphen (63)	a well∧stocked fridge	a well-stocked fridge
∿	transpose letter or word	transpose word this	transpose this word
≡	use a capital letter (63)	washington	Washington
/	use a lower case letter	Northern U.S.	northern U.S.
¶	begin a new paragraph	¶Even though an . . .	Even though an . . .
⌐	do not start a new paragraph	. . . only occasionally. Once we started	only occasionally. Once we started . . .
⊃	join	he was out spoken	he was outspoken
stet	let it remain as it was; change made was wrong	"Come on to My House" is a 1950s song.	"Come on to My House" is a 1950s song.
sp	spelling error (61)	misteak	mistake
ID	incorrect idiom (37, 64)	the answer to the problem	the answer to the question
Jarg	unnecessary jargon (64)	Have a peer-feedback session.	Have a peer-editing session.
WW	wrong word (64)	its now or never	it's now or never
u	usage (64)	I did good	I did well
Ros	run-on sentence (56)	It was my first day even I was happy.	It was my first day; even I was happy.